MINIX FOR THE IBM PC, XT, AND AT

MINIX FOR THE IBM PC, XT, AND AT

ANDREW S. TANENBAUM

Vrije Universiteit
Amsterdam, The Netherlands

PRENTICE HALL
ENGLEWOOD CLIFFS, N.J. 07632

Editorial/production supervision: *Maureen Lopez*
Cover design:
Manufacturing buyer: *Ron Chapman/Richard Washburn*

 © 1988 by Prentice-Hall, Inc.
A Division of Simon & Schuster
Englewood Cliffs, New Jersey 07632

Printed in the United States of America

10 9 8 7 6 5 4 3 2 1

ISBN 0-13-584400-2   025

Prentice-Hall International (UK) Limited, *London*
Prentice-Hall of Australia Pty. Limited, *Sydney*
Prentice-Hall Canada Inc., *Toronto*
Prentice-Hall Hispanoamericana, S.A., *Mexico*
Prentice-Hall of India Private Limited, *New Delhi*
Prentice-Hall of Japan, Inc., *Tokyo*
Simon & Schuster Southeast Asia Pte. Ltd., *Singapore*
Editora Prentice-Hall do Brasil, Ltda., *Rio de Janeiro*

To Suzanne, Barbara, Marvin, Muis, and the memory of Sweetie π

CONTENTS

PART TWO: HOW MINIX WORKS INSIDE

PART THREE: THE MINIX SOURCE CODE

PREFACE

For years the UNIX† operating system has enjoyed an enormous popularity at universities and at government and industrial research laboratories. It has been less popular on personal computers because to run well it requires a large, sophisticated processor with a lot of memory and expensive disk drives. Another problem is that the source code has been tightly controlled by AT&T, making it unavailable to students, hobbyists, and programmers who want to study or modify it.

With the advent of MINIX, all that is changed. MINIX is a new operating system that is compatible with the Seventh Edition of the UNIX operating system (popularly known as Version 7), but which has been written from scratch especially for the IBM PC, XT, and AT. It does not contain any AT&T code, not in the kernel and not in the utility programs such as *grep*, *cc*, and *make*. MINIX offers three major advantages to the IBM PC, XT, or AT owner:

1. MINIX is very inexpensive.

2. MINIX comes with full source code for the kernel and most utilities.

3. MINIX does not require a hard disk, but can use one if available.

As a result, MINIX is the ideal system for people who are looking for a low-cost

---

† UNIX is a registered trademark of AT&T Bell Laboratories.

operating system that is similar to the UNIX system and for which source code is available for study and experiment.

MINIX contains a large number of utility programs that are functionally similar to their counterparts in the UNIX system. For example, there is a full Kernighan and Ritchie compatible C compiler derived from the Amsterdam Compiler Kit (see the *Communications of the ACM*, Sept. 1983, pp. 654-660). There is also a *make*. A full-screen editor loosely pattern on Emacs (but much smaller and simpler) is provided. And of course, the standard utilities such as *cat*, *cp*, *grep*, *ls*, *mv*, *rm*, *sort*, *uniq* and *wc* are present, among many others.

This book contains three parts. The first part tells you how to boot MINIX and run it on your IBM PC, XT, or AT. This part presumes that you already are familiar with the UNIX operating system. If you are not, there are many suitable introductory books available that provide the necessary background.

Part one also contains all the manual "pages." Each page describes one utility program, listing the command syntax, flags, and options, as well as giving several examples of the how the command is used in practice. A description of what the command does is also provided.

The last chapter in part one provides detailed information for people who wish to modify the MINIX sources, to improve it, to add new drivers, or just to experiment with it. Step by step directions are given telling how to reconstruct the kernel, how to integrate new drivers, and what to do if problems arise.

Part two contains a detailed discussion of how MINIX works inside. Its organization, algorithms, and data structures are described in detail. The process management, I/O management, memory management, and file management are all covered at length. An entire chapter is devoted to each topic. The chapters begin with an overview of the subject, and then move on to a discussion of the actual code, discussing the system procedure by procedure.

Part three consists of the complete listing of the MINIX kernel, in C (except for two short files dealing with interrupt handling, etc. in assembly language). A cross reference map of the major symbols is also provided for reference.

I have been extremely fortunate in having the help of many people during the course of this project. I would especially like to thank Dick Grune, Wiebren de Jonge, Jan Looyen, Jim van Keulen, Hans van Staveren, Jennifer Steiner, and Peter Weinberger for reading parts of the manuscript and making many helpful suggestions. Special thanks also go to Brian Kernighan for 1.4 readings and constantly reminding me about rule 13.

Although I personally wrote the entire 12,000 lines of the operating system proper, a number of other people have contributed utility programs that are included in the distribution. Without their help, MINIX would have been far less useful. In particular, I would like to thank Martin Atkins, Erik Baalbergen, Charles Forsyth, Richard Gregg, Paul Polderman, and Robbert van Renesse. Paul Ogilvie ported the system to MS-DOS. Michiel Huisjes, Patrick van Kleef, and Adri Koppes provided immensely valuable help with many aspects of the software, far above and beyond the call of duty.

The only pieces of MINIX software not included on the diskettes in this box are the compiler sources. These were made using the Amsterdam Compiler Kit (see *Communications of the ACM*, Sept. 1983, pp. 654-660), which has also been used to make compilers for many other languages and machines. The compiler sources can be ordered from the following companies:

In North and South America: In Europe and elsewhere

UniPress Software   Transmediair Utrecht BV
2025 Lincoln Highway   Melkweg 3
Edison, NJ 08817   3721 RG Bilthoven
U.S.A.   Holland
Telephone: (201) 985-8000   Telephone: (30) 78 18 20

Note: MINIX itself is available from **Prentice-Hall**, not the above companies. In addition to the diskette versions, there is also one on industry standard 9-track magnetic tape. The tape also contains an IBM PC simulator and other software for classroom use.

Finally, I would like to thank Suzanne for her endless patience while I spent untold hours hiding in front of my PC. Without her support and understanding I would never have made it. I also want to thank Barbara and Marvin for using Suzanne's computer, instead of mine, thus making this book possible. I am better at *jove*, but they are better at *Donald Duck's Playground*.

Andrew S. Tanenbaum

MINIX FOR THE IBM PC, XT, AND AT

PART ONE

1

INTRODUCTION

In little more than a decade, the UNIX† operating system has developed from a laboratory curiosity to one of the most widely used operating systems in the world. It runs on more different computer types, ranging from tiny personal computers to giant supercomputers, than any other operating system ever written. It is the de facto standard among computer science departments at universities throughout the world. Nevertheless, it has a few properties that make it unattractive for certain users.

First, its licensing is stringently controlled by its owner, AT&T. The source code is only available to organizations that sign a multipage legal contract that specifies in enormous detail precisely what is and what is not allowed. Second, the licensing fee can run into tens of thousands of dollars for just a single copy. Third, the UNIX system is quite large, and requires moderately expensive hardware to run well.

In order to make an elegant and pleasant to use system more widely available under less restrictive conditions, I have written a new operating system, called **MINIX**, from scratch in such a way that to the user it appears very much like the UNIX system, but inside it is completely new (and better structured). Since MINIX does not contain even a single line of AT&T code, it is possible to make the full source code available to students, programmers, hobbyists, and others to study and modify as they wish. (A full source code listing is given in Chap. 8.) This new system—how to use it and how it works inside—is the subject of this book.

---

† UNIX is a registered trademark of AT&T Bell Laboratories.

1.1. OVERVIEW OF THE MINIX PROJECT

In the following sections we will take a quick look at the history of MINIX and the goals of the whole MINIX project. The first computers, back in the 1940s, had no operating systems at all. Their programmers worked right down on the bare metal, in absolute machine language. This was no fun at all, so they invented assemblers, compilers and operating systems.

The first operating systems were **batch systems**. In a batch system, all the users prepared their programs on punched cards, and brought them into the machine room. Every once in a while the operator came in and took a batch of cards to read in. A few hours later the output was printed and placed in little cubbyholes for the programmers to pick up. Frequently a run would be wasted because a missing semicolon caused the compilation to fail. Batch systems were only popular with people old enough to remember what it was like before batch systems.

In the early 1960s time-sharing was invented at M.I.T. and Dartmouth College. With a time-sharing system, many users could work interactively at terminals, with the computer giving each user a short burst of CPU time and then switching to another user. The first time-sharing system at M.I.T. was called CTSS (Compatible Time Sharing System). It was a tremendous success and had an enormous impact on future operating systems.

Based on their experience with CTSS, researchers at M.I.T., General Electric, and Bell Labs decided to design a second-generation time-sharing system to be called MULTICS the MULTiplexed Information and Computing System. It was designed to support hundreds of users and run 24 hours a day, 365 days a year, just like the electric power distribution network. That machines as powerful as their GE 645 would be sold as personal computers within 20 years was totally inconceivable at the time.

To make a long story short, building MULTICS was harder than anyone had expected. Bell Labs quit the project and General Electric left the computer business altogether. M.I.T. eventually got the system running, and it ran as a production system at the M.I.T. computer center and a few other sites for a number of years, but the concept of the computer utility never caught on.

Meanwhile, one of the Bell Labs researchers who had been working on the MULTICS project, Ken Thompson, found an abandoned PDP-7 that nobody wanted and decided to write a stripped down version of MULTICS in PDP-7 assembly language. Brian Kernighan somewhat jokingly called this system UNICS, the "UNIplexed Information and Computing System," because it could support only one user, instead of the hundreds that MULTICS was supposed to support. The spelling eventually got changed to UNIX.

Thompson then teamed up with another Bell Labs researcher, Dennis Ritchie, to rewrite the system for a PDP-11 in a new language, called C, invented and implemented by Ritchie. That system was so successful that many universities asked Bell Labs if they could have a copy of it. Bell Labs agreed to license it to universities, and its fame spread far and wide. Many universities taught courses about UNIX. John Lions of the University of New South Wales wrote a little booklet describing the source code line by line.

As UNIX became more popular, Bell Labs and its parent company, AT&T, began to realize that the system had commercial value, so as new releases came out, they came equipped with increasingly restrictive licenses. It was no longer permitted to teach UNIX in classes and it was forbidden to let students have easy access to the source code. This development was perhaps inevitable, but many people pined for the earlier days when there were shorter licenses and fewer restrictions. Since then, AT&T and others have made UNIX much larger and more complicated, and have developed it into a highly successful product.

As a result, there was a void in the area of a simple operating system that was available with source code for educational and other uses, both in academic settings and for use outside the classroom. It was in this environment that I decided to write a new system that would be similar to the UNIX operating system on the outside, but smaller, simpler, and better structured on the inside. Since this system was functionally a subset of the UNIX system, it was called MINIX (for mini-UNIX).

Writing a completely new system from scratch had not only the advantage of avoiding the licensing restrictions, but it also presented another opportunity. The UNIX system was originally written in the early 1970s, before structured programming was widespread. Furthermore, it was originally written for a slow computer, a PDP-7, in assembly language, with the emphasis on squeezing every last drop of performance out of the hardware. Through the years, it has evolved through subsequent versions written by large numbers of people who were not involved in the original design. All this activity has led to a system whose internal organization is less structured than it might otherwise have been.

MINIX, in contrast, was designed and written by a single person (AST) in the late 1980s. Because hardware has gotten much faster, there was much more emphasis on producing a modular system, rather than trying to save every last microsecond. The MINIX file system and memory manager, for example, are not part of the kernel at all, but run as user programs, making it possible to study, modify, and recompile them without even looking at, let alone modifying, the kernel.

As an aside, MINIX is system-call compatible with the *Seventh Edition* (Version 7) of the UNIX operating system for both practical and ideological reasons. On the practical side, I was unable to figure out how to make either 4.3 BSD or System V run on a 256K IBM PC with only 1 floppy disk, one of the design goals. On the ideological front, many people (myself included) strongly believe that Version 7 (the last released version done by Thompson and Ritchie) was not only an improvement on all of its predecessors, but also on all of its successors, certainly in terms of simplicity, coherence and elegance.

For completeness sake, it should be pointed out that MINIX does not implement a small number of Version 7 system calls that are rarely used, such as

ACCT, NICE, PHYS, and PKON. All the major calls are present, however. Similarly, the utility programs provided with MINIX are similar to their Version 7 counterparts. Again, not every program is provided, but nearly all the frequently used ones and some of the less frequently used ones are present.

1.2. THE USER VIEW OF MINIX

In this section, we will briefly look at some of the properties of MINIX as seen by the user. In subsequent sections we will take a look at its internal structure.

1.2.1. The Shell

The MINIX command interpreter is functionally identical to the Version 7 command interpreter, known as the **shell** (or the **Bourne shell** in honor of its inventor, S. R. Bourne). When a user logs in, the shell starts out by displaying the **prompt**, a character such as a dollar sign, which tells the user that the shell is waiting to accept a command. If the user now types

```
date
```

for example, the shell sees to it that the *date* program is run. When *date* finishes, the shell types the prompt again and tries to read the next input line.

The user can specify that standard output be redirected to a file by typing, for example,

```
date >file
```

Similarly, standard input can be redirected, as in

```
sort <file1 >file2
```

which invokes the sort program with input taken from *file1* and output sent to *file2*.

The output of one program can be used as the input for another program by connecting them with a pipe. Thus

```
cat file1 file2 file3 | sort >outfile
```

invokes the *cat* program to concatenate three files and send the output to *sort* to arrange all the lines in alphabetical order. The output of *sort* is redirected to the file *outfile*.

If a user puts an ampersand after a command, the shell does not wait for it to complete. Instead it just gives a prompt immediately. Consequently,

```
cat file1 file2 file3 | sort >outfile &
```

starts up the sort as a background job, allowing the user to continue working normally while the sort is going on.

It is possible to collect several commands together in a file called a **shell script** and have them executed by just typing the name of the shell script. The shell also recognizes some programming constructs, such as *if, for, while*, and *case*, so it is possible to write shell scripts that act like programs. For more information about the MINIX shell, consult any book about the UNIX system because the two shells are indistinguishable to the user (although they are very different internally).

1.2.2. The Editor

MINIX comes with a full-screen editor called *mined*. This program is one of the very few places where MINIX differs from UNIX. The editor that was standard with Version 7, *ed*, was a line-oriented editor designed for use with slow (10 char/sec), hardcopy terminals. Since the time Version 7 was released, many screen editors have been written, the two most popular ones being *vi* and *emacs*. Both of these are huge, have a vast number of commands, and are hard to learn. Neither one fits in with the "small is beautiful" philosophy of MINIX.

With none of the standard editors being appropriate, the only solution was to design a new editor. This editor was inspired by *emacs*, but it much smaller and can be learned in a few minutes. When you type an ordinary ASCII character, that character is inserted on the screen (and in the file being edited) at the position of the cursor. This may sound obvious, but *vi* requires you to first enter a special "insert mode," enter the text, and then leave insert mode.

Commands to the editor, such as moving the cursor or terminating the edit session, are handled by control characters, such as CTRL-F (go forward one word) or by the keys such as the four arrows on the numeric keypad at the right-hand side of the IBM PC keyboard. There are about three dozen commands in all, mostly chosen for their mnemonic value (e.g., CTRL-A moves the cursor to the start of the current line; CTRL-Z moves it to the end of the line).

Some of the commands move the cursor around the screen, scroll the screen forward or backward, or position it at the beginning or end of the file. Other commands delete text around the cursor (e.g., delete the word to the left or right of the cursor, or delete the tail of the current line). There are also commands available to manipulate blocks of text, such as deleting a block of text or saving it in a buffer to be copied to another part of the file. Finally, there are commands for searching forward or backward for a given text pattern, where the text pattern may contain a mixture of ordinary ASCII characters and "wild card" characters for matching sets of characters, end-of-line, and so on. The specific list of editor commands is given in the **mined** section in Chap. 2.

1.2.3. The C Compiler

MINIX comes with a C compiler that accepts programs written in C as described in the Kernighan and Ritchie book. It also accepts many nonstandard features that are commonly used, but gives a warning message about each of them when asked to. The command

```
cc prog.c
```

compiles the program on the file *prog.c* and leaves the executable binary program on a file called *a.out*.

The compiler knows about most of the standard C compiler flags, including **–c** (compile but do not link), **–o** (put the compiler output on a specific file instead of *a.out*), **–D** (define a macro), and **–I** (search a given directory for include files). Like the Version 7 compiler, this one also has a preprocessor for *#define*, *#include*, and *#ifdef* statements.

One minor difference between the MINIX compiler and most other ones is that this one produces *.s* rather than *.o* files as a result of the **–c** flag. Furthermore, the assembler and linker are combined into a single program, *asld*, that reads a list of *.s* files and possibly some library archives, and produces an executable file. The members of the library archives are also *.s* files, although both they and the compiler output are compacted to save time and space. The programs *libpack* and *libupack* are provided to convert assembly language files from ASCII to compact format and back.

1.2.4. Communication with MS-DOS

Like UNIX, MINIX is a complete operating system. It does not require any other operating system to help it. In particular, MINIX users do not need MS-DOS† to help them, just as UNIX users on a VAX do not need VMS* (DEC's operating system for the VAX) to help them.

Nevertheless, some MINIX users may wish to transport files back and forth between MINIX and MS-DOS, so three utility programs have been provided to assist them. (Actually, there is only one program; the three programs described below are just links to the same executable file.) All three utilities reside in */usr/bin* and are invoked in the usual way, by just typing their names and arguments. The first program, *dosdir*, reads an MS-DOS diskette and tells what is on it. The program can also be told to list a specific directory on the diskette.

The second program, *dosread*, reads a file from an MS-DOS diskette and copies it to standard output, which, of course, can be redirected to a file. When the **–a** flag is given, the MS-DOS conventions for ASCII files are converted to the MINIX conventions, so the resulting file appears to be a normal text file.

The third program, *doswrite*, copies its standard input to a diskette containing an MS-DOS file system, again doing format conversion if requested. It does not create directories, however, so all the necessary directories must be in place on the diskette when it is inserted into the drive.

---

† MS-DOS is a trademark of Microsoft, Inc.
* VMS is a trademark of Digital Equipment Corporation

Another way in which MINIX and MS-DOS can co-exist is on the hard disk. It is possible to set up a hard disk with several partitions. Some of these can be allocated as MS-DOS partitions, other ones as MINIX partitions. Files can be moved back and forth by using a diskette as an intermediate device by using *dosread* and *doswrite*.

1.2.5. The Utility Programs

MINIX comes with more than 60 utility programs. One rough grouping is to classify them into five categories as follows:

1. Compiler utilities.
2. File and directory manipulation.
3. Text file processing.
4. System administration.
5. Miscellaneous.

The compiler utilities are programs such as *make*, for keeping track of interdependent source and object files; *ar*, for maintaining libraries; and *size*, for determining the size of the various segments in a binary program.

The file and directory manipulation programs include *cat*, *cp*, *dd*, *mv*, and *pr*, for moving files around; *mkdir*, *rmdir*, and *ls*, for managing directories; and *chmod*, and *chown*, for dealing with protection.

A variety of programs are present for working with text files in addition to the editor, including the well-known filters *grep*, *rev*, *sort*, *tr*, *uniq*, and *wc*. The progam *gres* searches a set of files for a pattern, and replaces occurrences with a given pattern. The MINIX text justifier is *roff*, which has a wide variety of commands for controlling page layout.

Some utility programs deal with system administration. These include *df*, for determining how much space a file system has, *mkfs*, for making new file systems, *mount* and *umount* for attaching and detaching file systems to the main file tree, *passwd* for changing passwords, and *su* for becoming super-user.

The last category is for programs that do not fit in anywhere else. Among these are *date*, for setting and displaying the date and time, *pwd*, for printing the working directory, and *stty*, for setting the terminal parameters.

1.2.6. The Library Procedures

MINIX also comes with over 100 library procedures that can be called from C programs. Like the utilities, these can also be divided into several rough groups:

1. System calls.
2. Standard I/O.
3. Miscellaneous.

The system call procedures allow C programs to issue system calls. There are more than 40 system calls available, including OPEN, READ, WRITE, CLOSE, LSEEK, PIPE, FORK, and EXEC. For each system call, there is a library procedure with exactly the same parameters and results as in Version 7. It should be possible to take almost any C program that runs under Version 7 and compile and run it on MINIX. Furthermore, most reasonable C programs written for other versions of UNIX should also work on MINIX, provided that they do not use any of the more bizarre system calls available in other versions.

The second category is the standard I/O library. All the usual standard I/O calls such as *fopen*, *fread*, *fwrite*, *fclose*, *printf*, *fprintf*, *gets*, *putc*, *putchar*, *puts*, and *fputc* are all present, some as true library procedures and some as macros defined in *stdio.h*, which should be included in C programs that use the standard I/O package, just as in UNIX.

The last category consists of a mixture of other procedures, which span a wide range, from ASCII to binary conversion (*atoi*), memory allocation (*malloc*), string handling (*strcpy*), and temporary file creation (*mktemp*).

1.3. PROCESSES AND FILES IN MINIX

The interface between MINIX and the user programs is defined by the set of system calls that the operating system provides. To really understand what operating systems do, we must examine these calls closely. Before we look at the actual system calls (in Sec. 1.4), however, it worth taking a bird's-eye view of MINIX, to get a general feel for what an operating system is all about.

The MINIX system calls fall roughly in two broad categories: those dealing with processes and those dealing with the file system. We will now examine each of these in turn.

1.3.1. Processes

A key concept in MINIX, and in all operating systems, is the **process**. A process is basically a program in execution. It consists of the executable program, the program's data and stack, its program counter, stack pointer, and other registers, and all the other information needed to run the program.

The easiest way to get a good intuitive feel for a process is to think about time-sharing systems. Periodically, the operating system decides to stop running one process and start running another, for example, because the first one has had more than its share of CPU time in the past second.

When a process is temporarily suspended like this, it must later be restarted in exactly the same state it had when it was stopped. This means that all information about the process must be explicitly saved somewhere during the suspension. For example, if the process has several files open, the exact position in the files where the process was must be recorded somewhere, so that a subsequent

READ given after the process is restarted will read the proper data. In many operating systems, all the information about each process, other than the contents of its own address space, is stored in an operating system table called the **process table**, which is an array (or linked list) of structures, one for each process currently in existence.

Thus, a (suspended) process consists of its address space, usually called the **core image** (in honor of the magnetic core memories used in days of yore), and its process table entry, which contains its registers, among other things.

The key process management system calls are those dealing with the creation and termination of processes. Consider a typical example. The shell reads commands from a terminal. The user has just typed a command requesting that a program be compiled. The shell must now create a new process that will run the compiler. When that process has finished the compilation, it executes a system call to terminate itself.

If a process can create one or more other processes (referred to as **child processes**) and these processes in turn can create child processes, we quickly arrive at the process tree structure of Fig. 1-1.

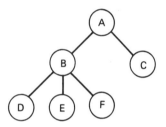

Fig. 1-1. A process tree. Process *A* created two child processes, *B* and *C*. Process *B* created three child processes, *D*, *E*, and *F*.

Other process system calls are available to request more memory (or release unused memory), wait for a child process to terminate, and overlay its program with a different one.

Occasionally, there is a need to convey information to a running process that is not sitting around waiting for it. For example, a process that is communicating with another process on a different computer does so by sending messages over a network. To guard against the possibility that a message or its reply is lost, the sender may request that its own operating system notify it after a specified number of seconds, so that it can retransmit the message if no acknowledgement has been received yet. After setting this timer, the program may continue doing other work.

When the specified number of seconds has elapsed, the operating system sends a **signal** to the process. The signal causes the process to temporarily suspend whatever it was doing, save its registers on the stack, and start running a special signal handling procedure, for example, to retransmit a presumably lost message. When the signal handler is done, the running process is restarted in the state it was just before the signal. Signals are the software analog of hardware interrupts, and can be generated by a variety of causes in addition to timers expiring. Many traps detected by hardware, such as executing an illegal instruction or using an invalid address, are also converted into signals to the guilty process.

Each person authorized to use MINIX is assigned a **uid** (user identification) by the system administrator. Every process started in MINIX has the uid of the person who started it. A child process has the same uid as its parent. One uid, called the **super-user**, has special power, and may violate many of the protection rules. In large installations, only the system administrator knows the password needed to become super-user, but many of the ordinary users (especially students) devote considerable effort to trying to find flaws in the system that allow them to become super-user without the password.

1.3.2. Files

The other broad category of system calls relates to the file system. As noted before, a major function of the operating system is to hide the peculiarities of the disks and other I/O devices, and present the programmer with a nice, clean abstract model of device-independent files. System calls are obviously needed to create files, remove files, read files, and write files. Before a file can be read, it must be opened, and after it has been read it should be closed, so calls are provided to do these things.

In order to provide a place to keep files, MINIX has the concept of a **directory** as a way of grouping files together. A student, for example, might have one directory for each course he was taking (for the programs needed for that course), another directory for his electronic mail, and still another directory for his computer games. System calls are then needed to create and remove directories. Calls are also provided to put an existing file in a directory, and to remove a file from a directory. Directory entries may be either files or other directories. This model also gives rise to a hierarchy—the file system, as shown in Fig. 1-2.

The process and file hierarchies both are organized as trees, but the similarity stops there. Process hierarchies usually are not very deep (more than three levels is unusual), whereas file hierarchies are commonly four, five, or even more levels deep. Process hierarchies are typically short-lived, generally a few minutes at most, whereas the directory hierarchy may exist for years. Ownership and protection also differ for processes and files. Typically, only a parent process may control or even access a child process, but mechanisms nearly always exist to allow files and directories to be read by a wider group than just the owner.

Every file within the directory hierarchy can be specified by giving its **path name** from the top of the directory hierarchy, the **root directory**. Such absolute path names consist of the list of directories that must be traversed from the root directory to get to the file, with slashes separating the components. In Fig. 1-2,

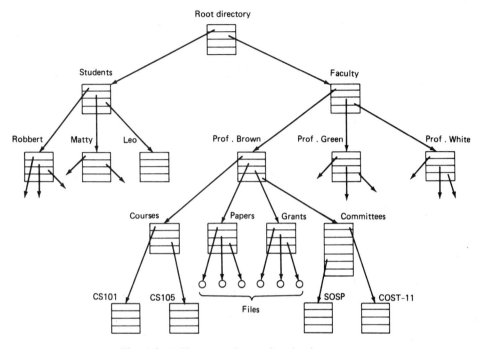

Fig. 1-2. A file system for a university department.

the path for file *CS101* is */Faculty/Prof.Brown/Courses/CS101*. The leading slash indicates that the path is absolute, that is, starting at the root directory.

At every instant, each process has a current **working directory**, in which path names not beginning with a slash are looked for. In Fig. 1-2, if */Faculty/Prof.Brown* were the working directory, then use of the path name *Courses/CS101* would yield the same file as the absolute path name given above. Processes can change their working directory by issuing a system call specifying the new working directory.

Files and directories in MINIX are protected by assigning each one a 9-bit binary protection code. The protection code consists of three 3-bit fields, one for the owner, one for other members of the owner's group (users are divided into groups by the system administrator), and one for everyone else. Each field has a bit for read access, a bit for write access, and a bit for execute access. These 3 bits are known as the **rwx bits**. For example, the protection code *rwxr-x--x* means that the owner can read, write, or execute the file, other group members can read or execute (but not write) the file, and everyone else can execute (but not read or write) the file. For a directory, *x* indicates search permission. A dash means that the corresponding permission is absent.

Before a file can be read or written, it must be opened, at which time the permissions are checked. If the access is permitted, the system returns a small integer called a **file descriptor** to use in subsequent operations. If the access is prohibited, an error code is returned.

Another important concept in MINIX is the mounted file system. Nearly all microcomputers have one or more floppy disk drives into which floppy disks can be inserted and removed. To provide a clean way to deal with these removable media, MINIX allows the file system on a floppy disk to be attached to the main tree. Consider the situation of Fig. 1-3(a). Before the MOUNT call, the RAM disk (simulated disk in main memory) contains the primary, or **root file system**, and drive 0 contains a floppy disk containing another file system.

However, the file system on drive 0 cannot be used, because there is no way to specify path names on it. MINIX does not allow path names to be prefixed by a drive name or number; that would be precisely the kind of device dependence that operating systems ought to eliminate. Instead, the MOUNT system call allows the file system on drive 0 to be attached to the root file system wherever the program wants it to be. In Fig. 1-3(b) the file system on drive 0 has been mounted on directory *b*, thus allowing access to files */b/x* and */b/y*. If directory *b* had contained any files they would not be accessible while drive 0 was mounted, since */b* would refer to the root directory of drive 0. (Not being able to access these files is not as serious as it at first seems: file systems are nearly always mounted on empty directories.)

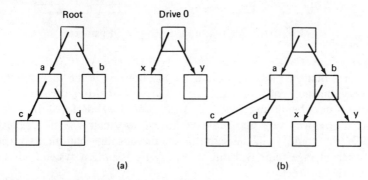

Fig. 1-3. (a) Before mounting, the files on drive 0 are not accessible. (b) After mounting, they are part of the file hierarchy.

Another important concept in MINIX is the **special file**. Special files are provided in order to make I/O devices look like files. That way, they can be read and written using the same system calls as are used for reading and writing files. Two kinds of special files exist: **block special files** and **character special files**. Block special files are used to model devices that consist of a collection of randomly addressable blocks, such as disks. By opening a block special file and reading, say, block 4, a program can directly access the fourth block on the device, without regard to the structure of the file system contained on it. Programs that do system maintenance often need this facility. Access to special files is controlled by the same *rwx* bits used to protect all files, so the power to directly access I/O devices can be restricted to the system administrator, for example.

Character special files are used to model devices that consist of character streams, rather than fixed-size randomly addressable blocks. Terminals, line printers, and network interfaces are typical examples of character special devices. The normal way for a program to read and write on the user's terminal is to read and write the corresponding character special file. When a process is started up, file descriptor 0, called **standard input**, is normally arranged to refer to the terminal for the purpose of reading. File descriptor 1, called **standard output**, refers to the terminal for writing. File descriptor 2, called **standard error**, also refers to the terminal for output, but normally is used only for writing error messages.

All special files have a **major device number** and a **minor device number**. The major device number specifies the device class, such as floppy disk, hard disk, or terminal. The minor device number specifies which of the devices in the class is being addressed, for example, which floppy disk drive. All devices with the same major device number share the same device driver code within the operating system. The minor device number is passed as a parameter to the device driver to tell it which device to read or write. The device numbers can be seen by listing */dev*.

The last feature we will discuss in this overview is one that relates to both processes and files: pipes. A **pipe** is a sort of pseudo-file that can be used to connect two processes together, as shown in Fig. 1-4. When process *A* wants to send data to process *B*, it writes on the pipe as though it were an output file. Process *B* can read the data by reading from the pipe as though it were an input file. Thus, communication between processes in MINIX looks very much like ordinary file reads and writes. Stronger yet, the only way a process can discover that the output file it is writing on is not really a file, but a pipe, is by making a special system call.

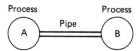

Fig. 1-4. Two processes connected by a pipe.

1.4. SYSTEM CALLS

Armed with our general knowledge of how MINIX deals with processes and files, we can now begin to look at the system calls in detail. To make the system call mechanism clearer, let us take a quick look at READ. It has three parameters, the first one specifying the file, the second one specifying the buffer, and the third one specifying the number of bytes to read. A call to READ from a C program might look like this:

```
count = read(file, buffer, nbytes);
```

The system call (and the library procedure) return the number of bytes actually read in *count*. This value is normally the same as *nbytes*, but may be smaller, if, for example, end-of-file is encountered while reading.

If the system call cannot be carried out, either due to an invalid parameter or a disk error, *count* is set to −1, and the error number is put in a global variable, *errno*. Programs should always check the results of a system call to see if an error occurred.

MINIX has a total of 41 system calls, all of them identical to UNIX V7 calls in terms of name, function, and parameters. They are listed in Fig. 1-5, grouped for convenience in six categories. In the following sections we will briefly examine each call to see what it does. For more detail, see the UNIX manual or one of the books about UNIX that discusses the system calls. To a large extent, the services offered by these calls determine most of what the operating system has to do, since the resource management on personal computers is minimal (at least compared to big machines with many users).

1.4.1. System Calls for Process Management

The first group of calls deals with process management. FORK is a good place to start the discussion. FORK is the only way to create a new process. It creates an exact duplicate of the original process, including all the file descriptors, registers—everything. After the FORK, the original process and the copy (the parent and child) go their separate ways. All the variables have identical values at the time of the FORK, but since the entire parent core image is copied to create the child, subsequent changes in one of them do not affect the other one. The FORK call returns a value, which is zero in the child, and equal to the child's process identifier or **pid** in the parent. Using the returned pid, the two processes can see which is the parent and which is the child.

In most cases, after a FORK, the child will need to execute different code from the parent. Consider the case of the shell. It reads a command from the terminal, forks off a child process, waits for the child to execute the command and then reads the next command when the child terminates. To wait for the child to finish, the parent executes a WAIT system call, which just waits until the child terminates (any child if more than one exists). WAIT has one parameter, the address of a variable that will be set to the child's exit status (normal or abnormal termination and exit value).

In the case of the shell, the child process must execute the command typed by the user. It does this by using the EXEC system call, which causes its entire core image to be replaced by the file named in its first parameter. A highly simplified shell illustrating the use of FORK, WAIT, and EXEC is shown in Fig. 1-6.

```
Process Management
pid = fork( ) — create a child process identical to the parent
s = wait(&status) — wait for a child to terminate and get its exit status
s = execve(name,argv,envp) — replace a process' core image
exit(status) — terminate process execution and return exit status
size = brk(addr) — set the size of the data segment to "addr"
pid = getpid( ) — return the caller's process id

Signals
oldfunc = signal(sig,func) — arrange for some signal to be caught, ignored etc.
s = kill(pid, sig) — send a signal to a process
residual = alarm(seconds) — schedule a SIGALRM signal after a certain time
s = pause( ) — suspend the caller until the next signal

File Management
fd = creat(name,mode) — create a new file or truncate an existing file
fd = mknod(name,mode,addr) — create a regular, special, or directory i-node
fd = open(file,how) — open a file for reading, writing or both
s = close(fd) — close an open file
n = read(fd,buffer,nbytes) — read data from a file into a buffer
n = write(fd,buffer,nbytes) — write data from a file into a buffer
pos = lseek(fd,offset,whence) — move the file pointer somewhere in the file
s = stat(name,&buf) — read and return a file's status from its i-node
s = fstat(fd,buf) — read and return a file's status from its i-node
fd = dup(fd1) — allocate another file descriptor for an open file
s = pipe(&fd[0]) — create a pipe
s = ioctl(fd,request,argp) — perform special operations on special files

Directory and File System Management
s = link(name1,name2) — create a new directory entry, name2,for file name1
s = unlink(name) — remove a directory entry
s = mount(special,name,rwflag) — mount a file system
s = umount(special) — unmount a file system
s = sync( ) — flush all disk blocks cached in memory to the disk
s = chdir(dirname) — change the working directory
s = chroot(dirname) — change the root directory

Protection
s = chmod(name,mode) — change the protection bits associated with a file
uid = getuid( ) — get the caller's uid
gid = getgid( ) — get the caller's gid
s = setuid(uid) — set the caller's uid
s = setgid(gid) — set the caller's gid
s = chown(name,owner,group) — change a file's owner and group
oldmask = umask(complmode) — set a mask used to mask off protection bits

Time Management
seconds = time(&seconds) — get the elapsed time in seconds since Jan. 1, 1970
s = stime(tp) — set the elapsed time since Jan. 1, 1970
s = utime(file, timep) — set the "last access" time for the file
s = times(buffer) — get the user and system times used so far
```

Fig. 1-5. The MINIX system calls. The return code s is -1 if an error has occurred; fd is a file descriptor, n is a byte count. The other return codes are what the name suggests.

In the most general case, EXEC has three parameters: the name of the file to be executed, a pointer to the argument array, and a pointer to the environment array. These will be described shortly. Various library routines, including *execl*, *execv*, *execle*, and *execve* are provided to allow the parameters to be omitted or specified in various ways. Throughout this book we will use the name EXEC to represent the system call invoked by all of these.

```
while (TRUE) {                                /* repeat forever */
     read_command(command, parameters);       /* read input from terminal */

     if (fork() != 0) {                       /* fork off child process */
            wait(&status);                    /* parent code */
     } else {
            execve(command, parameters, 0);   /* child  code */
     }
}
```

Fig. 1-6. A stripped-down shell. Throughout this book, *TRUE* is assumed to be defined as the constant 1, thus providing for an infinite loop.

Let us consider the case of a command such as

```
cp file1 file2
```

used to copy *file1* to *file2*. After the shell has forked, the child locates and executes the file *cp* and passes it information about the files to be copied.

The main program of *cp* (and many other programs) contains the declaration

```
main(argc, argv, envp)
```

where *argc* is a count of the number of items on the command line, including the program name. For the example above, *argc* is 3.

The second parameter, *argv*, is a pointer to an array. Element *i* of that array is a pointer to the *i*-th string on the command line. In our example, *argv*[0] would point to the string "cp." (As an aside, the string pointed to contains *two* characters, a "c" and a "p," although, if you look closely at the previous sentence you will also see a period inside the quotes. The period ends the sentence, but the rules of English punctuation require most punctuation marks to be *inside* the quotes, even though this is totally illogical. Hopefully, this will not cause any confusion.) Similarly, *argv*[1] would point to the 5-character string "file1" and *argv*[2] would point to the 5-character string "file2."

The third parameter of *main*, *envp*, is a pointer to the environment, an array of strings of the form *name = value* used to pass information such as the terminal type and home directory name to a program. In Fig. 1-6, no environment is passed to the child, so the third parameter of *execve* is a zero.

If EXEC seems complicated, do not despair; it is the most complex system call. All the rest are much simpler. As an example of a simple one, consider EXIT, which processes should use when they are finished executing. It has one parameter, the exit status (0 to 255), which is returned to the parent in the variable *status* of the WAIT system call. The low-order byte of *status* contains the termination status, with 0 being normal termination and the other values being various error conditions. The high-order byte contains the child's exit status (0 to 255). For example, if a parent process executes the statement

```
n = wait(&status);
```

it will be suspended until some child process terminates. If the child exits with, say, 4 as the parameter to *exit*, the parent will be awakened with *n* set to the child's pid and *status* set to 0x0400 (the C convention of prefixing hexadecimal constants with 0x will be used throughout this book).

Processes in MINIX have their memory divided up into three segments: the **text segment** (i.e., the program code), the **data segment**, and the **stack segment**. The data segment grows upward and the stack grows downward, as shown in Fig. 1-7. Between them is a gap of unused address space. The stack grows into the gap automatically, as needed, but expansion of the data segment is done explicitly by using the BRK system call. It has one parameter, giving the address where the data segment is to end. This address may be more than the current value (data segment is growing) or less than the current value (data segment is shrinking). The parameter must, of course, be less than the stack pointer or the data and stack segments would overlap, something that is forbidden. MINIX supports separate instruction and data spaces, so a program on the IBM PC, for example, can have 64K bytes of text and another 64K bytes for the data and stack segments combined, for a total of 128K bytes for text, data, and stack, total.

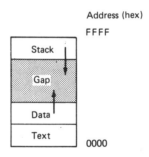

Fig. 1-7. Processes have three segments: text, data, and stack. In this example, all three are in one address space, but separate instruction and data space is also supported.

As a convenience to the programmer, a library routine *sbrk* is provided that also changes the size of the data segment, only its parameter is the number of bytes to add to the data segment (negative parameters make the data segment smaller). It works by keeping track of the current size of the data segment, which is the value returned by BRK, computing the new size, and making a call asking for that number of bytes.

The last process system call is also the simplest, GETPID. It just returns the caller's pid. Remember that in FORK, only the parent was given the child's pid. If the child wants to find out its own pid, it must use GETPID. A common use of GETPID is generating unique names for temporary files. A compiler that needs a scratch file, for example, can create a file whose name is the caller's pid. If two instances of the compiler are running at once, they will use different files.

1.4.2. System Calls for Signaling

Certain situations exist in which processes need to handle software interrupts. For example, if a user accidently tells a text editor to print the entire contents of a very long file, and then realizes the error, some way is needed to interrupt the editor. In MINIX, the user can hit the DEL key on the keyboard, which sends a signal to the editor. The editor catches the signal and stops the print-out. Signals can also be used to report certain traps detected by the hardware, such as illegal instruction or floating point overflow.

When a signal is sent to a process that has not announced its willingness to accept that signal, the process is simply killed without further ado. To avoid this fate, a process can use the SIGNAL system call to announce that it is prepared to accept some signal type, and to provide the address of the signal handling procedure. After a SIGNAL call, if a signal of the relevant type (e.g., the DEL key) is generated, the state of the process is pushed onto its own stack, and then the signal handler is called. It may run for as long as it wants to and perform any system calls it wants to. In practice, though, signal handlers are usually fairly short. When the signal handling procedure is done, it just returns in the usual way. The run time system in the user's address space then restores the process' state from the stack and continues execution from the point where it was interrupted.

The signal types are shown in Fig. 1-8. The ones in parentheses are UNIX signals that are not supported by MINIX, mostly because they are not generated by the IBM PC hardware. They are easy to add, however, if the need arises in the future.

(1)	SIGHUP	Modem has detected broken phone connection
2	SIGINT	DEL key has been hit on keyboard
3*	SIGQUIT	Quit signal from keyboard
(4)*	SIGILL	Illegal instruction
(5)*	SIGTRAP	Trace trap
(6)*	SIGIOT	IOT instruction
(7)*	SIGEMT	EMT instruction
(8)*	SIGFPE	Floating point overflow/underflow
9	SIGKILL	Kill
(10)*	SIGBUS	Bus error
(11)*	SIGSEGV	Segmentation violation
(12)*	SIGSYS	Bad argument to system call
13	SIGPIPE	Write on pipe with no reader
14	SIGALRM	Alarm
15	SIGTERM	Software generated termination signal
16	unassigned	

Fig. 1-8. Signal types. The signals in parentheses are not supported by MINIX. The asterisks denote signals that cause core dumps if not caught or ignored.

After a signal has been caught, it is necessary to re-enable the signal catching with another SIGNAL call. If another signal of the same type arrives before the signal catching has been re-enabled, the default action is taken (i.e.,the process is killed). If you try very hard, you may be able to hit DEL fast enough in succession to cause the shell to get a second signal before it has finished processing the first one, thus killing the shell (and logging yourself out).

Instead of providing a function to catch a signal, the program may also specify the constant SIG_IGN to have all subsequent signals of the specified type ignored, or SIG_DFL to restore the default action of killing the process when a signal occurs. As an example of how SIG_IGN is used, consider what happens when the shell forks off a background process as a result of

```
command &
```

It would be undesirable for a DEL signal from the keyboard to affect the background process, so after the FORK but before the EXEC, the shell does

```
signal(SIGINT, SIG_IGN);
```

and

```
signal(SIGQUIT, SIG_IGN);
```

to disable the DEL and quit signals. (The quit signal is generated by CTRL-\; it is the same as DEL except that if it is not caught or ignored, it makes a core dump of the process killed.) For foreground processes (no ampersand), these signals are not ignored.

Hitting the DEL key is not the only way to send a signal. The KILL system call allows a process to signal another process (provided they have the same uid—unrelated processes cannot signal each other). Getting back to the example of background processes used above, suppose a background process is started up, but later it is decided that the process should be terminated. SIGINT and SIGQUIT have been disabled, so something else is needed. The solution is to use the *kill* program, which uses the KILL system call to send a signal to any process. By sending signal 9 (SIGKILL), to a background process, that process can be killed. SIGKILL cannot be caught or ignored.

For many real-time applications, a process needs to be interrupted after a specific time interval to do something, such as to retransmit a potentially lost packet over an unreliable communication line. To handle this situation, the ALARM system call has been provided. The parameter specifies an interval, in seconds, after which a SIGALRM signal is sent to the process. A process may only have one alarm outstanding at any instant. If an ALARM call is made with a parameter of 10 seconds, and then 3 seconds later another ALARM call is made with a parameter of 20 seconds, only one signal will be generated, 20 seconds after the second call. The first signal is canceled by the second call to ALARM. If the parameter to ALARM is zero, any pending alarm signal is canceled. If an alarm signal is not caught, the default action is taken and the signaled process is killed. Technically, alarm signals may be ignored, but that is a pointless thing to do.

It sometimes occurs that a process has nothing to do until a signal arrives.

For example, consider a computer aided instruction program that is testing reading speed and comprehension. It displays some text on the screen and then calls ALARM to signal it after 30 seconds. While the student is reading the text, the program has nothing to do. It could sit in a tight loop doing nothing, but that would waste CPU time that a background process or other user might need. A better solution is to use the PAUSE system call, which tells MINIX to suspend the process until the next signal arrives.

1.4.3. System Calls for File Management

Many system calls relate to files and the file system. In this section we will look at the system calls that operate on individual files; in the next one we will examine those that involve directories or the file system as a whole. To create a new file, the CREAT call is used (why the call is CREAT and not CREATE has been lost in the mists of time). Its parameters provide the name of the file and the protection mode. Thus

```
fd = creat("abc", 0751);
```

creates a file called *abc* with mode 0751 octal (in C, a leading zero means that a constant is in octal). The low-order 9 bits of 0751 specify the *rwx* bits for the owner (7 means read-write-execute permission), his group (5 means read-execute), and others (1 means execute only).

CREAT not only creates a new file, but also opens it for writing, regardless of the file's mode. The file descriptor returned, *fd*, can be used to write the file. If a CREAT is done on an existing file, that file is truncated to length 0, provided, of course, that the permissions are all right.

Special files are created using MKNOD rather than CREAT. A typical call is

```
fd = mknod("/dev/tty2", 020744, 0x0402);
```

which creates a file named */dev/tty2* (the usual name for terminal 2), and gives it mode 020744 octal (a directory with protection bits *rwxr--r--*). The third parameter contains the major device (4) in the high-order byte and the minor device (2) in the low-order byte. The major device could have been anything, but a file named */dev/tty2* ought to be minor device 2. Calls to MKNOD fail unless the caller is the super-user.

To read or write an existing file, the file must first be opened using OPEN. This call specifies the file name to be opened, either as an absolute path name or relative to the working directory, and a code of 0, 1, or 2, meaning open for reading, writing, or both. The file descriptor returned can then be used for reading or writing. Afterward, the file can be closed by CLOSE, which makes the file descriptor available for reuse on a subsequent CREAT or OPEN.

The most heavily used calls are undoubtedly READ and WRITE. We saw READ earlier. WRITE has the same parameters.

Although most programs read and write files sequentially, for some applications programs need to be able to access any part of a file at random. Associated with each file is a pointer that indicates the current position in the file. When reading (writing) sequentially, it normally points to the next byte to be read (written). The LSEEK call changes the value of the position pointer, so that subsequent calls to READ or WRITE can begin anywhere in the file, or even beyond the end of it.

LSEEK has three parameters: the first one is the file descriptor for the file, the second one is a file position, and the third one tells whether the file position is relative to the beginning of the file, the current position, or the end of the file. The value returned by LSEEK is the absolute position in the file after the file pointer was changed.

For each file, MINIX keeps track of the file mode (regular file, special file, directory, and so on), size, time of last modification, and other information. Programs can ask to see this information via the STAT and FSTAT system calls. These differ only in that the former specifies the file by name, whereas the latter takes a file descriptor, making it useful for inherited files whose names are not known. Both calls provide as the second parameter a pointer to a structure where the information is to be put. The structure is shown in Fig. 1-9. In MINIX the three times are identical. Three of them are provided for compatibility with UNIX, where they are different.

```
struct stat {
    short st_dev;              /* device where i-node belongs */
    unsigned short st_ino;     /* i-node number */
    unsigned short st_mode;    /* mode word */
    short st_nlink;            /* number of links */
    short st_uid;              /* user id */
    short st_gid;              /* group id */
    short st_rdev;             /* major/minor device for special files */
    long st_size;              /* file size */
    long st_atime;             /* same as st_mtime */
    long st_mtime;             /* time of last modification */
    long st_ctime;             /* same as st_mtime */
};
```

Fig. 1-9. The structure used to return information for the STAT and FSTAT system calls. Three times are present for UNIX compatibility.

When manipulating file descriptors, the DUP call is occasionally helpful. Consider, for example, a program that needs to close standard output (file descriptor 1), substitute another file as standard output, call a function that writes some output onto standard output, and then restore the original situation. Just closing file descriptor 1 and then opening a new file will make the new file standard output (assuming standard input, file descriptor 0, is in use), but it will be impossible to restore the original situation later.

The solution is first to execute the statement

```
fd = dup(1);
```

which uses the DUP system call to allocate a new file descriptor, *fd*, and arrange for it to correspond to the same file as standard output. Then standard output can be closed and a new file opened and used. When it is time to restore the original situation, file descriptor 1 can be closed, and then

```
n = dup(fd);
```

executed to assign the lowest file descriptor, namely, 1, to the same file as *fd*. Finally, *fd* can be closed and we are back where we started.

The DUP call has a variant that allows an arbitrary unassigned file descriptor to be made to refer to a given open file. It is called by

```
dup2(fd, fd2);
```

where *fd* refers to an open file and *fd2* is the unassigned file descriptor that is to be made to refer to the same file as *fd*. Thus if *fd* refers to standard input (file descriptor 0) and *fd2* is 4, after the call, file descriptors 0 and 4 will both refer to standard input.

Interprocess communication in MINIX uses pipes, as described earlier. When a user types

```
cat filel file2 | sort
```

the shell creates a pipe and arranges for standard output of the first process to write to the pipe, so standard input of the second process can read from it. The PIPE system call creates a pipe and returns two file descriptors, one for writing and one for reading. The call is

```
pipe(&fd[0]);
```

where *fd* is an array of two integers and *fd* [0] is the file descriptor for reading and *fd* [1] is the one for writing.

Figure 1-10 depicts a skeleton procedure that creates two processes, with the output of the first one piped into the second one. (A more realistic example would do error checking and handle arguments.) First a pipe is created, and then the procedure forks, with the parent eventually becoming the first process in the pipeline and the child process becoming the second one. Since the files to be executed, *process1* and *process2*, do not know that they are part of a pipeline, it is essential that the file descriptors be manipulated so that the first process' standard output be the pipe and the second one's standard input be the pipe. The parent first closes off the file descriptor for reading from the pipe. Then it closes standard output and does a DUP call that allows file descriptor 1 to write on the pipe. It is important to realize that DUP always returns the lowest available file descriptor, in this case, 1. Then the program closes the other pipe file descriptor.

After the EXEC call, the process started will have file descriptors 0 and 2 be unchanged, and file descriptor 1 for writing on the pipe. The child code is analogous. The parameter to *execl* is repeated because the first one is the file to be executed and the second one is the first parameter, which most programs expect to be the file name.

```
#define STD_INPUT   0          /* file descriptor for standard input */
#define STD_OUTPUT  1          /* file descriptor for standard output */

pipeline(process1, process2)
char *process1, *process2;     /* pointers to program names */
{
  int fd[2];

  pipe(&fd[0]);                /* create a pipe */
  if (fork() != 0) {
        /* The parent process executes these statements. */
        close(fd[0]);          /* process 1 does not need to read from pipe */
        close(STD_OUTPUT);     /* prepare for new standard output */
        dup(fd[1]);            /* set standard output to fd[1] */
        close(fd[1]);          /* pipe not needed any more */
        execl(process1, process1, 0);
  } else {
        /* The child process executes these statements. */
        close(fd[1]);          /* process 2 does not need to write to pipe */
        close(STD_INPUT);      /* prepare for new standard input */
        dup(fd[0]);            /* set standard input to fd[0] */
        close(fd[0]);          /* pipe not needed any more */
        execl(process2, process2, 0);
  }
}
```

Fig. 1-10. A skeleton for setting up a two-process pipeline.

The last system call we will describe in this section, IOCTL, is applicable only to special character files, primarily terminals. It is used to change the characters used for correcting typing errors on the terminal, changing the terminal mode, and so forth. In **cooked mode**, the erase and kill characters work normally, CRTL-S and CRTL-Q can be used for stopping and starting terminal output, CTRL-D means end of file, DEL generates an interrupt signal, and CRTL-\ generates a quit signal to force a core dump.

In **raw mode**, all of these functions are disabled; every character is passed directly to the program with no special processing. Furthermore, in raw mode, a read from the terminal will give the program any characters that have been typed, even a partial line, rather than waiting for a complete line as in cooked mode.

Cbreak mode is in between. The erase and kill characters for editing are disabled, as is CRTL-D, but CRTL-S, CTRL-Q, DEL, and CTRL-\ are enabled. Like raw mode, partial lines can be returned to programs (if intraline editing is turned off, there is no need to wait until a whole line has been received—the user cannot change his mind and delete it, as he can in cooked mode).

IOCTL has three parameters, for example

```
ioctl(fd, TIOCSETP, &sgttyb);
```

The first parameter specifies a file, the second one specifies an operation, and the third one is the address of a structure containing various flags. MINIX supports the operation TIOCSETP for setting the terminal parameters to the values in the structure, and TIOCGETP for filling the structure with the current values. The structure is defined in the header file *sgtty.h*, as shown in Fig. 1-11.

```
/* Data structures for IOCTL calls TIOCGETP/TIOCSETP calls. */

struct sgttyb {
  char sg_ispeed;              /* input speed (not used at present) */
  char sg_ospeed;             /* output speed (not used at present) */
  char sg_erase;              /* erase character */
  char sg_kill;               /* kill character */
  int  sg_flags;              /* mode flags */
};

/* Fields in sg_flags. */
#define XTABS       0006000   /* set to cause tab expansion */
#define RAW         0000040   /* set to enable raw mode */
#define CRMOD       0000020   /* set to map lf to cr + lf */
#define ECHO        0000010   /* set to enable echoing of typed input */
#define CBREAK      0000002   /* set to enable cbreak mode */
#define COOKED      0000000   /* neither CBREAK nor RAW */

#define TIOCGETP (('t'<<8) | 8)
#define TIOCSETP (('t'<<8) | 9)
```

Fig. 1-11. The data structure used as the third parameter in IOCTL.

Bits in *sg_flags* can be set to enter raw or cbreak mode. The XTABS bit should be turned on to have MINIX replace tabs on output with the proper number of spaces. CRMOD should normally be on to cause line feeds sent to the terminal to also produce carriage returns. Finally, ECHO should be turned on to have the terminal echo characters, except when passwords and other secrets are being typed in.

IOCTL also has another call with an analogous structure, *tchars*, for changing the interrupt character, quit character, terminal start and stop characters, and terminal end-of-file character.

1.4.4. System Calls for Directory Management

In this section we will look at some system calls that relate more to directories or the file system as a whole, rather than just to one specific file as in the previous section. LINK is a good place to start. Although it only refers to one file, it does so under two path names. The purpose of LINK is to allow the same file to appear under two or more names, often in different directories. A typical use is to allow several members of the same programming team to share a common file, with each of them having the file appear in his own directory, possibly under different names. Sharing a file is not the same as giving every team member a private copy, because having a shared file means that changes that any member of the team makes are instantly visible to the other members—there is only one file. When copies are made of a file, subsequent changes made to one copy do not affect the other ones.

To see how LINK works, consider the situation of Fig. 1-12(a). Here are two users, *ast* and *jim*, each having their own directories with some files. If ast now executes a program containing the system call

```
link("/usr/jim/memo", "/usr/ast/note");
```

the file *memo* in *jim*'s directory is now entered into *ast*'s directory under the name *note*.

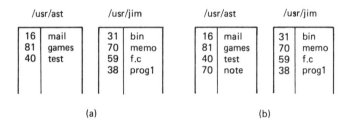

Fig. 1-12. (a) Two directories before linking */usr/jim/memo* to ast's directory. (b) The same directories after linking.

Understanding how LINK works will probably make it clearer what it does. Every file in MINIX has a unique number, its i-number, that identifies it. A directory is simply a file containing a set of (i-number, ASCII name) pairs. In Fig. 1-12, *mail* has i-number 16, and so on. What LINK does is simply create a new directory entry with a (possibly new) name, using the i-number of an existing file. In Fig. 1-12(b), two entries have the same i-number (70), and thus refer to the same file. If either one is later removed, using the UNLINK system call, the other one remains. If both are removed, MINIX sees that no entries to the file exist (a field in the i-node keeps track of the number of directory entries pointing to the file), so the file is removed from the disk.

As we have mentioned earlier, the MOUNT system call allows two file systems to be merged into one. A common situation is to have the **root file system**, containing the binary (executable) versions of the common commands and other heavily used files, on the RAM disk. The user can then insert a floppy disk, for example, containing user programs, into drive 0.

By executing the MOUNT system call, the drive 0 file system can be attached to the root file system, as shown in Fig. 1-13. A typical statement in C to perform the mount is

```
mount("/dev/fd0", "/mnt", 0);
```

where the first parameter is the name of a block special file for drive 0 and the second parameter is the place in the tree where it is to be mounted.

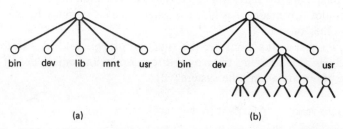

(a)   (b)

Fig. 1-13. (a) File system before the mount. (b) File system after the mount.

After the MOUNT call, a file on drive 0 can be accessed by just using its path from the root directory or the working directory, without regard to which drive it is on. In fact, second, third and fourth drives can also be mounted anywhere in the tree. The MOUNT command makes it possible to integrate removable media into a single integrated file hierarchy, without having to worry about which device a file is on. Although this example involves floppy disks, hard disks or portions of hard disks (often called **partitions** or **minor devices**) can also be mounted this way. When a file system is no longer needed, it can be unmounted with the UMOUNT system call.

MINIX maintains a cache of recently used blocks in main memory to avoid having to read them from the disk if they are used again quickly. If a block in the cache is modified (by a WRITE on a file) and the system crashes before the modified block is written out to disk, the file system will be damaged. To limit the potential damage, it is important to flush the cache periodically, so that the amount of data lost by a crash will be small. The system call SYNC tells MINIX to write out all the cache blocks that have been modified since being read in. When MINIX is started up, a program called *update* is started as a background process to do a SYNC every 30 seconds, to keep flushing the cache.

Two other calls that relate to directories are CHDIR and CHROOT. The former changes the working directory and the latter changes the root directory. After the call

```
chdir("/usr/ast/test");
```

an open on the file *xyz* will open */usr/ast/test/xyz*. CHROOT works in an analogous way. Once a process has told the system to change its root directory, all absolute path names (path names beginning with a "/") will start at the new root. Only super-users may execute CHROOT, and even super-users do not do it very often.

1.4.5. System Calls for Protection

In MINIX every file has an 11-bit mode used for protection. Nine of these bits are the read-write-execute bits for the owner, group and others. The CHMOD system call makes it possible to change the mode of a file. For example, to make a file read-only by everyone except the owner, one could execute

```
chmod("file", 0644);
```

The other two protection bits, 02000 and 04000, are the SETGID (set-group-id) and SETUID (set-user-id) bits, respectively. When any user executes a program with the SETUID bit on, for the duration of that process the user's effective uid is changed to that of the file's owner. This feature is heavily used to allow users to execute programs that perform super-user only functions, such as creating directories. Creating a directory uses MKNOD, which is for the super-user only. By arranging for the *mkdir* program to be owned by the superuser and have mode 04755, ordinary users can be given the power to execute MKNOD but in a highly restricted way.

When a process executes a file that has the SETUID or SETGID bit on in its mode, it acquires an effective uid or gid different from its real uid or gid. It is sometimes important for a process to find out what its real and effective uid or gid is. The system calls GETUID and GETGID have been provided to supply this information. Each call returns both the real and effective uid or gid, so four library routines are needed to extract the proper information: *getuid*, *getgid*, *geteuid*, and *getegid*. The first two get the real uid/gid, and the last two the effective ones.

Ordinary users cannot change their uid, except by executing programs with the SETUID bit on, but the super-user has another possibility: the SETUID system call, which sets both the effective and real uids. SETGID sets both gids. The super-user can also change the owner of a file with the CHOWN system call. In short, the super-user has plenty of opportunity for violating all the protection rules, which explains why so many students devote so much of their time to trying to become super-user.

The last two system calls in this category can be executed by ordinary user processes. The first one, UMASK, sets an internal bit mask within the system, which is used to mask off mode bits when a file is created. After the call

```
umask(022);
```

the mode supplied by CREAT and MKNOD will have the 022 bits masked off before being used. Thus the call

```
creat("file", 0777);
```

will set the mode to 0755 rather than 0777. Since the bit mask is inherited by child processes, if the shell does a UMASK just after login, none of the user's processes will accidently create files that other people can write on.

When a program owned by the root has the SETUID bit on, it can access any file, because its effective uid is the super-user. Frequently it is useful for the program to know if the person who called the program has permission to access a given file. If the program just tries the access, it will always succeed, and thus learn nothing.

What is needed is a way to see if the access is permitted for the real uid. The ACCESS system call provides a way to find out. The *mode* parameter is 4 to check for read access, 2 for write access, and 1 for execute access. Combinations are also allowed, for example, with *mode* equal to 6, the call returns 0 if both read and write access are allowed for the real uid; otherwise −1 is returned. With *mode* equal to 0, a check is made to see if the file exists and the directories leading up to it can be searched.

1.4.6. System Calls for Time Management

MINIX has four system calls that involve the time-of-day clock. TIME just returns the current time in seconds, with 0 corresponding to Jan. 1, 1970 at midnight (just as the day was starting, not ending). Of course the system clock must be set at some point in order to allow it to be read later, so STIME has been provided to let the clock be set (by the super-user). The third time call is UTIME, which allows the owner of a file (or the super-user) to change the time stored in a file's inode. Application of this system call is fairly limited, but a few programs need it, for example, *touch*, which sets the file's time to the current time. Finally, we have TIMES, which returns the accounting information to a process, so it can see how much CPU time it has used directly, and how much CPU time the system itself has expended on its behalf. The accumulated user and system times for its children are also returned.

1.5. HOW MINIX WORKS INSIDE

In this section we will give an outline of how MINIX is structured internally. We will look at the various parts and see how they relate to one another. In succeeding chapters we will come back to the individual pieces in more detail.

1.5.1. The MINIX System Architecture

UNIX is organized as a single executable program that is loaded into memory at system boot time and then run. MINIX is structured in a much more modular way, with the operating system itself being a collection of processes that communicate with each other and with user processes by sending and receiving messages. There are separate processes for the memory manager, the file system, for each device driver, and for certain other system functions. This structure enforces a better interface between the pieces. The file system cannot, for example, accidentally change the memory manager's tables because the file system and memory manager each have their own private address spaces.

These system processes are each full-fledged processes, with their own memory allocation, process table entry and state. They can be run, blocked, and send messages, just as the user processes. In fact, the memory manager and file system each run in user space as ordinary processes. The device drivers are all linked together with the kernel into the same binary program, but they communicate with each other and with the other processes by message passing.

When the system is compiled, four binary programs are independently created: the kernel (including the driver processes), the memory manager, the file system, and *init* (which reads */etc/ttys* and forks off the login processes). In other words, compiling the system results in four distinct *a.out* files. When the system is booted, all four of these are read into memory from the boot diskette.

It is possible, and in fact, normal, to modify, recompile, and relink, say, the file system, without having to relink the other three pieces. This design provides a high degree of modularity by dividing the system up into independent pieces, each with a well-defined function and interface to the other pieces. The pieces communicate by sending and receiving messages.

The various processes are structured in four layers:

4. The user processes (top layer).
3. The server processes (memory manager and file system).
2. The device drivers, one process per device.
1. Process and message handling (bottom layer).

Let us now briefly summarize the function of each layer.

Layer 1 is concerned with doing process management including CPU scheduling and interprocess communication. When a process does a SEND or RECEIVE, it traps to the kernel, which then tries to execute the command. If the command cannot be executed (e.g., a process does a RECEIVE and there are no messages waiting for it), the caller is blocked until the command can be executed, at which time the process is reactivated. When an interrupt occurs, layer 1 converts it into a message to the appropriate device driver, which will normally be blocked waiting for it. The decision about which process to run when is also made in layer 1. A priority algorithm is used, giving device drivers higher priority over ordinary user processes, for example.

Layer 2 contains the device drivers, one process per major device. These processes are part of the kernel's address space because they must run in kernel mode to access I/O device registers and execute I/O instructions. Although the IBM PC does not have user mode/kernel mode, most other machines do, so this decision has been made with an eye toward the future. To distinguish the processes within the kernel from those in user space, the kernel processes are called **tasks**.

Layer 3 contains only two processes, the memory manager and the file system. They are both structured as **servers**, with the user processes as **clients**. When a user process (i.e., a client) wants to execute a system call, it calls, for example, the library procedure *read* with the file descriptor, buffer, and count. The library procedure builds a message containing the system call number and the parameters and sends it to the file system. The client then blocks waiting for a reply. When the file system receives the message, it carries it out and sends back a reply containing the number of bytes read or the error code. The library procedure gets the reply and returns the result to the caller in the usual way. The user is completely unaware of what is going on here, making it easy to replace the local file system with a remote one.

Layer 4 contains the user programs. When the system comes up, *init* forks off login processes, which then wait for input. On a successful login, the shell is executed. Processes can fork, resulting in a tree of processes, with *init* at the root. When CTRL-D is typed to a shell, it exits, and *init* replaces the shell with another login process.

1.5.2. Layer 1 – Processes and Messages

The two basic concepts on which MINIX is built are processes and messages. A process is an independently schedulable entity with its own process table entry. A message is a structure containing the sender's process number, a message type field, and a variable part (a union) containing the parameters or reply codes of the message. Message size is fixed, depending on how big the union happens to be on the machine in question. On the IBM PC it is 24 bytes.

Three kernel calls are provided:

- RECEIVE(source, &message)
- SEND(destination, &message)
- SENDREC(process, &message)

These are the only true system calls (i.e., traps to the kernel). RECEIVE announces the willingness of the caller to accept a message from a specified process, or ANY, if the RECEIVER will accept any message. (From here on, "process" also includes the tasks.) If no message is available, the receiving process is blocked. SEND attempts to transmit a message to the destination process. If the destination process is currently blocked trying to receive from the sender, the kernel copies the message from the sender's buffer to the receiver's buffer, and then marks them both as runnable. If the receiver is not waiting for a message from the sender, the sender is blocked.

The SENDREC primitive combines the functions of the other two. It sends a message to the indicated process, and then blocks until a reply has been received. The reply overwrites the original message. User processes use SENDREC to execute system calls by sending messages to the servers and then blocking until the reply arrives.

There are two ways to enter the kernel. One way is by the trap resulting from a process' attempt to send or receive a message. The other way is by an interrupt. When an interrupt occurs, the registers and machine state of the currently running process are saved in its process table entry. Then a general interrupt handler is called with the interrupt number as parameter. This procedure builds a message of type INTERRUPT, copies it to the buffer of the waiting task, marks that task as runnable (unblocked), and then calls the scheduler to see who to run next.

The scheduler maintains three queues, corresponding to layers 2, 3, and 4, respectively. The driver queue has the highest priority, the server queue has middle priority, and the user queue has lowest priority. The scheduling algorithm is simple: find the highest priority queue that has at least one process on it, and run the first process on that queue. In this way, a clock interrupt will cause a process switch if the file system was running, but not if the disk driver was running. If the disk driver was running, the clock task will be put at the end of the highest priority queue, and run when its turn comes.

In addition to this rule, once every 100 msec, the clock task checks to see if the current process is a user process that has been running for at least 100 msec. If so, that user is removed from the front of the user queue and put on the back. In effect, compute bound user processes are run using a round robin scheduler. Once started, a user process runs until either it blocks trying to send or receive a message, or it has had 100 msec of CPU time. This algorithm is simple, fair, and easy to implement.

1.5.3. Layer 2 – Device Drivers

Like all versions of UNIX for the IBM PC, MINIX does not use the ROM BIOS for input or output because the BIOS does not support interrupts. Suppose a user forks off a compilation in the background and then calls the editor. If the editor tried to read from the terminal using the BIOS, the compilation (and any other background jobs such as printing) would be stopped dead in their tracks waiting for the the next character to be typed. Such behavior may be acceptable in the MS-DOS world, but it certainly is not in the UNIX world. As a result, MINIX contains a complete set of drivers that duplicate the functions of the BIOS. Like the rest of MINIX, these drivers are written in C, not assembly language.

This design has important implications for running MINIX on PC clones. A clone whose hardware is not compatible with the PC down to the chip level, but which tries to hide the differences by making the BIOS calls functionally identical to IBM's will not run an unmodified MINIX because MINIX does not use the BIOS.

Each device driver is a separate process in MINIX. At present, the drivers include the clock driver, terminal driver, various disk drivers (e.g., RAM disk, floppy disk), and printer driver. Each driver has a main loop consisting of three actions:

1. Wait for an incoming message.
2. Perform the request contained in the message.
3. Send a reply message.

Request messages have a standard format, containing the opcode (e.g., READ, WRITE, or IOCTL), the minor device number, the position (e.g., disk block number), the buffer address, the byte count, and the number of the process on whose behalf the work is being done.

As an example of where device drivers fit in, consider what happens when a user wants to read from a file. The user sends a message to the file system. If the file system has the needed data in its buffer cache, they are copied back to the user. Otherwise, the file system sends a message to the disk task requesting that the block be read into a buffer within the file system's address space (in its cache). Users may not send messages to the tasks directly. Only the servers may do this.

MINIX supports a RAM disk. In fact, the RAM disk is always used to hold the root device. When the system is booted, after the operating system has been loaded, the user is instructed to insert the root file system diskette. The file system then sees how big it is, allocates the necessary memory, and copies the diskette to the RAM disk. Other file systems can then be mounted on the root device.

This organization puts important directories such as /bin and /tmp on the fastest device, and also makes it easy to work with either floppy disks or hard disks or a mixture of the two by mounting them on /usr or /user or elsewhere. In any event, the root device is always in the same place.

In the standard distribution, the RAM disk is about 240K, most of which is full of parts of the C compiler. In the 256K system, a much smaller RAM disk has to be used, which explains why this version has no C compiler: there is no place to put it. (The /usr diskette is completely full with the other utility programs and one of the design goals was to make the system run on a 256K PC with 1 floppy disk.) Users with an unusual configuration such as 256K and three hard disks are free to juggle things around as they see fit.

The terminal driver is compatible with the standard V7 terminal driver. It supports cooked mode, raw mode, and cbreak mode. It also supports several escape sequences, such as cursor positioning and reverse scrolling because the screen editor needs them.

The printer driver copies its input to the printer character for character without modification. It does not even convert line feed to carriage return + line feed. This makes it possible to send escape sequences to graphics printers without the driver messing things up. MINIX does not spool output because floppy disk systems rarely have enough spare disk space for the spooling directory. Instead one normally would print a file f by saying

```
lpr <f &
```

to do the printing in the background. The *lpr* program insert carriage returns, expands tabs, and so on, so it should only be used for straight ASCII files. On hard disk systems, a spooler would not be difficult to write.

1.5.4. Layer 3 – Servers

Layer 3 contains two server processes: the memory manager and the file system. They are both structured in the same way as the device drivers, that is a main loop that accepts requests, performs them, and then replies. We will now look at each of these in turn.

The memory manager's job is to handle those system calls that affect memory allocation, as well as a few others. These include FORK, EXEC, WAIT, KILL, and BRK. The memory model used by MINIX is exceptionally simple in order to accommodate computers without any memory management hardware. When the shell forks off a process, a copy of the shell is made in memory. When the child does an EXEC, the new core image is placed in memory. Thereafter it is never moved. MINIX does not swap or page.

The amount of memory allocated to the process is determined by a field in the header of the executable file. A program, *chmem*, has been provided to manipulate this field. When a process is started, the text segment is set at the very bottom of the allocated memory area, followed by the data and bss. The stack starts at the top of the allocated memory and grows downward. The space between the bottom of the stack and the top of the data segment is available for both segments to grow into as needed. If the two segments meet, the process is killed.

In the past, before paging was invented, all memory allocation schemes worked like this. In the future, when even small microcomputers will use 32-bit CPUs and 1M x 1 bit memory chips, the minimum feasible memory will be 4 megabytes and this allocation scheme will probably become popular again due to its inherent simplicity. Thus the MINIX scheme can be regarded as either hopelessly outdated or amazingly futuristic, as you prefer.

The memory manager keeps track of memory using a list of holes. When new memory is needed, either for FORK or for EXEC, it searches the hole list and takes the first hole that is big enough (first fit). When a process terminates, if it is adjacent to a hole on either side, the process' memory and the hole are merged into a bigger hole.

The file system is really a remote file server that happens to be running on the user's machine. However it is straightforward to convert it into a true network file server. All that needs to be done is change the message interface and provide some way of authenticating requests. (In MINIX, the source field in the incoming message is trustworthy because it is filled in by the kernel.) When running remote, the MINIX file server maintains state information, like RFS and unlike NFS.

The MINIX file system is similar to that of V7 UNIX. The i-node is slightly different, containing only 9 disk addresses instead of 13, and only 1 time instead of 3. These changes reduce the i-node from 64 bytes to 32 bytes, to store more i-nodes per disk block and reduce the size of the in-core i-node table.

Free disk blocks and free inodes are kept track of using bit maps rather than free lists. The bit maps for the root device and all mounted file systems are kept in memory. When a file grows, the system makes a definite effort to allocate the new block as close as possible to the old ones, to minimize arm motion. Disk storage is not necessarily allocated one block at a time. A minor device can be configured to allocate 2, 4 (or more) contiguous blocks whenever a block is allocated. Although this wastes disk space, these multiblock **zones** improve disk performance by keeping file blocks close together. The standard parameters for MINIX as distributed are 1K blocks and 1K zones (i.e., just 1 block per zone).

MINIX maintains a buffer cache of recently used blocks. A hashing algorithm is used to look up blocks in the cache. When an i-node block, directory block, or other critical block is modified, it is written back to disk immediately. Data blocks are only written back at the next SYNC or when the buffer is needed for something else.

The MINIX directory system and format is identical to that of V7 UNIX. File names are strings of up to 14 characters, and directories can be arbitrarily long.

1.5.5. Layer 4 – User Processes

This layer contains *init*, the shell, the editor, the compiler, the utilities, and all the user processes. These processes may only send messages to the memory manager and the file system, and these servers only accept valid system call requests. Thus the user processes do not perceive MINIX to be a general-purpose message passing system. However, removing the one line of code that checks if the message destination is valid would convert it into a much more general system (but less UNIX-like).

1.6. OUTLINE OF THE REST OF THIS BOOK

Like MINIX itself, this book is also structured. It has three parts. Part one tells how to use MINIX. Chap. 1 is the introduction, Chap. 2 is the user manual, including all the "man pages," and Chap. 3 tells how to modify the system and recompile it from the sources provided.

Part two describes how the system works inside. It consist of four chapters, corresponding to the four major pieces of the system: process management (layer 1), I/O management (layer 2), memory management (layer 3), and file management (also layer 3). User programs (layer 4) are not discussed.

Each chapter begins with an overview of the subject, including a description of the architecture, data structure, and algorithms. Then comes a detailed exposition of the relevant code, file by file and procedure by procedure. The text contains many references to specific line numbers in the code for easy reference.

Part three contains a listing of the full MINIX source code (Chap. 8) and a cross reference map of all the global variables, procedure names, and macros. Local variables are not included because their inclusion would have tripled the number of pages required.

So much for the introduction. Now let's go see how to use MINIX.

2

MINIX USERS GUIDE

This chapter tells you how to run MINIX. If you are an experienced UNIX user, there will be relatively little new here. Using MINIX is very similar to using UNIX. If you are not familiar with UNIX at all, it is suggested that you first read one of the many books available on the subject, as this chapter is more of a reference manual than a tutorial for beginners.

This chapter is intended to provide enough information to get you started, and to point out some of the differences between MINIX and UNIX. To begin with, MINIX was designed with the idea of being similar to Version 7 UNIX, the last version of UNIX produced by Ken Thompson, Dennis Ritchie, and the other members of the Computing Science Research Center at Bell Labs. For a detailed description of Version 7 UNIX (as opposed to the various other versions), the best place to look is the official Bell Labs *UNIX Programmer's Manual*, published as a book by Holt, Rinehart, and Winston (1983). By and large though, most garden-variety commands are pretty much the same in all versions of UNIX. Still, the best way to tell if some feature is present in MINIX is to try it.

This chapter is divided into six sections. The first section tells how to boot the PC to get MINIX running. The second section tells how to use MINIX, with particular emphasis on ideas that are important and should not be missed. The third section discusses system administration. The fourth section consists of the MINIX manual "pages." The fifth section describes the MINIX library, especially a few procedures that differ slightly from their UNIX counterparts. Finally, the sixth section talks about some important file formats.

36

2.1. HOW TO START MINIX

The first step in running MINIX is to acquire an IBM PC, XT, AT, or true compatible. The latter point deserves some explanation. Many manufacturers have brought out machines that are similar to the IBM PC in some ways, but different in other ways. MINIX will not run on all these machines. Like all versions of UNIX for the IBM PC, MINIX does not use the BIOS (because the BIOS is not interrupt-driven, making it totally unsuitable for time-sharing). Instead, it programs all the I/O chips directly. Therefore it will only run on machines using the same I/O chips as the IBM PC.

MINIX comes in several versions, for different memory sizes. Be sure that the version you have is appropriate for your machine. The smallest configuration on which MINIX will run is 256K RAM and one 360K floppy drive, but not all programs will run on this configuration. A system with 640K RAM and two floppy disk drives is better. For information about running MINIX with a hard disk, see the *doc* directory in the software distribution on the */user* diskette (PC version).

Before running MINIX for the first time, make a backup of all the floppy disks, to prevent disaster if one of them should be subsequently damaged. They are not copy protected.

To boot MINIX, proceed as follows.

1. Turn off the PC and then insert the boot diskette in drive 0. You can also type CRTL-ALT-DEL to boot a running PC, but sometimes the PC is in a peculiar state and the boot message fails to appear or appears in a peculiar way. It does not matter that you cannot see it. Wait 15 seconds and then proceed with step 3. Alternatively, just turn off the PC and start again.

2. You should get a message like: "Booting MINIX 1.1" as soon as the power-on self-tests have finished.

3. About 15 seconds after the above message, you will get a menu on the screen offering you several options. Remove the boot diskette from drive 0, insert the root file system in its place, and hit the = (equal sign) key.

4. MINIX will now erase the screen and display a line at the top telling how much memory the machine has, how large the operating system (including all its tables and buffers) is, how large the RAM disk is, and how much memory is available for user programs (the first number minus the next two). Check to see that the available memory is at least positive. MINIX will not run with negative memory. To do anything useful, however, at least 100K is needed.

5. Now the root file system will be copied from drive 0 to the RAM disk. The MINIX root device is always on the RAM disk, no matter how many disks of what kind are being used.

6. When the RAM disk has been loaded, the system initialization file, */etc/rc*, is executed. It asks you to remove the root file system and then insert the */usr* file system in drive 0 and type a carriage return. Do so.

7. After */usr* has been mounted, you will next be requested to enter the date (and time). Enter a 12-digit number in the form MMDDYYhhmmss, followed by a carriage return. For example, 3:35 p.m. on July 4, 1976 was 070476153500.

8. You will now get the message

   ```
   login:
   ```

   on the screen. Type

   ```
   ast
   ```

   and wait for the system to ask for your password. Then type

   ```
   Wachtwoord
   ```

   being careful to type the first letter in upper case. Lower and upper case letters are always distinct in MINIX.

9. If you have successfully logged in, the shell will display a prompt (dollar sign) on the screen. Try typing

   ```
   ls -l
   ```

   to see what is in your directory. Then type

   ```
   ls -l /bin
   ```

   to see what is in the */bin* directory on the root device. After that, try

   ```
   ls -l /usr/bin
   ```

   to see what is on the drive 0 diskette. To stop the display from scrolling out of view, type CTRL-S; to restart it, type CTRL-Q. (Note that CTRL-S means depress the "control" key on the keyboard and then hit the *S* key while "control" is still depressed.)

10. If you have two drives, you can mount the */user* diskette by inserting it into drive 1 and typing

    ```
    /etc/mount /dev/fd1 /user
    ```

    Use *ls* to inspect it. The shell script */user/test/run* runs some tests to see if MINIX is working properly. To use it, first back up the diskette as described in Section 2.2.4. Then remove all the source code and documentation (to create more free space) and type

    ```
    cd /user/test; run
    ```

The tests take a number of minutes. After they have been completed, you can remove the entire *test* directory, leaving only */user/bin*. The rest of the diskette space is for your own files.

11. You can now edit files, compile programs, or do many other things. The reference manuals given later in this chapter give a brief description of the programs available. On the standard */usr* diskette, there is very little free space. If you have only one 360K drive, it will probably be necessary to delete some files to create more space.

12. When you are finished working, and want to log out, type CTRL-D. The

    ```
    login:
    ```

    message will appear, and you or another user can log in again.

13. When you want to shut the computer down, make sure all processes have finished, if need be, by killing them with *kill*. Then type sync or just log out. When the disk light goes out, you can turn the computer power off. Never turn the system off without first running *sync* or logging out (which does an implied *sync*). Failure to obey this rule will generally result in a garbled file system and lost data.

2.2. HOW TO USE MINIX

In the following sections we will look at some aspects of MINIX that will be of interest to many users. These include the standard file system, mounted file systems, working with disks, printing files, and so on.

2.2.1. Introduction

As a general rule, most aspects of MINIX work the same way as they do in UNIX. When you log in, you get a shell, which is functionally similar to the standard V7 shell (Bourne shell). Most programs are called the same way as in UNIX, have the same flags, and perform the same functions as their UNIX counterparts.

The MINIX shell, for example, recognizes redirection of standard input and standard output, pipes, magic characters in file names, semicolons to separate multiple commands on a line, and the ampersand, to indicate a background process. The (default) keyboard editing conventions are also similar to UNIX: the backspace key (CTRL-H) is used to correct typing errors, the @ symbol is used to erase the current input line, CTRL-S is used to stop the screen from scrolling out of view, CTRL-Q is used to start the screen moving again, and CTRL-D is used to indicate end-of-file from the keyboard. These key bindings can be changed using the IOCTL system call and *stty* program, the same way as they can be changed in UNIX.

One major difference between MINIX and UNIX is the editor. The standard UNIX editor, *ed*, was designed with slow, mechanical, hardcopy terminals in mind. More modern editors, such as *vi* and *emacs* were designed for computers with megabytes of memory and large disks. The MINIX editor, *mined*, was designed and implemented especially for MINIX. It is a small, fast, and easy to learn full-screen editor. Its commands are described later in this chapter.

2.2.2. A Tour Through the MINIX File System

The MINIX file tree is organized the same way as the standard UNIX file tree. The root directory (which is always located on the RAM disk, in memory) contains the following subdirectories:

/bin   - contains the most important binary (executable) programs
/dev   - contains the special files for the I/O devices
/etc   - contains various files and programs for system administration
/lib   - contains some programs called by other programs
/tmp   - used to hold temporary files
/user   - the user file system is mounted here
/usr   - the system disk is mounted here

Let us briefly examine these directories one at a time. In */bin* we find the most heavily used programs such as *cat*, *cp*, and *ls* as well as some programs such as *login* and *sh* needed to bring the system up. Because access to the RAM disk is much faster than to the rotating disks, */bin* should be used to hold programs that are frequently used. In principle, MINIX will run with only the root file system (i.e., no disks at all), but the amount of space available for user files will be extremely limited.

The directory */dev* contains the special files for the I/O devices, including:

/dev/ram   - the RAM disk
/dev/mem   - absolute memory
/dev/kmem   - kernel memory
/dev/null   - null device (data written to it are discarded)
/dev/fd0   - floppy disk drive 0
/dev/fd1   - floppy disk drive 1
/dev/hd0   - hard disk minor device 0
/dev/hd1   - hard disk minor device 1
/dev/lp   - line printer
/dev/tty   - current terminal
/dev/tty0   - terminal 0 (console)

When */dev/ram* is opened and read, for example, by the command

```
od -x /dev/ram
```

the contents of the RAM disk are read out, byte by byte, starting at byte 0. Similarly, reading */dev/mem* reads out absolute memory, starting at address 0 (the interrupt vectors). The file */dev/kmem* is similar to */dev/mem*, except that it starts at the address in memory where the kernel is located (0x600). The next file, */dev/null*, is the null device. It is used as a place for redirecting program output that is not needed. Data copied to */dev/null* are lost forever.

The next two files are for floppy disk drives 0 and 1, respectively. Reading or writing from one of these files reads or writes on the corresponding floppy disk, without regard to the structure of the file system on it. They are normally only used for operations such as copying complete floppy disks, block by block or creating fresh file systems.

The character special file */dev/lp* is for the line printer. It is write only. Bytes written to this file are sent to the line printer without modification (to make it possible to send escape sequences to graphics printers). Users normally print files by using the *lpr* program, rather than copying files directly to */dev/lp*. The latter method takes care of converting line feed to carriage return plus line feed, expanding tabs to spaces, etc., whereas the former method does not.

The final group of special files is for the terminal. Both */dev/tty* and */dev/tty0* refer to the terminal (console). In a system with only one terminal, there is no difference, but MINIX has been designed to make it easy to expand to multiple terminals, in which case */dev/tty1*, */dev/tty2*, etc. should be added for the new terminals. When more than one terminal is present, a specific terminal can be read or written by using one of the special files of the form */dev/ttyn*. In contrast, */dev/tty* always accesses the terminal associated with the process making the system call. In this way, a process can refer to its terminal without having to know the terminal number.

Another important directory is */etc*. This directory contains files and programs used for mounting and unmounting file systems, making new file systems, and other forms of system management. We will look at them later.

The directory */lib* holds two pieces of the C compiler that are not normally directly called by users: the C preprocessor, *cpp*, and the front end, *cem*.

The */tmp* directory is used by many programs for temporary files. By putting this directory on the RAM disk, these programs are speeded up.

The directories */user* and */usr* are empty. They should be used for mounting the user disk and system disk, respectively. When the standard */usr* file system is mounted, the directory */usr/bin* is where most of the executable binary programs are kept, and */usr/lib* is where the rest of the C compiler and its libraries are stored.

2.2.3. Mounted File Systems

When MINIX is started up, the only device present is the root device (on the RAM disk). After the files and directories that belong on the root device are copied there from the root file system diskette, MINIX prints a message asking the user to remove the diskette. It then executes the shell script */etc/rc* as the final step in bringing up the system.

The file */etc/rc* first prints a message asking the user to put the */usr* diskette in drive 0. Then it pauses to allow the diskette to be inserted and the date entered. The shell script now executes the command

```
/etc/mount /dev/fd0 /usr
```

to mount the system disk on */usr*. From this point on, all the files in */usr*, including the binary programs in */usr/bin*, are available.

On PCs with two floppy disk drives, the user should insert a user file system diskette (or any other file system diskette) in drive 1 and type:

```
/etc/mount /dev/fd1 /user
```

Users planning to mount the same diskette in drive 1 whenever the system is brought up can modify */etc/rc* to perform the mount on drive 1 analogously to the mount on drive 0. Note, however, that changes made to */etc/rc* on the RAM disk will be lost when the system is next booted unless they are also made to the root file system diskette, which can be mounted and modified, just like any other diskette.

If it is desired to remove the diskette in drive 1 during operation, first type the command:

```
/etc/umount /dev/fd1
```

and wait until it types "ok" before removing the diskette. (Note that the program is called *umount*, just as it is in UNIX, not *unmount.*)

If you remove a diskette while it is still mounted, the system may hang, but it can be brought back to life by simply re-inserting the same diskette. If you remove a diskette while it is still mounted and insert another in its place, the contents of both file systems will be seriously damaged and information may be irretrievably lost (see below about repairing damaged file systems). During normal MINIX operation, the diskettes are mounted when the system is booted, and not touched thereafter. Experienced MS-DOS users who are used to constantly switching diskettes without telling the operating system should post discrete KEEP OFF signs on their drives as a reminder.

Although it is permitted to *insert* a non-MINIX diskette in a drive (e.g., to read an MS-DOS diskette), only MINIX file system diskettes can be *mounted*. Attempts to mount a diskette not containing a MINIX file system will be detected and rejected.

2.2.4. Helpful Hints

In this section we will point out several aspects of MINIX that will frequently be useful. As a starter, it is wise to back up floppy disks periodically. To make a backup, first format a floppy disk with 9 sectors/track. MINIX does not have a format program, but the MS-DOS 2.0 and subsequent format programs can be used. Formatting a floppy disk writes timing information, sector preambles, and similar information on it. The MS-DOS formatter also puts an MS-DOS file system on the floppy disk, but that will be erased when the backup is made. The important thing is getting the timing and preambles onto the disk.

Next, unmount the file systems in drives 0 and 1. It is possible to back up a mounted file system, but only if no background processes are running. To be doubly safe, give a *sync* command. Insert the newly formatted diskette in drive 1, and then type

```
cp /dev/fd0 /dev/fd1
```

to copy information from drive 0 to drive 1. When the drive lights go out, the floppy disks can be removed.

Files can be printed using the *lpr* program. It can be given an explicit list of files, as in

```
lpr file1 file2 file3 &
```

If no arguments are supplied, *lpr* prints its standard input, for example

```
pr file1 file2 file3 | lpr &
```

Note that *lpr* is not a spooling daemon. It sits in a loop copying files to */dev/lp*. For this reason, it should be started off in the background with the ampersand, so the user can continue working while printing is going on. Only one *lpr* at a time may be running.

Disk space is always in short supply on floppy disk systems. To find out how much space and how many i-nodes are left on drive 0, type

```
df /dev/fd0
```

Similar commands can be used for other devices, including */dev/ram*.

When you log in, the shell checks to see if there is a file *.profile* in your home directory. If it finds one, it executes the file as a shell script. This file is commonly used to set shell variables, *stty* parameters, and so on. See */usr/ast/.profile* as a simple example.

It is possible to copy files from an MS-DOS disk to MINIX or vice versa. See the description of *dosread* and *doswrite* for details.

The ASCII codes produced by the IBM PC keyboard are determined by software, not hardware. A mapping has been chosen to try to produce a unique value for each key, so programs can see the difference between, for example, the + in the top row and the + in the numeric keypad. The codes 1 through 255 are used. To see which code a given key produces, use *od –b*, and then type the key or keys followed by a return and a CTRL-D.

The IBM PC does not have any protection hardware. As a result, if a program's stack overruns the area available for it, it will overwrite the data segment. This usually results in a system crash. When a program crashes unexpectedly or acts strange, it is probably worthwhile to find out how much memory is allocated for it (the "memory" column in the output of *size*). If this is less than 64K, it can be increased using *chmem*. When working with unreliable programs, doing *sync*s frequently is advisable.

The 640K version of MINIX can be used on 512K machines, although there are some limitations and problems to watch out for. The main problem is the small amount of memory available for user programs. It will be difficult to run several programs at once. When using the C compiler, it will be necessary to use the **–F** flag to avoid having the preprocessor and front end run at the same time, connected by a pipe. Running them separately means that enough disk space must be available for the intermediate file. If a program cannot be executed due to its size, *chmem* can sometimes be used to reduce the stack size, to allow it to run with less memory. If the stack is made too small, however, the program may go berserk or crash the system due to stack overrun. Unfortunately the hardware does not detect stack overrun.

The problems with memory allocation are due to a large chunk of memory being taken up by the operating system, its buffers, and the RAM disk, plus the fact that multiple programs can be running at once. This, plus the lack of hardware protection, requires that a more economical approach be taken to memory use than the standard MS-DOS method of just giving each program the whole machine to itself. In practice, once the sizes have been set right for a given configuration, they need not be fiddled with any more.

Even on 640K machines, it sometimes happens that a program (or a compiler pass) cannot be executed due to lack of memory for it. When this happens, the shell prints a message of the form *program: cannot execute*. The solution is to run fewer programs at once, or reduce the program's size with *chmem*. The amount of stack space assigned to the shell, *make*, etc. in the standard distribution may not be optimal for all applications. Change it if problems arise. To see how much is currently assigned, type

```
size /bin/* /usr/bin/* | mined
```

Several of the utility programs, including the C compiler, create their temporary files in */tmp*, on the RAM disk. If the RAM disk fills up, a message will be printed on the terminal. The first thing to do is check */tmp* to see if there is any debris left over from previous commands, and if so, remove it. If that does not solve the problem, temporarily removing some of the larger files from */bin* or */lib* will usually be enough. These files can be restored later by mounting the root file system on any drive and copying the needed files from it.

MINIX, like UNIX, will not break off a system call part way through just because the DEL key has been struck. When the system call in question happens to be an EXEC, which is loading a long program from a slow floppy disk, it can take a few seconds before the shell prompt appears. Be patient. Hitting DEL again makes things worse, rather than better.

Although it is really intended as a debugging aid, rather than a permanent part of the system, the F1 and F2 function keys cause dumps of some of the internal tables to be printed on the screen. F1 gives a dump like the UNIX *ps* command, which is not present in MINIX. Frequently, the system appears to be stopped, but it is actually thinking its little head off and using the RAM disk, which, unlike the other disks, is not accompanied by whirring and clicking noises and flashing lights. The nervous user can press F1 to see the internal process table to verify that progress is still being made. The F1 and F2 keys are intercepted directly by the keyboard driver, so they always work, no matter what the computer is doing. The values in the columns *user* and *sys* are the number of clock ticks charged to each process. By hitting F1 twice, a few seconds apart, it is possible to see where the CPU time is going.

Additional documentation can be found in the */doc* directory on the */user* disk.

2.3. HOW TO BEHAVE LIKE A SUPER-USER

Your days as an ordinary user are over. You will now have to learn how to be a system administrator as well. In fact, within a minute you will learn how to become a super-user. Fortunately, being a super-user is not difficult. However, super-users have more power than ordinary users. They can violate nearly all of the system's protection rules. Although there is no Hippocratic Oath for super-users (yet), tradition requires them to exercise their great power with care and responsibility. Super-users get a special prompt (#), to remind them of their awesome power.

To become super-user, login as *root* using the password *Geheim*. (Notice the capital *G*). Alternatively, use the *su* program with the same password. Hackers will no doubt enjoy trying to become super-user the hard way—by logging in as *ast* and hunting for loopholes in the system that allow one to become super-user without using the super-user password. In fact, I am prepared to offer a *rijksdaalder* to the first person reporting each successful new method.

2.3.1. Making New File Systems

One of the things that super-users do is make new file systems. Two ways are provided. First, when MINIX is booted, the initial menu offers several options. To run the system, type = (equal sign). Another possibility is making an empty file system. This option is exercised by typing the letter *m* instead of =. This file system can be subsequently mounted and files copied to it.

It is often convenient to make a file system during normal MINIX operation. This is possible using the program *mkfs* (make file system). To make an empty 360 block file system on drive 1, type

```
mkfs /dev/fd1 360
```

When the program finishes, the file system will be ready to mount. On a system with only one disk drive, *mkfs* will first have to be copied to */bin*, the */dev/fd0* file system unmounted, a blank diskette inserted into drive 0 and then the file system made using */dev/fd0* as the second argument to *mkfs*.

It is also possible to make a file system that is initialized with files and directories. A command for doing this is

```
mkfs /dev/fd1 proto
```

where *proto* is a prototype file. The description of *mkfs* later in this chapter gives an example of a prototype file.

2.3.2. File System Checking

File systems can be damaged by system crashes, by accidently removing a mounted file system, by forgetting to run *sync* before shutting the system down and in other ways. Repairing a file system by hand is a tricky business (see the discussion in Chap. 5), so a program has been provided to automate the job.

When MINIX is booted, one of the choices on the initial menu is to check a file system. To use this option, first insert the file system to be checked in drive 0, and then type *f*. The file system checker, *fsck*, then reads the i-nodes, bit maps, and directories to see if the file system is consistent. If it is, *fsck* prints some statistics and then redisplays the menu. At this point another file system can be checked, or MINIX can be started (after first inserting the root file system diskette in drive 0).

If *fsck* finds a problem, it will display a message. Before making changes to the file system, it always asks permission. In general, if you type *y* (followed by a carriage return), *fsck* will do its best to repair the system. It will always yield a correct file system, but if the file system has been badly damaged, files may be lost.

2.3.3. The /etc Directory

The */etc* directory contains several files that super-users should know about. One of these is the password file, */etc/passwd*. You can enter new users by editing this file and adding a line for each new user. The entry for a user named *kermit* might be

```
kermit::15:1:Kermit the Frog:/user/kermit:/bin/sh
```

The entry contains seven fields, separated by colons. These fields contain the login name, password (initially null), uid, gid, name, home directory, and shell for the new user. When a new user is entered, the corresponding home directory must also be created, using *mkdir*, and its owner set correctly, using *chown*. Each user must have a unique uid, but the numerical values are unimportant. It is probably adequate to put all ordinary users in group 3, unless there really are distinct groups of users. When the new user logs in for the first time, he should choose a password and enter it using *passwd*.

Another important file is /*etc*/*rc*. Each time the system is booted, this file is run as a shell script just before the login: message is printed. It can be used to mount file systems, request the date, erase temporary files, and anything else that needs to be done before starting the system. It also forks off *update*, which runs in the background and issues a SYNC system call every 30 seconds to flush the buffer cache.

If you have two drives, it may be convenient to modify /*etc*/*rc* to mount /*dev*/*fd1* on /*user* during system boot. If you do this, you can also change /*etc*/*passwd* to put your home directory on /*user* instead of /*usr*.

The file /*etc*/*ttys* contains one line for each terminal in the system. During startup, *init* reads this file and forks off a login process for each terminal. When the console is the only terminal, *ttys* contains only 1 line.

Also contained in /*etc* are the programs *mount*, and *umount* for mounting and unmounting file systems, respectively.

When any of the files on the RAM disk, such as /*etc*/*passwd*, are modified, the changes will be lost when the system is shut down unless the modified files are explicitly copied back to the root file system. This can be done by mounting the root file system diskette and then copying the files with *cp*.

2.3.4. Modifying File Systems

As distributed, MINIX comes with three file system diskettes: the root file system, /*usr*, and /*user*. When the system is booted, the root file system diskette is copied to the RAM disk, and not used thereafter. One implication of this design is that changes made to the RAM disk during system operation will be lost when the system is shut down. To modify the root file system, it should be mounted, for example, by putting it in drive 1 and typing

```
/etc/mount /dev/fd1 /user
```

Programs can then be copied to or from it, files can be removed, and so on. When the modification is done, it must be unmounted and removed from the drive.

More generally, the contents of the three file systems can be reorganized by mounting and copying. Programs that are heavily used should be put on the root file system, but at least 50K should be left unused for /*tmp*. Once a root file system diskette has been made, its size cannot be changed, but a new one can always be made using *mkfs*, as discussed in Chap. 3.

One simple way to build a new /*usr* or /*user* file system is to make an empty file system using the "m" option of the initial menu, or *mkfs*, mount this file system, and then copy files to it from one or more other file systems, possibly mounting and unmounting several of them during the process.

For systems containing only one floppy disk drive, a careful choice has to be made about which programs will be on the root file system and which will be on /usr since together they are too small to hold all the programs.

One way to build a file system is to start with an empty file system. Programs that are currently on the root device that are to go on the new file system are copied to it. Then, /lib and /bin, are emptied, except for rm and cp, to make more space on the root device. Next, the file system being built is unmounted, and another one mounted in its place. Useful programs from it are copied to the now-empty root device. Then the file system being built is remounted, and files copied to it from the root device. This process may have to be repeated several times, depending on how many files are being copied and from where.

2.3.5. Miscellaneous Notes

A number of MINIX programs can only be executed by the super-user. These include: *mkfs, chown,* and *mknod.* Other programs, such as *mkdir*, can be executed by any user, but are owned by the root and have the SETUID bit on, so that when they are executed, the effective uid is that of the super-user, even though the real uid is not.

In general, if a program, *prog*, needs to run as the super-user but is to be made generally available to all users, it can be made into a SETUID program owned by the root by the command line:

```
chown root prog;   chmod 4755 prog
```

Needless to say, only the super-user can execute these commands.

2.4. MINIX COMMANDS

In this section the MINIX commands (programs) that are supplied with the system are summarized. Books on UNIX should be consulted for more detail, especially the *UNIX Programmer's Manual* published by Holt, Rinehart and Winston. Most MINIX commands have the same flags and arguments as their UNIX counterparts. A few of the programs listed below are on the /user diskette, and will not be available unless that diskette is mounted.

In the notation used, square brackets denote optional quantities and the ellipsis (...) is used to indicate that the previous item may be present 1 or more times. In the **Syntax** lines, words and flags printed in **boldface** type must be entered exactly as shown. Words and symbols printed in lightface type are arguments, and must be replaced by file names, numeric arguments, and so forth. In the examples, all the information following a number sign (#) is comment.

Command: ar – archiver
Syntax: ar [adprtvx] archive file ...
Flags: a   Append files to the archive
            d   Delete files from the archive
            p   Print the files on standard output
            r   Replace files (append when not present)
            t   List archive's table of contents
            v   Verbose mode (give more information)
            x   Extract files from the archive
Examples: ar r clib *.c   # Replace all the C files
            ar d lib.a file.s   # Remove *file.s* from the archive

Ar maintains archives and libraries. An archive can be created with the **–r** flag by listing a nonexistent archive name. Members of the archive can be replaced, deleted, printed, or extracted.

Command: asld – assembler-loader
Syntax: asld [–d] [–s] [–o name] file ...
Flags: –L A listing is produced on standard output
            –T Used to specify a directory for the temporary file
            –o Output goes to file named by next argument
            –s A symbol table is produced on standard output
Examples: asld –s file.s   # Assemble *file.s and* list symbols
            asld –o output file.s   # Assemble *file.s*, put binary on *output*
            asld –T. file1.s file2.s # Use current directory for temporary file

Asld is the MINIX assembler and loader combined. It accepts a language similar to that accepted by the PC-IX assembler. Symbols are made up of letters, digits and underscores. The machine instructions and addressing modes are the same as those used by PC-IX, except that modes using multiple registers are written like this example: *mov ax,(bx_si)*. Constant operands are denoted by a number sign. Local labels are permitted in the usual UNIX style: the instruction *jmp 1f* jumps forward to the closest label *1:*

The pseudoinstructions accepted by the assembler are listed below:

.align n   Align to a multiple of *n* bytes
.ascii str   Assemble a string
.asciz str   Assemble a zero-terminated string
.bss   What follows goes in the bss segment
.byte n   Assemble one or more bytes
.data   What follows goes in the data segment
.define sym   Export *sym* from the file
.errnz n   Force error if *n* is nonzero
.even   Align to an even address
.extern sym   Declare *sym* external

.globl sym	Same as **extern**
.long n	Assemble *n* as a long
.org adr	Set address within current segment
.short n	Assemble *n* as a short
.space n	Skip *n* bytes
.text	What follows goes in the text segment
.word n	Assemble *n* as a word
.zerow n	Assemble *n* words of zeros

In the above pseudoinstructions, *adr* is an expression yielding a machine address, *n* is a numeric expression, *str* is a quoted string, and *sym* is a symbol. The library */usr/lib/libc.a* is a packed archive of assembly code. To see some examples of it, extract some files from the archive with *ar* and then use the filter *libupack* to convert them to readable ASCII.

MINIX does not use *.o* files. Compiler output is packed assembly language, as are the modules in an archive. This scheme requires reassembling archive modules all the time, but it saves precious diskette space. Unfortunately, the strategy also makes assembling and linking slow.

It is not possible at present to have the assembler (hence the C compiler) produce separate I & D program, even though the operating system supports such programs compiled with other compilers.

Command: basename – strip off file prefixes and suffixes
Syntax: basename file [suffix]
Flags: (none)
Examples: basename /user/ast/file   # Strips path to yield *file*
                    basename /user/file.c .c   # Strips path and *.c* to yield *file*

The initial directory names (if any) are removed yielding the name of the file itself. If a second argument is present, it is interpreted as a suffix and is also stripped, if present. This program is primarily used in shell scripts.

Command: cat – concatenate files and write them to standard output
Syntax: cat [–u] file ...
Flags: –u Unbuffered output
Examples: cat file   # Display file on the terminal
                    cat file1 file2 │ lpr   # Concatenate 2 files and print result

Cat concatenates its input files and copies the result to standard output. If no input file is named, or – is encountered as a file name, standard input is used. Output is buffered in 512 byte blocks unless the **–u** flag is given.

Command: cc – C compiler
Syntax: **cc** [option] ... file ...
Flags: **–D** The flag **–D**x=y defines a macro x with value y
              –F Use a file instead of a pipe for preprocessor output
              –I **–I**dir searches dir for include files
              –LIB Produce a library module
              –R Complain about all non Kernighan & Ritchie code
              –S Produce an assembly code file, then stop
              –T The flag **–T**dir tells cem to use dir for temporary files
              –U Undefine a macro
              –c Compile only. Do not link. (Same as **–S**)
              –o Put output on file named by next arg
              –v Verbose. Print pass names
              –w Suppress warning messages
Examples: cc –c file.c   # Compile *file.c*
              cc –Di8088 file.c   # Treat the symbol *i8088* as defined
              cc –c —LIB file.c   # Make a module for the library
              cc –R –o out file.c   # Check for K & R; output to *out*
       This is the C compiler. It has five passes, as follows:

Program	Input	Output	Operation performed
/lib/cpp	prog.c	prog.i	C preprocessor: #include, #define, #ifdef
/lib/cem	prog.i	prog.k	Parsing and semantic analysis
/usr/lib/opt	prog.k	prog.m	Optimization of the intermediate code
/usr/lib/cg	prog.m	prog.s	Code generation
/usr/lib/asld	prog.s	a.out	Assembly and linking

The main program, *cc*, forks appropriately to call the passes, transmitting flags and arguments. The **–v** flag causes the passes to be listed as they are called.

The **–c** or **–S** flags stop compilation when *cg* has produced an assembly code file (in packed format) because the current assembler-loader expects that (see under File Formats later in this chapter). The libraries are also archives of packed assembly code files, except that defined symbols must be declared by *.define* statements at the beginning. To make modules for inclusion in the library, use the **–c** and **–LIB** options. There is no way to get *.o* files; the packed assembly language files are used as a substitute. They can be unpacked with the filter *libupack*.

The **–R** flag gives warnings about all constructions not permitted by official Kernighan and Ritchie C. The average garden-variety C program that has been flawlessly acceptedly by most C compilers contains surprisingly many illegal constructions. Try it.

The compiler normally keeps *cpp* and *cem* in memory at the same time, transferring the output of *cpp* to *cem* using a pipe. However, if there is insufficient memory available to hold both at once, the **–F** flag can be given to cause these two passes to be run strictly sequentially, with the preprocessor output being stored on a file in */tmp* (unless **–T** is used). When available memory is very limited (e.g., a 512K machine), it may be necessary to run *chmem* to reduce the sizes of the compiler passes that do not fit, typically *cem*.

The other passes, especially *asld*, can create large temporary files in */tmp*. To compile very large programs, first type

```
cc -c *.c
```

to get *.s* files. Then remove */lib/cpp* and */lib/cem* and possibly other files from the RAM disk to make more space for */tmp*. Finally, type

```
cc *.s
```

which results in

```
asld /usr/lib/crtso.s *.s /usr/lib/libc.a /usr/lib/end.s
```

to produce the *a.out* file. The files removed from the RAM disk can be restored by mounting the root file system and copying them from there, or the system can be shut down and rebooted.

If the compiler (or, in fact, almost any program) begins acting strange, it is almost always due to its running out of space, either stack space or scratch file space. The relevant pass can be given more stack space using *chmem*. More space for scratch files can be obtained by removing other files on the device.

The compiler is derived from the ACK system (Tanenbaum et al., *CACM*, Sept. 1983) not from the AT&T portable C compiler. It has been shoehorned onto the PC with some loss of performance.

Command: **chmem – change memory allocation**
Syntax: **chmem [+] [–] [=] amount file ...**
Flags: **(none)**
Examples: chmem =50000 a.out   # Give *a.out* 50K of stack space
chmem –4000 a.out   # Reduce the stack space by 4000 bytes
chmem +1000 file1 file2 # Increase each stack by 1000 bytes

When a program is loaded into memory, it is allocated enough memory for the text and data+bss segments, plus an area for the stack. Data segment growth using *malloc*, *brk*, or *sbrk* eats up stack space from the low end. The amount of stack space to allocate is derived from a field in the executable program's file header. If the combined stack and data segment growth exceeds the stack space allocated, the program will be terminated.

It is therefore important to set the amount of stack space carefully. If too little is provided, the program may crash. If too much is provided, memory will be wasted, and fewer programs will be able to fit in memory and run simultaneously. MINIX does not swap, so that when memory is full, subsequent attempts to fork will fail. The compiler sets the stack space to the largest possible value (64K – text – data). For many programs, this value is far too large.

Nonrecursive programs that do not call *brk*, *sbrk*, or *malloc*, and do not have any local arrays usually do not need more than 1K of stack space.

The *chmem* command changes the value of the header field that determines the stack allocation, and thus indirectly the total memory required to run the program. The = option sets the stack size to a specific value; the + and – options increment and decrement the current value by the indicated amount. The old and new stack sizes are printed.

Command: chmod – change file mode
Syntax: chmod mode file ...
Flags: (none)
Examples: chmod 754 file   # Owner: rwx; Group r–x; Others r--
              chmod 4755 file1 file2   # Turn on SETUID bit

The permission bits for each file are set to *mode* (octal). The 04000 bit is the SETUID bit. The 02000 bit is the SETGID bit. The low-order 9 bits are the *rwx* bits for the owner, group, and others.

Command: chown – change owner
Syntax: chown user file ...
Flags: (none)
Example: chown ast file1 file2   # Make *ast* the owner of the files

The owner field of the named files is changed to *user* (i.e., login name specified). Only the super-user may execute this command.

Command: clr – clear the screen
Syntax: clr
Flags: (none)
Example: clr   # Clear the screen

The screen is cleared to blanks.

Command: cmp – compare two files
Syntax: cmp –ls file1 file2
Flags: –l Loud mode. Print bytes that differ (in octal)
              –s Silent mode. Print nothing, just return exit status
Examples: cmp file1 file2   # Tell whether the files are the same
              cmp –l file1 file2   # Print all corresponding bytes that differ

Two files are compared. If they are identical, exit status 0 is returned. If they differ, exit status 1 is returned. If the files cannot be opened, exit status 2 is returned. If *file1* is – , standard input is compared to *file2*.

Command: comm – print lines common to two sorted files
Syntax: **comm** [– [123]] file1 file2
Flags: **–1** Suppress column 1 (lines only in *file1*)
                   –2 Suppress column 2 (lines only in *file2*)
                   –3 Suppress column 3 (lines in both files)
Examples: comm file1 file2   # Print all three columns
              comm –12 file1 file2   # Print only lines common to both files
Two sorted files are read and compared. A three column listing is produced. Files only in *file1* are in column 1; files only in *file2* are in column 2; files common to both files are in column 3. The file name – means standard input.

Command: cp – copy file
Syntax: **cp** file1 file2
             cp file ... directory
Flags: (none)
Examples: cp oldfile newfile   # Copy *oldfile* to *newfile*
              cp file1 file2 /user/ast   # Copy two files to a directory
Cp copies one file to another, or copies one or more files to a directory. A file cannot be copied to itself.

Command: date – print or set the date and time
Syntax: **date** [[MMDDYY]hhmm[ss]]
Flags: **–q** Read the date from standard input
Examples: date   # Print the date and time
              date 0221881610   # Set date to Feb 21, 1988 at 4:10 p.m.
Without an argument, *date* prints the current date and time. With an argument, it sets the date and time. *MMDDYY* refers to the month, day, and year; *hhmmss* refers to the hour, minute and second. Each of the six fields must be two digits.

Command: dd – disk dumper
Syntax: **dd** [option = value] ...
Flags: (none)

Examples: dd if=/dev/fd0 of=/dev/fd1   # Copy disk 0 to disk 1
                  dd if=x of=y bs=1w skip=4   # Copy *x* to *y*, skipping 4 words
                  dd if=x of=y count=3   # Copy three 512–byte blocks

This command is intended for copying partial files. The block size, skip count, and number of blocks to copy can be specified. The options are:

if = file	- Input file (default is standard input)
of = file	- Output file (default is standard output)
ibs = n	- Input block size (default 512 bytes)
obs = n	- Output block size (default is 512 bytes)
bs = n	- Block size; sets *ibs* and *obs* (default is 512 bytes)
skip = n	- Skip *n* input blocks before reading
seek = n	- Skip *n* output blocks before writing
count = n	- Copy only *n* input blocks
conv = **lcase**	- Convert upper case letters to lower case
conv = **ucase**	- Convert lower case letters to upper case
conv = **swab**	- Swap every pair of bytes
conv = **noerror**	- Ignore errors and just keep going

Where sizes are expected, they are in bytes. However, the letters **w**, **b**, or **k** may be appended to the number to indicate words (2 bytes), blocks (512 bytes), or K (1024 bytes), respectively. When *dd* is finished, it reports the number of full and partial blocks read and written.

Command: df – report on free disk space and i-nodes
Syntax: **df** special ...
Flags: **(none)**
Examples: df /dev/ram   # Report on free RAM disk space
                 df /dev/fd0 /dev/fd1   # Report on floppy disk space

The amount of disk space and number of i-nodes, both free and used is reported.

Command: dosdir – list an MS-DOS diskette directory
Syntax: **dosdir [–lr]** drive
Flags: **–l** Long listing
                 –r Recursively descend and print subdirectories
Examples: dosdir 1 –l   # List root directory on drive 1
                 dosdir 0 –r x/y   # Recursively list directory *x/y*

Dosdir reads standard IBM PC diskettes in MS-DOS format and lists their contents on standard output. Directory names should contain slashes to separate components, even though MS-DOS uses backslashes. The names *dosdir*, *dosread*, and *doswrite* are all links to the same program. The program sees which function to perform by seeing how it was called.

Command: dosread – read a file from an MS-DOS diskette
Syntax: **dosread**
Flags: **–a**   ASCII file
Examples: dosread 1 g/adv >adv   # Read file *g/adv* from drive 1
                 dosread 0 –a prog.c >x   # Read ASCII file *prog.c* from drive 0

Dosread reads one file from an MS-DOS diskette and writes it on standard output. The file name should use slash, not backslash as a separator. ASCII files have the final CTRL-Z stripped, and carriage return plus line feed is mapped to line feed only, the usual MINIX convention.

Command: doswrite – write a file onto an MS-DOS diskette
Syntax: **doswrite [–a]** drive file
Flags: **–a**   ASCII file
Examples: doswrite 1 x/y <z   # Write file *z* to disk as *x/y*
                 doswrite –a 0 f   # Copy standard input to MS-DOS file *f*

Doswrite writes its standard input to an MS-DOS diskette. The diskette must be formatted and have an MS-DOS file system already in place, including all the directories leading up to the file.

Command: echo – print the arguments
Syntax: **echo [–n]** argument ...
Flags: **–n**   No line feed is output when done
Examples: echo Start Phase 1   # "Start Phase 1" is printed
                 echo –n Hello   # "Hello"

Echo writes its arguments to standard output. They are separated by blanks and terminated with a line feed unless **–n** is present. This command is used mostly in shell scripts.

Command: getlf – wait until a line has been typed
Syntax: **getlf** [argument]
Flags: **(none)**
Example: getlf   # Wait for a line

In shell scripts it is sometimes necessary to pause to give the user a chance to perform some action, such as inserting a diskette. This command prints its argument, if any, and then waits until a carriage return has been typed, at which time it terminates. It is used in */etc/rc*.

Command: **grep – search a file for lines containing a given pattern**
Syntax: **grep [–ensv] pattern [file] ...**
Flags: **–e**   –e *pattern* is the same as *pattern*
                 –n   Print line numbers
                 –s   Status only, no printed output
                 –v   Select lines that do not match
Examples: grep mouse file   # Find lines in *file* containing *mouse*
                 grep [0–9] file   # Print lines containing a digit

Grep searches one or more files (by default, standard input) and selects out all the lines that match the pattern. All the regular expressions accepted by *mined* are allowed. In addition, + can be used instead of * to mean 1 or more occurrences, ? can be used to mean 0 or 1 occurrences, and | can be used between two regular expressions to mean either one of them. Parentheses can be used for grouping. If a match is found, exit status 0 is returned. If no match is found, exit status 1 is returned. If an error is detected, exit status 2 is returned.

Command: **gres – grep and substitute**
Syntax: **gres [–g] pattern string [file] ...**
Flags: **–g**   Only change the first occurrence per line
Examples: gres bug insect   # Replace *bug* with *insect*
                 gres "^[A-Z]+$" CAPS   # Replace capital-only lines with *CAPS*

Gres is a poor man's *sed*. It looks for the same patterns as *grep*, and replaces each one by the given string.

Command: **head – print the first few lines of a file**
Syntax: **head [–n] [file] ...**
Flags: *–n*   How many lines to print
Examples: head –6   # Print first 6 lines of standard input
                 head –1 file1 file2   # Print first line of two files

The first few lines of one or more files are printed. The default count is 10 lines. The default file is standard input.

Command: **kill – send a signal to a process**
Syntax: **kill [–signal] process**
Flags: **(none)**
Examples: kill 35   # Send signal 15 to process 35
                 kill –9 40   # Send signal 9 to process 40
                 kill –2 0   # Send signal 2 to whole process group

A signal is sent to a given process. By default signal 15 (SIGTERM) is sent. Process 0 means all the processes in the sender's process group.

Command: libpack – pack an ASCII assembly code file
Syntax: **libpack**
Flags: **(none)**
Example: libpack <x.s >y.s   # Pack *x.s*

This program is a filter that reads an ASCII assembly code file from standard input and writes the corresponding packed file on standard output. The compiler libraries are archives of packed assembly code files.

Command: libupack – convert a packed assembly code file to ASCII
Syntax: **libupack**
Flags: **(none)**
Example: libupack <y.s >x.s   # Unpack *y.s*

This program is a filter that reads a packed assembly code file from standard input and writes the corresponding ASCII file on standard output.

Command: ln – create a link to a file
Syntax: **ln** file [name]
Flags: **(none)**
Examples: ln file newname   # Make *newname* a synonym for *file*
                    ln /usr/games/chess   # Create a link called *chess*

A directory entry is created for *name*. The entry points to *file*. Henceforth, *name* and *file* can be used interchangeably. If *name* is not supplied, the last component of *file* is used as the link name.

Command: lpr – copy a file to the line printer
Syntax: **lpr** [file] ...
Flags: **(none)**
Examples: lpr file &   # Print *file* on the line printer
                    pr file | lpr &   # Print standard input (*pr*'s output)

Each argument is interpreted as a file to be printed. *Lpr* copies each file to */dev/lp*, without spooling. It inserts carriage returns and expands tabs. Only one *lpr* at a time may be running.

Command: ls – list the contents of a directory
Syntax: ls [–adfgilrst] name ...
Flags: –a All entries are listed, even . and ..
                 –d Do not list contents of directories
                 –f List argument as unsorted directory
                 –g Group id given instead of user id
                 –i I-node number printed in first column
                 –l Long listing: mode, links, owner, size and time
                 –r Reverse the sort order
                 –s Give size in blocks (including indirect blocks)
                 –t Sort by time, latest first
Examples: ls –l   # List files in working directory
                 ls –lis   # List with i-nodes and sizes

For each file argument, list it. For each directory argument, list its contents, unless **–d** is present. When no argument is present, the working directory is listed.

Command: make – a program for maintaining large programs
Syntax: make [–f file] [–ikns] [option] ... [target]
Flags: –f Use *file* as the makefile
                 –i Ignore status returned by commands
                 –k Kill branch on error
                 –n Report, but do not execute
                 –s Silent mode
Examples: make kernel   # Make *kernel* up to date
                 make –n –f file   # Tell what needs to be done

Make is a program that is normally used for developing large programs consisting of multiple files. It keeps track of which object files depend on which source and header files. When called, it does the minimum amount of recompilation to bring the target file up to date.

The file dependencies are expected in *makefile* or *Makefile*, unless another file is specified with **–f**. *Make* has some default rules built in, for example, it knows how to make *.s* files from *.c* files. Here is a sample *makefile*.

```
d=/user/ast                            # d is a macro
program: head.s tail.s                 # program depends on these
        cc -o program head.s tail.s    # tells how to make program
        echo Program done.             # announce completion
head.s:    $d/def.h head.c             # head.s depends on these
tail.s:    $d/var.h tail.c             # tail.s depends on these
```

A complete description of *make* would require too much space here. However, many books on UNIX discuss *make*.

Command: mined – MINIX editor
Syntax: mined [file]
Flags: (none)
Examples: mined /user/ast/book.3   # Edit an existing file
              mined   # Call editor to create a new file
              ls –l | mined   # Use *mined* as a pager to inspect listing

Mined (pronounced min-ed) is a simple full-screen editor. When editing a file, it holds the file in memory, thus speeding up editing, but limiting the editor to files of up to about 43K. Larger files must first be cut into pieces by *split*. Lines may be arbitrarily long. Output from a command may be piped into *mined* so it can be viewed without scrolling off the screen.

At any instant, a window of 24 lines is visible on the screen. The current position in the file is shown by the cursor. Ordinary characters typed in are inserted at the cursor. Control characters and keys on the numeric keypad (at the right-hand side of the keyboard) are used to move the cursor and perform other functions.

Commands exist to move forward and backward a word, and delete words. A word in this context is a sequence of characters delimited on both ends by white space (space, tab, line feed, start of file, or end of file). The commands for deleting characters and words also work on line feeds, making it possible to join two consecutive lines by deleting the line feed between them.

The editor maintains one save buffer (not displayed). Commands are present to move text from the file to the buffer, from the buffer to the file, and to write the buffer onto a new file. If the edited text cannot be written out due to a full disk, it may still be possible to copy the whole text to the save buffer and then write it to a different file on a different disk with CTRL-Q. It may also be possible to escape from the editor with CTRL-S and remove some files.

Some of the commands prompt for arguments (file names, search patterns, etc.). All commands that might result in loss of the file being edited prompt to ask for confirmation.

A key (command or ordinary character) can be repeated *n* times by typing *ESC n key* where *ESC* is the "escape" key.

Forward and backward searching requires a regular expression as the search pattern. Regular expressions follow the same rules as in the UNIX editor, *ed*:

1. Any displayable character matches itself.

2. . (period) matches any character except line feed.

3. ^ (circumflex) matches the start of the line.

4. $ (dollar sign) matches the end of the line.

5. \c matches the character *c* (including period, circumflex, etc).

6. [string] matches any of the characters in the string.

7. [^string] matches any of the characters except those in the string.

8. [x–y] matches any characters between *x* and *y* (e.g., [a–z]).

9. Pattern* matches any number of occurrences of *pattern*.

Some examples of regular expressions are:

The boy	matches the string "The boy"
^$	matches any empty line.
^A.*\.$	matches any line starting with an *A*, ending with a period.
^[A–Z]*$	matches any line containing only capital letters (or empty).
[A–Z0–9]	matches any line containing either a capital letter or a digit.

Control characters cannot be entered into a file simply by typing them because all of them are editor commands. To enter a control character, depress the ALT key, and then while holding it down, hit the ESC key. Release both ALT and ESC and type the control character. Control characters are displayed in reverse video.

The *mined* commands are as follows.

CURSOR MOTION

arrows	Move the cursor in the indicated direction
CTRL-A	Move cursor to start of current line
CTRL-Z	Move cursor to end of current line
CTRL-^	Move cursor to top of screen
CTRL-_	Move cursor to end of screen
CTRL-F	Move cursor forward to start of next word
CTRL-B	Move cursor backward to start of previous word

SCREEN MOTION

Home key	Move to first character of the file
End key	Move to last character of the file
PgUp key	Scroll window up 23 lines (closer to start of the file)
PgDn key	Scroll window down 23 lines (closer to end of the file)
CTRL-U	Scroll window up 1 line
CTRL-D	Scroll window down 1 line

MODIFYING TEXT

Del key	Delete the character under the cursor
Backspace	Delete the character to left of the cursor
CTRL-N	Delete the next word
CTRL-P	Delete the previous word
CTRL-T	Delete tail of line (all characters from cursor to end of line)
CTRL-O	Open up the line (insert line feed and back up)
CTRL-G	Get and insert a file at the cursor position

BUFFER OPERATIONS

CTRL-@	Set mark at current position for use with CTRL-C and CTRL-K
CTRL-C	Copy the text between the mark and the cursor into the buffer
CTRL-K	Delete text between mark and cursor; also copy it to the buffer
CTRL-Y	Yank contents of the buffer out and insert it at the cursor
CTRL-Q	Write the contents of the buffer onto a file

MISCELLANEOUS

numeric +	Search forward (prompts for regular expression)
numeric —	Search backward (prompts for regular expression)
numeric 5	Display the file status
CTRL-]	Go to specific line
CTRL-R	Global replace *pattern* with *string* (from cursor to end)
CTRL-L	Line replace *pattern* with *string*
CTRL-W	Write the edited file back to the disk
CTRL-X	Exit the editor
CTRL-S	Fork off a shell (use CTRL-D to get back to the editor)
CTRL-	Abort whatever the editor was doing and wait for command
CTRL-E	Erase screen and redraw it
CTRL-V	Visit (edit) a new file

Command: mkdir – make a directory
Syntax: **mkdir** directory ...
Flags: **(none)**
Examples: mkdir dir   # Create *dir* in the current directory
              mkdir /user/ast/dir   # Create the specified directory

The specified directory or directories are created. The entries . and .. are inserted into the new directory.

Command: mkfs – make a file system
Syntax: **mkfs** special prototype
Flags: **–L** Make a listing on standard output
Examples: mkfs /dev/fd1 proto   # Make a file system on */dev/fd1*
              mkfs /dev/fd1 360   # Make empty 360 block file system

Mkfs builds a file system and copies specified files to it. The prototype file tells which directories and files to copy to it. If the prototype file cannot be opened, and its name is just a string of digits, an empty file system will be made with the specified number of blocks. A sample prototype file follows. The text following the # sign is comment. In the real prototype file, comments are not allowed.

```
boot                              # boot block file (ignored)
360 63                            # blocks and i-nodes
d--755 1 1                        # root directory
   bin d--755 2 1                 # bin dir: mode (755), uid (2), gid (1)
      sh    ---755 2 1 /user/ast/shell  # shell has mode rwxr-xr-x
      mv    -u-755 2 1 /user/ast/mv     # u = SETUID bit
      login -ug755 2 1 /user/ast/login  # SETUID and SETGID
   $                              # end of /bin
   dev d--755 2 1                 # special files: tty (char), fd0 (block)
      tty   c--777 2 1 4 0        # uid=2, gid=1, major=4, minor=0
      fd0   b--644 2 1 2 0 360    # uid, gid, major, minor, blocks
   $                              # end of /dev
   user d--755 12 1               # user dir: mode (755), uid (12), gid (1)
      ast   d--755 12 1           # /user/ast
      $                           # /user/ast is empty
   $                              # end of /user
$                                 # end of root directory
```

The first entry on each line (except the first 3 and the $ lines, which terminate directories) is the name the file or directory will get on the new file system. Next comes its mode, with the first character being **–dbc** for regular files, directories, block special files and character special files, respectively. The next two characters are used to specify the SETUID and SETGID bits, as shown above. The last three characters of the mode are the *rwx* protection bits.

Following the mode are the uid and gid. For special files, the major and minor devices are needed. The size in blocks must also be specified for block special files (the MINIX block size is 1K; this can only be changed by changing *BLOCK_SIZE* and then recompiling the operating system).

Command: mknod – create a special file
Syntax: **mknod** file [**b**] [**c**] major minor
Flags: **(none)**
Example: mknod /dev/plotter c 7 0 # Create special file for a plotter
  Mknod creates a special file named *file*, with the indicated major and minor device numbers. The second argument specifies a block or character file.

Command: mount – mount a file system
Syntax: **/etc/mount** special file [**–r**]
Flags: **–r** File system is mounted read-only
Example: /etc/mount /dev/fd1 /user# Mount floppy disk 1 on /user

The file system contained on the special file is mounted on *file*. In the example above, the root directory of the file system in drive 1 can be accessed as */user* after the mount. When the file system is no longer needed, it must be unmounted before being removed from the drive.

Command: mv – move or rename a file
Syntax: **mv** file1 file2
                 mv file ... directory
Flags: **(none)**
Examples: mv oldname newname   # Move *oldname* to *newname*
                 mv file1 file2 /user/ast   # Move two files to */user/ast*

Mv moves one or more files from one place in the file system to another. If the old path and new path are on the same device, it is done by linking and unlinking, otherwise by copying.

Command: od – octal dump
Syntax: **od [–bcdhox] [file] [[+] offset [.][b]]**
Flags: **–b** Dump bytes in octal
                 –c Dump bytes as ASCII characters
                 –d Dump words in decimal
                 –h Print addresses in hex (default is octal)
                 –o Dump words in octal (default)
                 –x Dump words in hex
Examples: od –ox file   # Dump *file* in octal and hex
                 od –d file +1000   # Dump *file* starting at byte 01000
                 od –c file +10.b   # Dump *file* starting at block 10

Od dumps a file in one or more formats. If *file* is missing, standard input is dumped. The *offset* argument tells *od* to skip a certain number of bytes or blocks before starting. The offset is in octal bytes, unless it is followed by a "." for decimal or **b** for blocks or both.

Command: passwd – change a login password
Syntax: **passwd [name]**
Flags: **(none)**
Examples: passwd   # Change current user's password
                 passwd ast   # Change ast's password (super–user only)

Passwd is used to change your password. It prompts for the old and new passwords. It asks for the new password twice, to reduce the effect of a typing error. Do not forget to copy the modified password file back to the root file system diskette, or the changes will be lost when the system is rebooted.

Command: pr – print a file
Syntax: **pr** [option] ... [–columns] [+page] [file] ...
Flags: **–h** Take next argument as page header
                 –l Sets page length in lines
                 –n Number the output lines
                 –t Do not print page header or trailer
                 –w Sets line length in characters
Examples: pr –w72 –l60 file   # Use 72 character line, 60 line page
               pr –3 file   # List *file* three columns to a page
               pr +4 file   # Start printing with page 4
     Pr formats one or more files for printing. If no files are specified, standard input is printed. Options are provided for setting the width and height of the page, the number of columns to use (default 1), and the page to start with, among others.

Command: pwd – print working directory
Syntax: **pwd**
Flags: **(none)**
Example: pwd   # Print the name of the working directory
     The full path name of the current working directory is printed.

Command: rev – reverse the characters on each line of a file
Syntax: **rev** [file] ...
Flags: **(none)**
Example: rev file   # Reverse each line
     Each file is copied to standard output with all the characters of each line reversed, last one first and first one last.

Command: rm – remove a file
Syntax: **rm** [–fir] name ...
Flags: **–f** Forced remove: no questions asked
                 –i Interactive remove: ask before removing
                 –r Remove directories too

Examples: rm file   # Remove *file*
                rm -i *.c   # Remove *.c* files, asking about each
Rm removes one or more files. If a file has no write permission, *rm* asks for permission (type "y" or "n") unless **-f** is specified. If the file is a directory, it will be recursively descended and removed if and only if the **-r** flag is present.

Command: rmdir - remove a directory
Syntax: **rmdir** directory ...
Flags: **(none)**
Examples: rmdir /user/ast/foobar   # Remove directory *foobar*
                rmdir /user/ast/f*   # Remove 0 or more directories
The specified directories are removed. Ordinary files are not removed.

Command: roff - text formatter
Syntax: **roff** [**-hs**] [+n] [-n] file ...
Flags: **-h** Expand tabs to spaces in output
                -s Stop before each page; continue on DEL
                +*n* Start printing with page *n*
                n Stop after page *n*
Examples: roff file   # Run off *file*
                roff +5 file   # Run off *file* starting at page 5
Roff is a text formatter. Its input consists of the text to be output, intermixed with formatting commands. A formatting command is a line containing the control character followed by a two character command name, and possibly one or arguments. The control character is initially "." (dot). The formatted output is produced on standard output.

The formatting commands are listed below, with *n* being a number, *c* being a character, and *t* being a title. A + before *n* means it may be signed, indicating a positive or negative change from the current value. Initial values for *n*, where relevant, are given in parentheses.

.ad	Adjust right margin.
.ar	Arabic page numbers.
.br	Line break. Subsequent text will begin on a new line.
.bl n	Insert *n* blank lines.
.bp +n	Begin new page and number it *n*. No *n* means +1.
.cc c	Control character is set to *c*.
.ce n	Center the next *n* input lines.
.de zz	Define a macro called *zz*. A line with ".." ends definition.
.ds	Double space the output. Same as **.ls 2**.
.ef t	Even page footer title is set to *t*.
.eh t	Even page header title is set to *t*.
.fi	Begin filling output lines as full as possible.

.fo t	Footer titles (even and odd) are set to *t*.
.hc c	The character *c* (e.g., %) tells *roff* where hyphens are permitted.
.he t	Header titles (even and odd) are set to *t*.
.hx	Header titles are suppressed.
.hy n	Hyphenation is done if *n* is 1, suppressed if it is 0. Default is 1.
.ig	Ignore input lines until a line beginning with ".." is found.
.in n	Indent *n* spaces from the left margin; force line break.
.ix n	Same as *.in* but continue filling output on current line.
.li n	Literal text on next *n* lines. Copy to output unmodified.
.ll +n	Line length (including indent) is set to *n* (65).
.ls +n	Line spacing: *n* (1) is 1 for single spacing, 2 for double, etc.
.m1 n	Insert *n* (2) blank lines between top of page and header.
.m2 n	Insert *n* (2) blank lines between header and start of text.
.m3 n	Insert *n* (1) blank lines between end of text and footer.
.m4 n	Insert *n* (3) blank lines between footer and end of page.
.na	No adjustment of the right margin.
.ne n	Need *n* lines. If fewer are left, go to next page.
.nn +n	The next *n* output lines are not numbered.
.n1	Number output lines in left margin starting at 1.
.n2 n	Number output lines starting at *n*. If 0, stop numbering.
.ni +n	Indent line numbers by *n* (0) spaces.
.nf	No more filling of lines.
.nx f	Switch input to file *f*.
.of t	Odd page footer title is set to *t*.
.oh t	Odd page header title is set to *t*.
.pa +n	Page adjust by *n* (1). Same as .bp
.pl +n	Paper length is *n* (66) lines.
.po +n	Page offset. Each line is started with *n* (0) spaces.
.ro	Page numbers are printed in Roman numerals.
.sk n	Skip *n* pages (i.e., make them blank), starting with next one.
.sp n	Insert *n* blank lines, except at top of page.
.ss	Single spacing. Equivalent to .ls 1.
.ta	Set tab stops, e.g., .ta 9 17 25 33 41 49 57 65 73 (default).
.tc c	Tabs are expanded into *c*. Default is space.
.ti n	Indent next line *n* spaces; then go back to previous indent.
.tr ab	Translate *a* into *b* on output.
.ul n	Underline the letters and numbers in the next *n* lines.

Command: sh – shell
Syntax: **sh** [file]
Flags: **(none)**
Example: sh < script   # Run a shell script

Sh is the shell. It permits redirection of input and output, pipes, magic characters, background processes, shell scripts and most of the other features of the V7 (Bourne) shell. A few of the more common commands are listed below:

```
date                    # Regular command
sort <file              # Redirect input
sort <file1  >file2     # Redirect input and output
cc file.c 2>error       # Redirect  standard error
a.out >f 2>&1           # Combine standard output and standard error
sort <file1  >>file2    # Append output to file2
sort <file1  >file2 &   # Background job
(ls -l; a.out) &        # Run two background commands sequentially
sort <file | wc         # Two-process pipeline
sort <f | uniq | wc     # Three-process pipeline
ls -l *.c               # List all files ending in .c
ls -l [a-c]*            # List all files beginning with a, b, or c
ls -l ?                 # List all one-character file names
ls \?                   # List the file whose name is question mark
ls '???'                # List the file whose name is three question marks
v=/usr/ast              # Set shell variable v
ls -l $v                # Use shell variable v
PS1='Hi! '              # Change the primary prompt to Hi!
PS2='More: '            # Change the secondary prompt to More:
ls -l $HOME             # List the home directory
echo $PATH              # Echo the search path
if ... then ... else ... fi  # If statement
for ... do ... done     # Iterate over argument list
while ... do ... done   # Repeat while condition holds
case ... esac           # Select clause based on condition
echo $?                 # Echo exit status of previous command
echo $$                 # Echo shell's pid
echo $#                 # Echo number of parameters (shell script)
echo $2                 # Echo second parameter (shell script)
echo $*                 # Echo all parameters (shell script)
```

Command: shar – shell archiver
Syntax: **shar** file ...
Flags: **(none)**
Examples: shar *.c >s   # Collect C programs in shell archive
           sh <s   # Extract files from a shell archive

The named files are collected together into a shell archive written onto standard output. The individual files can be extracted by redirecting the shell archive into the shell. The advantage of *shar* over *ar* is that *shar* archives can be read on almost any UNIX system, whereas numerous, incompatible versions of *ar* are in widespread use. Extracting the files from a shell archive requires that *gres* is accessible. In the distribution, *gres* is in */user/bin* rather than */usr/bin*.

Command: size – print text, data, and bss size of a program
Syntax: **size** [file] ...
Flags: **(none)**
Example: size file   # Print the size of *file*
    The text, data, bss, and total sizes for each argument are printed. If no arguments are present, *a.out* is assumed. The amount of memory available for combined stack and data segment growth is printed in the column "stack." This is the value manipulated by the *chmem* command. The total amount of memory allocated to the program when it is loaded is listed under "memory." This value is just the sum of the other four columns.

Command: sleep – suspend execution for a given number of seconds
Syntax: **sleep** seconds
Flags: **(none)**
Example: sleep 10   # Suspend execution for 10 sec.
    The caller is suspended for the indicated number of seconds. This command is typically used in shell scripts.

Command: sort – sort a file of ASCII lines
Syntax: **sort** [**–bcdfimnru**] [**–t**x] [**–o** name] [+pos1] [–pos2] file ...
Flags: **–b** Skip leading blanks when making comparisons
                –c Check to see if a file is sorted
                –d Dictionary order: ignore punctuation
                –f Fold upper case onto lower case
                –i Ignore nonASCII characters
                –m Merge presorted files
                –n Numeric sort order
                –o Next argument is output file
                –r Reverse the sort order
                –t Following character is field separator
                –u Unique mode (delete duplicate lines)
Examples: sort –nr file   # Sort keys numerically, reversed
                sort +2 –4 file   # Sort using fields 2 and 3 as key
                sort +2 –t: –o out   # Field separator is :
                sort +.3 –.6   # Characters 3 through 5 form the key

Sort sorts one or more files. If no files are specified, standard input is sorted. Output is written on standard output, unless –o is specified. The options +*pos1* –*pos2* use only fields *pos1* up to but not including *pos2* as the sort key, where a field is a string a characters delimited by spaces and tabs, unless a different field delimiter is specified with –t. Both *pos1* and *pos2* have the form *m.n* where *m* tells the number of fields and *n* tells the number of characters. Either *m* or *n* may be omitted.

Command: split – split a large file into several smaller files
Syntax: **split [–n] [file [prefix]]**
Flags: –*n* Number of lines per piece (default: 1000)
Examples: split –200 file   # Split *file* into pieces of 200 lines each
              split file z   # Split *file* into *zaa*, *zab*, etc.
       Split reads *file* and writes it out in *n*-line pieces. By default, the pieces are called *xaa*, *xab*, etc. The optional second argument can be used to provide an alternative prefix for the output file names.

Command: stty – set terminal parameters
Syntax: **stty [option ...]**
Flags: **(none)**
Examples: stty –echo   # Suppress echoing of input
              stty erase #   # Set the erase character to #
       When given no arguments, *stty* prints the current terminal parameters. It can also be used to set the parameters, as follows:

cbreak	- Enter *cbreak* mode; erase and kill disabled
echo	- Echo input on the terminal
nl	- Accept only line feed to end lines
raw	- Enter *raw* mode; no input processing at all
tabs	- Output tabs (do not expand to spaces)
erase c	- Set erase character (initially backspace)
int c	- Set interrupt (SIGINT) character (initially DEL)
kill c	- Set kill line character (initially @)
quit c	- Set quit (SIGQUIT) character (initially CTRL-\)
default	- Set options back to original values

The first five options may be prefixed by – as in –**tabs** to turn the option off. The next four options each have a single character parameter separated by a space from the option. The **default** option sets the mode and the four settable characters back to the values they had when the system was booted. It is useful when a rogue program has messed them up.

Command: su – temporarily log in as super-user or another user
Syntax: **su** [name]
Flags: **(none)** ·
Examples: su   # Become super-user
                su ast   # Become *ast*

Su can be used to temporarily login as another user. It prompts for the super-user password. If the correct password is entered, *su* creates a shell with the desired uid. If no name is specified, *root* is assumed. To exit the temporary shell, type CTRL-D.

Command: sum – compute the checksum and block count of a file
Syntax: **sum** file
Flags: **(none)**
Examples: sum /user/ast/xyz   # Checksum */user/ast/xyz*
Sum computes the checksum of one or more files. It is most often used to see if a file copied from another machine has been correctly received. This program works best when both machines use the same checksum algorithm.

Command: sync – flush the cache to disk
Syntax: **sync**
Flags: **(none)**
Example: sync   # Write out all modified cache blocks
MINIX maintains a cache of recently used disk blocks. The *sync* command writes any modified cache blocks back to the disk. This is essential before stopping the system, and should be done before running any *a.out* program that might crash the system.

Command: tail – print the last few lines of a file
Syntax: **tail** [–n] [file] ...
Flags: –*n* How many lines to print
Examples: tail –6   # Print last 6 lines of standard input
                tail –1 file1 file2   # Print last line of two files
The last few lines of one or more files are printed. The default count is 10 lines. The default file is standard input.

Command: tar – tape archiver
Syntax: **tar [cxtv]** tarfile file ...
Flags: **–c** Create a new archive
                –t Print a table listing the archive's contents
                –v Verbose mode-tell what is going on as it happens
                –x The named files are extracted from the archive
Examples: tar c /dev/fd1 file1 file2   # Create a two-file archive
                tar xv /dev/fd1 file1 file2 # Extract two files from the archive

Tar is an archiver in the style of the standard tape archiver, except that it does not use tape. It's primary advantage over *ar* is that the *tar* format is somewhat more standardized than the *ar* format, making it theoretically possible to transport MINIX files to another computer, but do not bet on it. If the target machine runs MS-DOS, try *doswrite*.

Command: tee – divert standard input to a file
Syntax: **tee [–ai]** file ...
Flags: **–a** Append to the files, rather than overwriting
                –i Ignore interrupts
Examples: cat file1 file2 | tee x   # Save and display two files
                pr file | tee x | lpr   # Save the output of *pr* on *x*

Tee copies standard input to standard output. It also makes copies on all the files listed as arguments.

Command: time – report how long a command takes
Syntax: **time** command
Flags: **(none)**
Examples: time a.out   # Report how long *a.out* takes
                time ls –l *.c   # Report how long the command takes

The command is executed and the real time, user time, and system time (in seconds) are printed.

Command: touch – update a file's time of last modification
Syntax: **touch [–c]** file ...
Flags: **–c** Do not create the file
Example: touch *.h   # Make the .*h* files look recent

The time of last modification is set to the current time. This command is mostly used to trick *make* into thinking that a file is more recent than it really is. If the file being touched does not exist, it is created, unless the **–c** flag is present.

Command: **tr – translate character codes**
Syntax: **tr [–cds]** [string1] [string2]
Flags: **–c** Complement the set of characters in *string1*
                 –d Delete all characters specified in *string1*
                 –s Squeeze all runs of characters in *string1* to one character
Examples: tr "[a–z]" "[A–Z]" <x >y   # Convert upper case to lower case
                 tr –d "0123456789" <f1 >f2 # Delete all digits from *f1*

Tr performs simple character translation. When no flag is specified, each character in *string1* is mapped onto the corresponding character in *string2*.

Command: **true – exit with the value true**
Syntax: **true**
Flags: **(none)**
Example: while true   # List the directory until DEL is hit
                 do ls –l
                 done

This command returns the value *true*. It is used for shell programming.

Command: **umount – unmount a mounted file system**
Syntax: **/etc/umount** special
Flags: **(none)**
Example: /etc/umount /dev/fd1   # Unmount floppy disk 1

A mounted file system is unmounted after the cache has been flushed to disk. A floppy disk should never be removed while it is mounted. If this happens, and is discovered before another floppy disk is inserted, the original one can be replaced without harm. Attempts to unmount a file system holding working directories or open files will be rejected with a "device busy" message.

Command: **uniq – delete consecutive identical lines in a file**
Syntax: **uniq [–cdu]** [+n] [–n] [input [output]]
Flags: **–c** Give count of identical lines in the input
                 –d Only duplicate lines are written to output
                 –u Only unique lines are written to output
Examples: uniq +2 file   # Ignore first 2 fields when comparing
                 uniq –d inf outf   # Write duplicate lines to *outf*

Uniq examines a file for consecutive lines that are identical. All but duplicate entries are deleted, and the file is written to output. The $+n$ option skips the first n fields, where a field is defined as a run of characters separated by white space. The $-n$ option skips the first n spaces. Fields are skipped first.

Command: update – periodically write the buffer cache to disk
Syntax: **/etc/update**
Flags: **(none)**
Example: /etc/update &   # Start a process that flushes the cache
    When the system is booted, *update* is started up in the background from
/etc/rc to issue a SYNC system call every 30 sec.

Command: wc – count characters, words, and lines in a file
Syntax: **wc [–clw] file ...**
Flags: **–c**   Print character count
                 –l   Print line count
                 –w   Print word count
Examples: wc file1 file2   # Print all three counts for both files
                 wc –l file   # Print line count only
    Wc reads each argument and computes the number of characters, words and
lines it contains. A word is delimited by white space (space, tab, or line feed).
If no flags are present, all three counts are printed.

2.5. LIBRARIES

    The MINIX distribution contains a substantial number of library procedures,
including the system call library, stdio, and many others. The procedures are
contained in the archive */usr/lib/libc.a*.
    The archive contains several kinds of procedures, among them procedures
called by the compiler that are not normally explicitly called by user programs.
For example, when the compiler has to generate code to do multiplication or
division on longs, it does not generate in-line code. It calls library procedures
instead.
    The archive also calls user-callable procedures. The ones corresponding to
the system calls have the same parameters as their UNIX counterparts, as do the
stdio procedures for the most part. However, there are a few minor exceptions
to this rule.
    For one thing, to keep them small, many of the standard MINIX programs do
not use *stdio*. To avoid having the *stdio* package loaded with these (and all) programs, the C run-time start-off routine, *crtso*, (which is loaded with all C programs), does not flush *stdio*'s internal buffers when the main program returns to
it after completion. User programs that use *stdio* should therefore make the call

```
_cleanup();
```

before exiting or returning from the main program. (Note the underscore, which
is part of the name.)

Another minor difference between MINIX *stdio* and UNIX *stdio* is how buffering of *stdout* is done. The MINIX version collects all the characters generated by each call to *printf* (or *fprintf*) and makes one WRITE system call per *printf*.

For noninteractive programs such as *ls* it is more efficient not to flush the buffer per *printf*, but to wait until it fills up. To disable the flushing of *stdout* on each *printf*, put the statement

```
setbuf(stdout, buffer);
```

at the beginning of the program, where *buffer* is an array of characters of size *BUFSIZ* (defined in *stdio.h*). When the program exits, it is then essential to make the call

```
fflush(stdout);
```

to flush the final bytes, or alternatively, to call *_cleanup* to flush all the buffers if more than one output file has been used.

The header file *stdio.h* is located in */usr/include*, along with several other common header files.

The version of *printf* provided lacks some of the more exotic options of V7. One clear difference however, is that V7 accepts both %D and %ld for printing longs. MINIX only accepts the former. Similarly, MINIX only accepts %O and %X for printing longs in octal and hex.

The other library procedures, such as *abs*, *malloc*, and *strcmp*, have the same parameters as the corresponding V7 procedures, and they perform the same function. Space limitations make it impossible to provide detailed documentation here about them. To see which procedures are available, type

```
ar tv /usr/lib/libc.a | mined
```

2.6. FILE FORMATS

In this section we will describe the format of several important files: executable files, archives, and library modules.

2.6.1. Executable File Format (a.out files)

An executable file consists of three parts: a header, the program text and the initialized data. The uninitialized data (the so-called bss segment) is not present in the executable file.

Two memory models are supported by the operating system. The small model has up to 64K memory total, for text, data, and stack. The separate I and D space model has 64K for the text and an additional 64K for data plus stack.

There is no space between the header and text or between the text and data, except that for a separate I and D program, the text size must be a multiple of 16 bytes, the last 0 to 15 of which may be padding. The normal header is 32 bytes and is the same as that of PC-IX. It consists of eight longs as follows:

0: 0x04100301L (small model), or 0x04200301L (separate I and D)
1: 0x00000020L (32-byte header), or 0x00000030L (48-byte header)
2: size of text segment in bytes
3: size of initialized data in bytes
4: size of bss in bytes
5: 0x00000000L
6: total memory allocated to program
7: 0x00000000L

An alternative 48-byte header is also acceptable, and consists of the standard header followed by 16 bytes that are ignored. The longs are stored with the low-order byte first, so the first byte of the file is 0x01 and the next one is 0x03.

One of the fields in the header is the total amount of space that the program will be allocated when it is executed. It is equal to the sum of the text, data, bss, and dynamic allocation. (For separate I and D programs, it is the sum of the data, bss, and dynamic allocation only). The dynamic allocation is the total amount of memory reserved for the stack plus growth of the data segment. The dynamic allocation can be changed with the *chmem* command, which just updates long 6 in the header.

2.6.2. Archive Format

The archive format consists of a sequence of (header, file) pairs, with the magic number 0177545 prepended to the beginning of the file. Each file header consists of 26 bytes as follows (sizes in parentheses):

name   (14)   - File name
time   (4)   - Time of last modification
uid   (1)   - Used id (truncated to 1 byte)
gid   (1)   - Group id
mode   (2)   - File mode (protection bits)
size   (4)   - File length

If a file has an odd number of bytes, a zero byte is added at the end so that each header begins at an even address. The zero byte is not included in the size field. The two longs in the header are stored with the high-order word first, in order to be V7 compatible.

2.6.3. Library Format

The MINIX library format consists of an archive of compact assembly code files. Each file in the archive normally contains just one procedure, although in a few cases two or three closely related procedures are in the same file. Each symbol that is to be visible outside the file must be declared in a *.define* statement. All the *.define* statements must occur at the start of the file, with no other statements before them. These statements are generated only when the C compiler is called with the **–LIB** flag.

Compact assembly code can be generated from ordinary ASCII assembly code by using the filter *libpack*. Compact assembly code can be turned back into ASCII by using the filter *libupack*. If a file is packed and then unpacked, the result will not be identical to the original because comments and excess white space are removed during the packing and cannot be restored. The resulting file will assemble into exactly the same binary file, however.

The packing algorithm relies on the fact that input to the assembler is a sequence of bytes, but only codes 0 to 127 (the ASCII character set) are used. What *libpack* does is recognize commonly occurring strings, and replace them with codes 128 to 255. For example, code 128 is *push ax*, code 129 is *ret*, code 130 is *mov bp,sp*, and so on. The exact list of strings mapped can be found by looking at the source of *libpack* or *libupack*. In theory, any file can be compacted, but if none of the approximately 120 built in strings occur in the file, the output will be identical to the input.

The advantage of this scheme over, say, a Huffman code is that an archive may contain some packed files and some unpacked files. They need not be distinguished in any way. *Asld* has been programmed to expand code 128 into *push ax* whenever it occurs, and so forth. If only ASCII codes appear in the input, no expansion occurs and no harm is done.

3

MINIX IMPLEMENTERS GUIDE

This chapter is intended for those readers who wish to modify MINIX or its utilities. In the following pages we will tell what the various files do and how the pieces are put together to form the whole.

One major problem is that some readers will undoubtedly want to use MINIX itself as the development system, others will want to use MS-DOS, and yet others will want to use one of the many UNIX systems available for the IBM PC (or even for other computers). Unfortunately, these systems all differ slightly, which gives rise to problems.

As a simple example, no two C compilers accept exactly the same dialect of C, and no two of them produce the same *a.out* file format. Furthermore, each assembler for the 8088 has its own input syntax and pseudoinstructions. Consequently this chapter is not a cookbook (*Joy of MINIX*). All we can do is try to provide enough background information to enable the aspiring implementer to tackle any problems that arise.

MINIX was developed on an IBM PC-XT using PC-IX. If that system is used as the development system, few problems will be encountered. If a 640K PC with two 360K drives is available, MINIX itself can be used as the development system. With a little bit of work, other systems can also be used. MS-DOS is not needed, except for formatting new diskettes.

Before modifying MINIX it is strongly recommended that you gain experience using it. Try running the programs in Chap. 2, especially *cp*, *df*, *mkdir*, *mkfs*, *mount*, *rm*, and *umount*, all of which will be heavily used during implementation.

Try to recompile the original system in your own environment, to see how that is done. Only then is it sensible to begin modifying MINIX. It is probably easiest to work as root when modifying the system.

3.1. INTRODUCTION

A running MINIX system consists of three or four diskettes: the boot diskette, the root file system, the /usr file system (normally mounted on drive 0), and optionally the /user file system (mounted on drive 1, if available). All of these pieces are independent. You can construct one or more new file systems to use with the original operating system, which is on the boot diskette, or you can build a new operating system to use with the original file systems. You can also modify some, but not all, of the file systems. Each one is self contained.

The boot diskette contains the executable image of the operating system, as well as the file system checker, *fsck*. When the PC is booted from it, the operating system is loaded into memory at address 1536 and *fsck* is loaded just after it, typically at an address of about 85K.

Control is initially passed to *fsck*, which displays the menu and waits for a command. If the command specifies that a file system is to be checked or an empty file system is to be built, *fsck* performs the work and then displays the menu again. If the command is an equal sign, *fsck* jumps to address 1536 to start MINIX. The memory occupied by *fsck* will shortly be overwritten by the root file system on the RAM disk.

The boot diskette is built by a program called *build*, which concatenates six programs in a special way, removing headers, padding pieces out to multiples of 16 bytes, and making certain patches to the resulting file. The six programs are: (1) the boot block, (2) the kernel, (3) the memory manager, (4) the file system, (5) the system initializer, and (6) the file system checker. Each of these programs is compiled and linked independently of the others. It is thus possible to change the file system, for example, without having to touch the kernel at all, not even to relink it. We will discuss how each of these programs is made and how *build* works later in this chapter.

File systems, including the root file system, /usr, and /user, can be made using *mkfs*. It is also possible to make an empty file system using the *fsck* menu, mount the file system, and then copy files to it. Existing file systems can be modified by mounting them, and then copying files to them or removing files from them.

The only difference between a file system intended as the root file system and one intended as /usr or /user is the size. When a file system is created, either by *mkfs* or by *fsck*, the number of blocks and i-nodes is written into its super-block and cannot be changed. A file system intended for /usr or /user will normally use 360 blocks, but one intended as the root file system will usually be smaller, to avoid tying up so much memory for RAM disk. The RAM disk size is determined dynamically when the system is booted by simply reading the root file system's super-block to see how big it is. (Throughout this chapter it will be assumed that both the block size and zone size are 1K, and little distinction will be made between blocks and zones.)

The MINIX sources contain nine directories with code and header files, and one directory, *doc*, containing some documentation. The code and header directories are as follows:

kernel   - process, message, and I/O device handling
mm   - the memory manager
fs   - the file system
h   - the headers used by the operating system
lib   - the library routines
tools   - miscellaneous tools and utilities
commands   - the commands (e.g., *cp*, *grep*, *ls*)
test   - programs for testing MINIX
include   - the headers used by the commands

We will look at each of these directories in detail as we need them. Some of the directories contain subdirectories containing assembly code or other files specific to one compiler or operating system.

Setting Up

Before trying to carry out the instructions contained in this chapter, you should read it all the way through to get a reasonable grasp of what you have to do and why. In fact, it is a good idea to run *build* to make a new boot diskette using the binaries supplied (see Sec. 3.5) before trying to recompile any of the parts of the operating system.

It will be tacitly assumed throughout this chapter that the development is being done on a PC with two 360K diskettes. For PC/ATs with a single 1.2M diskette, the procedure is slightly different, as noted in a few places. Furthermore, all references to diskette sizes of 360 blocks should be replaced by 1200 blocks for 1.2M diskettes.

MINIX is a large program. Unless you are a professional software developer, it is likely to be an order of magnitude larger than any program you have ever written. Many of the complications involved in recompiling it occur because the sources do not fit on a single diskette. This fact permeates every facet of the implementer's work.

To start with, you will need a large number of blank diskettes to hold the sources, intermediate files, executable programs, and new file systems. These diskettes should be standard IBM-compatible, double-sided, double-density, 360K diskettes. Before starting, format at least 10 diskettes with the format program of MS-DOS 2.0 or a later version. Format more diskettes as you need them. All diskettes must be formatted before being used.

The MINIX sources as distributed contain 9 directories with programs in them. As mentioned above, they are called *kernel, mm, fs, h, lib, tools, commands, test,* and *include.* To rebuild the operating system, you will need the first six; to rebuild the file systems you will need the last six. The directories *h, lib,* and *tools* are needed for both.

Before starting work, you should copy the information from the source diskettes to the newly formatted blank diskettes in a special way. The originals can then be put away for safe keeping. For each source diskette, make as many copies of it as there are directories on it. For example, for a diskette containing directories *a, b, c,* make three copies of it. This can be done by inserting the source diskette in drive 0 and the blank diskette in drive 1 (unmounted), and typing

```
cp /dev/fd0 /dev/fd1
```

Now remove directories *b* and *c* from the first copy, directories *a* and *c* from the second copy, and directories *a* and *b* from the third copy. The result will be that each directory will be on a diskette all by itself. Finally, copy the *h* directory and all its files to the *kernel, mm,* and *fs* diskettes. The *h* directory should be at the top level, not a subdirectory of *kernel* etc. because files are included as *../h/const.h* and so on.

On a system with only 1 drive, first put an empty MINIX file system on each blank diskette using *mkfs.* Then remove everything from the root file system except *cp,* mount a source diskette, and copy as much of it as possible to the RAM disk. The *df* program can be put in */bin* to keep track of available space. Then unmount the source diskette and mount the new (empty) diskette in its place, copying the files from the root device to it. Repeat several times until everything has been copied.

When doing the development on a single drive PC/AT, it will also be necessary to create directories *bin* and *lib* on each source diskette, and copy some files from */usr/bin* and */usr/lib* to each one. That way, no matter which source diskette is mounted on */usr* at any instant, all the necessary binaries and libraries will be available.

Some directories contain subdirectories called *MINIX, PCIX,* and *C86.* These directories contain assembly language files, makefiles, etc. that differ from system to system. If you are going to use MINIX as the development system, move all the files in the *MINIX* directory into the directory one level above it. For example, *kernel/MINIX/makefile* becomes *kernel/makefile.*

Similarly, if you are going to use PC-IX (or some other version of UNIX such as XENIX), use the files from *PCIX.* If you plan to use MS-DOS, use the *C86* directory. Although these files are specifically for the Computer Innovations C86 compiler, they are a better starting point for other MS-DOS compilers than the MINIX or PC-IX files. If you are using a system other than MINIX, PC-IX or MS-DOS with the C86 compiler, you will probably have to make minor changes to some of these files.

Once you have made a choice of subdirectory and moved its files one level up, remove all the subdirectories because every block of space will be needed later.

We now encounter the first obstacle thrown up by the large size of MINIX. The *commands* directory is too large to fit on a single diskette. Logically, it is a single directory, but when using floppy‑disks it will be necessary to split it up onto multiple diskettes, each one having a single directory, *commands*, at the top level, and holding some of the programs. Do not fill the diskettes completely full; at least 100K should be left unused on each one. The choice of which commands go on which diskette is unimportant.

A few programs need files from the *include* directory that are not contained in */usr/lib/include*. These are contained on one of the source diskettes. Other programs need files from *h*. These should be copied to the relevant diskette when their absence is noted by the compiler.

Implementers with a hard disk should create a directory *minix* on the hard disk and then create and load the nine subdirectories. As with the floppy disk systems, for each directory with subdirectories, one of them should be chosen and its contents placed in the directory. None of the subdirectories should be created on the hard disk.

The *tools* directory contains two or three programs that may be needed during the development process: *dos2out*, *build*, and *mkfs*. The first one, *dos2out*, converts MS-DOS *.EXE* files to MINIX format. It is only needed when MS-DOS is being used as the development system. The second one, *build*, puts together the compiled and linked pieces of MINIX to form the boot diskette. The third one, *mkfs*, builds MINIX file systems. To build a MINIX file system, you must use *this* version of *mkfs*. Accept no substitutes. Although *mkfs* is needed in both *commands* and in *tools*, its source is only included in the distribution once, so you have to get it into both directories by copying it.

Compile these programs to run on your development system, and use as directed. If your development system is MINIX or PC-IX, you will not need *dos2out*. If it is MS-DOS, compile these three programs with the flag *-DDOS*, for example,

```
cc -c -DDOS mkfs.c
```

After all these steps have been carried out, the original diskette distribution should be put away and all subsequent work done with the directory-per-diskette copies.

3.2. THE LIBRARY

The operating system and many of the commands use library procedures. These procedures must be linked in when the binary (i.e., executable) program is made. To speed up linking, they are precompiled, and kept in a library from which the linker extracts them. The following sections deal with how the library is built and maintained.

If you are using MINIX as the development system, it is not necessary to build the library. A complete, properly ordered MINIX library is already present as the archive */usr/lib/libc.a*. Just use it.

3.2.1. Internal Compiler Procedures

The necessary library procedures can be divided into two disjoint categories: user-callable procedures and internal compiler procedures. The user-callable procedures include the system call library procedures such as *open*, *read*, and *fork*, the standard I/O library procedures, such as *fopen*, *getc*, and *printf*, and miscellaneous procedures, such as *atoi*, *isatty*, and *strcmp*. The sources for all these procedures are provided in the distribution. They merely need to be compiled and put in the library.

The other category is much harder to deal with. Nearly all C compilers use library procedures as part of the generated code. For example, many C compilers do not compile in-line code for multiplication and division on longs. Instead they call the library routines *lmul* and *ldiv*. Similarly, the first or second instruction of each compiled C procedure is often a call to *csv*, which saves the registers and reserves storage for the local variables on the stack.

These internal procedures are written for use with one specific compiler. The version of *lmul* provided in the library that comes with compiler X is almost guaranteed not to work with compiler Y due to different calling conventions, assumptions about which registers it may and may not destroy, and so on. For this reason, none of the sources for the internal procedures are provided in the distribution. You have to use those that come with your compiler.

However, using the library that comes with your compiler can lead to serious problems. That library not only contains the small internal procedures, such as *lmul*, which are basically harmless, but it also contains the system call procedures such as *read*, which make foreign operating system calls. For example, if you were to compile and link one of the MINIX utilities with an MS-DOS compiler, the binary program produced might contain MS-DOS system calls, which would not work when the program ran on MINIX.

Thus we are faced with a situation in which the user-callable procedures must be derived from the supplied sources, but the internal procedures must be those that go with the particular compiler being used. The solution is to first compile the MINIX library sources and put them in the MINIX library. Then the necessary internal compiler procedures are extracted from the library supplied with the compiler and added to the MINIX library. When a MINIX program is linked, only the MINIX library is specified, thus preventing accidental use of a procedure that might make a foreign system call.

One problem with this approach is that in order to extract the compiler's internal procedures from the library, you must know which ones they are. For the PC-IX and C86 compilers, the necessary procedures are listed below. For other compilers, the only way to find out is to initially assume that none are needed, and try compiling some programs. If the compiler generates calls to internal procedures, these will be flagged by the linker as undefined external symbols. The necessary procedures can then be extracted from the compiler's library, inspected to make sure they contain no system calls, and added to the MINIX library. This process may have to be iterated several times before all of them have been pinpointed. To speed up the process, write a test program that does addition, subtraction, multiplication, division, and modulo on short integers, unsigned integers, and long integers, and try compiling and linking it.

This is an important point, so we will repeat it. Never link a MINIX program with any library other than the MINIX library, and never put any procedure in the MINIX library unless you are sure that it makes no system calls. Accidentally linking into a MINIX program a procedure that makes an MS-DOS, PC-IX, XENIX, or other foreign system call will lead to sure disaster. (Modifying MINIX so that it can handle not only all its own system calls, but also those of MS-DOS, PC-IX, and XENIX as well is left as an exercise for the reader who has a spare decade to kill.)

The directory */usr/lib* contains three assembly language files, *crtso.s*, *end.s*, and *head.s*. The first one, *crtso.s*, is the C run-time start-off procedure. It must be the first procedure in any binary program. When a program gets control after an EXEC system call, execution always begins at address 0, which must be the start of *crtso*. This little routine puts *argc*, *argv*, and *envp* on the stack properly, and calls *_main*.

It also defines some compiler-dependent labels needed to mark the start of the text, data, and bss segments. The file *end.s* defines the labels needed at the end of these segments. When *cc* is called with the argument *file.s*, the command that is actually executed is

```
asld /usr/lib/crtso.s file.s /usr/lib/libc.a /usr/lib/end.s
```

The file *head.s* is analogous to *crtso.s*, but is only used for linking the memory manager, the file system, and *init*, because they are started off directly by the kernel, not by an EXEC system call.

3.2.2. Ordering the Procedures in the Library

Another issue that arises when building the library is the ordering of the procedures in it. Some linkers do not care about the order, but others do. Most linkers are one pass, which means that as the linker examines each procedure in the library, it makes the decision to extract it or not based on the information it has at that instant.

To see what consequences this strategy has for library ordering, consider a program that calls *getc* to get the next input character. The procedure *getc* calls *read*. If *read* happens to be placed before *getc* in the library, when the linker processes *read* while scanning the library, it will not extract it because it is not used in the user's program. When the linker comes to *getc*, it will extract it and see that *getc* calls *read*. As it continues to scan the library, the linker will keep an eye out for *read*, but it will never find it and will eventually terminate the link with a message saying that *read* is an undefined symbol.

The obvious solution is to order all library procedures in such a way that if *X* calls *Y*, then *X* is located before *Y* in the library. It is easy to dream up situations where such an ordering is impossible, for example, *X* calls *Y*, *Y* calls *Z*, and *Z* calls *X*. Fortunately, in practice such situations rarely occur. On UNIX systems, the *lorder* command can be used to order the modules in a library.

Another factor to be taken into account when ordering the library is performance. Some linkers stop scanning a library when they have found all the procedures that they need. This observation leads to the goal of placing the most commonly used procedures as early as possible in the library.

3.2.3. Assembly Language Procedures

Although nearly all of the MINIX library is written in C, a handful of procedures had to be written in assembly language. Some of these procedures are not located in the directory *lib* itself, but in one of its subdirectories. If you have followed the instructions given above, you will have already copied the files from one of the subdirectories into *lib*.

Another point concerning the assembly code is the peculiar property that some C compilers have of not handling long names the same way as their own assemblers. When confronted with the name *catchsig*, for example, virtually all C compilers will prepend an underscore and then truncate the result to eight characters, yielding *_catchsi* as the external symbol. When the name *_catchsig* is used in an assembly routine, most assemblers will also truncate it to eight characters, yielding the same name, but a few of them do not truncate it, resulting in an undefined symbol *_catchsig* used by the assembly language file but defined nowhere. If you discover undefined symbols of this kind, the solution is to edit the assembly code files and truncate all symbols to eight characters by hand.

At least one compiler does not prepend the underscore, but attaches it *after* the name. In the above example, the external symbol would be *catchsig_*. Again, the assembly code files must then be manually edited to make the names agree with what the C compiler generates.

3.2.4. Step-by-Step Instructions

The library sources are contained in the archive *libsrc.a* rather than as separate files (to save space on the distribution diskette). Extract them and delete the archive by typing:

```
ar x libsrc.a; rm libsrc.a
```

Compile all the C files and assemble all the assembly code files in *lib*, but do not link them. If the work is being done on UNIX, the shell script *run* can be used. If the work is being done on MINIX, nothing needs to be done. The library */usr/lib/libc.a* on the */usr* diskette is complete and ready for use.

At this point you will have over 100 object files. The next step is to augment this collection by extracting the necessary internal compiler routines from the compiler's own library. Below is a list of files that probably need to be extracted for the PC-IX and C86 compilers:

PC-IX   - *ldiv.o, lmul.o, lrem.o, aldiv.o, almul.o, alrem.o, divsub.o*

C86   - *zldivmod, ziswitch, zfloatpp, zlrsshift, zllshift, zlmul, zlrushift*
          zsswitch, zentry

If the MINIX C compiler is being used, no procedures need to be extracted since everything that is needed is already in the library.

The procedures *csv* and *cret* need special care. Some compilers use them for procedure entry and exit, and others do not. If your compiler uses them, be sure to check to see that they do not make system calls. Some versions of *csv* check for stack overflow, and call *write* to report the problem. If this is the case, you will have to program new versions that do not do the checking. In most cases these procedures are only a few instructions. An example is given in the file *csv.s*, which can be used with PC-IX.

Once all the object files have been assembled, the order must be determined based on who calls whom. The command

```
ar t /usr/lib/libc.a >listing
```

gives the order of the MINIX library, which is a good starting point for other compilers. With UNIX the library, */usr/lib/libc.a*, is built using the archiver, *ar*.

One last note. Most compilers produce .o files as the final compilation step. The MINIX C compiler produces only .s (assembly code) files, which are then put in the library. The MINIX assembler-loader expects .s files rather than o files. When using the MINIX compiler, for example, to recompile library procedures that have been modified, the **–LIB** and **–c** flags are required in order to get the proper .*define* pseudoinstructions into the output files.

3.3. MAKING NEW FILE SYSTEMS

MINIX uses several file systems: the root file system, */usr*, and possibly */user*. All of these are constructed the same way. The following sections describe how to make new file systems for MINIX.

3.3.1. Concepts

There are no hard and fast rules about which programs should go on the root file system diskette and which should go elsewhere, except that *login* and *sh* must go in */bin* because *init* expects them there. In general, programs that are heavily used should be put in the root file system, because the root file system goes on the RAM disk. At least 50K should be left free so temporary files can be created in */tmp*.

An important issue is how large to make the root file system. The larger it is, the less room there is in memory for user programs. For 640K computers, a 240K RAM disk is reasonable. The only difference between the distributions for 256K and 640K PC's is the size of the root file system and its consequences, such as the impossibility of having all the utilities online with only 256K.

The general strategy for making new file systems is to first compile and link all the programs that are to go on the new file system. If need be, the executable files will have to be converted to MINIX format. Then the *mkfs* program is run to build a new file system, usually on a diskette, but possibly as a hard disk file.

MINIX supports two memory models: small model and separate instruction and data space model. In the former, a maximum of 64K is allowed for the entire program. In the latter, a maximum of 64K is allowed for the program text, and an additional 64K is allowed for the data and stack combined. No other models are supported, to encourage programmers to write small, modular programs. The current assembler-loader does not generate separate I and D space programs, but when large programs are set up with separate I and D space by another compiler (e.g., on PC-IX), the operating system can handle them.

Any C compiler can be used to compile the commands, but it is essential that they be linked only with the MINIX library, as discussed in the previous section. Accidentally linking in a library procedure that makes a foreign system call will almost certainly lead to an unexpected kernel trap.

When MINIX executes a program, it loads the program into memory and then transfers control to address 0. Address 0 must contain the C run-time start-off procedure, *crtso*. This procedure arranges for *argc*, *argv*, and *envp* to be pushed onto the stack using the standard C calling sequence so that *main* can access them. Because *crtso* is the first procedure that the linker sees, it must contain directives to define the various segments used. These differ from compiler to compiler so several versions are provided.

All executable programs must be in MINIX format, as described in Chap. 2. If an MS-DOS compiler is used, the resulting *.EXE* file will not be in MINIX format and thus cannot be executed by MINIX. A program, *dos2out* is provided in the *tools* directory to read a *.EXE* file and write a new file in MINIX format.

This conversion is not entirely trivial. The header format used for *.EXE* files does not include the text size, which MINIX needs. In order to force this information into the *.EXE* header, the *crtso* file used for MS-DOS (C68 compiler) forces the symbol *DGROUP* to be relocatable, thus getting its origin into the header. Since *DGROUP* is at the start of the data, its value is the size of the text. The utility *dos2out* expects *DGROUP* to be the only relocatable symbol.

It is normal in the UNIX world for C compilers to gather all the uninitialized variables, structures, and arrays together into the bss part of the data segment, following the initialized data. This scheme results in an executable program file whose size is equal to the sum of the sizes of the header, text, and initialized data. For example, a program with 3K text, 1K initialized data, and an uninitialized 50K array will have an executable file of about 4K. The bss area is set to zero by MINIX when the program is executed.

Unfortunately, some MS-DOS compilers do not distinguish between initialized and uninitialized data. They treat all variables as initialized data. If the above program were compiled with one of these compilers, the executable program would occupy about 54K of space on the disk, rather than 4K. Use of such a compiler will greatly limit the number of programs that can be kept in /*bin* and /*usr/bin*. If your compiler has this property, you are advised to replace it with one that does not.

The general strategy for making a new file system is to first compile all the commands that are to be put on it. These may well be spread over several diskettes. When all the compilations have been completed, and all the files converted to MINIX format, if need be, the resulting executable MINIX files should be gathered together in a single directory, conventionally *commands/bin*. On a system without a hard disk, a new diskette should be formatted and the directory *commands/bin* made on it. Then all the executable files should be copied there. A directory *tools* should also be put on the diskette, and loaded with *mkfs* and the prototype file.

A file system is made by running *mkfs*. If you are working on PC-IX, MS-DOS, or some other system, be sure to run the MINIX version of *mkfs* compiled for that system, not the version compiled for MINIX, and certainly not the *mkfs* that came with the development system. *Mkfs* takes a prototype file as described in Chap. 2, and builds the new file system. The new file system is normally generated on a diskette, but when using a hard disk, it can also be written onto a file, and copied to a diskette later.

The above process should be repeated for each file system to be made. Once all the file systems have been constructed, MINIX can be run, and several file systems merged by copying the files. This last step may be required in order to make a file system that is full down to the last block because a diskette containing executable programs and *mkfs* cannot hold a full 360K worth of programs— *mkfs* also takes up some space.

3.3.2. Step-by-Step Instructions

The first step is to make the library, as described in 3.2. Next, the programs to be compiled should be gathered together in the directory *commands*. On a system without a hard disk, the programs will have to be spread over several diskettes in order to leave enough room on each for the *h* and *include* directories, as well as space for the compiler and linker temporary files.

When using MINIX as the development system, a program can be compiled by typing

```
cc -I/usr/lib/include prog.c
```

(assuming the include files are located in */usr/lib/include*, where they normally are). The proper run-time start-off routine and libraries are automatically used.

When using PC-IX or another UNIX system for building the file system, the procedure is slightly different, in order to use the MINIX run-time start-off routine and the MINIX library instead of the native one. Compile, but do not link each program in *commands*, by typing

```
cc -c -O prog.c
```

To link *commands/prog.o* from inside the *commands* directory and put the resulting executable file on *bin/prog*, type

```
ld -s -o bin/prog ../lib/crtso.o prog.o ../lib/libc.a ../lib/end.o
```

The **–s** flag strips off the symbol table to make the binary file smaller. Alternatively, the flag can be omitted and *strip* used to get rid of the symbol table. An **–i** flag may be used to specify separate I and D space.

On PC-IX, *chmem* can now be used to reduce the dynamic allocation size. For many nonrecursive programs that have no local arrays and do not use the BRK system call, directly or indirectly, 1K is adequate for the stack. The command

```
chmem =1024 bin/prog
```

sets it to 1K. Using *chmem* does not affect the amount of disk space occupied by the program, but does change the amount of memory occupied when the program is executed. Smaller programs mean that more background processes can be running simultaneously. If a program crashes or acts strange, try giving it more stack space with *chmem*.

With MS-DOS, the exact command used to compile the program depends on the compiler being used. After compilation, linking can be typically performed by the command

```
link ..\lib\crtso.obj+prog.obj,prog,listing,..\lib\lib.a
```

After the *.EXE* file has been built, it must be converted to MINIX form by the command

```
dos2out -d prog
```

which reads *PROG.EXE* and writes the output on *PROG.OUT*. The flag **–d**, which is optional, specifies that *PROG.EXE* is to be deleted after *PROG.OUT* has been made.

The subdirectories in *commands* contain the files *makefile* and *make.bat* for use with *make* and MS-DOS, respectively. To compile and link *prog.c* on UNIX or MINIX, the call to make is

```
make f=prog
```

The macro *f* used in *makefile* is assumed to contain the name of the program, without the *.c* suffix. Unlike the *make* version, the MS-DOS batch file can handle several compilations on a single call, for example

```
make prog1 prog2 prog3
```

When all the programs that will go on the new file system have been compiled and linked, they should be gathered together in a single directory, for example, *commands/bin*. On a system with only floppy disks, this directory will normally be on a fresh diskette, not the ones containing the sources. An executable version of the program *mkfs* should also be present.

The directory must also contain the prototype file, as described in Chap. 2 under the listing for *mkfs*. This file tells how big the new file system is to be (e.g., 360 blocks for PC diskettes), and how many i-nodes it is to have. Since 32 i-nodes fit in a 1K block, and i-node 0 is not used but occupies space, the number of i-nodes should be one less than a multiple of 32. Typical values are 63, 95, or 127. Examples of prototype files can be found in the distribution as *tools/proto.ram* (root file system), *tools/proto.usr* (*/usr*), and *tools/proto.user* (*/user*).

The final step in making a file system is straightforward: just type

```
mkfs -L special proto >logfile
```

where *special* is a special file, such as */dev/fd0* and *proto* is the prototype file. The **–L** flag causes a description of the new file system to be produced on standard output.

After the file system has been made, but before it is put into production, it is a good idea to run MINIX and use *chmem* to reduce the dynamic allocation area of programs, if this step has not already been taken prior to making the file system.

Not all compilers produce equally good code. Before replacing all the binary programs that come with MINIX, determine whether your compiler produces smaller or larger code by compiling a few programs. If your compiler produces smaller code, it may be worthwhile to recompile all programs to replace the originals. However, if your compiler produces larger code, only recompile programs that you have modified.

3.4. RECOMPILING MINIX

Recompiling the operating system itself is not technically difficult, but its relatively large size requires some care when using a system having only two 360K floppy disks and no hard disk. Before modifying the system, it is strongly recommended that you try recompiling the system as distributed, to learn how to do it. Using a floppy disk based MINIX system, it takes two to three hours to compile and build the entire operating system from scratch.

The bootable image is composed of six parts: the kernel, memory manager, file system, initializer, boot block, and file system checker. You need only recompile those parts you have modified. The binaries of the other parts are already present in *tools*, and can be used as is. The instructions below tell how to recompile all the parts. Normally only some of them will have to be recompiled.

3.4.1. Concepts

The operating system is contained in three directories: *kernel*, *mm*, and *fs*. In addition, the directory *h* contains header files used by all three of these. The directory *kernel* contains the lowest two layers of the system, which do interrupt handling, process management, message passing, and I/O. All the files in this directory are linked into a single executable, binary program, *kernel*.

Although nearly all of the kernel is written in C, two assembly language files are also needed. They are *mpx88.s*, which contains the interrupt handlers (i.e., process multiplexing) and *klib88.s*, which holds several small library routines used only in the kernel.

As mentioned earlier, some compilers truncate long names different from their own assemblers, so if your linker complains about undefined symbols, it may be necessary to edit *mpx88.s* and *klib88.s* to truncate all the long names by hand.

If you are using an assembler that does not accept any of the assembly language versions provided, pick the closest one and modify it as need be. Most of the pseudoinstructions are present in all assemblers, sometimes with a different name however. The only one that may not be available everywhere is *.ASCIZ*, which generates a string terminated by a zero byte. In this case, the zero byte should be made explicit in the argument.

3.4.2. Step-by-Step Instructions

By now you should already have moved *mpx88.s* and *klib88.s* from one of the subdirectories to *kernel* and removed the subdirectories. When using a system with only 360K floppy disks, remove all other directories except *kernel* and *h* from the diskette, to provide room for the object files and compiler temporary files.

Now compile or assemble each of the files. On a PC with two diskette drives, the standard /usr file system should be in drive 0 and the kernel diskette should be in drive 1 (mounted on /user). When using MINIX as the development system, the easiest way is just to type

```
make
```

Alternatively the compilations can be done "by hand" by typing

```
cc -c -Di8088 -w *.c
```

The −w flag suppresses some irrelevant warning messages that occur because the source code is a compromise between what various compilers expect. This route is somewhat faster because the presence of *make* itself in memory means that there is not enough space left for both *cpp* and *cem* simultaneously. Consequently, the *makefile* uses the −F and −T. flags to direct the preprocessor output to disk instead of piping it into *cem*.

With MS-DOS, the *make.bat* file can also be used, but it should be checked first to see if it is appropriate for the configuration and compiler being used.

If the compilations have been done "by hand," link all the object files into a single executable binary program by just typing

```
make
```

For this step, the library described in Sec. 3.2 will be needed, but the source files will not be. The assembler-linker, *asld*, is smaller than *cem*, so there is no shortage of memory here. However, it produces a large temporary file, so the *makefile* removes /lib/cem to make room for it. It can be restored later by mounting the root file system and copying the file from it to /lib.

If the development system is MS-DOS, the kernel binary must now be converted to MINIX format by running *dos2out*, which can be found in the *tools* directory of the distribution. The executable kernel file should be named simply *kernel*.

In a similar manner, compile and link the memory manager. It has no assembly code files, just C files. If /lib/cem has been removed, restore it manually before starting. Then mount the diskette with the *mm* directory on /user. Copy the *h* directory there if it is not already present and use the *makefile* or *make.bat* file to compile and link the memory manager. Alternatively, do it by hand with the command

```
cc -c -Di8088 -w *.c
```

Again, link and convert the final output to MINIX format, if necessary, and call it *mm*.

Repeat the above process for the file system. Then compile, link, and convert *tools/init*, putting the result on the file *init*. At this point you will have four independently compiled and linked files: *kernel*, *mm*, *fs*, and *init*. Ultimately, these four files will form the operating system.

However, before the boot diskette can be built, two more programs, *fsck* and *bootblok* must be prepared. Both are located in *tools*. *Fsck* has two files, a C file, *fsck.c*, and an assembly language file, *fsck1.s*. *Bootblok* is entirely contained in the assembly code file *bootblok.s*. (The MS-DOS versions of the assembly language files have extension *.asm* rather than *.s*).

To compile *fsck.c*, you need the include files *h/const.h*, *h/type.h*, *fs/const.h*, and *fs/type.h*. Furthermore, *fsck.c* is the largest single file in MINIX, and its compilation strains the system the space resources to the utmost. Be sure that */lib/cem* has enough stack space (about 51K) and that there are no unnecessary files anywhere taking up precious disk blocks. The command

```
cc -c -T. fsck.c
```

compiles *fsck.c* using the current directory for the (large) intermediate files. Link *fsck* with the command

```
asld -T. fsck1.s fsck.s /usr/lib/libc.a /usr/lib/end.s
```

Alternatively, just type

```
make fsck
```

Normally it will not be necessary to reassemble *bootblok* since changes to the operating system rarely require changes to the boot block. However, if the boot block must be changed, after assembling and linking it remove the header, for example, using *dd*, so that the first byte of the file is the first instruction. See *tools/makefile* for the command sequence.

3.5. BUILDING THE BOOT DISKETTE

In this section we will describe how the six independently compiled and linked programs, *bootblok*, *kernel*, *mm*, *fs*, *init*, and *fsck* are forged together to make the boot diskette. The first time you try making a new operating system, use the six binaries provided in *tools*, rather than making new ones.

3.5.1. Concepts

The boot diskette contains the six programs mentioned above, in the order given. The boot block occupies the first 512 bytes on the disk. When the computer is turned on, the ROM gets control and tries to read the boot block from drive 0 into memory at address 0x7C00. If this read succeeds, the ROM jumps to address 0x7C00 to start the boot program.

The MINIX boot program first copies itself to an address just below 192K, to get itself out of the way. Then it calls the BIOS repeatedly to load 16 cylinders full of data into memory starting at address 0x600 (1536). This data is the core image of the operating system, followed directly by *fsck*. When the loading is finished, the boot program jumps to the start of *fsck*, which then displays the initial menu. If the user types an equal sign, *fsck* jumps to 1536 to start MINIX.

The boot diskette is generated by *tools/build*. It takes the six programs listed above and concatenates them in a special way. The first 512 bytes of the boot diskette come from *bootblok*. If need be, some zero bytes are added to pad *bootblok* out to 512. *Bootblok* does not have a header, and neither does the boot diskette because when the ROM loads the boot block to address 0x7C00, it expects the first byte to be the start of the first instruction.

At position 512, the boot diskette contains the kernel, again without a header. Byte 512 of the boot diskette will be placed at memory address 1536 by the boot program, and will be executed as the first MINIX instruction when *fsck* terminates. After the kernel comes *mm*, *fs*, *init*, and *fsck*, each padded out to a multiple of 16 bytes so that the next one begins at a click boundary.

Each of the programs may be compiled either with or without separate I and D space. The two models are different, but *build* explicitly checks to see which model each program uses and handles it. In short, what *build* does is read six files, stripping the headers off the last five of them, and concatenate them onto the output, rounding the first one up to 512 bytes and the rest up to a multiple of 16 bytes.

After having completed the concatenation of the six files, *build* makes three patches to the output.

1. The last 4 words of the boot block are set to the number of cylinders to load, and the DS, PC, and CS values to use for running *fsck*. The boot program needs this information so that it can jump to *fsck* after it has finished loading. Without this information, the boot program would not know where to jump.

2. *Build* loads the first 8 words of the kernel's data segment with the CS and DS segment register values for *kernel*, *mm*, *fs*, and *init*. Without this information, the kernel could not run these programs when the time came: it would not know where they were. It also sets word 4 of the kernel's text segment to the DS value needed to run the kernel.

3. The origin and size of *init* are inserted at address 4 of the file system's data space. The file system needs this information to know where to put the RAM disk, which begins just after the end of *init*, exactly overwriting the start of *fsck*.

3.5.2. Step-by-Step Instructions

First, compile, link, and if need be, convert to MINIX format *bootblok*, *kernel*, *mm*, *fs*, *init*, and *fsck* as described above, or better yet, use the ones provided where possible. The file *bootblok* provided in the distribution has already been stripped of its header and is ready to use. If for any reason you need to reassemble it, do not forget to strip off the header, as is done in *makefile*.

If you have not already done so, compile *build* to run on the development system (see *makefile* and *make.bat*). If you are using a computer without a hard disk, collect the six parts of the operating system and *build* in *tools* in drive 1.

Next unmount */usr* and insert a blank diskette in drive 0. This will be the boot diskette. Now type

```
build bootblok kernel mm fs init fsck /dev/fd0
```

On a hard disk system, the command given from *tools* will probably be

```
build bootblok ../kernel/kernel ../mm/mm ../fs/fs init fsck /dev/fd0
```

When *build* finishes running, the boot diskette will be ready in drive 0 and a printout of the sizes will appear on standard output.

Alternatively, you can just type

```
make image
```

to produce a bootable operating system on */dev/fd0*. At the time you give the command, you need */usr* in drive 0 so *make* itself can be loaded. Just before *build*, is called */dev/fd0*, is unmounted and you are asked to insert a blank (formatted) diskette in drive 0, and pauses until you hit the return key.

If you wish to use *make*, you will have to create dummy files *fsck.s* and *init.s* to prevent *make* from trying to reconstruct *fsck* and *init*. Before running it for real, give the command

```
make -n image
```

to see what *make* intends to do. If need be, use *touch* to trick *make* into doing what *you* want, rather than what *it* wants.

3.6. TESTING MINIX

After having built a new version of MINIX, it is a good idea to test it. To aid in this testing, a collection of test programs have been provided on the */user* diskette. To use the test programs, bring up the system, except that when it asks you to insert */usr* in drive 0, insert */user* instead. Now change to */user/test* and list the files there. You should find a shell script called *run*, and a series of executable files called *test0*, *test1*, and so on, as well as a few other files used by the test programs. You can run any of the tests individually, or type

```
run
```

to run them all. If any errors are encountered, they will be reported. You will have to refer to the source code to see what each error means. The tests are quite comprehensive, and take more than 10 minutes to finish.

3.7. INSTALLING NEW DEVICE DRIVERS

Once you have successfully reached this point, you will now be able to modify MINIX. In general, if a modification only affects, say, the file system, you will not have to recompile the memory manager or kernel. If a modification affects any of the files in *h*, you should recompile the entire system, just to be safe.

One common modification is adding new I/O devices and drivers. To add a new I/O device to MINIX, it is necessary to write a driver for it. The new driver should use the same message interface as the existing ones. The driver should be put in the directory *kernel* and *makefile* or *make.bat* updated, if they are used. In addition, the entry point of the new task must be added to the list contained in the array *task* in *kernel/table.c*. If *dmp.c* is still in use, an entry also has to be made for it in *nayme*.

Two changes are also required in the *h* directory. In *h/const.h*, the constant *NR_TASKS* has to be increased by 1, and the new task has to be given a name in *h/com.h*.

A new special file will have to be created for the driver. This can be done by adding a line to the directory */dev* in *tools/proto.ram*.

To tell the file system which task is handling the new special file, a line has to be added to the array *dmap* in *fs/table.c*.

3.8. TROUBLESHOOTING

If you modify the system, there is always the possibility that you will introduce an error. In this section, we will discuss some of the more common problems and how to track them down.

To start with, if something is acting strange, turn the computer off and reboot from scratch. This gets everything into a known state. Rebooting with CTRL-ALT-DEL may leave the system in a peculiar state, which may be the cause of the trouble.

If a message like

```
Booting MINIX 1.1
```

does not appear on the screen after the power-on self-tests have completed, something is wrong with the boot block. The boot block prints this message by calling the BIOS. Make a dump of the first block of the boot diskette and examine it by hand to see if it contains the proper program.

If the above message appears, but the initial menu does not, it is likely that *fsck* is not being started, since the first thing *fsck* does is print the menu. Check the last 6 bytes of the boot block to see if the segment and offset put there by *build* correspond to the address at which *fsck* is located (right after *init*).

If the menu appears, but the system does not respond to the equal sign,

MINIX is probably being started, but crashing during initialization. One possible cause is the introduction of print statements into the kernel. However, it is not permitted to display anything until after the terminal task has run to initialize itself. Be careful about where you put the print statements.

If the screen has been cleared and the message giving the sizes has appeared, the kernel has initialized itself, the memory manager has run and blocked waiting for a message, and the file system has started running. This message is printed as soon as the file system has read the super-block of the root file system.

If the system appears to hang before or after reading the root file system, some help can be obtained by hitting the F1 or F2 function keys (unless the dump routines have been removed). By hitting F1 twice a few seconds apart and noting the times in the display, it may be possible to see which processes are running. If, for example, *init* is unable to fork, for whatever reason, or cannot open */etc/ttys*, or cannot execute */bin/sh* or */bin/login*, the system will hang, but process 2 (*init*) may continue to use CPU cycles. If the F1 display shows that process 2 is constantly running, it is a good bet that *init* is unable to make a system call or open a file that is essential. The problem can usually be localized by putting statements in the main loops of the file system and memory manager to print a line describing each incoming message and each outgoing reply. Recompile and test the system using the new output as a guide.

PART TWO

4

PROCESSES IN MINIX

We are now about to embark on a detailed study of how MINIX works inside. Like all operating systems, MINIX is based on the concept of a process. A **process** is just a program in execution. It has a memory image, a program counter, a stack pointer, other registers, open files, and other aspects that keep track of where it is in the computation. Each command typed to the shell from the terminal, such as *ls*, *grep*, or *cc* starts off a separate process. Several processes may be running in the machine at the same time, with the operating system rapidly switching back and forth between them, first running one process for 100 msec, then another one for 100 msec, and so on. When a pipeline is started up, for example, by the command

```
sort file | uniq | wc
```

three processes are started up, one for *sort*, one for *uniq*, and one for *grep*.

Sometimes a process started up by a single command itselfs creates other processes. The command *cc*, for example, is a small program that just calls the various passes of the C compiler in the proper order, each pass running as a separate process in its own address space.

In MINIX the various parts of the operating system itself are also organized as processes. The file system, the memory manager, and each of the device drivers is a separate process (the device drivers all share a common address space, but the file system and memory manager each have their own private address space). The user processes and the operating system processes communicate with each other by sending and receiving fixed-size messages. The purpose of this chapter is to explain how MINIX processes and interprocess communication work internally.

4.1. OVERVIEW OF PROCESSES IN MINIX

As mentioned above (and unlike UNIX, whose kernel is a monolithic program not split up into modules), MINIX itself is a collection of processes that communicate with each other and with user processes using a single interprocess communication primitive—message passing. This design gives a more modular and flexible structure, making it easy, for example, to replace the entire file system by a completely different one.

4.1.1. The Internal Structure of MINIX

Let us begin our study of MINIX by taking a bird's-eye view of the system. MINIX is structured in four layers, with each layer performing a well-defined function. The four layers are illustrated in Fig. 4-1.

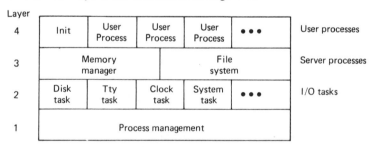

Fig. 4-1. MINIX is structured in four layers.

The bottom layer catches all interrupts and traps, and provides higher layers with a model of independent sequential processes that communicate using messages. The code in this layer has two major activities. The first is catching the traps and interrupts, saving and restoring registers, and the general nuts and bolts of actually making the process abstraction provided to the higher layers work. The second is handling the mechanics of messages; checking for legal destinations, locating send and receive buffers in physical memory, and copying bytes from sender to receiver. That part of the layer dealing with the lowest level of interrupt handling is written in assembly language. The rest of the layer and all of the higher layers, are written in C.

Layer 2 contains the I/O processes, one per device type. To distinguish them from ordinary user processes, we will call them **tasks**, but the differences between tasks and processes are minimal. In many systems the I/O tasks are called **device drivers**; we will use the terms "task" and "device driver" interchangeably. A task is needed for each device type, including disk, printer, terminal, and clock. If other I/O devices are present, a task is needed for each one of those too. One task, the system task, is a little different, since it does not correspond to any I/O device. We will discuss the tasks in the next chapter.

All the tasks in layer 2 and all the code in layer 1 are linked together into a single binary program called the **kernel**. On a machine with kernel mode and user mode, the kernel would run in kernel mode. Despite being linked together in the same object program, the tasks in layer 2 are all completely independent from one another, are scheduled independently, and communicate using messages. They are linked together into a single binary to make it easier to port MINIX to machines with two modes where only the kernel is allowed to do I/O.

Layer 3 contains two processes that provide useful services to the user processes. The **memory manager** (MM) carries out all the MINIX system calls that involve memory management, such as FORK, EXEC, and BRK. The **file system** (FS) carries out all the file system calls, such as READ, MOUNT, and CHDIR. As we noted at the start of Chap. 1, operating systems do two things: manage resources and provide an extended machine by implementing system calls. In MINIX the resource management is largely in the kernel (layers 1 and 2), and system call interpretation is in layer 3. The file system has been designed as a file "server" and can be moved to a remote machine with almost no changes. This also holds for the memory manager, although remote memory servers are not as useful as remote file servers.

Finally, layer 4 contains all the user processes—shells, editors, compilers, and user-written *a.out* programs.

4.1.2. Process Management in MINIX

Processes in MINIX follow the general process model given in this chapter. Processes can create subprocesses, which in turn can create more subprocesses, yielding a tree of processes. In fact, all the user processes in the whole system are part of a single tree with *init* (see Fig. 4-1) at the root.

To see how this situation comes about, we have to take a look at how MINIX is booted from floppy disk. When the computer is turned on, the hardware reads the first sector of the first track into memory and jumps to it. This sector contains a **bootstrap** program that loads the entire operating system (and the file system checker) into memory and starts it running. After the kernel, memory manager and file system have run and initialized themselves, control is passed to *init*.

Init starts out by reading the file */etc/ttys*, to see how many terminals are currently installed (in the standard distribution, just the console). It then forks off a child process for each terminal. Each of these children executes */bin/login* to wait until someone logs in.

After a successful login, */bin/login* executes the user's shell (specified in */etc/passwd*, normally */bin/sh*). The shell waits for commands to be typed and then forks off a new process for each command. In this way, the shells are the children of *init*, the user processes are the grandchildren, and all the processes in the system are part of a single tree.

The two principal system calls in MINIX for process management are FORK and EXEC. FORK, as we have seen, is the only way to create a new process. EXEC allows a process to execute a specified program. When a program is executed, it is allocated a portion of memory whose size is specified in the program file's header. It retains this memory allocation throughout its execution, although the distribution among data segment, stack segment, and unused can vary as the process runs.

All the information about a process is kept in the process table, which is divided up among the kernel, memory manager, and file system, with each one having those fields that it needs. When a new process comes into existence, by FORK, or an old process terminates, by EXIT or a signal, the memory manager first updates its part of the process table and then sends messages to the file system and kernel telling them to do likewise.

4.1.3. Interprocess Communication in MINIX

Interprocess communication within MINIX itself is by exchanging fixed-size messages. The size of the messages is determined by the size of a structure called *message*. On the 8088 it is 24 bytes, but if MINIX were moved to a CPU with 4-byte integers, the struct would become larger. Three primitives are provided for sending and receiving messages. They are called by the C library procedures

```
send(dest, &message);
```

to send a message to process *dest*,

```
receive(source, &message);
```

to receive a message from process *source* (or *ANY*), and

```
send_rec(src_dst, &message);
```

to send a message and wait for a reply from the same process. The reply overwrites the original message. Each process or task can send and receive messages from processes and tasks in its own layer, and from those in the layer directly below it. User processes may not communicate directly with the I/O tasks. The system enforces this restriction.

When a process (which also includes the tasks as a special case) sends a message to a process that is not currently waiting for a message, the sender blocks until the destination does a RECEIVE. In other words, MINIX uses the rendezvous method to avoid the problems of buffering sent, but not yet received, messages. Although less flexible than a scheme with buffering, it turns out to be adequate for this system, and much simpler because no buffer management is needed.

4.1.4. Process Scheduling in MINIX

The MINIX scheduler uses a multilevel queueing system with three levels, corresponding to layers 2, 3, and 4 in Fig. 4-1. Within each level, round robin is used. Tasks have the highest priority, the memory manager and file server are next, and user processes are last.

When picking a process to run, the scheduler checks to see if any tasks are ready. If one or more are ready, the one at the head of the queue is run. If no tasks are ready, a server (MM or FS) is chosen, if possible, otherwise a user is run. If no process is ready, the system sits in an idle loop waiting for the next interrupt.

At each clock tick, a check is made to see if the current process is a user process that has run more than 100 msec. If it is, the scheduler is called to see if another user process is waiting for the CPU. If one is found, the current process is moved to the end of its scheduling queue, and the process now at the head is run. Tasks, the memory manager, and the file system are never preempted by the clock, no matter how long they have been running.

4.2. IMPLEMENTATION OF PROCESSES IN MINIX

We are now moving closer to looking at the actual code, so a few words about the notation we will use to describe it are in order. The terms "procedure," "function," and "routine" will be used interchangeably. Variable names will be written in italics, as in *rw_flag*. When a variable or procedure name starts a sentence it will be capitalized, but the actual names all begin with lower case letters. System calls will be in small caps, for example, READ.

The book and the software, both of which are continuously evolving, did not "go to press" on the same day, so there may be minor discrepancies between the references to the code, the listing, and the disk or tape version. Such differences generally only affect a line or two, however.

4.2.1. Organization of the MINIX Source Code

Logically, the source code is organized as a single directory, *minix*, containing a few files and ten subdirectories:

1. *h* - header files used by the operating system

2. *kernel* - layers 1 and 2 (processes, messages, drivers)

3. *mm* - the code for the memory manager

4. *fs* - the code for the file system

5. *lib* - the library procedures (e.g., *open*, *read*)

6. *tools* - a collection of special programs needed to build MINIX

7. *commands* - the utility programs (e.g., *cat*, *cp*, *date*, *ls*, *pwd*)

8. *include* - header files used by the commands

9. *test* - programs to give MINIX a thorough testing

10. *doc* - documentation and manuals

The code for layers 1 and 2 is contained in the directory *kernel*. In this chapter we will study two key files, *mpx88.s* and *proc.c*, which handle the process management and message passing, respectively. In Chap. 5 we will look at the rest of the files in this directory, which are structured with one file per task. In this way, all the data and code for each I/O device are together in one place. In Chap. 6 we will look at the memory manager. In Chap. 7 we will study the file system.

When MINIX is compiled, all the source code files in *kernel*, *mm*, and *fs* are compiled to object files. Then all the object files in *kernel* are linked together to form a single executable program, *kernel*. The object files in *mm* are also linked together to form a single executable program, *mm*. The same holds for *fs*. A fourth executable program, *init*, is built in *tools*. The program *build* (also in *tools*) strips these four programs of their headers, pads each one out so that each is a multiple of 16 bytes, and concatenates them onto a new file. This new file is the binary of the operating system that is copied onto the boot diskette, and later loaded into memory and executed. Fig. 4-2 shows what memory looks like after the four concatenated programs are loaded into it.

It is important to realize that MINIX consists of four totally independent programs that communicate only by passing messages. A procedure called *panic* in *fs* does not conflict with a procedure called *panic* in *mm* because they ultimately are linked into different executable files. The only procedures that the four pieces of the operating system have in common are a few of the library routines in *lib*. This modular structure makes it very easy to modify, say, the file system, without having these changes affect the memory manager. It also makes it straightforward to remove the file system altogether, and put it on a different machine as a remote file server, communicating with the user machines by sending messages over a network.

As an aside, throughout this book we will be referring frequently to specific procedures in the code. As an aid to finding procedures quickly, a cross reference listing of procedure names and macros (but not local variables) is provided in Chap. 9. We suggest that you color the edge of the first page of that chapter with a felt-tipped marking pen, so that it can be located quickly when the book is closed.

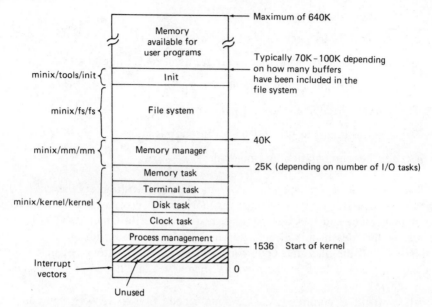

Fig. 4-2. Memory layout after MINIX has been loaded from the disk into memory. The four independently compiled and linked parts are clearly distinct. The sizes are approximate, depending on the configuration.

4.2.2. The Common Header Files

The directory *h* contains a collection of files defining constants, types, and macros used in more than one of the four pieces of MINIX. Let us take a brief look at these files, starting with *const.h* (line 0000). In this file we find a variety of constant definitions. Definitions that are used only in the kernel are included in the file *kernel/const.h*. Definitions that are used only in the file system are included in the file *fs/const.h*. The memory manager also has a file *mm/const.h* for its local definitions. Those definitions that are used in more than one of the directories are included in *h/const.h*.

A few of the definitions in *const.h* are especially noteworthy. *EXTERN* is defined as a macro expanding into *extern*. All global variables that are declared in header files and included in two or more files are declared *EXTERN*, as in

```
EXTERN int who;
```

If the variable were declared just as

```
int who;
```

and included in two or more files, some linkers would complain about a multiply defined variable. Furthermore, the C reference manual by Kernighan and Ritchie explicitly forbids this construction.

To avoid this problem, it is necessary to have the declaration read

```
extern int who;
```

in all places but one. Using *EXTERN* prevents this problem by having it expand into *extern* everywhere except in the file *table.c* where it is redefined as the null string on lines 5129 and 5130. When the header files are included and expanded as part of the compilation of *table.c*, *extern* is not inserted anywhere (because *EXTERN* is now defined as the null string). Thus, storage for the global variables is actually reserved only in one place, in the object file *table.o*. The same trick is used in the file system and memory manager.

The file *table.c* is also used for the declaration of the array *task*, which contains the mapping between task numbers and the associated procedures. It has been put here because the trick used above to prevent multiple declarations does not work with variables that are initialized; that is, you may not say

```
extern int x = 3;
```

anywhere.

If you are new to C programming and do not quite understand what is going on here, fear not; the details are really not important. C allows something, include files, that almost no other language allows. This feature can cause problems for some linkers because it can lead to multiple declarations for included variables. The *EXTERN* business is simply a way to make MINIX more portable so it can be linked on machines whose linkers will not accept multiply defined variables.

PRIVATE is defined as a synonym for static. Procedures and data that are not referenced outside the file in which they are declared are always declared as *PRIVATE* to prevent their names from being visible outside the file in which they are declared. As a general rule, all variables and procedures should be declared with as local a scope as possible. *PUBLIC* is defined as the null string. Thus, the declaration

```
PUBLIC free_zone()
```

comes out of the C preprocessor as

```
free_zone()
```

which, according to the C scope rules, means that the name *free_zone* is exported from the file and can be used in other files. *PRIVATE* and *PUBLIC* are not necessary, but are attempts to undo the damage caused by the C scope rules (default is that names are exported outside the file; it should be just the reverse). The rest of *const.h* defines numerical constants used throughout the system.

Now let us examine the file *callnr.h* (line 0100). Processes execute the MINIX system calls by sending messages to the memory manager (MM for short) or the file system (FS for short). Each message contains the number of the system call desired. These numbers are defined in *callnr.h*.

The file *com.h* (line 0150) mostly contains common definitions used in messages from MM and FS to the I/O tasks. The task numbers are also defined. To distinguish them from process numbers, task numbers are negative. The header file also defines the message types (function codes) that can be sent to each task. For example, the clock task accepts codes *SET_ALARM* (to set a timer), *CLOCK_TICK* (when a clock interrupt has occurred), *GET_TIME* (request for the real time), and *SET_TIME* (to set the current time of day). The value *REAL_TIME* is the message type for the reply to the *GET_TIME* request.

The next file is *error.h* (line 0250). It contains the error messages that are returned to user programs in *errno* when a system call fails, as well as some internal errors, such as trying to send to a nonexistent task. They are negative to mark them as error codes. The values are made positive before being returned to user programs.

The file *sgtty.h* (line 0350) defines two structures used in the IOCTL system call, along with some constants also used in IOCTL.

The file *signal.h* (line 0400) defines the standard signal names. The file *stat.h* (line 0450) contains the structure returned by the STAT and FSTAT system calls. All three of *sgtty.h*, *signal.h*, and *stat.h* are used not only by the operating system itself, but also by some of the commands. They are duplicated in the directory *include*.

The last of the common header files is *type.h* (line 0500). It contains a number of key type definitions, along with related numerical values. It also contains the macros *MAX* and *MIN*, so we can say

```
z = MAX(x, y);
```

to assign the larger of x and y to z.

The most important definition in this file is *message* on lines 0554 to 0565. While we could have defined *message* to be an array of some number of bytes, it is better programming practice to have it be a structure containing union of the various message types that are possible. Six message formats, *mess_1* through *mess_6*, are defined. A message is a structure containing a field *m_source*, telling who sent the message, a field *m_type*, telling what the message type is (e.g., *GET_TIME* to the clock task) and the data fields. The six message types are shown in Fig. 4-3.

When it is necessary to send a message containing, say, three integers and three pointers (or three integers and two pointers), then the first format in Fig. 4-3 is the one to use. The same applies to the other formats. How does one assign a value to the first integer in the first format? Suppose the message is called x. Then $x.m\_u$ refers to the union portion of the message struct. To refer to the first of the six alternatives in the union, we use $x.m\_u.m\_m1$. Finally, to get at the first integer in this struct we say $x.m\_u.m\_m1.m1i1$. This is quite a mouthful, so somewhat shorter field names are defined as macros after the definition of *message* itself. Thus $x.m1\_i1$ can be used instead of $x.m\_u.m\_m1.m1i1$. The short names all have the form of the letter *m*, the format number, an underscore, one or two letters indicating whether the field is an

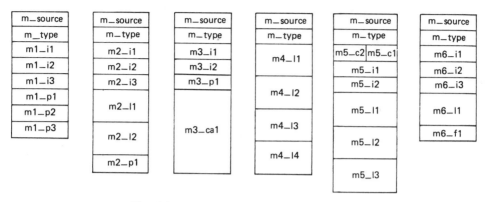

Fig. 4-3. The six message types used in MINIX.

integer, pointer, long, character, character array, or function, and a sequence number to distinguish multiple instances of the same type within a message.

4.2.3. Process Data Structures and Header Files

The ideas described above are straightforward, so let us dive in and see what the code looks like. Just as we have files *const.h* and *type.h* in the common header directory *minix/h*, we also have files *const.h* and *type.h* in *minix/kernel*. The file *const.h* (line 0650) contains a number of machine dependent values, that is, values that apply to the Intel 8088, but are likely to be different if MINIX is moved to a different machine. These values are enclosed between

```
#ifdef i8088
```

and

```
#endif
```

statements. (See lines 0652 to 0681).

When compiling MINIX the compiler is called with

```
cc -c -Di8088 file.c
```

to force the symbol i8088 to be defined, and the machine dependent code to be compiled. If MINIX is ported to, say, a Motorola 68000, the people doing the port will probably add sections of code bracketed by

```
#ifdef m68000
```

and

```
#endif
```

and call the compiler with

```
cc -c -Dm68000 file.c
```

to select out the 68000-dependent code. In this way, MINIX can deal with constants and code that are specific to one particular system. This construction does not especially enhance readability, so it should be used as little as possible.

A few of the definitions in *const.h* deserve special mention. The important interrupt vectors are defined here, as are some field values used for resetting the interrupt controller chip after each interrupt.

Each task within the kernel has its own stack, of size *TASK_STACK_BYTES*. While handling interrupts, a special stack of size *K_STACK_BYTES* is used.

The MINIX scheduler has *NQ* (3) priority queues, named *TASK_Q* (highest priority), *SERVER_Q* (middle priority), and *USER_Q* (lowest priority).

In the file *glo.h* (line 0700) we find the kernel's global variables. *Realtime* is the number of clock ticks since the system was booted. It is incremented 60 times a second by a crystal oscillator, independent of the line frequency. *Lost_ticks* is a counter that keeps track of how many clock ticks have been lost because the clock task was not waiting for a message when a clock interrupt occurred. The interrupt is just ignored and *lost_ticks* incremented so that the time of day can be corrected later.

Cur_proc is the number of the currently scheduled process. *Prev_proc* is the number of the previous process. It is needed for accounting purposes. *Sig_procs* counts the number of processes that have signals pending that have not yet been sent to the memory manager for processing.

When an interrupt occurs, a message is sent to the task associated with the interrupt. The message is built in the message buffer *int_mess*. Finally, we have the stacks. Each task has its own stack, in the array *t_stack*. During interrupt handling, the kernel uses a temporary stack, *k_stack*.

The final kernel header file, *proc.h* (line 0750), contains the process table. It contains storage for the process' registers, stack pointer, state, memory map, stack limit, process id, accounting, alarm time, and message information. When a process cannot complete a SEND because the destination is not waiting, the sender is put onto a queue pointed to by the destination's *p_callerq* field. That way, when the destination finally does a RECEIVE, it is easy to find all the processes wanting to send to it. The *p_sendlink* field is used to link the members of the queue together.

When a process does a RECEIVE and there is no message waiting for it, it blocks and the number of the process it wants to RECEIVE from is stored in *p_getfrom*. The address of the message buffer is stored in *p_messbuf*.

The last two fields are *p_nextready* and *p_pending*. The former is used to link processes together on the scheduler queues, and the latter is a bit map used to keep track of signals that have not yet been passed to the memory manager (because the memory manager is not waiting for a message).

The flag bits in *p_flags* define the state of each table entry. If any of the bits is set, the process cannot be run. If the slot is not in use, *P_SLOT_FREE* is set. After a FORK, *NO_MAP* is set to prevent the child process from running until its memory map has been set up. The other two flags indicate that the process is blocked trying to send or receive a message.

The macro *proc_addr* is provided because it is not possible to have negative subscripts in C. Logically, the array *proc* should go from $-NR\_TASKS$ to $+NR\_PROCS$. Unfortunately, it must start at 0, so *proc*[0] refers to the most negative task, and so forth. To make it easier to keep track of which slot goes with which process, we can write

```
rp = proc_addr(n);
```

to assign to *rp* the address of the process slot for process *n*, either positive or negative.

The variable *proc_ptr* points to the process table entry for the current process. When a system call or interrupt occurs, it tells where to store the registers and processor state. *Bill_ptr* points to the process being charged for the CPU. When a user process calls the file system, and the file system is running, *proc_ptr* will point to the file system process. However *bill_ptr* will point to the user making the call, since CPU time used by the file system is charged as system time to the caller.

The two arrays *rdy_head* and *rdy_tail* are used to maintain the scheduling queues. The first process on, say, the task queue is pointed to by *rdy_head[TASK_Q]*. Finally, *busy_map* and *task_mess* are used for handling interrupt messages to tasks that are busy when the message arrives and cannot accept them.

The file *type.h* (line 0800) contains only two type definitions, both machine dependent and both relating to interrupts. The struct *pc_psw* represents the three words, PSW (Program Status Word), CS (Code Segment register), and PC (Program Counter) pushed onto the stack by the interrupt hardware. The struct *sig_info* is the data structure pushed onto the stack of a user process when it catches a signal. It contains the same three words that the hardware pushes, and also the signal number.

4.2.4. System Initialization

Now it is time to start looking at the executable code. Let us begin at the beginning. When the PC is booted, the hardware reads the first sector of the floppy disk in drive 0 into memory and executes it. This **bootstrap** program loads the operating system and jumps to it. The operating system begins at the label *MINIX* in assembly code, sets up a few registers, and then calls *main* on line 0880 in *main.c*.

Main is responsible for initializing the system and then starting it up. It initializes the process table so that when the first tasks and processes are scheduled, their memory maps and registers will be set correctly. Part of the information for initialization comes from the array *sizes*, which contains the text and data sizes in clicks (a click is 16 bytes) for the kernel, memory manager, file system, and *init*. This information is patched into the system binary by a program called *build*, which concatenates the various system pieces to make the boot diskette. The first two elements of *sizes* are the kernel's text and data sizes; the next two are the memory manager's, and so on. If any of the four programs does not use separate I and D space, the text size is 0 and the text and data are lumped together as data.

Main also saves all the interrupt vectors, so if CRTL-ALT-DEL is ever typed, it will be possible to reboot the system with the vectors restored to their original situation.

The interrupt vectors are then changed to point to the MINIX interrupt handling routines. The vectors that are not used by MINIX are set to invoke the procedures *unexpected_int* (vectors below 16) or *trap* (vectors at or above 16). The unused vectors are sometimes trapped to by accident. The handling routines just print a message and then continue.

Part of the initialization done by *main* consists of calling *ready* (line 0915) to put all the tasks, the memory manager, and the file system onto their respective scheduling queues. When *main* exits, the task queued first (the one using slot 0 of the process table, i.e., the one with the most negative number) is run until it blocks trying to receive a message. Then the next task is run until it, too, blocks. Eventually all the tasks are blocked, so the memory manager and file system can run, and also block. Finally *init* runs to fork off a login process for each terminal. These processes block until input is typed at some terminal, at which point the first user can log in and get the show on the road.

The procedure *panic* (line 1012) in the file *main.c* is called when the system has discovered a condition that makes it impossible to continue. Typical panic conditions are a critical disk block being unreadable or one part of the system calling another part with invalid parameters.

The last procedure in *main.c* is *set_vec* (line 1036). It takes care of the mechanics of setting interrupt vectors.

4.2.5. Interrupt Handling in MINIX

Running processes may be interrupted by clock interrupts, disk interrupts, terminal interrupts, or other interrupts. It is the job of the lowest layer of MINIX to hide these interrupts by turning them into messages. As far as the processes are concerned, when an I/O device completes an operation, it sends a message to some process, waking it up and making it runnable. Only a tiny part of the MINIX kernel actually sees hardware interrupts.

That code is in the file *mpx88.s*. Typical interrupt procedures are *tty_int* (line 1187), *lpr_int* (line 1196), *disk_int* (line 1203), and *clock_int* (line 1217). (The leading underscores present in the assembly code are due to the convention that all variable and procedure names generated by the C compiler begin with an underscore so that library procedures in assembly language not starting with an underscore will never conflict with user-chosen names.)

These procedures are structurally similar. Each begins by calling *save* to store all the registers (including the segment registers) in the process table slot belonging to the currently running process. The variable *proc_ptr* makes this slot easy to find. The actual code of *save* is a bit tricky because all the segment registers except CS have unknown values when the procedure starts. When it is finished, they all have been set to point to the start of the kernel.

Disk_int and *clock_int* build a message and call *interrupt* in file *proc.c* to take care of sending the message and calling the scheduler. Keyboard interrupts require more processing before *interrupt* is called, so *tty_int* calls a C procedure *keyboard* to do the initial processing and then call *interrupt* if necessary. Keyboard interrupts are generated both when a key is struck and when it is released. The processing needed when most keys are released is so simple that *keyboard* can do it directly, without the overhead of switching to the terminal task.

For clock interrupts, disk interrupts, and some keyboard and line printer interrupts, the next step in the interrupt processing is the procedure *interrupt* on line 1878. This procedure has two parameters passed to it by the assembly code: the task to send to and a pointer to the message. It starts off by reenabling the interrupt controller chip. This chip must be explicitly reenabled to allow subsequent interrupts after the interrupt processing is finished. Any interrupts that occur before processing is finished are kept pending by the interrupt controller chip. They are not lost.

After taking care of the interrupt controller, *interrupt* calls *mini_send* to actually send the message. If the send is successful (i.e., the task was waiting for a message), the corresponding bit in *busy_map* is turned off. If the send is unsuccessful, the corresponding bit in *busy_map* is turned on, to indicate that a message to that task is pending. The pointer to the message is stored in *task_mess*.

Either way, a check is now made (line 1909) to see if any tasks with pending messages are now ready to accept their messages. For example, if two keyboard interrupts happen in rapid succession, on the second one the terminal task may not yet be done with the first one, so a bit is set in *busy_map*. If the next interrupt is for the clock or disk, a check will be made to see if the terminal task is now ready to accept a message. If it is, the message is sent on line 1914.

This code is needed because the message system does not provide any buffering: you cannot send a message to someone unless he is waiting for it (rendezvous principle). For normal processes, the unsuccessful sender is just suspended for a while. With interrupts this strategy is impossible. In effect, the use of *busy_map* and *task_mess* forms a limited kind of buffering to avoid losing messages. For most devices, such as disks, it is technically impossible for the device to generate a second interrupt until the task has run and issued another command. For the clock, lost interrupts do not matter because they are counted on line 1897 and are compensated for later. Only the keyboard can give multiple unexpected interrupts, but the characters typed are recorded in a buffer before *interrupt* is called. The same message pointer is used for each keyboard interrupt, so lost keyboard interrupts do not result in lost characters. When the terminal task is finally called, it gets a message containing a pointer to the buffer where *keyboard* has safely stored all the characters.

When the message processing has been finished, a check is made on line 1921 to see if a higher priority process is now runnable. If so, *pick_proc* is called to schedule that process. Either way, when *interrupt* returns to its assembly code caller, *cur_proc* and *proc_ptr* will be set up for the process to be run.

The assembly language interrupt procedures all call *restart* to reload the current process' registers and start it running.

We make no claim that interrupt processing is easy to fully understand. It requires a little study. In fact, the whole concept of the process abstraction was invented precisely to hide all the messy details of interrupt handling in a very thin layer at the bottom of the system.

Now a quick word or two about *s_call* (line 1173). When a process wants to send or receive a message, it calls a little assembly language library procedure to put the source or destination number in AX, the message pointer in BX, and the SEND or RECEIVE code in CX, followed by a trap instruction. The trap is treated by the hardware the same as an interrupt, and is vectored to *s_call*. This procedure calls *save* and builds a message, just as the interrupt procedures do.

Instead of calling *interrupt*, *s_call* calls *sys_call* to do the work, starting by checking for invalid parameters, illegal calls and destinations, and so on. If everything is all right, it does the send on line 1957 or the receive on line 1963. If the operation can be done immediately, the status code *OK* is returned in *RET_REG* (AX) and control is returned to the assembly code to restart the caller. If the operation cannot complete, the process is blocked in *mini_send* or *mini_rec* and a new process is designated as the next one to run. When control passes back to the assembly code, the new process will be started. If no process is now runnable, the idle routine (line 1319) runs.

It is important to realize that the value of *cur_proc* may be different on exit from *sys_call* from what it was on entry. The same is true for *interrupt*. After *save* has run in the assembly code, all of the current process' state has been safely stored away, so *cur_proc* can be changed with no ill effects. In essence, after a trap or interrupt, the current process is stopped, and the operating system itself is run with its own stack. When the operating system is finished, it does not matter whether the next process is the same one as the previous one. The work to be done is identical: load the registers and start it off.

Study *mpx88.s* carefully. It is important. The only other comments we will make here concern *surprise* and *trp*. Programs can (but should not) execute the INT instruction to cause any interrupt. These are caught by *surprise* or *trp*, depending on the number of the vector.

4.2.6. The Kernel's Assembly Code Utilities

While we are on the subject of assembly code routines, let us briefly look at the file *klib88.s*. This file contains about a dozen utility routines that are in assembly code, either for efficiency or because they cannot be written in C at all. The first one is *phys_copy* (line 1387). It is called in C by

```
phys_copy(source_address, destination_address, bytes);
```

and copies a block of data from anywhere in physical memory to anywhere else. Both addresses are absolute, that is, address 0 really means the first interrupt vector, and all three parameters are longs.

Although *phys_copy* could have been used for copying messages, a faster, specialized procedure has been provided for that purpose (line 1490). It is called by

```
cp_mess(source, src_clicks, src_offset, dest_clicks, dest_offset);
```

where *source* is the sender's process number, which is copied into the *m_source* field of the receiver's buffer. Both the source and destination addresses are specified by giving a click number, typically the base of the segment containing the buffer, and an offset from that click. (A click is a multiple of 16 bytes on the IBM PC. Clicks are important because the PC hardware requires all segments to begin at a click.) This form of specifying the source and destination is more efficient than the 32-bit addresses used by *phys_copy*.

Values are output to I/O ports in C using the assembly language procedure *port_out* (line 1529). For example,

```
port_out(0x3F2, 0x1C);
```

writes the byte 0x1C to port 0x3F2 to set floppy disk motors on and off. Values are read from I/O ports by the analogous procedure, *port_in* (line 1547). The call

```
port_in(0x60, &code);
```

for example, reads the number of the key just struck on the keyboard and stores it in the variable *code*.

Occasionally it is necessary for a task to disable interrupts temporarily. It does this by calling *lock* (line 1567). When interrupts can be reenabled, the task can call either *unlock* (line 1578) to enable interrupts or *restore* (line 1587) to put them back the way they were before *lock* was called.

Build_sig (line 1612) is a highly specialized procedure that is used only to simulate an interrupt when sending a process a signal.

The next two procedures, *csv* (line 1638) and *cret* (line 1660), are highly compiler dependent and may have to be modified when any compiler other than the PC-IX compiler is used. Some compilers do not use them at all. When a procedure compiled by the PC-IX compiler (and many other compilers) starts running, the first thing it does is put the number of bytes of local variables in AX. Then it calls *csv* to save BP, SI, DI, and advance the stack by the number of bytes of locals. While doing this work, *csv* also checks to see if the stack has grown beyond the memory allocated for it. When a procedure wants to return, it calls *cret* to reset the stack pointer and restore the registers. The *csv* and *cret* routines provided in the compiler's library cannot be used because they check for stack overflow and make non-MINIX system calls to report them. The purpose of rewriting them is to get rid of the calls to *printf*.

The last two assembly code procedures shown are *get_chrome* (line 1673) and *vid_copy* (line 1701). The former makes a BIOS call to see whether the console screen is monochrome or color. It matters because they are programmed slightly differently. It returns 1 for color, 0 for monochrome. *Vid_copy* takes care of the actual mechanics of displaying text on the console. We will see how it is used in the next chapter.

4.2.7. Interprocess Communication in MINIX

Processes (including tasks) in MINIX communicate by messages using the rendezvous principle. When a process does a SEND, the lowest layer of the kernel checks to see if the destination is waiting for a message from the sender (or from *ANY* sender). If so, the message is copied from the sender's buffer to the receiver's buffer, and both processes are marked as runnable. If the destination is not waiting for a message from the sender, the sender is marked as blocked and put onto a queue of processes waiting to send to the receiver.

When a process does a RECEIVE, the kernel checks to see if any process is queued trying to send to it. If so, the message is copied from the blocked sender to the receiver, and both are marked as runnable. If no process is queued trying to send to it, the receiver blocks until a message arrives.

The implementation of SEND and RECEIVE, as well as SENDREC, which is just a SEND to some process followed immediately by a RECEIVE from the same process, is handled in the file *proc.c*. Let us start with the implementation of SEND, which is done by *mini_send* (line 1971). It has three parameters: the caller, the process to be sent to, and a pointer to the buffer where the message is. It starts out by making sure that user processes cannot send messages to tasks. The parameter *caller*, supplied by the assembly code routine via *interrupt* or *sys_call*, is greater than or equal to *LOW_USER* if the caller is a user. For a hardware interrupt it is *HARDWARE* (-1). For a task it is less than -1.

After checking the destination address, *mini_send* checks to see if the message falls entirely within the user's data segment. If not, an error code is returned.

The key test in *mini_send* is on lines 2001 and 2002. Here a check is made to see if the destination is blocked on a RECEIVE, as shown by the *RECEIVING* bit in the *p_flags* field of its process table entry. If it is waiting, then the next question is: "Who is it waiting for?" If it is waiting for the sender, or for *ANY*, the code on lines 2004 to 2007 is executed to copy the message and ready the receiver (put it on the scheduling queues as runnable).

If, on the other hand, the receiver is not blocked, or is blocked but waiting for a message from someone else, the code on lines 2010 to 2023 is executed to block and queue the sender (except for sends done by interrupts). All processes wanting to send to a given destination are strung together on a linked list, with the destination's *p_callerq* field pointing to the process table entry of the process at the head of the queue. The example of Fig. 4-4(a) shows what happens when process 3 is unable to send to process 0. If process 4 is subsequently also unable to send to process 0, we get the situation of Fig. 4-4(b).

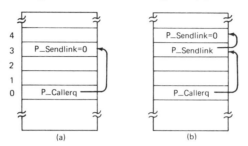

Fig. 4-4. Queueing of processes trying to send to process 0.

The RECEIVE call is carried out by *mini_rec*. The loop on line 2051 searches through all the processes queued waiting to send to the receiver to see if any are acceptable. If one is found, the message is copied from sender to receiver, then the sender is unblocked, made ready to run, and removed from the queue of processes trying to send to the receiver.

If no suitable sender is found, the source and buffer address are saved in its process table entry, and the receiver is marked as blocked on a RECEIVE call. The call to *unready* on line 2073 removes the receiver from the scheduler's queue of runnable processes.

The statement on line 2078 has to do with how kernel-generated signals (SIG-INT, SIGQUIT, and SIGALRM) are handled. When one of these occurs, a message is sent to the memory manager, if it is waiting for a message from *ANY*. If not, the signal is remembered in the kernel until the memory manager finally tries to receive from *ANY*. Then it is informed of pending signals.

4.2.8. Scheduling in MINIX

MINIX uses a multilevel scheduling algorithm that closely follows the structure of Fig. 4-1. In that figure we see I/O tasks in layer 2, server processes in layer 3, and user processes in layer 4. The scheduler maintains three queues of runnable processes, one for each layer, as shown in Fig. 4-5. The array *rdy_head* has one entry for each queue, with that entry pointing to the process at the head of the queue. Similarly, *rdy_tail* is an array whose entries point to the last process on each queue.

Whenever a blocked process is awakened, it is put on the end of its queue. The array *rdy_tail* makes adding a process at the end of a queue efficient. Whenever a running process becomes blocked, or a runnable process is killed by

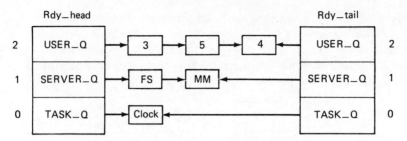

Fig. 4-5. The scheduler maintains three queues, one per priority level.

a signal, that process is removed from the scheduler's queues. Only runnable processes are queued.

Given the queue structures just described, the scheduling algorithm is simple: find the highest priority queue that is not empty and pick the process at the head of that queue. If all the queues are empty, the idle routine is run. In Fig. 4-5 *TASK_Q* has the highest priority. The queue is chosen in *pick_proc*, on lines 2092 to 2094. The process chosen to run next is not removed from its queue merely because it has been selected.

The procedures *ready* (line 2122) and *unready* (line 2153) are called to enter a runnable process on its queue and remove a no-longer runnable process from its queue, respectively. Any change to the queues that might affect the choice of which process to run next requires *pick_proc* to be called to set *cur_proc* again. Whenever the current process blocks on a SEND or a RECEIVE, *pick_proc* is called to reschedule the CPU. Also, after every interrupt, a check is made on line 1921 to see if a newly awakened task should now be scheduled. If a task was running at the time of the interrupt, then it continues to run after the interrupt processing is finished. All tasks are of equal priority, so the new one does not get preference over the old one.

Although most scheduling decisions are made when a process blocks or unblocks, there is one other situation in which scheduling is also done. When the clock task notices that the current user process has exceeded its quantum, it calls *sched* (line 2186) to move the process at the head of *USER_Q* to the end of that queue. This algorithm results in running the user processes in a straight round-robin fashion. The file system, memory manager, and I/O tasks are never put on the end of their queues because they have been running too long. They are trusted to work properly, and to block after having finished their work.

In summary, the scheduling algorithm maintains three priority queues, one for I/O tasks, one for the two server processes, and one for the user processes. The first process on the highest priority queue is always run next. If a user process uses up its quantum, it is put at the end of its queue, thus achieving a simple round-robin scheduling among the competing user processes.

5

INPUT/OUTPUT IN MINIX

One of the main functions of an operating system is to control all the computer's input/output devices. It must issue commands to the devices, catch interrupts, and handle errors. It should also provide an interface between the devices and the rest of the system that is simple and easy to use. To the extent possible, the interface should be the same for all devices (device independence). This is not completely possible because terminals and disks have inherently different operations. The I/O code represents a significant fraction of the total operating system. How MINIX manages I/O is the subject of this chapter.

5.1. OVERVIEW OF I/O IN MINIX

Each of the four layers of Fig. 4-1 relates to I/O in some way. Layer 1 handles the raw interrupts and turns them into messages. Above layer 1 interrupts are not visible. Layer 2 contains the device drivers, one driver for each device class. Layer 3 handles the device-independent part of the I/O. Layer 4 contains the user-level I/O, such as binary to ASCII formatting and (in principle) spoolers, although MINIX does not come with any spoolers initially. In the following sections we will look briefly at each of the layers, with the emphasis on the device drivers. Interrupt handling was covered in the previous chapter, and the device-independent I/O will be discussed when we come to the file system, in Chap. 7.

5.1.1. Interrupt Handlers in MINIX

Many of the device drivers start some I/O device and then block, waiting for a message to arrive. That message is generated by the interrupt handler, as we have seen. Other device drivers do not start any physical I/O (e.g., reading from RAM disk), and do not wait for a message from an I/O device. Since, as we have mentioned, the subject of interrupts has been gone over in great detail in the previous chapter, we will say no more about it here.

5.1.2. Device Drivers in MINIX

For each class of I/O device present in a MINIX system, a separate I/O task (device driver) is present. These drivers are full-fledged processes, each with its own state, registers, memory map, and so on. Device drivers communicate with each other (where necessary) and with the file system using the standard message passing mechanism used by all MINIX processes. Furthermore, each device driver is written as a single source file, such as *clock.c*, *tty.c*, or *floppy.c*. The only difference between the device drivers and the other processes is that the device drivers are linked together in the kernel, and thus all share a common address space.

This design is highly modular and moderately efficient. It is also one of the few places where MINIX differs from UNIX in an essential way. In MINIX a process reads a file by sending a message to the file system process. The file system, in turn, may send a message to the disk driver asking it to read the needed block. This sequence (slightly simplified from reality) is shown in Fig. 5-1(a). By making these interactions via the message mechanism, we force various parts of the system to interface in standard ways with other parts. Nevertheless, by putting all the device drivers in the kernel address space, they have easy access to the process table and other key data structures when needed.

In UNIX all processes have two parts: a user-space part and a kernel-space part, as shown in Fig. 5-1(b). When a system call is made, the operating system switches from the user-space part to the kernel-space part in a somewhat magical way. This structure is a remnant of the MULTICS design, in which the switch was just an ordinary procedure call, rather than a trap followed by saving the state of the user-part, as it is in UNIX.

Device drivers in UNIX are simply kernel procedures that are called by the kernel-space part of the process. When a driver needs to wait for an interrupt, it calls a kernel procedure that puts it to sleep until some interrupt handler wakes it up. Note that it is the user process itself that is being put to sleep here, because the kernel and user parts are really different parts of the same process.

Among operating system designers, arguments about the merits of monolithic systems, as in UNIX, versus process-structured systems, as in MINIX, are endless. The MINIX approach is better structured (more modular), has cleaner interfaces between the pieces, and extends easily to distributed systems in which the various

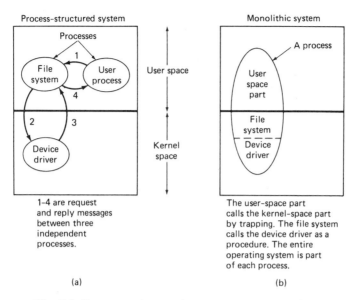

Fig. 5-1. Two ways of structuring user-system communication.

processes run on different computers. The UNIX approach is more efficient, because procedure calls are much faster than sending messages. MINIX was split into many processes because I believe that with increasingly powerful microcomputers available, cleaner software structure was worth making the system somewhat slower. Be warned that many operating system designers do not share this belief.

The MINIX configuration described in this book contains drivers for RAM disk, floppy disk, clock, and terminal. (The MINIX software distribution contains additional drivers, such as printer and hard disk.) The request messages sent to these tasks contain a variety of fields used to hold the operation code (e.g., READ or WRITE) and its parameters.

For block devices, the fields of the request and reply messages are shown in Fig. 5-2. The fields for the character devices are basically similar but can vary slightly from task to task. Messages to the clock task, for example, contain times, and messages to the terminal task specify the characters to use for the intraline editing functions erase-character and kill-line.

The function of each task is to accept requests from other processes, normally the file system, and carry them out. All tasks have been written to get a message, carry it out, and send a reply. Among other things, this decision means that tasks are strictly sequential and do not contain any internal multiprogramming to keep them simple. When a hardware request has been issued, the task does a RECEIVE operation specifying that it is interested only in accepting interrupt messages, not new requests for work. Any new request messages are just kept waiting until the current work has been done because a message is only

REQUESTS

Field	Type	Meaning
m.m_type	int	Operation requested
m.DEVICE	int	Minor device to use
m.POSITION	long	Position on the minor device
m.PROC_NR	int	User process requesting the I/O
m.ADDRESS	char*	Address within PROC_NR
m.COUNT	int	Bytes to transfer

REPLIES

Field	Type	Meaning
m.m_type	int	Always TASK_REPLY
m.REP_PROC_NR	int	Same as PROC_NR in request
m.REP_STATUS	int	# Bytes transferred or error number

Fig. 5-2. Fields of the message *m*, sent to and by block device drivers.

transferred when the sender is ready to send it *and* the receiver is ready to receive it (called the **rendezvous principle**).

The main program for each driver is structurally the same and is outlined in Fig. 5-3. When the system first comes up, each of the drivers is started up in turn to give them a chance to initialize internal tables and similar things. Then each one blocks by trying to get a message. When a message comes in, the identity of the caller is saved, and a procedure is called to carry out the work, with a different procedure invoked for each operation available. After the work has been finished, a reply is sent back to the caller, and the task then goes back to the top of the loop to wait for the next request.

Each of the *do_xxx* procedures handles one of the operations of which the driver is capable. It returns a status code telling what happened. The status code, which is included in the reply message as the field *REP_STATUS*, is the count of bytes transferred (zero or positive) if all went well, or the error number (negative) if something went wrong. This count may differ from the number of bytes requested. On terminals, for example, at most one line is returned, even if the count requested is larger.

5.1.3. Device-Independent I/O Software in MINIX

The MINIX file system process contains all the device-independent I/O code. The I/O system is so closely related to the file system that they were merged into one process. In addition to handling the interface with the drivers, buffering, block allocation and the like, the file system also handles protection and the management of i-nodes, directories, and mounted file systems. The file system will be covered in detail in Chap. 7.

```
message mess;                      /* message buffer */

io_task()
{
  int r, caller;

  initialize();                    /* only done once, during system init. */

  while (TRUE) {
        receive(ANY, &mess);       /* wait for a request for work */
        caller = mess.m_source;    /* process from whom message came */

        switch(mess.m_type) {      /* handle each possible request type */
                case READ:        r = do_read();   break;
                case WRITE:       r = do_write();  break;
                case OTHER:       r = do_other();  break;
                default:          r = ERROR;
        }

        mess.m_type = TASK_REPLY;
        mess.REP_STATUS = r;       /* result code */
        send(caller, &mess);       /* send reply message back to caller */
  }
}
```

Fig. 5-3. Outline of the main procedure of an I/O task.

5.1.4. User-level I/O Software in MINIX

Library procedures are available for making system calls and for converting from binary to ASCII and ASCII to binary. The standard MINIX configuration does not contain any spooler daemons, but since they are just user processes, it is easy to add them as needed later.

5.2. RAM DISKS

Now let us get back to device drivers, the main topic of this chapter, to study several of them. The drivers to be covered are the RAM disk, floppy disk, clock, and terminal. Each of these is interesting for a different reason. The RAM disk is a good example to study because it has all the properties of block devices in general—except the actual I/O (because the "disk" is actually just a portion of memory). This simplicity makes it a good place to start. The floppy disk shows what a real disk driver looks like, warts and all. The clock is important because every system has one, and because it is completely different from all the other drivers. The terminal driver is important in its own right, and furthermore, is a good example of a character device driver.

5.2.1. Overview of the RAM Disk Driver in MINIX

A RAM disk is a portion of memory that is used as if it were a disk. It is managed by the RAM disk driver, which accepts messages to read and write specific blocks of the RAM disk. Programs do not access the RAM disk directly, but only via the file system, which sends messages to the driver to read and write blocks as needed. The root file system in MINIX is always kept on the RAM disk to provide fast access.

The RAM disk driver is actually four closely related drivers in one. Each message to it specifies a minor device as follows:

0: /dev/ram   1: /dev/mem   2: /dev/kmem   3: /dev/null

The first special file listed above, *dev/ram*, is a true RAM disk. Neither its size nor its origin is built in to the driver. They are determined by the file system by booting the root file system when MINIX is booted. This strategy makes it possible to increase or reduce the amount of RAM disk present without having to recompile the operating system. All one needs to do is use a different root file system diskette.

The next two minor devices are used to read and write physical memory and kernel memory, respectively. When *dev/mem* is opened and read, it yields the contents of physical memory locations starting at absolute 0 (the interrupt vectors). Ordinary user programs will never do this, but a system program concerned with debugging the system might need this facility. Opening */dev/mem* and writing on it will change the interrupt vectors. Needless to say, this should only be done with the greatest of caution by an advanced wizard who likes to live dangerously.

The special file */dev/kmem* is like */dev/mem*, except that byte 0 of this file is byte 0 of the kernel's memory (physical address 0x600 or 1536 decimal in MINIX). It too is used mostly for debugging and very special programs. Note that the RAM disk areas covered by these two minor devices overlap. Opening */dev/mem* and seeking to 1536 is the same as reading from */dev/kmem*, except that the latter will continue to work even if in a subsequent version of MINIX the kernel is moved somewhere else in memory. Both of these special files are protected to prevent everyone except the super-user from using them. The last file in this group, */dev/null*, is a special file that accepts data and throws them away. It is commonly used in shell commands when the program being called generates output that is not needed. For example,

```
a.out >/dev/null
```

runs *a.out*, but discards its output. The RAM disk driver effectively treats this minor device as having zero size, so no data are ever copied to or from it.

The overall structure of the RAM disk driver follows the model of Fig. 5-3. The main loop accepts messages and dispatches to either *do_mem* for reading and writing, or to *do_setup* for the special message telling the driver where the RAM disk is located. When MINIX is booted, the kernel runs, then the memory manager, and then the file system. One of the first things the file system does is to see how far up in memory the operating system extends. Then it reads the super-block of the root file system to see how big it is (and thus how big the RAM disk must be to hold it). Once the file system knows where the operating system ends and how much memory the RAM disk needs, it sends the message to the RAM disk driver telling it the lower and upper limits of the RAM disk.

The code for handling /dev/ram, /dev/mem, and /dev/kmem is identical. The only difference among them is that each one corresponds to a different portion of memory, indicated by the arrays ram_origin and ram_limit, each indexed by minor device number.

5.2.2. Implementation of the RAM Disk Driver in MINIX

The implementation is straightforward and requires little comment. The main procedure, on line 2292, gets messages, dispatches to the appropriate procedure, and sends the replies. The procedure do_mem (line 2337) computes two key variables: mem_phys, the physical location in memory of the RAM disk block to be read or written, and user_phys, the physical location where the block is to go to or come from. Both of these absolute addresses are 32-bit quantities. The procedure umap (line 5021) computes the physical address corresponding to a given virtual address within a given process' address space. It is used throughout the kernel for this purpose.

Once mem_phys and user_phys have been computed, the only thing left to do is call phys_copy, the assembly code copy routine to move the block from RAM disk to the caller or vice versa. Normally, the only process to send messages to the RAM disk driver is the file system, which requests blocks to be copied to or from its buffer cache, not directly to user processes.

The procedure do_setup (line 2377) takes the parameters in the message and sets up the starting and ending points of the RAM disk, so they can be used in subsequent calls. The limits of the other minor devices are fixed and cannot be set.

5.3. DISKS

The RAM disk is a good introduction to disk drivers (because it is so simple), but real disks have a number of issues that we have not touched on yet. These include seeks, motor control, soft errors, drive recalibration, and handling balky controllers that refuse to accept commands. In the following sections we will look at the floppy disk driver as a more complex example of a disk driver.

5.3.1. Overview of the Floppy Disk Driver in MINIX

The floppy disk driver accepts and processes two messages: for reading a block and for writing a block. A block is of size *BLOCK_SIZE*, which is defined in *h/type.h*, and is 1024 bytes in the standard distribution, although it can be easily changed. The sector size on the disk is 512 bytes, so two consecutive sectors are always read or written together. The advantage of the larger block size is a reduction in the number of disk accesses required, and thus an improvement in performance. The price paid is that a file of only 1 character nevertheless ties up 1024 bytes of disk space.

The messages accepted by the floppy disk driver use the format of Fig. 5-2. These messages are normally sent by the file system, and request data to be transferred to or from buffers internal to the file system. The file system takes care of the transfer to or from the address space of the process making the system call. The reply messages also follow the form of Fig. 5-2, with the *REP_STATUS* field containing the number of bytes actually transferred or an error code if the request could not be carried out (e.g., disk error, invalid buffer address supplied).

The floppy disk driver does not use the elevator algorithm. It is strictly sequential, accepting a request and carrying it out before even accepting the next request (FCFS). The reason for using this simple strategy has to do with the environment for which MINIX was intended—a personal computer. On a personal computer, most of the time only one process is active; once in a while there are one or two background processes. Having five processes running at once is highly unusual. With only a small number of processes, the chance that a disk request will come in while another disk request is being carried out is slight, so the potential gain from reordering requests is small. This small gain is not enough to offset the considerable increase in software complexity required for queueing requests. A driver for a large time-sharing system would undoubtedly be written differently.

The main procedure of the floppy disk driver, *floppy_task*, is similar to that of the RAM disk driver and also that of Fig. 5-3. It accepts messages, calls procedures to do the work, and sends replies, all in an endless loop. The work that needs to be done for reading and writing is virtually identical, so both are handled by the same procedure, *do_rdwt*.

Figure 5-4 shows the relation between the major procedures within the driver. Under normal conditions (i.e., no errors), *do_rdwt* calls five other procedures, each of which does part of the work of a transfer. The first one, *dma_setup*, sets up the registers of the DMA chip so that on a read, after the controller has read the data into its internal buffer, the DMA chip will take care of requesting bus cycles to transfer the data to memory without bothering the CPU.

The next procedure, *start_motor*, checks to see if the motor is running. If it is, the procedure just returns. If it is off, the motor is turned on.

Seek checks to see if the drive happens to be positioned on the right cylinder

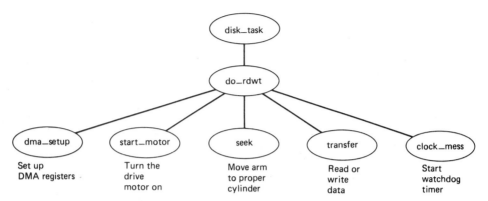

Fig. 5-4. The major procedures forming the floppy disk driver.

already. If it is not, it commands the controller to seek, and then does a RECEIVE to wait for the interrupt message sent when the seek is done.

The actual command to read or write the disk is issued by *transfer*. It too, does a RECEIVE after issuing the command to wait for it to complete. When the command has completed, *transfer* inspects the controller's status registers to see if any errors occurred. If a checksum error occurred, the procedure returns an error code to *do_rdwt*, so the transfer can be tried again.

The final procedure in Fig. 5-4 sends a message to the clock task asking it to call a certain procedure (part of the disk driver) in 3 sec. This mechanism is needed for motor control. Floppy disks cannot be read or written unless their motors are on. Turning the motors on or off is slow. Leaving the motors on all the time causes the drive and diskette to wear out very quickly. The compromise chosen for MINIX is to leave a drive motor on for 3 sec after a drive is used. If the drive is used again within 3 sec, the timer is extended for another 3 sec. If the drive is not used in this interval, the motor is turned off.

Some subsidiary procedures used in the disk driver are listed below:

1. *stop_motor* - stop a drive motor.
2. *fdc_out* - issue a command to the controller.
3. *fdc_results* - extract the results of command from the controller.
4. *recalibrate* - recalibrate a drive after a seek error.
5. *reset* - reset the controller after a serious error.
6. *send_mess* - take care of actually sending a message.

5.3.2. Implementation of the Floppy Disk Driver in MINIX

The floppy disk driver is 13 pages long, despite the fact that conceptually it is hardly any more complicated than the RAM disk driver. It simply must manage a lot of detail. The first two pages contain a large number of definitions for constants. These could be removed to shorten the driver, but the resulting shorter driver would be much harder to understand than the present one.

The main data structure used in the floppy disk driver is *floppy* (line 2508), which is an array of structures, one per drive. Each structure holds information about the state of its drive and the command currently pending. It contains the disk address, memory address, controller status information and calibration state of the drive. On lines 2525 to 2530 we find the declarations for several variables global to the whole disk driver.

The main procedure is on line 2540. It is completely straightforward, basically the same as Fig. 5-3, with the addition of a little bit of error checking. It gets a message, processes the message, and sends a reply.

The procedure that controls the real work is *do_rdwt* on line 2576. It has one parameter, a pointer to the message just received. The first thing the procedure does (lines 2585 to 2587) is compute *fp*, the pointer to the *floppy* slot of the drive to be used. Then it dissects the message and converts the block number into cylinder, track, sector, and head positions, storing all the pieces in the *floppy* array. From this point on, *fp* is used to refer to the drive, since it now contains all the relevant information. The array *interleave* is provided to allow software interleave, if desired; at present this feature is not used.

The loop starting on line 2604 is used to allow the operation now stored in *fp* to be repeated if checksum errors occur. The code on lines 2610 to 2617 is not strictly necessary, but makes the driver more robust. If the standard double-density MINIX diskette should be run on a machine containing a quad-density drive, this code notices that many errors are occurring right at the start of operation. It then adjusts *steps_per_cyl* to have the controller issue more pulses to the arm when seeking, so that the arm takes larger steps, thus allowing the coarser double-density diskettes to be read and written anyway. In effect, the driver discovers empirically whether the drive is double- or quad-density, and adjusts its parameters accordingly.

On line 2620 a check is made to see if the flag *need_reset* is set. If it is, *reset* is called to reset the controller. If any of the procedures called by *do_rdwt* discover that the controller is no longer responding, they set *need_reset* so that next time through the loop it will be reset.

Now the DMA chip is set up with the user buffer address and count taken from the message and put in *floppy*. Next, the motor is started, if necessary, and the seek command issued, again, if necessary. If the seek fails, for example, due to a controller that is not responding, the current attempt is cut off on line 2631, and the whole process started again. The next time through the loop the controller will be reset by the call on line 2620, if that is needed.

The actual data transfer is initiated by the call on line 2633. If it succeeds, the loop is exited. The loop is also exited if a write fails because the diskette is write protected (retries will not help here).

The code following the loop (lines 2640 and 2641) sets the watchdog timer by sending a message to the clock task, asking it to call the procedure *stop_motor* in 3 sec to stop the motor. If the timer runs out, the variable *motor_goal* tells *stop_motor* what status to set the motors to.

The rest of the driver contains procedures that help *do_rdwt*. *Dma_setup* loads the memory address and count into the DMA chip. The only thing peculiar about it is the check to make sure that a DMA buffer does not cross a 64K boundary. That is, a 1K DMA buffer may begin at 64510, but not at 64514 because the latter extends just beyond the 64K boundary at 65536.

This annoying rule occurs because the IBM PC uses an old DMA chip, the Intel 8237A, which contains a 16-bit counter, whereas a counter of at least 20 bits is needed because DMA uses absolute addresses, not addresses relative to a segment register. The low-order 16 bits of the DMA address are loaded into the 8237A, and the high-order 4 bits are loaded into a 4-bit latch. When the 8237A goes from 0xFFFF to 0x0000 it does not generate a carry into the 4-bit latch, so the DMA address suddenly jumps down by 64K in memory. Unexpected hardware "features" like this can cause weeks of time spent looking for exceedingly obscure bugs (all the more so when, like this one, the technical reference manual says nary a word about them).

Start_motor (line 2703) manages the motors. It calls *lock* to disable interrupts temporarily while checking the motor status, and computes the new motor goal. The 2 low-order bits of *motor_goal* contain the drive being selected. The next 2 bits set the controller in normal (interrupt enabled) mode. The high-order 4 bits control the motors for the four drives the controller can handle, 1 meaning motor on and 0 meaning motor off.

If the motor is off, it is necessary to delay while it is starting up. This delay is achieved on line 2732 by sending the clock a message, requesting that it call the function *send_mess* after 250 msec. That function (line 3003) sends the message received on line 2733.

Stopping the motor works a little differently. When the timer runs out for killing the motor, the procedure *stop_motor* (line 2740) is called by the clock task. Instead of going to the trouble of sending a message to the disk task, it just outputs the desired motor status to the hardware directly.

The procedure *seek* (line 2757) first checks to see if the drive is uncalibrated, a condition that happens when a seek error occurs. If it is uncalibrated, it is first recalibrated. If the current cylinder is the one needed (line 2769), *seek* just returns immediately. Otherwise it issues a seek and waits for the interrupt message on line 2776. The test on line 2775 is needed because if the controller refused to accept the seek command, waiting for the interrupt would be fatal: it would never happen.

After the interrupt comes in, *seek* checks the status reported by calling *fdc_results* on line 2780 to ask the floppy disk controller (FDC) to report back what happened. Unfortunately, even the status reporting may fail, since asking for the status is itself a command that the controller may refuse to accept. If the status is reported back properly, but indicates that there was a seek error, then the drive must be recalibrated.

For someone used to ordinary application programs, it may appear that an inordinate amount of the code in the driver deals with balky controllers and drives that refuse to go where they are told to go. In truth, the controller and drives are fairly reliable, but not having all this checking would mean that every once in a while MINIX would just crash for no apparent reason. To spare the user from this unpleasantry, the driver must be on guard against all kinds of unlikely, but theoretically possible events. It is also worth mentioning that the IBM PC's floppy disk controller, the NEC PD765 (a single chip costing less than 10 dollars), is about as simple as they come. More sophisticated (and expensive) controllers do much more of the error handling themselves.

The procedure *transfer* actually issues the command to the controller to initiate the read or write. Issuing the command consists of successively outputting 9 bytes of information (lines 2805 to 2813). After the command has been issued, *transfer* waits for the interrupt message, gets the results, and checks for errors.

Getting the results from the controller is not just a matter of reading a register or two. It requires a complex negotiation protocol with the controller in *fdc_results* (line 2843). All kinds of things may go wrong and must be checked for. As if this were not enough, the timing of the negotiation protocol is also important.

Even outputting a byte to the controller is complicated and requires a whole procedure, *fdc_out* (line 2872). The problem is that the controller has a mind of its own. You cannot force it to accept a command. There has to be a complex negotiation to determine whether it is in the mood or not. Recalibrating a drive and resetting the controller are handled by *recalibrate* (line 2903) and *reset* (line 2945), respectively.

The final two procedures in *floppy.c* take care of sending messages. *Clock_mess* (line 2986) sends a message to the clock task requesting a time out. *Send_mess* (line 3003) is called by the clock task itself when the motor has gotten up to speed. The message sent here is received on line 2733 to wake up the disk task.

All in all, the disk task is conceptually simple but full of detail, some of it inherent in running a real I/O device and some of it due to the fact that the PD765 is a very primitive controller. (On the other hand, a look *inside* the PD765 will quickly reveal how complex it is and how many things it does do by itself.) We will not study any more block devices in this book. Conceptually, they are all the same, differing only in the gory details, which, as we have seen, are plentiful.

5.4. CLOCKS

Clocks (also called **timers**) are essential to the operation of any time-sharing system for a variety of reasons. They maintain the time of day and prevent one process from monopolizing the CPU, among other things. The clock software generally takes the form of a device driver, even though a clock is neither a block device, like a disk, nor a character device, like a terminal. In the following sections we will take a look at how the MINIX clock driver works.

5.4.1. Overview of the Clock Driver in MINIX

The MINIX clock driver is contained in the file *clock.c*. It accepts these four message types, with the parameters shown:

1. SET_ALARM(process number, procedure to call, delay)

2. GET_TIME

3. SET_TIME(new time in seconds)

4. CLOCK_TICK

SET_ALARM allows a process to set a timer that goes off in a specified number of clock ticks. When a user process does an ALARM call, it sends a message to the memory manager, which then sends a message to the clock driver. When the alarm goes off, the clock driver sends a message back to the memory manager, which then takes care of making the signal happen.

SET_ALARM is also used by tasks that need to start a watchdog timer. When the timer goes off, the procedure provided is simply called. The clock driver has no knowledge of what the procedure does.

GET_TIME just returns the current real time as the number of seconds elapsed since Jan. 1, 1970 at 12:00 A.M.. *SET_TIME*, sets the real time. It can only be invoked by the super-user. Internal to the clock driver, the time is kept track of using two variables: the boot time in seconds and the real time since boot in ticks. When the time is set, the driver computes when the system was booted. It can make this computation because it has the current real time and it also knows how many ticks the system has been running. The system stores the real time of the boot in a variable. Later, when *GET_TIME* is called, it converts the current value of the tick counter to seconds and adds it to the stored boot time.

CLOCK_TICK is the message sent to the driver when a clock interrupt occurs. It has no parameters. When the driver receives this message, it updates the real time, checks to see if it is time for the next signal or watchdog call, charges the current tick to some process, and checks to see if the quantum is up. MINIX does not currently support profiling.

The driver has a few global variables, but no major data structures. The variable *realtime* (line 0703) is a counter incremented at every clock tick. Together with the variable *boot_time* (line 3099) it allows the current time of day to be computed. *Next_alarm* records the time when the next signal or watchdog call may happen. The driver has to be careful here, because the process requesting the signal may exit or be killed before the signal happens. When it is time for the signal, a check is made to see if it is still needed. If it is not needed, it is not carried out. *Sched_ticks* keeps track of the number of ticks left until the scheduler is called. When it becomes zero, it is time to schedule a new process.

Each user process is allowed to have only one outstanding alarm timer. Executing an ALARM call while a timer is still running cancels the first timer. Therefore, a convenient way to store the timers is to reserve one word in the process table entry for each process for its timer, if any. For tasks, the function to be called must also be stored somewhere, so an array, *watch_dog*, has been provided for this purpose.

The overall logic of the clock driver follows the same pattern as the disk drivers. The main program is an endless loop that gets messages, dispatches on the message type, and then sends a reply (except for *CLOCK_TICK*). Each message type is handled by a separate procedure, following our standard naming convention of naming all the procedures called from the main loop *do_xxx*, where *xxx* is different for each one, of course. As an aside, many linkers truncate procedure names to seven or eight characters, so the names *do_set_time* and *do_set_alarm* are potentially in conflict. The latter has been renamed *do_setalarm*. This problem occurs throughout MINIX, and is usually solved by mangling one of the names.

5.4.2. Implementation of the Clock Driver in MINIX

When MINIX starts up, all the drivers are called. Most of them just try to get a message and block. The clock driver does that too, but first it calls *init_clock* (line 3117) to initialize the programmable clock frequency to 60 Hz. Then it enters the main loop. The main loop of the clock driver is essentially the same as the other drivers, so we will not comment on it further.

The procedure *do_setalarm* (line 3142) extracts the parameters from the message and stores the alarm time in the process table on line 3161. After setting the alarm, it scans the entire process table to find the next one.

Do_get_time (line 3175) is only two lines. It computes the current real time from the two variables *boot_time* (the system boot time in seconds) and *realtime* (the number of ticks since boot).

The procedure *do_set_time* (line 3187) is even simpler—just one line. It computes the boot time based on the given current real time and number of ticks since booting.

The procedure *do_clocktick* (line 3199) is more interesting. It first updates the real time. Remember that if a clock interrupt occurs and the clock task is not waiting for a message, the procedure *interrupt* adds one to *lost_ticks* and forgets the whole thing, knowing that another interrupt will occur soon. It is here that these lost ticks are compensated for.

Next a check is made to see if a signal or watchdog timer has gone off. If one has, all the alarm entries are inspected. Because lost ticks are compensated for all at once, several alarms may go off in one pass over the table. The procedure *cause_sig* checks to see if the memory manager is currently waiting for a message. If so, it sends a message telling about the alarm. If the memory manager is busy, a note is made to inform it at the first opportunity. For tasks, the watchdog procedure is just called directly on line 3228.

After taking care of the alarms, *accounting* is called to charge someone one clock tick.

Finally a check is made to see if it is time to call the scheduler. The variable *sched_ticks* is not reset whenever a new process is scheduled (because the file system and memory manager are allowed to run to completion). Instead it is just reset after every *SCHED_RATE* ticks. The comparison on line 3243 is to make sure that the current process has actually run at least one full scheduler tick before taking the CPU away from it.

Accounting in MINIX keeps track of both user time and system time. User time is charged against a process if it is running when the clock ticks. System time is charged if the file system or memory manager is running. The variable *bill_ptr* always points to the last user process scheduled (the two servers do not count), so the procedure *accounting* (line 3253) will know whom to charge.

5.5. TERMINALS

Every computer has one or more terminals used to communicate with it. The IBM PC has a keyboard and a display that are an integral part of the computer, unlike the RS-232 terminals used on minicomputers and mainframes. In the following sections we will discuss how the MINIX terminal driver is structured internally.

5.5.1. Overview of the Terminal Driver in MINIX

The terminal driver is far and away the largest source file in MINIX, being almost twice as long as the floppy disk driver, which is the second largest. The size of the terminal driver is partly explained by the observation that the driver handles both the keyboard and the display, each of which is a complicated device in its own right. Still, it comes as a surprise to most people to learn that terminal I/O requires thirty times as much code as the scheduler. (This feeling is reinforced by looking at the numerous books on operating systems that devote thirty times as much space to scheduling as to all I/O combined.)

The terminal driver accepts five messages:

1. Read characters from the terminal (from the file system on behalf of a user process).

2. Write characters to the terminal (from the file system on behalf of a user process).

3. Set terminal parameters for IOCTL (from the file system on behalf of a user process).

4. Character available (from the interrupt procedure).

5. Cancel previous read request (from the file system when a signal occurs).

(In the code a sixth message is mentioned, for signaling that output is completed; it is intended for future terminals whose output is interrupt driven. It is provided as an aid to future modifications of the driver.) The messages for reading and writing have the same format as shown in Fig. 5-2, except that no *POSITION* field is needed. With a disk, the program has to specify which block it wants to read. With a terminal, there is no choice: the program always gets the next character typed in. Terminals do not support seeks and random access.

The message sent to the driver when the IOCTL system call is made contains a function code (are the terminal parameters to be read or to be written?), a mode word, and a long that may contain up to four characters. For one of the request types, *TIOCSETP*, only two of the characters are used: erase and kill. For another, *TIOCSETC*, all four characters are used: the SIGINT and SIGQUIT characters (DEL and CTRL-\), and the stop and start characters (CTRL-S and CTRL-Q). The message used to cancel requests specifies the terminal and process involved, and the message used for character arrival interrupts points to the input.

The terminal driver uses one main data structure, *tty_struct*, which is an array of structures, one per terminal. Even though the IBM PC generally has only one keyboard and display, the driver has been written to make it easy to add additional terminals, which is especially important if MINIX is ever ported to larger systems.

Tty_struct keeps track of both input and output. For input, it holds all characters that have been typed but not yet read by the program, requests to read characters that have not yet been typed, and the erase, kill, interrupt, quit, start, and stop characters. For output, it holds the parameters of write requests that are not yet finished, the current position on the screen and in the video RAM, the current attribute byte for the display, and information about escape sequences currently being processed. It also holds various general variables, such as the terminal mode and the I/O port, if any, corresponding to the terminal.

Terminal Input

To better understand how the driver works, let us first look at how characters typed in on the terminal work their way through the system to the program that wants them.

When a user logs in (e.g., on terminal 0), a shell is created for him with */dev/tty0* as standard input, standard output, and standard error. The shell starts up by trying to read from standard input by calling the library procedure *read*. This procedure sends a message that contains the file descriptor, buffer address and count to the file system. This message is shown as (1) in Fig. 5-5. After sending the message, the shell blocks, waiting for the reply. (User processes execute only the SEND_REC primitive, which combines a SEND with a RECEIVE from the process sent to.)

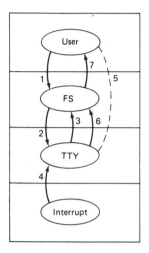

Fig. 5-5. Read request from terminal when no characters are pending. FS is the file system. TTY is the terminal task. Interrupt is the interrupt routine.

The file system gets the message and locates the i-node corresponding to the specified file descriptor. This i-node is for the character special file */dev/tty0*, and contains the major and minor device numbers for the terminal. The major device type for terminals in the standard distribution is 4; for terminal 0, the minor device number is 0.

The file system indexes into its device map, *dmap*, to find the number of the terminal task. Then it sends a message to the terminal task, shown as (2) in Fig. 5-5. Normally, the user will not have typed anything yet, so the terminal driver will be unable to satisfy the request. It sends a reply back immediately to unblock the file system and report that no characters are available, shown as (3). The file system records the fact that a process is waiting for terminal input in its tables, and then goes off to get the next request for work. The shell remains blocked, of course.

When a character is finally typed, it causes two interrupts, one when the key is depressed and one when it is released. This rule also applies to keys such as CTRL and SHIFT, which do not transmit any data by themselves, but still cause two interrupts per key hit. The interrupt routine in the assembly code file *mpx88.s* calls a C procedure, *keyboard* (line 4113) to extract the character from the keyboard hardware and put it in an array called *tty_driver_buf* along with the number of the line it came in on. *Keyboard* then calls *interrupt*, which, as we have seen in the previous chapter, sends a message to the terminal task (4) in the Fig. 5-5.

When enough characters have come in (meaning one character in raw or cbreak mode, or a line feed or CTRL-D in cooked mode), the terminal task calls the assembly language procedure *phys_copy* to copy the data to the address requested by the shell. This operation is not message passing and is shown by the dashed line in Fig. 5-5. Then the terminal driver sends a true message to the file system telling it that the work has been done (6). The file system reacts to this message by sending a message back to the shell to unblock it (7).

Note that the terminal driver copies the actual characters directly from its own address space to that of the shell. It does not first go through the file system. With block I/O, data do pass through the file system to allow it to maintain a buffer cache of the most recently used blocks. If a requested block happens to be in the cache, the request can be satisfied directly by the file system, without doing any disk I/O.

For terminal I/O, a cache makes no sense. Furthermore, a request from the file system to a disk driver can always be satisfied in at most a few hundred millisec, so there is no real harm in having the file system just wait. Terminal I/O may take hours to complete (it waits until something is typed in), so it is unacceptable to have the file system block that long.

Later on, it may happen that the user has typed ahead, and the characters are available before they have been requested. In that case, events 1, 2, 5, 6, and 7 all happen in quick succession after the read request; 3 and 4 do not occur.

When characters are typed in, they are put in the array *tty_driver_buf* as mentioned above. If the terminal task happens to be running at the time of the interrupt, no message can be sent to it because it is not waiting for one. Instead, a bit is set in the kernel variable *busy_map* in *interrupt*.

When the terminal task finally blocks, the bit is checked, and the message is sent then. If two or more terminal interrupts occur before the terminal driver finishes what it is doing, all the characters are stored in *tty_driver_buf*, and the bit in *busy_map* is repeatedly set. Ultimately, the terminal task gets one message; the rest are lost. But since all the characters are safely stored in *tty_driver_buf*, no typed input is lost.

The problem of what to do in an unbuffered message system (rendezvous principle) when an interrupt routine wants to send a message to a process that is busy is inherent in this kind of design. For most devices, such as disks, interrupts occur only in response to commands issued by the driver, so only one interrupt can be pending at any instant. The only devices that generate interrupts on their own are the clock and the terminal. The clock is handled by just counting lost interrupts, so they can be exactly compensated for later. The terminal is handled by having the interrupt routine accumulate the characters in a fixed buffer, so losing the second, third, and subsequent messages in a series is unimportant, as long as the first one is not lost. In MINIX the bit in *busy_map* guarantees that the first one is never lost.

In all fairness, this is not a part of the system that we are most proud of, but it does the job without too much additional software complexity and no loss in performance. The obvious alternative, to throw away the rendezvous principle and have the system buffer all messages sent to destinations not waiting for them, is much more complicated and also slower.

While it was not our primary purpose to air our dirty linen in public, real system designers are often faced with a tradeoff between using the general case, which is elegant all the time but slow, and using a simpler technique, which is usually fast but in one or two cases requires a trick to make it work properly. Experience is really the only guide to which approach is better under given circumstances.

When a message comes into the terminal task requesting characters, the main procedure, *tty_task* (line 3500) calls *do_read* (line 3784) to handle the request (see Fig. 5-6). *Do_read* stores the parameters of the call in *tty_struct*, just in case there are insufficient characters already buffered to satisfy the request now.

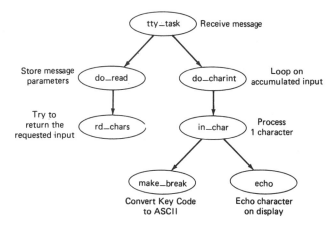

Fig. 5-6. Input handling in the terminal driver. The left branch of the tree is taken to process a request to read characters. The right branch is taken when a character-has-been-typed message is sent to the driver.

Then it calls *rd_chars* (line 3813) to check to see if enough input is available. If it is, the input is copied to the user. If no input is available, nothing is copied. In both cases, *rd_chars* returns a code to *do_read* reporting what happened, so that *do_read* can tell the file system.

When a character is typed, the interrupt procedure sends a message to the terminal driver telling it that one or more characters are now available in *tty_driver_buf*. Upon receiving this message, *tty_task* calls *do_charint* (line 3528) to loop on the characters accumulated in *tty_driver_buf* (almost always just one, but in theory, two or more are also possible) and call *in_char* (line 3581) for each character found (see Fig. 5-6).

Before doing any processing, *in_char* converts the key codes (scan codes) generated by the hardware into ASCII characters by calling *make_break* to look them up in the appropriate table. After that, *in_char* distinguishes between cooked mode, cbreak mode, and raw mode, and handles all the characters that need special processing. It also calls *echo* (line 3746) to have the characters displayed on the screen.

Terminal Output

Terminal output in MINIX is simpler than terminal input because the display is memory mapped. When a process wants to print something, it generally calls *printf* to format a line. *Printf* calls WRITE to send a message to the file system. The message contains a pointer to the characters to be printed (not the characters themselves). The file system then sends a message to the terminal driver, which fetches them and copies them to the video RAM.

When a message comes in to the terminal task to write on the screen, *do_write* (line 3905) is called to store the parameters in *tty_struct*. It then calls the output procedure for memory-mapped displays. (If RS-232 terminals are added later, a different procedure will be called for them.) This output procedure, called *console* (line 4178), consists mainly of a loop that fetches one byte directly from the user process and calls *out_char* (line 4217) to print it. Figure 5-7 shows the main procedures involved in output.

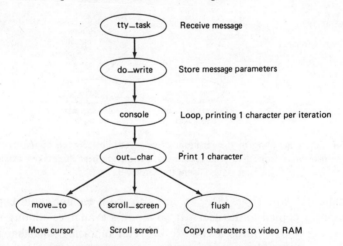

Fig. 5-7. Major procedures used on terminal output.

Logically, the bytes fetched from the user process could be written into the video RAM one per loop iteration. Unfortunately, writing into the video RAM while the 6845 is fetching characters from it interferes with the 6845's critical timing and may generate visual garbage all over the screen. Only during vertical retrace of the CRT beam is it always safe to write in the video RAM. Vertical retrace periods occur 50 or 60 times a second, each one lasting a few msec. To deal with this problem, *out_char* accumulates characters in *tty_ramqueue* rather than writing them directly into the video RAM.

When this buffer fills up, or a character involving cursor motion has to be printed, *flush* (line 4326) is called to output the buffer to the screen. *Flush* calls the assembly language procedure *vid_copy* to wait until the vertical retrace bit comes on, and then it quickly copies the buffer to the screen.

Out_char also checks for characters that need special handling, such as the bell, line feed, carriage return, tab, backspace, some cursor motion keys, and the escape sequences. If one of these is found, it is processed directly.

The current cursor position is stored in *tty_struct* in the fields *tty_row* and *tty_column*. The coordinate (0, 0) is in the lower left-hand corner of the screen, even though the hardware fills the screen starting in the upper left-hand corner. Each video scan begins at the address given by *tty_org* and continues for $160 \times 25 = 4000$ bytes, wrapping around the video RAM, if necessary.

In other words, the 6845 chip pulls the word at offset *tty_org* from the video RAM, and displays the character in the upper left-hand corner using the attribute byte to control color, blinking, reverse video, underlining, intensity, and so forth. Then it fetches the next word and displays the character at coordinate (0, 24). This process continues until it gets to (79, 0), at which time it begins again. Adding 160 to *tty_org* and then loading it into the 6845 causes the screen to scroll upward by one line.

The position of the cursor relative to the start of the video RAM can be derived from *tty_row* and *tty_column*, but it is faster to store it explicitly, which is done in the field *tty_vid*. When a character is to be printed, it is put into the video RAM at location *tty_vid*, which is then updated, as is *tty_column*. Figure 5-8 summarizes the fields of *tty_struct* that affect the current position and the display origin.

tty_row	Current row (0-24) with 0 at bottom
tty_column	Current column (0-79) with 0 at left
tty_vid	Offset into video RAM for cursor
tty_org	Position in video RAM where scan begins

Fig. 5-8. Fields of the tty structure that relate to the current screen position.

The characters that affect the cursor position (e.g., line feed, backspace) are handled by simply adjusting the values of *tty_row*, *tty_column*, and *tty_vid*. This work is done by *move_to* (line 4343). When a line feed is to be printed on the bottom line of the screen, *scroll_screen* (line 4304) is called to add 160 to *tty_org* and scroll the screen. It must also copy a row of blanks to the video RAM to ensure that the new line that suddenly appears at the bottom of the screen is empty.

The terminal driver supports a few escape sequences to allow screen editors and other interactive programs to update the screen in a flexible way. These escape sequences are all 3 bytes long and are shown in Fig. 5-9. By having ESC 32 32 correspond to moving to (0, 0), we have arranged that the parameters for cursor motion are printable characters. (When output to the screen, the escape sequences are not printed, but when they appear in programs they can be seen.)

Byte 1	Byte 2	Byte 3	
ESC	n1	n2	Move cursor to (n1–32, n2–32)
ESC	z	n1	Set attribute byte to n1
ESC	~	0	Clear screen from cursor to end
ESC	~	1	Scroll screen 1 line backward

Fig. 5-9. The escape sequences accepted by the terminal driver on output. ESC denotes the ASCII escape character (033).

5.5.2. Implementation of the Terminal Driver in MINIX

In this section we will inspect the actual code of the terminal driver in detail, first doing the input part and then doing the output part. The main loop of the driver (line 3508) is similar to that of the other drivers, except that the replies are sent by the procedures that are called here, rather than in *tty_task* itself.

Terminal Input

After our study of the other drivers, the only part of the terminal driver that is genuinely new is the way characters are processed as they are typed. When a key is struck or released, the CPU interrupts to line 1187, which saves the registers and calls the C procedure *keyboard* on line 4113. This procedure first plucks the key code (scan code) from the hardware and acknowledges this fact to the keyboard hardware. If the high-order bit of the key code is set, the key in question was released; otherwise, it was struck. Key releases, other than case shifts such as SHIFT, CTRL, and ALT, are just ignored and do not cause messages to be sent to the terminal task. This optimization reduces the message traffic within the system.

On lines 4144 to 4150 a check is made to see if the character is CTRL-S, which freezes the display. If it is, the *tty_inhibited* field is set to *STOPPED*, which causes the output loop in *console* (line 4196) to stop, if it is running.

On line 4145 a check is made to see if CTRL-ALT-DEL has been typed. If it has, the computer is rebooted. The code for *reboot* is in *klib88.s*. The rest of *keyboard* deals with storing the key code in the array *tty_driver_buf* and sending a message to the terminal task to have it process the stored characters.

When that message is received later, it is handled in *do_charint* (line 3528), which is mostly concerned with looping over the characters in *tty_driver_buf* and passing them to *in_char* one at a time. After each character is processed, a check is made to see if a previously incomplete read request can now be satisfied. In cooked mode this happens when a line feed is processed. In the other modes it happens on any character. If the read request can be completed now, *rd_chars* is called on line 3566 to copy the data to the user process.

The basic processing of each character typed in is done by *in_char* (line 3581). Early on it calls *make_break* (line 3695) to convert the key code received from the keyboard to an ASCII code by table lookup. Four tables are used, corresponding to lower and upper case for the IBM PC and for the Olivetti M24. The flag *olivetti* is set when the system is initialized, depending on which key code was typed in when the system asked for an equal sign.

Make_break keeps track of the state of five different case shifts in software. These shifts are SHIFT, CTRL, ALT, CAPS LOCK, and NUM LOCK. The entries above 0200 in the tables are used to indicate that the key code is for one of these shifts. Because the code output for each key is completely determined by software, we have been able to use a more flexible approach than most keyboard drivers. The basic idea is simple: each key outputs a unique code, so, for example, the software can distinguish between the "+" in the numeric pad and the "+" in the top row of keys, if it so desires. All the values between 1 and 255 are used.

Getting back to *in_char*, the tests on lines 3607 to 3653 check for the characters that are handled specially in cooked mode. The tests on lines 3655 to 3678 process those characters that are special in both cooked and cbreak mode. In raw mode, all of these characters are passed through to the user without any special processing. The actual queueing of characters is done at the end of *in_char*.

When a key is struck, neither the hardware nor the interrupt routine puts the character just typed on the display. It is up to the terminal driver to display it. The last thing *in_char* does before finishing up is call *echo* (line 3746) to print the character on the screen. All *echo* does is check to see if ECHO mode is enabled and the character is displayable. If so, it calls *out_char* to have it copied to *tty_ramqueue*, and then it calls *flush* to have that queue actually copied to the screen.

The procedure *chuck* (line 3761) is used for the erase and kill local editing characters to remove characters already typed from the input queue. We have now finished the story of how input characters are processed.

The procedure *do_read* (line 3784), as we have already seen, is concerned with handling read requests from user programs. It stores the message parameters in *tty_struct* because it may not be possible to satisfy the request now. When enough characters finally come in, the driver needs to have the information about the request so it can carry it out then.

The actual transfer of data from the driver to user space is done by *rd_chars*. It computes the physical address within user space where the data are to go, *user_phys*, by calling *umap*. It also computes the physical address of the input buffer, *tty_phys*. Given these two addresses, the two nested loops starting on line 3841 perform the actual copying, one buffer at a time. The inner loop fills up one buffer, a character at a time, and copies it to user space. The outer loop repeats this process, copying as many buffer loads as necessary to satisfy the request. When it is finished, *rd_chars* returns *cum*, which is the number of characters actually transferred. Note that a read from a terminal never returns more than one line, no matter how many characters are requested, so it is important to report how many characters have been put in the user's buffer.

The next procedure, *finish* (line 3884), is used to terminate output and reply to the file system. It is used for normal output termination, but also when a DEL or CTRL-\ is typed, to stop all output immediately and tell the file system that output has been completed.

Terminal Output

Having finished looking at how input works, let us look at output. The procedure *do_write* is called from *tty_task*, just as *do_read* is, and like *do_read*, does little more than store the message parameters in *tty_struct*. It also computes the physical address within user space of the data to be printed.

On line 3934 *do_write* calls a device-dependent procedure to perform the output. For terminal 0, this procedure is *console* (line 4178), but if RS-232 terminals are added later, it will call a different procedure for them. The device-dependent code is listed at the end of *tty.c*, starting at line 4050.

The heart of *console* is the loop on lines 4196 to 4201. Each iteration of that loop uses the assembly code procedure *get_byte* to fetch one byte from the user's output buffer into the local variable *c*. The byte is then output by calling *out_char*, specifying the terminal and the character. Finally, the pointer is advanced to the next character and the count of remaining bytes is decremented.

The output loop terminates either when the entire buffer has been printed, or when *tty_inhibited* comes on. Normally, this flag is off, but when CTRL-S is typed, the interrupt handler sets it (line 4147). This strategy has been chosen because once the driver starts doing output, it does not accept any more messages until it has finished its work. If the CTRL-S character were to be sent to the driver in a message, it would always have to wait until the current output was finished. With the implementation actually used, CTRL-S stops the output instantly. When CTRL-Q is typed, *console* is called (line 3676) to pick up where it left off.

Every character printed on the screen passes through *out_char*, including characters being echoed (line 3753). It contains a simple finite state machine to handle escape sequences, all of which are exactly three characters long, to keep things simple. The finite state machine, shown in Fig. 5-10, has three states, depending on whether the field *tty_esc_state* is 0, 1, or 2.

Normally, *tty_esc_state* is 0. When an ASCII ESC character (033) is output, the state switches to 1. After another character arrives, the character is saved in *tty_echar* and the state switches to 2. When the next character arrives, *escape* (line 4362) is called with both characters to handle it, and the state is reset to 0.

If the character being output is not part of an escape sequence, a check is made on line 4241 to see if it is a printable character or something special. The bell (CTRL-G) is handled by *beep* (line 4427), which generates a tone by directing one of the clock channels to the built-in loudspeaker. The characters

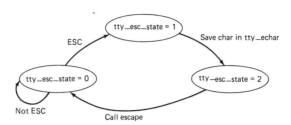

Fig. 5-10. Escape sequences are three characters long.

involving cursor motion, such as carriage return, backspace, and line feed, all call *move_to* (line 4343) to update the current row, column, and position within the video RAM.

Printable characters are handled on lines 4291 to 4296. As discussed earlier, they are stored in the buffer *tty_ramqueue* along with their attribute byte so that the number of times the video RAM has to be accessed can be reduced. In this manner, each vertical retrace interval can be used to deposit perhaps tens of characters in the video RAM, instead of just a few.

Scroll_screen (line 4304) can scroll the screen one line in either direction, depending on *dir*. Scrolling is accomplished by adding or subtracting 160 bytes from *tty_org* and then updating the 6845. The 6845's registers that are used by MINIX are shown in Fig. 5-11.

Registers	Function
10 - 11	Cursor size
12 - 13	Start address for drawing screen
14 - 15	Cursor position

Fig. 5-11. Some of the 6845's registers.

Each register is 8 bits wide, but they work in pairs to form 16-bit registers. All of them address the video RAM in words, rather than bytes. For this reason, *tty_org* (which is in bytes) is shifted right to convert it to words on line 4319. The 6845 registers not shown in Fig. 5-11 control the sync pulses that determine the width, height, and offset of the displayable area on the screen. They are set by the ROM when the IBM PC is booted and not touched by MINIX.

Flush (line 4326) calls *vid_copy* to copy the accumulated characters from the queue to the screen. Then it moves the cursor and clears the queue.

Move_to (line 4343) updates the row, column, and video RAM position, and moves the cursor. It is called whenever the cursor is explicitly moved. Before doing its work it flushes the buffer, to prevent the queued characters from being eventually displayed in the wrong place.

Escape sequences are detected in *out_char* but processed by *escape* (line 4362). Each of the four possibilities of Fig. 5-9 is checked for and handled.

The 6845 registers shown in Fig. 5-11 are set by calls to *set_6845* (line 4403). A 16-bit value is output as two 8-bit values, to consecutive registers. A value is loaded into a register by first loading the register number into an I/O port, and then loading the value into another I/O port.

Ringing the bell for CTRL-G is done in *beep* (line 4427). It is accomplished by programming channel 2 of the timer chip. Interrupts are disabled on line 4438 because it sounds funny otherwise. The frequency and duration of the beep tone are completely programmable, and can be changed by modifying the constants *BEEP_FREQ* and *B_TIME*.

When MINIX starts up, each task is called to give it the opportunity to initialize itself. On line 3507, the terminal task calls *tty_init* (line 4453) to do the initialization. First it sets up the default mode and special characters, such as erase, kill, and interrupt. Then it sets some of the 6845 display parameters, which differ for color and monochrome displays.

The global variable *color* used on line 4474 is set in *main.c* by calling the assembly language procedure *get_chrome*, which makes a BIOS call to find out. The BIOS finds out by reading an I/O port connected to the DIP switches on the PC's motherboard. This call is the only place in MINIX that the BIOS is used.

The cursor shape is set on line 4487. As you can see, the IBM PC is extremely flexible: the meaning of each key, the sound of the bell, the shape of the cursor, and many other things are all programmable. The keyboard type is set on line 4495 by looking at the number corresponding to the equals sign typed to start MINIX. It is different on the IBM PC and Olivetti M24.

In a few places in the kernel, the procedure *printf* is called. The MINIX version of *printf* is part of the standard I/O library, which sends messages to the file system to print its strings. A simpler procedure is needed within the kernel, and is provided in the form of the procedure *printk*, which calls the kernel version of *putc* directly. All occurrences of the string "printf" are changed into "printk" by the macro on line 0696.

The final procedure in the driver is temporary and used only for helping to debug MINIX. At the start of *in_char*, a check is made to see if the key is a function key. If it is, *func_key* (line 4519) is called to provide some debug information on the screen. This feature has been included to help people who plan to modify MINIX. It can be removed when this assistance is no longer needed. The dump procedures are in the file *dmp.c*, which is not really a permanent part of MINIX and is not shown in this book.

5.6. THE SYSTEM TASK IN MINIX

One consequence of making the file system and memory manager user processes outside the kernel is that occasionally they have some piece of information that the kernel needs. This structure, however, forbids them from just writing it into a kernel table. For example, the FORK system call is handled by the memory manager. When a new process is created, the kernel must know about it, in order to schedule it. How can the memory manager tell the kernel?

The solution to this problem is to have a kernel task that communicates with the file system and memory manager via the standard message mechanism, and which also has access to all the kernel tables. This task, called the **system task**, is in layer 2 in Fig. 4-1, and functions like the other tasks we have studied in this chapter. The only difference is that it does not control any I/O device. Nevertheless, it makes more sense to study it here than in any other chapter.

The system task accepts nine kinds of messages, shown in Fig. 5-12. The main program of the system task, *sys_task* (line 4627), is structured the same way as the other tasks. It gets a message, dispatches to the appropriate service procedure, and then sends a reply. We will now look at each of these messages and its service procedure.

Message type	From	Meaning
SYS_FORK	MM	A process has forked
SYS_NEWMAP	MM	Install memory map for a new process
SYS_EXEC	MM	Set stack pointer after EXEC call
SYS_XIT	MM	A process has exited
SYS_GETSP	MM	MM wants a process' stack pointer
SYS_TIMES	FS	FS wants a process' execution times
SYS_ABORT	Both	Panic: MINIX is unable to continue
SYS_SIG	MM	Interrupt a process with a signal
SYS_COPY	Both	Copy data between processes

Fig. 5-12. The nine message types accepted by the system task.

SYS_FORK is used by the memory manager to tell the kernel that a new process has come into existence. The kernel needs to know this in order to schedule it. The message contains the slot numbers within the process table corresponding to the parent and child. The memory manager and file system also have process tables, with entry *k* referring to the same process in all three. In this manner, the memory manager can specify just the parent and child slot numbers, and the kernel will know which processes are meant.

The procedure *do_fork* (line 4658) copies the parent's process table entry to the child's slot and zeros the accounting information. The check on line 4674 to see if the memory manager is feeding the kernel garbage is pure paranoia, but a little internal consistency checking does no harm. Similar checks are made in a number of other places in the system as well.

After a FORK, the memory manager allocates memory for the child. The kernel must know where the child is located in memory so it can set up the segment registers properly when running the child. The *SYS_NEWMAP* message allows the memory manager to give the kernel any process' memory map. This message can also be used after a BRK system call changes the map.

The message is handled by *do_newmap* (line 4698), which must first copy the new map from the memory manager's address space. The map is not contained in the message itself because it is too big. In theory, the memory manager could tell the kernel that the map is at address *m*, where *m* is an illegal address. The memory manager is not supposed to do this, but the kernel checks anyway. The 18-byte map is copied directly into the process table's *p_map* field. Information from it is also extracted and loaded into the *p_reg* fields that hold the segment registers.

When a process does an EXEC system call, the memory manager sets up a new stack for it containing the arguments and environment. It passes the resulting stack pointer to the kernel using *SYS_EXEC*, which is handled by *do_exec* (line 4746). In addition to setting the stack pointer, *do_exec* kills off the alarm timer, if any, by storing a zero on top of it. It is for this reason that the clock task always checks when a timer has run out to see if anybody is still interested.

The EXEC call causes a slight anomaly. The process invoking the call sends a message to the memory manager and blocks. With other system calls, the resulting reply unblocks it. With EXEC there is no reply, because the newly loaded core image is not expecting a reply. Therefore, *do_exec* unblocks the process itself on line 4762.

Processes can exit in MINIX either by doing an EXIT system call, which sends a message to the memory manager, or by being killed by a signal. In both cases, the memory manager tells the kernel by the *SYS_XIT* message. The work is done by *do_xit* (line 4771), which is more complicated than you might expect. Taking care of the accounting information is straightforward. The tricky part is that the process might have been queued trying to send or receive at the time it was killed. The code on lines 4796 to 4816 checks for this possibility, and, if found, carefully removes it from all the queues it is on.

In contrast to the previous message, which is slightly complicated, *SYS_GETSP* is completely trivial. It is used by the memory manager to find out the value of the current stack pointer for some process. This value is needed for the BRK and SBRK system calls to see if the data segment and stack segment have collided. The code is in *do_getsp* (line 4825).

Now we come to the only message type used exclusively by the file system, *SYS_TIMES*. It is needed to implement the TIMES system call, which returns the accounting times to the caller. All *do_times* (line 4844) does is put the requested times into the reply message.

It can happen that either the memory manager or the file system discovers an error that makes it impossible to continue operation. For example, if upon first starting up, the file system sees that the super-block on the root device has been corrupted, it panics and sends a *SYS_ABORT* message to the kernel. All *do_abort* (line 4868) does is call *panic* to terminate MINIX immediately.

Most of the signal handling is done in the memory manager. It checks to see if the process to be signaled is enabled to catch or ignore the signal, if the sender of the signal is entitled to do so, and so on. The one thing the memory manager cannot do is actually cause the signal, that is, push the PSW, CS register, program counter, and signal number onto the stack of the signaled process. That work is done by sending the *SYS_SIG* message to the system task.

The message is handled by *do_sig* (line 4880). After extracting the parameters of the message, *do_sig* calls the assembly language procedure *build_sig* to construct an 8-byte array containing the interrupt information. The array, *sig_stuff*, is copied onto the stack of the signaled process by *phys_copy* on line 4910. The process's stack pointer is then decremented by the size of the block of information just copied.

The final message, *SYS_COPY*, is the most heavily used one. It is needed to allow the file system and memory manager to copy information to and from user processes.

When a user does a READ call, the file system checks its cache to see if it has the block needed. If not, it sends a message to the appropriate disk task to load it into the cache. Then the file system sends a message to the system task telling it to copy the block to the user process. In the worst case, seven messages are needed to read a block; in the best case four messages are needed. Both cases are shown in Fig. 5-13. These messages are a significant source of overhead in MINIX, and are the price paid for the highly modular design.

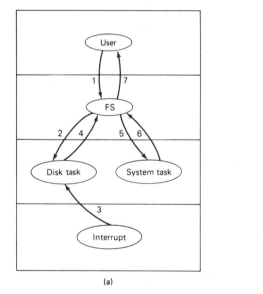
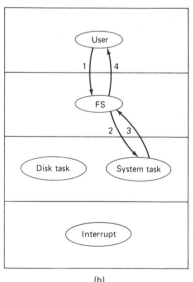

Fig. 5-13. (a) Worst case for reading a block requires seven messages. (b) Best case for reading a block requires four messages.

As an aside, on the 8088, which has no protection, it would be easy enough to cheat and let the file system copy the data to the caller's address space, but this would violate the design principle. Anyone interested in improving the performance of MINIX should look carefully at this mechanism to see how much improper behavior one can tolerate for how much gain in performance. The implementation of this procedure is straightforward. It is done by *do_copy* (line 4922) and consists of little more than extracting the message parameters and calling *phys_copy*.

At the end of *system.c* are three utility procedures used in various places throughout the kernel. When a task needs to cause a signal (e.g., the clock task needs to cause a SIGALRM signal, or the terminal task needs to cause a SIGINT signal), it calls *cause_sig* (line 4960). This procedure sets a bit in the *p_pending* field of the process table entry for the process to be signaled, and then calls *inform* to tell the memory manager to handle the signal.

Inform (line 4987) checks to see if the memory manager is currently waiting for a message from *ANY*, that is, if it is idle and waiting for the next request to process. If it is idle, *inform* builds a message of type *KSIG* and sends it the message. The task calling *cause_sig* continues running as soon as the message has been copied into the memory manager's receive buffer. It does not wait for the memory manager to run.

When the signaling task finishes, the scheduler will be called. If the memory manager is the highest priority runnable process, it will run and process the signal.

The procedure *umap* (line 5021) is a generally useful procedure that maps a virtual address onto a physical address. Its parameters are a pointer to the process table entry for the process or task whose virtual address space is to be mapped, a flag specifying the text, data, or stack segment, the virtual address itself, and a byte count. The byte count is useful because *umap* checks to make sure that the entire buffer starting at the virtual address is within the process' address space. For this reason, it must know how big the buffer is. The byte count is not used for the mapping itself, just this check. All the tasks that copy data to or from user space compute the physical address of the buffer using *umap*.

6

MEMORY MANAGEMENT IN MINIX

Memory is an important resource that must be carefully managed. While the average home computer nowadays has ten times as much memory as the IBM 7094, the largest computer in the world in the early 1960s, programs are getting bigger just as fast as memories. To paraphrase Parkinson's law, "Programs expand to fill the memory available to hold them." In this chapter we will study how MINIX manages its memory and carries out the system calls relating to memory management, especially FORK and EXEC.

6.1. OVERVIEW OF MEMORY MANAGEMENT IN MINIX

Memory management in MINIX is simple: neither paging nor swapping is used. The memory manager maintains a list of holes sorted in memory address order. When memory is needed, due either to a FORK or an EXEC system call, the hole list is searched using first fit for a piece that is big enough to hold the new process. Once a process has been placed in memory, it remains in exactly the same place until it terminates. It is never swapped out and also never moved to another place in memory. Nor does allocated area ever grow. Neither does it shrink.

This strategy deserves some explanation. It derives from three factors: (1) the idea that MINIX is for personal computers, rather than for large time-sharing systems, (2) the desire to have MINIX work on the IBM PC, and (3) an attempt to make the system straightforward to implement on other small, personal computers in the future.

The first factor means that, on the average, the number of running processes will be small, so that typically enough memory will be available to hold all the processes with room left over. Swapping will generally not be needed. Since it adds considerable complexity to the system, not swapping makes the code much smaller. Furthermore, many personal computers do not have a hard disk, and a floppy disk is not exactly the ideal swapping device.

The desire to have MINIX run on the IBM PC also had substantial impact on the memory management design. The 8088's memory management architecture is very primitive. It does not support virtual memory in any form and does not even detect stack overflow, a defect that has major implications for the way processes are laid out in memory.

The portability issue argues for as simple a memory management scheme as possible. If MINIX used paging or segmentation, it would be difficult, if not impossible to port it to machines not having these features. By making a minimal number of assumptions about what the hardware can do, the number of machines to which MINIX can be ported is increased.

Another unusual aspect of MINIX is the way the memory management is implemented. It is not part of the kernel. Instead, it is handled by the memory manager process, which runs in user space and communicates with the kernel by the standard message mechanism. The position of the memory manager is shown in Fig. 6-1.

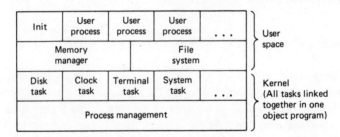

Fig. 6-1. The memory manager runs outside the kernel, in user space.

Moving the memory manager out of the kernel is an example of the separation of **policy** and **mechanism**. The decisions about which process will be placed where in memory (policy) are made by the memory manager. The actual setting of memory maps for processes (mechanism) is done by the system task within the kernel. This split makes it relatively easy to change the memory management policy (algorithms, etc.) without having to modify the lowest layers of the operating system.

Most of the memory manager code is devoted to handling the MINIX system calls that involve memory management, primarily FORK and EXEC, rather than just manipulating lists of processes and holes. In the next section we will look at the memory layout, and then in the ones following it we will take a bird's-eye view of how the memory management system calls are processed.

6.1.1. Memory Layout

Memory is allocated in MINIX on two occasions. First, when a process forks, an amount of memory equal in size to what the parent has is allocated for the child. Second, when a process changes its memory image via the EXEC system call, the old image is returned to the free list as a hole, and memory is allocated for the new one. Memory is released whenever a process terminates, either by exiting or by being killed by a signal.

Figure 6-2 shows both ways of allocating memory. In Fig. 6-2(a) we see two processes, *A* and *B*, in memory. If *A* forks, we get the situation of Fig. 6-2(b). If the child now executes the file *C*, the memory looks like Fig. 6-2(c).

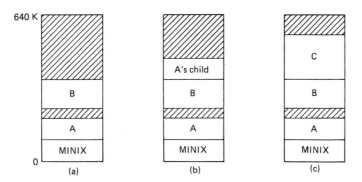

Fig. 6-2. Memory allocation. (a) Originally. (b) After a FORK. (c) After the child does an EXEC. The shaded regions are unused memory.

Note that the old memory for the child is released before the new memory for *C* is allocated, so that *C* can use the child's memory. In this way, a series of FORK and EXEC pairs (such as the shell setting up a pipeline) results in all the processes being adjacent, with no holes between them, as would have been the case had the new memory been allocated before the old memory had been released.

When memory is allocated, either by the FORK or EXEC system calls, a certain amount of it is taken for the new process. In the former case, the amount taken is identical to what the parent process has. In the latter case, the memory manager takes the amount specified in the header of the file executed. Once this allocation has been made, under no conditions is the process ever allocated any more total memory.

Figure 6-3 shows the internal memory layout used for a single MINIX process. For a program not using separate I and D space, the total amount of memory allocated is specified by a field in the header. If, for example, a program has 4K of text, 2K of data, and 1K of stack, and the header says to allocate 40K total, the gap of unused memory between the data segment and the stack segment will be 33K.

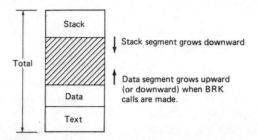

Fig. 6-3. Internal memory layout for a single process.

If the programmer knows that the total memory needed for the combined growth of the data and stack segments for the file *a.out* is at most 10K, he can give the command

```
chmem =10240 a.out
```

which changes the header field so that upon EXEC the memory manager allocates a space 10240 bytes more than the sum of the initial text and data segments. For the above example, a total of 16K would be allocated on all subsequent EXECs of the file. Of this amount, the topmost 1K would be used for the stack.

For a program using separate I and D space (indicated by a bit in the header that is set by the linker), the total field in the header applies to the data space only. A program with 4K of text, 2K of data, 1K of stack, and a total size of 64K would be allocated 68K (4K instruction space, 64K data space), leaving 61K for the data segment and stack to consume during execution. The boundary of the data segment can be moved only by the BRK system call. All BRK does is check to see if the new data segment bumps into the current stack pointer, and if not, note the change in some internal tables. No memory is allocated. If the new data segment bumps into the stack, the call fails.

This strategy has been chosen to make it possible to run MINIX on the IBM PC, which does not check for stack overflow in hardware. A user program can push as many words as it wants to on the stack without the operating system being aware of it. On computers with more sophisticated memory management hardware, the stack is allocated a certain amount of memory initially. If it attempts to grow beyond this amount, a trap to the operating system occurs, and the system allocates another piece of memory to the stack, if possible. This trap does not exist on the 8088, making it dangerous to have the stack adjacent to anything except a large chunk of unused memory, since the stack can grow quickly and without warning. MINIX has been designed so that if it is moved to a computer with better memory management, the better memory management can be used.

6.1.2. Message Handling

Like all the other components of MINIX, the memory manager is message driven. After the system has been initialized, the memory manager enters its main loop, which consists of waiting for a message, carrying out the request contained in the message, and sending a reply. Figure 6-4 gives the list of legal message types, their input parameters, and the value sent back in the reply message. FORK, EXIT, WAIT, BRK, and EXEC are clearly closely related to memory allocation and deallocation. The four signal calls, SIGNAL, KILL, ALARM, and PAUSE, also can affect what is in memory, because a signal that kills a process also causes its memory to be deallocated. The five GET/SET calls have nothing to do with memory management at all. They also have nothing to do with the file system. But they had to go either in the file system or the memory manager, since each system call is handled by one or the other. They were put here simply because the file system was large enough already.

The final two messages, KSIG and BRK2 are not system calls. KSIG is the message type used by the kernel to inform the memory manager of a signal originating in the kernel, such as SIGINT, SIGQUIT, or SIGALRM. BRK2 is used during system initialization to tell the memory manager how big the system is.

Message type	Input parameters	Reply value
FORK	(none)	Child's pid
EXIT	Exit status	(No reply)
WAIT	(none)	Status code
BRK	New size	New size
EXEC	Pointer to initial stack	(No reply)
SIGNAL	Signal number and function	Old function
KILL	Process identifier and signal	0 if OK
ALARM	Number of seconds to wait	Residual time
PAUSE	(none)	0 if OK
GETPID	(none)	Pid
GETUID	(none)	Uid
GETGID	(none)	Gid
SETUID	New uid	0 if OK
SETGID	New gid	0 if OK
KSIG	Process slot and signals	(No reply)
BRK2	Init and total sizes	0 if OK

Fig. 6-4. The message types, input parameters, and reply values used for communicating with the memory manager.

Although there is a library routine *sbrk*, there is no system call SBRK. The library routine computes the amount of memory needed by adding the increment or decrement specified as parameter to the current size, and makes a BRK call to set the size. Similarly, there are no separate system calls for *geteuid* and *getegid*.

The calls GETUID and GETGID return both the effective and real identifiers. The library procedures select out the proper values.

A key data structure used for message processing is the table *mm_callvec* declared in *table.c* (line 7400). It contains pointers to the procedures that handle the various message types. When a message comes in to the memory manager, the main loop extracts the message type and puts it in the global variable *mm_call*. This value is then used to index into *mm_callvec* to find the pointer to the procedure that handles the newly arrived message. That procedure is then called to execute the system call. The value that it returns is sent back to the caller in the reply message to report on the success or failure of the call.

6.1.3. Memory Manager Data Structures and Algorithms

The memory manager has two key data structures: the process table and the hole table. We will now look at each of these in turn. The process table has one entry per process. Some of its fields are needed for process management, others for memory management, and yet others for the file system. In MINIX, each of these three pieces of the operating system has its own process table, containing just those fields that it needs. The entries correspond exactly, to keep things simple. Thus, slot *k* of the memory manager's table refers to the same process as slot *k* of the file system's table. When a process is created or destroyed, all three parts update their tables to reflect the new situation, in order to keep them synchronized.

The memory manager's process table is called *mproc*. It contains all the fields related to a process' memory allocation, as well as some additional items. The most important field is the array *mp_seg*, which has three entries, for the text, data, and stack segments, respectively. Each entry is a structure containing the virtual address, physical address, and length of the segment, all measured in clicks rather than in bytes. All segments must start on a click boundary and occupy an integral number of clicks.

The method used for recording memory allocation is shown in Fig. 6-5. In this figure we have a process with 3K of text, 4K of data, a gap of 1K, and then a 2K stack, for a total memory allocation of 10K. In Fig. 6-5(b) we see what the virtual, physical, and length fields for each of the three segments are, assuming that the process does not have separate I and D space. In this model, the text segment is always empty, and the data segment contains both text and data. When a process references virtual address 0, either to jump to it or to read it (i.e., as instruction space or as data space), physical address 0x32000 (in decimal, 200K) will be used. This address is at click 0x3200.

Note that the virtual address at which the stack begins depends initially on the total amount of memory allocated to the process. If the *chmem* command were used to modify the file header to provide a larger dynamic allocation area (bigger gap between data and stack segments), the next time the file was executed, the stack would start at a higher virtual address. If the stack grows longer by one

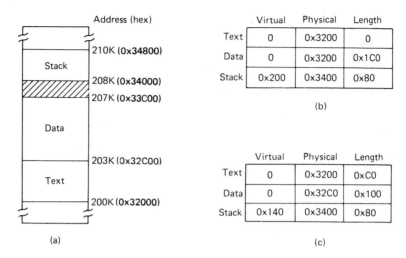

Fig. 6-5. (a) A process in memory. (b) Its memory representation for non-separate I and D space. (c) Its memory representation for separate I and D space.

click, the stack entry *should* change from the triple (0x200, 0x3400, 0x80) to the triple (0x1FF, 0x33FF, 0x81).

Because the 8088 hardware does not have a stack limit trap, this change will not be made until the next BRK system call, at which point the operating system explicitly reads SP and recomputes the segment entries. On a machine with a stack trap, the stack segment's entry would be updated as soon as the stack outgrew its segment.

Fig. 6-5(c) shows the segment entries for the memory layout of Fig. 6-5(a) for separate I and D space. Here both the text and data segments are nonzero in length.

The *mp_seg* array shown in Fig. 6-5(b) or (c) is primarily used to map virtual addresses onto physical memory addresses. Given a virtual address and the space to which it belongs, it is a simple matter to see whether the virtual address is legal or not (i.e., falls inside a segment), and if legal, what the corresponding physical address is. The kernel procedure *umap* performs this mapping for the I/O tasks and for copying to and from user space, for example.

In addition to the segment information, *mproc* also holds the process id (pid) of the process itself and of its parent, the uids and gids (both real and effective), information about signals, and the exit status, if the process has already terminated but its parent has not yet done a WAIT for it.

The other major memory manager table is the hole table, *hole*, which lists every hole in memory in order of increasing memory address. The gaps between the data and stack segments are not considered holes since they have already been allocated. They are not contained in the free hole list. Each hole list entry has three fields: the base address of the hole, in clicks; the length of the hole, in clicks; and a pointer to the next entry on the list. The list is singly linked, so it is easy to find the next hole starting from any given hole, but to find the previous hole, you have to search the entire list from the beginning until you come to the given hole.

The reason for recording everything about segments and holes in clicks rather than bytes is simple: it is much more efficient. On the 8088, using byte addresses would require 20 bits per address, whereas recording addresses in clicks requires only 16 bits per address. Similar arguments hold for paging machines. A computer with a page size of 1K and 64M of memory needs only 16 bits to hold a page number, but 26 bits to hold a full memory address.

The principal operations on the hole list are allocating a piece of memory of a given size and returning an existing allocation. To allocate memory, the entire hole list is searched, starting at the hole with the lowest address, until a hole that is large enough is found (first fit). The segment is then allocated by reducing the hole by the amount needed for the segment, or in the rare case of an exact fit, removing the hole from the list. This scheme is fast and simple, but suffers from both internal fragmentation (up to 15 bytes may be wasted in the final click, since an integral number of clicks is always taken) and external fragmentation.

When a process terminates and is cleaned up, its memory is returned to the free list. If either or both of the memory's neighbors are holes, they are merged, so adjacent holes never occur. In this way, the number, location, and sizes of the holes vary continuously as the system runs. Whenever all user processes have terminated, all of available memory is once again in a single hole, ready for allocation.

6.1.4. The FORK, EXIT, and WAIT System Calls

When processes are created or destroyed, memory must be allocated or deallocated. Also, the process table must be updated, including the parts held by the kernel and the file system. It is the memory manager that coordinates all of this activity. Process creation is done by FORK, which is carried out as a series of steps, as shown in Fig. 6-6.

```
1. Check to see if process table is full.
2. Try to allocate memory for the child.
3. Copy the parent's image to the child's memory.
4. Find a free process slot and copy parent's slot to it.
5. Enter child's memory map in process table.
6. Choose a pid for the child.
7. Tell kernel and file system about child.
8. Report child's memory map to kernel.
9. Send reply messages to parent and child.
```

Fig. 6-6. The steps required to carry out the FORK system call.

It is difficult and inconvenient to stop a FORK call part way through, so the memory manager maintains a count at all times of the number of processes currently in existence in order to see easily if a process table slot is available. If the table is not full, an attempt is made to allocate memory for the child. If this step also succeeds, the FORK is guaranteed to work. The newly allocated memory is then filled in, a process slot is located and filled in, a pid is chosen, and the other parts of the system informed that a new process has been created.

A process fully terminates when two events happen: (1) the process itself has exited (or has been killed by a signal), and (2) its parent has executed a WAIT system call to find out what happened. A process that has exited or has been killed, but whose parent has not (yet) done a WAIT for it, enters a kind of suspended animation, sometimes known as **zombie state**. It is prevented from being scheduled and has its alarm timer turned off (if it was on), but it is not removed from the process table. Its memory is not freed, although it could have been. (Zombie state is unusual and rarely lasts long, and it was easier to program this way.) When the parent finally does the WAIT, the memory and process table slot are freed, and the file system and kernel are informed.

A problem arises if the parent of an exiting process is already dead. If no special action were taken, the exiting process would remain a zombie forever. Instead, the tables are changed to make it a child of the *init* process. When the system comes up, *init* reads the */etc/ttys* file to get a list of all terminals, and then forks off a login process to handle each one. It then spends most of its time waiting for processes to terminate. In this way, orphan zombies are cleaned up.

6.1.5. The EXEC System Call

When a command is typed at the terminal, the shell forks off a new process, which then executes the command requested. It would have been possible to have a single system call to do both FORK and EXEC at once, but they were provided as two distinct calls for a very good reason: to make it easy to implement redirection. When the shell forks, the child process closes standard input and output if they are redirected, and then opens the redirected files. Then it executes the command, which inherits the redirected standard input and output.

EXEC is the most complex system call in MINIX. It must replace the current memory image with a new one, including setting up a new stack. It carries out its job in a series of steps, as shown in Fig. 6-7.

```
1. Check permissions — is the file executable?
2. Read the header to get the segment and total sizes.
3. Fetch the arguments and environment from the caller.
4. Release the old memory and allocate the new one.
5. Copy stack to new memory image.
6. Copy text and data segments to new memory image.
7. Check for and handle setuid, setgid bits.
8. Fix up process table entry.
9. Tell kernel that process is now runnable.
```

Fig. 6-7. The steps required to carry out the EXEC system call.

Each step consists, in turn, of yet smaller steps, some of which can fail. For example, there might be insufficient memory available. The order in which the tests are made has been carefully chosen to make sure the old memory image is not released until it is certain that the EXEC will succeed, to avoid the embarrassing situation of not being able to set up a new memory image, but not having the old one to go back to, either. Normally EXEC does not return, but if it fails, the calling process must get control again, with an error indication.

There are a few steps in Fig. 6-7 that deserve some more comment. First is the question of whether there is enough room or not. Checking to see if there is sufficient physical memory is done by searching the hole list *before* freeing the old memory—if the old memory were freed first and there was insufficient memory, it would be hard to get the old image back again.

However, this test is overly strict. It sometimes rejects EXEC calls that, in fact, could succeed. Suppose, for example, the process doing the EXEC call occupies 20K. Further suppose that there is a 30K hole available and that the new image requires 50K. By testing before releasing, we will discover that only 30K is available and reject the call. If we had released first, we might have succeeded, depending on whether or not the new 20K hole was adjacent to, and thus now merged with, the 30K hole. A more sophisticated implementation could handle this situation a little better.

A more subtle issue is whether the executable file fits in the *virtual* address space. The problem is that memory is allocated not in bytes, but in clicks (16 bytes on the 8088, 1 page on a virtual memory system). Each click must belong to a single segment, and may not be, for example, half data, half stack, because the entire memory administration is in clicks.

To see how this restriction can give trouble, note that the 64K address space of the 8088 can be divided into 4096 clicks. Suppose a separate I and D space program has 40,000 bytes of text, 32,770 bytes of data, and 32,760 bytes of stack. The data segment occupies 2049 clicks, of which the last one is only partially used; still, the whole click is part of the data segment. The stack segment is 2048 clicks. Together they exceed 4096 clicks, and thus cannot co-exist, even though the number of *bytes* needed fits in the virtual address space (barely). This problem exists on all machines whose click size is larger than 1 byte.

Another important issue is how the initial stack is set up. The library call normally used to invoke EXEC with arguments and an environment is

execve(name, argv, envp);

where *name* is a pointer to the name of the file to be executed, *argv* is a pointer to an array of pointers, each one pointing to an argument, and *envp* is a pointer to an array of pointers, each one pointing to an environment string.

It would be easy enough to implement EXEC by just putting the three pointers in the message to the memory manager, and letting it fetch the file name and two arrays by itself. Then it would have to fetch each argument and each string one at a time. Doing it this way requires at least one message to the system task per argument or string and probably more, since the memory manager has no way of knowing how big each one is in advance.

To avoid the overhead of multiple messages to read all these pieces, a completely different strategy has been chosen. The *execve* library procedure builds the entire initial stack inside itself and passes its base address and size to the memory manager. Building the new stack within the user space is highly efficient, because references to the arguments and strings are just local memory references, not references to a different address space.

To make this mechanism clearer, let us consider an example. When a user types

```
ls -l f.c g.c
```

to the shell, the shell makes the call

```
execve("/bin/ls", argv, envp);
```

to the library procedure. The contents of the two pointer arrays are shown in Fig. 6-8(a). The procedure *execve*, within the shell's address space, now builds the initial stack, as shown in Fig. 6-8(b). This stack is eventually copied intact to the memory manager during the processing of the EXEC call.

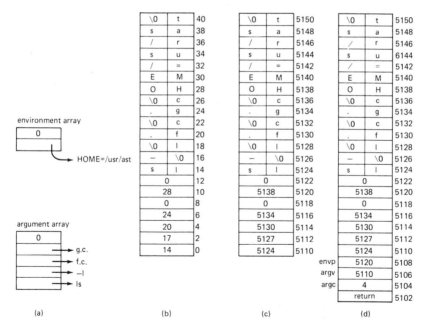

Fig. 6-8. (a) The arrays passed to *execve*. (b) The stack built by *execve*. (c) The stack after relocation by the memory manager. (d) The stack as it appears to *main* at the start of execution.

When the stack is finally copied to the user process, it will not be put at virtual address 0. Instead, it will be put at the end of the memory allocation, as determined by total memory size field in the executable file's header. As an example, let us arbitrarily assume that the stack begins at address 5110. It is up to the memory manager to relocate the pointers within the stack so that when deposited into the new address, the stack looks like Fig. 6-8(c).

When the EXEC call completes and the program starts running, the stack will indeed look exactly like Fig. 6-8(c), with the stack pointer having the value 5110. However, another problem is yet to be dealt with. The main program of the executed file is probably declared something like this:

```
main(argc, argv, envp);
```

As far as the C compiler is concerned, *main* is just another function. It does not know that *main* is special, so it compiles code to access the three parameters on the assumption that they will be passed according to the standard C calling convention, last parameter first. With one integer and two pointers, the three parameters are expected to occupy the three words just before the return address. Of course, the stack of Fig. 6-8(c) does not look like that at all.

The solution is that newly executed files do not begin with *main*. Instead, a small, assembly language routine called the C run-time, start-off procedure, is always linked in at text address 0 so it gets control first. Its job is to push three more words onto the stack and then to call *main* using the standard call instruction. This results in the stack of Fig. 6-8(d) at the time that *main* starts executing. Thus, *main* is tricked into thinking it was called in the usual way (actually, it is not really a trick; it *is* called that way).

If the programmer neglects to call *exit* at the end of *main*, control will pass back to the C run-time, start-off routine when main is finished. Again, the compiler just sees *main* as an ordinary procedure, and generates the usual code to return from it after the last statement. Thus *main* returns to its caller, the C run-time, start-off routine which then calls *exit* itself. The MINIX C run-time, start-off routine is called *crtso* and is located in the directory *lib* and its subdirectories, for various compilers.

6.1.6. The BRK System Call

The library procedures *brk* and *sbrk* are used to adjust the upper bound of the data segment. The former takes an absolute size and calls BRK. The latter takes a positive or negative increment to the current size, computes the new data segment size, and then calls BRK. There is no SBRK system call.

An interesting question is: "How does *sbrk* keep track of the current size, so it can compute the new size?" The answer is that a variable, *brksize*, always holds the current size so *sbrk* can find it. This variable is initialized to a compiler generated symbol giving the initial size of text plus data (nonseparate I and

D) or just data (separate I and D). The name, and, in fact, very existence of such a symbol is compiler dependent.

Carrying out BRK is easy for the memory manager. All that must be done is to check to see that everything still fits in the address space, adjust the tables, and tell the kernel.

6.1.7. Signal Handling

Signals can be generated in two ways: by the KILL system call, and by the kernel. The kernel generated signals currently implemented are SIGINT, SIGQUIT, and SIGALRM, but if MINIX is ever ported to a machine that traps on illegal instructions, detects illegal addresses, or notices other hardware violations, the corresponding signals will also be generated by the kernel.

Whatever their origin, the memory manager processes all signals the same way. For each process to be signaled, a variety of checks are made to see if the signal is feasible. One process can signal another if both have the same uid, and were started from the same terminal. Furthermore, neither zombies nor processes that have explicitly called SIGNAL to ignore the signal can be signaled.

If all the conditions are met, the signal can be sent. If the signal is to be caught, a message is sent to the system task within the kernel, requesting that it push the 4 words of Fig. 6-9 onto the signaled process' stack. The exact layout of the words pushed is designed to be identical to what a hardware trap pushes (plus the signal number), so porting MINIX to a different system implies changing the layout of Fig. 6-9 accordingly.

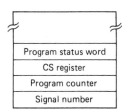

Fig. 6-9. The four words pushed onto the stack of a signaled process on the 8088.

After the process has received the interrupt, a run time system routine, *catchsig*, is called. This routine first saves all the registers on the stack. Then it uses the signal number as an index into a local table to find the C function to be called. When the user executes a SIGNAL call, the pointer to the function to be called is stored in a local table; the memory manager is merely told which signal is being enabled. It is also given the address of *catchsig*, which it traps to on all signals. After *catchsig* has found the pointer to the signal handler, it calls the handler.

When the handler is done, it returns to *catchsig*, which restores the registers and does a RETURN FROM INTERRUPT instruction to resume processing at the point it was prior to the interrupt. Interrupts are completely invisible to the interrupted program.

If a signal is sent to a process that has not been enabled to handle it, the memory manager kills the process. If the parent is waiting for it, it is cleaned up and removed from the process table. If the parent is not waiting, it becomes a zombie. For certain signal numbers (e.g., SIGQUIT), the memory manager also writes a core dump of the process to the current directory.

It can easily happen that a signal is sent to a process that is currently blocked waiting for a READ on a terminal for which no input is available. If the process has not specified that the signal is to be caught, it is just killed in the usual way. If, however, the signal is caught, the issue arises of what to do after the signal interrupt has been processed. Should the process go back to waiting, or should it continue with the next statement?

What MINIX does is this: the system call is terminated in such a way as to return the error code EINTR, so the process can see that the call was broken off by a signal. Determining that a signaled process was blocked on a system call is not entirely trivial. The memory manager must ask the file system to check.

6.1.8. Other System Calls

The memory manager also handles a few more simple system calls: GETPID, GETUID, GETGID, SETUID, and SETGID. The first three calls just look up and return the requested information. GETUID returns both the real and effective uid. Depending on whether *getuid* or *geteuid* was called, one or the other is extracted from the message and returned to the user. The same holds for the gid. These five calls are the simplest MINIX system calls.

6.2. IMPLEMENTATION OF MEMORY MANAGEMENT IN MINIX

Armed with a general overview of how the memory manager works, let us now turn to the code itself. The memory manager is written entirely in C, is straightforward and contains a substantial amount of comment in the code itself, so our treatment of most parts need not be long or involved. We will first look briefly at the header files, then the main program, and finally the files for the various system call groups discussed previously.

6.2.1. The Header Files

The file *const.h* (line 5150) defines a few constants used by the memory manager. The conditional declaration of *MM_STACK_BYTES* is needed primarily for the array *mbuf* in *exec.c*. The array is used for several purposes and has to be large enough for all of them.

The memory manager's global variables are declared in *glo.h* (line 5200). The same trick used in the kernel with *EXTERN* is used here, namely, that

EXTERN is normally a macro that expands to *extern*, except in the file *table.c*, where it becomes the null string so storage is actually reserved for them. As in the kernel, it is essential that storage only be reserved in one place.

The first variable, *mp*, is a pointer to the *mproc* structure for the process whose system call is now being processed. The second variable, *dont_reply*, is initialized to *FALSE* when each new request arrives, but can be set to *TRUE* during the call if it is discovered that no reply message should be sent. No replies are sent for a successful EXEC, for example. The third variable, *procs_in_use*, keeps track of how many process slots are currently in use, making it easy to see if a FORK call is feasible.

The message buffers *mm_in* and *mm_out* are for the request and reply messages, respectively. *Who* is the index of the current process and is related to *mp* by

```
mp = &mproc[who];
```

When a message comes in, the system call number is extracted from it and put in *mm_call*.

The three variables *err_code*, *result2*, and *res_ptr* are used to hold values returned to the caller in the reply message. The most important one is *err_code*, which generally is set to *OK* if the call was completed without error.

The array *mm_stack* holds the memory manager's stack. The stack pointer is initialized to point to it in a tiny assembly code routine, called *head*, that is called before *main* starts. In a sense, *head* is analogous to *crtso*, which is not linked with the memory manager or file system, because they do not have arguments.

The file *mproc.h* (line 5250) contains the memory manager's version of the process table. Most of the fields are adequately described by their comments. The two bit maps, *mp_ignore* and *mp_catch*, each contain 16 bits, 1 bit per signal, with signal 1 being the rightmost bit. The *mp_flags* field is used to hold a miscellaneous collection of bits, as indicated at the end of the file.

Next comes *param.h* (line 5300), which contains macros for many of the system call parameters contained in the request message. It also contains three macros for fields in the reply message. If the statement

```
k = pid;
```

were to appear in any file in which *param.h* were included, the preprocessor would convert it to

```
k = mm_in.m1_i1;
```

before feeding it to the compiler proper.

The final header file is *type.h* (line 5350). All it does is include the global type definition file. It is merely included for symmetry, since the kernel and file system have nonempty *type.h* files.

6.2.2. The Main Program

The memory manager is compiled and linked independently from the kernel and the file system. Consequently, it has its own main program, which is started up after the kernel has finished initializing itself. The main program is in *main.c* (line 5400). After doing its own initialization (line 5441), the memory manager enters its loop on line 5444. In this loop, it calls *get_work* to wait for an incoming request message, calls one of its *do_XXX* procedures via the *mm_callvec* table to carry out the request, and finally sends a reply, if needed. This structure should be familiar by now: it is the same used by the I/O tasks.

The procedures *get_work* (line 5471) and *reply* (line 5485) handle the actual receiving and sending, respectively. The remaining procedures in this file are all concerned with initializing the memory manager. They are not used after the system has started running.

6.2.3. Implementation of FORK, EXIT, and WAIT

The FORK, EXIT, and WAIT system calls are implemented by the procedures *do_fork*, *do_mm_exit*, and *do_wait* in the file *forkexit.c*. The procedure *do_fork* (line 5683) follows the steps shown in Fig. 6-6. Notice that it reserves the last few process table slots for the super-user. After computing how much memory the child needs, including the gap between the data and stack segments on the 8088, *mem_copy* is called to send a message to the system task to get the copying done.

Now a slot is found in the process table. The test involving *procs_in_use* earlier guarantees that one will exist. After the slot has been found, it is filled in, first by copying the parent's slot there, and afterward by updating the *mp_parent*, *mp_seg*, *mp_exitstatus*, and *mp_sigstatus* fields.

The next step is assigning a pid to the child. The variable *next_pid* keeps track of the next pid to be assigned. However, the following problem could conceivably occur. After assigning, say, pid 20 to a very long-lived process, 30,000 more processes might be created and destroyed, and *next_pid* might come back to 20 again. Assigning a pid that was still in use would be a disaster (suppose someone later tried to signal process 20), so we search the whole process table to make sure that the pid to be assigned is not already in use. This only happens if a very old process (65,536 processes ago) is still running.

The calls to *sys_fork* and *tell_fs* inform the kernel and file system, respectively, that a new process has been created, so they can update their process tables. (All the procedures beginning with *sys_* are library routines that send a message to the system task in the kernel to request a service from the system task.) Process creation and destruction are always initiated by the memory manager and then propagated to the kernel and file system when completed.

The reply message to the child is sent explicitly at the end of *do_fork*. The reply to the parent, containing the child's pid, is sent by the loop in *main*, as the normal reply to a request.

The next system call handled by the memory manager is EXIT. The procedure *do_mm_exit* (line 5767) accepts the call, but most of the work is done by *mm_exit*, a few lines further down. The reason for this division of labor is that *mm_exit* is also called to take care of processes terminated by a signal. The work is the same, but the parameters are different, so it is convenient to split things up this way.

The action taken by *mm_exit* depends on whether the parent is already waiting or not. If so, *cleanup* is called to release the memory and process table slot, and to get rid of the process entirely. If the parent is not waiting, the process becomes a zombie, indicated by the *HANGING* bit in the *mp_flags* word. Either way, if it has a running timer, the timer is killed. The call to the library procedure *sys_xit* sends a message to the system task telling it to mark the process as no longer runnable, so it will not be scheduled any more.

When the parent process does a WAIT, control comes to *do_wait* on line 5809. The loop in *do_wait* scans the entire process table to see if the process has any children at all, and if so, checks to see if any are zombies that can now be cleaned up. If a zombie is found (line 5828), it is cleaned up. The flag *dont_reply* is set because the reply to the parent is sent from inside *cleanup*, not from the loop in *main*.

If the process doing the WAIT has no children, it simply gets an error return (line 5842). If it has children, but none are zombies, then a bit is set on line 5838 to indicate that it is waiting, and the parent is suspended until a child terminates.

When a process has exited and its parent is waiting for it, in whichever order these events occur, the procedure *cleanup* (line 5849) is called to perform the last rites. The parent is awakened from its WAIT call and is given the pid of the terminated child, as well as its exit and signal status. The file system is told to mark the child's entry as free. (The kernel is told when the process terminates, as it must suspend scheduling immediately.) Then the child's memory is freed and the parent's and child's flags are updated.

The last step has to do with the problem discussed earlier of what happens to a process if its parent dies. To see if any existing process is a child of the process trying to exit, all the processes are inspected. If the test on line 5890 succeeds, the exiting process has children.

It is possible that a situation such as shown in Fig. 6-10(a) occurs. In this figure we see that process 12 is about to exit, and that its parent, 7, is waiting for it. *Cleanup* will be called to get rid of 12, so 52 and 53 are turned into children of *init*, as shown in Fig. 6-10(b). Now we have the situation that 53, which has already exited, is the child of a process doing a WAIT. Consequently, it can also be cleaned up. The code on lines 5893 to 5897 takes care of this. We see here one of the very few recursive calls in MINIX.

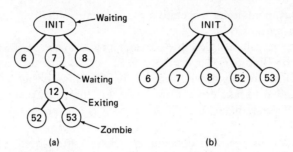

Fig. 6-10. (a) The situation as process 12 is about to exit. (b) The situation after it has exited.

6.2.4. Implementation of EXEC

The code for EXEC follows the outline of Fig. 6-7. It is contained in the procedure *do_exec* (line 5934). After making a few simple validity checks, the memory manager fetches the name of the file to be executed from the user space. On line 5965 it sends a special message to the file system, to switch to the user's directory, so that the path just fetched will be interpreted relative to the user's, rather than to MM's, working directory.

If the file is present and executable, the memory manager reads the header to extract the segment sizes. Then it fetches the stack from user space (line 5981), allocates memory for the new image (line 5988), patches up the pointers [see the differences between Fig. 6-8(b) and (c)], and reads in the text and data segments (lines 6003 and 6004). Finally, it processes the setuid and setgid bits, updates the process table entry, and tells the kernel that it is finished, so that the process can be scheduled again.

Although the control of all the steps is in *do_exec*, many of the details are carried out by subsidiary procedures within *exec.c*. *Read_header*, for example, not only reads the header and returns the segment sizes, but also verifies that all the segments fit in the virtual address space.

Procedure *new_mem* checks to see if sufficient memory is available for the new memory image. If so, the old memory is released and the new memory acquired. If insufficient memory is available, the EXEC call fails. After the new memory is allocated, *new_mem* updates the memory map (in *mp_seg*) and reports it to the kernel by calling the library procedure *sys_newmap*.

The remainder of *new_map* is concerned with zeroing the bss segment, gap, and stack segment. (The bss segment is that part of the data segment that contains all the uninitialized global variables.) Many compilers generate explicit code to zero the bss segment, but doing it here allows MINIX to work even with compilers that do not explicitly zero the bss. The gap between data and stack segments is also zeroed, so that when the data segment is extended by BRK, the newly acquired memory will contain zeros.

The next procedure is *patch_ptr* (line 6183), which does the job of relocating the pointers of Fig. 6-8(b) to the form of Fig.6-8(c). The work is simple: Examine the stack to find all the pointers, and add the base address to each one.

The final procedure in *exec.c* is *load_seg* (line 6216), which is called twice per EXEC, once to load the text segment and once to load the data segment. Rather than just reading the file block by block and then copying the blocks to the user, a trick is used to allow the file system to load the entire segment directly to the user space. Loading is appreciably speeded up by this maneuver. In effect, the call is decoded by the file system in a slightly special way so that it appears to be a read of the entire segment by the user process itself. Only a few lines at the beginning of the file system's read routine know that some monkey business is going on here.

6.2.5. Implementation of BRK

As we have just seen, the memory model used by MINIX is quite simple. Each process is given a single contiguous allocation when it is created. It is never moved around in memory, it is never swapped out of memory, it never grows, and it never shrinks. All that can happen is that the data segment can eat away at the gap from the low end, and the stack can eat away at it from the high end. Under these circumstances, the implementation of the BRK call is especially easy. It consists of verifying that the new sizes are feasible, and then updating the tables to reflect them.

The top-level procedure is *do_brk* (line 6283), but most of the work is done in *adjust*. The latter checks to see if the stack and data segments have collided. If they have, the BRK call cannot be carried out, but the process is not killed immediately. It gets control back (with an error message), so it can print appropriate messages and shut down gracefully.

If *adjust* has to adjust the data segment, all it does is update the length field. If it also notices that the stack pointer, which is given to it as a parameter, has grown beyond the stack segment, both the origin and length are updated.

The procedure *size_ok* makes the test to see if the segment sizes fit within the address space, in clicks as well as in bytes. The last procedure in this file, *stack_fault*, is not used at present. If MINIX is ever ported to a machine that traps when the stack pointer moves outside the stack segment, then the memory manager will have to handle stack growth, analogous to data segment growth. This procedure will then be of use.

6.2.6. Implementation of Signal Handling

The four system calls relating to signals, SIGNAL, KILL, ALARM, and PAUSE, as well as the signals themselves, are processed in the file *signal.c*. Let us start with the SIGNAL call, since it is the easiest (line 6488). First the memory manager checks to see that the signal number is valid. If it is, the two bit maps, one for signals to be ignored and one for signals to be caught, are updated.

Each bit map has 16 bits, one for each of signals 1 to 16, with signal 1 the right-most bit.

Next come two procedures, *do_kill* (line 6519) and *do_ksig* (line 6530), that are conceptually similar. Both are used to cause the memory manager to send a signal. *Do_kill* is called when a user process issues a KILL system call. *Do_ksig* is called when a message arrives from the kernel with one or more signals.

Although *do_ksig* has code to handle stack faults, the kernel does not gen-erate them at present. This feature may be useful on other machines, however. Messages from the kernel may contain multiple signals, which are examined and processed one bit at a time by the loop on line 6564. Each signal bit set results in a call to *check_sig*, just as *do_kill*.

The procedure *check_sig* is where the memory manager checks to see if the signal can be sent. The call

```
kill(0, sig);
```

causes the indicated signal to be sent to all the processes in the caller's group (i.e., all the processes started from the same terminal). For this reason, *check_sig* contains a loop on line 6602 to scan through the process table to find all the processes to which a signal should be sent. The loop contains a large number of tests. Only if all of them are passed is the signal sent, by calling *sig_proc* on line 6627.

Now we come to *sig_proc* (line 6640), which actually does the signaling. The key test here is to distinguish processes that have been enabled to catch sig-nals from those that have not. Those processes that want to catch signals but do not have enough stack space left for the interrupt information, are not signaled. If the signal is to be caught, the call to *sys_sig* on line 6663 sends a message to the system task requesting it to cause the signal.

If the signal is not to be caught (or cannot be caught due to lack of stack space), control passes to line 6668 to allow *mm_exit* to terminate the process as though it had exited, and then tries to dump core if that is appropriate for the signal class.

The third system call handled in *signal.c* is ALARM, which is controlled by *do_alarm* (line 6679). The work, done by *set_alarm* (line 6695), consists of sending a message to the clock task telling it to start the timer. When the timer runs out, the kernel announces the fact by sending the memory manager a mes-sage of type KSIG, which causes *do_ksig* to run, as discussed above. The com-plete sequence of events for a SIGALRM signal is shown in Fig. 6-11.

The final system call is PAUSE. All that is necessary for *do_pause* (line 6723) to do is set a bit and refrain from replying, thus keeping the caller blocked. The kernel need not even be informed, since the kernel knows that the caller is blocked.

The procedure *unpause* (line 6736) has to do with signals that are sent to processes suspended on READ, WRITE, PAUSE, and WAIT calls. The latter two can be checked directly, but the former two require asking the file system.

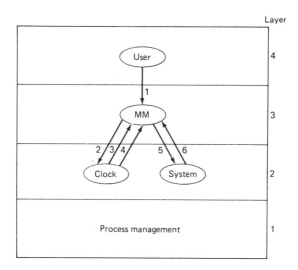

Fig. 6-11. Messages for an alarm. (1) User does ALARM. (2) MM sends request to clock task. (3) Clock task replies. (4) Signal arrives. (5) MM tells system task to copy interrupt block to user space. (6) Reply.

The final procedure in this file is *dump_core* (line 6774), which writes core dumps, block by block, to the disk.

6.2.7. Implementation of the Other System Calls

The file *getset.c* contains one procedure, *do_getset* (line 6867), which carries out the five remaining memory manager calls: GETPID, GETUID, GETGID, SETUID, and SETGID. They are all so simple that they are not worth an entire procedure each. The GETUID and GETGID calls both return the real and effective uid or gid.

Setting the uid or gid is slightly more complex than just reading it. A check has to be made to see if the caller is authorized to set the uid or gid. If the caller passes the test, the file system must be informed of the new uid or gid, since file protection depends on it.

6.2.8. Memory Manager Utilities

The remaining files contain utility routines and tables. The file *alloc.c* is where the system keeps track of which parts of memory are in use and which are free. It has four entry points:

alloc_mem	- request a block of memory of a given size.
free_mem	- return memory that is no longer needed.
max_hole	- compute the size of the largest available hole.
mem_init	- initialize the free list when the memory manager starts running.

As we have said before, *alloc_mem* (line 6987) just uses first fit on a list of holes sorted by memory address. If it finds a piece that is too big, it takes what it needs and leaves the rest on the free list, but reduced in size by the amount taken. If an entire hole is needed, *del_slot* (line 7072) is called to remove the entry from the free list.

Free_mem's job is to check if a newly released piece of memory can be merged with holes on either side. If it can, *merge* (line 7095) is called to join the holes and update the lists.

Max_hole (line 7131) scans the hole list and returns the largest item it finds. *Mem_init* (line 7153) builds the initial free list, consisting of all available memory in one big hole.

The next file is *utility.c*, which holds a few miscellaneous procedures used in various places in the memory manager. The procedure *allowed* (line 7224) checks to see if a given access is allowed to a file.

For example, *do_exec* needs to know if a file is executable. *Mem_copy* is the interface to the system task for copying data around in memory. It is used to copy the parent image to the child for FORK, and similar things.

The procedure *no_sys* (line 7298) should never be called. It is provided just in case a user ever calls the memory manager with a system call number that is invalid or is not handled by the memory manager.

Panic (line 7309) is called only when the memory manager has detected an error from which it cannot recover. It reports the error to the system task, which then brings MINIX to a screeching halt. It is not called lightly.

The two procedures in the file *putc.c* are also utilities, although of quite a different character from the previous ones. From time to time, calls to *printf* are inserted into the memory manager, mostly for debugging. Also, *panic* calls *printf*. The name *printf* is actually a macro defined as *printk*, so that calls to *printf* do not use the standard I/O library procedure that sends messages to the file system. *Printk* calls *putc* to communicate directly with the terminal task, something that is forbidden to ordinary users.

Our final file is *table.c*. It contains key statements on lines 7408 and 7409. Together, these redefine the macro *EXTERN* to be the null string, so that when all the include files are expanded during the compilation of *table.c*, the word *extern* will not be present, and storage will be allocated for all the variables.

The other major feature of *table.c* is the array *mm_callvec*. When a request message arrives, the system call number is extracted from it and used as an index into *mm_callvec* to locate the procedure that carries out that system call (see line 5458). System call numbers that are not valid calls all invoke *no_sys*, which just returns an error code.

7

THE MINIX FILE SYSTEM

The most visible part of any operating system is the file system. Most programs read or write at least one file, and users are always aware of the existence of files and their properties. For many people, the convenience and usability of the operating system is largely determined by the interface, structure, and reliability of the file system. In this chapter we will describe how the MINIX file system is implemented.

7.1. OVERVIEW OF THE MINIX FILE SYSTEM

Like all file systems, the MINIX file system must allocate and deallocate space for files, keep track of disk blocks and free space, provide some way to protect files against unauthorized usage, an so on. In this chapter we will look closely at MINIX to see how it accomplishes these goals.

The MINIX file system is just a big C program that runs in user space (see Fig. 4-1). To read and write files, user processes send messages to the file system telling what they want done. The file system does the work and then sends back a reply. The file system is, in fact, a network file server that happens to be running on the same machine as the caller.

This design has some important implications. For one thing, the file system can be modified, experimented with, and tested almost completely independently of the rest of MINIX. For another, it is very easy to move the whole file system to any computer that has a C compiler, compile it there, and use it as a free-standing UNIX-like remote file server. The only changes that need to be made are in the area of how messages are sent and received, which differs from system to system.

In the following sections, we will present an overview of many of the key areas of the file system design. Specifically, we will look at messages, the file system layout, i-nodes, the block cache, the bit maps, directories and path names, the process table, and special files (plus pipes). After studying all of these topics, we will show a simple example of how the pieces fit together by tracing what happens when a user process executes the READ system call.

7.1.1. Messages

The file system accepts 29 types of messages requesting work. All but two are for MINIX system calls. The two exceptions are for messages generated by other parts of MINIX. All the messages, their parameters, and results are shown in Fig. 7-1. The file system also gets messages from the memory manager telling about work that the latter has done on behalf of a few other system calls, such as FORK and EXIT. These are not listed in the figure since they are primarily handled by the memory manager.

The structure of the file system is basically the same as that of the memory manager and all the I/O tasks. It has a main loop that waits for a message to arrive. When a message arrives, its type is extracted and used as an index into a table containing pointers to the procedures within the file system that handle all the types. Then the appropriate procedure is called, it does its work and returns a status value. The file system then sends a reply back to the caller and goes back to the top of the loop to wait for the next message.

7.1.2. File System Layout

A MINIX file system is a logical, self-contained entity with i-nodes, directories, and data blocks. It can be stored on any block device, such as a floppy disk or a (portion of a) hard disk. In all cases, the layout of the file system has the same structure. Figure 7-2 shows this layout for a 360K floppy disk with 127 i-nodes and a 1K block size. Larger file systems, or those with more or fewer i-nodes or a different block size, will have the same six components in the same order, but their relative sizes may be different.

Each file system begins with a **boot block**. When the computer is turned on, the hardware reads the boot block into memory and jumps to it. Not every disk drive can be used as a boot device, but to keep the structure uniform, every device has a boot block. Once the system has been booted, the boot block is not used any more.

The **super-block** contains information describing the layout of the file system. It is illustrated in Fig. 7-3.

Message type	Input parameters	Reply value
ACCESS	File name, access mode	status
CHDIR	Name of new working directory	status
CHMOD	File name, new mode	status
CHOWN	File name, new owner, new group	status
CHROOT	Name of new root directory	status
CLOSE	File descriptor of file to close	status
CREAT	Name of file to be created, mode	File descriptor
DUP	File descriptor (for DUP2, two of them)	New file descr
FSTAT	Name of file whose status is wanted, buffer	status
IOCTL	File descriptor, function code, argument	status
LINK	Name of file to link to, name of link	status
LSEEK	File descriptor, offset, whence	New position
MKNOD	Name of dir or special file, mode, address	status
MOUNT	Special file, where to mount it, ro–flag	status
OPEN	Name of file to open, read/write flag	File descriptor
PIPE	(none)	File descriptor
READ	File descriptor, buffer, how many bytes	# bytes read
STAT	File name, status buffer	status
STIME	Pointer to current time	status
SYNC	(none)	Always OK
TIME	Pointer to place where current time goes	Real time
TIMES	Pointer to buffer for process and child times	status
UMASK	Complement of mode mask	Always OK
UMOUNT	Name of special file to unmount	status
UNLINK	Name of file to unlink	status
UTIME	File name, file times	Always OK
WRITE	File descriptor, buffer, how many bytes	# bytes written
REVIVE	Process to revive	(no reply)
UNPAUSE	Process to check	(see text)

Fig. 7-1. The principal message types accepted by the file system. File name parameters are always pointers to the name. The code *status* as reply value means OK or ERROR.

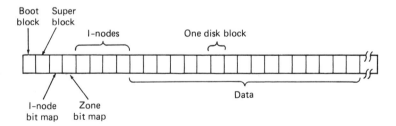

Fig. 7-2. Disk layout for a typical 360K floppy disk, with 127 i-nodes and a 1K block size (i.e., two consecutive 512-byte sectors are treated as a single block).

The main function of the super-block is to tell the file system how big the various pieces of Fig. 7-2 are. Given the block size and the number of i-nodes, it is easy to calculate the size of the i-node bit map and the number of blocks of i-nodes. For example, for a 1K block, each block of the bit map has 1K bytes

(8K bits), and thus can keep track of the status of up to 8191 i-nodes (i-node 0 always contains zeros and is effectively unused). For 10,000 i-nodes, two bit map blocks are needed. Since i-nodes are 32 bytes, a 1K block holds up to 32 i-nodes. With 127 usable i-nodes, 4 disk blocks are needed to contain them all.

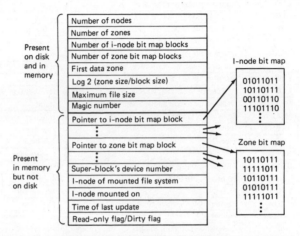

Fig. 7-3. The MINIX super-block.

We will explain the difference between zones and blocks in detail later, but for the time being it is sufficient to say that disk storage can be allocated in units (zones) of 1, 2, 4, 8, or in general 2^n blocks. The zone bit map keeps track of free storage in zones, not blocks. For the standard 360K floppy disk MINIX distribution, the zone and block sizes are the same (1K), so for a first approximation a zone is the same as a block on these devices. Until we come to the details of storage allocation later in the chapter, it is adequate to think "block" whenever you see "zone."

Note that the number of blocks per zone is not stored in the super-block, as it is never needed. All that is needed is the base 2 logarithm of the zone to block ratio, which is used as the shift count to convert zones to blocks and vice versa. For example, with 8 blocks per zone, $\log_2 8 = 3$, so to find the zone containing block 128 we shift 128 right 3 bits to get zone 16. Zone 0 is the boot block, but the zone bit map includes only the data zones.

The information in the super-block is redundant because sometimes it is needed in one form and sometimes in another. With 1K devoted to the super-block, it makes sense to compute this information in all the forms it is needed, rather than having to recompute it frequently during execution. The zone number of the first data zone on the disk, for example, can be calculated from the block size, zone size, number of i-nodes, and number of zones, but it is faster just to keep it in the super-block. The rest of the super-block is wasted anyhow, so using up another word of it costs nothing.

When MINIX is booted, the super-block for the root device is read into a table in memory. Similarly, as other file systems are mounted, their super-blocks are also brought into memory. The super-block table holds a few fields not present on the disk, such as the device from which it came, a field telling whether it has been mounted read-only or not, and a field that is set whenever the memory version is modified.

Before a disk can be used as a MINIX file system, it must be given the structure of Fig. 7-2. The utility program *mkfs* has been provided to build file systems. This program can be called either by a command like

```
mkfs /dev/fd1 360
```

to build an empty 360 block file system on the floppy disk in drive 1, or it can be given a prototype file listing directories and files to include in the new file system. Attempts to mount a file system not in MINIX format, such as an MS-DOS diskette will be rejected by the MOUNT system call, which checks the super-block for the magic number and other things.

7.1.3. Bit Maps

MINIX keeps tracks of which i-nodes and zones are free by using two bit maps (see Fig. 7-3). When the system is booted, the super-block and bit maps for the root device are loaded into memory. As mentioned, the super-block table in memory holds some fields not present on the disk. One of these fields is an array whose k-th entry is a pointer to the k-th i-node bit map block (in memory).

When a file is removed, it is then a simple matter to calculate which block of the bit map contains the bit for the i-node being freed, and to find it via pointer array. Once the block is found, the bit corresponding to the freed i-node is set to 1. A similar set of pointers is used for the zone bit map.

When a file is created, the file system searches through the bit map blocks, one at a time, until it finds a free i-node. This i-node is then allocated for the new file. If every i-node slot on the disk is full, the search routine returns a 0, which is why i-node 0 is not used. (When *mkfs* creates a new file system, it zeros i-node 0 and sets the lowest bit in the bit map to 1, so the file system will never attempt to allocate it.)

With this background, we can now explain the difference between zones and blocks. The idea behind zones is to help ensure that disk blocks that belong to the same file are located on the same cylinder, to improve performance when the file is read sequentially. The approach chosen is to make it possible to allocate several blocks at a time. If, for example, the block size is 1K and the zone size is 4K, the zone bit map keeps track of zones, not blocks. A 20M disk has 5K zones of 4K, hence 5K bits in its zone map.

Most of the file system works with blocks. Disk transfers are always a block at a time, and the buffer cache also works with individual blocks. Only a few parts of the system that keep track of physical disk addresses (e.g., the zone bit map and the i-nodes) know about zones.

Another reason for having zones has to do with the desire to keep disk addresses to 16 bits, primarily to be able to store lots of them in the indirect blocks. However, with a 16-bit zone number and a 1K zone, only 64K zones can be addressed, limiting disks to 64M. As disks get larger, it is easy to switch to 2K or 4K zones, without changing the block size. Most files are smaller than 1K, so increasing the block size means wasting disk bandwidth reading and writing mostly empty blocks, and wastes precious main memory storing them in the buffer cache. Of course, a larger zone size means more wasted disk space, but since large zones are needed only with large disks, the problem of disk space efficiency is not so acute.

Zones also introduce an unexpected problem, best illustrated by a simple example, again with 4K zones and 1K blocks. Suppose a file is of length 1K, meaning that 1 zone has been allocated for it. The blocks between 1K and 4K contain garbage (residue from the previous owner), but no harm is done because the file size is clearly marked in the i-node as 1K. Reads beyond the end of a file always return a count of 0 and no data.

Now someone seeks to address 32768 and writes 1 byte. The file size is now changed to 32769. Subsequent seeks to 1K followed by attempts to read the data will now be able to read the previous contents of the block, which is a serious security breach.

The solution is to check for this situation when a write is done beyond the end of a file, and explicitly zero all the not-yet-allocated blocks in the zone that was previously the last one. Although this situation rarely occurs, the code has to deal with it, making the system slightly more complex. In retrospect, it is not clear whether having zones is worth the extra trouble. In the standard distribution of MINIX the zone size and block size are both set to 1K, so the problem does not arise.

7.1.4. I-nodes

The layout of the MINIX i-node is given in Fig. 7-4. It differs from the UNIX i-node in several ways. First, shorter disk pointers are used (2 bytes vs. 3 bytes). Second, fewer pointers are stored (9 vs. 13). Third, MINIX only records one time, whereas UNIX records three of them. Finally, the *links* and *gid* fields have been reduced to 1 byte in MINIX. These changes reduce the size from 64 bytes to 32 bytes, to reduce the disk and memory space needed to store i-nodes.

When a file is opened, its i-node is located and brought into the *inode* table in memory, where it remains until the file is closed. The *inode* table has a few additional fields not present on the disk, such as the i-node's device and number, so the file system knows where to rewrite it if it is modified while in memory. It also has a counter per i-node. If the same file is opened more than once, only one copy of the i-node is kept in memory, but the counter is incremented each

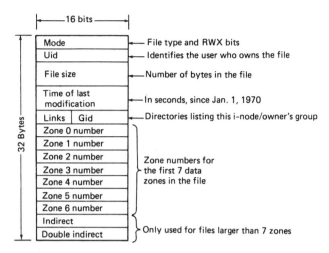

Fig. 7-4. The MINIX i-node.

time the file is opened and decremented each time it is closed. Only when the counter goes to zero is the i-node removed from the table (and rewritten to the disk, if it has been modified).

The main function of a file's i-node is to tell where the data blocks are. The first seven zone numbers are given right in the i-node itself. For the standard distribution, with zones and blocks both 1K, files up to 7K do not need indirect blocks. Beyond 7K, indirect zones are needed, using the scheme of Fig. 7-4. With 1K blocks and zones and 16-bit zone numbers, a single indirect block holds 512 entries, representing half a megabyte of storage. A double indirect block points to 512 single indirect blocks, giving up to 256 megabytes. (Actually this limit is not reachable, because with 16-bit zone numbers and 1K zones, we can address only 64K zones, which is 64 megabytes; for a larger disk we would have to go to a 2K zone.)

The i-node also holds the mode information, which tells what kind of a file it is (regular, directory, block special, character special, or pipe), and gives the protection and SETUID and SETGID bits. The *link* field in the i-node records how many directory entries point to the i-node, so the file system knows when to release the file's storage. This field should not be confused with the counter (present only in the *inode* table in memory, not on the disk) that tells how many times the file is currently open.

7.1.5. The Block Cache

MINIX uses a block cache to improve its performance. The cache is implemented as an array of buffers, each consisting of a header containing pointers, counters, and flags, and a body with room for one disk block. All the blocks are chained together in a double-linked list, from most recently used (MRU) to least recently used (LRU) as shown in Fig. 7-5.

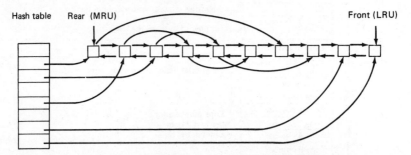

Fig. 7-5. The linked lists used by the block cache.

In addition, to be able to quickly determine if a given block is in the cache or not, a hash table is used. All the blocks that have hash code *k* are linked together on a single-linked list pointed to by entry *k* in the hash table. At present, the hash function just extracts the low-order *n* bits from the block number, so blocks from different devices appear on the same hash chain.

When the file system needs a block, it calls a procedure, *get_block*, which computes the hash code for that block and searches the appropriate list. If the block is found, a counter in the block's header is incremented to show that the block is in use, and a pointer to it is returned. If the block is not found, the LRU list is searched to find a block to evict from the cache. If the block at the front (the least recently used block) has count 0, it is chosen, otherwise the next block is inspected, and so on. It is important to check the counter because some blocks, such as the bit maps, must never be evicted while they are still in use, no matter how infrequently they are used.

Once a block has been chosen for eviction, another flag in its header is checked to see if the block has been modified since being read in. If so, it is rewritten to the disk. At this point the block needed is read in by sending a message to the disk task. The file system is suspended until the block arrives, at which time it continues and a pointer to the block is returned to the caller.

When the procedure that requested the block has done its job, it calls another procedure, *put_block*, to free the block. One of the parameters to *put_block* tells what class of block (e.g., i-nodes, directory, data) is being freed. Depending on the class, two key decisions are made:

1. Whether to put the block on the front or rear of the LRU list.

2. Whether to write the block (if modified) to disk immediately or not.

Blocks that are not likely to be needed again soon, such as double indirect blocks, go on the front of the list so they will be claimed the next time a free buffer is needed. Blocks that are likely to be needed again soon go on the rear of the list in true LRU fashion.

When a directory has been modified, it is written to disk immediately, to reduce the chance of corrupting the file system in the event of a crash. An ordinary data block that has been modified is not rewritten until either one of two events occurs: (1) it reaches the front of the LRU chain and is evicted, or (2) a SYNC system call is executed.

Note that the header flag indicating that a block has been modified is set by the procedure within the file system that requested and used the block. The procedures *get_block* and *put_block* are concerned just with manipulating all the linked lists. They have no idea which file system procedure wants which block or why.

7.1.6. Directories and Paths

Another important subsystem within the file system is the management of directories and path names. Many system calls, such as OPEN, have a file name as a parameter. What is really needed is the i-node for that file, so it is up to the file system to look up the file in the directory tree and locate its i-node.

A MINIX directory consists of a file containing 16-byte entries. The first 2 bytes form a 16-bit i-node number, and the remaining 14 bytes are the file name. To look up the path */user/ast/mbox* the system first looks up *user* in the root directory, then it looks up *ast* in */user*, and finally it looks up *mbox* in */user/ast*. The actual lookup proceeds one path component at a time.

As an aside, the standard MINIX configuration uses */usr* for floppy disk 0 (system files) and */user* for floppy disk 1 (user files). Most UNIX systems have the whole file tree under */usr*. In the following examples, we will use */user/ast* as an example of a typical user directory.

The only complication is what happens when a mounted file system is encountered. To see how that works, we must look at how mounting is done. When the user types the command

```
/etc/mount /dev/fdl /user
```

on the terminal, the file system contained on floppy disk 1 is mounted on top of */user* in the root file system. The file systems before and after mounting are shown in Fig. 7-6.

The key to the whole mount business is a flag set in the i-node of */user* after a successful mount. This flag indicates that the i-node is mounted on. The MOUNT call also loads the super-block for the newly mounted file system into the *super_block* table and sets two pointers in it. Furthermore, it puts the root i-node of the mounted file system in the *inode* table.

In Fig. 7-3 we see that super-blocks in memory contain two fields related to mounted file systems. The first of these, the *i-node-of-the-mounted-file-system*, is set to point to the root i-node of the newly mounted file system. The second, the *i-node-mounted-on*, is set to point to the i-node mounted on, in this case, the i-node for */user*. These two pointers serve to connect the mounted file system to

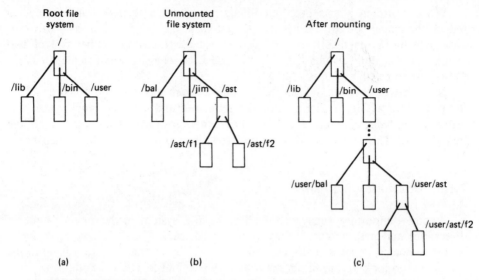

Fig. 7-6. (a) Root file system. (b) An unmounted file system. (c) The result of mounting the file system of (b) on /user.

the root, and, represent the "glue" that holds the mounted file system to the root [shown as the dots in Fig. 7-6(c)].

When a path such as /user/ast/f2 is being looked up, the file system will see a flag in the i-node for /user and realize that it must continue searching at the root i-node of the file system mounted on /user. The question is: "How does it find this root i-node?"

The answer is straightforward. The system searches all the super-blocks in memory until it finds the one whose *i-node mounted on* field points to /user. This must be the super-block for the file system mounted on /user. Once it has the super-block, it is easy to follow the other pointer to find the root i-node for the mounted file system. Now the file system can continue searching. In this example, it looks for *ast* in the root directory of floppy disk 1.

7.1.7. File Descriptors

Once a file has been opened, a file descriptor is returned to the user process for use in subsequent READ and WRITE calls. In this section we will look at how file descriptors are managed within the file system.

Like the kernel and the memory manager, the file system maintains part of the process table within its address space. Three of its fields are of particular interest. The first two are pointers to the i-nodes for the root directory and the working directory. Path searches always begin at one or the other, depending on whether the path is absolute or relative. These pointers are changed by the

CHROOT and CHDIR system calls to point to the new root or new working directory, respectively.

The third interesting field in the process table is an array indexed by file descriptor number. It is used to locate the proper file when a file descriptor is presented. At first glance, it might seem sufficient to have the k-th entry in this array just point to the i-node for the file belonging to file descriptor k. After all, the i-node is fetched into memory when the file is opened and kept there until it is closed, so it is sure to be available.

Unfortunately, this simple plan fails because files can be shared in subtle ways in MINIX (as well as in UNIX). The trouble arises because associated with each file is a 32-bit number that indicates the next byte to be read or written. It is this number, called the **file position**, that is changed by the LSEEK system call. The problem can be stated easily: "Where should the file pointer be stored?"

The first possibility is to put it in the i-node. Unfortunately, if two or more processes have the same file open at once, they must all have their own file pointers, since it would hardly do to have an LSEEK by one process affect the next read of a different process. Thus the file position cannot go in the i-node.

What about putting it in the process table? Why not have a second array, paralleling the file descriptor array, giving the current position of each file? This idea does not work either, but the reasoning is more subtle. Basically, the trouble comes from the semantics of the FORK system call. When a process forks, both the parent and the child are required to share a single pointer giving the current position of each open file.

To understand the problem better, consider the case of a shell script whose output has been redirected to a file. When the shell forks off the first program, its file position for standard output is 0. This position is then inherited by the child, which writes, say, 1K of output. When the child terminates, the shared file position must now be 1K.

Now the shell reads some more of the shell script and forks off another child. It is essential that the second child inherit a file position of 1K from the shell, so it will begin writing at the place where the first program left off. If the shell did not share the file position with its children, the second program would overwrite the output from the first one, instead of appending to it.

As a result, it is not possible to put the file position in the process table. It really must be shared. The solution used in MINIX is to introduce a new, shared table, *filp*, which contains all the file positions. Its use is illustrated in Fig. 7-7. By having the file position truly shared, the semantics of FORK can be implemented correctly, and shell scripts work properly.

Although the only thing that the *filp* table really must contain is the shared file position, it is convenient to put the i-node pointer there as well. In this way, all that the file descriptor array in the process table contains is a pointer to a *filp* entry. The *filp* entry also contains a count of the number of processes using it, so the file system can tell when the last process using the entry has terminated, in order to reclaim the slot.

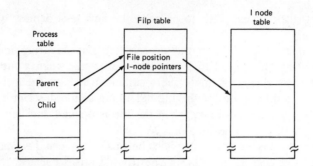

Fig. 7-7. How file positions are shared between a parent and a child.

7.1.8. Pipes and Special Files

Pipes and special files differ from ordinary files in an important way. When a process tries to read or write from a disk file, it is certain that the operation will complete within a few hundred milliseconds at most. In the worst case, two or three disk accesses might be needed. When reading from a pipe, the situation is different: if the pipe is empty, the reader will have to wait until some other process puts data in the pipe, which might take hours. Similarly, when reading from a terminal, a process will have to wait until somebody types something.

As a consequence, the file system's normal rule of handling a request until it is finished does not work. It is necessary to suspend these requests and restart them later. When a process tries to read or write from a pipe, the file system can check the state of the pipe immediately to see if the operation can be completed. If it can be, it is, but if it cannot be, the file system records the parameters of the system call in the process table, so it can restart the process later.

Note that the file system need not take any action to have the caller suspended. All it has to do is refrain from sending a reply, leaving the caller blocked waiting for the reply. Thus, after suspending a process, the file system goes back to its main loop to wait for the next system call. As soon as another process modifies the pipe's state so that the suspended process can complete, the file system sets a flag so that next time through the main loop it extracts the suspended process' parameters from the process table and executes the call.

The situation with terminals and other character special files is slightly different. The i-node for each special file contains two numbers, the major device and the minor device. The major device number indicates the device class (e.g., RAM disk, floppy disk, hard disk, terminal). It is used as an index into a file system table that maps it onto the number of the corresponding task (i.e., I/O driver). In effect, the major device determines which I/O driver to call. The minor device number is passed to the driver as a parameter. It specifies which device is to be used, for example, terminal 2 or drive 1.

When a process reads from a special file, the file system extracts the major and minor device numbers from the file's i-node, and uses the major device number as an index in a file system table to map it onto the corresponding task number. Then the file system sends the task a message, including as parameters the minor device, the operation to be performed, the caller's process number and buffer address, and the number of bytes to be transferred. The format is the same as in Fig. 5-2, except that *POSITION* is not used.

If the driver is able to carry out the work immediately (e.g., a line of input has already been typed on the terminal), it copies the data from its own internal buffers to the user and sends the file system a reply message saying that the work is done. The file system then sends a reply message to the user, and the call is finished. Note that the driver does not copy the data to the file system. Data from block devices go through the block cache, but data from character special files do not.

On the other hand, if the driver is not able to carry out the work, it records the message parameters in its internal tables, and immediately sends a reply to the file system saying that the call could not be completed. At this point, the file system is in the same situation as having discovered that someone is trying to read from an empty pipe. It records the fact that the process is suspended, and waits for the next message.

When the driver has acquired enough data to complete the call, it transfers it to the buffer of the still-blocked user, and then sends the file system a message reporting what it has done. All the file system has to do is send a reply message to the user to unblock it and report the number of bytes transferred.

7.1.9. An Example: The READ System Call

As we shall see shortly, most of the code of the file system is devoted to carrying out system calls. Therefore, it is appropriate that we conclude this overview with a brief sketch of how the most important call, READ, works.

When a user program executes the statement

```
n = read(fd, buffer, nbytes);
```

to read an ordinary file, the library procedure *read* is called with three parameters. It builds a message containing these parameters, along with the code for READ as the message type, sends the message to the file system, and blocks waiting for the reply. When the message arrives, the file system uses the message type as an index into its tables to call the procedure that handles reading.

This procedure extracts the file descriptor from the message, and uses it to locate the *filp* entry and then the i-node for the file to be read (see Fig. 7-7). The request is then broken up into pieces such that each piece fits within a block. For example, if the current file position is 600 and 1K bytes have been requested, the request is split into two parts, for 600 to 1023, and for 1024 to 1623 (assuming 1K blocks).

For each of these pieces in turn, a check is made to see if the relevant block is in the cache. If it is not, the file system picks the least recently used buffer not currently in use and claims it, sending a message to the disk task to rewrite it if it is dirty. Then the disk task is asked to fetch the block to be read.

Once the block is in the cache, the file system sends a message to the system task asking it to copy the data to the appropriate place in the user's buffer (i.e., bytes 600 to 1023 to the start of the buffer, and bytes 1024 to 1623 to offset 424 within the buffer). After the copy has been done, the file system sends a reply message to the user specifying how many bytes have been copied.

When the reply comes back to the user, the library function *read* extracts the reply code and returns it as the function value to the caller.

7.2. IMPLEMENTATION OF THE MINIX FILE SYSTEM

The MINIX file system is relatively large (more than 100 pages of C) but quite straightforward. Requests to carry out system calls come in, are carried out, and replies are sent. In the following sections we will go through it a file at a time, pointing out the highlights. The code itself contains many comments to aid the reader.

7.2.1. The Header Files

Like the kernel and memory manager, the file system has some header files that define various data structures and tables. Let us begin our study of the file system with them.

The file *const.h* (line 7500) defines some constants, such as table sizes and flags, that are used throughout the file system. Some of them, such as *NR_BUFS* and *NR_BUF_HASH*, can be changed to tune the system's performance. Others, such as *BOOT_BLOCK* and *SUPER_BLOCK*, do not affect the performance.

The next file, *buf.h* (line 7550), defines the block cache. The array *buf* holds all the buffers, each of which contains a block, *b*, and a header full of pointers, flags, and counters. The data part is declared as a union of 5 types (line 7565) because sometimes it is convenient to refer to the block as a character array, sometimes as a directory, and so on.

The proper way to refer to the data part of buffer 3 as a character array is *buf[3].b.b__data* because *buf[3].b* refers to the union as a whole, from which the *b__data* field is selected. Although this syntax is correct, it is a little cumbersome, so on line 7588 we define a macro *b_data*, which allows us to write *buf[3].b_data* instead. Note that *b__data* (the field of the union) contains two underscores, whereas *b_data* (the macro) contains just one, to distinguish them. Macros for other ways of accessing the block are contained in lines 7588 to 7592.

Another interesting aspect of this file is the use of *EXTERN* for all the arrays and variables. When this file is included in code files, *EXTERN* has the value *extern*, as defined on line 0009. However, in the file *table.c*, it is defined as the null string, to cause storage to be allocated. The rules of C (Kernighan and Ritchie book, p. 206) clearly specify that global variables must be declared as *extern* in all files except one, although some compilers and many programmers do not understand this point. We saw the same issue in the kernel and memory manager.

The macros at the end of the file (lines 7601 to 7610) define different block types. When a block is returned to the buffer cache after use, one of these values is supplied to tell the cache manager whether to put the block on the front or rear of the LRU list, and whether to write it to disk immediately or not.

The file *dev.h* (line 7650) provides the definition of the *dmap* table. The table itself is declared in *table.c* with initial values, so that version cannot be included in several files. This is why *dev.h* is needed. The table provides the mapping between the major device number and the corresponding task.

The file *file.h* (line 7700) contains the intermediate table used to hold the current file position and i-node pointer (see Fig. 7-7). It also tells whether the file was opened for reading, writing, or both, and how many file descriptors are currently pointing to the entry.

The file system's part of the process table is contained in *fproc.h* (line 7750). It holds the mode mask, pointers to the i-nodes for the current root directory and working directory, the file descriptor array, uid, gid, and terminal number. The remaining fields are used to store the parameters of system calls that are suspended part way through, such as reading from an empty pipe. The fields *fp_suspended* and *fp_revived* actually require only single bits, but nearly all compilers generate better code for characters than bit fields.

Next comes the file with the global variables, *glo.h*. The message buffers for the incoming and reply messages are also here, as is the file system's stack. When the file system starts up for the first time after MINIX is booted, a tiny assembly code procedure sets the stack pointer to the top of *fstack*.

Now we come to the i-node table in *inode.h* (line 7850). As we have said several times, when a file is opened, its i-node is read into memory and kept there until the file is closed. These i-nodes are kept in this table. Most of the fields should be self-explanatory at this point. However, *i_seek* deserves some comment. As an optimization, when the file system notices that a file is being read sequentially, it tries to read blocks into the cache even before they are asked for. For randomly accessed files there is no read ahead. When an LSEEK call is made, the field *i_seek* is set to inhibit read ahead.

The file *param.h* (line 7900) is analogous to the file of the same name in the memory manager. It defines names for message fields containing parameters, so the code can refer to, for example, *buffer*, instead of *m.m1_p1*, which selects one of the fields of the message buffer *m*.

In *super.h* (line 7950), we have the declaration of the super-block table. When the system is booted, the super-block for the root device is loaded here. As file systems are mounted, their super-blocks go here as well.

Finally, we come to the type declarations, in *type.h* (line 8000). Two types are defined, the directory entry and the disk i-node.

7.2.2. Table Management

Associated with each of the main tables—blocks, i-nodes, super-blocks, and so forth—is a file that contains procedures that manage the table. These procedures are heavily used by the rest of the file system, and form the principal interface between tables and the file system. For this reason, it is appropriate to begin our study of the file system code with them.

Block Management

The block cache is managed by the procedures in the file *cache.c*. This file contains five procedures, which are listed in Fig. 7-8. The first one, *get_block* (line 8079), is the standard way the file system acquires data blocks. When a file system procedure needs to read a user data block, a directory block, a super-block, or any other kind of block, it calls *get_block*, specifying the device and block number desired.

get_block	Fetch a block for reading or writing
put_block	Return a block previously requested with get_block
alloc_zone	Allocate a new zone (to make a file longer)
free_zone	Release a zone (when a file is removed)
rw-block	Transfer a block between disk and cache
invalidate	Purge all the cache blocks for some device

Fig. 7-8. Procedures used for block management.

When *get_block* is called, it first looks in the block cache to see if the requested block is present. If so, it returns a pointer to it. Otherwise, it has to read the block in. The blocks in the cache are linked together on *NR_BUF_HASH* (32) linked lists. All the blocks on each list have block numbers that end with the same string of 5 bits, that is 00000, 00001, ..., or 11111.

The statement on line 8099 sets *bp* to point to the start of the list on which the requested block would be, if it were in the cache. The loop on line 8101 searches this list to see if the block can be found. If so, the pointer to it is returned to the caller on line 8106.

If the block is not on the list, it is not in the cache, so the least recently used block that is not currently in use is taken. Bit maps and similar blocks that are still in use are never chosen for eviction. The buffer chosen is removed from its hash chain, since it is about to acquire a new block number and hence belongs on a different hash chain. If it is dirty, it is rewritten to the disk on line 8139.

As soon as the buffer is available, the new parameters are filled in and the block is read in from the disk, with one exception. If the file system needs a block just to rewrite all of it, it is wasteful to first read the old version in. In this case, the disk read is omitted (line 8149). When the new block has been read in, *get_block* returns to its caller with a pointer to it.

Suppose that the file system needs a directory block temporarily, to look up a file name. It calls *get_block* to acquire the directory block. When it has looked up its file name, it makes a call to *put_block* (line 8157) to return the block to the cache, thus making the buffer available in case it is needed later for a different block.

The procedure *put_block* takes care of putting the newly returned block on the LRU list, and in some cases, rewriting it to the disk. First (lines 8179 to 8189), it removes the block from its current position on the LRU list. Next it puts it on the front or rear of the LRU list, depending on *block_type*, a flag provided by the caller telling what kind of a block it is. Blocks that are not likely to be needed again soon are put on the front, where they will be reused quickly. Blocks that may be needed again soon go on the rear, so they will stay around for a while.

After the block has been repositioned on the LRU list, another check is made (lines 8224 and 8225) to see if the block should be rewritten to disk immediately. I-nodes, directory blocks, and other blocks that are essential for the correct functioning of the file system itself fall into this category and are rewritten on the spot.

As a file grows, from time to time a new zone must be allocated to hold the new data. The procedure *alloc_zone* (line 8235) takes care of allocating new zones. It does this by causing the zone bit map to be searched for a free zone. An attempt is made to find a zone close to zone 0 of the current file, in order to keep the zones of a file together. The mapping between bit number in the bit map and zone number is handled on line 8268, with bit 1 corresponding to the first data zone.

When a file is removed, its zones must be returned to the bit map. *Free_zone* (line 8275) is responsible for returning these zones. All it does is call *free_bit*, passing the zone map and the bit number as parameters. *Free_bit* is also used to return free i-nodes, but then with the i-node map as the first parameter, of course.

Managing the cache requires reading and writing blocks. To provide a simple interface to the disk, the procedure *rw_block* (line 8295) has been provided. It reads or writes a single block. Similar procedures *rw_inode* and *rw_super* exist to read and write i-nodes and super-blocks as well.

The last procedure in the file is *invalidate* (line 8326). It is called when a disk is unmounted, for example, to remove from the cache all the blocks belonging to the file system just unmounted. If this were not done, then when the device were reused (with a different floppy disk), the file system might find the old blocks instead of the new ones.

I-node Management

The block cache is not the only table that needs support procedures. The i-node table does too. Many of the procedures are similar in function to the block management procedures. They are listed in Fig. 7-9.

get—inode	Fetch an i-node into memory
put—inode	Return an i-node that is no longer needed
alloc—inode	Allocate a new i-node (for a new file)
wipe—inode	Clear some fields in an i-node
free—inode	Release an i-node (when a file is removed)
rw—inode	Transfer an i-node between memory and disk
dup—inode	Indicate that someone else is using an i-node

Fig. 7-9. Procedures used for i-node management.

The procedure *get_inode* (line 8379) is analogous to *get_block*. When any part of the file system needs an i-node, it calls *get_inode* to acquire it. *Get_inode* first searches the *inode* table to see if the i-node is already present. If so, it increments the usage counter and returns a pointer to it. This search is contained on lines 8390 to 8406. If the i-node is not present in memory, the i-node is loaded by calling *rw_inode*.

When the procedure that needed the i-node is finished with it, the i-node is returned by calling the procedure *put_inode* (line 8421), which decrements the usage count *i_count*. If the count is then zero, the file is no longer in use, and the i-node can be removed from the table. If it is dirty, it is rewritten to disk.

If the *i_link* field is zero, no directory entry is pointing to the file, so all its zones can be freed. Note that the usage count going to zero and the number of links going to zero are different events, with different causes and consequences.

When a new file is created, an i-node must be allocated for it. This work is done by *alloc_inode* (line 8446). Unlike zones, where an attempt is made to keep the zones of a file close together, any i-node will do.

After the i-node has been acquired, *get_inode* is called to fetch the i-node into the table in memory. Then its fields are initialized, partly in-line (lines 8482 to 8486) and partly using *wipe_inode* (line 8503). This split has been made because *wipe_inode* is also needed elsewhere in the file system.

When a file is removed, its i-node is freed by calling *free_inode* (line 8525). All that happens is that the corresponding bit in the i-node bit map is set to 1.

The procedure *rw_inode* (line 8543) is analogous to *rw_block*. Its job is to fetch an i-node from the disk. It does its work in the following steps:

1. Calculate which block contains the required i-node.

2. Read in the block by calling *get_block*.

3. Extract the i-node and copy it to the *inode* table .

4. Return the block by calling *put_block*.

The procedure *dup_inode* (line 8579) just increments the usage count of the i-node.

Super-block Management

The file *super.c* contains procedures that manage the super-block and the bit maps. There are seven procedures in this file, listed in Fig. 7-10.

load_bit_maps	Fetch the bit maps for some file system
unload_bit_maps	Return the bit maps after a file system is unmounted
alloc_bit	Allocate a bit from the zone or i-node map
free_bit	Free a bit in the zone or i-node map
get_super	Search the super-block table for a device
scale_factor	Look up the zone-to-block conversion factor
rw_super	Transfer a super-block between memory and disk

Fig. 7-10. Procedures used to manage the super-block and bit maps.

Load_bit_maps (line 8631) is called when the root device is loaded, or when a new file system is mounted. It reads in all the bit map blocks, and sets up the super-block to point to them. The arrays *s_imap* and *s_zmap* in the super-block point to the i-node bit map blocks and zone bit map blocks, respectively.

When a file system is unmounted, its bit maps are copied back to disk by *unload_bit_maps* (line 8669).

When an i-node or zone is needed, *alloc_inode* or *alloc_zone* is called, as we have seen above. Both of these call *alloc_bit* (line 8689) to actually search the relevant bit map. The search involves three nested loops, as follows:

1. The outer one loops on all the blocks of a bit map.

2. The middle one loops on all the words of a block.

3. The inner one loops on all the bits of a word.

The middle loop works by seeing if the current word is equal to the one's complement of zero, that is, a complete word full of 1s. If so, it has no free i-nodes or zones, so the next word is tried. When a word with a different value is found, it must have at least one 0 bit in it, so the inner loop is entered to find the free (i.e., 0) bit. If all the blocks have been tried without success, there are no free i-nodes or zones, so the code *NO_BIT* (0) is returned.

Freeing a bit is simpler than allocating one, because no search is needed. *Free_bit* (line 8747) calculates which bit map block contains the bit to free, and sets the proper bit to 1. The block itself is always in memory, and can be found by following the *s_imap* or *s_zmap* pointers in the super-block.

The next procedure *get_super* (line 8771), is used to search the super-block table for a specific device. For example, when a file system is to be mounted, it is necessary to check that it is not already mounted. This check can be performed by asking *get_super* to find the file system's device. If it does not find the device, then the file system is not mounted.

The conversion between block and zone is done by shifting block numbers left or zone numbers right. The amount to shift depends on the number of blocks per zone, which can be different for each file system. The procedure *scale_factor* (line 8810) does the lookup.

Finally, we have *rw_super* (line 8824), which is analogous to *rw_block* and *rw_inode*, as we have mentioned. It is called to read and write super-blocks.

File Descriptor Management

MINIX contains special procedures to manage file descriptors and the *filp* table (see Fig. 7-7). They are contained in the file *filedes.c*. When a file is created or opened, a free file descriptor and a free *filp* slot are needed. The procedure *get_fd* (line 8871) is used to find them. They are not marked as in use, however, because many checks must first be made before it is known for sure that the CREAT or OPEN will succeed.

Get_filp (line 8916) is used to see if a file descriptor is in range, and if so, returns its *filp* pointer.

The last procedure in this file is *find_filp* (line 8930). It is needed to find out when a process is writing on a broken pipe (i.e., a pipe not open for reading by any other process). It locates potential readers by a brute force search of the *filp* table.

7.2.3. The Main Program

The main loop of the file system is contained in file *main.c*, starting at line 8992. Structurally, it is very similar to the main loop of the memory manager and the I/O tasks. The call to *get_work* waits for the next request message to arrive (unless a process previously suspended on a pipe or terminal can now be handled). It also sets a global variable, *who*, to the caller's process table slot number and another global variable, *fs_call*, to the number of the system call to be carried out.

Once back in the main loop, three flags are set: *fp* points to the caller's process table slot, *super_user* tells whether the caller is the super-user or not, and *dont_reply* is initialized to *FALSE*. Then comes the main attraction—the call to the procedure that carries out the system call. The procedure to call is selected by using *fs_call* as an index into the array of procedure pointers, *call_vector*.

When control comes back to the main loop, if *dont_reply* has been set, the reply is inhibited (e.g., a process has blocked trying to read from an empty pipe). Otherwise a reply is sent. The final statement in the main loop has been designed to detect that a file is being read sequentially, and to load the next block into the cache before it is actually requested, to improve performance.

The procedure *get_work* (line 9016) checks to see if any previously blocked procedures have now been revived. If so, these have priority over new messages. Only if there is no internal work to do does the file system call the kernel to get a message, on line 9042.

After a system call has been completed, successfully or otherwise, a reply is sent back to the caller by *reply* (line 9053). In principle, *send* should never fail, but the kernel returns a status code, so we might as well check it.

Before the file system starts running, it initializes itself by calling *fs_init* (line 9069). This procedure builds the linked lists used by the block cache, deleting any buffers that happen to lie across a 64K boundary (because the IBM PC's DMA chip cannot cross 64K boundaries). It then loads the RAM disk from the boot diskette, initializes the super-block table, and reads in the super-block and root i-node for the root device. If everything appears to be in good shape, the i-node and zone bit maps are loaded. Finally, some tests are made on the constants, to see if they make sense.

When a boot diskette is created, a bit-for-bit copy of the RAM disk image is included on it after the MINIX binary. The procedure *load_ram* copies this image, block by block, to the RAM disk, after first doing some housekeeping (including telling the RAM disk driver where the RAM disk will go and how big it is).

The Dispatch Table

The file *table.c* (line 9300) contains the pointer array used in the main loop for determining which procedure handles which system call number. We saw a similar table inside the memory manager.

Something new, however, is the table *dmap* on line 9416. This table has one row for each major device, starting at zero. When a device is opened, closed, read, or written, it is this table that provides the name of the procedure to call to handle the operation. All of these procedures are located in the file system's address space. Many of these procedures do nothing, but some call a task to actually request I/O. The task number corresponding to each major device is also provided by the table.

Whenever a new major device is added to MINIX, a line must be appended to this table telling what action, if any, is to be taken when the device is opened, closed, read, or written. As a simple example, if a tape drive is added to MINIX, when its special file is opened, the procedure in the table could check to see if the tape is already in use.

7.2.4. Operations on Individual Files

In this section we will look at the system calls that operate on files (as opposed to, say, directories). We will start with how files are created, opened, and closed, and then see how they are read and written.

Creating, Opening, and Closing Files

The file *open.c* contains the code for five system calls: CREAT, MKNOD, OPEN, CLOSE, and LSEEK. We will examine each of these in turn. Creating a file involves three steps:

1. Allocating and initializing an i-node for the new file.

2. Entering the new file in the proper directory.

3. Setting up and returning a file descriptor for the new file.

The procedure that handles CREAT is *do_creat* (line 9479). As in the memory manager, the convention is used in the file system that system call XXX is performed by procedure *do_xxx*.

Do_creat starts out by fetching the name of the new file, and making sure that free file descriptor and *filp* table slots are available. The new i-node is actually created by the procedure *new_node*, which is called on line 9496. If the i-node cannot be created, *new_node* sets the global variable *err_code*.

The specific actions carried out by *do_creat* depend on whether the file already exists. If the file does not exist, lines 9504 to 9521 are skipped, the table slots claimed, and the file descriptor returned.

If the file does exist, then the file system must test to see what kind of a file it is, what its mode is, and so on. Doing a CREAT on an ordinary file causes it to be truncated to length zero; doing it on a special file that is writable causes it to be opened for writing; doing it on a directory is always rejected.

The code of *do_creat*, as well as many other file system procedures, contains a substantial amount of code that checks for various errors and illegal combinations. While not glamorous, this code is essential to having an error-free, robust file system. If everything is in order, the file descriptor and *filp* slot located at the beginning are now marked as allocated and the file descriptor is returned. They were not marked as allocated in the beginning in order to make it easier to exit part way through if that had been needed.

The MKNOD call is handled by *do_mknod* (line 9541). This procedure is similar to *do_creat*, except that it justs creates the i-node and makes a directory entry for it. If the i-node already exists, the call terminates with an error. The case-by-case analysis we saw in *do_creat* is not needed here.

The allocation of the i-node and the entering of the path name into the file system are done by *new_node* (line 9557). The statement on line 9575 parses the path name (i.e., looks it up component by component) as far as the final directory; the call to *advance* three lines later tries to see if the final component can be opened.

For example, on the call

```
fd = creat("/user/ast/foobar", 0755);
```

last_dir tries to load the i-node for */user/ast* into the tables and return a pointer to it. If the file does not exist, we will need this i-node shortly in order to add *foobar* to the directory. All the other system calls that add or delete files also use *last_dir* to first open the final directory in the path.

If *new_node* discovers that the file does not exist, it calls *alloc_inode* on line 9581 to allocate and load a new i-node, returning a pointer to it. If no free i-nodes are left, *new_node* fails, and returns *NIL_INODE*.

If an i-node can be allocated, we continue at line 9591, filling in some of the fields, writing it back to the disk, and entering the file name in the final directory (on line 9596). Again we see that the file system must constantly check for errors, and upon encountering one, carefully release all the resources, such as i-nodes and blocks that it is holding. If we were prepared to just let MINIX panic when we ran out of, say, i-nodes, rather than undoing all the effects of the current call, and returning an error code to the caller, the file system would be appreciably simpler.

The next procedure is *do_open* (line 9622). After making a variety of checks, it calls *eat_path* to parse the file name and fetch the i-node into memory. Once the i-node is available, the mode can be checked to see if the file may be opened. The call to *forbidden* on line 9645 does the *rwx* bit checking. Directories and special files are handled afterward. Finally, the file descriptor is returned as the function value.

Closing a file is even easier than opening one. The work is done by *do_close* (line 9680). Pipes and special files need some attention, but for regular files, all that needs to be done is to decrement the *filp* counter and check to see if it is zero, in which case the i-node is returned with *put_inode*.

Note that returning an i-node means that its counter in the *inode* table is decremented, so it can be removed from the table eventually. This operation has nothing to do with freeing the i-node (i.e., setting a bit in the bit map saying that it is available). The i-node is only freed when the file has been removed from all directories.

The final procedure in this file is *do_lseek* (line 9721). When a seek is done, this procedure is called to set the file position to a new value.

Reading a File

Once a file has been opened, it can be read or written. First we will discuss reading, then writing. They differ in a number of ways, but have enough similarities that both *do_read* (line 9784) and *do_write* (line 10125) call a common procedure *read_write* (line 9794), to do most of the work.

The code on lines 9811 to 9818 is used by the memory manager to have the file system load entire segments in user space for it. Normal calls are processed starting on line 9821, where validity checks are made (e.g., reading on a file opened only for writing) and variables are initialized. Reads from character special files do not use the block cache, so they are filtered out on line 9836.

The tests on lines 9844 to 9854 apply only to writes, and have to do with files that may get bigger than the device can hold, or writes that will create a hole in the file by writing *beyond* the end-of-file. As we discussed in the MINIX overview, the presence of multiple blocks per zone causes problems that must be dealt with explicitly. Pipes are also special and are checked for.

The heart of the read mechanism, at least for ordinary files, is the loop starting on line 9861. This loop breaks the request up into chunks, each of which fits in a single disk block. A chunk begins at the current position and extends until one of the following conditions is met:

1. All the bytes have been read.

2. A block boundary is encountered.

3. The end-of-file is hit.

These rules mean that a chunk never requires two disk blocks to satisfy it. Figure 7-11 shows three examples of how the chunk size is determined. The actual calculation is done on lines 9862 to 9871.

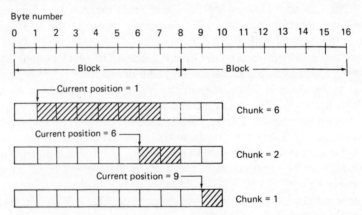

Fig. 7-11. Three examples of how the first chunk size is determined for a 10-byte file. The block size is 8 bytes, and the number of bytes requested is 6. The chunk is shown shaded.

The actual reading of the chunk is done by *rw_chunk* (line 9874). When control comes back, various counters and pointers are incremented, and the next iteration begins. When the loop terminates, the file position and other variables may be updated (e.g., pipe pointers).

Finally, if read ahead is called for, the i-node to read from and the position to read from are stored in global variables, so that after the reply message is sent to the user, the file system can start working on getting the next block. In many cases the file system will block, waiting for the next disk block, during which time the user process will be able to work on the data it already has. Read ahead allows I/O and computing to occur together.

The procedure *rw_chunk* (line 9919) is concerned with taking an i-node and a file position, converting them into a physical disk block number, and requesting the transfer of that block (or a portion of it) to the user space. The mapping of the relative file position to the physical disk address is done by *read_map*, which understands about i-nodes and indirect blocks. For an ordinary file, the variables *b* and *dev* on lines 9944 and 9945 contain the physical block number and device number, respectively. The call to *get_block* on line 9964 is where the cache handler is asked to find the block, reading it in if need be.

Once we have a pointer to the block, the call to *rw_user* on line 9972 takes care of transferring the required portion of it to the user space. The block is then released by *put_block*, so that it can be evicted from the cache later, when the time comes. (After being acquired by *get_block*, the counter in the block's header will show that it is in use, so it will be exempt from eviction; *put_block* decrements the counter.)

Read_map (line 9984) converts a logical file position to the physical block number by inspecting the i-node. For blocks close enough to the beginning of the file that they fall within one of the first seven zones (the ones right in the i-node), a simple calculation is sufficient to determine which zone is needed, and then which block. For blocks further into the file, one or more indirect blocks may have to be read.

The procedure *rw_user* (line 10042) just formats a message for the system task and sends it. The actual copying is done by the kernel. The file system could hardly do the copying; it does not even know where the user is located in memory. This extra overhead is the price that must be paid for the highly modular design.

Finally, *read_ahead* (line 10082) converts the logical position to a physical block number, calls *get_block* to make sure the block is in the cache, and then returns the block immediately. It cannot do anything with the block, after all. It just wants to improve the chance that the block is around if it should be used soon.

Note that *read_ahead* is called only from the main loop in *main*. It is not called as part of the processing of the READ system call. It is important to realize that the call to *readahead* is performed *after* the reply is sent, so that the user will be able to continue running even if the file system has to wait for a disk block while reading ahead. Figure 7-12 shows the relations between some of the major procedures involved in reading a file.

Writing a File

Writing a file is similar to reading one, except that writing requires allocating new disk blocks. One difference is *write_map* (line 10135), which is analogous to *read_map*, only instead of looking up physical block numbers in the i-node and its indirect blocks, it enters new ones there (to be precise, it enters zone numbers, not block numbers).

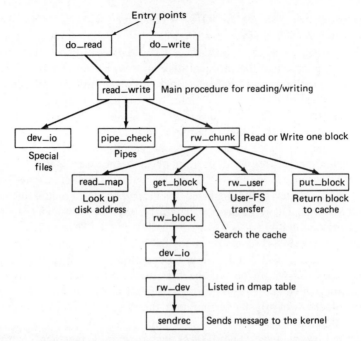

Fig. 7-12. Some of the procedures involved in reading a file.

The code of *write_map* is somewhat long and detailed because it must deal with several cases. If the zone to be inserted is close to the beginning of the file, it is just inserted into the i-node on (line 10160).

The worst case is when the file is at the maximum size that can be handled by a single-indirect block, so a double-indirect block must be allocated. Next, a single-indirect block must be allocated and its address put into the double-indirect block. If the double-indirect block is successfully allocated, but the single-indirect block cannot be allocated (i.e., disk full), then the double one must be carefully released so as not to corrupt the bit map.

Again, if we could just toss in the sponge and panic at this point, the code would be much simpler. However, from the user's point of view it is much nicer that running out of disk space just returns an error from WRITE, rather than crashing the computer with a corrupted file system.

The next procedure in *write.c* is *clear_zone*, which takes care of the problem of erasing blocks that are suddenly in the middle of a file, when a seek is done beyond the end of file, followed by a write of some data. Fortunately, this situation does not occur very often.

New_block (line 10265) is called by *rw_chunk* on line 9955 whenever a new block is needed. Figure 7-13 shows six successive stages of the growth of a sequential file. The block size is 1K and the zone size is 2K in this example.

The first time *new_block* is called, it allocates zone 12 (blocks 24 and 25). The next time it uses block 25, which has already been allocated but is not yet in

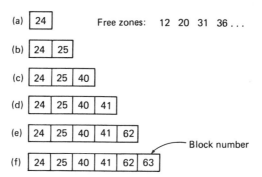

Fig. 7-13. (a) - (f) The successive allocation of 1K blocks. The zone size is 2K.

use. On the third call, zone 20 (blocks 40 and 41) is allocated, and so on.
Zero_block (line 10318) clears a block, erasing its previous contents.

Pipes

Pipes are similar to ordinary files in many respects. In this section we will
focus on the differences. First of all, they are created differently, by the PIPE
call, rather than the CREAT call. The PIPE call is handled by *do_pipe* (line
10384) in file *pipe.c*. All *do_pipe* really does is allocate an i-node for the pipe,
and return two file descriptors for it.

Reading and writing a pipe is slightly different from reading and writing a
file, because a pipe has a finite capacity. An attempt to write to a pipe that is
already full will cause the writer to be suspended. Similarly, reading from an
empty pipe will suspend the reader. In effect, a pipe has two pointers, the
current position (used by readers) and the size (used by writers), to determine
where data comes from or goes to.

The various checks to see if an operation on a pipe is possible are carried out
by *pipe_check* (line 10433). In addition to the above tests, which may lead to
the caller being suspended, *pipe_check* calls *release* to see if a process previously
suspended due to no data or too much data can now be revived. These revivals
are done on line 10457 and line 10478, for sleeping writers and readers, respectively. Writing on a broken pipe (no readers) is also detected here.

The act of suspending a process is done by *suspend* (line 10488). All it does
is save the parameters of the call in the process table, and set the flag *dont_reply*
to *TRUE*, to inhibit the file system's reply message.

The procedure *release* (line 10510) is called to check to see if a process that
was suspended on a pipe can now be allowed to continue. If it finds one, it calls
revive to set a flag so that the main loop will notice it later.

The last procedure in *pipe.c* is *do_unpause* (line 10572). When the memory
manager is trying to signal a process, it must find out if that process is hanging
on a pipe or special file (in which case it must be awakened with an *EINTR*

error). Since the memory manager knows nothing about pipes or special files, it sends a message to the file system to ask. That message is processed by *do_unpause*, which revives the process, if it is blocked.

7.2.5. Directories and Paths

We have now finished looking at how files are read and written. Our next task is to see how path names and directories are handled.

Converting a Path to an I-node

Many system calls (e.g., OPEN, UNLINK, and MOUNT) have path names (i.e., file names) as a parameter. Most of these calls must fetch the i-node for the named file before they can start working on the call itself. How a path name is converted to an i-node is a subject we will now look at in detail.

The parsing of path names is done in the file *path.c*. The first procedure, *eat_path* (line 10675), accepts a pointer to a path name, parses it, arranges for its i-node to be loaded into memory, and returns a pointer to the i-node. It does its work by calling *last_dir* to get the i-node to the final directory, and then calling *advance* to get the final component of the path. If the search fails, for example, because one of the directories along the path does not exist, *NIL_INODE* is returned instead of a pointer to the i-node.

Pathnames may be absolute or relative, and may have arbitrarily many components, separated by slashes. These issues are dealt with by *last_dir* (line 10703). It begins (line 10722) by examining the first character of the path name to see if it is an absolute path or a relative one. For absolute paths, *rip* is set to point to the root i-node; for relative ones, it is set to point to the i-node for the current working directory.

At this point, *last_dir* has the path name and a pointer to the i-node of the directory to look up the first component in. It enters a loop on line 10726 now, parsing the path name, component by component. When it gets to the end, it returns a pointer to the final directory.

Get_name (line 10749) is a utility procedure that extracts components from strings. More interesting is *advance* (line 10792), which takes as parameters a directory pointer and a string, and looks up the string in the directory. If it finds the string, *advance* returns a pointer to its i-node. The details of transferring across mounted file systems are handled here.

Although *advance* controls the string lookup, the actual comparison of the string against the directory entries is done in *search_dir*, which is the only place in the file system where directory files are actually examined. It contains two nested loops, one to loop over the blocks in a directory, and one to loop over the entries in a block. The procedure *search_dir* is also used to enter and delete names from directories. Figure 7-14 gives the relations between some of the major procedures used in looking up path names.

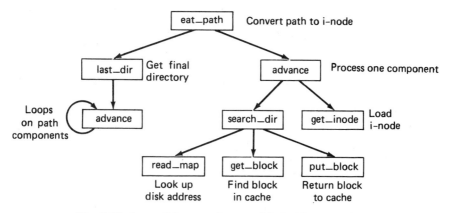

Fig. 7-14. Some of the procedures used in looking up path names.

Mounting File Systems

Two system calls that affect the file system as a whole are MOUNT and UMOUNT. They allow independent file systems on different minor devices to be "glued" together to form a single naming tree. Mounting is effectively achieved by reading in the root i-node and super-block of the file system to be mounted, and setting two pointers in its super-block. One of them points to the i-node mounted on, and the other points to the root i-node of the mounted file system.

The setting of these pointers is done in the file *mount.c* by *do_mount* on lines 11116 and 11117. The two pages of code that precede setting the pointers are almost entirely concerned with checking for all the errors that can occur while mounting a file system, among them:

1. The special file given is not a block device.

2. The special file is a block device, but is already mounted.

3. The file system to be mounted has a rotten magic number.

4. The file system to be mounted is invalid (e.g., no i-nodes).

5. The file to be mounted on does not exist or is a special file.

6. There is no room for the mounted file system's bit maps.

7. There is no room for the mounted file system's super-block.

8. There is no room for the mounted file system's root i-node.

Perhaps it seems inappropriate to keep harping on this point, but the reality of any practical operating system is that a substantial fraction of the code is devoted to doing minor chores that are not intellectually very exciting, but are crucial to making a system usable. If a user attempts to mount the wrong floppy disk by accident, say, once a month, and this leads to a crash and a corrupted file system, the user will perceive the system as being unreliable and blame the designer, not himself.

Thomas Edison once made a remark that is relevant here. He said that "genius" is one percent inspiration and 99 percent perspiration. The difference between a good system and a mediocre one is not the brilliance of the former's scheduling algorithm, but its attention to getting all the details right.

Unmounting a file system is easier than mounting one—there are fewer things that can go wrong. The only real issue is making sure that no process has any open files or working directories on the file system to be removed. This check is straightforward: just scan the whole i-node table to see if any i-nodes in memory belong to the file system to be removed (other than the root i-node). If so, the UMOUNT call fails.

The last procedure in *mount.c* is *name_to_dev* (line 11180), which takes a special file, gets its i-node, and extracts its major and minor device numbers. These are stored in the i-node itself, in the place where the first zone would normally go. This slot is available because special files do not have zones.

Linking and Unlinking Files

The next file is *link.c*, which deals with linking and unlinking files. The procedure *do_link* (line 11275) is very much like *do_mount* in that nearly all of the code is concerned with error checking. Here are some of the possible errors that can occur in the call

link(file_name, link_name);

1. *File_name* does not exist or cannot be accessed.

2. *File_name* already has the maximum number of links.

3. *File_name* is a directory (only super-user can link to it).

4. *Link_name* already exists.

5. *File_name* and *link_name* are on different devices.

If no errors are present, a new directory entry is made with the string *link_name* and the i-node number of *file_name*. The actual entry is made by *search_dir*, called from *do_link* on line 11324.

Files are removed by unlinking them. The work is done by *do_unlink* (line 11342). Again, a variety of checks are made first. If no errors are found, the directory entry is cleared and the link count in the i-node is reduced by one.

If the link count is now zero, all the zones are freed by *truncate* (line 11388). This procedure works by simply stepping through the i-node a zone at a time, freeing all the zones it finds.

7.2.6. Other System Calls

The last group of system calls is a mixed bag of things involving status, directories, protection, time, and other services.

Changing Directories and File Status

The file *stadir.c* contains the code for four system calls: CHDIR, CHROOT, STAT, and FSTAT. In *last_dir*, on line 10722, we saw how path searches start out by looking at the first character of the path, to see if it is a slash or not. Depending on the result, a pointer is then set to the working directory or the root directory.

Changing from one working directory (or root directory) to another is just a matter of changing these two pointers within the caller's process table. These changes are made by *do_chdir* (line 11475) and *do_chroot* (line 11500). Both of them do the necessary checking, and then call *change* (line 11515) to open the new directory to replace the old one.

The code on lines 11483 to 11490 is not executed on CHDIR calls made by user processes. It is specifically for calls made by the memory manager, to change to a user's directory for the purpose of handling EXEC calls. When a user tries to execute a file, say, *a.out* in his working directory, it is easier for the memory manager to change to that directory than to try to figure out where it is.

The remaining two system calls handled in this file, STAT and FSTAT, are basically the same, except for how the file is specified. The former gives a path name, whereas the latter provides the file descriptor of an open file. The top-level procedures, *do_stat* and *do_fstat*, both call *stat_inode* to do the work. Before calling *stat_inode*, *do_stat* opens the file to get its i-node. In this way, both *do_stat* and *do_fstat* pass an i-node pointer to *stat_inode*.

All *stat_inode* does is extract information from the i-node and copy it into a buffer. The buffer must be explicitly copied to user space by *rw_user* on line 11624 because it is too large to fit in a message.

Protection

The MINIX protection mechanism uses the *rwx* bits. Three sets of bits are present for each file: for the owner, for his group, and for others. The bits are set by the CHMOD system call, which is carried out by *do_chmod* (line 11677). After making a series of validity checks, the mode is changed on line 11704.

The CHOWN system call is similar to CHMOD in that both of them change an internal i-node field in some file. The implementation is also similar although *do_chown* (line 11715) is available only to the super-user.

The UMASK system call allows the user to set a mask (stored in the process table), which then masks out bits in subsequent CREAT system calls. The complete implementation would be only one statement, line 11752, except that the call must return the old mask value as its result. This additional burden triples the number of lines of code required (lines 11751 to 11753).

The ACCESS system call makes it possible for a process to find out if it can access a file in a specified way (e.g., for reading). It is implemented by *do_access* (line 11760), which fetches the file's i-node and calls the internal procedure, *forbidden* (line 11782), to see if the access is forbidden. *Forbidden* checks the uid and gid, as well as the information in the i-node. Depending on what it finds, it selects one of the three *rwx* groups and checks the access.

Read_only (line 11830) is a little internal procedure that tells whether the file system on which its i-node parameter is located is mounted read-only or read-write. It is needed to prevent writes on file systems mounted read-only.

Time

MINIX has several system calls that involve time: UTIME, TIME, STIME, and TIMES. They are summarized in Fig. 7-15. They are handled by the file system for no good reason. They just had to go somewhere.

UTIME	Set a file's "time of last modification"
TIME	Get the current real time in seconds
STIME	Set the real time clock
TIMES	Get the process accounting times

Fig. 7-15. The four system calls involving time.

Associated with each file is a 32-bit number that records the time when the file was last modified. This time is kept in the i-node. With the UTIME system call, this time can be set by the owner of the file or the super-user. The procedure *do_utime* (line 11877) performs the system call by fetching the i-node and storing the user-specified time in it.

The real time is not maintained by the file system. It is maintained by the clock task within the kernel. Consequently, the only way to get or set the real time is to send a message to the clock task. This is, in fact, what *do_time* and *do_stime* both do. The real time is in seconds, since Jan 1, 1970.

The accounting information is also maintained by the kernel. At each clock tick it charges one tick to some process. This information can be retrieved by sending a message to the system task, which is what *do_tims* (line 11937) does. The procedure is not named *do_times* because most C compilers add an underscore to the front of all external symbols, and most linkers truncate symbols to eight characters, thus making *do_time* indistinguishable from *do_times*.

Leftovers

The file *misc.c* contains procedures for a few system calls that do not fit in anywhere else. The DUP system call duplicates a file descriptor. In other words, it creates a new file descriptor that points to the same file as its argument.

The call has a variant that is slightly different. It is invoked by the call

```
dup2(fd, fd2);
```

in which *fd* is a file descriptor referring to an open file, and *fd2* is an integer that has no file assigned to it yet. The call makes *fd2* a valid file descriptor for the same file as *fd*.

The two system calls share the same message type. They are distinguished by the 0100 bit, which is set in *fd* for DUP2. Both versions of the call are handled by *do_dup* (line 11981). The work to be done is straightforward, consisting of manipulating file descriptors and *filp* entries.

The next system call is SYNC, which copies all blocks, i-nodes, and super-blocks that have been modified since being loaded back to the disk. The call is processed by *do_sync* (line 12018). It simply searches through all the tables looking for dirty entries.

The system calls FORK, EXIT, and SETUID are really memory manager calls, but the results have to be posted here as well. When a process forks, it is essential that the kernel, memory manager, and file system all know about it. These "system calls" do not come from user processes, but from the memory manager. Their job consists of recording the relevant information.

The last nonsystem call is handled by *do_revive* (line 12149). It is called when a task that was previously unable to complete work that the file system had requested, such as providing input data for a user process, has now completed the work. The file system now revives the process and sends it the reply message.

7.2.7. The I/O Device Interface

I/O in MINIX is done by sending messages to the tasks within the kernel. The file system's interface with these tasks is contained in the file *device.c*, which also contains procedures that do special things for special files. As a starter, when a special file is opened, the procedure *dev_open* (line 12233) is called, just in case some special processing is needed. This procedure extracts the major and minor device numbers for the special file, and uses the major device number as an index into the *dmap* table in file *table.c* to call a procedure within the file system for special processing (line 12240). Normally this entry is *no_call*, which does nothing, but other procedures can be entered into *dmap* as needed.

Closing a device is similar, with the work being done by *dev_close* (line 12248) in this case.

When actual device I/O is needed, *dev_io* (line 12261) is called. It builds a standard message (see Fig. 5-2) and sends it to the specified task. It is called from *read_write* to handle character special files, and from *rw_block* for block special files. While *dev_io* is waiting for a reply from the task, the file system waits. It has no internal multiprogramming. Usually these waits are quite short though (a few hundred milliseconds at worst).

One system call is handled in *device.c*, IOCTL. That call has been put here because it is closely tied to the task interface. When an IOCTL is done, *do_ioctl* is called to build a message and send it to the proper task.

Find_dev (line 12328) is a little helper procedure that extracts the major and minor device numbers from a full device number. The final three procedures in *device.c* are not mentioned explicitly in the file system. All three are procedures that are called indirectly, via *dmap*. Reads and writes use either *rw_dev* or *rw_dev2* (see Fig. 7-12 for the call hierarchy). When a null routine is needed, *no_call* is used.

7.2.8. General Utilities

The file system contains a few general purpose utility procedures that are used in various places. They are collected together in the file *utility.c*. The first procedure is *clock_time*. It sends messages to the clock task to find out what the current real time is. The next one is *cmp_string*. It compares two strings to see if they are the same. Then comes *copy*. It copies a block of data from one part of the file system's address space to another.

The procedure *fetch_name* is needed because many system calls have a file name as parameter. If the file name is short, it is included in the message from the user to the file system. If it is long, a pointer to the name in user space is put in the message. *Fetch_name* checks for both cases, and either way, gets the name.

No_sys is the error handler that is called when the file system receives a system call that is not one of its calls. Finally, *panic* prints a message and tells the kernel to throw in the towel when something catastrophic happens.

The last file is *putc.c*. It contains two procedures, both of which have to do with printing messages. The standard library procedures cannot be used, because they send messages to the file system. These procedures send messages directly to the terminal task.

PART THREE

8

THE MINIX SOURCE CODE LISTING

```
0000   /* Copyright (C) 1987 by Prentice-Hall, Inc.  The author and publisher
0001    * of this software have used their best efforts in preparing it.
0002    * However, they make no warranty of any kind, express or implied,
0003    * with regard to this software or its documentation.  The author and
0004    * publisher shall not be liable in any event for incidental or
0005    * consequential damages in connection with, or arising out of, the
0006    * furnishing, performance, or use of this software or documentation.
0007    */
0008
0009   #define EXTERN        extern    /* used in *.h files */
0010   #define PRIVATE       static    /* PRIVATE x limits the scope of x */
0011   #define PUBLIC                  /* PUBLIC is the opposite of PRIVATE */
0012   #define FORWARD                 /* some compilers require this to be 'static' */
0013
0014   #define TRUE             1      /* used for turning integers into Booleans */
0015   #define FALSE            0      /* used for turning integers into Booleans */
0016
0017   #define HZ              60      /* clock freq (software settable on IBM-PC) */
0018   #define BLOCK_SIZE    1024      /* # bytes in a disk block */
0019   #define SUPER_USER  (uid) 0     /* uid of superuser */
0020
0021   #define MAJOR            8      /* major device = (dev>>MAJOR) & 0377 */
0022   #define MINOR            0      /* minor device = (dev>>MINOR) & 0377 */
0023
0024   #define NR_TASKS         8      /* number of tasks in the transfer vector */
0025   #define NR_PROCS        16      /* number of slots in proc table */
0026   #define NR_SEGS          3      /* # segments per process */
0027   #define T                0      /* proc[i].mem_map[T] is for text */
```

```
0028    #define D                 1    /* proc[i].mem_map[D] is for data */
0029    #define S                 2    /* proc[i].mem_map[S] is for stack */
0030
0031    #define MAX_P_LONG  2147483647  /* maximum positive long, i.e. 2**31 - 1 */
0032
0033    /* Memory is allocated in clicks. */
0034    #define CLICK_SIZE      0020    /* unit in which memory is allocated */
0035    #define CLICK_SHIFT        4    /* log2 of CLICK_SIZE */
0036
0037    /* Process numbers of some important processes */
0038    #define MM_PROC_NR         0    /* process number of memory manager */
0039    #define FS_PROC_NR         1    /* process number of file system */
0040    #define INIT_PROC_NR       2    /* init -- the process that goes multiuser */
0041    #define LOW_USER           2    /* first user not part of operating system */
0042
0043    /* Miscellaneous */
0044    #define BYTE            0377    /* mask for 8 bits */
0045    #define TO_USER            0    /* flag telling to copy from fs to user */
0046    #define FROM_USER          1    /* flag telling to copy from user to fs */
0047    #define READING            0    /* copy data to user */
0048    #define WRITING            1    /* copy data from user */
0049    #define ABS             -999    /* this process means absolute memory */
0050
0051    #define WORD_SIZE          2              /* number of bytes per word */
0052
0053    #define NIL_PTR    (char *) 0   /* generally useful expression */
0054
0055    #define NO_NUM        0x8000 /* used as numerical argument to panic() */
0056    #define MAX_PATH         128 /* max length of path names */
0057    #define SIG_PUSH_BYTES     8 /* how many bytes pushed by signal */
0058    #define MAX_ISTACK_BYTES 1024 /* maximum initial stack size for EXEC */
0059
0060    /* Device numbers of root (RAM) and boot (fd0) devices. */
0061    #define ROOT_DEV (dev_nr)   256 /* major-minor device number of root dev */
0062    #define BOOT_DEV (dev_nr)   512 /* major-minor device number of boot diskette */
0063
0064    /* Flag bits for i_mode in the inode. */
0065    #define I_TYPE         0170000 /* this field gives inode type */
0066    #define I_REGULAR      0100000 /* regular file, not dir or special */
0067    #define I_BLOCK_SPECIAL 0060000 /* block special file */
0068    #define I_DIRECTORY    0040000 /* file is a directory */
0069    #define I_CHAR_SPECIAL 0020000 /* character special file */
0070    #define I_SET_UID_BIT  0004000 /* set effective uid on exec */
0071    #define I_SET_GID_BIT  0002000 /* set effective gid on exec */
0072    #define ALL_MODES      0006777 /* all bits for user, group and others */
0073    #define RWX_MODES      0000777 /* mode bits for RWX only */
0074    #define R_BIT          0000004 /* Rwx protection bit */
0075    #define W_BIT          0000002 /* rWx protection bit */
0076    #define X_BIT          0000001 /* rwX protection bit */
0077    #define I_NOT_ALLOC    0000000 /* this inode is free */
```

```
0100    #define NCALLS          69      /* number of system calls allowed */
0101
0102    #define EXIT            1
0103    #define FORK            2
0104    #define READ            3
0105    #define WRITE           4
0106    #define OPEN            5
0107    #define CLOSE           6
0108    #define WAIT            7
0109    #define CREAT           8
0110    #define LINK            9
0111    #define UNLINK         10
0112    #define CHDIR          12
0113    #define TIME           13
0114    #define MKNOD          14
0115    #define CHMOD          15
0116    #define CHOWN          16
0117    #define BRK            17
0118    #define STAT           18
0119    #define LSEEK          19
0120    #define GETPID         20
0121    #define MOUNT          21
0122    #define UMOUNT         22
0123    #define SETUID         23
0124    #define GETUID         24
0125    #define STIME          25
0126    #define ALARM          27
0127    #define FSTAT          28
0128    #define PAUSE          29
0129    #define UTIME          30
0130    #define ACCESS         33
0131    #define SYNC           36
0132    #define KILL           37
0133    #define DUP            41
0134    #define PIPE           42
0135    #define TIMES          43
0136    #define SETGID         46
0137    #define GETGID         47
0138    #define SIGNAL         48
0139    #define IOCTL          54
0140    #define EXEC           59
0141    #define UMASK          60
0142    #define CHROOT         61
0143
0144    /* The following are not system calls, but are processed like them. */
0145    #define KSIG           64      /* kernel detected a signal */
0146    #define UNPAUSE        65      /* to MM or FS: check for EINTR */
0147    #define BRK2           66      /* to MM: used to say how big FS & INIT are */
0148    #define REVIVE         67      /* to FS: revive a sleeping process */
0149    #define TASK_REPLY     68      /* to FS: reply code from tty task */
```

```
0150   /* System calls. */
0151   #define SEND            1       /* function code for sending messages */
0152   #define RECEIVE         2       /* function code for receiving messages */
0153   #define BOTH            3       /* function code for SEND + RECEIVE */
0154   #define ANY     (NR_PROCS+100)  /* receive(ANY, buf) accepts from any source */
0155
0156   /* Task numbers, function codes and reply codes. */
0157   #define HARDWARE       -1       /* used as source on interrupt generated msgs */
0158
0159   #define SYSTASK        -2       /* internal functions */
0160   #      define SYS_XIT     1       /* fcn code for sys_xit(parent, proc) */
0161   #      define SYS_GETSP   2       /* fcn code for sys_sp(proc, &new_sp) */
0162   #      define SYS_SIG     3       /* fcn code for sys_sig(proc, sig) */
0163   #      define SYS_FORK    4       /* fcn code for sys_fork(parent, child) */
0164   #      define SYS_NEWMAP  5       /* fcn code for sys_newmap(procno, map_ptr) */
0165   #      define SYS_COPY    6       /* fcn code for sys_copy(ptr) */
0166   #      define SYS_EXEC    7       /* fcn code for sys_exec(procno, new_sp) */
0167   #      define SYS_TIMES   8       /* fcn code for sys_times(procno, bufptr) */
0168   #      define SYS_ABORT   9       /* fcn code for sys_abort() */
0169
0170   #define CLOCK          -3       /* clock class */
0171   #      define SET_ALARM   1       /* fcn code to CLOCK, set up alarm */
0172   #      define CLOCK_TICK  2       /* fcn code for clock tick */
0173   #      define GET_TIME    3       /* fcn code to CLOCK, get real time */
0174   #      define SET_TIME    4       /* fcn code to CLOCK, set real time */
0175   #      define REAL_TIME   1       /* reply from CLOCK: here is real time */
0176
0177   #define MEM            -4       /* /dev/ram, /dev/(k)mem and /dev/null class */
0178   #      define RAM_DEV     0       /* minor device for /dev/ram */
0179   #      define MEM_DEV     1       /* minor device for /dev/mem */
0180   #      define KMEM_DEV    2       /* minor device for /dev/kmem */
0181   #      define NULL_DEV    3       /* minor device for /dev/null */
0182
0183   #define FLOPPY         -5       /* floppy disk class */
0184   #define WINCHESTER     -6       /* winchester (hard) disk class */
0185   #      define DISKINT     1       /* fcn code for disk interupt */
0186   #      define DISK_READ   3       /* fcn code to DISK (must equal TTY_READ) */
0187   #      define DISK_WRITE  4       /* fcn code to DISK (must equal TTY_WRITE) */
0188   #      define DISK_IOCTL  5       /* fcn code for setting up RAM disk */
0189
0190   #define TTY            -7       /* terminal I/O class */
0191   #define PRINTER        -8       /* printer  I/O class */
0192   #      define TTY_CHAR_INT 1      /* fcn code for tty input interrupt */
0193   #      define TTY_O_DONE  2       /* fcn code for tty output done */
0194   #      define TTY_READ    3       /* fcn code for reading from tty */
0195   #      define TTY_WRITE   4       /* fcn code for writing to tty */
0196   #      define TTY_IOCTL   5       /* fcn code for ioctl */
0197   #      define SUSPEND   -998      /* used in interrupts when tty has no data */
0198
0199   /* Names of message fields for messages to CLOCK task. */
```

```
0200    #define DELTA_TICKS     m6_l1    /* alarm interval in clock ticks */
0201    #define FUNC_TO_CALL    m6_f1    /* pointer to function to call */
0202    #define NEW_TIME        m6_l1    /* value to set clock to (SET_TIME) */
0203    #define CLOCK_PROC_NR   m6_i1    /* which proc (or task) wants the alarm? */
0204    #define SECONDS_LEFT    m6_l1    /* how many seconds were remaining */
0205
0206    /* Names of message fields used for messages to block and character tasks. */
0207    #define DEVICE          m2_i1    /* major-minor device */
0208    #define PROC_NR         m2_i2    /* which (proc) wants I/O? */
0209    #define COUNT           m2_i3    /* how many bytes to transfer */
0210    #define POSITION        m2_l1    /* file offset */
0211    #define ADDRESS         m2_p1    /* core buffer address */
0212
0213    /* Names of message fields for messages to TTY task. */
0214    #define TTY_LINE        m2_i1    /* message parameter: terminal line */
0215    #define TTY_REQUEST     m2_i3    /* message parameter: ioctl request code */
0216    #define TTY_SPEK        m2_l1    /* message parameter: ioctl speed, erasing */
0217    #define TTY_FLAGS       m2_l2    /* message parameter: ioctl tty mode */
0218
0219    /* Names of messages fields used in reply messages from tasks. */
0220    #define REP_PROC_NR     m2_i1    /* # of proc on whose behalf I/O was done */
0221    #define REP_STATUS      m2_i2    /* bytes transferred or error number */
0222
0223    /* Names of fields for copy message to SYSTASK. */
0224    #define SRC_SPACE       m5_c1    /* T or D space (stack is also D) */
0225    #define SRC_PROC_NR     m5_i1    /* process to copy from */
0226    #define SRC_BUFFER      m5_l1    /* virtual address where data come from */
0227    #define DST_SPACE       m5_c2    /* T or D space (stack is also D) */
0228    #define DST_PROC_NR     m5_i2    /* process to copy to */
0229    #define DST_BUFFER      m5_l2    /* virtual address where data go to */
0230    #define COPY_BYTES      m5_l3    /* number of bytes to copy */
0231
0232    /* Field names for accounting, SYSTASK and miscellaneous. */
0233    #define USER_TIME       m4_l1    /* user time consumed by process */
0234    #define SYSTEM_TIME     m4_l2    /* system time consumed by process */
0235    #define CHILD_UTIME     m4_l3    /* user time consumed by process' children */
0236    #define CHILD_STIME     m4_l4    /* system time consumed by proces children */
0237
0238    #define PROC1           m1_i1    /* indicates a process */
0239    #define PROC2           m1_i2    /* indicates a process */
0240    #define PID             m1_i3    /* process id passed from MM to kernel */
0241    #define STACK_PTR       m1_p1    /* used for stack ptr in sys_exec, sys_getsp */
0242    #define PR              m6_i1    /* process number for sys_sig */
0243    #define SIGNUM          m6_i2    /* signal number for sys_sig */
0244    #define FUNC            m6_f1    /* function pointer for sys_sig */
0245    #define MEM_PTR         m1_p1    /* tells where memory map is for sys_newmap */
0246    #define CANCEL          0        /* general request to force a task to cancel */
0247    #define SIG_MAP         m1_i2    /* used by kernel for passing signal bit map */
```

```
0250    /* Error codes.  They are negative since a few system calls, such as READ, can
0251     * either return a positive number indicating success, or an error code.
0252     */
0253
0254    #define NERROR          34
0255    #define OK               0
0256    #define ERROR           -1
0257    #define EPERM           -1
0258    #define ENOENT          -2
0259    #define ESRCH           -3
0260    #define EINTR           -4
0261    #define EIO             -5
0262    #define ENXIO           -6
0263    #define E2BIG           -7
0264    #define ENOEXEC         -8
0265    #define EBADF           -9
0266    #define ECHILD         -10
0267    #define EAGAIN         -11
0268    #define ENOMEM         -12
0269    #define EACCES         -13
0270    #define EFAULT         -14
0271    #define ENOTBLK        -15
0272    #define EBUSY          -16
0273    #define EEXIST         -17
0274    #define EXDEV          -18
0275    #define ENODEV         -19
0276    #define ENOTDIR        -20
0277    #define EISDIR         -21
0278    #define EINVAL         -22
0279    #define ENFILE         -23
0280    #define EMFILE         -24
0281    #define ENOTTY         -25
0282    #define ETXTBSY        -26
0283    #define EFBIG          -27
0284    #define ENOSPC         -28
0285    #define ESPIPE         -29
0286    #define EROFS          -30
0287    #define EMLINK         -31
0288    #define EPIPE          -32
0289    #define EDOM           -33
0290    #define ERANGE         -34
0291
0292    #define E_LOCKED      -101
0293    #define E_BAD_CALL    -102
0294    #define E_LONG_STRING -103
0295
0296    /* The following error codes are generated by the kernel itself. */
0297    #define E_BAD_DEST      -1   /* destination address illegal */
0298    #define E_BAD_SRC       -2   /* source address illegal */
0299    #define E_TRY_AGAIN     -3   /* can't send-- tables full */
```

```
0300  #define E_OVERRUN       -4    /* interrupt for task that is not waiting */
0301  #define E_BAD_BUF       -5    /* message buf outside caller's addr space */
0302  #define E_TASK          -6    /* can't send to task */
0303  #define E_NO_MESSAGE    -7    /* RECEIVE failed: no message present */
0304  #define E_NO_PERM       -8    /* ordinary users can't send to tasks */
0305  #define E_BAD_FCN       -9    /* only valid fcns are SEND, RECEIVE, BOTH */
0306  #define E_BAD_ADDR      -10   /* bad address given to utility routine */
0307  #define E_BAD_PROC      -11   /* bad proc number given to utility */
```

```
0350    /* Data structures for IOCTL. */
0351
0352    struct sgttyb {
0353      char sg_ispeed;                /* input speed (not used at present) */
0354      char sg_ospeed;                /* output speed (not used at present) */
0355      char sg_erase;                 /* erase character */
0356      char sg_kill;                  /* kill character */
0357      int  sg_flags;                 /* mode flags */
0358    };
0359
0360    struct tchars {
0361      char t_intrc;                  /* character that generates SIGINT */
0362      char t_quitc;                  /* character that generates SIGQUIT */
0363      char t_startc;                 /* start output (initially CTRL-Q) */
0364      char t_stopc;                  /* stop output  (initially CTRL-S) */
0365      char t_eofc;                   /* end-of-file  (initially CTRL-D) */
0366      char t_brkc;                   /* input delimiter (like nl) */
0367    };
0368
0369    /* Fields in sg_flags. */
0370    #define XTABS      0006000       /* set to cause tab expansion */
0371    #define RAW        0000040       /* set to enable raw mode */
0372    #define CRMOD      0000020       /* set to map lf to cr + lf */
0373    #define ECHO       0000010       /* set to enable echoing of typed input */
0374    #define CBREAK     0000002       /* set to enable cbreak mode */
0375    #define COOKED     0000000       /* neither CBREAK nor RAW */
0376
0377    #define TIOCGETP (('t'<<8) | 8)
0378    #define TIOCSETP (('t'<<8) | 9)
0379    #define TIOCGETC (('t'<<8) | 18)
0380    #define TIOCSETC (('t'<<8) | 17)
```

```
0400     #define NR_SIGS              16    /* number of signals used */
0401
0402     #define SIGHUP                1    /* hangup */
0403     #define SIGINT                2    /* interrupt (DEL) */
0404     #define SIGQUIT               3    /* quit (ASCII FS) */
0405     #define SIGILL                4    /* illegal instruction (not reset when caught)*/
0406     #define SIGTRAP               5    /* trace trap (not reset when caught) */
0407     #define SIGIOT                6    /* IOT instruction */
0408     #define SIGEMT                7    /* EMT instruction */
0409     #define SIGFPE                8    /* floating point exception */
0410     #define SIGKILL               9    /* kill (cannot be caught or ignored) */
0411     #define SIGBUS               10    /* bus error */
0412     #define SIGSEGV              11    /* segmentation violation */
0413     #define SIGSYS               12    /* bad argument to system call */
0414     #define SIGPIPE              13    /* write on a pipe with no one to read it */
0415     #define SIGALRM              14    /* alarm clock */
0416     #define SIGTERM              15    /* software termination signal from kill */
0417
0418     #define STACK_FAULT          16    /* used by kernel to signal stack fault */
0419
0420     int     (*signal())();
0421     #define SIG_DFL (int (*)())0
0422     #define SIG_IGN (int (*)())1
```

```
0450    struct stat {
0451        short int st_dev;
0452        unsigned short st_ino;
0453        unsigned short st_mode;
0454        short int st_nlink;
0455        short int st_uid;
0456        short int st_gid;
0457        short int st_rdev;
0458        long st_size;
0459        long st_atime;
0460        long st_mtime;
0461        long st_ctime;
0462    };
0463
0464    /* Some common definitions. */
0465    #define S_IFMT  0170000         /* type of file */
0466    #define S_IFDIR 0040000         /* directory */
0467    #define S_IFCHR 0020000         /* character special */
0468    #define S_IFBLK 0060000         /* block special */
0469    #define S_IFREG 0100000         /* regular */
0470    #define S_ISUID   04000         /* set user id on execution */
0471    #define S_ISGID   02000         /* set group id on execution */
0472    #define S_ISVTX   01000         /* save swapped text even after use */
0473    #define S_IREAD   00400         /* read permission, owner */
0474    #define S_IWRITE  00200         /* write permission, owner */
0475    #define S_IEXEC   00100         /* execute/search permission, owner */
```

```
0500    /* Macros */
0501    #define MAX(a,b)        (a > b ? a : b)
0502    #define MIN(a,b)        (a < b ? a : b)
0503
0504    /* Type definitions */
0505    typedef unsigned short unshort; /* must be 16-bit unsigned */
0506    typedef unshort block_nr;       /* block number */
0507    #define NO_BLOCK (block_nr) 0   /* indicates the absence of a block number */
0508    #define MAX_BLOCK_NR (block_nr) 0177777
0509
0510    typedef unshort inode_nr;       /* inode number */
0511    #define NO_ENTRY (inode_nr) 0   /* indicates the absence of a dir entry */
0512    #define MAX_INODE_NR (inode_nr) 0177777
0513
0514    typedef unshort zone_nr;        /* zone number */
0515    #define NO_ZONE   (zone_nr) 0   /* indicates the absence of a zone number */
0516    #define HIGHEST_ZONE (zone_nr) 0177777
0517
0518    typedef unshort bit_nr;         /* if inode_nr & zone_nr both unshort,
0519                                       then also unshort, else long */
0520
0521    typedef long zone_type;         /* zone size */
0522    typedef unshort mask_bits;      /* mode bits */
0523    typedef unshort dev_nr;         /* major | minor device number */
0524    #define NO_DEV    (dev_nr) ~0   /* indicates absence of a device number */
0525
0526    typedef char links;             /* number of links to an inode */
0527    #define MAX_LINKS       0177
0528
0529    typedef long real_time;         /* real time in seconds since Jan 1, 1970 */
0530    typedef long file_pos;          /* position in, or length of, a file */
0531    #define MAX_FILE_POS 017777777777L
0532    typedef short int uid;          /* user id */
0533    typedef char gid;               /* group id */
0534
0535    typedef unsigned vir_bytes;     /* virtual addresses and lengths in bytes */
0536    typedef unsigned vir_clicks;    /* virtual addresses and lengths in clicks */
0537    typedef long phys_bytes;        /* physical addresses and lengths in bytes */
0538    typedef unsigned phys_clicks;   /* physical addresses and lengths in clicks */
0539    typedef int signed_clicks;      /* same length as phys_clicks, but signed */
0540
0541    /* Types relating to messages. */
0542    #define M1              1
0543    #define M3              3
0544    #define M4              4
0545    #define M3_STRING       14
0546
0547    typedef struct {int m1i1, m1i2, m1i3; char *m1p1, *m1p2, *m1p3;} mess_1;
0548    typedef struct {int m2i1, m2i2, m2i3; long m2l1, m2l2; char *m2p1;} mess_2;
0549    typedef struct {int m3i1, m3i2; char *m3p1; char m3ca1[M3_STRING];} mess_3;
```

```
0550    typedef struct {long m4l1, m4l2, m4l3, m4l4;} mess_4;
0551    typedef struct {char m5c1, m5c2; int m5i1, m5i2; long m5l1, m5l2, m5l3;} mess_5;
0552    typedef struct {int m6i1, m6i2, m6i3; long m6l1; int (*m6f1)();} mess_6;
0553
0554    typedef struct {
0555      int m_source;                     /* who sent the message */
0556      int m_type;                       /* what kind of message is it */
0557      union {
0558            mess_1 m_m1;
0559            mess_2 m_m2;
0560            mess_3 m_m3;
0561            mess_4 m_m4;
0562            mess_5 m_m5;
0563            mess_6 m_m6;
0564      } m_u;
0565    } message;
0566
0567    #define MESS_SIZE (sizeof(message))
0568    #define NIL_MESS (message *) 0
0569
0570    /* The following defines provide names for useful members. */
0571    #define m1_i1   m_u.m_m1.m1i1
0572    #define m1_i2   m_u.m_m1.m1i2
0573    #define m1_i3   m_u.m_m1.m1i3
0574    #define m1_p1   m_u.m_m1.m1p1
0575    #define m1_p2   m_u.m_m1.m1p2
0576    #define m1_p3   m_u.m_m1.m1p3
0577
0578    #define m2_i1   m_u.m_m2.m2i1
0579    #define m2_i2   m_u.m_m2.m2i2
0580    #define m2_i3   m_u.m_m2.m2i3
0581    #define m2_l1   m_u.m_m2.m2l1
0582    #define m2_l2   m_u.m_m2.m2l2
0583    #define m2_p1   m_u.m_m2.m2p1
0584
0585    #define m3_i1   m_u.m_m3.m3i1
0586    #define m3_i2   m_u.m_m3.m3i2
0587    #define m3_p1   m_u.m_m3.m3p1
0588    #define m3_ca1  m_u.m_m3.m3ca1
0589
0590
0591    #define m4_l1   m_u.m_m4.m4l1
0592    #define m4_l2   m_u.m_m4.m4l2
0593    #define m4_l3   m_u.m_m4.m4l3
0594    #define m4_l4   m_u.m_m4.m4l4
0595
0596    #define m5_c1   m_u.m_m5.m5c1
0597    #define m5_c2   m_u.m_m5.m5c2
0598    #define m5_i1   m_u.m_m5.m5i1
0599    #define m5_i2   m_u.m_m5.m5i2
```

```
0600     #define m5_l1   m_u.m_m5.m5l1
0601     #define m5_l2   m_u.m_m5.m5l2
0602     #define m5_l3   m_u.m_m5.m5l3
0603
0604     #define m6_i1   m_u.m_m6.m6i1
0605     #define m6_i2   m_u.m_m6.m6i2
0606     #define m6_i3   m_u.m_m6.m6i3
0607     #define m6_l1   m_u.m_m6.m6l1
0608     #define m6_f1   m_u.m_m6.m6f1
0609
0610     struct mem_map {
0611       vir_clicks mem_vir;             /* virtual address */
0612       phys_clicks mem_phys;           /* physical address */
0613       vir_clicks mem_len;             /* length */
0614     };
0615
0616     struct copy_info {                /* used by sys_copy(src, dst, bytes) */
0617             int cp_src_proc;
0618             int cp_src_space;
0619             vir_bytes cp_src_vir;
0620             int cp_dst_proc;
0621             int cp_dst_space;
0622             vir_bytes cp_dst_vir;
0623             vir_bytes cp_bytes;
0624     };
```

```
0650    /* General constants used by the kernel. */
0651
0652    #ifdef i8088
0653    /* p_reg contains: ax, bx, cx, dx, si, di, bp, es, ds, cs, ss in that order. */
0654    #define NR_REGS         11      /* number of general regs in each proc slot */
0655    #define INIT_PSW        0x0200  /* initial psw */
0656    #define INIT_SP (int*)0x0010    /* initial sp: 3 words pushed by kernel */
0657
0658    /* The following values are used in the assembly code.  Do not change the
0659     * values of 'ES_REG', 'DS_REG', 'CS_REG', or 'SS_REG' without making the
0660     * corresponding changes in the assembly code.
0661     */
0662    #define ES_REG          7       /* proc[i].p_reg[ESREG] is saved es */
0663    #define DS_REG          8       /* proc[i].p_reg[DSREG] is saved ds */
0664    #define CS_REG          9       /* proc[i].p_reg[CSREG] is saved cs */
0665    #define SS_REG          10      /* proc[i].p_reg[SSREG] is saved ss */
0666
0667    #define VECTOR_BYTES    260     /* bytes of interrupt vectors to save */
0668    #define MEM_BYTES       655360L /* memory size for /dev/mem */
0669
0670    /* Interrupt vectors */
0671    #define CLOCK_VECTOR    8       /* clock interrupt vector */
0672    #define KEYBOARD_VECTOR 9       /* keyboard interrupt vector */
0673    #define FLOPPY_VECTOR   14      /* floppy disk interrupt vector */
0674    #define PRINTER_VECTOR  15      /* line printer interrupt vector */
0675    #define SYS_VECTOR      32      /* system calls are made with int SYSVEC */
0676
0677    /* The 8259A interrupt controller has to be re-enabled after each interrupt. */
0678    #define INT_CTL         0x20    /* I/O port for interrupt controller */
0679    #define INT_CTLMASK     0x21    /* setting bits in this port disables ints */
0680    #define ENABLE          0x20    /* code used to re-enable after an interrupt */
0681    #endif
0682
0683    #define TASK_STACK_BYTES 256    /* how many bytes for each task stack */
0684    #define K_STACK_BYTES   256     /* how many bytes for the kernel stack */
0685
0686    #define RET_REG         0       /* system call return codes go in this reg */
0687    #define IDLE            -999    /* 'cur_proc' = IDLE means nobody is running */
0688
0689    /* The following items pertain to the 3 scheduling queues. */
0690    #define NQ              3       /* # of scheduling queues */
0691    #define TASK_Q          0       /* ready tasks are scheduled via queue 0 */
0692    #define SERVER_Q        1       /* ready servers are scheduled via queue 1 */
0693    #define USER_Q          2       /* ready users are scheduled via queue 2 */
0694
0695    #define printf          printk  /* the kernel really uses printk, not printf */
```

```
0700    /* Global variables used in the kernel. */
0701
0702    /* Clocks and timers */
0703    EXTERN real_time realtime;          /* real time clock */
0704    EXTERN int lost_ticks;              /* incremented when clock int can't send mess*/
0705
0706    /* Processes, signals, and messages. */
0707    EXTERN int cur_proc;                /* current process */
0708    EXTERN int prev_proc;               /* previous process */
0709    EXTERN int sig_procs;               /* number of procs with p_pending != 0 */
0710    EXTERN message int_mess;            /* interrupt routines build message here */
0711
0712    /* The kernel and task stacks. */
0713    EXTERN struct t_stack {
0714      int stk[TASK_STACK_BYTES/sizeof(int)];
0715    } t_stack[NR_TASKS - 1];            /* task stacks; task = -1 never really runs */
0716
0717    EXTERN char k_stack[K_STACK_BYTES];     /* The kernel stack. */
```

```
0750    /* Here is the declaration of the process table.  Three assembly code routines
0751     * reference fields in it.  They are restart(), save(), and csv().  When
0752     * changing 'proc', be sure to change the field offsets built into the code.
0753     * It contains the process' registers, memory map, accounting, and message
0754     * send/receive information.
0755     */
0756
0757    EXTERN struct proc {
0758      int p_reg[NR_REGS];              /* process' registers */
0759      int *p_sp;                       /* stack pointer */
0760      struct pc_psw p_pcpsw;                 /* pc and psw as pushed by interrupt */
0761      int p_flags;                     /* P_SLOT_FREE, SENDING, RECEIVING, etc. */
0762      struct mem_map p_map[NR_SEGS];/* memory map */
0763      int *p_splimit;                  /* lowest legal stack value */
0764      int p_pid;                       /* process id passed in from MM */
0765
0766      real_time user_time;             /* user time in ticks */
0767      real_time sys_time;              /* sys time in ticks */
0768      real_time child_utime;           /* cumulative user time of children */
0769      real_time child_stime;           /* cumulative sys time of children */
0770      real_time p_alarm;               /* time of next alarm in ticks, or 0 */
0771
0772      struct proc *p_callerq;          /* head of list of procs wishing to send */
0773      struct proc *p_sendlink;         /* link to next proc wishing to send */
0774      message *p_messbuf;              /* pointer to message buffer */
0775      int p_getfrom;                   /* from whom does process want to receive? */
0776
0777      struct proc *p_nextready;        /* pointer to next ready process */
0778      int p_pending;                   /* bit map for pending signals 1-16 */
0779    } proc[NR_TASKS+NR_PROCS];
0780
0781    /* Bits for p_flags in proc[].  A process is runnable iff p_flags == 0 */
0782    #define P_SLOT_FREE      001    /* set when slot is not in use */
0783    #define NO_MAP           002    /* keeps unmapped forked child from running */
0784    #define SENDING          004    /* set when process blocked trying to send */
0785    #define RECEIVING        010    /* set when process blocked trying to recv */
0786
0787    #define proc_addr(n) &proc[NR_TASKS + n]
0788    #define NIL_PROC (struct proc *) 0
0789
0790    EXTERN struct proc *proc_ptr;    /* &proc[cur_proc] */
0791    EXTERN struct proc *bill_ptr;    /* ptr to process to bill for clock ticks */
0792    EXTERN struct proc *rdy_head[NQ];        /* pointers to ready list headers */
0793    EXTERN struct proc *rdy_tail[NQ];        /* pointers to ready list tails */
0794
0795    EXTERN unsigned busy_map;                 /* bit map of busy tasks */
0796    EXTERN message *task_mess[NR_TASKS+1]; /* ptrs to messages for busy tasks */
```

```
0800    /* The 'pc_psw' struct is machine dependent.  It must contain the information
0801     * pushed onto the stack by an interrupt, in the same format as the hardware
0802     * creates and expects.  It is used for storing the interrupt status after a
0803     * trap or interrupt, as well as for causing interrupts for signals.
0804     */
0805
0806
0807    #ifdef i8088
0808    struct pc_psw {
0809      int (*pc)();                     /* storage for program counter */
0810      phys_clicks cs;                  /* code segment register */
0811      unsigned psw;                    /* program status word */
0812    };
0813
0814    /* This struct is used to build data structure pushed by kernel upon signal. */
0815    struct sig_info {
0816      int signo;                       /* sig number at end of stack */
0817      struct pc_psw sigpcpsw;
0818    };
0819    #endif
```

```
0850      /* This file contains the main program of MINIX.  The routine main()
0851       * initializes the system and starts the ball rolling by setting up the proc
0852       * table, interrupt vectors, and scheduling each task to run to initialize
0853       * itself.
0854       *
0855       * The entries into this file are:
0856       *   main:              MINIX main program
0857       *   unexpected_int:    called when an interrupt to an unused vector < 16 occurs
0858       *   trap:              called when an unexpected trap to a vector >= 16 occurs
0859       *   panic:             abort MINIX due to a fatal error
0860       */

0862      #include "../h/const.h"
0863      #include "../h/type.h"
0864      #include "../h/callnr.h"
0865      #include "../h/com.h"
0866      #include "../h/error.h"
0867      #include "const.h"
0868      #include "type.h"
0869      #include "glo.h"
0870      #include "proc.h"

0872      #define SAFETY           8      /* margin of safety for stack overflow (ints)*/
0873      #define VERY_BIG     39328      /* must be bigger than kernel size (clicks) */
0874      #define BASE          1536      /* address where MINIX starts in memory */
0875      #define SIZES            8      /* sizes array has 8 entries */

0877      /*===========================================================================*
0878       *                              main                                         *
0879       *===========================================================================*/
0880      PUBLIC main()
0881      {
0882      /* Start the ball rolling. */

0884        register struct proc *rp;
0885        register int t;
0886        vir_clicks size;
0887        phys_clicks base_click, mm_base, previous_base;
0888        phys_bytes phys_b;
0889        extern unsigned sizes[8];      /* table filled in by build */
0890        extern int color, vec_table[], get_chrome(), (*task[])();
0891        extern int s_call(), disk_int(), tty_int(), clock_int(), disk_int();
0892        extern int lpr_int(), surprise(), trp();
0893        extern phys_bytes umap();

0895        /* Set up proc table entry for user processes.  Be very careful about
0896         * sp, since the 3 words prior to it will be clobbered when the kernel pushes
0897         * pc, cs, and psw onto the USER's stack when starting the user the first
0898         * time.  This means that with initial sp = 0x10, user programs must leave
0899         * the words at 0x000A, 0x000C, and 0x000E free.
```

```
0900        */
0901
0902        lock();                         /* we can't handle interrupts yet */
0903        base_click = BASE >> CLICK_SHIFT;
0904        size = sizes[0] + sizes[1];     /* kernel text + data size in clicks */
0905        mm_base = base_click + size;    /* place where MM starts (in clicks) */
0906
0907        for (rp = &proc[0]; rp <= &proc[NR_TASKS+LOW_USER]; rp++) {
0908            for (t=0; t< NR_REGS; t++) rp->p_reg[t] = 0100*t;        /* DEBUG */
0909            t = rp - proc - NR_TASKS;          /* task number */
0910            rp->p_sp = (rp < &proc[NR_TASKS] ? t_stack[NR_TASKS+t+1].stk : INIT_SP);
0911            rp->p_splimit = rp->p_sp;
0912            if (rp->p_splimit != INIT_SP)
0913                    rp->p_splimit -= (TASK_STACK_BYTES - SAFETY)/sizeof(int);
0914            rp->p_pcpsw.pc = task[t + NR_TASKS];
0915            if (rp->p_pcpsw.pc != 0 || t >= 0) ready(rp);
0916            rp->p_pcpsw.psw = INIT_PSW;
0917            rp->p_flags = 0;
0918
0919            /* Set up memory map for tasks and MM, FS, INIT. */
0920            if (t < 0) {
0921                    /* I/O tasks. */
0922                    rp->p_map[T].mem_len  = VERY_BIG;
0923                    rp->p_map[T].mem_phys = base_click;
0924                    rp->p_map[D].mem_len  = VERY_BIG;
0925                    rp->p_map[D].mem_phys = base_click + sizes[0];
0926                    rp->p_map[S].mem_len  = VERY_BIG;
0927                    rp->p_map[S].mem_phys = base_click + sizes[0] + sizes[1];
0928                    rp->p_map[S].mem_vir = sizes[0] + sizes[1];
0929            } else {
0930                    /* MM, FS, and INIT. */
0931                    previous_base = proc[NR_TASKS + t - 1].p_map[S].mem_phys;
0932                    rp->p_map[T].mem_len  = sizes[2*t + 2];
0933                    rp->p_map[T].mem_phys = (t == 0 ? mm_base : previous_base);
0934                    rp->p_map[D].mem_len  = sizes[2*t + 3];
0935                    rp->p_map[D].mem_phys = rp->p_map[T].mem_phys + sizes[2*t + 2];
0936                    rp->p_map[S].mem_vir  = sizes[2*t + 3];
0937                    rp->p_map[S].mem_phys = rp->p_map[D].mem_phys + sizes[2*t + 3];
0938            }
0939
0940    #ifdef i8088
0941            rp->p_reg[CS_REG] = rp->p_map[T].mem_phys;
0942            rp->p_reg[DS_REG] = rp->p_map[D].mem_phys;
0943            rp->p_reg[SS_REG] = rp->p_map[D].mem_phys;
0944            rp->p_reg[ES_REG] = rp->p_map[D].mem_phys;
0945    #endif
0946        }
0947
0948      proc[NR_TASKS+(HARDWARE)].p_sp = (int *) k_stack;
0949      proc[NR_TASKS+(HARDWARE)].p_sp += K_STACK_BYTES/2;
```

```
0950        proc[NR_TASKS+(HARDWARE)].p_splimit = (int *) k_stack;
0951        proc[NR_TASKS+(HARDWARE)].p_splimit += SAFETY/2;
0952
0953        for (rp = proc_addr(LOW_USER+1); rp < proc_addr(NR_PROCS); rp++)
0954              rp->p_flags = P_SLOT_FREE;
0955
0956        /* Determine if display is color or monochrome. */
0957        color = get_chrome();            /* 0 = mono, 1 = color */
0958
0959        /* Save the old interrupt vectors. */
0960        phys_b = umap(proc_addr(HARDWARE), D, (vir_bytes) vec_table, VECTOR_BYTES);
0961        phys_copy(0L, phys_b, (long) VECTOR_BYTES);   /* save all the vectors */
0962
0963        /* Set up the new interrupt vectors. */
0964        for (t = 0; t < 16; t++) set_vec(t, surprise, base_click);
0965        for (t = 16; t < 256; t++) set_vec(t, trp, base_click);
0966        set_vec(SYS_VECTOR, s_call, base_click);
0967        set_vec(CLOCK_VECTOR, clock_int, base_click);
0968        set_vec(KEYBOARD_VECTOR, tty_int, base_click);
0969        set_vec(FLOPPY_VECTOR, disk_int, base_click);
0970        set_vec(PRINTER_VECTOR, lpr_int, base_click);
0971
0972        /* Put a ptr to proc table in a known place so it can be found in /dev/mem */
0973        set_vec( (BASE - 4)/4, proc, (phys_clicks) 0);
0974
0975        bill_ptr = proc_addr(HARDWARE);       /* it has to point somewhere */
0976        pick_proc();
0977
0978        /* Now go to the assembly code to start running the current process. */
0979        port_out(INT_CTLMASK, 0);    /* do not mask out any interrupts in 8259A */
0980        restart();
0981    }


0984    /*===========================================================================*
0985     *                              unexpected_int                               *
0986     *===========================================================================*/
0987    PUBLIC unexpected_int()
0988    {
0989    /* A trap or interrupt has occurred that was not expected. */
0990      panic("Unexpected trap or interrupt.  cur_proc =", cur_proc);
0991    }


0994    /*===========================================================================*
0995     *                                 trap                                      *
0996     *===========================================================================*/
0997    PUBLIC trap()
0998    {
0999    /* A trap (vector >= 16) has occurred.  It was not expected. */
```

```
1000
1001        printf("\nUnexpected trap. ");
1002        printf("This may be due to accidentally including in your program\n");
1003        printf("a non-MINIX library routine that is trying to make a system call.\n");
1004        printf("pc = 0x%x    size of program = 0x%x\n",proc_ptr->p_pcpsw.pc,
1005                                            proc_ptr->p_map[D].mem_len<<4);
1006    }


1009    /*===========================================================================*
1010     *                                panic                                      *
1011     *===========================================================================*/
1012    PUBLIC panic(s,n)
1013    char *s;
1014    int n;
1015    {
1016    /* The system has run aground of a fatal error.  Terminate execution.
1017     * If the panic originated in MM or FS, the string will be empty and the
1018     * file system already syncked.  If the panic originates in the kernel, we are
1019     * kind of stuck.
1020     */
1021
1022      if (*s != 0) {
1023            printf("\nKernel panic: %s",s);
1024            if (n != NO_NUM) printf(" %d", n);
1025            printf("\n");
1026      }
1027      printf("\nType space to reboot\n");
1028      wreboot();
1029
1030    }

1032    #ifdef i8088
1033    /*===========================================================================*
1034     *                              set_vec                                       *
1035     *===========================================================================*/
1036    PRIVATE set_vec(vec_nr, addr, base_click)
1037    int vec_nr;                     /* which vector */
1038    int (*addr)();                  /* where to start */
1039    phys_clicks base_click;         /* click where kernel sits in memory */
1040    {
1041    /* Set up an interrupt vector. */
1042
1043      unsigned vec[2];
1044      unsigned u;
1045      phys_bytes phys_b;
1046      extern unsigned sizes[8];
1047
1048      /* Build the vector in the array 'vec'. */
1049      vec[0] = (unsigned) addr;
```

```
1050        vec[1] = (unsigned) base_click;
1051        u = (unsigned) vec;
1052
1053        /* Copy the vector into place. */
1054        phys_b = ( (phys_bytes) base_click + (phys_bytes) sizes[0]) << CLICK_SHIFT;
1055        phys_b += u;
1056        phys_copy(phys_b, (phys_bytes) 4*vec_nr, (phys_bytes) 4);
1057    }
1058    #endif
```

```
1100    This file is part of the lowest layer of the MINIX kernel.  All processing
1101    switching and message handling is done here and in file "proc.c".  This file
1102    is entered on every transition to the kernel, both for sending/receiving
1103    messages and for all interrupts.  In all cases, the trap or interrupt
1104    routine first calls save() to store the machine state in the proc table.
1105    Then the stack is switched to k_stack.  Finally, the real trap or interrupt
1106    handler (in C) is called.  When it returns, the interrupt routine jumps to
1107    restart, to run the process or task whose number is in 'cur_proc'.
1108
1109    The external entry points into this file are:
1110       s_call:    process or task wants to send or receive a message
1111       tty_int:   interrupt routine for each key depression and release
1112       lpr_int:   interrupt routine for each line printer interrupt
1113       disk_int:  disk interrupt routine
1114       clock_int: clock interrupt routine (HZ times per second)
1115       surprise:  all other interrupts < 16 are vectored here
1116       trp:       all traps with vector >= 16 are vectored here
1117       restart:   start running a task or process
1118
1119  #include "const.h"
1120  #include "../h/const.h"
1121  #include "../h/com.h"
1122
1123  | The following procedures are defined in this file and called from outside it.
1124  .globl _tty_int, _lpr_int, _clock_int, _disk_int
1125  .globl _s_call, _surprise, _trp, _restart
1126
1127  | The following external procedures are called in this file.
1128  .globl _main, _sys_call, _interrupt, _keyboard, _panic, _unexpected_int, _trap
1129  .globl _pr_char
1130
1131  | Variables and data structures.
1132  .globl _cur_proc, _proc_ptr, _scan_code, _int_mess, _k_stack, splimit
1133  .globl _sizes
1134
1135  | The following constants are offsets into the proc table.
1136  esreg = 14
1137  dsreg = 16
1138  csreg = 18
1139  ssreg = 20
1140  SP    = 22
1141  PC    = 24
1142  PSW   = 28
1143  SPLIM = 50
1144  OFF   = 18
1145  ROFF  = 12
1146
1147  .text
1148
1149
```

```
1150   |*==============================================================================*
1151   |*                              MINIX                                           *
1152   |*==============================================================================*
1153   MINIX:                            | this is the entry point for the MINIX kernel.
1154          jmp M.0                    | skip over the next few bytes
1155          .word 0,0                  | build puts DS at kernel text address 4
1156   M.0:   cli                        | disable interrupts
1157          mov ax,cs                  | set up segment registers
1158          mov ds,ax                  | set up ds
1159          mov ax,4                   | build has loaded this word with ds value
1160          mov ds,ax                  | ds now contains proper value
1161          mov ss,ax                  | ss now contains proper value
1162          mov _scan_code,bx          | save scan code for '=' key from bootstrap
1163          mov sp,#_k_stack           | set sp to point to the top of the
1164          add sp,#K_STACK_BYTES      |    kernel stack
1165
1166          call _main                 | start the main program of MINIX
1167   M.1:   jmp M.1                    | this should never be executed
1168
1169
1170   |*==============================================================================*
1171   |*                              s_call                                          *
1172   |*==============================================================================*
1173   _s_call:                          | System calls are vectored here.
1174          call save                  | save the machine state
1175          mov bp,_proc_ptr           | use bp to access sys call parameters
1176          push 2(bp)                 | push(pointer to user message) (was bx)
1177          push (bp)                  | push(src/dest) (was ax)
1178          push _cur_proc             | push caller
1179          push 4(bp)                 | push(SEND/RECEIVE/BOTH) (was cx)
1180          call _sys_call             | sys_call(function, caller, src_dest, m_ptr)
1181          jmp _restart               | jump to code to restart proc/task running
1182
1183
1184   |*==============================================================================*
1185   |*                              tty_int                                         *
1186   |*==============================================================================*
1187   _tty_int:                         | Interrupt routine for terminal input.
1188          call save                  | save the machine state
1189          call _keyboard             | process a keyboard interrupt
1190          jmp _restart               | continue execution
1191
1192
1193   |*==============================================================================*
1194   |*                              lpr_int                                         *
1195   |*==============================================================================*
1196   _lpr_int:                         | Interrupt routine for terminal input.
1197          call save                  | save the machine state
1198          call _pr_char              | process a line printer interrupt
1199          jmp _restart               | continue execution
```

```
1200    |*========================================================================*
1201    |*                              disk_int                                  *
1202    |*========================================================================*
1203    _disk_int:                      | Interrupt routine for the floppy disk.
1204            call save               | save the machine state
1205            mov _int_mess+2,*DISKINT| build message for disk task
1206            mov ax,#_int_mess       | prepare to call interrupt(FLOPPY, &intmess)
1207            push ax                 | push second parameter
1208            mov ax,*FLOPPY          | prepare to push first parameter
1209            push ax                 | push first parameter
1210            call _interrupt         | this is the call
1211            jmp _restart            | continue execution
1212
1213
1214    |*========================================================================*
1215    |*                              clock_int                                 *
1216    |*========================================================================*
1217    _clock_int:                     | Interrupt routine for the clock.
1218            call save               | save the machine state
1219            mov _int_mess+2,*CLOCK_TICK | build message for clock task
1220            mov ax,#_int_mess       | prepare to call interrupt(CLOCK, &intmess)
1221            push ax                 | push second parameter
1222            mov ax,*CLOCK           | prepare to push first parameter
1223            push ax                 | push first parameter
1224            call _interrupt         | this is the call
1225            jmp _restart            | continue execution
1226
1227
1228    |*========================================================================*
1229    |*                              surprise                                  *
1230    |*========================================================================*
1231    _surprise:                      | This is where unexpected interrupts come.
1232            call save               | save the machine state
1233            call _unexpected_int    | go panic
1234            jmp _restart            | never executed
1235
1236
1237    |*========================================================================*
1238    |*                               trp                                      *
1239    |*========================================================================*
1240    _trp:                           | This is where unexpected traps come.
1241            call save               | save the machine state
1242            call _trap              | print a message
1243            jmp _restart            | this error is not fatal
1244
1245
1246    |*========================================================================*
1247    |*                               save                                     *
1248    |*========================================================================*
1249    save:                           | save the machine state in the proc table.
```

```
1250            push ds                      | stack: psw/cs/pc/ret addr/ds
1251            push cs                      | prepare to restore ds
1252            pop ds                       | ds has now been set to cs
1253            mov ds,4                     | word 4 in kernel text space contains ds value
1254            pop ds_save                  | stack: psw/cs/pc/ret addr
1255            pop ret_save                 | stack: psw/cs/pc
1256            mov bx_save,bx               | save bx for later ; we need a free register
1257            mov bx,_proc_ptr             | start save set up; make bx point to save area
1258            add bx,*OFF                  | bx points to place to store cs
1259            pop PC-OFF(bx)               | store pc in proc table
1260            pop csreg-OFF(bx)            | store cs in proc table
1261            pop PSW-OFF(bx)              | store psw
1262            mov ssreg-OFF(bx),ss         | store ss
1263            mov SP-OFF(bx),sp            | sp as it was prior to interrupt
1264            mov sp,bx                    | now use sp to point into proc table/task save
1265            mov bx,ds                    | about to set ss
1266            mov ss,bx                    | set ss
1267            push ds_save                 | start saving all the registers, sp first
1268            push es                      | save es between sp and bp
1269            mov es,bx                    | es now references kernel memory too
1270            push bp                      | save bp
1271            push di                      | save di
1272            push si                      | save si
1273            push dx                      | save dx
1274            push cx                      | save cx
1275            push bx_save                 | save original bx
1276            push ax                      | all registers now saved
1277            mov sp,#_k_stack             | temporary stack for interrupts
1278            add sp,#K_STACK_BYTES        | set sp to top of temporary stack
1279            mov splimit,#_k_stack        | limit for temporary stack
1280            add splimit,#8               | splimit checks for stack overflow
1281            mov ax,ret_save              | ax = address to return to
1282            jmp (ax)                     | return to caller; Note: sp points to saved ax
1283
1284
1285    |*===========================================================================*
1286    |*                            restart                                        *
1287    |*===========================================================================*
1288    _restart:                            | This routine sets up and runs a proc or task.
1289            cmp _cur_proc,#IDLE          | restart user; if cur_proc = IDLE, go idle
1290            je idle                      | no user is runnable, jump to idle routine
1291            cli                          | disable interrupts
1292            mov sp,_proc_ptr             | return to user, fetch regs from proc table
1293            pop ax                       | start restoring registers
1294            pop bx                       | restore bx
1295            pop cx                       | restore cx
1296            pop dx                       | restore dx
1297            pop si                       | restore si
1298            pop di                       | restore di
1299            mov lds_low,bx               | lds_low contains bx
```

```
1300            mov bx,sp                  | bx points to saved bp register
1301            mov bp,SPLIM-ROFF(bx)      | splimit = p_splimit
1302            mov splimit,bp             | ditto
1303            mov bp,dsreg-ROFF(bx)      | bp = ds
1304            mov lds_low+2,bp           | lds_low+2 contains ds
1305            pop bp                     | restore bp
1306            pop es                     | restore es
1307            mov sp,SP-ROFF(bx)         | restore sp
1308            mov ss,ssreg-ROFF(bx)      | restore ss using the value of ds
1309            push PSW-ROFF(bx)          | push psw
1310            push csreg-ROFF(bx)        | push cs
1311            push PC-ROFF(bx)           | push pc
1312            lds bx,lds_low             | restore ds and bx in one fell swoop
1313            iret                       | return to user or task
1314
1315
1316    |*===========================================================================*
1317    |*                              idle                                         *
1318    |*===========================================================================*
1319    idle:                              | executed when there is no work
1320            sti                        | enable interrupts
1321    L3:     wait                       | just idle while waiting for interrupt
1322            jmp L3                     | loop until interrupt
1323
1324
1325
1326    |*===========================================================================*
1327    |*                              data                                         *
1328    |*===========================================================================*
1329    .data
1330    _sizes: .word 0x526F               | this must be the first data entry (magic #)
1331            .zerow 7                   | build table uses prev word and this space
1332    bx_save: .word 0                   | storage for bx
1333    ds_save: .word 0                   | storage for ds
1334    ret_save:.word 0                   | storage for return address
1335    lds_low: .word 0,0                 | storage used for restoring bx
1336    ttyomess: .asciz "RS232 interrupt"
1337
1338    .bss
1339    begbss:
```

```
1350   | This file contains a number of assembly code utility routines needed by the
1351   | kernel.  They are:
1352   |
1353   |     phys_copy:  copies data from anywhere to anywhere in memory
1354   |     cp_mess:    copies messages from source to destination
1355   |     port_out:   outputs data on an I/O port
1356   |     port_in:    inputs data from an I/O port
1357   |     lock:       disable interrupts
1358   |     unlock:     enable interrupts
1359   |     restore:    restore interrupts (enable/disabled) as they were before lock()
1360   |     build_sig:  build 4 word structure pushed onto stack for signals
1361   |     csv:        procedure prolog to save the registers
1362   |     cret:       procedure epilog to restore the registers
1363   |     get_chrome: returns 0 is display is monochrome, 1 if it is color
1364   |     vid_copy:   copy data to video ram (on color display during retrace only)
1365   |     get_byte:   reads a byte from a user program and returns it as value
1366   |     reboot:     reboot for CTRL-ALT-DEL
1367   |     wreboot:    wait for character then reboot
1368
1369   | The following procedures are defined in this file and called from outside it.
1370   .globl _phys_copy, _cp_mess, _port_out, _port_in, _lock, _unlock, _restore
1371   .globl _build_sig, csv, cret, _get_chrome, _vid_copy, _get_byte, _reboot
1372   .globl _wreboot
1373
1374   | The following external procedure is called in this file.
1375   .globl _panic
1376
1377   | Variables and data structures
1378   .globl _color, _cur_proc, _proc_ptr, splimit, _vec_table
1379
1380
1381   |*===========================================================================*
1382   |*                            phys_copy                                      *
1383   |*===========================================================================*
1384   | This routine copies a block of physical memory.  It is called by:
1385   |     phys_copy( (long) source, (long) destination, (long) bytecount)
1386
1387   _phys_copy:
1388           pushf                   | save flags
1389           cli                     | disable interrupts
1390           push bp                 | save the registers
1391           push ax                 | save ax
1392           push bx                 | save bx
1393           push cx                 | save cx
1394           push dx                 | save dx
1395           push si                 | save si
1396           push di                 | save di
1397           push ds                 | save ds
1398           push es                 | save es
1399           mov bp,sp               | set bp to point to saved es
```

```
1400
1401   L0:     mov ax,28(bp)         | ax = high-order word of 32-bit destination
1402           mov di,26(bp)         | di = low-order word of 32-bit destination
1403           mov cx,*4             | start extracting click number from dest
1404   L1:     rcr ax,*1             | click number is destination address / 16
1405           rcr di,*1             | it is used in segment register for copy
1406           loop L1               | 4 bits of high-order word are used
1407           mov es,di             | es = destination click
1408
1409           mov ax,24(bp)         | ax = high-order word of 32-bit source
1410           mov si,22(bp)         | si = low-order word of 32-bit source
1411           mov cx,*4             | start extracting click number from source
1412   L2:     rcr ax,*1             | click number is source address / 16
1413           rcr si,*1             | it is used in segment register for copy
1414           loop L2               | 4 bits of high-order word are used
1415           mov ds,si             | ds = source click
1416
1417           mov di,26(bp)         | di = low-order word of dest address
1418           and di,*0x000F        | di = offset from paragraph # in es
1419           mov si,22(bp)         | si = low-order word of source address
1420           and si,*0x000F        | si = offset from paragraph # in ds
1421
1422           mov dx,32(bp)         | dx = high-order word of byte count
1423           mov cx,30(bp)         | cx = low-order word of byte count
1424
1425           test cx,#0x8000       | if bytes >= 32768, only do 32768
1426           jnz L3               | per iteration
1427           test dx,#0xFFFF       | check high-order 17 bits to see if bytes
1428           jnz L3               | if bytes >= 32768 then go to L3
1429           jmp L4               | if bytes < 32768 then go to L4
1430   L3:     mov cx,#0x8000        | 0x8000 is unsigned 32768
1431   L4:     mov ax,cx            | save actual count used in ax; needed later
1432
1433           test cx,*0x0001       | should we copy a byte or a word at a time?
1434           jz L5                | jump if even
1435           rep                  | copy 1 byte at a time
1436           movb                 | byte copy
1437           jmp L6               | check for more bytes
1438
1439   L5:     shr cx,*1            | word copy
1440           rep                  | copy 1 word at a time
1441           movw                 | word copy
1442
1443   L6:     mov dx,32(bp)         | decr count, incr src & dst, iterate if needed
1444           mov cx,30(bp)         | dx || cx is 32-bit byte count
1445           xor bx,bx            | bx || ax is 32-bit actual count used
1446           sub cx,ax            | compute bytes - actual count
1447           sbb dx,bx            | dx || cx is # bytes not yet processed
1448           or cx,cx             | see if it is 0
1449           jnz L7               | if more bytes then go to L7
```

```
1450              or dx,dx                  | keep testing
1451              jnz L7                    | if loop done, fall through
1452
1453              pop es                    | restore all the saved registers
1454              pop ds                    | restore ds
1455              pop di                    | restore di
1456              pop si                    | restore si
1457              pop dx                    | restore dx
1458              pop cx                    | restore cx
1459              pop bx                    | restore bx
1460              pop ax                    | restore ax
1461              pop bp                    | restore bp
1462              popf                      | restore flags
1463              ret                       | return to caller
1464
1465    L7:       mov 32(bp),dx             | store decremented byte count back in mem
1466              mov 30(bp),cx             | as a long
1467              add 26(bp),ax             | increment destination
1468              adc 28(bp),bx             | carry from low-order word
1469              add 22(bp),ax             | increment source
1470              adc 24(bp),bx             | carry from low-order word
1471              jmp L0                    | start next iteration
1472
1473
1474    |*===========================================================================*
1475    |*                              cp_mess                                      *
1476    |*===========================================================================*
1477    | This routine is makes a fast copy of a message from anywhere in the address
1478    | space to anywhere else.  It also copies the source address provided as a
1479    | parameter to the call into the first word of the destination message.
1480    | It is called by:
1481    |    cp_mess(src, src_clicks, src_offset, dst_clicks, dst_offset)
1482    | where all 5 parameters are shorts (16-bits).
1483
1484    | Note that the message size, 'Msize' is in WORDS (not bytes) and must be set
1485    | correctly.  Changing the definition of message the type file and not changing
1486    | it here will lead to total disaster.
1487    | This routine destroys ax.  It preserves the other registers.
1488
1489    Msize = 12                          | size of a message in 16-bit words
1490    _cp_mess:
1491              push bp                   | save bp
1492              push es                   | save es
1493              push ds                   | save ds
1494              mov bp,sp                 | index off bp because machine can't use sp
1495              pushf                     | save flags
1496              cli                       | disable interrupts
1497              push cx                   | save cx
1498              push si                   | save si
1499              push di                   | save di
```

```
1500
1501          mov ax,8(bp)              | ax = process number of sender
1502          mov di,16(bp)             | di = offset of destination buffer
1503          mov es,14(bp)             | es = clicks of destination
1504          mov si,12(bp)             | si = offset of source message
1505          mov ds,10(bp)             | ds = clicks of source message
1506          seg es                    | segment override prefix
1507          mov (di),ax               | copy sender's process number to dest message
1508          add si,*2                 | don't copy first word
1509          add di,*2                 | don't copy first word
1510          mov cx,*Msize-1           | remember, first word doesn't count
1511          rep                       | iterate cx times to copy 11 words
1512          movw                      | copy the message
1513
1514          pop di                    | restore di
1515          pop si                    | restore si
1516          pop cx                    | restore cs
1517          popf                      | restore flags
1518          pop ds                    | restore ds
1519          pop es                    | restore es
1520          pop bp                    | restore bp
1521          ret                       | that's all folks!
1522
1523
1524    |*===========================================================================*
1525    |*                              port_out                                     *
1526    |*===========================================================================*
1527    | port_out(port, value) writes 'value' on the I/O port 'port'.
1528
1529    _port_out:
1530          push bx                    | save bx
1531          mov bx,sp                 | index off bx
1532          push ax                    | save ax
1533          push dx                    | save dx
1534          mov dx,4(bx)              | dx = port
1535          mov ax,6(bx)              | ax = value
1536          out                        | output 1 byte
1537          pop dx                     | restore dx
1538          pop ax                     | restore ax
1539          pop bx                     | restore bx
1540          ret                        | return to caller
1541
1542
1543    |*===========================================================================*
1544    |*                              port_in                                      *
1545    |*===========================================================================*
1546    | port_in(port, &value) reads from port 'port' and puts the result in 'value'.
1547    _port_in:
1548          push bx                    | save bx
1549          mov bx,sp                 | index off bx
```

```
1550          push ax                  | save ax
1551          push dx                  | save dx
1552          mov dx,4(bx)             | dx = port
1553          in                       | input 1 byte
1554          xorb ah,ah               | clear ah
1555          mov bx,6(bx)             | fetch address where byte is to go
1556          mov (bx),ax              | return byte to caller in param
1557          pop dx                   | restore dx
1558          pop ax                   | restore ax
1559          pop bx                   | restore bx
1560          ret                      | return to caller
1561
1562
1563  |*===========================================================================*
1564  |*                             lock                                          *
1565  |*===========================================================================*
1566  | Disable CPU interrupts.
1567  _lock:
1568          pushf                    | save flags on stack
1569          cli                      | disable interrupts
1570          pop lockvar              | save flags for possible restoration later
1571          ret                      | return to caller
1572
1573
1574  |*===========================================================================*
1575  |*                             unlock                                        *
1576  |*===========================================================================*
1577  | Enable CPU interrupts.
1578  _unlock:
1579          sti                      | enable interrupts
1580          ret                      | return to caller
1581
1582
1583  |*===========================================================================*
1584  |*                             restore                                       *
1585  |*===========================================================================*
1586  | Restore enable/disable bit to the value it had before last lock.
1587  _restore:
1588          push lockvar             | push flags as they were before previous lock
1589          popf                     | restore flags
1590          ret                      | return to caller
1591
1592
1593  |*===========================================================================*
1594  |*                             build_sig                                     *
1595  |*===========================================================================*
1596  |* Build a structure that is pushed onto the stack for signals.  It contains
1597  |* pc, psw, etc., and is machine dependent. The format is the same as generated
1598  |* by hardware interrupts, except that after the "interrupt", the signal number
1599  |* is also pushed.  The signal processing routine within the user space first
```

```
1600    | * pops the signal number, to see which function to call.  Then it calls the
1601    | * function.  Finally, when the function returns to the low-level signal
1602    | * handling routine, control is passed back to where it was prior to the signal
1603    | * by executing a return-from-interrupt instruction, hence the need for using
1604    | * the hardware generated interrupt format on the stack.  The call is:
1605    | *      build_sig(sig_stuff, rp, sig)
1606
1607    | Offsets within proc table
1608    PC    = 24
1609    csreg = 18
1610    PSW   = 28
1611
1612    _build_sig:
1613            push bp                 | save bp
1614            mov bp,sp               | set bp to sp for accessing params
1615            push bx                 | save bx
1616            push si                 | save si
1617            mov bx,4(bp)            | bx points to sig_stuff
1618            mov si,6(bp)            | si points to proc table entry
1619            mov ax,8(bp)            | ax = signal number
1620            mov (bx),ax             | put signal number in sig_stuff
1621            mov ax,PC(si)           | ax = signalled process' PC
1622            mov 2(bx),ax            | put pc in sig_stuff
1623            mov ax,csreg(si)        | ax = signalled process' cs
1624            mov 4(bx),ax            | put cs in sig_stuff
1625            mov ax,PSW(si)          | ax = signalled process' PSW
1626            mov 6(bx),ax            | put psw in sig_stuff
1627            pop si                  | restore si
1628            pop bx                  | restore bx
1629            pop bp                  | restore bp
1630            ret                     | return to caller
1631
1632
1633    | *===========================================================================*
1634    | *                         csv & cret                                        *
1635    | *===========================================================================*
1636    | This version of csv replaces the standard one.  It checks for stack overflow
1637    | within the kernel in a simpler way than is usually done. cret is standard.
1638    csv:
1639            pop bx                  | bx = return address
1640            push bp                 | stack old frame pointer
1641            mov bp,sp               | set new frame pointer to sp
1642            push di                 | save di
1643            push si                 | save si
1644            sub sp,ax               | ax = # bytes of local variables
1645            cmp sp,splimit          | has kernel stack grown too large
1646            jbe csv.1               | if sp is too low, panic
1647            jmp (bx)                | normal return: copy bx to program counter
1648
1649    csv.1:
```

```
1650              mov  splimit,#0              | prevent call to panic from aborting in csv
1651              mov  bx,_proc_ptr            | update rp->p_splimit
1652              mov  50(bx),#0               | rp->sp_limit = 0
1653              push _cur_proc               | task number
1654              mov  ax,#stkoverrun          | stack overran the kernel stack area
1655              push ax                      | push first parameter
1656              call _panic                  | call is: panic(stkoverrun, cur_proc)
1657              jmp  csv.1                   | this should not be necessary
1658
1659
1660      cret:
1661              lea   sp,*-4(bp)             | set sp to point to saved si
1662              pop   si                     | restore saved si
1663              pop   di                     | restore saved di
1664              pop   bp                     | restore bp
1665              ret                          | end of procedure
1666
1667      |*===========================================================================*
1668      |*                              get_chrome                                   *
1669      |*===========================================================================*
1670      | This routine calls the BIOS to find out if the display is monochrome or
1671      | color.  The drivers are different, as are the video ram addresses, so we
1672      | need to know.
1673      _get_chrome:
1674              int  0x11                    | call the BIOS to get equipment type
1675              andb al,#0x30                | isolate color/mono field
1676              cmpb al,*0x30                | 0x30 is monochrome
1677              je   getchr1                 | if monochrome then go to getchr1
1678              mov  ax,#1                    | color = 1
1679              ret                          | color return
1680      getchr1: xor ax,ax                   | mono = 0
1681              ret                          | monochrome return
1682
1683
1684      |*===========================================================================*
1685      |*                              vid_copy                                     *
1686      |*===========================================================================*
1687      | This routine takes a string of (character, attribute) pairs and writes them
1688      | onto the screen.  For a color display, the writing only takes places during
1689      | the vertical retrace interval, to avoid displaying garbage on the screen.
1690      | The call is:
1691      |      vid_copy(buffer, videobase, offset, words)
1692      | where
1693      |      'buffer'   is a pointer to the (character, attribute) pairs
1694      |      'videobase' is 0xB800 for color and 0xB000 for monochrome displays
1695      |      'offset'   tells where within video ram to copy the data
1696      |      'words'    tells how many words to copy
1697      | if buffer is zero, the fill char (BLANK) is used
1698
1699      BLANK = 0x0700                        | controls color of cursor on blank screen
```

```
1700
1701    _vid_copy:
1702            push bp                  | we need bp to access the parameters
1703            mov bp,sp                | set bp to sp for indexing
1704            push si                  | save the registers
1705            push di                  | save di
1706            push cx                  | save cx
1707            push dx                  | save dx
1708            push es                  | save es
1709            mov si,4(bp)             | si = pointer to data to be copied
1710            mov di,8(bp)             | di = offset within video ram
1711            mov cx,10(bp)            | cx = word count for copy loop
1712            mov dx,#0x3DA            | prepare to see if color display is retracing
1713
1714            test _color,*1           | skip vertical retrace test if display is mono
1715            jz vid.3                 | if monochrome then go to vid.2
1716
1717    |vid.1: in                       | with a color display, you can only copy to
1718    |       test al,*010             | the video ram during vertical retrace, so
1719    |       jnz vid.1                | wait for start of retrace period.  Bit 3 of
1720    vid.2:  in                       | 0x3DA is set during retrace.  First wait
1721            testb al,*010            | until it is off (no retrace), then wait
1722            jz vid.2                 | until it comes on (start of retrace)
1723
1724    vid.3:  pushf                    | copying may now start; save flags
1725            cli                      | interrupts just get in the way: disable them
1726            mov es,6(bp)             | load es now: int routines may ruin it
1727
1728            cmp si,#0                | si = 0 means blank the screen
1729            je vid.5                 | jump for blanking
1730            lock                     | this is a trick for the IBM PC simulator only
1731            nop                      | 'lock' indicates a video ram access
1732            rep                      | this is the copy loop
1733            movw                     | ditto
1734
1735    vid.4:  popf                     | restore flags
1736            pop es                   | restore registers
1737            pop dx                   | restore dx
1738            pop cx                   | restore cx
1739            pop di                   | restore di
1740            pop si                   | restore si
1741            pop bp                   | restore bp
1742            ret                      | return to caller
1743
1744    vid.5:  mov ax,#BLANK            | ax = blanking character
1745            rep                      | copy loop
1746            stow                     | blank screen
1747            jmp vid.4                | done
1748
1749
```

```
1750     |*===========================================================================*
1751     |*                              get_byte                                     *
1752     |*===========================================================================*
1753     | This routine is used to fetch a byte from anywhere in memory.
1754     | The call is:
1755     |       c = get_byte(seg, off)
1756     | where
1757     |       'seg' is the value to put in es
1758     |       'off' is the offset from the es value
1759     _get_byte:
1760             push bp                 | save bp
1761             mov bp,sp               | we need to access parameters
1762             push es                 | save es
1763             mov es,4(bp)            | load es with segment value
1764             mov bx,6(bp)            | load bx with offset from segment
1765             seg es                  | go get the byte
1766             movb al,(bx)            | al = byte
1767             xorb ah,ah              | ax = byte
1768             pop es                  | restore es
1769             pop bp                  | restore bp
1770             ret                     | return to caller
1771
1772
1773
1774
1775     |*===========================================================================*
1776     |*                         reboot & wreboot                                  *
1777     |*===========================================================================*
1778     | This code reboots the PC
1779
1780     _reboot:
1781             cli                     | disable interrupts
1782             mov ax,#0x20            | re-enable interrupt controller
1783             out 0x20
1784             call resvec             | restore the vectors in low core
1785             int 0x19                | reboot the PC
1786
1787     _wreboot:
1788             cli                     | disable interrupts
1789             mov ax,#0x20            | re-enable interrupt controller
1790             out 0x20
1791             call resvec             | restore the vectors in low core
1792             xor ax,ax               | wait for character before continuing
1793             int 0x16                | get char
1794             int 0x19                | reboot the PC
1795
1796     | Restore the interrupt vectors in low core.
1797     resvec: cld
1798             mov cx,#2*65
1799             mov si,#_vec_table
```

```
1800              xor di,di
1801              mov es,di
1802              rep
1803              movw
1804              ret
1805
1806      .data
1807      lockvar:        .word 0          | place to store flags for lock()/restore()
1808      splimit:        .word 0          | stack limit for current task (kernel only)
1809      stkoverrun:     .asciz "Kernel stack overrun, task = "
1810      _vec_table:     .zerow 130       | storage for interrupt vectors
```

```
1850    /* This file contains essentially all of the process and message handling.
1851     * It has two main entry points from the outside:
1852     *
1853     *   sys_call:   called when a process or task does SEND, RECEIVE or SENDREC
1854     *   interrupt: called by interrupt routines to send a message to task
1855     *
1856     * It also has five minor entry points:
1857     *
1858     *   ready:     put a process on one of the ready queues so it can be run
1859     *   unready:   remove a process from the ready queues
1860     *   sched:     a process has run too long; schedule another one
1861     *   mini_send: send a message (used by interrupt signals, etc.)
1862     *   pick_proc: pick a process to run (used by system initialization)
1863     */
1864
1865    #include "../h/const.h"
1866    #include "../h/type.h"
1867    #include "../h/callnr.h"
1868    #include "../h/com.h"
1869    #include "../h/error.h"
1870    #include "const.h"
1871    #include "type.h"
1872    #include "glo.h"
1873    #include "proc.h"
1874
1875    /*===========================================================================*
1876     *                              interrupt                                    *
1877     *===========================================================================*/
1878    PUBLIC interrupt(task, m_ptr)
1879    int task;                       /* number of task to be started */
1880    message *m_ptr;                 /* interrupt message to send to the task */
1881    {
1882    /* An interrupt has occurred.  Schedule the task that handles it. */
1883
1884      int i, n, old_map, this_bit;
1885
1886    #ifdef i8088
1887      /* Re-enable the 8259A interrupt controller. */
1888      port_out(INT_CTL, ENABLE);    /* this re-enables the 8259A controller chip */
1889    #endif
1890
1891      /* Try to send the interrupt message to the indicated task. */
1892      this_bit = 1 << (-task);
1893      if (mini_send(HARDWARE, task, m_ptr) != OK) {
1894            /* The message could not be sent to the task; it was not waiting. */
1895            old_map = busy_map;     /* save original map of busy tasks */
1896            if (task == CLOCK) {
1897                    lost_ticks++;
1898            } else {
1899                    busy_map |= this_bit;           /* mark task as busy */
```

```
1900                       task_mess[-task] = m_ptr;        /* record message pointer */
1901             }
1902       } else {
1903             /* Hardware interrupt was successfully sent as a message. */
1904             busy_map &= ~this_bit;  /* turn off the bit in case it was on */
1905             old_map = busy_map;
1906       }
1907
1908       /* See if any tasks that were previously busy are now listening for msgs. */
1909       if (old_map != 0) {
1910             for (i = 2; i <= NR_TASKS; i++) {
1911                   /* Check each task looking for one with a pending interrupt. */
1912                   if ( (old_map>>i) & 1) {
1913                         /* Task 'i' has a pending interrupt. */
1914                         n = mini_send(HARDWARE, -i, task_mess[i]);
1915                         if (n == OK) busy_map &= ~(1 << i);
1916                   }
1917             }
1918       }
1919
1920       /* If a task has just been readied and a user is running, run the task. */
1921       if (rdy_head[TASK_Q] != NIL_PROC && (cur_proc >= 0 || cur_proc == IDLE))
1922             pick_proc();
1923   }


1926   /*===========================================================================*
1927    *                              sys_call                                      *
1928    *===========================================================================*/
1929   PUBLIC sys_call(function, caller, src_dest, m_ptr)
1930   int function;                     /* SEND, RECEIVE, or BOTH */
1931   int caller;                       /* who is making this call */
1932   int src_dest;                     /* source to receive from or dest to send to */
1933   message *m_ptr;                   /* pointer to message */
1934   {
1935   /* The only system calls that exist in MINIX are sending and receiving
1936    * messages.  These are done by trapping to the kernel with an INT instruction.
1937    * The trap is caught and sys_call() is called to send or receive a message (or
1938    * both).
1939    */
1940
1941     register struct proc *rp;
1942     int n;
1943
1944     /* Check for bad system call parameters. */
1945     rp = proc_addr(caller);
1946     if (src_dest < -NR_TASKS || (src_dest >= NR_PROCS && src_dest != ANY) ) {
1947           rp->p_reg[RET_REG] = E_BAD_SRC;
1948           return;
1949     }
```

```
1950          if (function != BOTH && caller >= LOW_USER) {
1951                  rp->p_reg[RET_REG] = E_NO_PERM; /* users only do BOTH */
1952                  return;
1953          }
1954
1955          /* The parameters are ok. Do the call. */
1956          if (function & SEND) {
1957                  n = mini_send(caller, src_dest, m_ptr); /* func = SEND or BOTH */
1958                  if (function == SEND || n != OK) rp->p_reg[RET_REG] = n;
1959                  if (n != OK) return;      /* SEND failed */
1960          }
1961
1962          if (function & RECEIVE) {
1963                  n = mini_rec(caller, src_dest, m_ptr);        /* func = RECEIVE or BOTH */
1964                  rp->p_reg[RET_REG] = n;
1965          }
1966  }


1968  /*===========================================================================*
1969   *                              mini_send                                    *
1970   *===========================================================================*/
1971  PUBLIC int mini_send(caller, dest, m_ptr)
1972  int caller;                           /* who is trying to send a message? */
1973  int dest;                             /* to whom is message being sent? */
1974  message *m_ptr;                       /* pointer to message buffer */
1975  {
1976  /* Send a message from 'caller' to 'dest'.  If 'dest' is blocked waiting for
1977   * this message, copy the message to it and unblock 'dest'.  If 'dest' is not
1978   * waiting at all, or is waiting for another source, queue 'caller'.
1979   */
1980
1981          register struct proc *caller_ptr, *dest_ptr, *next_ptr;
1982          vir_bytes vb;                   /* message buffer pointer as vir_bytes */
1983          vir_clicks vlo, vhi;            /* virtual clicks containing message to send */
1984          vir_clicks len;                 /* length of data segment in clicks */
1985
1986          /* User processes are only allowed to send to FS and MM.  Check for this. */
1987          if (caller >= LOW_USER && (dest != FS_PROC_NR && dest != MM_PROC_NR))
1988                  return(E_BAD_DEST);
1989          caller_ptr = proc_addr(caller);        /* pointer to source's proc entry */
1990          dest_ptr = proc_addr(dest);     /* pointer to destination's proc entry */
1991          if (dest_ptr->p_flags & P_SLOT_FREE) return(E_BAD_DEST);       /* dead dest */
1992
1993          /* Check for messages wrapping around top of memory or outside data seg. */
1994          len = caller_ptr->p_map[D].mem_len;
1995          vb = (vir_bytes) m_ptr;
1996          vlo = vb >> CLICK_SHIFT;      /* vir click for bottom of message */
1997          vhi = (vb + MESS_SIZE - 1) >> CLICK_SHIFT;      /* vir click for top of message */
1998          if (vhi < vlo || vhi - caller_ptr->p_map[D].mem_vir >= len)return(E_BAD_ADDR);
1999
```

```
2000        /* Check to see if 'dest' is blocked waiting for this message. */
2001        if ( (dest_ptr->p_flags & RECEIVING) &&
2002                    (dest_ptr->p_getfrom == ANY || dest_ptr->p_getfrom == caller) )
2003            /* Destination is indeed waiting for this message. */
2004            cp_mess(caller, caller_ptr->p_map[D].mem_phys, m_ptr,
2005                            dest_ptr->p_map[D].mem_phys, dest_ptr->p_messbuf
2006            dest_ptr->p_flags &= ~RECEIVING;       /* deblock destination */
2007            if (dest_ptr->p_flags == 0) ready(dest_ptr);
2008        } else {
2009            /* Destination is not waiting.  Block and queue caller. */
2010            if (caller == HARDWARE) return(E_OVERRUN);
2011            caller_ptr->p_messbuf = m_ptr;
2012            caller_ptr->p_flags |= SENDING;
2013            unready(caller_ptr);
2014
2015            /* Process is now blocked.  Put in on the destination's queue. */
2016            if ( (next_ptr = dest_ptr->p_callerq) == NIL_PROC) {
2017                    dest_ptr->p_callerq = caller_ptr;
2018            } else {
2019                    while (next_ptr->p_sendlink != NIL_PROC)
2020                            next_ptr = next_ptr->p_sendlink;
2021                    next_ptr->p_sendlink = caller_ptr;
2022            }
2023            caller_ptr->p_sendlink = NIL_PROC;
2024        }
2025    return(OK);
2026 }


2029 /*===========================================================================*
2030  *                              mini_rec                                     *
2031  *===========================================================================*/
2032 PRIVATE int mini_rec(caller, src, m_ptr)
2033 int caller;                        /* process trying to get message */
2034 int src;                           /* which message source is wanted (or ANY) */
2035 message *m_ptr;                    /* pointer to message buffer */
2036 {
2037 /* A process or task wants to get a message.  If one is already queued,
2038  * acquire it and deblock the sender.  If no message from the desired source
2039  * is available, block the caller.  No need to check parameters for validity.
2040  * Users calls are always sendrec(), and mini_send() has checked already.
2041  * Calls from the tasks, MM, and FS are trusted.
2042  */
2043
2044    register struct proc *caller_ptr, *sender_ptr, *prev_ptr;
2045    int sender;
2046
2047    caller_ptr = proc_addr(caller);         /* pointer to caller's proc structure */
2048
2049    /* Check to see if a message from desired source is already available. */
```

```
2050        sender_ptr = caller_ptr->p_callerq;
2051        while (sender_ptr != NIL_PROC) {
2052              sender = sender_ptr - proc - NR_TASKS;
2053              if (src == ANY || src == sender) {
2054                    /* An acceptable message has been found. */
2055                    cp_mess(sender, sender_ptr->p_map[D].mem_phys, sender_ptr->p_messbuf,
2056                                      caller_ptr->p_map[D].mem_phys, m_ptr);
2057                    sender_ptr->p_flags &= ~SENDING;       /* deblock sender */
2058                    if (sender_ptr->p_flags == 0) ready(sender_ptr);
2059                    if (sender_ptr == caller_ptr->p_callerq)
2060                          caller_ptr->p_callerq = sender_ptr->p_sendlink;
2061                    else
2062                          prev_ptr->p_sendlink = sender_ptr->p_sendlink;
2063                    return(OK);
2064              }
2065              prev_ptr = sender_ptr;
2066              sender_ptr = sender_ptr->p_sendlink;
2067        }
2068
2069        /* No suitable message is available.  Block the process trying to receive. */
2070        caller_ptr->p_getfrom = src;
2071        caller_ptr->p_messbuf = m_ptr;
2072        caller_ptr->p_flags |= RECEIVING;
2073        unready(caller_ptr);
2074
2075        /* If MM has just blocked and there are kernel signals pending, now is the
2076         * time to tell MM about them, since it will be able to accept the message.
2077         */
2078        if (sig_procs > 0 && caller == MM_PROC_NR && src == ANY) inform(MM_PROC_NR);
2079        return(OK);
2080  }


2083  /*===========================================================================*
2084   *                              pick_proc                                    *
2085   *===========================================================================*/
2086  PUBLIC pick_proc()
2087  {
2088  /* Decide who to run now. */
2089
2090    register int q;                    /* which queue to use */
2091
2092    if (rdy_head[TASK_Q] != NIL_PROC) q = TASK_Q;
2093    else if (rdy_head[SERVER_Q] != NIL_PROC) q = SERVER_Q;
2094    else q = USER_Q;
2095
2096    /* Set 'cur_proc' and 'proc_ptr'. If system is idle, set 'cur_proc' to a
2097     * special value (IDLE), and set 'proc_ptr' to point to an unused proc table
2098     * slot, namely, that of task -1 (HARDWARE), so save() will have somewhere to
2099     * deposit the registers when a interrupt occurs on an idle machine.
```

```
2100        * Record previous process so that when clock tick happens, the clock task
2101        * can find out who was running just before it began to run.  (While the
2102        * clock task is running, 'cur_proc' = CLOCKTASK. In addition, set 'bill_ptr'
2103        * to always point to the process to be billed for CPU time.
2104        */
2105       prev_proc = cur_proc;
2106       if (rdy_head[q] != NIL_PROC) {
2107            /* Someone is runnable. */
2108            cur_proc = rdy_head[q] - proc - NR_TASKS;
2109            proc_ptr = rdy_head[q];
2110            if (cur_proc >= LOW_USER) bill_ptr = proc_ptr;
2111       } else {
2112            /* No one is runnable. */
2113            cur_proc = IDLE;
2114            proc_ptr = proc_addr(HARDWARE);
2115            bill_ptr = proc_ptr;
2116       }
2117    }

2119    /*===========================================================================*
2120     *                              ready                                         *
2121     *===========================================================================*/
2122    PUBLIC ready(rp)
2123    register struct proc *rp;          /* this process is now runnable */
2124    {
2125    /* Add 'rp' to the end of one of the queues of runnable processes. Three
2126     * queues are maintained:
2127     *    TASK_Q    - (highest priority) for runnable tasks
2128     *    SERVER_Q  - (middle priority) for MM and FS only
2129     *    USER_Q    - (lowest priority) for user processes
2130     */

2132       register int q;                  /* TASK_Q, SERVER_Q, or USER_Q */
2133       int r;

2135       lock();                          /* disable interrupts */
2136       r = (rp - proc) - NR_TASKS;    /* task or proc number */
2137       q = (r < 0 ? TASK_Q : r < LOW_USER ? SERVER_Q : USER_Q);

2139       /* See if the relevant queue is empty. */
2140       if (rdy_head[q] == NIL_PROC)
2141            rdy_head[q] = rp;           /* add to empty queue */
2142       else
2143            rdy_tail[q]->p_nextready = rp;  /* add to tail of nonempty queue */
2144       rdy_tail[q] = rp;               /* new entry has no successor */
2145       rp->p_nextready = NIL_PROC;
2146       restore();                       /* restore interrupts to previous state */
2147    }
```

```
2150     /*===========================================================================*
2151      *                              unready                                       *
2152      *===========================================================================*/
2153     PUBLIC unready(rp)
2154     register struct proc *rp;          /* this process is no longer runnable */
2155     {
2156     /* A process has blocked. */
2157
2158       register struct proc *xp;
2159       int r, q;
2160
2161       lock();                          /* disable interrupts */
2162       r = rp - proc - NR_TASKS;
2163       q = (r < 0 ? TASK_Q : r < LOW_USER ? SERVER_Q : USER_Q);
2164       if ( (xp = rdy_head[q]) == NIL_PROC) return;
2165       if (xp == rp) {
2166             /* Remove head of queue */
2167             rdy_head[q] = xp->p_nextready;
2168             pick_proc();
2169       } else {
2170             /* Search body of queue.  A process can be made unready even if it is
2171              * not running by being sent a signal that kills it.
2172              */
2173             while (xp->p_nextready != rp)
2174                     if ( (xp = xp->p_nextready) == NIL_PROC) return;
2175             xp->p_nextready = xp->p_nextready->p_nextready;
2176             while (xp->p_nextready != NIL_PROC) xp = xp->p_nextready;
2177             rdy_tail[q] = xp;
2178       }
2179       restore();                       /* restore interrupts to previous state */
2180     }


2183     /*===========================================================================*
2184      *                              sched                                         *
2185      *===========================================================================*/
2186     PUBLIC sched()
2187     {
2188     /* The current process has run too long.  If another low priority (user)
2189      * process is runnable, put the current process on the end of the user queue,
2190      * possibly promoting another user to head of the queue.
2191      */
2192
2193       lock();                          /* disable interrupts */
2194       if (rdy_head[USER_Q] == NIL_PROC) {
2195             restore();                 /* restore interrupts to previous state */
2196             return;
2197       }
2198
2199       /* One or more user processes queued. */
```

```
2200        rdy_tail[USER_Q]->p_nextready = rdy_head[USER_Q];
2201        rdy_tail[USER_Q] = rdy_head[USER_Q];
2202        rdy_head[USER_Q] = rdy_head[USER_Q]->p_nextready;
2203        rdy_tail[USER_Q]->p_nextready = NIL_PROC;
2204        pick_proc();
2205        restore();                       /* restore interrupts to previous state */
2206    }
```

```
2250   /* This file contains the drivers for four special files:
2251    *     /dev/null      - null device (data sink)
2252    *     /dev/mem       - absolute memory
2253    *     /dev/kmem      - kernel virtual memory
2254    *     /dev/ram       - RAM disk
2255    * It accepts three messages, for reading, for writing, and for
2256    * control. All use message format m2 and with these parameters:
2257    *
2258    *    m_type      DEVICE   PROC_NR    COUNT    POSITION  ADRRESS
2259    * ----------------------------------------------------------------
2260    * | DISK_READ  | device | proc nr | bytes  | offset  | buf ptr |
2261    * |------------+--------+---------+--------+---------+---------|
2262    * | DISK_WRITE | device | proc nr | bytes  | offset  | buf ptr |
2263    * |------------+--------+---------+--------+---------+---------|
2264    * | DISK_IOCTL | device |         | blocks | ram org |         |
2265    * ----------------------------------------------------------------
2266    *
2267    *
2268    * The file contains one entry point:
2269    *
2270    *    mem_task:  main entry when system is brought up
2271    *
2272    */
2273
2274   #include "../h/const.h"
2275   #include "../h/type.h"
2276   #include "../h/callnr.h"
2277   #include "../h/com.h"
2278   #include "../h/error.h"
2279   #include "const.h"
2280   #include "type.h"
2281   #include "proc.h"
2282
2283   #define NR_RAMS          4      /* number of RAM-type devices */
2284
2285   PRIVATE message mess;               /* message buffer */
2286   PRIVATE phys_bytes ram_origin[NR_RAMS]; /* origin of each RAM disk  */
2287   PRIVATE phys_bytes ram_limit[NR_RAMS];  /* limit of RAM disk per minor dev. */
2288
2289   /*===========================================================================*
2290    *                            mem_task                                       *
2291    *===========================================================================*/
2292   PUBLIC mem_task()
2293   {
2294   /* Main program of the disk driver task. */
2295
2296     int r, caller, proc_nr;
2297     extern unsigned sizes[8];
2298     extern phys_clicks get_base();
2299
```

```
2300
2301        /* Initialize this task. */
2302        ram_origin[KMEM_DEV] = (phys_bytes) get_base() << CLICK_SHIFT;
2303        ram_limit[KMEM_DEV] = (sizes[0] + sizes[1]) << CLICK_SHIFT;
2304        ram_limit[MEM_DEV] = MEM_BYTES;
2305
2306        /* Here is the main loop of the memory task.  It waits for a message, carries
2307         * it out, and sends a reply.
2308         */
2309        while (TRUE) {
2310            /* First wait for a request to read or write. */
2311            receive(ANY, &mess);
2312            if (mess.m_source < 0)
2313                    panic("mem task got message from ", mess.m_source);
2314            caller = mess.m_source;
2315            proc_nr = mess.PROC_NR;
2316
2317            /* Now carry out the work.  It depends on the opcode. */
2318            switch(mess.m_type) {
2319                case DISK_READ:     r = do_mem(&mess);      break;
2320                case DISK_WRITE:    r = do_mem(&mess);      break;
2321                case DISK_IOCTL:    r = do_setup(&mess);    break;
2322                default:            r = EINVAL;             break;
2323            }
2324
2325            /* Finally, prepare and send the reply message. */
2326            mess.m_type = TASK_REPLY;
2327            mess.REP_PROC_NR = proc_nr;
2328            mess.REP_STATUS = r;
2329            send(caller, &mess);
2330        }
2331    }


2334    /*===========================================================================*
2335     *                              do_mem                                        *
2336     *===========================================================================*/
2337    PRIVATE int do_mem(m_ptr)
2338    register message *m_ptr;            /* pointer to read or write message */
2339    {
2340    /* Read or write /dev/null, /dev/mem, /dev/kmem, or /dev/ram. */
2341
2342      int device, count;
2343      phys_bytes mem_phys, user_phys;
2344      struct proc *rp;
2345      extern phys_clicks get_base();
2346      extern phys_bytes umap();
2347
2348      /* Get minor device number and check for /dev/null. */
2349      device = m_ptr->DEVICE;
```

```
2350        if (device < 0 || device >= NR_RAMS) return(ENXIO);   /* bad minor device */
2351        if (device == NULL_DEV) return(m_ptr->m_type == DISK_READ ? 0 : m_ptr->COUNT);
2352
2353        /* Set up 'mem_phys' for /dev/mem, /dev/kmem, or /dev/ram. */
2354        if (m_ptr->POSITION < 0) return(ENXIO);
2355        mem_phys = ram_origin[device] + m_ptr->POSITION;
2356        if (mem_phys > ram_limit[device]) return(0);
2357        count = m_ptr->COUNT;
2358        if(mem_phys + count > ram_limit[device]) count = ram_limit[device] - mem_phys;
2359
2360        /* Determine address where data is to go or to come from. */
2361        rp = proc_addr(m_ptr->PROC_NR);
2362        user_phys = umap(rp, D, (vir_bytes) m_ptr->ADDRESS, (vir_bytes) count);
2363        if (user_phys == 0) return(E_BAD_ADDR);
2364
2365        /* Copy the data. */
2366        if (m_ptr->m_type == DISK_READ)
2367             phys_copy(mem_phys, user_phys, (long) count);
2368        else
2369             phys_copy(user_phys, mem_phys, (long) count);
2370      return(count);
2371    }


2374    /*===========================================================================*
2375     *                              do_setup                                      *
2376     *===========================================================================*/
2377    PRIVATE int do_setup(m_ptr)
2378    message *m_ptr;                        /* pointer to read or write message */
2379    {
2380    /* Set parameters for one of the disk RAMs. */
2381
2382      int device;
2383
2384      device = m_ptr->DEVICE;
2385      if (device < 0 || device >= NR_RAMS) return(ENXIO);   /* bad minor device */
2386      ram_origin[device] = m_ptr->POSITION;
2387      ram_limit[device] = m_ptr->POSITION + (long) m_ptr->COUNT * BLOCK_SIZE;
2388      return(OK);
2389    }
```

```
2400     /* This file contains a driver for a Floppy Disk Controller (FDC) using the
2401      * NEC PD765 chip.  The driver supports two operations: read a block and
2402      * write a block.  It accepts two messages, one for reading and one for
2403      * writing, both using message format m2 and with the same parameters:
2404      *
2405      *    m_type     DEVICE    PROC_NR    COUNT    POSITION  ADRRESS
2406      * ----------------------------------------------------------------
2407      * | DISK_READ  | device  | proc nr  | bytes  | offset  | buf ptr |
2408      * |------------+---------+----------+--------+---------+---------|
2409      * | DISK_WRITE | device  | proc nr  | bytes  | offset  | buf ptr |
2410      * ----------------------------------------------------------------
2411      *
2412      * The file contains one entry point:
2413      *
2414      *    floppy_task:       main entry when system is brought up
2415      *
2416      */
2417
2418     #include "../h/const.h"
2419     #include "../h/type.h"
2420     #include "../h/callnr.h"
2421     #include "../h/com.h"
2422     #include "../h/error.h"
2423     #include "const.h"
2424     #include "type.h"
2425     #include "proc.h"
2426
2427     /* I/O Ports used by floppy disk task. */
2428     #define DOR            0x3F2    /* motor drive control bits */
2429     #define FDC_STATUS     0x3F4    /* floppy disk controller status register */
2430     #define FDC_DATA       0x3F5    /* floppy disk controller data register */
2431     #define DMA_ADDR       0x004    /* port for low 16 bits of DMA address */
2432     #define DMA_TOP        0x081    /* port for top 4 bits of 20-bit DMA addr */
2433     #define DMA_COUNT      0x005    /* port for DMA count (count =  bytes - 1) */
2434     #define DMA_M2         0x00C    /* DMA status port */
2435     #define DMA_M1         0x00B    /* DMA status port */
2436     #define DMA_INIT       0x00A    /* DMA init port */
2437
2438     /* Status registers returned as result of operation. */
2439     #define ST0            0x00     /* status register 0 */
2440     #define ST1            0x01     /* status register 1 */
2441     #define ST2            0x02     /* status register 2 */
2442     #define ST3            0x00     /* status register 3 (return by DRIVE_SENSE) */
2443     #define ST_CYL         0x03     /* slot where controller reports cylinder */
2444     #define ST_HEAD        0x04     /* slot where controller reports head */
2445     #define ST_SEC         0x05     /* slot where controller reports sector */
2446     #define ST_PCN         0x01     /* slot where controller reports present cyl */
2447
2448     /* Fields within the I/O ports. */
2449     #define MASTER         0x80     /* used to see who is master */
```

```
2450    #define DIRECTION        0x40     /* is FDC trying to read or write? */
2451    #define CTL_BUSY         0x10     /* used to see when controller is busy */
2452    #define CTL_ACCEPTING    0x80     /* bit pattern FDC gives when idle */
2453    #define MOTOR_MASK       0xF0     /* these bits control the motors in DOR */
2454    #define ENABLE_INT       0x0C     /* used for setting DOR port */
2455    #define ST0_BITS         0xF8     /* check top 5 bits of seek status */
2456    #define ST3_FAULT        0x80     /* if this bit is set, drive is sick */
2457    #define ST3_WR_PROTECT   0x40     /* set when diskette is write protected */
2458    #define ST3_READY        0x20     /* set when drive is ready */
2459    #define TRANS_ST0        0x00     /* top 5 bits of ST0 for READ/WRITE */
2460    #define SEEK_ST0         0x20     /* top 5 bits of ST0 for SEEK */
2461    #define BAD_SECTOR       0x05     /* if these bits are set in ST1, recalibrate */
2462    #define BAD_CYL          0x1F     /* if any of these bits are set, recalibrate */
2463    #define WRITE_PROTECT    0x02     /* bit is set if diskette is write protected */
2464    #define CHANGE           0xC0     /* value returned by FDC after reset */
2465
2466    /* Floppy disk controller command bytes. */
2467    #define FDC_SEEK         0x0F     /* command the drive to seek */
2468    #define FDC_READ         0xE6     /* command the drive to read */
2469    #define FDC_WRITE        0xC5     /* command the drive to write */
2470    #define FDC_SENSE        0x08     /* command the controller to tell its status */
2471    #define FDC_RECALIBRATE  0x07     /* command the drive to go to cyl 0 */
2472    #define FDC_SPECIFY      0x03     /* command the drive to accept params */
2473
2474    /* DMA channel commands. */
2475    #define DMA_READ         0x46     /* DMA read opcode */
2476    #define DMA_WRITE        0x4A     /* DMA write opcode */
2477
2478    /* Parameters for the disk drive. */
2479    #define SECTOR_SIZE      512      /* physical sector size in bytes */
2480    #define NR_SECTORS       0x09     /* number of sectors per track */
2481    #define NR_HEADS         0x02     /* two heads (i.e., two tracks/cylinder) */
2482    #define GAP              0x2A     /* intersector gap size */
2483    #define DTL              0xFF     /* determines data length (sector size) */
2484    #define SPEC1            0xDF     /* first parameter to SPECIFY */
2485    #define SPEC2            0x02     /* second parameter to SPECIFY */
2486
2487    #define MOTOR_OFF        3*HZ     /* how long to wait before stopping motor */
2488    #define MOTOR_START      HZ/4     /* how long does it take motor to start up? */
2489
2490    /* Error codes */
2491    #define ERR_SEEK         -1       /* bad seek */
2492    #define ERR_TRANSFER     -2       /* bad transfer */
2493    #define ERR_STATUS       -3       /* something wrong when getting status */
2494    #define ERR_RECALIBRATE  -4       /* recalibrate didn't work properly */
2495    #define ERR_WR_PROTECT   -5       /* diskette is write protected */
2496    #define ERR_DRIVE        -6       /* something wrong with a drive */
2497
2498    /* Miscellaneous. */
2499    #define MOTOR_RUNNING    0xFF     /* message type for clock interrupt */
```

```
2500    #define MAX_ERRORS        10      /* how often to try rd/wt before quitting */
2501    #define MAX_RESULTS        8      /* max number of bytes controller returns */
2502    #define NR_DRIVES          2      /* maximum number of drives */
2503    #define DIVISOR          128      /* used for sector size encoding */
2504    #define MAX_FDC_RETRY    100      /* max # times to try to output to FDC */
2505    #define NR_BLOCKS        720      /* number of blocks on 9 sector diskette */
2506
2507    /* Variables. */
2508    PRIVATE struct floppy {           /* main drive struct, one entry per drive */
2509      int fl_opcode;                  /* DISK_READ or DISK_WRITE */
2510      int fl_curcyl;                  /* current cylinder */
2511      int fl_procnr;                  /* which proc wanted this operation? */
2512      int fl_drive;                   /* drive number addressed */
2513      int fl_cylinder;                /* cylinder number addressed */
2514      int fl_sector;                  /* sector addressed */
2515      int fl_head;                    /* head number addressed */
2516      int fl_count;                   /* byte count */
2517      vir_bytes fl_address;           /* user virtual address */
2518      char fl_results[MAX_RESULTS];   /* the controller can give lots of output */
2519      char fl_calibration;            /* CALIBRATED or UNCALIBRATED */
2520    } floppy[NR_DRIVES];
2521
2522    #define UNCALIBRATED       0      /* drive needs to be calibrated at next use */
2523    #define CALIBRATED         1      /* no calibration needed */
2524
2525    PRIVATE int motor_status;         /* current motor status is in 4 high bits */
2526    PRIVATE int motor_goal;           /* desired motor status is in 4 high bits */
2527    PRIVATE int prev_motor;           /* which motor was started last */
2528    PRIVATE int need_reset;           /* set to 1 when controller must be reset */
2529    PRIVATE int initialized;          /* set to 1 after first successful transfer */
2530    PRIVATE int steps_per_cyl = 1;    /* # pulses to give stepping motor per cyl */
2531
2532    PRIVATE message mess;             /* message buffer for in and out */
2533
2534    PRIVATE char len[] = {-1,0,1,-1,2,-1,-1,3,-1,-1,-1,-1,-1,-1,-1,4};
2535    PRIVATE char interleave[] = {1,2,3,4,5,6,7,8,9};
2536
2537    /*===========================================================================*
2538     *                              floppy_task                                  *
2539     *===========================================================================*/
2540    PUBLIC floppy_task()
2541    {
2542    /* Main program of the floppy disk driver task. */
2543
2544      int r, caller, proc_nr;
2545
2546      /* Here is the main loop of the disk task.  It waits for a message, carries
2547       * it out, and sends a reply.
2548       */
2549      while (TRUE) {
```

```
2550                /* First wait for a request to read or write a disk block. */
2551                receive(ANY, &mess);    /* get a request to do some work */
2552                if (mess.m_source < 0)
2553                        panic("disk task got message from ", mess.m_source);
2554                caller = mess.m_source;
2555                proc_nr = mess.PROC_NR;
2556
2557                /* Now carry out the work. */
2558                switch(mess.m_type) {
2559                    case DISK_READ:    r = do_rdwt(&mess);    break;
2560                    case DISK_WRITE:   r = do_rdwt(&mess);    break;
2561                    default:           r = EINVAL;            break;
2562                }
2563
2564                /* Finally, prepare and send the reply message. */
2565                mess.m_type = TASK_REPLY;
2566                mess.REP_PROC_NR = proc_nr;
2567                mess.REP_STATUS = r;    /* # of bytes transferred or error code */
2568                send(caller, &mess);    /* send reply to caller */
2569        }
2570    }


2573    /*===========================================================================*
2574     *                              do_rdwt                                       *
2575     *===========================================================================*/
2576    PRIVATE int do_rdwt(m_ptr)
2577    message *m_ptr;                      /* pointer to read or write message */
2578    {
2579    /* Carry out a read or write request from the disk. */
2580      register struct floppy *fp;
2581      int r, drive, errors, stop_motor();
2582      long block;
2583
2584      /* Decode the message parameters. */
2585      drive = m_ptr->DEVICE;
2586      if (drive < 0 || drive >= NR_DRIVES) return(EIO);
2587      fp = &floppy[drive];               /* 'fp' points to entry for this drive */
2588      fp->fl_drive = drive;              /* save drive number explicitly */
2589      fp->fl_opcode = m_ptr->m_type;         /* DISK_READ or DISK_WRITE */
2590      if (m_ptr->POSITION % BLOCK_SIZE != 0) return(EINVAL);
2591      block = m_ptr->POSITION/SECTOR_SIZE;
2592      if (block >= NR_BLOCKS) return(0);
2593      fp->fl_cylinder = (int) (block / (NR_HEADS * NR_SECTORS));
2594      fp->fl_sector = (int) interleave[block % NR_SECTORS];
2595      fp->fl_head = (int) (block % (NR_HEADS*NR_SECTORS) )/NR_SECTORS;
2596      fp->fl_count = m_ptr->COUNT;
2597      fp->fl_address = (vir_bytes) m_ptr->ADDRESS;
2598      fp->fl_procnr = m_ptr->PROC_NR;
2599      if (fp->fl_count != BLOCK_SIZE) return(EINVAL);
```

```
2600
2601        errors = 0;
2602
2603        /* This loop allows a failed operation to be repeated. */
2604        while (errors <= MAX_ERRORS) {
2605
2606                /* If a lot of errors occur when 'initialized' is 0, it probably
2607                 * means that we are trying at the wrong density.  Try another one.
2608                 * Increment 'errors' here since loop is aborted on error.
2609                 */
2610                errors++;                 /* increment count once per loop cycle */
2611                if (initialized == 0 && errors == MAX_ERRORS && fp->fl_cylinder > 0) {
2612                        if (steps_per_cyl > 1) {
2613                                panic("Unreadable diskette (drive density?)", NO_NUM);
2614                        } else {
2615                                steps_per_cyl++;
2616                                errors = 0;
2617                        }
2618                }
2619
2620                /* First check to see if a reset is needed. */
2621                if (need_reset) reset();
2622
2623                /* Now set up the DMA chip. */
2624                dma_setup(fp);
2625
2626                /* See if motor is running; if not, turn it on and wait */
2627                start_motor(fp);
2628
2629                /* If we are going to a new cylinder, perform a seek. */
2630                r = seek(fp);
2631                if (r != OK) continue;  /* if error, try again */
2632
2633                /* Perform the transfer. */
2634                r = transfer(fp);
2635                if (r == OK) break;     /* if successful, exit loop */
2636                if (r == ERR_WR_PROTECT) break; /* retries won't help */
2637
2638        }
2639
2640        /* Start watch_dog timer to turn motor off in a few seconds */
2641        motor_goal = ENABLE_INT;      /* when timer goes off, kill all motors */
2642        clock_mess(MOTOR_OFF, stop_motor);
2643        if (r == OK && fp->fl_cylinder > 0) initialized = 1;  /* seek works */
2644        return(r == OK ? BLOCK_SIZE : EIO);
2645    }
```

```
2650     /*===========================================================================*
2651      *                              dma_setup                                    *
2652      *===========================================================================*/
2653     PRIVATE dma_setup(fp)
2654     struct floppy *fp;                   /* pointer to the drive struct */
2655     {
2656     /* The IBM PC can perform DMA operations by using the DMA chip.  To use it,
2657      * the DMA (Direct Memory Access) chip is loaded with the 20-bit memory address
2658      * to be read from or written to, the byte count minus 1, and a read or write
2659      * opcode.  This routine sets up the DMA chip.  Note that the chip is not
2660      * capable of doing a DMA across a 64K boundary (e.g., you can't read a
2661      * 512-byte block starting at physical address 65520).
2662      */
2663
2664       int mode, low_addr, high_addr, top_addr, low_ct, high_ct, top_end;
2665       vir_bytes vir, ct;
2666       phys_bytes user_phys;
2667       extern phys_bytes umap();
2668
2669       mode = (fp->fl_opcode == DISK_READ ? DMA_READ : DMA_WRITE);
2670       vir = (vir_bytes) fp->fl_address;
2671       ct = (vir_bytes) fp->fl_count;
2672       user_phys = umap(proc_addr(fp->fl_procnr), D, vir, ct);
2673       low_addr  = (int) (user_phys >>  0) & BYTE;
2674       high_addr = (int) (user_phys >>  8) & BYTE;
2675       top_addr  = (int) (user_phys >> 16) & BYTE;
2676       low_ct  = (int) ( (ct - 1) >> 0) & BYTE;
2677       high_ct = (int) ( (ct - 1) >> 8) & BYTE;
2678
2679       /* Check to see if the transfer will require the DMA address counter to
2680        * go from one 64K segment to another.  If so, do not even start it, since
2681        * the hardware does not carry from bit 15 to bit 16 of the DMA address.
2682        * Also check for bad buffer address.  These errors mean FS contains a bug.
2683        */
2684       if (user_phys == 0) panic("FS gave floppy disk driver bad addr", (int) vir);
2685       top_end = (int) (((user_phys + ct - 1) >> 16) & BYTE);
2686       if (top_end != top_addr) panic("Trying to DMA across 64K boundary", top_addr);
2687
2688       /* Now set up the DMA registers. */
2689       lock();
2690       port_out(DMA_M2, mode);        /* set the DMA mode */
2691       port_out(DMA_M1, mode);        /* set it again */
2692       port_out(DMA_ADDR, low_addr); /* output low-order 8 bits */
2693       port_out(DMA_ADDR, high_addr);/* output next 8 bits */
2694       port_out(DMA_TOP, top_addr);  /* output highest 4 bits */
2695       port_out(DMA_COUNT, low_ct);  /* output low 8 bits of count - 1 */
2696       port_out(DMA_COUNT, high_ct); /* output high 8 bits of count - 1 */
2697       unlock();
2698       port_out(DMA_INIT, 2);        /* initialize DMA */
2699     }
```

```
2700   /*===========================================================================*
2701    *                            start_motor                                    *
2702    *===========================================================================*/
2703   PRIVATE start_motor(fp)
2704   struct floppy *fp;                  /* pointer to the drive struct */
2705   {
2706   /* Control of the floppy disk motors is a big pain.  If a motor is off, you
2707    * have to turn it on first, which takes 1/2 second.  You can't leave it on
2708    * all the time, since that would wear out the diskette.  However, if you turn
2709    * the motor off after each operation, the system performance will be awful.
2710    * The compromise used here is to leave it on for a few seconds after each
2711    * operation.  If a new operation is started in that interval, it need not be
2712    * turned on again.  If no new operation is started, a timer goes off and the
2713    * motor is turned off.  I/O port DOR has bits to control each of 4 drives.
2714    * Interrupts must be disabled temporarily to prevent clock interrupt from
2715    * turning off motors while we are testing the bits.
2716    */
2717
2718     int motor_bit, running, send_mess();
2719
2720     lock();                            /* no interrupts while checking out motor */
2721     motor_bit = 1 << (fp->fl_drive + 4);  /* bit mask for this drive */
2722     motor_goal = motor_bit | ENABLE_INT | fp->fl_drive;
2723     if (motor_status & prev_motor) motor_goal |= prev_motor;
2724     running = motor_status & motor_bit;   /* nonzero if this motor is running */
2725     port_out(DOR, motor_goal);
2726     motor_status = motor_goal;
2727     prev_motor = motor_bit;            /* record motor started for next time */
2728     unlock();
2729
2730     /* If the motor was already running, we don't have to wait for it. */
2731     if (running) return;               /* motor was already running */
2732     clock_mess(MOTOR_START, send_mess);  /* motor was not running */
2733     receive(CLOCK, &mess);             /* wait for clock interrupt */
2734   }


2737   /*===========================================================================*
2738    *                            stop_motor                                     *
2739    *===========================================================================*/
2740   PRIVATE stop_motor()
2741   {
2742   /* This routine is called by the clock interrupt after several seconds have
2743    * elapsed with no floppy disk activity.  It checks to see if any drives are
2744    * supposed to be turned off, and if so, turns them off.
2745    */
2746
2747     if ( (motor_goal & MOTOR_MASK) != (motor_status & MOTOR_MASK) ) {
2748           port_out(DOR, motor_goal);
2749           motor_status = motor_goal;
```

```
2750       }
2751    }


2754    /*===========================================================================*
2755     *                              seek                                          *
2756     *===========================================================================*/
2757    PRIVATE int seek(fp)
2758    struct floppy *fp;                 /* pointer to the drive struct */
2759    {
2760    /* Issue a SEEK command on the indicated drive unless the arm is already
2761     * positioned on the correct cylinder.
2762     */
2763
2764      int r;
2765
2766      /* Are we already on the correct cylinder? */
2767      if (fp->fl_calibration == UNCALIBRATED)
2768            if (recalibrate(fp) != OK) return(ERR_SEEK);
2769      if (fp->fl_curcyl == fp->fl_cylinder) return(OK);
2770
2771      /* No.  Wrong cylinder.  Issue a SEEK and wait for interrupt. */
2772      fdc_out(FDC_SEEK);                  /* start issuing the SEEK command */
2773      fdc_out( (fp->fl_head << 2) | fp->fl_drive);
2774      fdc_out(fp->fl_cylinder * steps_per_cyl);
2775      if (need_reset) return(ERR_SEEK);       /* if controller is sick, abort seek */
2776      receive(HARDWARE, &mess);
2777
2778      /* Interrupt has been received.  Check drive status. */
2779      fdc_out(FDC_SENSE);                 /* probe FDC to make it return status */
2780      r = fdc_results(fp);                /* get controller status bytes */
2781      if ( (fp->fl_results[ST0] & ST0_BITS) != SEEK_ST0) r = ERR_SEEK;
2782      if (fp->fl_results[ST1] != fp->fl_cylinder * steps_per_cyl) r = ERR_SEEK;
2783      if (r != OK)
2784            if (recalibrate(fp) != OK) return(ERR_SEEK);
2785      return(r);
2786    }


2789    /*===========================================================================*
2790     *                              transfer                                     *
2791     *===========================================================================*/
2792    PRIVATE int transfer(fp)
2793    register struct floppy *fp;      /* pointer to the drive struct */
2794    {
2795    /* The drive is now on the proper cylinder.  Read or write 1 block. */
2796
2797      int r, s, op;
2798
2799      /* Never attempt a transfer if the drive is uncalibrated or motor is off. */
```

```
2800        if (fp->fl_calibration == UNCALIBRATED) return(ERR_TRANSFER);
2801        if ( ( (motor_status>>(fp->fl_drive+4)) & 1) == 0) return(ERR_TRANSFER);
2802
2803        /* The command is issued by outputing 9 bytes to the controller chip. */
2804        op = (fp->fl_opcode == DISK_READ ? FDC_READ : FDC_WRITE);
2805        fdc_out(op);                    /* issue the read or write command */
2806        fdc_out( (fp->fl_head << 2) | fp->fl_drive);
2807        fdc_out(fp->fl_cylinder);       /* tell controller which cylinder */
2808        fdc_out(fp->fl_head);           /* tell controller which head */
2809        fdc_out(fp->fl_sector);         /* tell controller which sector */
2810        fdc_out( (int) len[SECTOR_SIZE/DIVISOR]);    /* sector size */
2811        fdc_out(NR_SECTORS);            /* tell controller how big a track is */
2812        fdc_out(GAP);                   /* tell controller how big sector gap is */
2813        fdc_out(DTL);                   /* tell controller about data length */
2814
2815        /* Block, waiting for disk interrupt. */
2816        if (need_reset) return(ERR_TRANSFER); /* if controller is sick, abort op */
2817        receive(HARDWARE, &mess);
2818
2819        /* Get controller status and check for errors. */
2820        r = fdc_results(fp);
2821        if (r != OK) return(r);
2822        if ( (fp->fl_results[ST1] & BAD_SECTOR) || (fp->fl_results[ST2] & BAD_CYL) )
2823             fp->fl_calibration = UNCALIBRATED;
2824        if (fp->fl_results[ST1] & WRITE_PROTECT) {
2825             printf("Diskette in drive %d is write protected.\n", fp->fl_drive);
2826             return(ERR_WR_PROTECT);
2827        }
2828        if ((fp->fl_results[ST0] & ST0_BITS) != TRANS_ST0) return(ERR_TRANSFER);
2829        if (fp->fl_results[ST1] | fp->fl_results[ST2]) return(ERR_TRANSFER);
2830
2831        /* Compare actual numbers of sectors transferred with expected number. */
2832        s =  (fp->fl_results[ST_CYL] - fp->fl_cylinder) * NR_HEADS * NR_SECTORS;
2833        s += (fp->fl_results[ST_HEAD] - fp->fl_head) * NR_SECTORS;
2834        s += (fp->fl_results[ST_SEC] - fp->fl_sector);
2835        if (s * SECTOR_SIZE != fp->fl_count) return(ERR_TRANSFER);
2836        return(OK);
2837  }


2840  /*===========================================================================*
2841   *                              fdc_results                                   *
2842   *===========================================================================*/
2843  PRIVATE int fdc_results(fp)
2844  register struct floppy *fp;     /* pointer to the drive struct */
2845  {
2846  /* Extract results from the controller after an operation. */
2847
2848      int i, j, status;
2849
```

```
2850          /* Loop, extracting bytes from FDC until it says it has no more. */
2851          for (i = 0; i < MAX_RESULTS; i++) {
2852                port_in(FDC_STATUS, &status);
2853                if ( (status & MASTER) == 0) return(ERR_STATUS);
2854                port_in(FDC_STATUS, &status);       /* read it again */
2855                if ( (status & DIRECTION) == 0) return(ERR_STATUS);
2856                port_in(FDC_DATA, &status);
2857                fp->fl_results[i] = status & BYTE;
2858                for (j = 0; j < 5; j++) ;            /* delay loop */
2859                port_in(FDC_STATUS, &status);
2860                if ( (status & CTL_BUSY) == 0) return(OK);
2861          }
2862
2863          /* FDC is giving back too many results. */
2864          need_reset = TRUE;              /* controller chip must be reset */
2865          return(ERR_STATUS);
2866      }


2869      /*===========================================================================*
2870       *                              fdc_out                                      *
2871       *===========================================================================*/
2872      PRIVATE fdc_out(val)
2873      int val;                            /* write this byte to floppy disk controller */
2874      {
2875      /* Output a byte to the controller.  This is not entirely trivial, since you
2876       * can only write to it when it is listening, and it decides when to listen.
2877       * If the controller refuses to listen, the FDC chip is given a hard reset.
2878       */
2879
2880        int retries, r;
2881
2882        if (need_reset) return;           /* if controller is not listening, return */
2883        retries = MAX_FDC_RETRY;
2884
2885        /* It may take several tries to get the FDC to accept a command. */
2886        while (retries-- > 0) {
2887                port_in(FDC_STATUS, &r);
2888                r &= (MASTER | DIRECTION);      /* just look at bits 2 and 3 */
2889                if (r != CTL_ACCEPTING) continue;      /* FDC is not listening */
2890                port_out(FDC_DATA, val);
2891                return;
2892        }
2893
2894        /* Controller is not listening.  Hit it over the head with a hammer. */
2895        need_reset = TRUE;
2896      }
```

```
2900    /*===========================================================================*
2901     *                              recalibrate                                  *
2902     *===========================================================================*/
2903    PRIVATE int recalibrate(fp)
2904    register struct floppy *fp;        /* pointer tot he drive struct */
2905    {
2906    /* The floppy disk controller has no way of determining its absolute arm
2907     * position (cylinder).  Instead, it steps the arm a cylinder at a time and
2908     * keeps track of where it thinks it is (in software).  However, after a
2909     * SEEK, the hardware reads information from the diskette telling where the
2910     * arm actually is.  If the arm is in the wrong place, a recalibration is done,
2911     * which forces the arm to cylinder 0.  This way the controller can get back
2912     * into sync with reality.
2913     */
2914
2915      int r;
2916
2917      /* Issue the RECALIBRATE command and wait for the interrupt. */
2918      start_motor(fp);                  /* can't recalibrate with motor off */
2919      fdc_out(FDC_RECALIBRATE);         /* tell drive to recalibrate itself */
2920      fdc_out(fp->fl_drive);            /* specify drive */
2921      if (need_reset) return(ERR_SEEK);    /* don't wait if controller is sick */
2922      receive(HARDWARE, &mess);         /* wait for interrupt message */
2923
2924      /* Determine if the recalibration succeeded. */
2925      fdc_out(FDC_SENSE);               /* issue SENSE command to see where we are */
2926      r = fdc_results(fp);              /* get results of the SENSE command */
2927      fp->fl_curcyl = -1;               /* force a SEEK next time */
2928      if (r != OK ||                    /* controller would not respond */
2929         (fp->fl_results[ST0]&ST0_BITS) != SEEK_ST0 || fp->fl_results[ST_PCN] !=0){
2930            /* Recalibration failed.  FDC must be reset. */
2931            need_reset = TRUE;
2932            fp->fl_calibration = UNCALIBRATED;
2933            return(ERR_RECALIBRATE);
2934      } else {
2935            /* Recalibration succeeded. */
2936            fp->fl_calibration = CALIBRATED;
2937            return(OK);
2938      }
2939    }


2942    /*===========================================================================*
2943     *                                 reset                                     *
2944     *===========================================================================*/
2945    PRIVATE reset()
2946    {
2947    /* Issue a reset to the controller.  This is done after any catastrophe,
2948     * like the controller refusing to respond.
2949     */
```

```
2950
2951        int i, r, status;
2952        register struct floppy *fp;
2953
2954        /* Disable interrupts and strobe reset bit low. */
2955        need_reset = FALSE;
2956        lock();
2957        motor_status = 0;
2958        motor_goal = 0;
2959        port_out(DOR, 0);                /* strobe reset bit low */
2960        port_out(DOR, ENABLE_INT);       /* strobe it high again */
2961        unlock();                        /* interrupts allowed again */
2962        receive(HARDWARE, &mess);        /* collect the RESET interrupt */
2963
2964        /* Interrupt from the reset has been received.  Continue resetting. */
2965        fp = &floppy[0];                 /* use floppy[0] for scratch */
2966        fp->fl_results[0] = 0;           /* this byte will be checked shortly */
2967        fdc_out(FDC_SENSE);              /* did it work? */
2968        r = fdc_results(fp);             /* get results */
2969        if (r != OK) panic("FDC won't reset", r);
2970        status = fp->fl_results[0] & BYTE;
2971        if (status != CHANGE)
2972            panic("FDC did not become ready after reset", fp->fl_results[0]);
2973
2974        /* Reset succeeded.  Tell FDC drive parameters. */
2975        fdc_out(FDC_SPECIFY);            /* specify some timing parameters */
2976        fdc_out(SPEC1);                  /* step-rate and head-unload-time */
2977        fdc_out(SPEC2);                  /* head-load-time and non-dma */
2978
2979        for (i = 0; i < NR_DRIVES; i++) floppy[i].fl_calibration = UNCALIBRATED;
2980    }


2983    /*===========================================================================*
2984     *                              clock_mess                                   *
2985     *===========================================================================*/
2986    PRIVATE clock_mess(ticks, func)
2987    int ticks;                          /* how many clock ticks to wait */
2988    int (*func)();                      /* function to call upon time out */
2989    {
2990    /* Send the clock task a message. */
2991
2992      mess.m_type = SET_ALARM;
2993      mess.CLOCK_PROC_NR = FLOPPY;
2994      mess.DELTA_TICKS = ticks;
2995      mess.FUNC_TO_CALL = func;
2996      sendrec(CLOCK, &mess);
2997    }
```

```
3000   /*===========================================================================*
3001    *                              send_mess                                    *
3002    *===========================================================================*/
3003   PRIVATE send_mess()
3004   {
3005   /* This routine is called when the clock task has timed out on motor startup.*/
3006
3007     mess.m_type = MOTOR_RUNNING;
3008     send(FLOPPY, &mess);
3009   }
```

```
3050    /* This file contains the code and data for the clock task.  The clock task
3051     * has a single entry point, clock_task().  It accepts four message types:
3052     *
3053     *   CLOCK_TICK:  a clock interrupt has occurred
3054     *   GET_TIME:    a process wants the real time
3055     *   SET_TIME:    a process wants to set the real time
3056     *   SET_ALARM:   a process wants to be alerted after a specified interval
3057     *
3058     * The input message is format m6.  The parameters are as follows:
3059     *
3060     *     m_type    CLOCK_PROC   FUNC    NEW_TIME
3061     * -------------------------------------------
3062     * | SET_ALARM | proc_nr  |f to call| delta  |
3063     * |-----------+----------+---------+---------|
3064     * | CLOCK_TICK |         |         |         |
3065     * |-----------+----------+---------+---------|
3066     * | GET_TIME  |          |         |         |
3067     * |-----------+----------+---------+---------|
3068     * | SET_TIME  |          |         | newtime |
3069     * -------------------------------------------
3070     *
3071     * When an alarm goes off, if the caller is a user process, a SIGALRM signal
3072     * is sent to it.  If it is a task, a function specified by the caller will
3073     * be invoked.  This function may, for example, send a message, but only if
3074     * it is certain that the task will be blocked when the timer goes off.
3075     */
3076
3077    #include "../h/const.h"
3078    #include "../h/type.h"
3079    #include "../h/callnr.h"
3080    #include "../h/com.h"
3081    #include "../h/error.h"
3082    #include "../h/signal.h"
3083    #include "const.h"
3084    #include "type.h"
3085    #include "glo.h"
3086    #include "proc.h"
3087
3088    /* Constant definitions. */
3089    #define MILLISEC          100      /* how often to call the scheduler (msec) */
3090    #define SCHED_RATE (MILLISEC*HZ/1000)   /* number of ticks per schedule */
3091
3092    /* Clock parameters. */
3093    #define TIMERO           0x40      /* port address for timer channel 0 */
3094    #define TIMER_MODE       0x43      /* port address for timer channel 3 */
3095    #define IBM_FREQ      1193182L     /* IBM clock frequency for setting timer */
3096    #define SQUARE_WAVE      0x36      /* mode for generating square wave */
3097
3098    /* Clock task variables. */
3099    PRIVATE real_time boot_time;       /* time in seconds of system boot */
```

```
3100   PRIVATE real_time next_alarm;   /* probable time of next alarm */
3101   PRIVATE int sched_ticks = SCHED_RATE;   /* counter: when 0, call scheduler */
3102   PRIVATE struct proc *prev_ptr;  /* last user process run by clock task */
3103   PRIVATE message mc;             /* message buffer for both input and output */
3104   PRIVATE int (*watch_dog[NR_TASKS+1])(); /* watch_dog functions to call */
3105
3106   /*===========================================================================*
3107    *                              clock_task                                   *
3108    *===========================================================================*/
3109   PUBLIC clock_task()
3110   {
3111   /* Main program of clock task.  It determines which of the 4 possible
3112    * calls this is by looking at 'mc.m_type'.   Then it dispatches.
3113    */
3114
3115     int opcode;
3116
3117     init_clock();                  /* initialize clock tables */
3118
3119     /* Main loop of the clock task.  Get work, process it, sometimes reply. */
3120     while (TRUE) {
3121        receive(ANY, &mc);          /* go get a message */
3122        opcode = mc.m_type;         /* extract the function code */
3123
3124        switch (opcode) {
3125           case SET_ALARM:  do_setalarm(&mc);      break;
3126           case GET_TIME:   do_get_time();         break;
3127           case SET_TIME:   do_set_time(&mc);      break;
3128           case CLOCK_TICK: do_clocktick();        break;
3129           default: panic("clock task got bad message", mc.m_type);
3130        }
3131
3132        /* Send reply, except for clock tick. */
3133        mc.m_type = OK;
3134        if (opcode != CLOCK_TICK) send(mc.m_source, &mc);
3135     }
3136   }


3139   /*===========================================================================*
3140    *                              do_setalarm                                  *
3141    *===========================================================================*/
3142   PRIVATE do_setalarm(m_ptr)
3143   message *m_ptr;                  /* pointer to request message */
3144   {
3145   /* A process wants an alarm signal or a task wants a given watch_dog function
3146    * called after a specified interval.  Record the request and check to see
3147    * it is the very next alarm needed.
3148    */
3149
```

```
3150          register struct proc *rp;
3151          int proc_nr;                          /* which process wants the alarm */
3152          long delta_ticks;                     /* in how many clock ticks does he want it? */
3153          int (*function)();                    /* function to call (tasks only) */
3154
3155          /* Extract the parameters from the message. */
3156          proc_nr = m_ptr->CLOCK_PROC_NR;         /* process to interrupt later */
3157          delta_ticks = m_ptr->DELTA_TICKS;       /* how many ticks to wait */
3158          function = m_ptr->FUNC_TO_CALL;         /* function to call (tasks only) */
3159          rp = proc_addr(proc_nr);
3160          mc.SECONDS_LEFT = (rp->p_alarm == 0L ? 0 : (rp->p_alarm - realtime)/HZ );
3161          rp->p_alarm = (delta_ticks == 0L ? 0L : realtime + delta_ticks);
3162          if (proc_nr < 0) watch_dog[-proc_nr] = function;
3163
3164          /* Which alarm is next? */
3165          next_alarm = MAX_P_LONG;
3166          for (rp = &proc[0]; rp < &proc[NR_TASKS+NR_PROCS]; rp++)
3167               if(rp->p_alarm != 0 && rp->p_alarm < next_alarm)next_alarm=rp->p_alarm;
3168
3169      }


3172      /*===========================================================================*
3173       *                              do_get_time                                  *
3174       *===========================================================================*/
3175      PRIVATE do_get_time()
3176      {
3177      /* Get and return the current clock time in ticks. */
3178
3179        mc.m_type = REAL_TIME;            /* set message type for reply */
3180        mc.NEW_TIME = boot_time + realtime/HZ;         /* current real time */
3181      }


3184      /*===========================================================================*
3185       *                              do_set_time                                  *
3186       *===========================================================================*/
3187      PRIVATE do_set_time(m_ptr)
3188      message *m_ptr;                        /* pointer to request message */
3189      {
3190      /* Set the real time clock.  Only the superuser can use this call. */
3191
3192        boot_time = m_ptr->NEW_TIME - realtime/HZ;
3193      }


3196      /*===========================================================================*
3197       *                              do_clocktick                                 *
3198       *===========================================================================*/
3199      PRIVATE do_clocktick()
```

```
3200     {
3201     /* This routine called on every clock tick. */
3202
3203          register struct proc *rp;
3204          register int t, proc_nr;
3205
3206          /* To guard against race conditions, first copy 'lost_ticks' to a local
3207           * variable, add this to 'realtime', and then subtract it from 'lost_ticks'.
3208           */
3209          t = lost_ticks;                    /* 'lost_ticks' counts missed interrupts */
3210          realtime += t + 1;                 /* update the time of day */
3211          lost_ticks -= t;                   /* these interrupts are no longer missed */
3212
3213          if (next_alarm <= realtime) {
3214              /* An alarm may have gone off, but proc may have exited, so check. */
3215              next_alarm = MAX_P_LONG;        /* start computing next alarm */
3216              for (rp = &proc[0]; rp < &proc[NR_TASKS+NR_PROCS]; rp++) {
3217                  if (rp->p_alarm != (real_time) 0) {
3218                      /* See if this alarm time has been reached. */
3219                      if (rp->p_alarm <= realtime) {
3220                          /* A timer has gone off.  If it is a user proc,
3221                           * send it a signal.  If it is a task, call the
3222                           * function previously specified by the task.
3223                           */
3224                          proc_nr = rp - proc - NR_TASKS;
3225                          if (proc_nr >= 0)
3226                                  cause_sig(proc_nr, SIGALRM);
3227                          else
3228                                  (*watch_dog[-proc_nr])();
3229                          rp->p_alarm = 0;
3230                      }
3231
3232                      /* Work on determining which alarm is next. */
3233                      if (rp->p_alarm != 0 && rp->p_alarm < next_alarm)
3234                          next_alarm = rp->p_alarm;
3235                  }
3236              }
3237          }
3238
3239          accounting();                      /* keep track of who is using the cpu */
3240
3241          /* If a user process has been running too long, pick another one. */
3242          if (--sched_ticks == 0) {
3243              if (bill_ptr == prev_ptr) sched();     /* process has run too long */
3244              sched_ticks = SCHED_RATE;              /* reset quantum */
3245              prev_ptr = bill_ptr;                   /* new previous process */
3246          }
3247
3248     }
```

```
3250     /*===========================================================================*
3251      *                              accounting                                   *
3252      *===========================================================================*/
3253     PRIVATE accounting()
3254     {
3255     /* Update user and system accounting times.  The variable 'bill_ptr' is always
3256      * kept pointing to the process to charge for CPU usage.  If the CPU was in
3257      * user code prior to this clock tick, charge the tick as user time, otherwise
3258      * charge it as system time.
3259      */
3260
3261       if (prev_proc >= LOW_USER)
3262             bill_ptr->user_time++;   /* charge CPU time */
3263       else
3264             bill_ptr->sys_time++;    /* charge system time */
3265     }


3268     #ifdef i8088
3269     /*===========================================================================*
3270      *                              init_clock                                   *
3271      *===========================================================================*/
3272     PRIVATE init_clock()
3273     {
3274     /* Initialize channel 2 of the 8253A timer to e.g. 60 Hz. */
3275
3276       unsigned int count, low_byte, high_byte;
3277
3278       count = (unsigned) (IBM_FREQ/HZ);        /* value to load into the timer */
3279       low_byte = count & BYTE;                 /* compute low-order byte */
3280       high_byte = (count >> 8) & BYTE;         /* compute high-order byte */
3281       port_out(TIMER_MODE, SQUARE_WAVE);       /* set timer to run continuously */
3282       port_out(TIMER0, low_byte);              /* load timer low byte */
3283       port_out(TIMER0, high_byte);             /* load timer high byte */
3284     }
3285     #endif
```

```
3300   /* This file contains the terminal driver, both for the IBM console and regular
3301    * ASCII terminals.  It is split into two sections, a device-independent part
3302    * and a device-dependent part.  The device-independent part accepts
3303    * characters to be printed from programs and queues them in a standard way
3304    * for device-dependent output.  It also accepts input and queues it for
3305    * programs. This file contains 2 main entry points: tty_task() and keyboard().
3306    * When a key is struck on a terminal, an interrupt to an assembly language
3307    * routine is generated.  This routine saves the machine state and registers
3308    * and calls keyboard(), which enters the character in an internal table, and
3309    * then sends a message to the terminal task.  The main program of the terminal
3310    * task is tty_task(). It accepts not only messages about typed input, but
3311    * also requests to read and write from terminals, etc.
3312    *
3313    * The device-dependent part interfaces with the IBM console and ASCII
3314    * terminals.  The IBM keyboard is unusual in that keystrokes yield key numbers
3315    * rather than ASCII codes, and furthermore, an interrupt is generated when a
3316    * key is depressed and again when it is released.  The IBM display is memory
3317    * mapped, so outputting characters such as line feed, backspace and bell are
3318    * tricky.
3319    *
3320    * The valid messages and their parameters are:
3321    *
3322    *    TTY_CHAR_INT: a character has been typed on a terminal (input interrupt)
3323    *    TTY_O_DONE:   a character has been output (output completed interrupt)
3324    *    TTY_READ:     a process wants to read from a terminal
3325    *    TTY_WRITE:    a process wants to write on a terminal
3326    *    TTY_IOCTL:    a process wants to change a terminal's parameters
3327    *    CANCEL:       terminate a previous incomplete system call immediately
3328    *
3329    *    m_type       TTY_LINE   PROC_NR    COUNT   TTY_SPEK TTY_FLAGS ADDRESS
3330    * -------------------------------------------------------------------------
3331    * | TTY_CHAR_INT|          |          |         |         |         |array ptr|
3332    * |-------------+----------+----------+---------+---------+---------+---------|
3333    * | TTY_O_DONE  |minor dev |          |         |         |         |         |
3334    * |-------------+----------+----------+---------+---------+---------+---------|
3335    * | TTY_READ    |minor dev | proc nr  | count   |         |         | buf ptr |
3336    * |-------------+----------+----------+---------+---------+---------+---------|
3337    * | TTY_WRITE   |minor dev | proc nr  | count   |         |         | buf ptr |
3338    * |-------------+----------+----------+---------+---------+---------+---------|
3339    * | TTY_IOCTL   |minor dev | proc nr  |func code|erase etc|  flags  |         |
3340    * |-------------+----------+----------+---------+---------+---------+---------|
3341    * | CANCEL      |minor dev | proc nr  |         |         |         |         |
3342    * -------------------------------------------------------------------------
3343    */
3344
3345   #include "../h/const.h"
3346   #include "../h/type.h"
3347   #include "../h/callnr.h"
3348   #include "../h/com.h"
3349   #include "../h/error.h"
```

```
3350    #include "../h/sgtty.h"
3351    #include "../h/signal.h"
3352    #include "const.h"
3353    #include "type.h"
3354    #include "proc.h"
3355
3356    #define NR_TTYS           1       /* how many terminals can system handle */
3357    #define TTY_IN_BYTES    200       /* input queue size */
3358    #define TTY_RAM_WORDS   320       /* ram buffer size */
3359    #define TTY_BUF_SIZE    256       /* unit for copying to/from queues */
3360    #define TAB_SIZE          8       /* distance between tabs */
3361    #define TAB_MASK         07       /* mask for tty_column when tabbing */
3362    #define MAX_OVERRUN      16       /* size of overrun input buffer */
3363
3364    #define ERASE_CHAR      '\b'      /* default erase character */
3365    #define KILL_CHAR       '@'       /* default kill character */
3366    #define INTR_CHAR (char)0177      /* default interrupt character */
3367    #define QUIT_CHAR (char) 034      /* default quit character */
3368    #define XOFF_CHAR (char) 023      /* default x-off character (CTRL-S) */
3369    #define XON_CHAR  (char) 021      /* default x-on character (CTRL-Q) */
3370    #define EOT_CHAR  (char) 004      /* CTRL-D */
3371    #define MARKER    (char) 000      /* non-escaped CTRL-D stored as MARKER */
3372    #define DEL_CODE  (char) 83       /* DEL for use in CTRL-ALT-DEL reboot */
3373    #define AT_SIGN          0220     /* code to yield for CTRL-@ */
3374
3375    #define F1               59       /* scan code for function key F1 */
3376    #define F2               60       /* scan code for function key F2 */
3377    #define F10              68       /* scan code for function key F10 */
3378    #define TOP_ROW          14       /* codes below this are shifted if CTRL */
3379
3380    PRIVATE struct tty_struct {
3381      /* Input queue.  Typed characters are stored here until read by a program. */
3382      char tty_inqueue[TTY_IN_BYTES];   /* array used to store the characters */
3383      char *tty_inhead;               /* pointer to place where next char goes */
3384      char *tty_intail;               /* pointer to next char to be given to prog */
3385      int tty_incount;                /* # chars in tty_inqueue */
3386      int tty_lfct;                   /* # line feeds in tty_inqueue */
3387
3388      /* Output section. */
3389      int tty_ramqueue[TTY_RAM_WORDS];      /* buffer for video RAM */
3390      int tty_rwords;                 /* number of WORDS (not bytes) in outqueue */
3391      int tty_org;                    /* location in RAM where 6845 base points */
3392      int tty_vid;                    /* current position of cursor in video RAM */
3393      char tty_esc_state;             /* 0=normal, 1 = ESC seen, 2 = ESC + x seen */
3394      char tty_echar;                 /* first character following an ESC */
3395      int tty_attribute;              /* current attribute byte << 8 */
3396      int (*tty_devstart)();          /* routine to start actual device output */
3397
3398      /* Terminal parameters and status. */
3399      int tty_mode;                   /* terminal mode set by IOCTL */
```

```
3400        int tty_column;                  /* current column number (O-origin) */
3401        int tty_row;                     /* current row (0 at bottom of screen) */
3402        char tty_busy;                   /* 1 when output in progress, else 0 */
3403        char tty_escaped;                /* 1 when '\' just seen, else 0 */
3404        char tty_inhibited;              /* 1 when CTRL-S just seen (stops output) */
3405        char tty_makebreak;              /* 1 for terminals that interrupt twice/key */
3406        char tty_waiting;                /* 1 when output process waiting for reply */
3407
3408        /* User settable characters: erase, kill, interrupt, quit, x-on; x-off. */
3409        char tty_erase;                  /* char used to erase 1 char (init ^H) */
3410        char tty_kill;                   /* char used to erase a line (init @) */
3411        char tty_intr;                   /* char used to send SIGINT   (init DEL) */
3412        char tty_quit;                   /* char used for core dump    (init CTRL-\) */
3413        char tty_xon;                    /* char used to start output (init CTRL-Q)*/
3414        char tty_xoff;                   /* char used to stop output  (init CTRL-S) */
3415        char tty_eof;                    /* char used to stop output  (init CTRL-D) */
3416
3417        /* Information about incomplete I/O requests is stored here. */
3418        char tty_incaller;               /* process that made the call (usually FS) */
3419        char tty_inproc;                 /* process that wants to read from tty */
3420        char *tty_in_vir;                /* virtual address where data is to go */
3421        int tty_inleft;                  /* how many chars are still needed */
3422        char tty_otcaller;               /* process that made the call (usually FS) */
3423        char tty_outproc;                /* process that wants to write to tty */
3424        char *tty_out_vir;               /* virtual address where data comes from */
3425        phys_bytes tty_phys;             /* physical address where data comes from */
3426        int tty_outleft;                 /* # chars yet to be copied to tty_outqueue */
3427        int tty_cum;                     /* # chars copied to tty_outqueue so far */
3428
3429        /* Miscellaneous. */
3430        int tty_ioport;                  /* I/O port number for this terminal */
3431    } tty_struct[NR_TTYS];
3432
3433    /* Values for the fields. */
3434    #define NOT_ESCAPED     0            /* previous character on this line not '\' */
3435    #define ESCAPED         1            /* previous character on this line was '\' */
3436    #define RUNNING         0            /* no CRTL-S has been typed to stop the tty */
3437    #define STOPPED         1            /* CTRL-S has been typed to stop the tty */
3438    #define INACTIVE        0            /* the tty is not printing */
3439    #define BUSY            1            /* the tty is printing */
3440    #define ONE_INT         0            /* regular terminals interrupt once per char */
3441    #define TWO_INTS        1            /* IBM console interrupts two times per char */
3442    #define NOT_WAITING     0            /* no output process is hanging */
3443    #define WAITING         1            /* an output process is waiting for a reply */
3444
3445    PRIVATE char tty_driver_buf[2*MAX_OVERRUN+2]; /* driver collects chars here */
3446    PRIVATE char tty_copy_buf[2*MAX_OVERRUN];  /* copy buf used to avoid races */
3447    PRIVATE char tty_buf[TTY_BUF_SIZE];       /* scratch buffer to/from user space */
3448    PRIVATE int shift1, shift2, capslock, numlock; /* keep track of shift keys */
3449    PRIVATE int control, alt;            /* keep track of key statii */
```

```
3450    PRIVATE int olivetti;              /* flag set for Olivetti M24 keyboard */
3451    PUBLIC scan_code;                  /* scan code for '=' saved by bootstrap */
3452
3453    /* Scan codes to ASCII for unshifted keys */
3454    PRIVATE char unsh[] = {
3455      0,033,'1','2','3','4','5','6',          '7','8','9','0','-','=','\b','\t',
3456      'q','w','e','r','t','y','u','i',        'o','p','[',']',015,0202,'a','s',
3457      'd','f','g','h','j','k','l',';',        047,0140,0200,0134,'z','x','c','v',
3458      'b','n','m',',','.','/',0201,'*',       0203,' ',0204,0241,0242,0243,0244,0245,
3459      0246,0247,0250,0251,0252,0205,0210,0267, 0270,0271,0211,0264,0265,0266,0214
3460      ,0261,  0262,0263,'0',0177
3461    };
3462
3463    /* Scan codes to ASCII for shifted keys */
3464    PRIVATE char sh[] = {
3465      0,033,'!','@','#','$','%','^',          '&','*','(',')','_','+','\b','\t',
3466      'Q','W','E','R','T','Y','U','I',        'O','P','{','}',015,0202,'A','S',
3467      'D','F','G','H','J','K','L',':',        042,'~',0200,'|','Z','X','C','V',
3468      'B','N','M','<','>','?',0201,'*',       0203,' ',0204,0221,0222,0223,0224,0225,
3469      0226,0227,0230,0231,0232,0204,0213,'7', '8','9',0211,'4','5','6',0214,'1',
3470      '2','3','0',177
3471    };
3472
3473
3474    /* Scan codes to ASCII for Olivetti M24 for unshifted keys. */
3475    PRIVATE char unm24[] = {
3476      0,033,'1','2','3','4','5','6',          '7','8','9','0','-','^','\b','\t',
3477      'q','w','e','r','t','y','u','i',        'o','p','@','[','\r',0202,'a','s',
3478      'd','f','g','h','j','k','l',';',        ':',']',0200,'\\','z','x','c','v',
3479      'b','n','m',',','.','/',0201,'*',       0203,' ',0204,0241,0242,0243,0244,0245,
3480      0246,0247,0250,0251,0252,023,0210,'7',  '8','9',0211,'4','5','6',0214,'1',
3481      '2','3','0','.',' ',014,0212,'\r',      '\b','\n','\f',013,032,0213,' ','/',
3482      0253,0254,0255,0256,0257,0215,0216,0217
3483    };
3484
3485    /* Scan codes to ASCII for Olivetti M24 for shifted keys. */
3486    PRIVATE char m24[] = {
3487      0,033,'!','"','#','$','%','&',          047,'(',')','_','=','~','\b','\t',
3488      'Q','W','E','R','T','Y','U','I',        'O','P',0140,'{','\r',0202,'A','S',
3489      'D','F','G','H','J','K','L','+',        '*','}',0200,'|','Z','X','C','V',
3490      'B','N','M','<','>','?',0201,'*',       0203,' ',0204,0221,0222,0223,0224,0225,
3491      0226,0227,0230,0231,0232,0270,023,036,  013,037,0211,'\b',036,'\f',0214,04,
3492      '\n',037,0207,0177,0271,014,0272,'\r',  '\b','\n','\f',036,032,0273,0274,'/',
3493      0233,0234,0235,0236,0237,0275,0276,0277
3494    };
3495
3496
3497 /*===========================================================================*
3498  *                              tty_task                                     *
3499  *===========================================================================*/
```

```
3500    PUBLIC tty_task()
3501    {
3502    /* Main routine of the terminal task. */
3503
3504      message tty_mess;                /* buffer for all incoming messages */
3505      register struct tty_struct *tp;
3506
3507      tty_init();                      /* initialize */
3508      while (TRUE) {
3509            receive(ANY, &tty_mess);
3510            tp = &tty_struct[tty_mess.TTY_LINE];
3511            switch(tty_mess.m_type) {
3512               case TTY_CHAR_INT:  do_charint(&tty_mess);          break;
3513               case TTY_READ:      do_read(tp, &tty_mess);          break;
3514               case TTY_WRITE:     do_write(tp, &tty_mess);         break;
3515               case TTY_IOCTL:     do_ioctl(tp, &tty_mess);         break;
3516               case CANCEL    :    do_cancel(tp, &tty_mess);        break;
3517               case TTY_O_DONE:    /* reserved for future use (RS-232 terminals)*/
3518               default:            tty_reply(TASK_REPLY, tty_mess.m_source,
3519                                        tty_mess.PROC_NR, EINVAL, OL, OL);
3520            }
3521      }
3522    }


3525    /*===========================================================================*
3526     *                              do_charint                                   *
3527     *===========================================================================*/
3528    PRIVATE do_charint(m_ptr)
3529    message *m_ptr;                  /* message containing pointer to char(s) */
3530    {
3531    /* A character has been typed.  If a character is typed and the tty task is
3532     * not able to service it immediately, the character is accumulated within
3533     * the tty driver.  Thus multiple chars may be accumulated.  A single message
3534     * to the tty task may have to process several characters.
3535     */
3536
3537      int m, n, count, replyee, caller;
3538      char *ptr, *copy_ptr, ch;
3539      struct tty_struct *tp;
3540
3541      lock();                          /* prevent races by disabling interrupts */
3542      ptr = m_ptr->ADDRESS;            /* pointer to accumulated char array */
3543      copy_ptr = tty_copy_buf;         /* ptr to shadow array where chars copied */
3544      n = *ptr;                        /* how many chars have been accumulated */
3545      count = n;                       /* save the character count */
3546      n = n + n;                       /* each char occupies 2 bytes */
3547      ptr += 2;                        /* skip count field at start of array */
3548      while (n-- > 0)
3549            *copy_ptr++ = *ptr++;      /* copy the array to safety */
```

```
3550        ptr = m_ptr->ADDRESS;
3551        *ptr = 0;                    /* accumulation count set to 0 */
3552        unlock();                    /* re-enable interrupts */
3553
3554        /* Loop on the accumulated characters, processing each in turn. */
3555        copy_ptr = tty_copy_buf;
3556        while (count-- > 0) {
3557                ch = *copy_ptr++;        /* get the character typed */
3558                n = *copy_ptr++;         /* get the line number it came in on */
3559                in_char(n, ch);          /* queue the char and echo it */
3560
3561                /* See if a previously blocked reader can now be satisfied. */
3562                tp = &tty_struct[n];     /* pointer to struct for this character */
3563                if (tp->tty_inleft > 0 ) {        /* does anybody want input? */
3564                        m = tp->tty_mode & (CBREAK | RAW);
3565                        if (tp->tty_lfct > 0 || (m != 0 && tp->tty_incount > 0)) {
3566                                m = rd_chars(tp);
3567
3568                                /* Tell hanging reader that chars have arrived. */
3569                                replyee = (int) tp->tty_incaller;
3570                                caller = (int) tp->tty_inproc;
3571                                tty_reply(REVIVE, replyee, caller, m, OL, OL);
3572                        }
3573                }
3574        }
3575    }


3578    /*===========================================================================*
3579     *                              in_char                                       *
3580     *===========================================================================*/
3581    PRIVATE in_char(line, ch)
3582    int line;                        /* line number on which char arrived */
3583    char ch;                         /* scan code for character that arrived */
3584    {
3585    /* A character has just been typed in.  Process, save, and echo it. */
3586
3587      register struct tty_struct *tp;
3588      int mode, sig;
3589      char make_break();
3590      tp = &tty_struct[line];        /* set 'tp' to point to proper struct */
3591      /* Function keys are temporarily being used for debug dumps. */
3592      if (ch >= Fl && ch <= FlO) {   /* Check for function keys Fl, F2, ... FlO */
3593           func_key(ch);             /* process function key */
3594           return;
3595      }
3596      if (tp->tty_incount >= TTY_IN_BYTES) return; /* no room, discard char */
3597      mode = tp->tty_mode & (RAW | CBREAK);
3598      if (tp->tty_makebreak)
3599           ch = make_break(ch);      /* console give 2 ints/ch */
```

```
3600      else
3601            if (mode != RAW) ch &= 0177;    /* 7-bit chars except in raw mode */
3602      if (ch == 0) return;
3603
3604      /* Processing for COOKED and CBREAK mode contains special checks. */
3605      if (mode == COOKED || mode == CBREAK) {
3606            /* Handle erase, kill and escape processing. */
3607            if (mode == COOKED) {
3608                  /* First erase processing (rub out of last character). */
3609                  if (ch == tp->tty_erase && tp->tty_escaped == NOT_ESCAPED) {
3610                        chuck(tp);      /* remove last char entered */
3611                        echo(tp, '\b'); /* remove it from the screen */
3612                        echo(tp, ' ');
3613                        echo(tp, '\b');
3614                        return;
3615                  }
3616
3617                  /* Now do kill processing (remove current line). */
3618                  if (ch == tp->tty_kill && tp->tty_escaped == NOT_ESCAPED) {
3619                        while( chuck(tp) == OK) /* keep looping */ ;
3620                        echo(tp, tp->tty_kill);
3621                        echo (tp, '\n');
3622                        return;
3623                  }
3624
3625                  /* Handle EOT and the escape symbol (backslash). */
3626                  if (tp->tty_escaped == NOT_ESCAPED) {
3627                        /* Normal case: previous char was not backslash. */
3628                        if (ch == '\\') {
3629                              /* An escaped symbol has just been typed. */
3630                              tp->tty_escaped = ESCAPED;
3631                              echo(tp, ch);
3632                              return; /* do not store the '\' */
3633                        }
3634                        /* CTRL-D means end-of-file, unless it is escaped. It
3635                         * is stored in the text as MARKER, and counts as a
3636                         * line feed in terms of knowing whether a full line
3637                         * has been typed already.
3638                         */
3639                        if (ch == tp->tty_eof) ch = MARKER;
3640                  } else {
3641                        /* Previous character was backslash. */
3642                        tp->tty_escaped = NOT_ESCAPED;  /* turn escaping off */
3643                        if (ch != tp->tty_erase && ch != tp->tty_kill &&
3644                                          ch != tp->tty_eof) {
3645                              /* Store the escape previously skipped over */
3646                              *tp->tty_inhead++ = '\\';
3647                              tp->tty_incount++;
3648                              if (tp->tty_inhead ==
3649                                          &tp->tty_inqueue[TTY_IN_BYTES])
```

```
3650                                          tp->tty_inhead = tp->tty_inqueue;
3651                          }
3652                  }
3653          }
3654          /* Both COOKED and CBREAK modes come here; first map CR to LF. */
3655          if (ch == '\r' && (tp->tty_mode & CRMOD)) ch = '\n';
3656
3657          /* Check for interrupt and quit characters. */
3658          if (ch == tp->tty_intr || ch == tp->tty_quit) {
3659                  sig = (ch == tp->tty_intr ? SIGINT : SIGQUIT);
3660                  tp->tty_inhibited = RUNNING;        /* do implied CRTL-Q */
3661                  finish(tp, EINTR);                  /* send reply */
3662                  echo(tp, '\n');
3663                  cause_sig(LOW_USER + 1 + line, sig);
3664                  return;
3665          }
3666
3667          /* Check for and process CTRL-S (terminal stop). */
3668          if (ch == tp->tty_xoff) {
3669                  tp->tty_inhibited = STOPPED;
3670                  return;
3671          }
3672
3673          /* Check for and process CTRL-Q (terminal start). */
3674          if (ch == tp->tty_xon) {
3675                  tp->tty_inhibited = RUNNING;
3676                  (*tp->tty_devstart)(tp);           /* resume output */
3677                  return;
3678          }
3679      }
3680
3681      /* All 3 modes come here. */
3682      if (ch == '\n' || ch == MARKER) tp->tty_lfct++;        /* count line feeds */
3683      *tp->tty_inhead++ = ch;         /* save the character in the input queue */
3684      if (tp->tty_inhead == &tp->tty_inqueue[TTY_IN_BYTES])
3685          tp->tty_inhead = tp->tty_inqueue;          /* handle wraparound */
3686      tp->tty_incount++;
3687      echo(tp, ch);
3688  }


3691  #ifdef i8088
3692  /*===========================================================================*
3693   *                              make_break                                    *
3694   *===========================================================================*/
3695  PRIVATE char make_break(ch)
3696  char ch;                        /* scan code of key just struck or released */
3697  {
3698  /* This routine can handle keyboards that interrupt only on key depression,
3699   * as well as keyboards that interrupt on key depression and key release.
```

```
3700      * For efficiency, the interrupt routine filters out most key releases.
3701      */
3702
3703      int c, make, code;
3704
3705
3706      c = ch & 0177;                  /* high-order bit set on key release */
3707      make = (ch & 0200 ? 0 : 1);   /* 1 when key depressed, 0 when key released */
3708      if (olivetti == FALSE) {
3709              /* Standard IBM keyboard. */
3710              code = (shift1 || shift2 || capslock ? sh[c] : unsh[c]);
3711              if (control && c < TOP_ROW) code = sh[c];         /* CTRL-(top row) */
3712              if (c > 70 && numlock) code = sh[c];      /* numlock depressed */
3713      } else {
3714              /* (Olivetti M24 or AT&T 6300) with Olivetti-style keyboard. */
3715              code = (shift1 || shift2 || capslock ? m24[c] : unm24[c]);
3716              if (control && c < TOP_ROW) code = sh[c];         /* CTRL-(top row) */
3717              if (c > 70 && numlock) code = m24[c];    /* numlock depressed */
3718      }
3719      code &= BYTE;
3720      if (code < 0200 || code >= 0206) {
3721              /* Ordinary key, i.e. not shift, control, alt, etc. */
3722              if (alt) code |= 0200;  /* alt key ORs 0200 into code */
3723              if (control) code &= 037;
3724              if (code == 0) code = AT_SIGN;  /* @ is 0100, so CTRL-@ = 0 */
3725              if (make == 0) code = 0;        /* key release */
3726              return(code);
3727      }
3728
3729      /* Table entries 0200 - 0206 denote special actions. */
3730      switch(code - 0200) {
3731        case 0:    shift1 = make;              break;  /* shift key on left */
3732        case 1:    shift2 = make;              break;  /* shift key on right */
3733        case 2:    control = make;             break;  /* control */
3734        case 3:    alt = make;                 break;  /* alt key */
3735        case 4:    if (make) capslock = 1 - capslock; break;       /* caps lock */
3736        case 5:    if (make) numlock  = 1 - numlock;  break;       /* num lock */
3737      }
3738      return(0);
3739    }
3740    #endif
3741
3742
3743    /*===========================================================================*
3744     *                                 echo                                       *
3745     *===========================================================================*/
3746    PRIVATE echo(tp, c)
3747    register struct tty_struct *tp; /* terminal on which to echo */
3748    register char c;                /* character to echo */
3749    {
```

```
3750      /* Echo a character on the terminal. */
3751
3752        if ( (tp->tty_mode & ECHO) == 0) return;        /* if no echoing, don't echo */
3753        if (c != MARKER) out_char(tp, c);
3754        flush(tp);                       /* force character out onto the screen */
3755      }


3758      /*========================================================================*
3759       *                               chuck                                    *
3760       *========================================================================*/
3761      PRIVATE int chuck(tp)
3762      register struct tty_struct *tp; /* from which tty should chars be removed */
3763      {
3764      /* Delete one character from the input queue.  Used for erase and kill. */
3765
3766        char *prev;
3767
3768        /* If input queue is empty, don't delete anything. */
3769        if (tp->tty_incount == 0) return(-1);
3770
3771        /* Don't delete '\n' or '\r'. */
3772        prev = (tp->tty_inhead != tp->tty_inqueue ? tp->tty_inhead - 1 :
3773                                        &tp->tty_inqueue[TTY_IN_BYTES-1]);
3774        if (*prev == '\n' || *prev == '\r') return(-1);
3775        tp->tty_inhead = prev;
3776        tp->tty_incount--;
3777        return(OK);                      /* char erasure was possible */
3778      }


3781      /*========================================================================*
3782       *                              do_read                                    *
3783       *========================================================================*/
3784      PRIVATE do_read(tp, m_ptr)
3785      register struct tty_struct *tp; /* pointer to tty struct */
3786      message *m_ptr;                        /* pointer to message sent to the task */
3787      {
3788      /* A process wants to read from a terminal. */
3789
3790        int code, caller;
3791
3792        if (tp->tty_inleft > 0) {      /* if someone else is hanging, give up */
3793            tty_reply(TASK_REPLY,m_ptr->m_source,m_ptr->PROC_NR, E_TRY_AGAIN,OL,OL);
3794            return;
3795        }
3796
3797        /* Copy information from the message to the tty struct. */
3798        tp->tty_incaller = m_ptr->m_source;
3799        tp->tty_inproc = m_ptr->PROC_NR;
```

```
3800        tp->tty_in_vir = m_ptr->ADDRESS;
3801        tp->tty_inleft = m_ptr->COUNT;
3802
3803        /* Try to get chars.  This call either gets enough, or gets nothing. */
3804        code = rd_chars(tp);
3805        caller = (int) tp->tty_inproc;
3806        tty_reply(TASK_REPLY, m_ptr->m_source, caller, code, OL, OL);
3807    }


3810    /*===========================================================================*
3811     *                              rd_chars                                     *
3812     *===========================================================================*/
3813    PRIVATE int rd_chars(tp)
3814    register struct tty_struct *tp; /* pointer to terminal to read from */
3815    {
3816    /* A process wants to read from a terminal.  First check if enough data is
3817     * available. If so, pass it to the user.  If not, send FS a message telling
3818     * it to suspend the user.  When enough data arrives later, the tty driver
3819     * copies it to the user space directly and notifies FS with a message.
3820     */
3821
3822        int cooked, ct, user_ct, buf_ct, cum, enough, eot_seen;
3823        vir_bytes in_vir, left;
3824        phys_bytes user_phys, tty_phys;
3825        char ch, *tty_ptr;
3826        struct proc *rp;
3827        extern phys_bytes umap();
3828
3829        cooked = ( (tp->tty_mode & (RAW | CBREAK)) ? 0 : 1); /* 1 iff COOKED mode */
3830        if (tp->tty_incount == 0 || (cooked && tp->tty_lfct == 0)) return(SUSPEND);
3831        rp = proc_addr(tp->tty_inproc);
3832        in_vir = (vir_bytes) tp-> tty_in_vir;
3833        left = (vir_bytes) tp->tty_inleft;
3834        if ( (user_phys = umap(rp, D, in_vir, left)) == 0) return(E_BAD_ADDR);
3835        tty_phys = umap(proc_addr(TTY), D, (vir_bytes) tty_buf, TTY_BUF_SIZE);
3836        cum = 0;
3837        enough = 0;
3838        eot_seen = 0;
3839
3840        /* The outer loop iterates on buffers, one buffer load per iteration. */
3841        while (tp->tty_inleft > 0) {
3842            buf_ct = MIN(tp->tty_inleft, tp->tty_incount);
3843            buf_ct = MIN(buf_ct, TTY_BUF_SIZE);
3844            ct = 0;
3845            tty_ptr = tty_buf;
3846
3847            /* The inner loop fills one buffer. */
3848            while(buf_ct-- > 0) {
3849                ch = *tp->tty_intail++;
```

```
3850                    if (tp->tty_intail == &tp->tty_inqueue[TTY_IN_BYTES])
3851                            tp->tty_intail = tp->tty_inqueue;
3852                    *tty_ptr++ = ch;
3853                    ct++;
3854                    if (ch == '\n' || ch == MARKER) {
3855                            tp->tty_lfct--;
3856                            if (cooked && ch == MARKER) eot_seen++;
3857                            enough++;          /* exit loop */
3858                            if (cooked) break;       /* only provide 1 line */
3859                    }
3860            }
3861
3862            /* Copy one buffer to user space.  Be careful about CTRL-D.  In cooked
3863             * mode it is not transmitted to user programs, and is not counted as
3864             * a character as far as the count goes, but it does occupy space in
3865             * the driver's tables and must be counted there.
3866             */
3867            user_ct = (eot_seen ? ct - 1 : ct);      /* bytes to copy to user */
3868            phys_copy(tty_phys, user_phys, (phys_bytes) user_ct);
3869            user_phys += user_ct;
3870            cum += user_ct;
3871            tp->tty_inleft -= ct;
3872            tp->tty_incount -= ct;
3873            if (tp->tty_incount == 0 || enough) break;
3874      }
3875
3876      tp->tty_inleft = 0;
3877      return(cum);
3878  }
3879
3880
3881  /*===========================================================================*
3882   *                              finish                                       *
3883   *===========================================================================*/
3884  PRIVATE finish(tp, code)
3885  register struct tty_struct *tp; /* pointer to tty struct */
3886  int code;                       /* reply code */
3887  {
3888  /* A command has terminated (possibly due to DEL).  Tell caller. */
3889
3890      int replyee, caller;
3891
3892      tp->tty_rwords = 0;
3893      tp->tty_outleft = 0;
3894      if (tp->tty_waiting == NOT_WAITING) return;
3895      replyee = (int) tp->tty_otcaller;
3896      caller = (int) tp->tty_outproc;
3897      tty_reply(TASK_REPLY, replyee, caller, code, 0L, 0L);
3898      tp->tty_waiting = NOT_WAITING;
3899  }
```

```
3902   /*===========================================================================*
3903    *                               do_write                                    *
3904    *===========================================================================*/
3905   PRIVATE do_write(tp, m_ptr)
3906   register struct tty_struct *tp; /* pointer to tty struct */
3907   message *m_ptr;                 /* pointer to message sent to the task */
3908   {
3909   /* A process wants to write on a terminal. */
3910
3911     vir_bytes out_vir, out_left;
3912     struct proc *rp;
3913     extern phys_bytes umap();
3914
3915     /* Copy message parameters to the tty structure. */
3916     tp->tty_otcaller = m_ptr->m_source;
3917     tp->tty_outproc = m_ptr->PROC_NR;
3918     tp->tty_out_vir = m_ptr->ADDRESS;
3919     tp->tty_outleft = m_ptr->COUNT;
3920     tp->tty_waiting = WAITING;
3921     tp->tty_cum = 0;
3922
3923     /* Compute the physical address where the data is in user space. */
3924     rp = proc_addr(tp->tty_outproc);
3925     out_vir = (vir_bytes) tp->tty_out_vir;
3926     out_left = (vir_bytes) tp->tty_outleft;
3927     if ( (tp->tty_phys = umap(rp, D, out_vir, out_left)) == 0) {
3928           /* Buffer address provided by user is outside its address space. */
3929           tp->tty_cum = E_BAD_ADDR;
3930           tp->tty_outleft = 0;
3931     }
3932
3933     /* Copy characters from the user process to the terminal. */
3934     (*tp->tty_devstart)(tp);        /* copy data to queue and start I/O */
3935   }


3938   /*===========================================================================*
3939    *                               do_ioctl                                    *
3940    *===========================================================================*/
3941   PRIVATE do_ioctl(tp, m_ptr)
3942   register struct tty_struct *tp; /* pointer to tty_struct */
3943   message *m_ptr;                 /* pointer to message sent to task */
3944   {
3945   /* Perform IOCTL on this terminal. */
3946
3947     long flags, erki, erase, kill, intr, quit, xon, xoff, eof;
3948     int r;
3949
```

```
3950        r = OK;
3951        flags = 0;
3952        erki = 0;
3953        switch(m_ptr->TTY_REQUEST) {
3954            case TIOCSETP:
3955                /* Set erase, kill, and flags. */
3956                tp->tty_erase = (char) ((m_ptr->TTY_SPEK >> 8) & BYTE); /* erase */
3957                tp->tty_kill  = (char) ((m_ptr->TTY_SPEK >> 0) & BYTE); /* kill */
3958                tp->tty_mode  = (int) m_ptr->TTY_FLAGS; /* mode word */
3959                break;
3960
3961            case TIOCSETC:
3962                /* Set intr, quit, xon, xoff, eof (brk not used). */
3963                tp->tty_intr = (char) ((m_ptr->TTY_SPEK >> 24) & BYTE); /* interrupt */
3964                tp->tty_quit = (char) ((m_ptr->TTY_SPEK >> 16) & BYTE); /* quit */
3965                tp->tty_xon  = (char) ((m_ptr->TTY_SPEK >>  8) & BYTE); /* CTRL-S */
3966                tp->tty_xoff = (char) ((m_ptr->TTY_SPEK >>  0) & BYTE); /* CTRL-Q */
3967                tp->tty_eof  = (char) ((m_ptr->TTY_FLAGS >> 8) & BYTE); /* CTRL-D */
3968                break;
3969
3970            case TIOCGETP:
3971                /* Get erase, kill, and flags. */
3972                erase = ((long) tp->tty_erase) & BYTE;
3973                kill  = ((long) tp->tty_kill) & BYTE;
3974                erki  = (erase << 8) | kill;
3975                flags = (long) tp->tty_mode;
3976                break;
3977
3978            case TIOCGETC:
3979                /* Get intr, quit, xon, xoff, eof. */
3980                intr = ((long) tp->tty_intr) & BYTE;
3981                quit = ((long) tp->tty_quit) & BYTE;
3982                xon  = ((long) tp->tty_xon)  & BYTE;
3983                xoff = ((long) tp->tty_xoff) & BYTE;
3984                eof  = ((long) tp->tty_eof)  & BYTE;
3985                erki = (intr << 24) | (quit << 16) | (xon << 8) | (xoff << 0);
3986                flags = (eof <<8);
3987                break;
3988
3989            default:
3990                r = EINVAL;
3991        }
3992
3993        /* Send the reply. */
3994        tty_reply(TASK_REPLY, m_ptr->m_source, m_ptr->PROC_NR, r, flags, erki);
3995    }
```

```
4000   /*===========================================================================*
4001    *                              do_cancel                                    *
4002    *===========================================================================*/
4003   PRIVATE do_cancel(tp, m_ptr)
4004   register struct tty_struct *tp;  /* pointer to tty_struct */
4005   message *m_ptr;                  /* pointer to message sent to task */
4006   {
4007   /* A signal has been sent to a process that is hanging trying to read or write.
4008    * The pending read or write must be finished off immediately.
4009    */
4010
4011     /* First check to see if the process is indeed hanging.  If it is not, don't
4012      * reply (to avoid race conditions).
4013      */
4014     if (tp->tty_inleft == 0 && tp->tty_outleft == 0) return;
4015
4016     /* Kill off input and output. */
4017     tp->tty_inhead = tp->tty_inqueue;      /* discard all input */
4018     tp->tty_intail = tp->tty_inqueue;
4019     tp->tty_incount = 0;
4020     tp->tty_lfct = 0;
4021     tp->tty_inleft = 0;
4022     tp->tty_outleft = 0;
4023     tp->tty_waiting = NOT_WAITING;         /* don't send reply */
4024     tp->tty_inhibited = RUNNING;
4025     tty_reply(TASK_REPLY, m_ptr->m_source, m_ptr->PROC_NR, EINTR, OL, OL);
4026   }


4028   /*===========================================================================*
4029    *                              tty_reply                                    *
4030    *===========================================================================*/
4031   PRIVATE tty_reply(code, replyee, proc_nr, status, extra, other)
4032   int code;                        /* TASK_REPLY or REVIVE */
4033   int replyee;                     /* destination address for the reply */
4034   int proc_nr;                     /* to whom should the reply go? */
4035   int status;                      /* reply code */
4036   long extra;                      /* extra value */
4037   long other;                      /* used for IOCTL replies */
4038   {
4039   /* Send a reply to a process that wanted to read or write data. */
4040
4041     message tty_mess;
4042
4043     tty_mess.m_type = code;
4044     tty_mess.REP_PROC_NR = proc_nr;
4045     tty_mess.REP_STATUS = status;
4046     tty_mess.TTY_FLAGS = extra;    /* used by IOCTL for flags (mode) */
4047     tty_mess.TTY_SPEK = other;     /* used by IOCTL for erase and kill chars */
4048     send(replyee, &tty_mess);
4049   }
```

```
4050   /**************************************************************************/
4051   /**************************************************************************/
4052   /**************************************************************************/
4053   /**************************************************************************/
4054   /**************************************************************************/
4055
4056   #ifdef i8088
4057   /* Now begins the code and data for the device-dependent tty drivers. */
4058
4059   /* Definitions used by the console driver. */
4060   #define COLOR_BASE      0xB800    /* video ram paragraph for color display */
4061   #define MONO_BASE       0xB000    /* video ram address for mono display */
4062   #define C_VID_MASK      0x3FFF    /* mask for 16K video RAM */
4063   #define M_VID_MASK      0x0FFF    /* mask for  4K video RAM */
4064   #define C_RETRACE       0x0300    /* how many characters to display at once */
4065   #define M_RETRACE       0x7000    /* how many characters to display at once */
4066   #define WORD_MASK       0xFFFF    /* mask for 16 bits */
4067   #define OFF_MASK        0x000F    /* mask for  4 bits */
4068   #define BEEP_FREQ       0x0533    /* value to put into timer to set beep freq */
4069   #define B_TIME          0x2000    /* how long to sound the CTRL-G beep tone */
4070   #define BLANK           0x0700    /* determines  cursor color on blank screen */
4071   #define LINE_WIDTH      80        /* # characters on a line */
4072   #define SCR_LINES       25        /* # lines on the screen */
4073   #define CTRL_S          31        /* scan code for letter S (for CRTL-S) */
4074   #define MONOCHROME      1         /* value for tty_ioport tells color vs. mono */
4075   #define CONSOLE         0         /* line number for console */
4076   #define GO_FORWARD      0         /* scroll forward */
4077   #define GO_BACKWARD     1         /* scroll backward */
4078   #define TIMER2          0x42      /* I/O port for timer channel 2 */
4079   #define TIMER3          0x43      /* I/O port for timer channel 3 */
4080   #define KEYBD           0x60      /* I/O port for keyboard data */
4081   #define PORT_B          0x61      /* I/O port for 8255 port B */
4082   #define KBIT            0x80      /* bit used to ack characters to keyboard */
4083
4084   /* Constants relating to the video RAM and 6845. */
4085   #define M_6845          0x3B0     /* port for 6845 mono */
4086   #define C_6845          0x3D0     /* port for 6845 color */
4087   #define INDEX           4         /* 6845's index register */
4088   #define DATA            5         /* 6845's data register */
4089   #define CUR_SIZE        10        /* 6845's cursor size register */
4090   #define VID_ORG         12        /* 6845's origin register */
4091   #define CURSOR          14        /* 6845's cursor register */
4092
4093   /* Definitions used for determining if the keyboard is IBM or Olivetti type. */
4094   #define KB_STATUS       0x64      /* Olivetti keyboard status port */
4095   #define BYTE_AVAIL      0x01      /* there is something in KEYBD port */
4096   #define KB_BUSY         0x02      /* KEYBD port ready to accept a command */
4097   #define DELUXE          0x01      /* this bit is set up iff deluxe keyboard */
4098   #define GET_TYPE        5         /* command to get keyboard type */
4099   #define OLIVETTI_EQUAL  12        /* the '=' key is 12 on olivetti, 13 on IBM */
```

```
4100
4101    /* Global variables used by the console driver. */
4102    PUBLIC  int color;                  /* 1 if console is color, 0 if it is mono */
4103    PUBLIC  message keybd_mess;         /* message used for console input chars */
4104    PRIVATE vid_retrace;                /* how many characters to display per burst */
4105    PRIVATE unsigned vid_base;          /* base of video ram (0xB000 or 0xB800) */
4106    PRIVATE int vid_mask;               /* 037777 for color (16K) or 07777 for mono */
4107    PRIVATE int vid_port;               /* I/O port for accessing 6845 */
4108
4109
4110    /*===========================================================================*
4111     *                                keyboard                                   *
4112     *===========================================================================*/
4113    PUBLIC keyboard()
4114    {
4115    /* A keyboard interrupt has occurred.  Process it. */
4116
4117      int val, code, k, raw_bit;
4118      char stopc;
4119
4120      /* Fetch the character from the keyboard hardware and acknowledge it. */
4121      port_in(KEYBD, &code);            /* get the scan code for the key struck */
4122      port_in(PORT_B, &val);            /* strobe the keyboard to ack the char */
4123      port_out(PORT_B, val | KBIT);     /* strobe the bit high */
4124      port_out(PORT_B, val);            /* now strobe it low */
4125
4126      /* The IBM keyboard interrupts twice per key, once when depressed, once when
4127       * released.  Filter out the latter, ignoring all but the shift-type keys.
4128       * The shift-type keys, 29, 42, 54, 56, and 69 must be processed normally.
4129       */
4130      k = code - 0200;                  /* codes > 0200 mean key release */
4131      if (k > 0) {
4132          /* A key has been released. */
4133          if (k != 29 && k != 42 && k != 54 && k != 56 && k != 69) {
4134              port_out(INT_CTL, ENABLE);      /* re-enable interrupts */
4135              return;                    /* don't call tty_task() */
4136          }
4137      } else {
4138          /* Check to see if character is CTRL-S, to stop output. Setting xoff
4139           * to anything other than CTRL-S will not be detected here, but will
4140           * be detected later, in the driver.  A general routine to detect any
4141           * xoff character here would be complicated since we only have the
4142           * scan code here, not the ASCII character.
4143           */
4144          raw_bit = tty_struct[CONSOLE].tty_mode & RAW;
4145          stopc = tty_struct[CONSOLE].tty_xoff;
4146          if (raw_bit == 0 && control && code == CTRL_S && stopc == XOFF_CHAR) {
4147              tty_struct[CONSOLE].tty_inhibited = STOPPED;
4148              port_out(INT_CTL, ENABLE);
4149              return;
```

```
4150                }
4151         }
4152
4153         /* Check for CTRL-ALT-DEL, and if found, reboot the computer. */
4154         if (control && alt && code == DEL_CODE) reboot();      /* CTRL-ALT-DEL */
4155
4156         /* Store the character in memory so the task can get at it later. */
4157         if ( (k = tty_driver_buf[0]) < tty_driver_buf[1]) {
4158                /* There is room to store this character; do it. */
4159                k = k + k;                        /* each entry contains two bytes */
4160                tty_driver_buf[k+2] = code;       /* store the scan code */
4161                tty_driver_buf[k+3] = CONSOLE;    /* tell which line it came from */
4162                tty_driver_buf[0]++;              /* increment counter */
4163
4164                /* Build and send the interrupt message. */
4165                keybd_mess.m_type = TTY_CHAR_INT;
4166                keybd_mess.ADDRESS = tty_driver_buf;
4167                interrupt(TTY, &keybd_mess);      /* send a message to the tty task */
4168         } else {
4169                /* Too many characters have been buffered.  Discard excess. */
4170                port_out(INT_CTL, ENABLE);        /* re-enable 8259A controller */
4171         }
4172    }


4175    /*===========================================================================*
4176     *                              console                                       *
4177     *===========================================================================*/
4178    PRIVATE console(tp)
4179    register struct tty_struct *tp; /* tells which terminal is to be used */
4180    {
4181    /* Copy as much data as possible to the output queue, then start I/O.  On
4182     * memory-mapped terminals, such as the IBM console, the I/O will also be
4183     * finished, and the counts updated.  Keep repeating until all I/O done.
4184     */
4185
4186      int count;
4187      char c;
4188      unsigned segment, offset, offset1;
4189
4190      /* Loop over the user bytes one at a time, outputting each one. */
4191      segment = (tp->tty_phys >> 4) & WORD_MASK;
4192      offset = tp->tty_phys & OFF_MASK;
4193      offset1 = offset;
4194      count = 0;
4195
4196      while (tp->tty_outleft > 0 && tp->tty_inhibited == RUNNING) {
4197            c = get_byte(segment, offset); /* fetch 1 byte from user space */
4198            out_char(tp, c);          /* write 1 byte to terminal */
4199            offset++;                 /* advance one character in user buffer */
```

```
4200                tp->tty_outleft--;        /* decrement count */
4201        }
4202        flush(tp);                        /* clear out the pending characters */
4203
4204        /* Update terminal data structure. */
4205        count = offset - offset1;      /* # characters printed */
4206        tp->tty_phys += count;         /* advance physical data pointer */
4207        tp->tty_cum += count;          /* number of characters printed */
4208
4209        /* If all data has been copied to the terminal, send the reply. */
4210        if (tp->tty_outleft == 0) finish(tp, tp->tty_cum);
4211   }


4214   /*===========================================================================*
4215    *                              out_char                                     *
4216    *===========================================================================*/
4217   PRIVATE out_char(tp, c)
4218   register struct tty_struct *tp; /* pointer to tty struct */
4219   char c;                         /* character to be output */
4220   {
4221   /* Output a character on the console. Check for escape sequences, including
4222    *    ESC 32+x 32+y to move cursor to (x, y)
4223    *    ESC ~ 0       to clear from cursor to end of screen
4224    *    ESC ~ 1       to reverse scroll the screen 1 line
4225    *    ESC z x       to set the attribute byte to x (z is a literal here)
4226    */
4227
4228        /* Check to see if we are part way through an escape sequence. */
4229        if (tp->tty_esc_state == 1) {
4230                tp->tty_echar = c;
4231                tp->tty_esc_state = 2;
4232                return;
4233        }
4234
4235        if (tp->tty_esc_state == 2) {
4236                escape(tp, tp->tty_echar, c);
4237                tp->tty_esc_state = 0;
4238                return;
4239        }
4240
4241        switch(c) {
4242            case 007:                  /* ring the bell */
4243                    flush(tp);         /* print any chars queued for output */
4244                    beep(BEEP_FREQ);/* BEEP_FREQ gives bell tone */
4245                    return;
4246
4247            case 013:                  /* CTRL-K */
4248                    move_to(tp, tp->tty_column, tp->tty_row + 1);
4249                    return;
```

```
4250
4251          case 014:                /* CTRL-L */
4252              move_to(tp, tp->tty_column + 1, tp->tty_row);
4253              return;
4254
4255          case 016:                /* CTRL-N */
4256              move_to(tp, tp->tty_column + 1, tp->tty_row);
4257              return;
4258
4259          case '\b':               /* backspace */
4260              move_to(tp, tp->tty_column - 1, tp->tty_row);
4261              return;
4262
4263          case '\n':               /* line feed */
4264              if (tp->tty_mode & CRMOD) out_char(tp, '\r');
4265              if (tp->tty_row == 0)
4266                      scroll_screen(tp, GO_FORWARD);
4267              else
4268                      tp->tty_row--;
4269              move_to(tp, tp->tty_column, tp->tty_row);
4270              return;
4271                      .
4272          case '\r':               /* carriage return */
4273              move_to(tp, 0, tp->tty_row);
4274              return;
4275
4276          case '\t':               /* tab */
4277              if ( (tp->tty_mode & XTABS) == XTABS) {
4278                      do {
4279                              out_char(tp, ' ');
4280                      } while (tp->tty_column & TAB_MASK);
4281                      return;
4282              }
4283              /* Ignore tab is XTABS is off--video RAM has no hardware tab */
4284              return;
4285
4286          case 033:                /* ESC - start of an escape sequence */
4287              flush(tp);        /* print any chars queued for output */
4288              tp->tty_esc_state = 1;  /* mark ESC as seen */
4289              return;
4290
4291          default:                 /* printable chars are stored in ramqueue */
4292              if (tp->tty_column >= LINE_WIDTH) return;        /* long line */
4293              if (tp->tty_rwords == TTY_RAM_WORDS) flush(tp);
4294              tp->tty_ramqueue[tp->tty_rwords++] = tp->tty_attribute | c;
4295              tp->tty_column++;       /* next column */
4296              return;
4297      }
4298  }
```

```
4301    /*===========================================================================*
4302     *                            scroll_screen                                  *
4303     *===========================================================================*/
4304    PRIVATE scroll_screen(tp, dir)
4305    register struct tty_struct *tp; /* pointer to tty struct */
4306    int dir;                        /* GO_FORWARD or GO_BACKWARD */
4307    {
4308      int amount, offset;
4309
4310      amount = (dir == GO_FORWARD ? 2 * LINE_WIDTH : -2 * LINE_WIDTH);
4311      tp->tty_org = (tp->tty_org + amount) & vid_mask;
4312      if (dir == GO_FORWARD)
4313            offset = (tp->tty_org + 2 * (SCR_LINES - 1) * LINE_WIDTH) & vid_mask;
4314      else
4315            offset = tp->tty_org;
4316
4317      /* Blank the new line at top or bottom. */
4318      vid_copy(NIL_PTR, vid_base, offset, LINE_WIDTH);
4319      set_6845(VID_ORG, tp->tty_org >> 1);  /* 6845 thinks in words */
4320    }


4323    /*===========================================================================*
4324     *                               flush                                       *
4325     *===========================================================================*/
4326    PRIVATE flush(tp)
4327    register struct tty_struct *tp; /* pointer to tty struct */
4328    {
4329    /* Have the characters in 'ramqueue' transferred to the screen. */
4330
4331      if (tp->tty_rwords == 0) return;
4332      vid_copy(tp->tty_ramqueue, vid_base, tp->tty_vid, tp->tty_rwords);
4333
4334      /* Update the video parameters and cursor. */
4335      tp->tty_vid += 2 * tp->tty_rwords;
4336      set_6845(CURSOR, tp->tty_vid >> 1);   /* cursor counts in words */
4337      tp->tty_rwords = 0;
4338    }


4340    /*===========================================================================*
4341     *                              move_to                                      *
4342     *===========================================================================*/
4343    PRIVATE move_to(tp, x, y)
4344    struct tty_struct *tp;              /* pointer to tty struct */
4345    int x;                              /* column (0 <= x <= 79) */
4346    int y;                              /* row (0 <= y <= 24, 0 at bottom) */
4347    {
4348    /* Move the cursor to (x, y). */
4349
```

```
4350        flush(tp);                          /* flush any pending characters */
4351        if (x < 0 || x >= LINE_WIDTH || y < 0 || y >= SCR_LINES) return;
4352        tp->tty_column = x;                 /* set x co-ordinate */
4353        tp->tty_row = y;                    /* set y co-ordinate */
4354        tp->tty_vid = (tp->tty_org + 2*(SCR_LINES-1-y)* LINE_WIDTH + 2*x);
4355        set_6845(CURSOR, tp->tty_vid >> 1);   /* cursor counts in words */
4356      }


4359    /*===========================================================================*
4360     *                              escape                                        *
4361     *===========================================================================*/
4362    PRIVATE escape(tp, x, y)
4363    register struct tty_struct *tp; /* pointer to tty struct */
4364    char x;                                 /* escape sequence is ESC x y; this is x */
4365    char y;                                 /* escape sequence is ESC x y; this is y */
4366    {
4367    /* Handle an escape sequence. */
4368
4369      int n, ct, vx;
4370
4371
4372      /* Check for ESC z attribute - used to change attribute byte. */
4373      if (x == 'z') {
4374            /* Set attribute byte */
4375            tp->tty_attribute = y << 8;
4376            return;
4377      }
4378      /* Check for ESC ~ n -  used for clear screen, reverse scroll. */
4379      if (x == '~') {
4380            if (y == '0') {
4381                    /* Clear from cursor to end of screen */
4382                    n = 2 * LINE_WIDTH * (tp->tty_row + 1) - 2 * tp->tty_column;
4383                    vx = tp->tty_vid;
4384                    while (n > 0) {
4385                            ct = MIN(n, vid_retrace);
4386                            vid_copy(NIL_PTR, vid_base, vx, ct/2);
4387                            vx += ct;
4388                            n -= ct;
4389                    }
4390            } else if (y == '1') {
4391                    /* Reverse scroll. */
4392                    scroll_screen(tp, GO_BACKWARD);
4393            }
4394            return;
4395      }
4396
4397      /* Must be cursor movement (or invalid). */
4398      move_to(tp, x - 32, y - 32);
4399    }
```

```
4400   /*===========================================================================*
4401    *                              set_6845                                      *
4402    *===========================================================================*/
4403   PRIVATE set_6845(reg, val)
4404   int reg;                          /* which register pair to set */
4405   int val;                          /* 16-bit value to set it to */
4406   {
4407   /* Set a register pair inside the 6845.
4408    * Registers 10-11 control the format of the cursor (how high it is, etc).
4409    * Registers 12-13 tell the 6845 where in video ram to start (in WORDS)
4410    * Registers 14-15 tell the 6845 where to put the cursor (in WORDS)
4411    *
4412    * Note that registers 12-15 work in words, i.e. 0x0000 is the top left
4413    * character, but 0x0001 (not 0x0002) is the next character.  This addressing
4414    * is different from the way the 8088 addresses the video ram, where 0x0002
4415    * is the address of the next character.
4416    */
4417     port_out(vid_port + INDEX, reg);        /* set the index register */
4418     port_out(vid_port + DATA, (val>>8) & BYTE);   /* output high byte */
4419     port_out(vid_port + INDEX, reg + 1);  /* again */
4420     port_out(vid_port + DATA, val&BYTE);  /* output low byte */
4421   }


4424   /*===========================================================================*
4425    *                               beep                                         *
4426    *===========================================================================*/
4427   PRIVATE beep(f)
4428   int f;                            /* this value determines beep frequency */
4429   {
4430   /* Making a beeping sound on the speaker (output for CRTL-G).  The beep is
4431    * kept short, because interrupts must be disabled during beeping, and it
4432    * is undesirable to keep them off too long.  This routine works by turning
4433    * on the bits in port B of the 8255 chip that drive the speaker.
4434    */
4435
4436     int x, k;
4437
4438     lock();                          /* disable interrupts */
4439     port_out(TIMER3,0xB6);           /* set up timer channel 2 mode */
4440     port_out(TIMER2, f&BYTE);        /* load low-order bits of frequency in timer */
4441     port_out(TIMER2,(f>>8)&BYTE);    /* now high-order bits of frequency in timer */
4442     port_in(PORT_B,&x);              /* acquire status of port B */
4443     port_out(PORT_B, x|3);           /* turn bits 0 and 1 on to beep */
4444     for (k = 0; k < B_TIME; k++);    /* delay loop while beeper sounding */
4445     port_out(PORT_B, x);             /* restore port B the way it was */
4446     unlock();                        /* re-enable interrupts */
4447   }
```

```
4450     /*===========================================================================*
4451      *                              tty_init                                     *
4452      *===========================================================================*/
4453     PRIVATE tty_init()
4454     {
4455     /* Initialize the tty tables. */
4456
4457       register struct tty_struct *tp;
4458
4459       for (tp = &tty_struct[0]; tp < &tty_struct[NR_TTYS]; tp++) {
4460             tp->tty_inhead = tp->tty_inqueue;
4461             tp->tty_intail = tp->tty_inqueue;
4462             tp->tty_mode = CRMOD | XTABS | ECHO;
4463             tp->tty_devstart = console;
4464             tp->tty_erase = ERASE_CHAR;
4465             tp->tty_kill  = KILL_CHAR;
4466             tp->tty_intr  = INTR_CHAR;
4467             tp->tty_quit  = QUIT_CHAR;
4468             tp->tty_xon   = XON_CHAR;
4469             tp->tty_xoff  = XOFF_CHAR;
4470             tp->tty_eof   = EOT_CHAR;
4471       }
4472
4473       tty_struct[0].tty_makebreak = TWO_INTS;          /* tty 0 is console */
4474       if (color) {
4475             vid_base = COLOR_BASE;
4476             vid_mask = C_VID_MASK;
4477             vid_port = C_6845;
4478             vid_retrace = C_RETRACE;
4479       } else {
4480             vid_base = MONO_BASE;
4481             vid_mask = M_VID_MASK;
4482             vid_port = M_6845;
4483             vid_retrace = M_RETRACE;
4484       }
4485       tty_struct[0].tty_attribute = BLANK;
4486       tty_driver_buf[1] = MAX_OVERRUN;        /* set up limit on keyboard buffering */
4487       set_6845(CUR_SIZE, 31);                 /* set cursor shape */
4488       set_6845(VID_ORG, 0);                   /* use page 0 of video ram */
4489       move_to(&tty_struct[0], 0, 0);          /* move cursor to lower left corner */
4490
4491       /* Determine which keyboard type is attached.  The bootstrap program asks
4492        * the user to type an '='.  The scan codes for '=' differ depending on the
4493        * keyboard in use.
4494        */
4495       if (scan_code == OLIVETTI_EQUAL) olivetti = TRUE;
4496     }
```

```
4500    /*=========================================================================*
4501     *                              putc                                        *
4502     *=========================================================================*/
4503    PUBLIC putc(c)
4504    char c;                         /* character to print */
4505    {
4506    /* This procedure is used by the version of printf() that is linked with
4507     * the kernel itself.  The one in the library sends a message to FS, which is
4508     * not what is needed for printing within the kernel.  This version just queues
4509     * the character and starts the output.
4510     */
4511
4512      out_char(&tty_struct[0], c);
4513    }


4516    /*=========================================================================*
4517     *                              func_key                                    *
4518     *=========================================================================*/
4519    PRIVATE func_key(ch)
4520    char ch;                        /* scan code for a function key */
4521    {
4522    /* This procedure traps function keys for debugging purposes.  When MINIX is
4523     * fully debugged, it should be removed.
4524     */
4525
4526      if (ch == F1) p_dmp();        /* print process table */
4527      if (ch == F2) map_dmp();      /* print memory map */
4528    }
4529    #endif
```

```
4550    /* This task handles the interface between file system and kernel as well as
4551     * between memory manager and kernel.  System services are obtained by sending
4552     * sys_task() a message specifying what is needed.  To make life easier for
4553     * MM and FS, a library is provided with routines whose names are of the
4554     * form sys_xxx, e.g. sys_xit sends the SYS_XIT message to sys_task.  The
4555     * message types and parameters are:
4556     *
4557     *    SYS_FORK     informs kernel that a process has forked
4558     *    SYS_NEWMAP   allows MM to set up a process memory map
4559     *    SYS_EXEC     sets program counter and stack pointer after EXEC
4560     *    SYS_XIT      informs kernel that a process has exited
4561     *    SYS_GETSP    caller wants to read out some process' stack pointer
4562     *    SYS_TIMES    caller wants to get accounting times for a process
4563     *    SYS_ABORT    MM or FS cannot go on; abort MINIX
4564     *    SYS_SIG      send a signal to a process
4565     *    SYS_COPY     requests a block of data to be copied between processes
4566     *
4567     * Message type m1 is used for all except SYS_SIG and SYS_COPY, both of
4568     * which need special parameter types.
4569     *
4570     *    m_type       PROC1       PROC2       PID      MEM_PTR
4571     * -----------------------------------------------------------
4572     * | SYS_FORK   | parent   | child    | pid     |           |
4573     * |------------+----------+----------+---------+---------- |
4574     * | SYS_NEWMAP | proc nr  |          |         | map ptr   |
4575     * |------------+----------+----------+---------+---------- |
4576     * | SYS_EXEC   | proc nr  |          | new sp  |           |
4577     * |------------+----------+----------+---------+---------- |
4578     * | SYS_XIT    | parent   | exitee   |         |           |
4579     * |------------+----------+----------+---------+---------- |
4580     * | SYS_GETSP  | proc nr  |          |         |           |
4581     * |------------+----------+----------+---------+---------- |
4582     * | SYS_TIMES  | proc nr  |          | buf ptr |           |
4583     * |------------+----------+----------+---------+---------- |
4584     * | SYS_ABORT  |          |          |         |           |
4585     * -----------------------------------------------------------
4586     *
4587     *
4588     *    m_type       m6_il       m6_i2       m6_i3      m6_fl
4589     * -----------------------------------------------------------
4590     * | SYS_SIG    | proc_nr  | sig      |         | handler  |
4591     * -----------------------------------------------------------
4592     *
4593     *
4594     *    m_type       m5_cl   m5_il   m5_ll   m5_c2   m5_i2   m5_l2   m5_l3
4595     * ------------------------------------------------------------------------
4596     * | SYS_COPY  |src seg|src proc|src vir|dst seg|dst proc|dst vir| byte ct |
4597     * ------------------------------------------------------------------------
4598     *
4599     * In addition to the main sys_task() entry point, there are three other minor
```

```
4600     * entry points:
4601     *    cause_sig: take action to cause a signal to occur, sooner or later
4602     *    inform:    tell MM about pending signals
4603     *    umap:      compute the physical address for a given virtual address
4604     */
4605
4606     #include "../h/const.h"
4607     #include "../h/type.h"
4608     #include "../h/callnr.h"
4609     #include "../h/com.h"
4610     #include "../h/error.h"
4611     #include "../h/signal.h"
4612     #include "const.h"
4613     #include "type.h"
4614     #include "glo.h"
4615     #include "proc.h"
4616
4617     #define COPY_UNIT    65534L     /* max bytes to copy at once */
4618
4619     extern phys_bytes umap();
4620
4621     PRIVATE message m;
4622     PRIVATE char sig_stuff[SIG_PUSH_BYTES]; /* used to send signals to processes */
4623
4624     /*===========================================================================*
4625      *                              sys_task                                     *
4626      *===========================================================================*/
4627     PUBLIC sys_task()
4628     {
4629     /* Main entry point of sys_task.  Get the message and dispatch on type. */
4630
4631       register int r;
4632
4633       while (TRUE) {
4634             receive(ANY, &m);
4635
4636             switch (m.m_type) {      /* which system call */
4637                 case SYS_FORK:    r = do_fork(&m);      break;
4638                 case SYS_NEWMAP:  r = do_newmap(&m);    break;
4639                 case SYS_EXEC:    r = do_exec(&m);      break;
4640                 case SYS_XIT:     r = do_xit(&m);       break;
4641                 case SYS_GETSP:   r = do_getsp(&m);     break;
4642                 case SYS_TIMES:   r = do_times(&m);     break;
4643                 case SYS_ABORT:   r = do_abort(&m);     break;
4644                 case SYS_SIG:     r = do_sig(&m);       break;
4645                 case SYS_COPY:    r = do_copy(&m);      break;
4646                 default:          r = E_BAD_FCN;
4647             }
4648
4649             m.m_type = r;            /* 'r' reports status of call */
```

```
4650                 send(m.m_source, &m);    /* send reply to caller */
4651         }
4652   }


4655   /*===========================================================================*
4656    *                              do_fork                                       *
4657    *===========================================================================*/
4658   PRIVATE int do_fork(m_ptr)
4659   message *m_ptr;                          /* pointer to request message */
4660   {
4661   /* Handle sys_fork().  'kl' has forked.  The child is 'k2'. */
4662
4663     register struct proc *rpc;
4664     register char *sptr, *dptr;    /* pointers for copying proc struct */
4665     int kl;                         /* number of parent process */
4666     int k2;                         /* number of child process */
4667     int pid;                        /* process id of child */
4668     int bytes;                      /* counter for copying proc struct */
4669
4670     kl = m_ptr->PROC1;              /* extract parent slot number from msg */
4671     k2 = m_ptr->PROC2;             /* extract child slot number */
4672     pid = m_ptr->PID;             /* extract child process id */
4673
4674     if (kl < 0 || kl >= NR_PROCS || k2 < 0 || k2 >= NR_PROCS)return(E_BAD_PROC);
4675     rpc = proc_addr(k2);
4676
4677     /* Copy parent 'proc' struct to child. */
4678     sptr = (char *) proc_addr(kl);        /* parent pointer */
4679     dptr = (char *) proc_addr(k2);        /* child pointer */
4680     bytes = sizeof(struct proc);          /* # bytes to copy */
4681     while (bytes--) *dptr++ = *sptr++;    /* copy parent struct to child */
4682
4683     rpc->p_flags |= NO_MAP;       /* inhibit the process from running */
4684     rpc->p_pid = pid;             /* install child's pid */
4685     rpc->p_reg[RET_REG] = 0;      /* child sees pid = 0 to know it is child */
4686
4687     rpc->user_time = 0;           /* set all the accounting times to 0 */
4688     rpc->sys_time = 0;
4689     rpc->child_utime = 0;
4690     rpc->child_stime = 0;
4691     return(OK);
4692   }


4695   /*===========================================================================*
4696    *                              do_newmap                                     *
4697    *===========================================================================*/
4698   PRIVATE int do_newmap(m_ptr)
4699   message *m_ptr;                          /* pointer to request message */
```

```
4700     {
4701     /* Handle sys_newmap().  Fetch the memory map from MM. */
4702
4703       register struct proc *rp, *rsrc;
4704       phys_bytes src_phys, dst_phys, pn;
4705       vir_bytes vmm, vsys, vn;
4706       int caller;                      /* whose space has the new map (usually MM) */
4707       int k;                           /* process whose map is to be loaded */
4708       int old_flags;                   /* value of flags before modification */
4709       struct mem_map *map_ptr;         /* virtual address of map inside caller (MM) */
4710
4711       /* Extract message parameters and copy new memory map from MM. */
4712       caller = m_ptr->m_source;
4713       k = m_ptr->PROC1;
4714       map_ptr = (struct mem_map *) m_ptr->MEM_PTR;
4715       if (k < -NR_TASKS || k >= NR_PROCS) return(E_BAD_PROC);
4716       rp = proc_addr(k);               /* ptr to entry of user getting new map */
4717       rsrc = proc_addr(caller);        /* ptr to MM's proc entry */
4718       vn = NR_SEGS * sizeof(struct mem_map);
4719       pn = vn;
4720       vmm = (vir_bytes) map_ptr;       /* careful about sign extension */
4721       vsys = (vir_bytes) rp->p_map;    /* again, careful about sign extension */
4722       if ( (src_phys = umap(rsrc, D, vmm, vn)) == 0)
4723             panic("bad call to sys_newmap (src)", NO_NUM);
4724       if ( (dst_phys = umap(proc_addr(SYSTASK), D, vsys, vn)) == 0)
4725             panic("bad call to sys_newmap (dst)", NO_NUM);
4726       phys_copy(src_phys, dst_phys, pn);
4727
4728 #ifdef i8088
4729       /* On 8088, set segment registers. */
4730       rp->p_reg[CS_REG] = rp->p_map[T].mem_phys;    /* set cs */
4731       rp->p_reg[DS_REG] = rp->p_map[D].mem_phys;    /* set ds */
4732       rp->p_reg[SS_REG] = rp->p_map[D].mem_phys;    /* set ss */
4733       rp->p_reg[ES_REG] = rp->p_map[D].mem_phys;    /* set es */
4734 #endif
4735
4736       old_flags = rp->p_flags;         /* save the previous value of the flags */
4737       rp->p_flags &= ~NO_MAP;
4738       if (old_flags != 0 && rp->p_flags == 0) ready(rp);
4739       return(OK);
4740     }


4743     /*===========================================================================*
4744      *                              do_exec                                       *
4745      *===========================================================================*/
4746     PRIVATE int do_exec(m_ptr)
4747     message *m_ptr;                    /* pointer to request message */
4748     {
4749     /* Handle sys_exec().  A process has done a successful EXEC. Patch it up. */
```

```
4750
4751        register struct proc *rp;
4752        int k;                          /* which process */
4753        int *sp;                        /* new sp */
4754
4755        k = m_ptr->PROC1;               /* 'k' tells which process did EXEC */
4756        sp = (int *) m_ptr->STACK_PTR;
4757        if (k < 0 || k >= NR_PROCS) return(E_BAD_PROC);
4758        rp = proc_addr(k);
4759        rp->p_sp = sp;                  /* set the stack pointer */
4760        rp->p_pcpsw.pc = (int (*)()) 0;      /* reset pc */
4761        rp->p_alarm = 0;                /* reset alarm timer */
4762        rp->p_flags &= ~RECEIVING;      /* MM does not reply to EXEC call */
4763        if (rp->p_flags == 0) ready(rp);
4764        return(OK);
4765    }


4768    /*===========================================================================*
4769     *                              do_xit                                       *
4770     *===========================================================================*/
4771    PRIVATE int do_xit(m_ptr)
4772    message *m_ptr;                     /* pointer to request message */
4773    {
4774    /* Handle sys_xit().  A process has exited. */
4775
4776        register struct proc *rp, *rc;
4777        struct proc *np, *xp;
4778        int parent;                     /* number of exiting proc's parent */
4779        int proc_nr;                    /* number of process doing the exit */
4780
4781        parent = m_ptr->PROC1;          /* slot number of parent process */
4782        proc_nr = m_ptr->PROC2;         /* slot number of exiting process */
4783        if (parent < 0 || parent >= NR_PROCS || proc_nr < 0 || proc_nr >= NR_PROCS)
4784            return(E_BAD_PROC);
4785        rp = proc_addr(parent);
4786        rc = proc_addr(proc_nr);
4787        rp->child_utime += rc->user_time + rc->child_utime;   /* accum child times */
4788        rp->child_stime += rc->sys_time + rc->child_stime;
4789        unready(rc);
4790        rc->p_alarm = 0;                /* turn off alarm timer */
4791
4792        /* If the process being terminated happens to be queued trying to send a
4793         * message (i.e., the process was killed by a signal, rather than it doing an
4794         * EXIT), then it must be removed from the message queues.
4795         */
4796        if (rc->p_flags & SENDING) {
4797            /* Check all proc slots to see if the exiting process is queued. */
4798            for (rp = &proc[0]; rp < &proc[NR_TASKS + NR_PROCS]; rp++) {
4799                if (rp->p_callerq == NIL_PROC) continue;
```

```
4800                        if (rp->p_callerq == rc) {
4801                                /* Exiting process is on front of this queue. */
4802                                rp->p_callerq = rc->p_sendlink;
4803                                break;
4804                        } else {
4805                                /* See if exiting process is in middle of queue. */
4806                                np = rp->p_callerq;
4807                                while ( ( xp = np->p_sendlink) != NIL_PROC)
4808                                        if (xp == rc) {
4809                                                np->p_sendlink = xp->p_sendlink;
4810                                                break;
4811                                        } else {
4812                                                np = xp;
4813                                        }
4814                        }
4815                }
4816        }
4817        rc->p_flags = P_SLOT_FREE;
4818        return(OK);
4819 }


4822 /*===========================================================================*
4823  *                              do_getsp                                     *
4824  *===========================================================================*/
4825 PRIVATE int do_getsp(m_ptr)
4826 message *m_ptr;                         /* pointer to request message */
4827 {
4828 /* Handle sys_getsp().  MM wants to know what sp is. */
4829
4830    register struct proc *rp;
4831    int k;                               /* whose stack pointer is wanted? */
4832
4833    k = m_ptr->PROC1;
4834    if (k < 0 || k >= NR_PROCS) return(E_BAD_PROC);
4835    rp = proc_addr(k);
4836    m.STACK_PTR = (char *) rp->p_sp;      /* return sp here */
4837    return(OK);
4838 }


4841 /*===========================================================================*
4842  *                              do_times                                     *
4843  *===========================================================================*/
4844 PRIVATE int do_times(m_ptr)
4845 message *m_ptr;                         /* pointer to request message */
4846 {
4847 /* Handle sys_times().  Retrieve the accounting information. */
4848
4849    register struct proc *rp;
```

```
4850        int k;
4851
4852        k = m_ptr->PROC1;               /* k tells whose times are wanted */
4853        if (k < 0 || k >= NR_PROCS) return(E_BAD_PROC);
4854        rp = proc_addr(k);
4855
4856        /* Insert the four times needed by the TIMES system call in the message. */
4857        m_ptr->USER_TIME    = rp->user_time;
4858        m_ptr->SYSTEM_TIME  = rp->sys_time;
4859        m_ptr->CHILD_UTIME  = rp->child_utime;
4860        m_ptr->CHILD_STIME  = rp->child_stime;
4861        return(OK);
4862    }


4865    /*===========================================================================*
4866     *                              do_abort                                      *
4867     *===========================================================================*/
4868    PRIVATE int do_abort(m_ptr)
4869    message *m_ptr;                 /* pointer to request message */
4870    {
4871    /* Handle sys_abort.  MINIX is unable to continue.  Terminate operation. */
4872
4873        panic("", NO_NUM);
4874    }


4877    /*===========================================================================*
4878     *                              do_sig                                        *
4879     *===========================================================================*/
4880    PRIVATE int do_sig(m_ptr)
4881    message *m_ptr;                 /* pointer to request message */
4882    {
4883    /* Handle sys_sig(). Signal a process.  The stack is known to be big enough. */
4884
4885        register struct proc *rp;
4886        phys_bytes src_phys, dst_phys;
4887        vir_bytes vir_addr, sig_size, new_sp;
4888        int proc_nr;                    /* process number */
4889        int sig;                        /* signal number 1-16 */
4890        int (*sig_handler)();           /* pointer to the signal handler */
4891
4892        /* Extract parameters and prepare to build the words that get pushed. */
4893        proc_nr = m_ptr->PR;            /* process being signalled */
4894        sig = m_ptr->SIGNUM;            /* signal number, 1 to 16 */
4895        sig_handler = m_ptr->FUNC;      /* run time system addr for catching sigs */
4896        if (proc_nr < LOW_USER || proc_nr >= NR_PROCS) return(E_BAD_PROC);
4897        rp = proc_addr(proc_nr);
4898        vir_addr = (vir_bytes) sig_stuff;       /* info to be pushed is in 'sig_stuff' */
4899        new_sp = (vir_bytes) rp->p_sp;
```

```
4900
4901        /* Actually build the block of words to push onto the stack. */
4902        build_sig(sig_stuff, rp, sig);        /* build up the info to be pushed */
4903
4904        /* Prepare to do the push, and do it. */
4905        sig_size = SIG_PUSH_BYTES;
4906        new_sp -= sig_size;
4907        src_phys = umap(proc_addr(SYSTASK), D, vir_addr, sig_size);
4908        dst_phys = umap(rp, S, new_sp, sig_size);
4909        if (dst_phys == 0) panic("do_sig can't signal; SP bad", NO_NUM);
4910        phys_copy(src_phys, dst_phys, (phys_bytes) sig_size); /* push pc, psw */
4911
4912        /* Change process' sp and pc to reflect the interrupt. */
4913        rp->p_sp = (int *) new_sp;
4914        rp->p_pcpsw.pc = sig_handler;
4915        return(OK);
4916    }


4919    /*===========================================================================*
4920     *                              do_copy                                       *
4921     *===========================================================================*/
4922    PRIVATE int do_copy(m_ptr)
4923    message *m_ptr;                         /* pointer to request message */
4924    {
4925    /* Handle sys_copy().  Copy data for MM or FS. */
4926
4927        int src_proc, dst_proc, src_space, dst_space;
4928        vir_bytes src_vir, dst_vir;
4929        phys_bytes src_phys, dst_phys, bytes;
4930
4931        /* Dismember the command message. */
4932        src_proc = m_ptr->SRC_PROC_NR;
4933        dst_proc = m_ptr->DST_PROC_NR;
4934        src_space = m_ptr->SRC_SPACE;
4935        dst_space = m_ptr->DST_SPACE;
4936        src_vir = (vir_bytes) m_ptr->SRC_BUFFER;
4937        dst_vir = (vir_bytes) m_ptr->DST_BUFFER;
4938        bytes = (phys_bytes) m_ptr->COPY_BYTES;
4939
4940        /* Compute the source and destination addresses and do the copy. */
4941        if (src_proc == ABS)
4942                src_phys = (phys_bytes) m_ptr->SRC_BUFFER;
4943        else
4944                src_phys = umap(proc_addr(src_proc),src_space,src_vir,(vir_bytes)bytes);
4945
4946        if (dst_proc == ABS)
4947                dst_phys = (phys_bytes) m_ptr->DST_BUFFER;
4948        else
4949                dst_phys = umap(proc_addr(dst_proc),dst_space,dst_vir,(vir_bytes)bytes);
```

```
4950
4951      if (src_phys == 0 || dst_phys == 0) return(EFAULT);
4952      phys_copy(src_phys, dst_phys, bytes);
4953      return(OK);
4954    }


4957    /*===========================================================================*
4958     *                              cause_sig                                     *
4959     *===========================================================================*/
4960    PUBLIC cause_sig(proc_nr, sig_nr)
4961    int proc_nr;                    /* process to be signalled */
4962    int sig_nr;                     /* signal to be sent in range 1 - 16 */
4963    {
4964    /* A task wants to send a signal to a process.  Examples of such tasks are:
4965     *    TTY wanting to cause SIGINT upon getting a DEL
4966     *    CLOCK wanting to cause SIGALRM when timer expires
4967     * Signals are handled by sending a message to MM.  The tasks don't dare do
4968     * that directly, for fear of what would happen if MM were busy.  Instead they
4969     * call cause_sig, which sets bits in p_pending, and then carefully checks to
4970     * see if MM is free.  If so, a message is sent to it.  If not, when it becomes
4971     * free, a message is sent.  The calling task always gets control back from
4972     * cause_sig() immediately.
4973     */
4974
4975      register struct proc *rp;
4976
4977      rp = proc_addr(proc_nr);
4978      if (rp->p_pending == 0) sig_procs++;  /* incr if a new proc is now pending */
4979      rp->p_pending |= 1 << (sig_nr - 1);
4980      inform(MM_PROC_NR);             /* see if MM is free */
4981    }


4984    /*===========================================================================*
4985     *                              inform                                        *
4986     *===========================================================================*/
4987    PUBLIC inform(proc_nr)
4988    int proc_nr;                    /* MM_PROC_NR or FS_PROC_NR */
4989    {
4990    /* When a signal is detected by the kernel (e.g., DEL), or generated by a task
4991     * (e.g. clock task for SIGALRM), cause_sig() is called to set a bit in the
4992     * p_pending field of the process to signal.  Then inform() is called to see
4993     * if MM is idle and can be told about it.  Whenever MM blocks, a check is
4994     * made to see if 'sig_procs' is nonzero; if so, inform() is called.
4995     */
4996
4997      register struct proc *rp, *mmp;
4998
4999      /* If MM is not waiting for new input, forget it. */
```

```
5000        mmp = proc_addr(proc_nr);
5001        if ( ((mmp->p_flags & RECEIVING) == 0) || mmp->p_getfrom != ANY) return;
5002
5003        /* MM is waiting for new input.  Find a process with pending signals. */
5004        for (rp = proc_addr(0); rp < proc_addr(NR_PROCS); rp++)
5005            if (rp->p_pending != 0) {
5006                    m.m_type = KSIG;
5007                    m.PROC1 = rp - proc - NR_TASKS;
5008                    m.SIG_MAP = rp->p_pending;
5009                    sig_procs--;
5010                    if (mini_send(HARDWARE, proc_nr, &m) != OK)
5011                            panic("can't inform MM", NO_NUM);
5012                    rp->p_pending = 0;       /* the ball is now in MM's court */
5013                    return;
5014            }
5015    }


5018    /*===========================================================================*
5019     *                              umap                                          *
5020     *===========================================================================*/
5021    PUBLIC phys_bytes umap(rp, seg, vir_addr, bytes)
5022    register struct proc *rp;       /* pointer to proc table entry for process */
5023    int seg;                        /* T, D, or S segment */
5024    vir_bytes vir_addr;             /* virtual address in bytes within the seg */
5025    vir_bytes bytes;                /* # of bytes to be copied */
5026    {
5027    /* Calculate the physical memory address for a given virtual address. */
5028      vir_clicks vc;                /* the virtual address in clicks */
5029      phys_bytes seg_base, pa;      /* intermediate variables as phys_bytes */
5030
5031      /* If 'seg' is D it could really be S and vice versa.  T really means T.
5032       * If the virtual address falls in the gap,  it causes a problem. On the
5033       * 8088 it is probably a legal stack reference, since "stackfaults" are
5034       * not detected by the hardware.  On 8088s, the gap is called S and
5035       * accepted, but on other machines it is called D and rejected.
5036       */
5037      if (bytes <= 0) return( (phys_bytes) 0);
5038      vc = (vir_addr + bytes - 1) >> CLICK_SHIFT;   /* last click of data */
5039
5040    #ifdef i8088
5041      if (seg != T)
5042            seg = (vc < rp->p_map[D].mem_vir + rp->p_map[D].mem_len ? D : S);
5043    #else
5044      if (seg != T)
5045            seg = (vc < rp->p_map[S].mem_vir ? D : S);
5046    #endif
5047
5048      if((vir_addr>>CLICK_SHIFT) >= rp->p_map[seg].mem_vir + rp->p_map[seg].mem_len)
5049            return( (phys_bytes) 0 );
```

```
5050        seg_base = (phys_bytes) rp->p_map[seg].mem_phys;
5051        seg_base = seg_base << CLICK_SHIFT;    /* segment orgin in bytes */
5052        pa = (phys_bytes) vir_addr;
5053        pa -= rp->p_map[seg].mem_vir << CLICK_SHIFT;
5054      return(seg_base + pa);
5055    }
```

```
5100   /* The object file of "table.c" contains all the data.  In the *.h files,
5101    * declared variables appear with EXTERN in front of them, as in
5102    *
5103    *     EXTERN int x;
5104    *
5105    * Normally EXTERN is defined as extern, so when they are included in another
5106    * file, no storage is allocated.  If the EXTERN were not present, but just
5107    * say,
5108    *
5109    *     int x;
5110    *
5111    * then including this file in several source files would cause 'x' to be
5112    * declared several times.  While some linkers accept this, others do not,
5113    * so they are declared extern when included normally.  However, it must
5114    * be declared for real somewhere.  That is done here, but redefining
5115    * EXTERN as the null string, so the inclusion of all the *.h files in
5116    * table.c actually generates storage for them.  All the initialized
5117    * variables are also declared here, since
5118    *
5119    * extern int x = 4;
5120    *
5121    * is not allowed.  If such variables are shared, they must also be declared
5122    * in one of the *.h files without the initialization.
5123    */
5124
5125   #include "../h/const.h"
5126   #include "../h/type.h"
5127   #include "const.h"
5128   #include "type.h"
5129   #undef   EXTERN
5130   #define  EXTERN
5131   #include "glo.h"
5132   #include "proc.h"
5133
5134   extern int sys_task(), clock_task(), mem_task(), floppy_task(),
5135             winchester_task(), tty_task(), printer_task();
5136
5137   /* The startup routine of each task is given below, from -NR_TASKS upwards.
5138    * The order of the names here MUST agree with the numerical values assigned to
5139    * the tasks in ../h/com.h.
5140    */
5141   int (*task[NR_TASKS+INIT_PROC_NR+1])() = {
5142   printer_task, tty_task, winchester_task, floppy_task, mem_task,
5143   clock_task, sys_task, 0, 0, 0, 0
5144   };
```

```
5150    /* Constants used by the Memory Manager. */
5151
5152    #define ZEROBUF_SIZE    1024    /* buffer size for erasing memory */
5153
5154    /* Size of MM's stack depends mostly on do_exec(). */
5155    #if ZEROBUF_SIZE > MAX_PATH
5156    #define MM_STACK_BYTES  MAX_ISTACK_BYTES + ZEROBUF_SIZE + 384
5157    #else
5158    #define MM_STACK_BYTES  MAX_ISTACK_BYTES + MAX_PATH + 384
5159    #endif
5160
5161    #define NO_MEM (phys_clicks)0   /* returned by alloc_mem() with mem is up */
5162
5163    #ifdef i8088
5164    #define PAGE_SIZE       16      /* how many bytes in a page */
5165    #define MAX_PAGES       4096    /* how many pages in the virtual addr space */
5166    #define HDR_SIZE        32      /* # bytes in the exec file header */
5167    #endif
5168
5169    #define printf          printk
```

```
5200    /* Global variables. */
5201    EXTERN struct mproc *mp;          /* ptr to 'mproc' slot of current process */
5202    EXTERN int dont_reply;           /* normally 0; set to 1 to inhibit reply */
5203    EXTERN int procs_in_use;         /* how many processes are marked as IN_USE */
5204
5205    /* The parameters of the call are kept here. */
5206    EXTERN message mm_in;            /* the incoming message itself is kept here. */
5207    EXTERN message mm_out;           /* the reply message is built up here. */
5208    EXTERN int who;                  /* caller's proc number */
5209    EXTERN int mm_call;              /* caller's proc number */
5210
5211    /* The following variables are used for returning results to the caller. */
5212    EXTERN int err_code;             /* temporary storage for error number */
5213    EXTERN int result2;              /* secondary result */
5214    EXTERN char *res_ptr;            /* result, if pointer */
5215
5216    EXTERN char mm_stack[MM_STACK_BYTES];   /* MM's stack */
5217
```

```
5250   /* This table has one slot per process.  It contains all the memory management
5251    * information for each process.  Among other things, it defines the text, data
5252    * and stack segments, uids and gids, and various flags.  The kernel and file
5253    * systems have tables that are also indexed by process, with the contents
5254    * of corresponding slots referring to the same process in all three.
5255    */
5256
5257   EXTERN struct mproc {
5258     struct mem_map mp_seg[NR_SEGS];      /* points to text, data, stack */
5259     char mp_exitstatus;                  /* storage for status when process exits */
5260     char mp_sigstatus;                   /* storage for signal # for killed processes */
5261     int mp_pid;                          /* process id */
5262     int mp_parent;                       /* index of parent process */
5263     int mp_procgrp;                      /* process group (used for signals) */
5264
5265     /* Real and effective uids and gids. */
5266     uid mp_realuid;                      /* process' real uid */
5267     uid mp_effuid;                       /* process' effective uid */
5268     gid mp_realgid;                      /* process' real gid */
5269     gid mp_effgid;                       /* process' effective gid */
5270
5271     /* Bit maps for signals. */
5272     unshort mp_ignore;                   /* 1 means ignore the signal, 0 means don't */
5273     unshort mp_catch;                    /* 1 means catch the signal, 0 means don't */
5274     int (*mp_func)();                    /* all signals vectored to a single user fcn */
5275
5276     unsigned mp_flags;                   /* flag bits */
5277   } mproc[NR_PROCS];
5278
5279   /* Flag values */
5280   #define IN_USE          001    /* set when 'mproc' slot in use */
5281   #define WAITING         002    /* set by WAIT system call */
5282   #define HANGING         004    /* set by EXIT system call */
5283   #define PAUSED          010    /* set by PAUSE system call */
5284   #define ALARM_ON        020    /* set when SIGALRM timer started */
5285   #define SEPARATE        040    /* set if file is separate I & D space */
```

```
5300    /* The following names are synonyms for the variables in the input message. */
5301    #define addr            mm_in.m1_p1
5302    #define exec_name       mm_in.m1_p1
5303    #define exec_len        mm_in.m1_i1
5304    #define func            mm_in.m6_f1
5305    #define grpid           (gid) mm_in.m1_i1
5306    #define kill_sig        mm_in.m1_i2
5307    #define namelen         mm_in.m1_i1
5308    #define pid             mm_in.m1_i1
5309    #define seconds         mm_in.m1_i1
5310    #define sig             mm_in.m6_i1
5311    #define stack_bytes     mm_in.m1_i2
5312    #define stack_ptr       mm_in.m1_p2
5313    #define status          mm_in.m1_i1
5314    #define usr_id          (uid) mm_in.m1_i1
5315
5316    /* The following names are synonyms for the variables in the output message. */
5317    #define reply_type      mm_out.m_type
5318    #define reply_i1        mm_out.m2_i1
5319    #define reply_p1        mm_out.m2_p1
```

```
5350    /* If there were any type definitions local to the Memory Manager, they would
5351     * be here.  This file is included only for symmetry with the kernel and File
5352     * System, which do have some local type definitions.
5353     */
5354
5355    #include "../h/type.h"
```

```
5400    /* This file contains the main program of the memory manager and some related
5401     * procedures. When MINIX starts up, the kernel runs for a little while,
5402     * initializing itself and its tasks, and then it runs MM.  MM at this point
5403     * does not know where FS is in memory and how big it is.  By convention, FS
5404     * must start at the click following MM, so MM can deduce where it starts at
5405     * least.  Later, when FS runs for the first time, FS makes a pseudo-call,
5406     * BRK2, to tell MM how big it is.  This allows MM to figure out where INIT
5407     * is.
5408     *
5409     * The entry points into this file are:
5410     *   main:      starts MM running
5411     *   reply:     reply to a process making an MM system call
5412     *   do_brk2:   pseudo-call for FS to report its size
5413     */
5414
5415    #include "../h/const.h"
5416    #include "../h/type.h"
5417    #include "../h/callnr.h"
5418    #include "../h/com.h"
5419    #include "../h/error.h"
5420    #include "const.h"
5421    #include "glo.h"
5422    #include "mproc.h"
5423    #include "param.h"
5424
5425    #define ENOUGH (phys_clicks) 4096       /* any # > max(FS size, INIT size) */
5426    #define CLICK_TO_K (1024L/CLICK_SIZE)   /* convert clicks to K */
5427
5428    PRIVATE phys_clicks tot_mem;
5429    extern (*mm_callvec[])();
5430    extern char *sp_limit;                  /* stack limit register; checked on calls */
5431
5432    /*===========================================================================*
5433     *                              main                                         *
5434     *===========================================================================*/
5435    PUBLIC main()
5436    {
5437    /* Main routine of the memory manager. */
5438
5439      int error;
5440
5441      mm_init();                            /* initialize memory manager tables */
5442
5443      /* This is MM's main loop- get work and do it, forever and forever. */
5444      while (TRUE) {
5445            /* Wait for message. */
5446            get_work();                     /* wait for an MM system call */
5447            mp = &mproc[who];
5448
5449            /* Set some flags. */
```

```
5450                error = OK;
5451                dont_reply = FALSE;
5452                err_code = -999;
5453
5454                /* If the call number is valid, perform the call. */
5455                if (mm_call < 0 || mm_call >= NCALLS)
5456                        error = E_BAD_CALL;
5457                else
5458                        error = (*mm_callvec[mm_call])();
5459
5460                /* Send the results back to the user to indicate completion. */
5461                if (dont_reply) continue;        /* no reply for EXIT and WAIT */
5462                if (mm_call == EXEC && error == OK) continue;
5463                reply(who, error, result2, res_ptr);
5464        }
5465   }


5468   /*===========================================================================*
5469    *                              get_work                                     *
5470    *===========================================================================*/
5471   PRIVATE get_work()
5472   {
5473   /* Wait for the next message and extract useful information from it. */
5474
5475      if (receive(ANY, &mm_in) != OK) panic("MM receive error", NO_NUM);
5476      who = mm_in.m_source;          /* who sent the message */
5477      if (who < HARDWARE || who >= NR_PROCS) panic("MM called by", who);
5478      mm_call = mm_in.m_type;        /* system call number */
5479   }


5482   /*===========================================================================*
5483    *                              reply                                        *
5484    *===========================================================================*/
5485   PUBLIC reply(proc_nr, result, res2, respt)
5486   int proc_nr;                      /* process to reply to */
5487   int result;                       /* result of the call (usually OK or error #)*/
5488   int res2;                         /* secondary result */
5489   char *respt;                      /* result if pointer */
5490   {
5491   /* Send a reply to a user process. */
5492
5493      register struct mproc *proc_ptr;
5494
5495      /* To make MM robust, check to see if destination is still alive. */
5496      proc_ptr = &mproc[proc_nr];
5497      if ( (proc_ptr->mp_flags&IN_USE) == 0 || (proc_ptr->mp_flags&HANGING)) return;
5498      reply_type = result;
5499      reply_il = res2;
```

```
5500        reply_p1 = respt;
5501        if (send(proc_nr, &mm_out) != OK) panic("MM can't reply", NO_NUM);
5502    }


5505    /*===========================================================================*
5506     *                              mm_init                                       *
5507     *===========================================================================*/
5508    PRIVATE mm_init()
5509    {
5510    /* Initialize the memory manager. */
5511
5512        extern phys_clicks get_tot_mem(), alloc_mem();
5513
5514        /* Find out how much memory the machine has and set up core map.  MM and FS
5515         * are part of the map.  Tell the kernel.
5516         */
5517        tot_mem = get_tot_mem();         /* # clicks in mem starting at absolute 0 */
5518        mem_init(tot_mem);               /* initialize tables to all physical mem */
5519
5520        /* Initialize MM's tables. */
5521        mproc[MM_PROC_NR].mp_flags  |= IN_USE;
5522        mproc[FS_PROC_NR].mp_flags  |= IN_USE;
5523        mproc[INIT_PROC_NR].mp_flags |= IN_USE;
5524        procs_in_use = 3;
5525
5526        /* Set stack limit, which is checked on every procedure call. */
5527        sp_limit = mm_stack - 32;
5528    }


5531    /*===========================================================================*
5532     *                              do_brk2                                       *
5533     *===========================================================================*/
5534    PUBLIC do_brk2()
5535    {
5536    /* This "call" is made once by FS during system initialization and then never
5537     * again by anyone.  It contains the origin and size of INIT, and the combined
5538     * size of the 1536 bytes of unused mem, MINIX and RAM disk.
5539     *    ml_il = size of INIT text in clicks
5540     *    ml_i2 = size of INIT data in clicks
5541     *    ml_i3 = number of bytes for MINIX + RAM DISK
5542     *    ml_pl = origin of INIT in clicks
5543     */
5544
5545        int mem1, mem2, mem3;
5546        register struct mproc *rmp;
5547        phys_clicks init_org, init_clicks, ram_base, ram_clicks, tot_clicks;
5548        phys_clicks init_text_clicks, init_data_clicks;
5549
```

```
5550        if (who != FS_PROC_NR) return(EPERM); /* only FS make do BRK2 */
5551
5552        /* Remove the memory used by MINIX and RAM disk from the memory map. */
5553        init_text_clicks = mm_in.m1_i1;        /* size of INIT in clicks */
5554        init_data_clicks = mm_in.m1_i2;        /* size of INIT in clicks */
5555        tot_clicks = mm_in.m1_i3;              /* total size of MINIX + RAM disk */
5556        init_org = (phys_clicks) mm_in.m1_p1; /* addr where INIT begins in memory */
5557        init_clicks = init_text_clicks + init_data_clicks;
5558        ram_base = init_org + init_clicks;     /* start of RAM disk */
5559        ram_clicks = tot_clicks - ram_base;    /* size of RAM disk */
5560        alloc_mem(tot_clicks);                 /* remove RAM disk from map */
5561
5562        /* Print memory information. */
5563        mem1 = tot_mem/CLICK_TO_K;
5564        mem2 = (ram_base + 512/CLICK_SIZE)/CLICK_TO_K;          /* MINIX, rounded */
5565        mem3 = ram_clicks/CLICK_TO_K;
5566        printf("%c 8%c~0",033, 033);  /* go to top of screen and clear screen */
5567        printf("Memory size = %dK      ", mem1);
5568        printf("MINIX = %dK      ", mem2);
5569        printf("RAM disk = %dK      ", mem3);
5570        printf("Available = %dK\n\n", mem1 - mem2 - mem3);
5571        if (mem1 - mem2 - mem3 < 32) {
5572            printf("\nNot enough memory to run MINIX\n\n", NO_NUM);
5573            sys_abort();
5574        }
5575
5576        /* Initialize INIT's table entry. */
5577        rmp = &mproc[INIT_PROC_NR];
5578        rmp->mp_seg[T].mem_phys = init_org;
5579        rmp->mp_seg[T].mem_len  = init_text_clicks;
5580        rmp->mp_seg[D].mem_phys = init_org + init_text_clicks;
5581        rmp->mp_seg[D].mem_len  = init_data_clicks;
5582        rmp->mp_seg[S].mem_vir  = init_clicks;
5583        rmp->mp_seg[S].mem_phys = init_org + init_clicks;
5584        if (init_text_clicks != 0) rmp->mp_flags |= SEPARATE;
5585
5586        return(OK);
5587    }


5590    /*===========================================================================*
5591     *                              set_map                                       *
5592     *===========================================================================*/
5593    PRIVATE set_map(proc_nr, base, clicks)
5594    int proc_nr;                            /* whose map to set? */
5595    phys_clicks base;                       /* where in memory does the process start? */
5596    phys_clicks clicks;                     /* total size in clicks (sep I & D not used) */
5597    {
5598    /* Set up the memory map as part of the system initialization. */
5599
```

```
5600      register struct mproc *rmp;
5601      vir_clicks vclicks;
5602
5603      rmp = &mproc[proc_nr];
5604      vclicks = (vir_clicks) clicks;
5605      rmp->mp_seg[T].mem_vir = 0;
5606      rmp->mp_seg[T].mem_len = 0;
5607      rmp->mp_seg[T].mem_phys = base;
5608      rmp->mp_seg[D].mem_vir = 0;
5609      rmp->mp_seg[D].mem_len = vclicks;
5610      rmp->mp_seg[D].mem_phys = base;
5611      rmp->mp_seg[S].mem_vir = vclicks;
5612      rmp->mp_seg[S].mem_len = 0;
5613      rmp->mp_seg[S].mem_phys = base + vclicks;
5614      sys_newmap(proc_nr, rmp->mp_seg);
5615   }
```

```
5650    /* This file deals with creating processes (via FORK) and deleting them (via
5651     * EXIT/WAIT).  When a process forks, a new slot in the 'mproc' table is
5652     * allocated for it, and a copy of the parent's core image is made for the
5653     * child.  Then the kernel and file system are informed.  A process is removed
5654     * from the 'mproc' table when two events have occurred: (1) it has exited or
5655     * been killed by a signal, and (2) the parent has done a WAIT.  If the process
5656     * exits first, it continues to occupy a slot until the parent does a WAIT.
5657     *
5658     * The entry points into this file are:
5659     *   do_fork:   perform the FORK system call
5660     *   do_mm_exit:        perform the EXIT system call (by calling mm_exit())
5661     *   mm_exit:   actually do the exiting
5662     *   do_wait:   perform the WAIT system call
5663     */
5664
5665    #include "../h/const.h"
5666    #include "../h/type.h"
5667    #include "../h/callnr.h"
5668    #include "../h/error.h"
5669    #include "const.h"
5670    #include "glo.h"
5671    #include "mproc.h"
5672    #include "param.h"
5673
5674    #define LAST_FEW            2   /* last few slots reserved for superuser */
5675
5676    PRIVATE next_pid = INIT_PROC_NR+1;      /* next pid to be assigned */
5677
5678    /* Some C compilers require static declarations to precede their first use. */
5679
5680    /*===========================================================================*
5681     *                              do_fork                                      *
5682     *===========================================================================*/
5683    PUBLIC int do_fork()
5684    {
5685    /* The process pointed to by 'mp' has forked.  Create a child process. */
5686
5687      register struct mproc *rmp;   /* pointer to parent */
5688      register struct mproc *rmc;   /* pointer to child */
5689      int i, child_nr, t;
5690      char *sptr, *dptr;
5691      long prog_bytes;
5692      phys_clicks prog_clicks, child_base;
5693      long parent_abs, child_abs;
5694      extern phys_clicks alloc_mem();
5695
5696      /* If tables might fill up during FORK, don't even start since recovery half
5697       * way through is such a nuisance.
5698       */
5699
```

```
5700        rmp = mp;
5701        if (procs_in_use == NR_PROCS) return(EAGAIN);
5702        if (procs_in_use >= NR_PROCS - LAST_FEW && rmp->mp_effuid != 0)return(EAGAIN);
5703
5704        /* Determine how much memory to allocate. */
5705        prog_clicks = (phys_clicks) rmp->mp_seg[T].mem_len + rmp->mp_seg[D].mem_len +
5706                                                    rmp->mp_seg[S].mem_len;
5707   #ifdef i8088
5708        prog_clicks += rmp->mp_seg[S].mem_vir - rmp->mp_seg[D].mem_len; /* gap too */
5709   #endif
5710        prog_bytes = (long) prog_clicks << CLICK_SHIFT;
5711        if ( (child_base = alloc_mem(prog_clicks)) == NO_MEM) return(EAGAIN);
5712
5713        /* Create a copy of the parent's core image for the child. */
5714        child_abs = (long) child_base << CLICK_SHIFT;
5715        parent_abs = (long) rmp->mp_seg[T].mem_phys << CLICK_SHIFT;
5716        i = mem_copy(ABS, 0, parent_abs, ABS, 0, child_abs, prog_bytes);
5717        if ( i < 0) panic("do_fork can't copy", i);
5718
5719        /* Find a slot in 'mproc' for the child process. A slot must exist. */
5720        for (rmc = &mproc[0]; rmc < &mproc[NR_PROCS]; rmc++)
5721             if ( (rmc->mp_flags & IN_USE) == 0) break;
5722
5723        /* Set up the child and its memory map; copy its 'mproc' slot from parent. */
5724        child_nr = rmc - mproc;         /* slot number of the child */
5725        procs_in_use++;
5726        sptr = (char *) rmp;            /* pointer to parent's 'mproc' slot */
5727        dptr = (char *) rmc;            /* pointer to child's 'mproc' slot */
5728        i = sizeof(struct mproc);       /* number of bytes in a proc slot. */
5729        while (i--) *dptr++ = *sptr++;/* copy from parent slot to child's */
5730
5731        rmc->mp_parent = who;           /* record child's parent */
5732        rmc->mp_seg[T].mem_phys = child_base;
5733        rmc->mp_seg[D].mem_phys = child_base + rmc->mp_seg[T].mem_len;
5734        rmc->mp_seg[S].mem_phys = rmc->mp_seg[D].mem_phys +
5735                             (rmp->mp_seg[S].mem_phys - rmp->mp_seg[D].mem_phys);
5736        rmc->mp_exitstatus = 0;
5737        rmc->mp_sigstatus = 0;
5738
5739        /* Find a free pid for the child and put it in the table. */
5740        do {
5741             t = 0;                     /* 't' = 0 means pid still free */
5742             next_pid = (next_pid < 30000 ? next_pid + 1 : INIT_PROC_NR + 1);
5743             for (rmp = &mproc[0]; rmp < &mproc[NR_PROCS]; rmp++)
5744                  if (rmp->mp_pid == next_pid) {
5745                       t = 1;
5746                       break;
5747                  }
5748             rmc->mp_pid = next_pid; /* assign pid to child */
5749        } while (t);
```

```
5750
5751        /* Tell kernel and file system about the (now successful) FORK. */
5752        sys_fork(who, child_nr, rmc->mp_pid);
5753        tell_fs(FORK, who, child_nr, 0);
5754
5755        /* Report child's memory map to kernel. */
5756        sys_newmap(child_nr, rmc->mp_seg);
5757
5758        /* Reply to child to wake it up. */
5759        reply(child_nr, 0, 0, NIL_PTR);
5760        return(next_pid);                    /* child's pid */
5761    }


5764    /*===========================================================================*
5765     *                              do_mm_exit                                   *
5766     *===========================================================================*/
5767    PUBLIC int do_mm_exit()
5768    {
5769    /* Perform the exit(status) system call. The real work is done by mm_exit(),
5770     * which is also called when a process is killed by a signal.
5771     */
5772
5773        mm_exit(mp, status);
5774        dont_reply = TRUE;              /* don't reply to newly terminated process */
5775        return(OK);                     /* pro forma return code */
5776    }


5779    /*===========================================================================*
5780     *                              mm_exit                                      *
5781     *===========================================================================*/
5782    PUBLIC mm_exit(rmp, exit_status)
5783    register struct mproc *rmp;     /* pointer to the process to be terminated */
5784    int exit_status;                /* the process' exit status (for parent) */
5785    {
5786    /* A process is done.  If parent is waiting for it, clean it up, else hang. */
5787
5788        /* How to terminate a process is determined by whether or not the
5789         * parent process has already done a WAIT.  Test to see if it has.
5790         */
5791        rmp->mp_exitstatus = (char) exit_status;        /* store status in 'mproc' */
5792
5793        if (mproc[rmp->mp_parent].mp_flags & WAITING)
5794            cleanup(rmp);               /* release parent and tell everybody */
5795        else
5796            rmp->mp_flags |= HANGING;   /* Parent not waiting.  Suspend proc */
5797
5798        /* If the exited process has a timer pending, kill it. */
5799        if (rmp->mp_flags & ALARM_ON) set_alarm(rmp - mproc, (unsigned) 0);
```

```
5800
5801        /* Tell the kernel that the process is no longer runnable. */
5802        sys_xit(rmp->mp_parent, rmp - mproc);
5803    }


5806    /*===========================================================================*
5807     *                              do_wait                                      *
5808     *===========================================================================*/
5809    PUBLIC int do_wait()
5810    {
5811    /* A process wants to wait for a child to terminate. If one is already waiting,
5812     * go clean it up and let this WAIT call terminate.  Otherwise, really wait.
5813     */
5814
5815      register struct mproc *rp;
5816      register int children;
5817
5818      /* A process calling WAIT never gets a reply in the usual way via the
5819       * reply() in the main loop.  If a child has already exited, the routine
5820       * cleanup() sends the reply to awaken the caller.
5821       */
5822
5823      /* Is there a child waiting to be collected? */
5824      children = 0;
5825      for (rp = &mproc[0]; rp < &mproc[NR_PROCS]; rp++) {
5826            if ( (rp->mp_flags & IN_USE) && rp->mp_parent == who) {
5827                    children++;
5828                    if (rp->mp_flags & HANGING) {
5829                            cleanup(rp);    /* a child has already exited */
5830                            dont_reply = TRUE;
5831                            return(OK);
5832                    }
5833            }
5834      }
5835
5836      /* No child has exited.  Wait for one, unless none exists. */
5837      if (children > 0) {            /* does this process have any children? */
5838            mp->mp_flags |= WAITING;
5839            dont_reply = TRUE;
5840            return(OK);              /* yes - wait for one to exit */
5841      } else
5842            return(ECHILD);          /* no - parent has no children */
5843    }


5846    /*===========================================================================*
5847     *                              cleanup                                      *
5848     *===========================================================================*/
5849    PRIVATE cleanup(child)
```

```
5850    register struct mproc *child;   /* tells which process is exiting */
5851    {
5852    /* Clean up the remains of a process.  This routine is only called if two
5853     * conditions are satisfied:
5854     *     1. The process has done an EXIT or has been killed by a signal.
5855     *     2. The process' parent has done a WAIT.
5856     *
5857     * It tells everyone about the process' demise and also releases the memory, if
5858     * that has not yet been done.  (Whether it has or has not been done depends on
5859     * the order the EXIT and WAIT were done in.)
5860     */
5861      register struct mproc *parent, *rp;
5862      int init_waiting, child_nr;
5863      unsigned int r;
5864      phys_clicks s;
5865
5866      child_nr = child - mproc;
5867      parent = &mproc[child->mp_parent];
5868
5869      /* Wakeup the parent and tell the file system that the process is dead. */
5870      r = child->mp_sigstatus & 0377;
5871      r = r | (child->mp_exitstatus << 8);
5872      reply(child->mp_parent, child->mp_pid, r, NIL_PTR);
5873      tell_fs(EXIT, child_nr, 0, 0);  /* file system can free the proc slot */
5874
5875      /* Release the memory occupied by the child. */
5876      s = (phys_clicks) child->mp_seg[S].mem_vir + child->mp_seg[S].mem_len;
5877      if (child->mp_flags & SEPARATE) s += child->mp_seg[T].mem_len;
5878      free_mem(child->mp_seg[T].mem_phys, s);        /* free the memory */
5879
5880      /* Update flags. */
5881      child->mp_flags &= ~HANGING;  /* turn off HANGING bit */
5882      parent->mp_flags &= ~WAITING; /* turn off WAITING bit */
5883      child->mp_flags &= ~IN_USE;   /* release the table slot */
5884      procs_in_use--;
5885
5886      /* If exiting process has children, disinherit them.  INIT is new parent. */
5887      init_waiting = (mproc[INIT_PROC_NR].mp_flags & WAITING ? 1 : 0);
5888      for (rp = &mproc[0]; rp < &mproc[NR_PROCS]; rp++) {
5889            if (rp->mp_parent == child_nr) {
5890                    /* 'rp' points to a child to be disinherited. */
5891                    rp->mp_parent = INIT_PROC_NR;   /* init takes over */
5892                    if (init_waiting && (rp->mp_flags & HANGING) ) {
5893                            /* Init was waiting. */
5894                            cleanup(rp);    /* recursive call */
5895                            init_waiting = 0;
5896                    }
5897            }
5898      }
5899    }
```

```
5900   /* This file handles the EXEC system call.  It performs the work as follows:
5901    *      - see if the permissions allow the file to be executed
5902    *      - read the header and extract the sizes
5903    *      - fetch the initial args and environment from the user space
5904    *      - allocate the memory for the new process
5905    *      - copy the initial stack from MM to the process
5906    *      - read in the text and data segments and copy to the process
5907    *      - take care of setuid and setgid bits
5908    *      - fix up 'mproc' table
5909    *      - tell kernel about EXEC
5910    *
5911    *    The only entry point is do_exec.
5912    */
5913
5914   #include "../h/const.h"
5915   #include "../h/type.h"
5916   #include "../h/callnr.h"
5917   #include "../h/error.h"
5918   #include "../h/stat.h"
5919   #include "const.h"
5920   #include "glo.h"
5921   #include "mproc.h"
5922   #include "param.h"
5923
5924   #define MAGIC      0x04000301L    /* magic number with 2 bits masked off */
5925   #define SEP        0x00200000L    /* value for separate I & D */
5926   #define TEXTB             2       /* location of text size in header */
5927   #define DATAB             3       /* location of data size in header */
5928   #define BSSB              4       /* location of bss size in header */
5929   #define TOTB              6       /* location of total size in header */
5930
5931   /*===========================================================================*
5932    *                              do_exec                                      *
5933    *===========================================================================*/
5934   PUBLIC int do_exec()
5935   {
5936   /* Perform the exece(name, argv, envp) call.  The user library builds a
5937    * complete stack image, including pointers, args, environ, etc.  The stack
5938    * is copied to a buffer inside MM, and then to the new core image.
5939    */
5940
5941     register struct mproc *rmp;
5942     int m, r, fd, ft;
5943     char mbuf[MAX_ISTACK_BYTES];  /* buffer for stack and zeroes */
5944     union u {
5945            char name_buf[MAX_PATH];        /* the name of the file to exec */
5946            char zb[ZEROBUF_SIZE];  /* used to zero bss */
5947     } u;
5948     char *new_sp;
5949     vir_bytes src, dst, text_bytes, data_bytes, bss_bytes, stk_bytes, vsp;
```

```
5950        phys_bytes tot_bytes;          /* total space for program, including gap */
5951        vir_clicks sc;
5952        struct stat s_buf;
5953
5954        /* Do some validity checks. */
5955        rmp = mp;
5956        stk_bytes = (vir_bytes) stack_bytes;
5957        if (stk_bytes > MAX_ISTACK_BYTES) return(ENOMEM);      /* stack too big */
5958        if (exec_len <= 0 || exec_len > MAX_PATH) return(EINVAL);
5959
5960        /* Get the exec file name and see if the file is executable. */
5961        src = (vir_bytes) exec_name;
5962        dst = (vir_bytes) u.name_buf;
5963        r = mem_copy(who, D, (long) src, MM_PROC_NR, D, (long) dst, (long) exec_len);
5964        if (r != OK) return(r);        /* file name not in user data segment */
5965        tell_fs(CHDIR, who, 0, 0);      /* temporarily switch to user's directory */
5966        fd = allowed(u.name_buf, &s_buf, X_BIT);       /* is file executable? */
5967        tell_fs(CHDIR, 0, 1, 0);      /* switch back to MM's own directory */
5968        if (fd < 0) return(fd);        /* file was not executable */
5969
5970        /* Read the file header and extract the segment sizes. */
5971        sc = (stk_bytes + CLICK_SIZE - 1) >> CLICK_SHIFT;
5972        m = read_header(fd, &ft, &text_bytes, &data_bytes, &bss_bytes, &tot_bytes,sc);
5973        if (m < 0) {
5974              close(fd);               /* something wrong with header */
5975              return(ENOEXEC);
5976        }
5977
5978        /* Fetch the stack from the user before destroying the old core image. */
5979        src = (vir_bytes) stack_ptr;
5980        dst = (vir_bytes) mbuf;
5981        r = mem_copy(who, D, (long) src, MM_PROC_NR, D, (long) dst, (long) stk_bytes);
5982        if (r != OK) {
5983              close(fd);               /* can't fetch stack (e.g. bad virtual addr) */
5984              return(EACCES);
5985        }
5986
5987        /* Allocate new memory and release old memory. Fix map and tell kernel. */
5988        r = new_mem(text_bytes, data_bytes, bss_bytes, stk_bytes, tot_bytes,
5989                                                       u.zb, ZEROBUF_SIZE);
5990        if (r != OK) {
5991              close(fd);               /* insufficient core or program too big */
5992              return(r);
5993        }
5994
5995        /* Patch up stack and copy it from MM to new core image. */
5996        vsp = (vir_bytes) rmp->mp_seg[S].mem_vir << CLICK_SHIFT;
5997        patch_ptr(mbuf, vsp);
5998        src = (vir_bytes) mbuf;
5999        r = mem_copy(MM_PROC_NR, D, (long) src, who, D, (long) vsp, (long) stk_bytes);
```

```
6000        if (r != OK) panic("do_exec stack copy err", NO_NUM);
6001
6002        /* Read in text and data segments. */
6003        load_seg(fd, T, text_bytes);
6004        load_seg(fd, D, data_bytes);
6005        close(fd);                      /* don't need exec file any more */
6006
6007        /* Take care of setuid/setgid bits. */
6008        if (s_buf.st_mode & I_SET_UID_BIT) {
6009             rmp->mp_effuid = s_buf.st_uid;
6010             tell_fs(SETUID, who, (int) rmp->mp_realuid, (int) rmp->mp_effuid);
6011        }
6012        if (s_buf.st_mode & I_SET_GID_BIT) {
6013             rmp->mp_effgid = s_buf.st_gid;
6014             tell_fs(SETGID, who, (int) rmp->mp_realgid, (int) rmp->mp_effgid);
6015        }
6016
6017        /* Fix up some 'mproc' fields and tell kernel that exec is done. */
6018        rmp->mp_catch = 0;              /* reset all caught signals */
6019        rmp->mp_flags &= ~SEPARATE;     /* turn off SEPARATE bit */
6020        rmp->mp_flags |= ft;            /* turn it on for separate I & D files */
6021        new_sp = (char *) vsp;
6022        sys_exec(who, new_sp);
6023        return(OK);
6024   }


6027   /*===========================================================================*
6028    *                              read_header                                  *
6029    *===========================================================================*/
6030   PRIVATE int read_header(fd, ft, text_bytes, data_bytes, bss_bytes, tot_bytes,sc)
6031   int fd;                         /* file descriptor for reading exec file */
6032   int *ft;                        /* place to return ft number */
6033   vir_bytes *text_bytes;          /* place to return text size */
6034   vir_bytes *data_bytes;          /* place to return initialized data size */
6035   vir_bytes *bss_bytes;           /* place to return bss size */
6036   phys_bytes *tot_bytes;          /* place to return total size */
6037   vir_clicks sc;                  /* stack size in clicks */
6038   {
6039   /* Read the header and extract the text, data, bss and total sizes from it. */
6040
6041        int m, ct;
6042        vir_clicks tc, dc, s_vir, dvir;
6043        phys_clicks totc;
6044        long buf[HDR_SIZE/sizeof(long)];
6045
6046        /* Read the header and check the magic number.  The standard MINIX header
6047         * consists of 8 longs, as follows:
6048         *    0: 0x04100301L (combined I & D space) or 0x04200301L (separate I & D)
6049         *    1: 0x00000020L
```

```
6050    *    2: size of text segments in bytes
6051    *    3: size of initialized data segment in bytes
6052    *    4: size of bss in bytes
6053    *    5: 0x00000000L
6054    *    6: total memory allocated to program (text, data and stack, combined)
6055    *    7: 0x00000000L
6056    * The longs are represented low-order byte first and high-order byte last.
6057    * The first byte of the header is always 0x01, followed by 0x03.
6058    * The header is followed directly by the text and data segments, whose sizes
6059    * are given in the header.
6060    */
6061
6062    if (read(fd, buf, HDR_SIZE) != HDR_SIZE) return(ENOEXEC);
6063    if ( (buf[0] & 0xFF0FFFFFL) != MAGIC) return(ENOEXEC);
6064    *ft = (buf[0] & SEP ? SEPARATE : 0);  /* separate I & D or not */
6065
6066    /* Get text and data sizes. */
6067    *text_bytes = (vir_bytes) buf[TEXTB]; /* text size in bytes */
6068    *data_bytes = (vir_bytes) buf[DATAB]; /* data size in bytes */
6069    if (*ft != SEPARATE) {
6070            /* If I & D space is not separated, it is all considered data. Text=0 */
6071            *data_bytes += *text_bytes;
6072            *text_bytes = 0;
6073    }
6074
6075    /* Get bss and total sizes. */
6076    *bss_bytes = (vir_bytes) buf[BSSB];   /* bss size in bytes */
6077    *tot_bytes = buf[TOTB];        /* total bytes to allocate for program */
6078    if (*tot_bytes == 0) return(ENOEXEC);
6079
6080    /* Check to see if segment sizes are feasible. */
6081    tc = (*text_bytes + CLICK_SHIFT - 1) >> CLICK_SHIFT;
6082    dc = (*data_bytes + *bss_bytes + CLICK_SHIFT - 1) >> CLICK_SHIFT;
6083    totc = (*tot_bytes + CLICK_SIZE - 1) >> CLICK_SHIFT;
6084    if (dc >= totc) return(ENOEXEC);      /* stack must be at least 1 click */
6085    dvir = (*ft == SEPARATE ? 0 : tc);
6086    s_vir = dvir + (totc - sc);
6087    m = size_ok(*ft, tc, dc, sc, dvir, s_vir);
6088    ct = buf[1] & BYTE;           /* header length */
6089    if (ct > HDR_SIZE) read(fd, buf, ct - HDR_SIZE);       /* skip unused hdr */
6090    return(m);
6091  }


6094  /*===========================================================================*
6095   *                            new_mem                                        *
6096   *===========================================================================*/
6097  PRIVATE int new_mem(text_bytes, data_bytes, bss_bytes,stk_bytes,tot_bytes,bf,zs)
6098  vir_bytes text_bytes;             /* text segment size in bytes */
6099  vir_bytes data_bytes;             /* size of initialized data in bytes */
```

```
6100     vir_bytes bss_bytes;              /* size of bss in bytes */
6101     vir_bytes stk_bytes;             /* size of initial stack segment in bytes */
6102     phys_bytes tot_bytes;            /* total memory to allocate, including gap */
6103     char bf[ZEROBUF_SIZE];           /* buffer to use for zeroing data segment */
6104     int zs;                          /* true size of 'bf' */
6105     {
6106     /* Allocate new memory and release the old memory.  Change the map and report
6107      * the new map to the kernel.  Zero the new core image's bss, gap and stack.
6108      */
6109
6110       register struct mproc *rmp;
6111       char *rzp;
6112       vir_bytes vzb;
6113       vir_clicks text_clicks, data_clicks, gap_clicks, stack_clicks, tot_clicks;
6114       phys_clicks new_base, old_clicks;
6115       phys_bytes bytes, base, count, bss_offset;
6116       extern phys_clicks alloc_mem();
6117       extern phys_clicks max_hole();
6118
6119       /* Acquire the new memory.  Each of the 4 parts: text, (data+bss), gap,
6120        * and stack occupies an integral number of clicks, starting at click
6121        * boundary.  The data and bss parts are run together with no space.
6122        */
6123
6124       text_clicks = (text_bytes + CLICK_SIZE - 1) >> CLICK_SHIFT;
6125       data_clicks = (data_bytes + bss_bytes + CLICK_SIZE - 1) >> CLICK_SHIFT;
6126       stack_clicks = (stk_bytes + CLICK_SIZE - 1) >> CLICK_SHIFT;
6127       tot_clicks = (tot_bytes + CLICK_SIZE - 1) >> CLICK_SHIFT;
6128       gap_clicks = tot_clicks - data_clicks - stack_clicks;
6129       if ( (int) gap_clicks < 0) return(ENOMEM);
6130
6131       /* Check to see if there is a hole big enough.  If so, we can risk first
6132        * releasing the old core image before allocating the new one, since we
6133        * know it will succeed.  If there is not enough, return failure.
6134        */
6135       if (text_clicks + tot_clicks > max_hole()) return(EAGAIN);
6136
6137       /* There is enough memory for the new core image.  Release the old one. */
6138       rmp = mp;
6139       old_clicks = (phys_clicks) rmp->mp_seg[S].mem_vir + rmp->mp_seg[S].mem_len;
6140       if (rmp->mp_flags & SEPARATE) old_clicks += rmp->mp_seg[T].mem_len;
6141       free_mem(rmp->mp_seg[T].mem_phys, old_clicks);        /* free the memory */
6142
6143       /* We have now passed the point of no return.  The old core image has been
6144        * forever lost.  The call must go through now.  Set up and report new map.
6145        */
6146       new_base = alloc_mem(text_clicks + tot_clicks);      /* new core image */
6147       if (new_base == NO_MEM) panic("MM hole list is inconsistent", NO_NUM);
6148       rmp->mp_seg[T].mem_vir = 0;
6149       rmp->mp_seg[T].mem_len = text_clicks;
```

```
6150        rmp->mp_seg[T].mem_phys = new_base;
6151        rmp->mp_seg[D].mem_vir = 0;
6152        rmp->mp_seg[D].mem_len = data_clicks;
6153        rmp->mp_seg[D].mem_phys = new_base + text_clicks;
6154        rmp->mp_seg[S].mem_vir = rmp->mp_seg[D].mem_vir + data_clicks + gap_clicks;
6155        rmp->mp_seg[S].mem_len = stack_clicks;
6156        rmp->mp_seg[S].mem_phys = rmp->mp_seg[D].mem_phys + data_clicks + gap_clicks;
6157        sys_newmap(who, rmp->mp_seg); /* report new map to the kernel */
6158
6159        /* Zero the bss, gap, and stack segment. Start just above text. */
6160        for (rzp = &bf[0]; rzp < &bf[zs]; rzp++) *rzp = 0;    /* clear buffer */
6161        bytes = (phys_bytes) (data_clicks + gap_clicks + stack_clicks) << CLICK_SHIFT;
6162        vzb = (vir_bytes) bf;
6163        base = (long) rmp->mp_seg[T].mem_phys + rmp->mp_seg[T].mem_len;
6164        base = base << CLICK_SHIFT;
6165        bss_offset = (data_bytes >> CLICK_SHIFT) << CLICK_SHIFT;
6166        base += bss_offset;
6167        bytes -= bss_offset;
6168
6169        while (bytes > 0) {
6170                count = (long) MIN(bytes, (phys_bytes) zs);
6171                if (mem_copy(MM_PROC_NR, D, (long) vzb, ABS, 0, base, count) != OK)
6172                        panic("new_mem can't zero", NO_NUM);
6173                base += count;
6174                bytes -= count;
6175        }
6176        return(OK);
6177  }


6180  /*===========================================================================*
6181   *                              patch_ptr                                    *
6182   *===========================================================================*/
6183  PRIVATE patch_ptr(stack, base)
6184  char stack[MAX_ISTACK_BYTES];    /* pointer to stack image within MM */
6185  vir_bytes base;                  /* virtual address of stack base inside user */
6186  {
6187  /* When doing an exec(name, argv, envp) call, the user builds up a stack
6188   * image with arg and env pointers relative to the start of the stack.  Now
6189   * these pointers must be relocated, since the stack is not positioned at
6190   * address 0 in the user's address space.
6191   */
6192
6193    char **ap, flag;
6194    vir_bytes v;
6195
6196    flag = 0;                      /* counts number of 0-pointers seen */
6197    ap = (char **) stack;          /* points initially to 'nargs' */
6198    ap++;                          /* now points to argv[0] */
6199    while (flag < 2) {
```

```
6200                    if (ap >= (char **) &stack[MAX_ISTACK_BYTES]) return;      /* too bad */
6201                    if (*ap != NIL_PTR) {
6202                            v = (vir_bytes) *ap;      /* v is relative pointer */
6203                            v += base;                /* relocate it */
6204                            *ap = (char *) v;         /* put it back */
6205                    } else {
6206                            flag++;
6207                    }
6208                    ap++;
6209            }
6210    }


6213    /*===========================================================================*
6214     *                              load_seg                                      *
6215     *===========================================================================*/
6216    PRIVATE load_seg(fd, seg, seg_bytes)
6217    int fd;                              /* file descriptor to read from */
6218    int seg;                             /* T or D */
6219    vir_bytes seg_bytes;                 /* how big is the segment */
6220    {
6221    /* Read in text or data from the exec file and copy to the new core image.
6222     * This procedure is a little bit tricky.  The logical way to load a segment
6223     * would be to read it block by block and copy each block to the user space
6224     * one at a time.  This is too slow, so we do something dirty here, namely
6225     * send the user space and virtual address to the file system in the upper
6226     * 10 bits of the file descriptor, and pass it the user virtual address
6227     * instead of a MM address.  The file system copies the whole segment
6228     * directly to user space, bypassing MM completely.
6229     */

6231      int new_fd, bytes;
6232      char *ubuf_ptr;

6234      if (seg_bytes == 0) return;   /* text size for combined I & D is 0 */
6235      new_fd = (who << 8) | (seg << 6) | fd;
6236      ubuf_ptr = (char *) (mp->mp_seg[seg].mem_vir << CLICK_SHIFT);
6237      bytes = (int) seg_bytes;
6238      read(new_fd, ubuf_ptr, bytes);
6239    }
```

```
6250    /* The MINIX model of memory allocation reserves a fixed amount of memory for
6251     * the combined text, data, and stack segments.  The amount used for a child
6252     * process created by FORK is the same as the parent had.  If the child does
6253     * an EXEC later, the new size is taken from the header of the file EXEC'ed.
6254     *
6255     * The layout in memory consists of the text segment, followed by the data
6256     * segment, followed by a gap (unused memory), followed by the stack segment.
6257     * The data segment grows upward and the stack grows downward, so each can
6258     * take memory from the gap.  If they meet, the process must be killed.  The
6259     * procedures in this file deal with the growth of the data and stack segments.
6260     *
6261     * The entry points into this file are:
6262     *   do_brk:     BRK/SBRK system calls to grow or shrink the data segment
6263     *   adjust:     see if a proposed segment adjustment is allowed
6264     *   size_ok:    see if the segment sizes are feasible
6265     *   stack_fault: grow the stack segment
6266     */

6268    #include "../h/const.h"
6269    #include "../h/type.h"
6270    #include "../h/error.h"
6271    #include "../h/signal.h"
6272    #include "const.h"
6273    #include "glo.h"
6274    #include "mproc.h"
6275    #include "param.h"

6277    #define DATA_CHANGED      1    /* flag value when data segment size changed */
6278    #define STACK_CHANGED     2    /* flag value when stack size changed */

6280    /*===========================================================================*
6281     *                              do_brk                                        *
6282     *===========================================================================*/
6283    PUBLIC int do_brk()
6284    {
6285    /* Perform the brk(addr) system call.
6286     *
6287     * The call is complicated by the fact that on some machines (e.g., 8088),
6288     * the stack pointer can grow beyond the base of the stack segment without
6289     * anybody noticing it.   For a file not using separate I & D space,
6290     * the parameter, 'addr' is to the total size, text + data.  For a file using
6291     * separate text and data spaces, it is just the data size. Files using
6292     * separate I & D space have the SEPARATE bit in mp_flags set.
6293     */

6295      register struct mproc *rmp;
6296      int r;
6297      vir_bytes v, new_sp;
6298      vir_clicks new_clicks;
6299
```

```
6300        rmp = mp;
6301        v = (vir_bytes) addr;          /* 'addr' is the new data segment size */
6302        new_clicks = (vir_clicks) ( ((long) v + CLICK_SIZE - 1) >> CLICK_SHIFT);
6303        sys_getsp(who, &new_sp);       /* ask kernel for current sp value */
6304        r = adjust(rmp, new_clicks, new_sp);
6305        res_ptr = (r == OK ? addr : (char *) -1);
6306        return(r);                     /* return new size or -1 */
6307   }



6310   /*===========================================================================*
6311    *                              adjust                                        *
6312    *===========================================================================*/
6313   PUBLIC int adjust(rmp, data_clicks, sp)
6314   register struct mproc *rmp;        /* whose memory is being adjusted? */
6315   vir_clicks data_clicks;            /* how big is data segment to become? */
6316   vir_bytes sp;                      /* new value of sp */
6317   {
6318   /* See if data and stack segments can coexist, adjusting them if need be.
6319    * Memory is never allocated or freed.  Instead it is added or removed from the
6320    * gap between data segment and stack segment.  If the gap size becomes
6321    * negative, the adjustment of data or stack fails and ENOMEM is returned.
6322    */
6323
6324     register struct mem_map *mem_sp, *mem_dp;
6325     vir_clicks sp_click, gap_base, lower, old_clicks;
6326     int changed, r, ft;
6327     long base_of_stack, delta;       /* longs avoid certain problems */
6328
6329     mem_dp = &rmp->mp_seg[D];         /* pointer to data segment map */
6330     mem_sp = &rmp->mp_seg[S];         /* pointer to stack segment map */
6331     changed = 0;                      /* set when either segment changed */
6332
6333     /* See if stack size has gone negative (i.e., sp too close to 0xFFFF...) */
6334     base_of_stack = (long) mem_sp->mem_vir + (long) mem_sp->mem_len;
6335     sp_click = sp >> CLICK_SHIFT;     /* click containing sp */
6336     if (sp_click >= base_of_stack) return(ENOMEM);        /* sp too high */
6337
6338     /* Compute size of gap between stack and data segments. */
6339     delta = (long) mem_sp->mem_vir - (long) sp_click;
6340     lower = (delta > 0 ? sp_click : mem_sp->mem_vir);
6341     gap_base = mem_dp->mem_vir + data_clicks;
6342     if (lower < gap_base) return(ENOMEM); /* data and stack collided */
6343
6344     /* Update data length (but not data orgin) on behalf of brk() system call. */
6345     old_clicks = mem_dp->mem_len;
6346     if (data_clicks != mem_dp->mem_len) {
6347         mem_dp->mem_len = data_clicks;
6348         changed |= DATA_CHANGED;
6349     }
```

```
6350
6351        /* Update stack length and origin due to change in stack pointer. */
6352        if (delta > 0) {
6353                mem_sp->mem_vir -= delta;
6354                mem_sp->mem_phys -= delta;
6355                mem_sp->mem_len += delta;
6356                changed |= STACK_CHANGED;
6357        }
6358
6359        /* Do the new data and stack segment sizes fit in the address space? */
6360        ft = (rmp->mp_flags & SEPARATE);
6361        r = size_ok(ft, rmp->mp_seg[T].mem_len, rmp->mp_seg[D].mem_len,
6362                rmp->mp_seg[S].mem_len, rmp->mp_seg[D].mem_vir, rmp->mp_seg[S].mem_vir);
6363        if (r == OK) {
6364                if (changed) sys_newmap(rmp - mproc, rmp->mp_seg);
6365                return(OK);
6366        }
6367
6368        /* New sizes don't fit or require too many page/segment registers. Restore.*/
6369        if (changed & DATA_CHANGED) mem_dp->mem_len = old_clicks;
6370        if (changed & STACK_CHANGED) {
6371                mem_sp->mem_vir += delta;
6372                mem_sp->mem_phys += delta;
6373                mem_sp->mem_len -= delta;
6374        }
6375        return(ENOMEM);
6376   }


6379   /*===========================================================================*
6380    *                                size_ok                                     *
6381    *===========================================================================*/
6382   PUBLIC int size_ok(file_type, tc, dc, sc, dvir, s_vir)
6383   int file_type;                      /* SEPARATE or 0 */
6384   vir_clicks tc;                      /* text size in clicks */
6385   vir_clicks dc;                      /* data size in clicks */
6386   vir_clicks sc;                      /* stack size in clicks */
6387   vir_clicks dvir;                    /* virtual address for start of data seg */
6388   vir_clicks s_vir;                   /* virtual address for start of stack seg */
6389   {
6390   /* Check to see if the sizes are feasible and enough segmentation registers
6391    * exist.  On a machine with eight 8K pages, text, data, stack sizes of
6392    * (32K, 16K, 16K) will fit, but (33K, 17K, 13K) will not, even though the
6393    * former is bigger (64K) than the latter (63K).  Even on the 8088 this test
6394    * is needed, since the data and stack may not exceed 4096 clicks.
6395    */
6396
6397     int pt, pd, ps;                   /* segment sizes in pages */
6398
6399     pt = ( (tc << CLICK_SHIFT) + PAGE_SIZE - 1)/PAGE_SIZE;
```

```
6400        pd = ( (dc << CLICK_SHIFT) + PAGE_SIZE - 1)/PAGE_SIZE;
6401        ps = ( (sc << CLICK_SHIFT) + PAGE_SIZE - 1)/PAGE_SIZE;
6402
6403        if (file_type == SEPARATE) {
6404                if (pt > MAX_PAGES || pd + ps > MAX_PAGES) return(ENOMEM);
6405        } else {
6406                if (pt + pd + ps > MAX_PAGES) return(ENOMEM);
6407        }
6408
6409        if (dvir + dc > s_vir) return(ENOMEM);
6410
6411        return(OK);
6412    }


6415    /*===========================================================================*
6416     *                              stack_fault                                   *
6417     *===========================================================================*/
6418    PUBLIC stack_fault(proc_nr)
6419    int proc_nr;                         /* tells who got the stack fault */
6420    {
6421    /* Handle a stack fault by growing the stack segment until sp is inside of it.
6422     * If this is impossible because data segment is in the way, kill the process.
6423     */
6424
6425        register struct mproc *rmp;
6426        int r;
6427        vir_bytes new_sp;
6428
6429        rmp = &mproc[proc_nr];
6430        sys_getsp(rmp - mproc, &new_sp);
6431        r = adjust(rmp, rmp->mp_seg[D].mem_len, new_sp);
6432        if (r == OK) return;
6433
6434        /* Stack has bumped into data segment.  Kill the process. */
6435        rmp->mp_catch = 0;                 /* don't catch this signal */
6436        sig_proc(rmp, SIGSEGV);            /* terminate process */
6437    }
```

```
6450    /* This file handles signals, which are asynchronous events and are generally
6451     * a messy and unpleasant business.  Signals can be generated by the KILL
6452     * system call, or from the keyboard (SIGINT) or from the clock (SIGALRM).
6453     * In all cases control eventually passes to check_sig() to see which processes
6454     * can be signalled.  The actual signalling is done by sig_proc().
6455     *
6456     * The entry points into this file are:
6457     *   do_signal: perform the SIGNAL system call
6458     *   do_kill:   perform the KILL system call
6459     *   do_ksig:   accept a signal originating in the kernel (e.g., SIGINT)
6460     *   sig_proc:  interrupt or terminate a signalled process
6461     *   do_alarm:  perform the ALARM system call by calling set_alarm()
6462     *   set_alarm: tell the clock task to start or stop a timer
6463     *   do_pause:  perform the PAUSE system call
6464     *   unpause:   check to see if process is suspended on anything
6465     */
6466
6467    #include "../h/const.h"
6468    #include "../h/type.h"
6469    #include "../h/callnr.h"
6470    #include "../h/com.h"
6471    #include "../h/error.h"
6472    #include "../h/signal.h"
6473    #include "../h/stat.h"
6474    #include "const.h"
6475    #include "glo.h"
6476    #include "mproc.h"
6477    #include "param.h"
6478
6479    #define DUMP_SIZE       256     /* buffer size for core dumps */
6480    #define CORE_MODE       0777    /* mode to use on core image files */
6481    #define DUMPED          0200    /* bit set in status when core dumped */
6482
6483    PRIVATE message m_sig;
6484
6485    /*===========================================================================*
6486     *                              do_signal                                    *
6487     *===========================================================================*/
6488    PUBLIC int do_signal()
6489    {
6490    /* Perform the signal(sig, func) call by setting bits to indicate that a signal
6491     * is to be caught or ignored.
6492     */
6493
6494      int mask;
6495
6496      if (sig < 1 || sig > NR_SIGS) return(EINVAL);
6497      if (sig == SIGKILL) return(OK);        /* SIGKILL may not ignored/caught */
6498      mask = 1 << (sig - 1);          /* singleton set with 'sig' bit on */
6499
```

```
6500      /* All this func does is set the bit maps for subsequent sig processing. */
6501      if (func == SIG_IGN) {
6502            mp->mp_ignore |= mask;
6503            mp->mp_catch &= ~mask;
6504      } else if (func == SIG_DFL) {
6505            mp->mp_ignore &= ~mask;
6506            mp->mp_catch &= ~mask;
6507      } else {
6508            mp->mp_ignore &= ~mask;
6509            mp->mp_catch |= mask;
6510            mp->mp_func = func;
6511      }
6512      return(OK);
6513   }


6516   /*===========================================================================*
6517    *                              do_kill                                      *
6518    *===========================================================================*/
6519   PUBLIC int do_kill()
6520   {
6521   /* Perform the kill(pid, kill_sig) system call. */
6522
6523      return check_sig(pid, kill_sig, mp->mp_effuid);
6524   }


6527   /*===========================================================================*
6528    *                              do_ksig                                      *
6529    *===========================================================================*/
6530   PUBLIC int do_ksig()
6531   {
6532   /* Certain signals, such as segmentation violations and DEL, originate in the
6533    * kernel.  When the kernel detects such signals, it sets bits in a bit map.
6534    * As soon is MM is awaiting new work, the kernel sends MM a message containing
6535    * the process slot and bit map.  That message comes here.  The File System
6536    * also uses this mechanism to signal writing on broken pipes (SIGPIPE).
6537    */
6538
6539      register struct mproc *rmp;
6540      int i, proc_id, proc_nr, id;
6541      unshort sig_map;                 /* bits 0 - 15 for sigs 1 - 16 */
6542
6543      /* Only kernel and FS may make this call. */
6544      if (who != HARDWARE && who != FS_PROC_NR) return(EPERM);
6545
6546      proc_nr = mm_in.PROC1;
6547      rmp = &mproc[proc_nr];
6548      if ( (rmp->mp_flags & IN_USE) == 0 || (rmp->mp_flags & HANGING) ) return(OK);
6549      proc_id = rmp->mp_pid;
```

```
6550        sig_map = (unshort) mm_in.SIG_MAP;
6551        mp = &mproc[0];                /* pretend kernel signals are from MM */
6552
6553        /* Stack faults are passed from kernel to MM as pseudo-signal 16. */
6554        if (sig_map == 1 << (STACK_FAULT - 1)) {
6555              stack_fault(proc_nr);
6556              return(OK);
6557        }
6558
6559        /* Check each bit in turn to see if a signal is to be sent.  Unlike
6560         * kill(), the kernel may collect several unrelated signals for a process
6561         * and pass them to MM in one blow.  Thus loop on the bit map. For SIGINT
6562         * and SIGQUIT, use proc_id 0, since multiple processes may have to signalled.
6563         */
6564        for (i = 0; i < NR_SIGS; i++) {
6565              id = (i+1 == SIGINT || i+1 == SIGQUIT ? 0 : proc_id);
6566              if ( (sig_map >> i) & 1) check_sig(id, i + 1, SUPER_USER);
6567        }
6568
6569        dont_reply = TRUE;             /* don't reply to the kernel */
6570        return(OK);
6571    }


6574    /*===========================================================================*
6575     *                            check_sig                                      *
6576     *===========================================================================*/
6577    PRIVATE int check_sig(proc_id, sig_nr, send_uid)
6578    int proc_id;                       /* pid of process to signal, or 0 or -1 */
6579    int sig_nr;                        /* which signal to send (1-16) */
6580    uid send_uid;                      /* identity of process sending the signal */
6581    {
6582    /* Check to see if it is possible to send a signal.  The signal may have to be
6583     * sent to a group of processes.  This routine is invoked by the KILL system
6584     * call, and also when the kernel catches a DEL or other signal. SIGALRM too.
6585     */
6586
6587      register struct mproc *rmp;
6588      int count, send_sig;
6589      unshort mask;
6590      extern unshort core_bits;
6591
6592      if (sig_nr < 1 || sig_nr > NR_SIGS) return(EINVAL);
6593      count = 0;                       /* count # of signals sent */
6594      mask = 1 << (sig_nr - 1);
6595
6596      /* Search the proc table for processes to signal.  Several tests are made:
6597       *    - if proc's uid != sender's, and sender is not superuser, don't signal
6598       *    - if specific process requested (i.e., 'procpid' > 0, check for match
6599       *    - if a process has already exited, it can't receive signals
```

```
6600        *    - if 'proc_id' is 0 signal everyone in same process group except caller
6601        */
6602      for (rmp = &mproc[INIT_PROC_NR + 1]; rmp < &mproc[NR_PROCS]; rmp++ ) {
6603            if ( (rmp->mp_flags & IN_USE) == 0) continue;
6604            send_sig = TRUE;        /* if it's FALSE at end of loop, don't signal */
6605            if (send_uid != rmp->mp_effuid && send_uid != SUPER_USER)send_sig=FALSE;
6606            if (proc_id > 0 && proc_id != rmp->mp_pid) send_sig = FALSE;
6607            if (rmp->mp_flags & HANGING) send_sig = FALSE;   /*don't wake the dead*/
6608            if (proc_id == 0 && mp->mp_procgrp != rmp->mp_procgrp) send_sig = FALSE;
6609            if (send_uid == SUPER_USER && proc_id == -1) send_sig = TRUE;
6610
6611            /* SIGALARM is a little special.  When a process exits, a clock signal
6612             * can arrive just as the timer is being turned off.  Also, turn off
6613             * ALARM_ON bit when timer goes off to keep it accurate.
6614             */
6615            if (sig_nr == SIGALRM) {
6616                    if ( (rmp->mp_flags & ALARM_ON) == 0) continue;
6617                    rmp->mp_flags &= ~ALARM_ON;
6618            }
6619
6620            if (send_sig == FALSE || rmp->mp_ignore & mask) continue;
6621
6622            /* If process is hanging on PAUSE, WAIT, tty, pipe, etc. release it. */
6623            unpause(rmp - mproc);   /* check to see if process is paused */
6624            count++;
6625
6626            /* Send the signal or kill the process, possibly with core dump. */
6627            sig_proc(rmp, sig_nr);
6628            if (proc_id > 0) break; /* only one process being signalled */
6629      }
6630
6631      /* If the calling process has killed itself, don't reply. */
6632      if ((mp->mp_flags & IN_USE) == 0 || (mp->mp_flags & HANGING))dont_reply =TRUE;
6633      return(count > 0 ? OK : ESRCH);
6634  }


6637  /*===========================================================================*
6638   *                              sig_proc                                     *
6639   *===========================================================================*/
6640  PUBLIC sig_proc(rmp, sig_nr)
6641  register struct mproc *rmp;      /* pointer to the process to be signalled */
6642  int sig_nr;                      /* signal to send to process (1-16) */
6643  {
6644  /* Send a signal to a process.  Check to see if the signal is to be caught.
6645   * If so, the pc, psw, and signal number are to be pushed onto the process'
6646   * stack.  If the stack cannot grow or the signal is not to be caught, kill
6647   * the process.
6648   */
6649
```

```
6650        unshort mask;
6651        int core_file;
6652        vir_bytes new_sp;
6653        extern unshort core_bits;
6654
6655        if ( (rmp->mp_flags & IN_USE) == 0) return;   /* if already dead forget it */
6656        mask = 1 << (sig_nr - 1);
6657        if (rmp->mp_catch & mask) {
6658                /* Signal should be caught. */
6659                rmp->mp_catch &= ~mask;         /* disable further signals */
6660                sys_getsp(rmp - mproc, &new_sp);
6661                new_sp -= SIG_PUSH_BYTES;
6662                if (adjust(rmp, rmp->mp_seg[D].mem_len, new_sp) == OK) {
6663                        sys_sig(rmp - mproc, sig_nr, rmp->mp_func);
6664                        return;          /* successful signal */
6665                }
6666        }
6667
6668        /* Signal should not or cannot be caught.  Take default action. */
6669        core_file = ( core_bits >> (sig_nr - 1 )) & 1;
6670        rmp->mp_sigstatus = (char) sig_nr;
6671        mm_exit(rmp, 0);                 /* terminate process */
6672        if (core_file) dump_core(rmp); /* dump core */
6673    }


6676    /*===========================================================================*
6677     *                              do_alarm                                     *
6678     *===========================================================================*/
6679    PUBLIC int do_alarm()
6680    {
6681    /* Perform the alarm(seconds) system call. */
6682
6683      register int r;
6684      unsigned sec;
6685
6686      sec = (unsigned) seconds;
6687      r = set_alarm(who, sec);
6688      return(r);
6689    }


6692    /*===========================================================================*
6693     *                              set_alarm                                    *
6694     *===========================================================================*/
6695    PUBLIC int set_alarm(proc_nr, sec)
6696    int proc_nr;                     /* process that wants the alarm */
6697    unsigned sec;                    /* how many seconds delay before the signal */
6698    {
6699    /* This routine is used by do_alarm() to set the alarm timer.  It is also
```

```
6700        * to turn the timer off when a process exits with the timer still on.
6701        */
6702
6703       int remaining;
6704
6705       m_sig.m_type = SET_ALARM;
6706       m_sig.PROC_NR = proc_nr;
6707       m_sig.DELTA_TICKS = HZ * sec;
6708       if (sec != 0)
6709               mproc[proc_nr].mp_flags |= ALARM_ON;     /* turn ALARM_ON bit on */
6710       else
6711               mproc[proc_nr].mp_flags &= ~ALARM_ON;    /* turn ALARM_ON bit off */
6712
6713       /* Tell the clock task to provide a signal message when the time comes. */
6714       if (sendrec(CLOCK, &m_sig) != OK) panic("alarm er", NO_NUM);
6715       remaining = (int) m_sig.SECONDS_LEFT;
6716       return(remaining);
6717     }


6720     /*===========================================================================*
6721      *                              do_pause                                     *
6722      *===========================================================================*/
6723     PUBLIC int do_pause()
6724     {
6725     /* Perform the pause() system call. */
6726
6727       mp->mp_flags |= PAUSED;          /* turn on PAUSE bit */
6728       dont_reply = TRUE;
6729       return(OK);
6730     }


6733     /*===========================================================================*
6734      *                              unpause                                      *
6735      *===========================================================================*/
6736     PUBLIC unpause(pro)
6737     int pro;                          /* which process number */
6738     {
6739     /* A signal is to be sent to a process.  It that process is hanging on a
6740      * system call, the system call must be terminated with EINTR.  Possible
6741      * calls are PAUSE, WAIT, READ and WRITE, the latter two for pipes and ttys.
6742      * First check if the process is hanging on PAUSE or WAIT.  If not, tell FS,
6743      * so it can check for READs and WRITEs from pipes, ttys and the like.
6744      */
6745
6746       register struct mproc *rmp;
6747
6748       rmp = &mproc[pro];
6749
```

```
6750        /* Check to see if process is hanging on PAUSE call. */
6751        if (rmp->mp_flags & PAUSED) {
6752             rmp->mp_flags &= ~PAUSED;         /* turn off PAUSED bit */
6753             reply(pro, EINTR, 0, NIL_PTR);
6754             return;
6755        }
6756
6757        /* Check to see if process is hanging on a WAIT call. */
6758        if (rmp->mp_flags & WAITING) {
6759             rmp->mp_flags &= ~ WAITING;       /* turn off WAITING bit */
6760             reply(pro, EINTR, 0, NIL_PTR);
6761             return;
6762        }
6763
6764        /* Process is not hanging on an MM call.  Ask FS to take a look. */
6765        tell_fs(UNPAUSE, pro, 0, 0);
6766
6767        return;
6768        }
6769
6770
6771        /*===========================================================================*
6772         *                              dump_core                                   *
6773         *===========================================================================*/
6774        PRIVATE dump_core(rmp)
6775        register struct mproc *rmp;      /* whose core is to be dumped */
6776        {
6777        /* Make a core dump on the file "core", if possible. */
6778
6779          struct stat s_buf, d_buf;
6780          char buf[DUMP_SIZE];
6781          int i, r, s, er1, er2, slot;
6782          vir_bytes v_buf;
6783          long len, a, c, ct, dest;
6784          struct mproc *xmp;
6785          extern char core_name[];
6786
6787
6788          /* Change to working directory of dumpee. */
6789          slot = rmp - mproc;
6790          tell_fs(CHDIR, slot, 0, 0);
6791
6792          /* Can core file be written? */
6793          if (rmp->mp_realuid != rmp->mp_effuid) return;
6794          xmp = mp;                        /* allowed() looks at 'mp' */
6795          mp = rmp;
6796          r = allowed(core_name, &s_buf, W_BIT);        /* is core_file writable */
6797          s = allowed(".", &d_buf, W_BIT);      /* is directory writable? */
6798          mp = xmp;
6799          if (r >= 0) close(r);
```

```
6800        if (s >= 0) close(s);
6801        if (rmp->mp_effuid == SUPER_USER) r = 0;        /* su can always dump core */
6802
6803        if (r >= 0 || (r == ENOENT && s >= 0)) {
6804                /* Either file is writable or it doesn't exist & dir is writable */
6805                r = creat(core_name, CORE_MODE);
6806                tell_fs(CHDIR, 0, 1, 0);            /* go back to MM's own dir */
6807                if (r < 0) return;
6808                rmp->mp_sigstatus |= DUMPED;
6809
6810                /* First loop through segments and write each length on core file. */
6811                for (i = 0; i < NR_SEGS; i++) {
6812                        len = rmp->mp_seg[i].mem_len << CLICK_SHIFT;
6813                        if (write(r, (char *) &len, sizeof len) < 0) {
6814                                close(r);
6815                                return;
6816                        }
6817                }
6818
6819                /* Now loop through segments and write the segments themselves out. */
6820                v_buf = (vir_bytes) buf;
6821                dest = (long) v_buf;
6822                for (i = 0; i < NR_SEGS; i++) {
6823                        a = (phys_bytes) rmp->mp_seg[i].mem_vir << CLICK_SHIFT;
6824                        c = (phys_bytes) rmp->mp_seg[i].mem_len << CLICK_SHIFT;
6825
6826                        /* Loop through a segment, dumping it. */
6827                        while (c > 0) {
6828                                ct = MIN(c, DUMP_SIZE);
6829                                er1 = mem_copy(slot, i, a, MM_PROC_NR, D, dest, ct);
6830                                er2 = write(r, buf, (int) ct);
6831                                if (er1 < 0 || er2 < 0) {
6832                                        close(r);
6833                                        return;
6834                                }
6835                                a += ct;
6836                                c -= ct;
6837                        }
6838                }
6839        } else {
6840                tell_fs(CHDIR, 0, 1, 0);            /* go back to MM's own dir */
6841                close(r);
6842                return;
6843        }
6844
6845        close(r);
6846    }
```

```
6850    /* This file handles the 4 system calls that get and set uids and gids.
6851     * It also handles getpid().  The code for each one is so tiny that it hardly
6852     * seemed worthwhile to make each a separate function.
6853     */
6854
6855    #include "../h/const.h"
6856    #include "../h/type.h"
6857    #include "../h/callnr.h"
6858    #include "../h/error.h"
6859    #include "const.h"
6860    #include "glo.h"
6861    #include "mproc.h"
6862    #include "param.h"
6863
6864    /*===========================================================================*
6865     *                              do_getset                                     *
6866     *===========================================================================*/
6867    PUBLIC int do_getset()
6868    {
6869    /* Handle GETUID, GETGID, GETPID, SETUID, SETGID.  The three GETs return
6870     * their primary results in 'r'.  GETUID and GETGID also return secondary
6871     * results (the effective IDs) in 'result2', which is returned to the user.
6872     */
6873
6874      register struct mproc *rmp = mp;
6875      register int r;
6876
6877      switch(mm_call) {
6878          case GETUID:
6879                  r = rmp->mp_realuid;
6880                  result2 = rmp->mp_effuid;
6881                  break;
6882
6883          case GETGID:
6884                  r = rmp->mp_realgid;
6885                  result2 = rmp->mp_effgid;
6886                  break;
6887
6888          case GETPID:
6889                  r = mproc[who].mp_pid;
6890                  result2 = mproc[rmp->mp_parent].mp_pid;
6891                  break;
6892
6893          case SETUID:
6894                  if (rmp->mp_realuid != usr_id && rmp->mp_effuid != SUPER_USER)
6895                          return(EPERM);
6896                  rmp->mp_realuid = usr_id;
6897                  rmp->mp_effuid = usr_id;
6898                  tell_fs(SETUID, who, usr_id, usr_id);
6899                  r = OK;
```

```
6900                        break;
6901
6902            case SETGID:
6903                        if (rmp->mp_realgid != grpid && rmp->mp_effuid != SUPER_USER)
6904                                return(EPERM);
6905                        rmp->mp_realgid = grpid;
6906                        rmp->mp_effgid = grpid;
6907                        tell_fs(SETGID, who, grpid, grpid);
6908                        r = OK;
6909                        break;
6910        }
6911
6912        return(r);
6913    }
```

```
6950     /* This file is concerned with allocating and freeing arbitrary-size blocks of
6951      * physical memory on behalf of the FORK and EXEC system calls. The key data
6952      * structure used is the hole table, which maintains a list of holes in memory.
6953      * It is kept sorted in order of increasing memory address. The addresses
6954      * it contains refer to physical memory, starting at absolute address 0
6955      * (i.e., they are not relative to the start of MM). During system
6956      * initialization, that part of memory containing the interrupt vectors,
6957      * kernel, and MM are "allocated" to mark them as not available and to
6958      * remove them from the hole list.
6959      *
6960      * The entry points into this file are:
6961      *   alloc_mem: allocate a given sized chunk of memory
6962      *   free_mem:  release a previously allocated chunk of memory
6963      *   mem_init:  initialize the tables when MM start up
6964      *   max_hole:  returns the largest hole currently available
6965      */
6966
6967     #include "../h/const.h"
6968     #include "../h/type.h"
6969     #include "const.h"
6970
6971     #define NR_HOLES        128     /* max # entries in hole table */
6972     #define NIL_HOLE (struct hole *) 0
6973
6974     PRIVATE struct hole {
6975       phys_clicks h_base;            /* where does the hole begin? */
6976       phys_clicks h_len;             /* how big is the hole? */
6977       struct hole *h_next;           /* pointer to next entry on the list */
6978     } hole[NR_HOLES];
6979
6980
6981     PRIVATE struct hole *hole_head; /* pointer to first hole */
6982     PRIVATE struct hole *free_slots;        /* ptr to list of unused table slots */
6983
6984     /*===========================================================================*
6985      *                              alloc_mem                                     *
6986      *===========================================================================*/
6987     PUBLIC phys_clicks alloc_mem(clicks)
6988     phys_clicks clicks;                     /* amount of memory requested */
6989     {
6990     /* Allocate a block of memory from the free list using first fit. The block
6991      * consists of a sequence of contiguous bytes, whose length in clicks is
6992      * given by 'clicks'. A pointer to the block is returned.  The block is
6993      * always on a click boundary. This procedure is called when memory is
6994      * needed for FORK or EXEC.
6995      */
6996
6997       register struct hole *hp, *prev_ptr;
6998       phys_clicks old_base;
6999
```

```
7000        hp = hole_head;
7001        while (hp != NIL_HOLE) {
7002              if (hp->h_len >= clicks) {
7003                      /* We found a hole that is big enough.  Use it. */
7004                      old_base = hp->h_base;  /* remember where it started */
7005                      hp->h_base += clicks;   /* bite a piece off */
7006                      hp->h_len -= clicks;    /* ditto */
7007
7008                      /* If hole is only partly used, reduce size and return. */
7009                      if (hp->h_len != 0) return(old_base);
7010
7011                      /* The entire hole has been used up.  Manipulate free list. */
7012                      del_slot(prev_ptr, hp);
7013                      return(old_base);
7014              }
7015
7016              prev_ptr = hp;
7017              hp = hp->h_next;
7018        }
7019        return(NO_MEM);
7020   }


7023   /*===========================================================================*
7024    *                              free_mem                                      *
7025    *===========================================================================*/
7026   PUBLIC free_mem(base, clicks)
7027   phys_clicks base;                    /* base address of block to free */
7028   phys_clicks clicks;                  /* number of clicks to free */
7029   {
7030   /* Return a block of free memory to the hole list.  The parameters tell where
7031    * the block starts in physical memory and how big it is.  The block is added
7032    * to the hole list.  If it is contiguous with an existing hole on either end,
7033    * it is merged with the hole or holes.
7034    */
7035
7036     register struct hole *hp, *new_ptr, *prev_ptr;
7037
7038     if ( (new_ptr = free_slots) == NIL_HOLE) panic("Hole table full", NO_NUM);
7039     new_ptr->h_base = base;
7040     new_ptr->h_len = clicks;
7041     free_slots = new_ptr->h_next;
7042     hp = hole_head;
7043
7044     /* If this block's address is numerically less than the lowest hole currently
7045      * available, or if no holes are currently available, put this hole on the
7046      * front of the hole list.
7047      */
7048     if (hp == NIL_HOLE || base <= hp->h_base) {
7049              /* Block to be freed goes on front of hole list. */
```

```
7050                new_ptr->h_next = hp;
7051                hole_head = new_ptr;
7052                merge(new_ptr);
7053                return;
7054          }
7055
7056          /* Block to be returned does not go on front of hole list. */
7057          while (hp != NIL_HOLE && base > hp->h_base) {
7058                prev_ptr = hp;
7059                hp = hp->h_next;
7060          }
7061
7062          /* We found where it goes.  Insert block after 'prev_ptr'. */
7063          new_ptr->h_next = prev_ptr->h_next;
7064          prev_ptr->h_next = new_ptr;
7065          merge(prev_ptr);                      /* sequence is 'prev_ptr', 'new_ptr', 'hp' */
7066    }


7069    /*===========================================================================*
7070     *                              del_slot                                      *
7071     *===========================================================================*/
7072    PRIVATE del_slot(prev_ptr, hp)
7073    register struct hole *prev_ptr; /* pointer to hole entry just ahead of 'hp' */
7074    register struct hole *hp;        /* pointer to hole entry to be removed */
7075    {
7076    /* Remove an entry from the hole list.  This procedure is called when a
7077     * request to allocate memory removes a hole in its entirety, thus reducing
7078     * the numbers of holes in memory, and requiring the elimination of one
7079     * entry in the hole list.
7080     */
7081
7082      if (hp == hole_head)
7083            hole_head = hp->h_next;
7084      else
7085            prev_ptr->h_next = hp->h_next;
7086
7087      hp->h_next = free_slots;
7088      free_slots = hp;
7089    }


7092    /*===========================================================================*
7093     *                                merge                                       *
7094     *===========================================================================*/
7095    PRIVATE merge(hp)
7096    register struct hole *hp;        /* ptr to hole to merge with its successors */
7097    {
7098    /* Check for contiguous holes and merge any found.  Contiguous holes can occur
7099     * when a block of memory is freed, and it happens to abut another hole on
```

```
7100      * either or both ends.  The pointer 'hp' points to the first of a series of
7101      * three holes that can potentially all be merged together.
7102      */
7103
7104      register struct hole *next_ptr;
7105
7106      /* If 'hp' points to the last hole, no merging is possible.  If it does not,
7107       * try to absorb its successor into it and free the successor's table entry.
7108       */
7109      if ( (next_ptr = hp->h_next) == NIL_HOLE) return;
7110      if (hp->h_base + hp->h_len == next_ptr->h_base) {
7111            hp->h_len += next_ptr->h_len;   /* first one gets second one's mem */
7112            del_slot(hp, next_ptr);
7113      } else {
7114            hp = next_ptr;
7115      }
7116
7117      /* If 'hp' now points to the last hole, return; otherwise, try to absorb its
7118       * succesor into it.
7119       */
7120      if ( (next_ptr = hp->h_next) == NIL_HOLE) return;
7121      if (hp->h_base + hp->h_len == next_ptr->h_base) {
7122            hp->h_len += next_ptr->h_len;
7123            del_slot(hp, next_ptr);
7124      }
7125 }


7128 /*===========================================================================*
7129  *                              max_hole                                     *
7130  *===========================================================================*/
7131 PUBLIC phys_clicks max_hole()
7132 {
7133 /* Scan the hole list and return the largest hole. */
7134
7135      register struct hole *hp;
7136      register phys_clicks max;
7137
7138      hp = hole_head;
7139      max = 0;
7140      while (hp != NIL_HOLE) {
7141            if (hp->h_len > max) max = hp->h_len;
7142            hp = hp->h_next;
7143      }
7144      return(max);
7145 }
```

```
7150     /*===========================================================================*
7151      *                              mem_init                                     *
7152      *===========================================================================*/
7153     PUBLIC mem_init(clicks)
7154     phys_clicks clicks;              /* amount of memory available */
7155     {
7156     /* Initialize hole lists.  There are two lists: 'hole_head' points to a linked
7157      * list of all the holes (unused memory) in the system; 'free_slots' points to
7158      * a linked list of table entries that are not in use.  Initially, the former
7159      * list has one entry, a single hole encompassing all of memory, and the second
7160      * list links together all the remaining table slots.  As memory becomes more
7161      * fragmented in the course of time (i.e., the initial big hole breaks up into
7162      * many small holes), new table slots are needed to represent them.  These
7163      * slots are taken from the list headed by 'free_slots'.
7164      */
7165
7166       register struct hole *hp;
7167
7168       for (hp = &hole[0]; hp < &hole[NR_HOLES]; hp++) hp->h_next = hp + 1;
7169       hole[0].h_next = NIL_HOLE;       /* only 1 big hole initially */
7170       hole[NR_HOLES-1].h_next = NIL_HOLE;
7171       hole_head = &hole[0];
7172       free_slots = &hole[1];
7173       hole[0].h_base = 0;
7174       hole[0].h_len = clicks;
7175     }
```

```
7200    /* This file contains some useful utility routines used by MM.
7201     *
7202     * The entries into the file are:
7203     *   allowed:    see if an access is permitted
7204     *   mem_copy:   copy data from somewhere in memory to somewhere else
7205     *   no_sys:     this routine is called for invalid system call numbers
7206     *   panic:      MM has run aground of a fatal error and cannot continue
7207     */
7208
7209    #include "../h/const.h"
7210    #include "../h/type.h"
7211    #include "../h/callnr.h"
7212    #include "../h/com.h"
7213    #include "../h/error.h"
7214    #include "../h/stat.h"
7215    #include "const.h"
7216    #include "glo.h"
7217    #include "mproc.h"
7218
7219    PRIVATE message copy_mess;
7220
7221    /*===========================================================================*
7222     *                              allowed                                      *
7223     *===========================================================================*/
7224    PUBLIC int allowed(name_buf, s_buf, mask)
7225    char *name_buf;                 /* pointer to file name to be EXECed */
7226    struct stat *s_buf;             /* buffer for doing and returning stat struct */
7227    int mask;                       /* R_BIT, W_BIT, or X_BIT */
7228    {
7229    /* Check to see if file can be accessed.  Return EACCES or ENOENT if the access
7230     * is prohibited.  If it is legal open the file and return a file descriptor.
7231     */
7232
7233      register int fd, shift;
7234      int mode;
7235      extern errno;
7236
7237      /* Open the file and stat it. */
7238      if ( (fd = open(name_buf, 0)) < 0) return(-errno);
7239      if (fstat(fd, s_buf) < 0) panic("allowed: fstat failed", NO_NUM);
7240
7241      /* Only regular files can be executed. */
7242      mode = s_buf->st_mode & I_TYPE;
7243      if (mask == X_BIT && mode != I_REGULAR) {
7244            close(fd);
7245            return(EACCES);
7246      }
7247      /* Even for superuser, at least 1 X bit must be on. */
7248      if (mp->mp_effuid == 0 && mask == X_BIT &&
7249            (s_buf->st_mode & (X_BIT << 6 | X_BIT << 3 | X_BIT))) return(fd);
```

```
7250
7251      /* Right adjust the relevant set of permission bits. */
7252      if (mp->mp_effuid == s_buf->st_uid) shift = 6;
7253      else if (mp->mp_effgid == s_buf->st_gid) shift = 3;
7254      else shift = 0;
7255
7256      if (s_buf->st_mode >> shift & mask)   /* test the relevant bits */
7257           return(fd);                      /* permission granted */
7258      else {
7259           close(fd);                       /* permission denied */
7260           return(EACCES);
7261      }
7262   }


7265   /*===========================================================================*
7266    *                              mem_copy                                     *
7267    *===========================================================================*/
7268   PUBLIC int mem_copy(src_proc,src_seg, src_vir, dst_proc,dst_seg, dst_vir, bytes)
7269   int src_proc;                     /* source process */
7270   int src_seg;                      /* source segment: T, D, or S */
7271   long src_vir;                     /* source virtual address (clicks for ABS) */
7272   int dst_proc;                     /* dest process */
7273   int dst_seg;                      /* dest segment: T, D, or S */
7274   long dst_vir;                     /* dest virtual address (clicks for ABS) */
7275   long bytes;                       /* how many bytes (clicks for ABS) */
7276   {
7277   /* Transfer a block of data.  The source and destination can each either be a
7278    * process (including MM) or absolute memory, indicate by setting 'src_proc'
7279    * or 'dst_proc' to ABS.
7280    */
7281
7282     if (bytes == 0L) return(OK);
7283     copy_mess.SRC_SPACE = (char) src_seg;
7284     copy_mess.SRC_PROC_NR = src_proc;
7285     copy_mess.SRC_BUFFER = src_vir;
7286
7287     copy_mess.DST_SPACE = (char) dst_seg;
7288     copy_mess.DST_PROC_NR = dst_proc;
7289     copy_mess.DST_BUFFER = dst_vir;
7290
7291     copy_mess.COPY_BYTES = bytes;
7292     sys_copy(&copy_mess);
7293     return(copy_mess.m_type);
7294   }
7295   /*===========================================================================*
7296    *                              no_sys                                       *
7297    *===========================================================================*/
7298   PUBLIC int no_sys()
7299   {
```

```
7300      /* A system call number not implemented by MM has been requested. */
7301
7302        return(EINVAL);
7303      }


7306      /*===========================================================================*
7307       *                                panic                                      *
7308       *===========================================================================*/
7309      PUBLIC panic(format, num)
7310      char *format;                        /* format string */
7311      int num;                             /* number to go with format string */
7312      {
7313      /* Something awful has happened.  Panics are caused when an internal
7314       * inconsistency is detected, e.g., a programm_ing error or illegal value of a
7315       * defined constant.
7316       */
7317
7318        printf("Memory manager panic: %s ", format);
7319        if (num != NO_NUM) printf("%d",num);
7320        printf("\n");
7321        tell_fs(SYNC, 0, 0, 0);            /* flush the cache to the disk */
7322        sys_abort();
7323      }
```

```
7350   /* MM must occasionally print some message.  It uses the standard library
7351    * routine prink().  (The name "printf" is really a macro defined as "printk").
7352    * Printing is done by calling the TTY task directly, not going through FS.
7353    */
7354
7355   #include "../h/const.h"
7356   #include "../h/type.h"
7357   #include "../h/com.h"
7358
7359   #define STD_OUTPUT         1   /* file descriptor for standard output */
7360   #define BUF_SIZE         100   /* print buffer size */
7361
7362   PRIVATE int buf_count;         /* # characters in the buffer */
7363   PRIVATE char print_buf[BUF_SIZE];     /* output is buffered here */
7364   PRIVATE message putch_msg;     /* used for message to TTY task */
7365
7366   /*===========================================================================*
7367    *                              putc                                         *
7368    *===========================================================================*/
7369   PUBLIC putc(c)
7370   char c;
7371   {
7372
7373     /* Accumulate another character.  If '\n' or buffer full, print it. */
7374     print_buf[buf_count++] = c;
7375     if (buf_count == BUF_SIZE) F_l_u_s_h();
7376     if (c == '\n')  F_l_u_s_h();
7377   }


7380   /*===========================================================================*
7381    *                              F_l_u_s_h                                    *
7382    *===========================================================================*/
7383   PRIVATE F_l_u_s_h()
7384   {
7385   /* Flush the print buffer by calling TTY task. */
7386
7387     if (buf_count == 0) return;
7388     putch_msg.m_type = TTY_WRITE;
7389     putch_msg.PROC_NR  = 0;
7390     putch_msg.TTY_LINE = 0;
7391     putch_msg.ADDRESS  = print_buf;
7392     putch_msg.COUNT = buf_count;
7393     sendrec(TTY, &putch_msg);
7394     buf_count = 0;
7395   }
```

```
7400    /* This file contains the table used to map system call numbers onto the
7401     * routines that perform them.
7402     */
7403
7404    #include "../h/const.h"
7405    #include "../h/type.h"
7406    #include "const.h"
7407
7408    #undef EXTERN
7409    #define EXTERN
7410
7411    #include "../h/callnr.h"
7412    #include "glo.h"
7413    #include "mproc.h"
7414    #include "param.h"
7415
7416    /* Miscellaneous */
7417    char core_name[] = {"core"};      /* file name where core images are produced */
7418    unshort core_bits = 0x0EFC;       /* which signals cause core images */
7419
7420    extern char mm_stack[];
7421    char *stackpt = &mm_stack[MM_STACK_BYTES];        /* initial stack pointer */
7422
7423    extern do_mm_exit(), do_fork(), do_wait(), do_brk(), do_getset(), do_exec();
7424    extern do_signal(), do_kill(), do_pause(), do_alarm();
7425    extern no_sys(), unpause(), do_ksig(), do_brk2();
7426
7427    int (*mm_callvec[NCALLS])() = {
7428            no_sys,         /*  0 = unused */
7429            do_mm_exit,     /*  1 = exit   */
7430            do_fork,        /*  2 = fork   */
7431            no_sys,         /*  3 = read   */
7432            no_sys,         /*  4 = write  */
7433            no_sys,         /*  5 = open   */
7434            no_sys,         /*  6 = close  */
7435            do_wait,        /*  7 = wait   */
7436            no_sys,         /*  8 = creat  */
7437            no_sys,         /*  9 = link   */
7438            no_sys,         /* 10 = unlink */
7439            no_sys,         /* 11 = exec   */
7440            no_sys,         /* 12 = chdir  */
7441            no_sys,         /* 13 = time   */
7442            no_sys,         /* 14 = mknod  */
7443            no_sys,         /* 15 = chmod  */
7444            no_sys,         /* 16 = chown  */
7445            do_brk,         /* 17 = break  */
7446            no_sys,         /* 18 = stat   */
7447            no_sys,         /* 19 = lseek  */
7448            do_getset,      /* 20 = getpid */
7449            no_sys,         /* 21 = mount  */
```

```
7450          no_sys,          /* 22 = umount  */
7451          do_getset,       /* 23 = setuid  */
7452          do_getset,       /* 24 = getuid  */
7453          no_sys,          /* 25 = stime   */
7454          no_sys,          /* 26 = (ptrace)*/
7455          do_alarm,        /* 27 = alarm   */
7456          no_sys,          /* 28 = fstat   */
7457          do_pause,        /* 29 = pause   */
7458          no_sys,          /* 30 = utime   */
7459          no_sys,          /* 31 = (stty)  */
7460          no_sys,          /* 32 = (gtty)  */
7461          no_sys,          /* 33 = access  */
7462          no_sys,          /* 34 = (nice)  */
7463          no_sys,          /* 35 = (ftime) */
7464          no_sys,          /* 36 = sync    */
7465          do_kill,         /* 37 = kill    */
7466          no_sys,          /* 38 = unused  */
7467          no_sys,          /* 39 = unused  */
7468          no_sys,          /* 40 = unused  */
7469          no_sys,          /* 41 = dup     */
7470          no_sys,          /* 42 = pipe    */
7471          no_sys,          /* 43 = times   */
7472          no_sys,          /* 44 = (prof)  */
7473          no_sys,          /* 45 = unused  */
7474          do_getset,       /* 46 = setgid  */
7475          do_getset,       /* 47 = getgid  */
7476          do_signal,       /* 48 = sig     */
7477          no_sys,          /* 49 = unused  */
7478          no_sys,          /* 50 = unused  */
7479          no_sys,          /* 51 = (acct)  */
7480          no_sys,          /* 52 = (phys)  */
7481          no_sys,          /* 53 = (lock)  */
7482          no_sys,          /* 54 = ioctl   */
7483          no_sys,          /* 55 = unused  */
7484          no_sys,          /* 56 = (mpx)   */
7485          no_sys,          /* 57 = unused  */
7486          no_sys,          /* 58 = unused  */
7487          do_exec,         /* 59 = exece   */
7488          no_sys,          /* 60 = umask   */
7489          no_sys,          /* 61 = chroot  */
7490          no_sys,          /* 62 = unused  */
7491          no_sys,          /* 63 = unused  */
7492
7493          do_ksig,         /* 64 = KSIG: signals originating in the kernel */
7494          no_sys,          /* 65 = UNPAUSE */
7495          do_brk2,         /* 66 = BRK2 (used to tell MM size of FS,INIT) */
7496          no_sys,          /* 67 = REVIVE  */
7497          no_sys           /* 68 = TASK_REPLY        */
7498    };
```

```
7500    /* Tables sizes */
7501    #define NR_ZONE_NUMS        9     /* # zone numbers in an inode */
7502    #define NR_BUFS            30     /* # blocks in the buffer cache */
7503    #define NR_BUF_HASH        32     /* size of buf hash table; MUST BE POWER OF 2*/
7504    #define NR_FDS             20     /* max file descriptors per process */
7505    #define NR_FILPS           64     /* # slots in filp table */
7506    #define I_MAP_SLOTS         4     /* max # of blocks in the inode bit map */
7507    #define ZMAP_SLOTS          6     /* max # of blocks in the zone bit map */
7508    #define NR_INODES          32     /* # slots in "in core" inode table */
7509    #define NR_SUPERS           3     /* # slots in super block table */
7510    #define NAME_SIZE          14     /* # bytes in a directory component */
7511    #define FS_STACK_BYTES    512     /* size of file system stack */
7512
7513    /* Miscellaneous constants */
7514    #define SUPER_MAGIC     0x137F    /* magic number contained in super-block */
7515    #define SU_UID        (uid) 0     /* super_user's uid */
7516    #define SYS_UID       (uid) 0     /* uid for processes MM and INIT */
7517    #define SYS_GID       (gid) 0     /* gid for processes MM and INIT */
7518    #define NORMAL              0     /* forces get_block to do disk read */
7519    #define NO_READ             1     /* prevents get_block from doing disk read */
7520
7521    #define XPIPE               0     /* used in fp_task when suspended on pipe */
7522    #define NO_BIT     (bit_nr) 0     /* returned by alloc_bit() to signal failure */
7523    #define DUP_MASK         0100     /* mask to distinguish dup2 from dup */
7524
7525    #define LOOK_UP             0     /* tells search_dir to lookup string */
7526    #define ENTER               1     /* tells search_dir to make dir entry */
7527    #define DELETE              2     /* tells search_dir to delete entry */
7528
7529    #define CLEAN               0     /* disk and memory copies identical */
7530    #define DIRTY               1     /* disk and memory copies differ */
7531
7532    #define BOOT_BLOCK (block_nr) 0 /* block number of boot block */
7533    #define SUPER_BLOCK (block_nr)1 /* block number of super block */
7534    #define ROOT_INODE (inode_nr) 1 /* inode number for root directory */
7535
7536    /* Derived sizes */
7537    #define ZONE_NUM_SIZE     sizeof(zone_nr)              /* # bytes in zone nr*/
7538    #define NR_DZONE_NUM      (NR_ZONE_NUMS-2)             /* # zones in inode */
7539    #define DIR_ENTRY_SIZE    sizeof(dir_struct)          /* # bytes/dir entry */
7540    #define INODES_PER_BLOCK  (BLOCK_SIZE/INODE_SIZE)      /* # inodes/disk blk */
7541    #define INODE_SIZE        (sizeof (d_inode))           /* bytes in disk inode*/
7542    #define NR_DIR_ENTRIES    (BLOCK_SIZE/DIR_ENTRY_SIZE)  /* # dir entries/blk*/
7543    #define NR_INDIRECTS      (BLOCK_SIZE/ZONE_NUM_SIZE)   /* # zones/indir blk */
7544    #define INTS_PER_BLOCK    (BLOCK_SIZE/sizeof(int))     /* # integers/blk */
7545    #define SUPER_SIZE        sizeof(struct super_block)   /* super_block size */
7546    #define PIPE_SIZE         (NR_DZONE_NUM*BLOCK_SIZE)    /* pipe size in bytes*/
7547    #define MAX_ZONES (NR_DZONE_NUM+NR_INDIRECTS+(long)NR_INDIRECTS*NR_INDIRECTS)
7548                                                  /* max # of zones in a file */
7549    #define printf printk
```

```
7550   /* Buffer (block) cache.  To acquire a block, a routine calls get_block(),
7551    * telling which block it wants.  The block is then regarded as "in use"
7552    * and has its 'b_count' field incremented.  All the blocks, whether in use
7553    * or not, are chained together in an LRU list, with 'front' pointing
7554    * to the least recently used block, and 'rear' to the most recently used
7555    * block.  A reverse chain, using the field b_prev is also maintained.
7556    * Usage for LRU is measured by the time the put_block() is done.  The second
7557    * parameter to put_block() can violate the LRU order and put a block on the
7558    * front of the list, if it will probably not be needed soon.  If a block
7559    * is modified, the modifying routine must set b_dirt to DIRTY, so the block
7560    * will eventually be rewritten to the disk.
7561    */
7562
7563   EXTERN struct buf {
7564     /* Data portion of the buffer. */
7565     union {
7566       char b__data[BLOCK_SIZE];           /* ordinary user data */
7567       dir_struct b__dir[NR_DIR_ENTRIES];  /* directory block */
7568       zone_nr b__ind[NR_INDIRECTS];       /* indirect block */
7569       d_inode b__inode[INODES_PER_BLOCK]; /* inode block */
7570       int b__int[INTS_PER_BLOCK];         /* block full of integers */
7571     } b;
7572
7573     /* Header portion of the buffer. */
7574     struct buf *b_next;           /* used to link bufs in a chain */
7575     struct buf *b_prev;           /* used to link bufs the other way */
7576     struct buf *b_hash;           /* used to link bufs on hash chains */
7577     block_nr b_blocknr;           /* block number of its (minor) device */
7578     dev_nr b_dev;                 /* major | minor device where block resides */
7579     char b_dirt;                  /* CLEAN or DIRTY */
7580     char b_count;                 /* number of users of this buffer */
7581   } buf[NR_BUFS];
7582
7583   /* A block is free if b_dev == NO_DEV. */
7584
7585   #define NIL_BUF (struct buf *) 0       /* indicates absence of a buffer */
7586
7587   /* These defs make it possible to use to bp->b_data instead of bp->b.b__data */
7588   #define b_data  b.b__data
7589   #define b_dir   b.b__dir
7590   #define b_ind   b.b__ind
7591   #define b_inode b.b__inode
7592   #define b_int   b.b__int
7593
7594   EXTERN struct buf *buf_hash[NR_BUF_HASH];      /* the buffer hash table */
7595
7596   EXTERN struct buf *front;      /* points to least recently used free block */
7597   EXTERN struct buf *rear;       /* points to most recently used free block */
7598   EXTERN int bufs_in_use;        /* # bufs currently in use (not on free list) */
7599
```

```
7600   /* When a block is released, the type of usage is passed to put_block(). */
7601   #define WRITE_IMMED       0100 /* block should be written to disk now */
7602   #define ONE_SHOT          0200 /* set if block not likely to be needed soon */
7603   #define INODE_BLOCK       0 + WRITE_IMMED              /* inode block */
7604   #define DIRECTORY_BLOCK   1 + WRITE_IMMED              /* directory block */
7605   #define INDIRECT_BLOCK    2 + WRITE_IMMED              /* pointer block */
7606   #define I_MAP_BLOCK       3 + WRITE_IMMED + ONE_SHOT   /* inode bit map */
7607   #define ZMAP_BLOCK        4 + WRITE_IMMED + ONE_SHOT   /* free zone map */
7608   #define ZUPER_BLOCK       5 + WRITE_IMMED + ONE_SHOT   /* super block */
7609   #define FULL_DATA_BLOCK   6                            /* data, fully used */
7610   #define PARTIAL_DATA_BLOCK 7                           /* data, partly used */
```

```
7650     /* Device table.  This table is indexed by major device number.  It provides
7651      * the link between major device numbers and the routines that process them.
7652      */
7653
7654     EXTERN struct dmap {
7655       int (*dmap_open)();
7656       int (*dmap_rw)();
7657       int (*dmap_close)();
7658       int dmap_task;
7659     } dmap[];
7660
```

```
7700    /* This is the filp table.  It is an intermediary between file descriptors and
7701     * inodes.  A slot is free if filp_count == 0.
7702     */
7703
7704    EXTERN struct filp {
7705      mask_bits filp_mode;          /* RW bits, telling how file is opened */
7706      int filp_count;               /* how many file descriptors share this slot? */
7707      struct inode *filp_ino;       /* pointer to the inode */
7708      file_pos filp_pos;            /* file position */
7709    } filp[NR_FILPS];
7710
7711    #define NIL_FILP (struct filp *) 0      /* indicates absence of a filp slot */
```

```
7750    /* This is the per-process information.  A slot is reserved for each potential
7751     * process. Thus NR_PROCS must be the same as in the kernel. It is not possible
7752     * or even necessary to tell when a slot is free here.
7753     */
7754
7755    EXTERN struct fproc {
7756      mask_bits fp_umask;              /* mask set by umask system call */
7757      struct inode *fp_workdir;        /* pointer to working directory's inode */
7758      struct inode *fp_rootdir;        /* pointer to current root dir (see chroot) */
7759      struct filp *fp_filp[NR_FDS];    /* the file descriptor table */
7760      uid fp_realuid;                  /* real user id */
7761      uid fp_effuid;                   /* effective user id */
7762      gid fp_realgid;                  /* real group id */
7763      gid fp_effgid;                   /* effective group id */
7764      dev_nr fs_tty;                   /* major/minor of controlling tty */
7765      int fp_fd;                       /* place to save fd if rd/wr can't finish */
7766      char *fp_buffer;                 /* place to save buffer if rd/wr can't finish */
7767      int  fp_nbytes;                  /* place to save bytes if rd/wr can't finish */
7768      char fp_suspended;               /* set to indicate process hanging */
7769      char fp_revived;                 /* set to indicate process being revived */
7770      char fp_task;                    /* which task is proc suspended on */
7771    } fproc[NR_PROCS];
7772
7773    /* Field values. */
7774    #define NOT_SUSPENDED      0    /* process is not suspended on pipe or task */
7775    #define SUSPENDED          1    /* process is suspended on pipe or task */
7776    #define NOT_REVIVING       0    /* process is not being revived */
7777    #define REVIVING           1    /* process is being revived from suspension */
```

```
7800    /* File System global variables */
7801    EXTERN struct fproc *fp;            /* pointer to caller's fproc struct */
7802    EXTERN int super_user;              /* 1 if caller is super_user, else 0 */
7803    EXTERN int dont_reply;              /* normally 0; set to 1 to inhibit reply */
7804    EXTERN int susp_count;              /* number of procs suspended on pipe */
7805    EXTERN int reviving;                /* number of pipe processes to be revived */
7806    EXTERN file_pos rdahedpos;          /* position to read ahead */
7807    EXTERN struct inode *rdahed_inode;      /* pointer to inode to read ahead */
7808
7809    /* The parameters of the call are kept here. */
7810    EXTERN message m;                   /* the input message itself */
7811    EXTERN message ml;                  /* the output message used for reply */
7812    EXTERN int who;                     /* caller's proc number */
7813    EXTERN int fs_call;                 /* system call number */
7814    EXTERN char user_path[MAX_PATH];/* storage for user path name */
7815
7816    /* The following variables are used for returning results to the caller. */
7817    EXTERN int err_code;                /* temporary storage for error number */
7818
7819    EXTERN char fstack[FS_STACK_BYTES];     /* the File System's stack. */
```

```
7850    /* Inode table.  This table holds inodes that are currently in use.  In some
7851     * cases they have been opened by an open() or creat() system call, in other
7852     * cases the file system itself needs the inode for one reason or another,
7853     * such as to search a directory for a path name.
7854     * The first part of the struct holds fields that are present on the
7855     * disk; the second part holds fields not present on the disk.
7856     * The disk inode part is also declared in "type.h" as 'd_inode'.
7857     */
7858
7859    EXTERN struct inode {
7860        unshort i_mode;                 /* file type, protection, etc. */
7861        uid i_uid;                      /* user id of the file's owner */
7862        file_pos i_size;                /* current file size in bytes */
7863        real_time i_modtime;            /* when was file data last changed */
7864        gid i_gid;                      /* group number */
7865        links i_nlinks;                 /* how many links to this file */
7866        zone_nr i_zone[NR_ZONE_NUMS];   /* zone numbers for direct, ind, and dbl ind */
7867
7868        /* The following items are not present on the disk. */
7869        dev_nr i_dev;                   /* which device is the inode on */
7870        inode_nr i_num;                 /* inode number on its (minor) device */
7871        short int i_count;              /* # times inode used; 0 means slot is free */
7872        char i_dirt;                    /* CLEAN or DIRTY */
7873        char i_pipe;                    /* set to I_PIPE if pipe */
7874        char i_mount;                   /* this bit is set if file mounted on */
7875        char i_seek;                    /* set on LSEEK, cleared on READ/WRITE */
7876    } inode[NR_INODES];
7877
7878
7879    #define NIL_INODE (struct inode *) 0    /* indicates absence of inode slot */
7880
7881    /* Field values.  Note that CLEAN and DIRTY are defined in "const.h" */
7882    #define NO_PIPE          0    /* i_pipe is NO_PIPE if inode is not a pipe */
7883    #define I_PIPE           1    /* i_pipe is I_PIPE if inode is a pipe */
7884    #define NO_MOUNT         0    /* i_mount is NO_MOUNT if file not mounted on */
7885    #define I_MOUNT          1    /* i_mount is I_MOUNT if file mounted on */
7886    #define NO_SEEK          0    /* i_seek = NO_SEEK if last op was not SEEK */
7887    #define ISEEK            1    /* i_seek = ISEEK if last op was SEEK */
```

```
7900    /* The following names are synonyms for the variables in the input message. */
7901    #define acc_time        m.m2_l1
7902    #define addr            m.m1_i3
7903    #define buffer          m.m1_p1
7904    #define cd_flag         m.m1_i2
7905    #define child           m.m1_i2
7906    #define co_mode         m.m1_i1
7907    #define eff_grp_id      m.m1_i3
7908    #define eff_user_id     m.m1_i3
7909    #define erki            m.m1_p1
7910    #define fd              m.m1_i1
7911    #define fd2             m.m1_i2
7912    #define ioflags         m.m1_i3
7913    #define group           m.m1_i3
7914    #define real_grp_id     m.m1_i2
7915    #define ls_fd           m.m2_i1
7916    #define mk_mode         m.m1_i2
7917    #define mode            m.m3_i2
7918    #define name            m.m3_p1
7919    #define name1           m.m1_p1
7920    #define name2           m.m1_p2
7921    #define name_length     m.m3_i1
7922    #define name1_length    m.m1_i1
7923    #define name2_length    m.m1_i2
7924    #define nbytes          m.m1_i2
7925    #define offset          m.m2_l1
7926    #define owner           m.m1_i2
7927    #define parent          m.m1_i1
7928    #define pathname        m.m3_ca1
7929    #define pro             m.m1_i1
7930    #define rd_only         m.m1_i3
7931    #define real_user_id    m.m1_i2
7932    #define request         m.m1_i2
7933    #define sig             m.m1_i2
7934    #define slot1           m.m1_i1
7935    #define tp              m.m2_l1
7936    #define update_time     m.m2_l2
7937    #define utime_file      m.m2_p1
7938    #define utime_length    m.m2_i1
7939    #define whence          m.m2_i2
7940
7941    /* The following names are synonyms for the variables in the output message. */
7942    #define reply_type      m1.m_type
7943    #define reply_l1        m1.m2_l1
7944    #define reply_i1        m1.m1_i1
7945    #define reply_i2        m1.m1_i2
7946    #define reply_t1        m1.m4_l1
7947    #define reply_t2        m1.m4_l2
7948    #define reply_t3        m1.m4_l3
7949    #define reply_t4        m1.m4_l4
```

```
7950    /* Super block table.  The root file system and every mounted file system
7951     * has an entry here.  The entry holds information about the sizes of the bit
7952     * maps and inodes.  The s_ninodes field gives the number of inodes available
7953     * for files and directories, including the root directory.  Inode 0 is
7954     * on the disk, but not used.  Thus s_ninodes = 4 means that 5 bits will be
7955     * used in the bit map, bit 0, which is always 1 and not used, and bits 1-4
7956     * for files and directories.  The disk layout is:
7957     *
7958     *      Item         # blocks
7959     *      boot block    1
7960     *      super block   1
7961     *      inode map     s_imap_blocks
7962     *      zone map      s_zmap_blocks
7963     *      inodes        (s_ninodes + 1 + INODES_PER_BLOCK - 1)/INODES_PER_BLOCK
7964     *      unused        whatever is needed to fill out the current zone
7965     *      data zones    (s_nzones - s_firstdatazone) << s_log_zone_size
7966     *
7967     * A super_block slot is free if s_dev == NO_DEV.
7968     */
7969
7970
7971    EXTERN struct super_block {
7972      inode_nr s_ninodes;            /* # usable inodes on the minor device */
7973      zone_nr s_nzones;              /* total device size, including bit maps etc */
7974      unshort s_imap_blocks;         /* # of blocks used by inode bit map */
7975      unshort s_zmap_blocks;         /* # of blocks used by zone bit map */
7976      zone_nr s_firstdatazone;       /* number of first data zone */
7977      short int s_log_zone_size;     /* log2 of blocks/zone */
7978      file_pos s_max_size;           /* maximum file size on this device */
7979      int s_magic;                   /* magic number to recognize super-blocks */
7980
7981      /* The following items are only used when the super_block is in memory. */
7982      struct buf *s_imap[I_MAP_SLOTS]; /* pointers to the in-core inode bit map */
7983      struct buf *s_zmap[ZMAP_SLOTS]; /* pointers to the in-core zone bit map */
7984      dev_nr s_dev;                  /* whose super block is this? */
7985      struct inode *s_isup;          /* inode for root dir of mounted file sys */
7986      struct inode *s_imount;        /* inode mounted on */
7987      real_time s_time;              /* time of last update */
7988      char s_rd_only;                /* set to 1 iff file sys mounted read only */
7989      char s_dirt;                   /* CLEAN or DIRTY */
7990    } super_block[NR_SUPERS];
7991
7992    #define NIL_SUPER (struct super_block *) 0
```

```
8000   /* Type definitions local to the File System. */
8001
8002   typedef struct {                  /* directory entry */
8003     inode_nr d_inum;                /* inode number */
8004     char d_name[NAME_SIZE];         /* character string */
8005   } dir_struct;
8006
8007   /* Declaration of the disk inode used in rw_inode(). */
8008   typedef struct {                  /* disk inode.  Memory inode is in "inotab.h" */
8009     mask_bits i_mode;               /* file type, protection, etc. */
8010     uid i_uid;                      /* user id of the file's owner */
8011     file_pos i_size;                /* current file size in bytes */
8012     real_time i_modtime;            /* when was file data last changed */
8013     gid i_gid;                      /* group number */
8014     links i_nlinks;                 /* how many links to this file */
8015     zone_nr i_zone[NR_ZONE_NUMS];   /* block nums for direct, ind, and dbl ind */
8016   } d_inode;
```

```
8050   /* The file system maintains a buffer cache to reduce the number of disk
8051    * accesses needed.  Whenever a read or write to the disk is done, a check is
8052    * first made to see if the block is in the cache.  This file manages the
8053    * cache.
8054    *
8055    * The entry points into this file are:
8056    *   get_block:    request to fetch a block for reading or writing from cache
8057    *   put_block:    return a block previously requested with get_block
8058    *   alloc_zone:   allocate a new zone (to increase the length of a file)
8059    *   free_zone:    release a zone (when a file is removed)
8060    *   rw_block:     read or write a block from the disk itself
8061    *   invalidate:   remove all the cache blocks on some device
8062    */
8063
8064   #include "../h/const.h"
8065   #include "../h/type.h"
8066   #include "../h/error.h"
8067   #include "const.h"
8068   #include "type.h"
8069   #include "buf.h"
8070   #include "file.h"
8071   #include "fproc.h"
8072   #include "glo.h"
8073   #include "inode.h"
8074   #include "super.h"
8075
8076   /*===========================================================================*
8077    *                              get_block                                    *
8078    *===========================================================================*/
8079   PUBLIC struct buf *get_block(dev, block, only_search)
8080   register dev_nr dev;              /* on which device is the block? */
8081   register block_nr block;          /* which block is wanted? */
8082   int only_search;                  /* if NO_READ, don't read, else act normal */
8083   {
8084   /* Check to see if the requested block is in the block cache.  If so, return
8085    * a pointer to it.  If not, evict some other block and fetch it (unless
8086    * 'only_search' is 1).  All blocks in the cache, whether in use or not,
8087    * are linked together in a chain, with 'front' pointing to the least recently
8088    * used block and 'rear' to the most recently used block.  If 'only_search' is
8089    * 1, the block being requested will be overwritten in its entirety, so it is
8090    * only necessary to see if it is in the cache; if it is not, any free buffer
8091    * will do.  It is not necessary to actually read the block in from disk.
8092    * In addition to the LRU chain, there is also a hash chain to link together
8093    * blocks whose block numbers end with the same bit strings, for fast lookup.
8094    */
8095
8096     register struct buf *bp, *prev_ptr;
8097
8098     /* Search the list of blocks not currently in use for (dev, block). */
8099     bp = buf_hash[block & (NR_BUF_HASH - 1)];      /* search the hash chain */
```

```
8100          if (dev != NO_DEV) {
8101                while (bp != NIL_BUF) {
8102                      if (bp->b_blocknr == block && bp->b_dev == dev) {
8103                            /* Block needed has been found. */
8104                            if (bp->b_count == 0) bufs_in_use++;
8105                            bp->b_count++;  /* record that block is in use */
8106                            return(bp);
8107                      } else {
8108                            /* This block is not the one sought. */
8109                            bp = bp->b_hash; /* move to next block on hash chain */
8110                      }
8111                }
8112          }
8113
8114          /* Desired block is not on available chain.  Take oldest block ('front').
8115           * However, a block that is aready in use (b_count > 0) may not be taken.
8116           */
8117          if (bufs_in_use == NR_BUFS) panic("All buffers in use", NR_BUFS);
8118          bufs_in_use++;                    /* one more buffer in use now */
8119          bp = front;
8120          while (bp->b_count > 0 && bp->b_next != NIL_BUF) bp = bp->b_next;
8121          if (bp == NIL_BUF || bp->b_count > 0) panic("No free buffer", NO_NUM);
8122
8123          /* Remove the block that was just taken from its hash chain. */
8124          prev_ptr = buf_hash[bp->b_blocknr & (NR_BUF_HASH - 1)];
8125          if (prev_ptr == bp) {
8126                buf_hash[bp->b_blocknr & (NR_BUF_HASH - 1)] = bp->b_hash;
8127          } else {
8128                /* The block just taken is not on the front of its hash chain. */
8129                while (prev_ptr->b_hash != NIL_BUF)
8130                      if (prev_ptr->b_hash == bp) {
8131                            prev_ptr->b_hash = bp->b_hash;  /* found it */
8132                            break;
8133                      } else {
8134                            prev_ptr = prev_ptr->b_hash;    /* keep looking */
8135                      }
8136          }
8137
8138          /* If the  block taken is dirty, make it clean by rewriting it to disk. */
8139          if (bp->b_dirt == DIRTY && bp->b_dev != NO_DEV) rw_block(bp, WRITING);
8140
8141          /* Fill in block's parameters and add it to the hash chain where it goes. */
8142          bp->b_dev = dev;              /* fill in device number */
8143          bp->b_blocknr = block;       /* fill in block number */
8144          bp->b_count++;               /* record that block is being used */
8145          bp->b_hash = buf_hash[bp->b_blocknr & (NR_BUF_HASH - 1)];
8146          buf_hash[bp->b_blocknr & (NR_BUF_HASH - 1)] = bp;     /* add to hash list */
8147
8148          /* Go get the requested block, unless only_search = NO_READ. */
8149          if (dev != NO_DEV && only_search == NORMAL) rw_block(bp, READING);
```

```
8150        return(bp);                    /* return the newly acquired block */
8151    }


8154    /*===========================================================================*
8155     *                              put_block                                     *
8156     *===========================================================================*/
8157    PUBLIC put_block(bp, block_type)
8158    register struct buf *bp;          /* pointer to the buffer to be released */
8159    int block_type;                   /* INODE_BLOCK, DIRECTORY_BLOCK, or whatever */
8160    {
8161    /* Return a block to the list of available blocks.   Depending on 'block_type'
8162     * it may be put on the front or rear of the LRU chain.  Blocks that are
8163     * expected to be needed again shortly (e.g., partially full data blocks)
8164     * go on the rear; blocks that are unlikely to be needed again shortly
8165     * (e.g., full data blocks) go on the front.  Blocks whose loss can hurt
8166     * the integrity of the file system (e.g., inode blocks) are written to
8167     * disk immediately if they are dirty.
8168     */

8170      register struct buf *next_ptr, *prev_ptr;

8172      if (bp == NIL_BUF) return;     /* it is easier to check here than in caller */

8174      /* If block is no longer in use, first remove it from LRU chain. */
8175      bp->b_count--;                 /* there is one use fewer now */
8176      if (bp->b_count > 0) return;   /* block is still in use */

8178      bufs_in_use--;                 /* one fewer block buffers in use */
8179      next_ptr = bp->b_next;         /* successor on LRU chain */
8180      prev_ptr = bp->b_prev;         /* predecessor on LRU chain */
8181      if (prev_ptr != NIL_BUF)
8182            prev_ptr->b_next = next_ptr;
8183      else
8184            front = next_ptr;        /* this block was at front of chain */

8186      if (next_ptr != NIL_BUF)
8187            next_ptr->b_prev = prev_ptr;
8188      else
8189            rear = prev_ptr;         /* this block was at rear of chain */

8191      /* Put this block back on the LRU chain.  If the ONE_SHOT bit is set in
8192       * 'block_type', the block is not likely to be needed again shortly, so put
8193       * it on the front of the LRU chain where it will be the first one to be
8194       * taken when a free buffer is needed later.
8195       */
8196      if (block_type & ONE_SHOT) {
8197            /* Block probably won't be needed quickly. Put it on front of chain.
8198             * It will be the next block to be evicted from the cache.
8199             */
```

```
8200                bp->b_prev = NIL_BUF;
8201                bp->b_next = front;
8202                if (front == NIL_BUF)
8203                        rear = bp;        /* LRU chain was empty */
8204                else
8205                        front->b_prev = bp;
8206                front = bp;
8207        } else {
8208                /* Block probably will be needed quickly.  Put it on rear of chain.
8209                 * It will not be evicted from the cache for a long time.
8210                 */
8211                bp->b_prev = rear;
8212                bp->b_next = NIL_BUF;
8213                if (rear == NIL_BUF)
8214                        front = bp;
8215                else
8216                        rear->b_next = bp;
8217                rear = bp;
8218        }
8219
8220        /* Some blocks are so important (e.g., inodes, indirect blocks) that they
8221         * should be written to the disk immediately to avoid messing up the file
8222         * system in the event of a crash.
8223         */
8224        if ((block_type & WRITE_IMMED) && bp->b_dirt==DIRTY && bp->b_dev != NO_DEV)
8225                rw_block(bp, WRITING);
8226
8227        /* Super blocks must not be cached, lest mount use cached block. */
8228        if (block_type == ZUPER_BLOCK) bp->b_dev = NO_DEV;
8229 }


8232  /*===========================================================================*
8233   *                              alloc_zone                                   *
8234   *===========================================================================*/
8235  PUBLIC zone_nr alloc_zone(dev, z)
8236  dev_nr dev;                           /* device where zone wanted */
8237  zone_nr z;                            /* try to allocate new zone near this one */
8238  {
8239  /* Allocate a new zone on the indicated device and return its number. */
8240
8241    bit_nr b, bit;
8242    struct super_block *sp;
8243    int major, minor;
8244    extern bit_nr alloc_bit();
8245    extern struct super_block *get_super();
8246
8247    /* Note that the routine alloc_bit() returns 1 for the lowest possible
8248     * zone, which corresponds to sp->s_firstdatazone.  To convert a value
8249     * between the bit number, 'b', used by alloc_bit() and the zone number, 'z',
```

```
8250         * stored in the inode, use the formula:
8251         *      z = b + sp->s_firstdatazone - 1
8252         * Alloc_bit() never returns 0, since this is used for NO_BIT (failure).
8253         */
8254         sp = get_super(dev);             /* find the super_block for this device */
8255         bit = (bit_nr) z - (sp->s_firstdatazone - 1);
8256         b = alloc_bit(sp->s_zmap, (bit_nr) sp->s_nzones - sp->s_firstdatazone + 1,
8257                                               sp->s_zmap_blocks, bit);
8258         if (b == NO_BIT) {
8259                 err_code = ENOSPC;
8260                 major = (int) (sp->s_dev >> MAJOR) & BYTE;
8261                 minor = (int) (sp->s_dev >> MINOR) & BYTE;
8262                 if (sp->s_dev == ROOT_DEV)
8263                         printf("No space on root device (RAM disk)\n");
8264                 else
8265                         printf("No space on device %d/%d\n", major, minor);
8266                 return(NO_ZONE);
8267         }
8268         return(sp->s_firstdatazone - 1 + (zone_nr) b);
8269 }


8272 /*===========================================================================*
8273  *                              free_zone                                    *
8274  *===========================================================================*/
8275 PUBLIC free_zone(dev, numb)
8276 dev_nr dev;                              /* device where zone located */
8277 zone_nr numb;                            /* zone to be returned */
8278 {
8279 /* Return a zone. */
8280
8281   register struct super_block *sp;
8282   extern struct super_block *get_super();
8283
8284   if (numb == NO_ZONE) return;   /* checking here easier than in caller */
8285
8286   /* Locate the appropriate super_block and return bit. */
8287   sp = get_super(dev);
8288   free_bit(sp->s_zmap, (bit_nr) numb - (sp->s_firstdatazone - 1) );
8289 }


8292 /*===========================================================================*
8293  *                              rw_block                                     *
8294  *===========================================================================*/
8295 PUBLIC rw_block(bp, rw_flag)
8296 register struct buf *bp;                 /* buffer pointer */
8297 int rw_flag;                             /* READING or WRITING */
8298 {
8299 /* Read or write a disk block. This is the only routine in which actual disk
```

```
8300      * I/O is invoked.  If an error occurs, a message is printed here, but the error
8301      * is not reported to the caller.  If the error occurred while purging a block
8302      * from the cache, it is not clear what the caller could do about it anyway.
8303      */
8304
8305      int r;
8306      long pos;
8307      dev_nr dev;
8308
8309      if (bp->b_dev != NO_DEV) {
8310            pos = (long) bp->b_blocknr * BLOCK_SIZE;
8311            r = dev_io(rw_flag, bp->b_dev, pos, BLOCK_SIZE, FS_PROC_NR, bp->b_data);
8312            if (r < 0) {
8313                  dev = bp->b_dev;
8314                  printf("Unrecoverable disk error on device %d/%d, block %d\n",
8315                        (dev>>MAJOR)&BYTE, (dev>>MINOR)&BYTE, bp->b_blocknr);
8316            }
8317      }
8318
8319      bp->b_dirt = CLEAN;
8320  }


8323  /*===========================================================================*
8324   *                              invalidate                                   *
8325   *===========================================================================*/
8326  PUBLIC invalidate(device)
8327  dev_nr device;                /* device whose blocks are to be purged */
8328  {
8329  /* Remove all the blocks belonging to some device from the cache. */
8330
8331      register struct buf *bp;
8332
8333      for (bp = &buf[0]; bp < &buf[NR_BUFS]; bp++)
8334            if (bp->b_dev == device) bp->b_dev = NO_DEV;
8335  }
```

```
8350   /* This file manages the inode table.  There are procedures to allocate and
8351    * deallocate inodes, acquire, erase, and release them, and read and write
8352    * them from the disk.
8353    *
8354    * The entry points into this file are
8355    *   get_inode:    search inode table for a given inode; if not there, read it
8356    *   put_inode:    indicate that an inode is no longer needed in memory
8357    *   alloc_inode:  allocate a new, unused inode
8358    *   wipe_inode:   erase some fields of a newly allocated inode
8359    *   free_inode:   mark an inode as available for a new file
8360    *   rw_inode:     read a disk block and extract an inode, or corresp. write
8361    *   dup_inode:    indicate that someone else is using an inode table entry
8362    */

8364   #include "../h/const.h"
8365   #include "../h/type.h"
8366   #include "../h/error.h"
8367   #include "const.h"
8368   #include "type.h"
8369   #include "buf.h"
8370   #include "file.h"
8371   #include "fproc.h"
8372   #include "glo.h"
8373   #include "inode.h"
8374   #include "super.h"

8376   /*===========================================================================*
8377    *                              get_inode                                     *
8378    *===========================================================================*/
8379   PUBLIC struct inode *get_inode(dev, numb)
8380   dev_nr dev;                    /* device on which inode resides */
8381   inode_nr numb;                 /* inode number */
8382   {
8383   /* Find a slot in the inode table, load the specified inode into it, and
8384    * return a pointer to the slot.  If 'dev' == NO_DEV, just return a free slot.
8385    */

8387     register struct inode *rip, *xp;

8389     /* Search the inode table both for (dev, numb) and a free slot. */
8390     xp = NIL_INODE;
8391     for (rip = &inode[0]; rip < &inode[NR_INODES]; rip++) {
8392           if (rip->i_count > 0) { /* only check used slots for (dev, numb) */
8393                   if (rip->i_dev == dev && rip->i_num == numb) {
8394                           /* This is the inode that we are looking for. */
8395                           rip->i_count++;
8396                           return(rip);    /* (dev, numb) found */
8397                   }
8398           } else
8399                   xp = rip;       /* remember this free slot for later */
```

```
8400          }
8401
8402          /* Inode we want is not currently in use.  Did we find a free slot? */
8403          if (xp == NIL_INODE) {          /* inode table completely full */
8404                err_code = ENFILE;
8405                return(NIL_INODE);
8406          }
8407
8408          /* A free inode slot has been located.  Load the inode into it. */
8409          xp->i_dev = dev;
8410          xp->i_num = numb;
8411          xp->i_count = 1;
8412          if (dev != NO_DEV) rw_inode(xp, READING);      /* get inode from disk */
8413
8414          return(xp);
8415    }


8418    /*===========================================================================*
8419     *                              put_inode                                    *
8420     *===========================================================================*/
8421    PUBLIC put_inode(rip)
8422    register struct inode *rip;      /* pointer to inode to be released */
8423    {
8424    /* The caller is no longer using this inode.  If no one else is using it either
8425     * write it back to the disk immediately.  If it has no links, truncate it and
8426     * return it to the pool of available inodes.
8427     */
8428
8429      if (rip == NIL_INODE) return; /* checking here is easier than in caller */
8430      if (--rip->i_count == 0) {    /* i_count == 0 means no one is using it now */
8431            if ((rip->i_nlinks & BYTE) == 0) {
8432                    /* i_nlinks == 0 means free the inode. */
8433                    truncate(rip); /* return all the disk blocks */
8434                    rip->i_mode = I_NOT_ALLOC;      /* clear I_TYPE field */
8435                    rip->i_pipe = NO_PIPE;
8436                    free_inode(rip->i_dev, rip->i_num);
8437            }
8438
8439            if (rip->i_dirt == DIRTY) rw_inode(rip, WRITING);
8440      }
8441    }


8443    /*===========================================================================*
8444     *                              alloc_inode                                  *
8445     *===========================================================================*/
8446    PUBLIC struct inode *alloc_inode(dev, bits)
8447    dev_nr dev;                      /* device on which to allocate the inode */
8448    mask_bits bits;                  /* mode of the inode */
8449    {
```

```
8450    /* Allocate a free inode on 'dev', and return a pointer to it. */
8451
8452    register struct inode *rip;
8453    register struct super_block *sp;
8454    int major, minor;
8455    inode_nr numb;
8456    bit_nr b;
8457    extern bit_nr alloc_bit();
8458    extern struct inode *get_inode();
8459    extern struct super_block *get_super();
8460
8461    /* Acquire an inode from the bit map. */
8462    sp = get_super(dev);          /* get pointer to super_block */
8463    b=alloc_bit(sp->s_imap, (bit_nr)sp->s_ninodes+1, sp->s_imap_blocks,(bit_nr)0);
8464    if (b == NO_BIT) {
8465          err_code = ENFILE;
8466          major = (int) (sp->s_dev >> MAJOR) & BYTE;
8467          minor = (int) (sp->s_dev >> MINOR) & BYTE;
8468          if (sp->s_dev == ROOT_DEV)
8469                printf("Out of i-nodes on root device (RAM disk)\n");
8470          else
8471                printf("Out of i-nodes on device %d/%d\n", major, minor);
8472          return(NIL_INODE);
8473    }
8474    numb = (inode_nr) b;
8475
8476    /* Try to acquire a slot in the inode table. */
8477    if ( (rip = get_inode(NO_DEV, numb)) == NIL_INODE) {
8478          /* No inode table slots available. Free the inode just allocated. */
8479          free_bit(sp->s_imap, b);
8480    } else {
8481          /* An inode slot is available. Put the inode just allocated into it. */
8482          rip->i_mode = bits;
8483          rip->i_nlinks = (links) 0;
8484          rip->i_uid = fp->fp_effuid;
8485          rip->i_gid = fp->fp_effgid;
8486          rip->i_dev = dev;          /* was provisionally set to NO_DEV */
8487
8488          /* The fields not cleared already are cleared in wipe_inode(). They have
8489           * been put there because truncate() needs to clear the same fields if
8490           * the file happens to be open while being truncated. It saves space
8491           * not to repeat the code twice.
8492           */
8493          wipe_inode(rip);
8494    }
8495
8496    return(rip);
8497    }
```

```
8500  /*===========================================================================*
8501   *                              wipe_inode                                   *
8502   *===========================================================================*/
8503  PUBLIC wipe_inode(rip)
8504  register struct inode *rip;      /* The inode to be erased. */
8505  {
8506  /* Erase some fields in the inode.  This function is called from alloc_inode()
8507   * when a new inode is to be allocated, and from truncate(), when an existing
8508   * inode is to be truncated.
8509   */
8510
8511    register int i;
8512    extern real_time clock_time();
8513
8514    rip->i_size = 0;
8515    rip->i_modtime = clock_time();
8516    rip->i_dirt = DIRTY;
8517    for (i = 0; i < NR_ZONE_NUMS; i++)
8518          rip->i_zone[i] = NO_ZONE;
8519  }


8522  /*===========================================================================*
8523   *                              free_inode                                   *
8524   *===========================================================================*/
8525  PUBLIC free_inode(dev, numb)
8526  dev_nr dev;                      /* on which device is the inode */
8527  inode_nr numb;                   /* number of inode to be freed */
8528  {
8529  /* Return an inode to the pool of unallocated inodes. */
8530
8531    register struct super_block *sp;
8532    extern struct super_block *get_super();
8533
8534    /* Locate the appropriate super_block. */
8535    sp = get_super(dev);
8536    free_bit(sp->s_imap, (bit_nr) numb);
8537  }


8540  /*===========================================================================*
8541   *                              rw_inode                                     *
8542   *===========================================================================*/
8543  PUBLIC rw_inode(rip, rw_flag)
8544  register struct inode *rip;      /* pointer to inode to be read/written */
8545  int rw_flag;                     /* READING or WRITING */
8546  {
8547  /* An entry in the inode table is to be copied to or from the disk. */
8548
8549    register struct buf *bp;
```

```
8550        register d_inode *dip;
8551        register struct super_block *sp;
8552        block_nr b;
8553        extern struct buf *get_block();
8554        extern struct super_block *get_super();
8555
8556        /* Get the block where the inode resides. */
8557        sp = get_super(rip->i_dev);
8558        b = (block_nr) (rip->i_num - 1)/INODES_PER_BLOCK +
8559                                   sp->s_imap_blocks + sp->s_zmap_blocks + 2;
8560        bp = get_block(rip->i_dev, b, NORMAL);
8561        dip = bp->b_inode + (rip->i_num - 1) % INODES_PER_BLOCK;
8562
8563        /* Do the read or write. */
8564        if (rw_flag == READING) {
8565            copy((char *)rip, (char *) dip, INODE_SIZE); /* copy from blk to inode */
8566        } else {
8567            copy((char *)dip, (char *) rip, INODE_SIZE); /* copy from inode to blk */
8568            bp->b_dirt = DIRTY;
8569        }
8570
8571        put_block(bp, INODE_BLOCK);
8572        rip->i_dirt = CLEAN;
8573    }


8576    /*========================================================================*
8577     *                           dup_inode                                    *
8578     *========================================================================*/
8579    PUBLIC dup_inode(ip)
8580    struct inode *ip;                /* The inode to be duplicated. */
8581    {
8582    /* This routine is a simplified form of get_inode() for the case where
8583     * the inode pointer is already known.
8584     */
8585
8586        ip->i_count++;
8587    }
```

```
8600    /* This file manages the super block table and the related data structures,
8601     * namely, the bit maps that keep track of which zones and which inodes are
8602     * allocated and which are free.  When a new inode or zone is needed, the
8603     * appropriate bit map is searched for a free entry.
8604     *
8605     * The entry points into this file are
8606     *    load_bit_maps:   get the bit maps for the root or a newly mounted device
8607     *    unload_bit_maps: write the bit maps back to disk after an UMOUNT
8608     *    alloc_bit:       somebody wants to allocate a zone or inode; find one
8609     *    free_bit:        indicate that a zone or inode is available for allocation
8610     *    get_super:       search the 'superblock' table for a device
8611     *    mounted:         tells if file inode is on mounted (or ROOT) file system
8612     *    scale_factor:    get the zone-to-block conversion factor for a device
8613     *    rw_super:        read or write a superblock
8614     */
8615
8616    #include "../h/const.h"
8617    #include "../h/type.h"
8618    #include "../h/error.h"
8619    #include "const.h"
8620    #include "type.h"
8621    #include "buf.h"
8622    #include "inode.h"
8623    #include "super.h"
8624
8625    #define INT_BITS (sizeof(int)<<3)
8626    #define BIT_MAP_SHIFT    13      /* (log2 of BLOCK_SIZE) + 3; 13 for 1k blocks */
8627
8628    /*===========================================================================*
8629     *                          load_bit_maps                                    *
8630     *===========================================================================*/
8631    PUBLIC int load_bit_maps(dev)
8632    dev_nr dev;                      /* which device? */
8633    {
8634    /* Load the bit map for some device into the cache and set up superblock. */
8635
8636      register int i;
8637      register struct super_block *sp;
8638      block_nr zbase;
8639      extern struct buf *get_block();
8640      extern struct super_block *get_super();
8641
8642      sp = get_super(dev);           /* get the superblock pointer */
8643      if (bufs_in_use + sp->s_imap_blocks + sp->s_zmap_blocks >= NR_BUFS - 3)
8644            return(ERROR);           /* insufficient buffers left for bit maps */
8645      if (sp->s_imap_blocks > I_MAP_SLOTS || sp->s_zmap_blocks > ZMAP_SLOTS)
8646            panic("too many map blocks", NO_NUM);
8647
8648      /* Load the inode map from the disk. */
8649      for (i = 0; i < sp->s_imap_blocks; i++)
```

```
8650            sp->s_imap[i] = get_block(dev, SUPER_BLOCK + 1 + i, NORMAL);
8651
8652        /* Load the zone map from the disk. */
8653        zbase = SUPER_BLOCK + 1 + sp->s_imap_blocks;
8654        for (i = 0; i < sp->s_zmap_blocks; i++)
8655            sp->s_zmap[i] = get_block(dev, zbase + i, NORMAL);
8656
8657        /* inodes 0 and 1, and zone 0 are never allocated.  Mark them as busy. */
8658        sp->s_imap[0]->b_int[0] |= 3; /* inodes 0, 1 busy */
8659        sp->s_zmap[0]->b_int[0] |= 1; /* zone 0 busy */
8660        bufs_in_use += sp->s_imap_blocks + sp->s_zmap_blocks;
8661        return(OK);
8662    }



8666    /*===========================================================================*
8667     *                              unload_bit_maps                               *
8668     *===========================================================================*/
8669    PUBLIC unload_bit_maps(dev)
8670    dev_nr dev;                        /* which device is being unmounted? */
8671    {
8672    /* Unload the bit maps so a device can be unmounted. */
8673
8674        register int i;
8675        register struct super_block *sp;
8676        struct super_block *get_super();
8677
8678        sp = get_super(dev);           /* get the superblock pointer */
8679        bufs_in_use -= sp->s_imap_blocks + sp->s_zmap_blocks;
8680        for (i = 0; i < sp->s_imap_blocks; i++) put_block(sp->s_imap[i], I_MAP_BLOCK);
8681        for (i = 0; i < sp->s_zmap_blocks; i++) put_block(sp->s_zmap[i], ZMAP_BLOCK);
8682        return(OK);
8683    }



8686    /*===========================================================================*
8687     *                                alloc_bit                                   *
8688     *===========================================================================*/
8689    PUBLIC bit_nr alloc_bit(map_ptr, map_bits, bit_blocks, origin)
8690    struct buf *map_ptr[];             /* pointer to array of bit block pointers */
8691    bit_nr map_bits;                   /* how many bits are there in the bit map? */
8692    unshort bit_blocks;                /* how many blocks are there in the bit map? */
8693    bit_nr origin;                     /* number of bit to start searching at */
8694    {
8695    /* Allocate a bit from a bit map and return its bit number. */
8696
8697        register unsigned k;
8698        register int *wptr, *wlim;
8699        int i, a, b, w, o, block_count;
```

```
8700        struct buf *bp;
8701
8702        /* Figure out where to start the bit search (depends on 'origin'). */
8703        if (origin >= map_bits) origin = 0;    /* for robustness */
8704        b = origin >> BIT_MAP_SHIFT;
8705        o = origin - (b << BIT_MAP_SHIFT);
8706        w = o/INT_BITS;
8707        block_count = (w == 0 ? bit_blocks : bit_blocks + 1);
8708
8709        /* The outer while loop iterates on the blocks of the map.  The inner
8710         * while loop iterates on the words of a block.  The for loop iterates
8711         * on the bits of a word.
8712         */
8713        while (block_count--) {
8714                /* If need be, loop on all the blocks in the bit map. */
8715                bp = map_ptr[b];
8716                wptr = &bp->b_int[w];
8717                wlim = &bp->b_int[INTS_PER_BLOCK];
8718                while (wptr != wlim) {
8719                        /* Loop on all the words of one of the bit map blocks. */
8720                        if ((k = (unsigned) *wptr) != (unsigned) ~0) {
8721                                /* This word contains a free bit.  Allocate it. */
8722                                for (i = 0; i < INT_BITS; i++)
8723                                        if (((k >> i) & 1) == 0) {
8724                                                a = i + (wptr - &bp->b_int[0])*INT_BITS
8725                                                        + (b << BIT_MAP_SHIFT);
8726                                                /* If 'a' beyond map check other blks*/
8727                                                if (a >= map_bits) {
8728                                                        wptr = wlim - 1;
8729                                                        break;
8730                                                }
8731                                                *wptr |= 1 << i;
8732                                                bp->b_dirt = DIRTY;
8733                                                return( (bit_nr) a);
8734                                        }
8735                        }
8736                        wptr++;         /* examine next word in this bit map block */
8737                }
8738                if (++b == bit_blocks) b = 0;   /* we have wrapped around */
8739                w = 0;
8740        }
8741        return(NO_BIT);                         /* no bit could be allocated */
8742 }

8744 /*===========================================================================*
8745  *                              free_bit                                     *
8746  *===========================================================================*/
8747 PUBLIC free_bit(map_ptr, bit_returned)
8748 struct buf *map_ptr[];                  /* pointer to array of bit block pointers */
8749 bit_nr bit_returned;                    /* number of bit to insert into the map */
```

```
8750    {
8751    /* Return a zone or inode by turning on its bitmap bit. */
8752
8753      int b, r, w, bit;
8754      struct buf *bp;
8755
8756      b = bit_returned >> BIT_MAP_SHIFT;    /* 'b' tells which block it is in */
8757      r = bit_returned - (b << BIT_MAP_SHIFT);
8758      w = r/INT_BITS;                 /* 'w' tells which word it is in */
8759      bit = r % INT_BITS;
8760      bp = map_ptr[b];
8761      if (((bp->b_int[w] >> bit)& 1)== 0)
8762          panic("trying to free unused block--check file sys", (int)bit_returned);
8763      bp->b_int[w] &= ~(1 << bit);  /* turn the bit on */
8764      bp->b_dirt = DIRTY;
8765    }


8768    /*===========================================================================*
8769     *                            get_super                                      *
8770     *===========================================================================*/
8771    PUBLIC struct super_block *get_super(dev)
8772    dev_nr dev;                        /* device number whose super_block is sought */
8773    {
8774    /* Search the superblock table for this device.  It is supposed to be there. */
8775
8776      register struct super_block *sp;
8777
8778      for (sp = &super_block[0]; sp < &super_block[NR_SUPERS]; sp++)
8779          if (sp->s_dev == dev) return(sp);
8780
8781      /* Search failed.  Something wrong. */
8782      panic("can't find superblock for device", (int) dev);
8783    }


8786    /*===========================================================================*
8787     *                            mounted                                        *
8788     *===========================================================================*/
8789    PUBLIC int mounted(rip)
8790    register struct inode *rip;     /* pointer to inode */
8791    {
8792    /* Report on whether the given inode is on a mounted (or ROOT) file system. */
8793
8794      register struct super_block *sp;
8795      register dev_nr dev;
8796
8797      dev = rip->i_dev;
8798      if (dev == ROOT_DEV) return(TRUE);    /* inode is on root file system */
8799
```

```
8800        for (sp = &super_block[0]; sp < &super_block[NR_SUPERS]; sp++)
8801              if (sp->s_dev == dev) return(TRUE);
8802
8803        return(FALSE);
8804    }


8807    /*===========================================================================*
8808     *                              scale_factor                                 *
8809     *===========================================================================*/
8810    PUBLIC int scale_factor(ip)
8811    struct inode *ip;                  /* pointer to inode whose superblock needed */
8812    {
8813    /* Return the scale factor used for converting blocks to zones. */
8814      register struct super_block *sp;
8815      extern struct super_block *get_super();
8816
8817      sp = get_super(ip->i_dev);
8818      return(sp->s_log_zone_size);
8819    }

8821    /*===========================================================================*
8822     *                              rw_super                                     *
8823     *===========================================================================*/
8824    PUBLIC rw_super(sp, rw_flag)
8825    register struct super_block *sp; /* pointer to a superblock */
8826    int rw_flag;                     /* READING or WRITING */
8827    {
8828    /* Read or write a superblock. */
8829
8830      register struct buf *bp;
8831      dev_nr dev;
8832      extern struct buf *get_block();
8833
8834      /* Check if this is a read or write, and do it. */
8835      if (rw_flag == READING) {
8836            dev = sp->s_dev;         /* save device; it will be overwritten by copy*/
8837            bp = get_block(sp->s_dev, (block_nr) SUPER_BLOCK, NORMAL);
8838            copy( (char *) sp, bp->b_data, SUPER_SIZE);
8839            sp->s_dev = dev;         /* restore device number */
8840      } else {
8841            /* On a write, it is not necessary to go read superblock from disk. */
8842            bp = get_block(sp->s_dev, (block_nr) SUPER_BLOCK, NO_READ);
8843            copy(bp->b_data, (char *) sp, SUPER_SIZE);
8844            bp->b_dirt = DIRTY;
8845      }
8846
8847      sp->s_dirt = CLEAN;
8848      put_block(bp, ZUPER_BLOCK);
8849    }
```

```
8850   /* This file contains the procedures that manipulate file descriptors.
8851    *
8852    * The entry points into this file are
8853    *   get_fd:    look for free file descriptor and free filp slots
8854    *   get_filp:  look up the filp entry for a given file descriptor
8855    *   find_filp: find a filp slot that points to a given inode
8856    */
8857
8858   #include "../h/const.h"
8859   #include "../h/type.h"
8860   #include "../h/error.h"
8861   #include "const.h"
8862   #include "type.h"
8863   #include "file.h"
8864   #include "fproc.h"
8865   #include "glo.h"
8866   #include "inode.h"
8867
8868   /*===========================================================================*
8869    *                              get_fd                                       *
8870    *===========================================================================*/
8871   PUBLIC int get_fd(bits, k, fpt)
8872   mask_bits bits;                    /* mode of the file to be created (RWX bits) */
8873   int *k;                            /* place to return file descriptor */
8874   struct filp **fpt;                 /* place to return filp slot */
8875   {
8876   /* Look for a free file descriptor and a free filp slot.  Fill in the mode word
8877    * in the latter, but don't claim either one yet, since the open() or creat()
8878    * may yet fail.
8879    */
8880
8881     register struct filp *f;
8882     register int i;
8883
8884     *k = -1;                         /* we need a way to tell if file desc found */
8885
8886     /* Search the fproc table for a free file descriptor. */
8887     for (i = 0; i < NR_FDS; i++) {
8888          if (fp->fp_filp[i] == NIL_FILP) {
8889               /* A file descriptor has been located. */
8890               *k = i;
8891               break;
8892          }
8893     }
8894
8895     /* Check to see if a file descriptor has been found. */
8896     if (*k < 0) return(EMFILE);   /* this is why we initialized k to -1 */
8897
8898     /* Now that a file descriptor has been found, look for a free filp slot. */
8899     for (f = &filp[0]; f < &filp[NR_FILPS]; f++) {
```

```
8900                if (f->filp_count == 0) {
8901                        f->filp_mode = bits;
8902                        f->filp_pos = 0L;
8903                        *fpt = f;
8904                        return(OK);
8905                }
8906        }
8907
8908    /* If control passes here, the filp table must be full.  Report that back. */
8909    return(ENFILE);
8910  }


8913  /*===========================================================================*
8914   *                              get_filp                                      *
8915   *===========================================================================*/
8916  PUBLIC struct filp *get_filp(fild)
8917  int fild;                       /* file descriptor */
8918  {
8919  /* See if 'fild' refers to a valid file descr.  If so, return its filp ptr. */
8920
8921    err_code = EBADF;
8922    if (fild < 0 || fild >= NR_FDS ) return(NIL_FILP);
8923    return(fp->fp_filp[fild]);      /* may also be NIL_FILP */
8924  }


8927  /*===========================================================================*
8928   *                              find_filp                                     *
8929   *===========================================================================*/
8930  PUBLIC struct filp *find_filp(rip, bits)
8931  register struct inode *rip;     /* inode referred to by the filp to be found */
8932  int bits;                       /* mode of the filp to be found (RWX bits) */
8933  {
8934  /* Find a filp slot that refers to the inode 'rip' in a way as described
8935   * by the mode bit 'bits'. Used for determining whether somebody is still
8936   * interested in either end of a pipe; other applications are conceivable.
8937   * Like 'get_fd' it performs its job by linear search through the filp table.
8938   */
8939
8940    register struct filp *f;
8941
8942    for (f = &filp[0]; f < &filp[NR_FILPS]; f++) {
8943            if (f->filp_count != 0 && f->filp_ino == rip && (f->filp_mode & bits))
8944                    return(f);
8945    }
8946
8947    /* If control passes here, the filp wasn't there.  Report that back. */
8948    return(NIL_FILP);
8949  }
```

```
8950    /* This file contains the main program of the File System.  It consists of
8951     * a loop that gets messages requesting work, carries out the work, and sends
8952     * replies.
8953     *
8954     * The entry points into this file are
8955     *   main:     main program of the File System
8956     *   reply:    send a reply to a process after the requested work is done
8957     */
8958
8959    #include "../h/const.h"
8960    #include "../h/type.h"
8961    #include "../h/callnr.h"
8962    #include "../h/com.h"
8963    #include "../h/error.h"
8964    #include "const.h"
8965    #include "type.h"
8966    #include "buf.h"
8967    #include "file.h"
8968    #include "fproc.h"
8969    #include "glo.h"
8970    #include "inode.h"
8971    #include "param.h"
8972    #include "super.h"
8973
8974    #define M64K      0xFFFF0000L   /* 16 bit mask for DMA check */
8975    #define INFO            2       /* where in data_org is info from build */
8976
8977    /*===========================================================================*
8978     *                              main                                         *
8979     *===========================================================================*/
8980    PUBLIC main()
8981    {
8982    /* This is the main program of the file system.  The main loop consists of
8983     * three major activities: getting new work, processing the work, and sending
8984     * the reply.  This loop never terminates as long as the file system runs.
8985     */
8986      int error;
8987      extern int (*call_vector[NCALLS])();
8988
8989      fs_init();
8990
8991      /* This is the main loop that gets work, processes it, and sends replies. */
8992      while (TRUE) {
8993            get_work();                /* sets who and fs_call */
8994
8995            fp = &fproc[who];          /* pointer to proc table struct */
8996            super_user = (fp->fp_effuid == SU_UID ? TRUE : FALSE);   /* su? */
8997            dont_reply = FALSE;        /* in other words, do reply is default */
8998
8999            /* Call the internal function that does the work. */
```

```
9000                if (fs_call < 0 || fs_call >= NCALLS)
9001                        error = E_BAD_CALL;
9002                else
9003                        error = (*call_vector[fs_call])();
9004
9005                /* Copy the results back to the user and send reply. */
9006                if (dont_reply) continue;
9007                reply(who, error);
9008                if (rdahed_inode != NIL_INODE) read_ahead(); /* do block read ahead */
9009        }
9010  }


9013  /*===========================================================================*
9014   *                              get_work                                     *
9015   *===========================================================================*/
9016  PRIVATE get_work()
9017  {
9018    /* Normally wait for new input.  However, if 'reviving' is
9019     * nonzero, a suspended process must be awakened.
9020     */
9021
9022    register struct fproc *rp;
9023
9024    if (reviving != 0) {
9025            /* Revive a suspended process. */
9026            for (rp = &fproc[0]; rp < &fproc[NR_PROCS]; rp++)
9027                    if (rp->fp_revived == REVIVING) {
9028                            who = rp - fproc;
9029                            fs_call = rp->fp_fd & BYTE;
9030                            fd = (rp->fp_fd >>8) & BYTE;
9031                            buffer = rp->fp_buffer;
9032                            nbytes = rp->fp_nbytes;
9033                            rp->fp_suspended = NOT_SUSPENDED; /* no longer hanging*/
9034                            rp->fp_revived = NOT_REVIVING;
9035                            reviving--;
9036                            return;
9037                    }
9038            panic("get_work couldn't revive anyone", NO_NUM);
9039    }
9040
9041    /* Normal case.  No one to revive. */
9042    if (receive(ANY, &m) != OK) panic("fs receive error", NO_NUM);
9043
9044    who = m.m_source;
9045    fs_call = m.m_type;
9046  }
```

```
9050    /*===========================================================================*
9051     *                              reply                                        *
9052     *===========================================================================*/
9053    PUBLIC reply(whom, result)
9054    int whom;                          /* process to reply to */
9055    int result;                        /* result of the call (usually OK or error #) */
9056    {
9057    /* Send a reply to a user process. It may fail (if the process has just
9058     * been killed by a signal, so don't check the return code.  If the send
9059     * fails, just ignore it.
9060     */
9061
9062      reply_type = result;
9063      send(whom, &m1);
9064    }


9066    /*===========================================================================*
9067     *                              fs_init                                      *
9068     *===========================================================================*/
9069    PRIVATE fs_init()
9070    {
9071    /* Initialize global variables, tables, etc. */
9072
9073      register struct inode *rip;
9074      int i;
9075      extern struct inode *get_inode();
9076
9077      buf_pool();                        /* initialize buffer pool */
9078      load_ram();                        /* Load RAM disk from root diskette. */
9079      load_super();                      /* Load super block for root device */
9080
9081      /* Initialize the 'fproc' fields for process 0 and process 2. */
9082      for (i = 0; i < 3; i+= 2) {
9083            fp = &fproc[i];
9084            rip = get_inode(ROOT_DEV, ROOT_INODE);
9085            fp->fp_rootdir = rip;
9086            dup_inode(rip);
9087            fp->fp_workdir = rip;
9088            fp->fp_realuid = (uid) SYS_UID;
9089            fp->fp_effuid = (uid) SYS_UID;
9090            fp->fp_realgid = (gid) SYS_GID;
9091            fp->fp_effgid = (gid) SYS_GID;
9092            fp->fp_umask = ~0;
9093      }
9094
9095      /* Certain relations must hold for the file system to work at all. */
9096      if (ZONE_NUM_SIZE != 2) panic("ZONE_NUM_SIZE != 2", NO_NUM);
9097      if (SUPER_SIZE > BLOCK_SIZE) panic("SUPER_SIZE > BLOCK_SIZE", NO_NUM);
9098      if(BLOCK_SIZE % INODE_SIZE != 0)panic("BLOCK_SIZE % INODE_SIZE != 0", NO_NUM);
9099      if (NR_FDS > 127) panic("NR_FDS > 127", NO_NUM);
```

```
9100        if (NR_BUFS < 6) panic("NR_BUFS < 6", NO_NUM);
9101        if (sizeof(d_inode) != 32) panic("inode size != 32", NO_NUM);
9102    }


9104    /*===========================================================================*
9105     *                              buf_pool                                      *
9106     *===========================================================================*/
9107    PRIVATE buf_pool()
9108    {
9109    /* Initialize the buffer pool.  On the IBM PC, the hardware DMA chip is
9110     * not able to cross 64K boundaries, so any buffer that happens to lie
9111     * across such a boundary is not used.  This is not very elegant, but all
9112     * the alternative solutions are as bad, if not worse.  The fault lies with
9113     * the PC hardware.
9114     */
9115      register struct buf *bp;
9116      vir_bytes low_off, high_off;
9117      phys_bytes org;
9118      extern phys_clicks get_base();
9119
9120      bufs_in_use = 0;
9121      front = &buf[0];
9122      rear = &buf[NR_BUFS - 1];
9123
9124      for (bp = &buf[0]; bp < &buf[NR_BUFS]; bp++) {
9125            bp->b_blocknr = NO_BLOCK;
9126            bp->b_dev = NO_DEV;
9127            bp->b_next = bp + 1;
9128            bp->b_prev = bp - 1;
9129      }
9130      buf[0].b_prev = NIL_BUF;
9131      buf[NR_BUFS - 1].b_next = NIL_BUF;
9132
9133      /* Delete any buffers that span a 64K boundary. */
9134    #ifdef i8088
9135      for (bp = &buf[0]; bp < &buf[NR_BUFS]; bp++) {
9136            org = get_base() << CLICK_SHIFT;          /* phys addr where FS is */
9137            low_off = (vir_bytes) bp->b_data;
9138            high_off = low_off + BLOCK_SIZE - 1;
9139            if (((org + low_off) & M64K) != ((org + high_off) & M64K)) {
9140                    if (bp == &buf[0]) {
9141                            front = &buf[1];
9142                            buf[1].b_prev = NIL_BUF;
9143                    } else if (bp == &buf[NR_BUFS - 1]) {
9144                            rear = &buf[NR_BUFS - 2];
9145                            buf[NR_BUFS - 2].b_next = NIL_BUF;
9146                    } else {
9147                            /* Delete a buffer in the middle. */
9148                            bp->b_prev->b_next = bp + 1;
9149                            bp->b_next->b_prev = bp - 1;
```

```
9150                         }
9151                 }
9152         }
9153     #endif
9154
9155       for (bp = &buf[0]; bp < &buf[NR_BUFS]; bp++) bp->b_hash = bp->b_next;
9156       buf_hash[NO_BLOCK & (NR_BUF_HASH - 1)] = front;
9157     }


9160     /*===========================================================================*
9161      *                              load_ram                                     *
9162      *===========================================================================*/
9163     PRIVATE load_ram()
9164     {
9165     /* The root diskette contains a block-by-block image of the root file system
9166      * starting at 0.  Go get it and copy it to the RAM disk.
9167      */
9168
9169       register struct buf *bp, *bp1;
9170       int count;
9171       long k_loaded;
9172       struct super_block *sp;
9173       block_nr i;
9174       phys_clicks ram_clicks, init_org, init_text_clicks, init_data_clicks;
9175       extern phys_clicks data_org[INFO + 2];
9176       extern struct buf *get_block();
9177
9178       /* Get size of INIT by reading block on diskette where 'build' put it. */
9179       init_org = data_org[INFO];
9180       init_text_clicks = data_org[INFO + 1];
9181       init_data_clicks = data_org[INFO + 2];
9182
9183       /* Get size of RAM disk by reading root file system's super block */
9184       bp = get_block(BOOT_DEV, SUPER_BLOCK, NORMAL);  /* get RAM super block */
9185       copy(super_block, bp->b_data, sizeof(struct super_block));
9186       sp = &super_block[0];
9187       if (sp->s_magic != SUPER_MAGIC)
9188               panic("Diskette in drive 0 is not root file system", NO_NUM);
9189       count = sp->s_nzones << sp->s_log_zone_size;  /* # blocks on root dev */
9190       ram_clicks = count * (BLOCK_SIZE/CLICK_SIZE);
9191       put_block(bp, FULL_DATA_BLOCK);
9192
9193       /* Tell MM the origin and size of INIT, and the amount of memory used for the
9194        * system plus RAM disk combined, so it can remove all of it from the map.
9195        */
9196       m1.m_type = BRK2;
9197       m1.m1_i1 = init_text_clicks;
9198       m1.m1_i2 = init_data_clicks;
9199       m1.m1_i3 = init_org + init_text_clicks + init_data_clicks + ram_clicks;
```

```
9200        ml.ml_pl = (char *) init_org;
9201        if (sendrec(MM_PROC_NR, &ml) != OK) panic("FS Can't report to MM", NO_NUM);
9202
9203        /* Tell RAM driver where RAM disk is and how big it is. */
9204        ml.m_type = DISK_IOCTL;
9205        ml.DEVICE = RAM_DEV;
9206        ml.POSITION = (long) init_org + (long) init_text_clicks + init_data_clicks;
9207        ml.POSITION = ml.POSITION << CLICK_SHIFT;
9208        ml.COUNT = count;
9209        if (sendrec(MEM, &ml) != OK) panic("Can't report size to MEM", NO_NUM);
9210
9211        /* Copy the blocks one at a time from the root diskette to the RAM */
9212        printf("Loading RAM disk from root diskette.      Loaded:   OK ");
9213        for (i = 0; i < count; i++) {
9214              bp = get_block(BOOT_DEV, (block_nr) i, NORMAL);
9215              bp1 = get_block(ROOT_DEV, i, NO_READ);
9216              copy(bp1->b_data, bp->b_data, BLOCK_SIZE);
9217              bp1->b_dirt = DIRTY;
9218              put_block(bp, I_MAP_BLOCK);
9219              put_block(bp1, I_MAP_BLOCK);
9220              k_loaded = ( (long) i * BLOCK_SIZE)/1024L;        /* K loaded so far */
9221              if (k_loaded % 5 == 0) printf("\b\b\b\b\b%3DK %c", k_loaded, 0);
9222        }
9223
9224        printf("\rRAM disk loaded.  Please remove root diskette.            \n\n");
9225  }


9228  /*===========================================================================*
9229   *                              load_super                                   *
9230   *===========================================================================*/
9231  PRIVATE load_super()
9232  {
9233    register struct super_block *sp;
9234    register struct inode *rip;
9235    extern struct inode *get_inode();
9236
9237  /* Initialize the super_block table. */
9238
9239        for (sp = &super_block[0]; sp < &super_block[NR_SUPERS]; sp++)
9240              sp->s_dev = NO_DEV;
9241
9242        /* Read in super_block for the root file system. */
9243        sp = &super_block[0];
9244        sp->s_dev = ROOT_DEV;
9245        rw_super(sp,READING);
9246        rip = get_inode(ROOT_DEV, ROOT_INODE);              /* inode for root dir */
9247
9248        /* Check super_block for consistency (is it the right diskette?). */
9249        if ( ( rip->i_mode & I_TYPE) != I_DIRECTORY || rip->i_nlinks < 3 ||
```

```
9250                                                 sp->s_magic != SUPER_MAGIC)
9251            panic("Root file system corrupted.  Possibly wrong diskette.", NO_NUM);
9252
9253        sp->s_imount = rip;
9254        dup_inode(rip);
9255        sp->s_isup = rip;
9256        sp->s_rd_only = 0;
9257        if (load_bit_maps(ROOT_DEV) != OK)
9258            panic("init: can't load root bit maps", NO_NUM);
9259    }
```

```
9300    /* This file contains the table used to map system call numbers onto the
9301     * routines that perform them.
9302     */
9303
9304    #include "../h/const.h"
9305    #include "../h/type.h"
9306    #include "../h/stat.h"
9307    #include "const.h"
9308    #include "type.h"
9309    #include "dev.h"
9310
9311    #undef EXTERN
9312    #define EXTERN
9313
9314    #include "../h/callnr.h"
9315    #include "../h/com.h"
9316    #include "../h/error.h"
9317    #include "buf.h"
9318    #include "file.h"
9319    #include "fproc.h"
9320    #include "glo.h"
9321    #include "inode.h"
9322    #include "super.h"
9323
9324    extern do_access(), do_chdir(), do_chmod(), do_chown(), do_chroot();
9325    extern do_close(), do_creat(), do_dup(), do_exit(), do_fork(), do_fstat();
9326    extern do_ioctl(), do_link(), do_lseek(), do_mknod(), do_mount(), do_open();
9327    extern do_pipe(), do_read(), do_revive(), do_set(), do_stat(), do_stime();
9328    extern do_sync(), do_time(), do_tims(), do_umask(), do_umount(), do_unlink();
9329    extern do_unpause(), do_utime(), do_write(), no_call(), no_sys();
9330
9331    extern char fstack[];
9332    char *stackpt = &fstack[FS_STACK_BYTES];          /* initial stack pointer */
9333
9334    int (*call_vector[NCALLS])() = {
9335            no_sys,         /*  0 = unused */
9336            do_exit,        /*  1 = exit   */
9337            do_fork,        /*  2 = fork   */
9338            do_read,        /*  3 = read   */
9339            do_write,       /*  4 = write  */
9340            do_open,        /*  5 = open   */
9341            do_close,       /*  6 = close  */
9342            no_sys,         /*  7 = wait   */
9343            do_creat,       /*  8 = creat  */
9344            do_link,        /*  9 = link   */
9345            do_unlink,      /* 10 = unlink */
9346            no_sys,         /* 11 = exec   */
9347            do_chdir,       /* 12 = chdir  */
9348            do_time,        /* 13 = time   */
9349            do_mknod,       /* 14 = mknod  */
```

```
9350            do_chmod,        /* 15 = chmod    */
9351            do_chown,        /* 16 = chown    */
9352            no_sys,          /* 17 = break    */
9353            do_stat,         /* 18 = stat     */
9354            do_lseek,        /* 19 = lseek    */
9355            no_sys,          /* 20 = getpid   */
9356            do_mount,        /* 21 = mount    */
9357            do_umount,       /* 22 = umount   */
9358            do_set,          /* 23 = setuid   */
9359            no_sys,          /* 24 = getuid   */
9360            do_stime,        /* 25 = stime    */
9361            no_sys,          /* 26 = (ptrace)*/
9362            no_sys,          /* 27 = alarm    */
9363            do_fstat,        /* 28 = fstat    */
9364            no_sys,          /* 29 = pause    */
9365            do_utime,        /* 30 = utime    */
9366            no_sys,          /* 31 = (stty)   */
9367            no_sys,          /* 32 = (gtty)   */
9368            do_access,       /* 33 = access   */
9369            no_sys,          /* 34 = (nice)   */
9370            no_sys,          /* 35 = (ftime)  */
9371            do_sync,         /* 36 = sync     */
9372            no_sys,          /* 37 = kill     */
9373            no_sys,          /* 38 = unused   */
9374            no_sys,          /* 39 = unused   */
9375            no_sys,          /* 40 = unused   */
9376            do_dup,          /* 41 = dup      */
9377            do_pipe,         /* 42 = pipe     */
9378            do_tims,         /* 43 = times    */
9379            no_sys,          /* 44 = (prof)   */
9380            no_sys,          /* 45 = unused   */
9381            do_set,          /* 46 = setgid   */
9382            no_sys,          /* 47 = getgid   */
9383            no_sys,          /* 48 = sig      */
9384            no_sys,          /* 49 = unused   */
9385            no_sys,          /* 50 = unused   */
9386            no_sys,          /* 51 = (acct)   */
9387            no_sys,          /* 52 = (phys)   */
9388            no_sys,          /* 53 = (lock)   */
9389            do_ioctl,        /* 54 = ioctl    */
9390            no_sys,          /* 55 = unused   */
9391            no_sys,          /* 56 = (mpx)    */
9392            no_sys,          /* 57 = unused   */
9393            no_sys,          /* 58 = unused   */
9394            no_sys,          /* 59 = exece    */
9395            do_umask,        /* 60 = umask    */
9396            do_chroot,       /* 61 = chroot   */
9397            no_sys,          /* 62 = unused   */
9398            no_sys,          /* 63 = unused   */
9399
```

```
9400            no_sys,        /* 64 = KSIG: signals originating in the kernel */
9401            do_unpause,    /* 65 = UNPAUSE */
9402            no_sys,        /* 66 = BRK2 (used to tell MM size of FS,INIT)  */
9403            do_revive,     /* 67 = REVIVE  */
9404            no_sys         /* 68 = TASK_REPLY      */
9405    };
9406
9407
9408    extern rw_dev(), rw_dev2();
9409
9410    /* The order of the entries here determines the mapping between major device
9411     * numbers and tasks.  The first entry (major device 0) is not used.  The
9412     * next entry is major device 1, etc.  Character and block devices can be
9413     * intermixed at random.  If this ordering is changed, BOOT_DEV and ROOT_DEV
9414     * must be changed to correspond to the new values.
9415     */
9416    struct dmap dmap[] = {
9417    /*  Open        Read/Write    Close       Task #       Device File
9418        ----        ----------    -----       -------      ------ ----     */
9419        0,          0,            0,          0,           /* 0 = not used  */
9420        no_call,    rw_dev,       no_call,    MEM,         /* 1 = /dev/mem  */
9421        no_call,    rw_dev,       no_call,    FLOPPY,      /* 2 = /dev/fd0  */
9422        no_call,    rw_dev,       no_call,    WINCHESTER,  /* 3 = /dev/hd0  */
9423        no_call,    rw_dev,       no_call,    TTY,         /* 4 = /dev/tty0 */
9424        no_call,    rw_dev2,      no_call,    TTY,         /* 5 = /dev/tty  */
9425        no_call,    rw_dev,       no_call,    PRINTER      /* 6 = /dev/lp   */
9426    };
9427
9428    int max_major = sizeof(dmap)/sizeof(struct dmap);
```

```
9450   /* This file contains the procedures for creating, opening, closing, and
9451    * seeking on files.
9452    *
9453    * The entry points into this file are
9454    *   do_creat:  perform the CREAT system call
9455    *   do_mknod:  perform the MKNOD system call
9456    *   do_open:   perform the OPEN system call
9457    *   do_close:  perform the CLOSE system call
9458    *   do_lseek:  perform the LSEEK system call
9459    */
9460
9461   #include "../h/const.h"
9462   #include "../h/type.h"
9463   #include "../h/callnr.h"
9464   #include "../h/error.h"
9465   #include "const.h"
9466   #include "type.h"
9467   #include "buf.h"
9468   #include "file.h"
9469   #include "fproc.h"
9470   #include "glo.h"
9471   #include "inode.h"
9472   #include "param.h"
9473
9474   PRIVATE char mode_map[] = {R_BIT, W_BIT, R_BIT|W_BIT, 0};
9475
9476   /*===========================================================================*
9477    *                              do_creat                                     *
9478    *===========================================================================*/
9479   PUBLIC int do_creat()
9480   {
9481   /* Perform the creat(name, mode) system call. */
9482
9483     register struct inode *rip;
9484     register int r;
9485     register mask_bits bits;
9486     struct filp *fil_ptr;
9487     int file_d;
9488     extern struct inode *new_node();
9489
9490     /* See if name ok and file descriptor and filp slots are available. */
9491     if (fetch_name(name, name_length, M3) != OK) return(err_code);
9492     if ( (r = get_fd(W_BIT, &file_d, &fil_ptr)) != OK) return(r);
9493
9494     /* Create a new inode by calling new_node(). */
9495     bits = I_REGULAR | (mode & ALL_MODES & fp->fp_umask);
9496     rip = new_node(user_path, bits, NO_ZONE);
9497     r = err_code;
9498     if (r != OK && r != EEXIST) return(r);
9499
```

```
9500        /* At this point two possibilities exist: the given path did not exist
9501         * and has been created, or it pre-existed.  In the later case, truncate
9502         * if possible, otherwise return an error.
9503         */
9504        if (r == EEXIST) {
9505                /* File exists already. */
9506                switch (rip->i_mode & I_TYPE) {
9507                    case I_REGULAR:              /* truncate regular file */
9508                        if ( (r = forbidden(rip, W_BIT, 0)) == OK) truncate(rip);
9509                        break;
9510
9511                    case I_DIRECTORY:   /* can't truncate directory */
9512                        r = EISDIR;
9513                        break;
9514
9515                    case I_CHAR_SPECIAL:         /* special files are special */
9516                    case I_BLOCK_SPECIAL:
9517                        if ( ( r = forbidden(rip, W_BIT, 0)) != OK) break;
9518                        r = dev_open( (dev_nr) rip->i_zone[0], W_BIT);
9519                        break;
9520                }
9521        }
9522
9523        /* If error, return inode. */
9524        if (r != OK) {
9525                put_inode(rip);
9526                return(r);
9527        }
9528
9529        /* Claim the file descriptor and filp slot and fill them in. */
9530        fp->fp_filp[file_d] = fil_ptr;
9531        fil_ptr->filp_count = 1;
9532        fil_ptr->filp_ino = rip;
9533        return(file_d);
9534    }



9538    /*===========================================================================*
9539     *                              do_mknod                                     *
9540     *===========================================================================*/
9541    PUBLIC int do_mknod()
9542    {
9543    /* Perform the mknod(name, mode, addr) system call. */
9544
9545        register mask_bits bits;
9546
9547        if (!super_user) return(EPERM);        /* only super_user may make nodes */
9548        if (fetch_name(namel, namel_length, M1) != OK) return(err_code);
9549        bits = (mode & I_TYPE) | (mode  & ALL_MODES & fp->fp_umask);
```

```
9550            put_inode(new_node(user_path, bits, (zone_nr) addr));
9551            return(err_code);
9552    }

9554    /*===========================================================================*
9555     *                              new_node                                     *
9556     *===========================================================================*/
9557    PRIVATE struct inode *new_node(path, bits, z0)
9558    char *path;                     /* pointer to path name */
9559    mask_bits bits;                 /* mode of the new inode */
9560    zone_nr z0;                     /* zone number 0 for new inode */
9561    {
9562    /* This function is called by do_creat() and do_mknod().  In both cases it
9563     * allocates a new inode, makes a directory entry for it on the path 'path',
9564     * and initializes it.  It returns a pointer to the inode if it can do this;
9565     * err_code is set to OK or EEXIST. If it can't, it returns NIL_INODE and
9566     * 'err_code' contains the appropriate message.
9567     */

9569        register struct inode *rlast_dir_ptr, *rip;
9570        register int r;
9571        char string[NAME_SIZE];
9572        extern struct inode *alloc_inode(), *advance(), *last_dir();

9574        /* See if the path can be opened down to the last directory. */
9575        if ((rlast_dir_ptr = last_dir(path, string)) == NIL_INODE) return(NIL_INODE);

9577        /* The final directory is accessible. Get final component of the path. */
9578        rip = advance(rlast_dir_ptr, string);
9579        if ( rip == NIL_INODE && err_code == ENOENT) {
9580                /* Last path component does not exist.  Make new directory entry. */
9581                if ( (rip = alloc_inode(rlast_dir_ptr->i_dev, bits)) == NIL_INODE) {
9582                        /* Can't creat new inode: out of inodes. */
9583                        put_inode(rlast_dir_ptr);
9584                        return(NIL_INODE);
9585                }

9587                /* Force inode to the disk before making directory entry to make
9588                 * the system more robust in the face of a crash: an inode with
9589                 * no directory entry is much better than the opposite.
9590                 */
9591                rip->i_nlinks++;
9592                rip->i_zone[0] = z0;
9593                rw_inode(rip, WRITING);          /* force inode to disk now */

9595                /* New inode acquired.  Try to make directory entry. */
9596                if ((r = search_dir(rlast_dir_ptr, string, &rip->i_num,ENTER)) != OK) {
9597                        put_inode(rlast_dir_ptr);
9598                        rip->i_nlinks--;         /* pity, have to free disk inode */
9599                        rip->i_dirt = DIRTY;     /* dirty inodes are written out */
```

```
9600                    put_inode(rip); /* this call frees the inode */
9601                    err_code = r;
9602                    return(NIL_INODE);
9603            }
9604
9605      } else {
9606          /* Either last component exists, or there is some problem. */
9607          if (rip != NIL_INODE)
9608                  r = EEXIST;
9609          else
9610                  r = err_code;
9611      }
9612
9613      /* Return the directory inode and exit. */
9614      put_inode(rlast_dir_ptr);
9615      err_code = r;
9616      return(rip);
9617  }


9619  /*===========================================================================*
9620   *                              do_open                                       *
9621   *===========================================================================*/
9622  PUBLIC int do_open()
9623  {
9624  /* Perform the open(name, mode) system call. */
9625
9626      register struct inode *rip;
9627      struct filp *fil_ptr;
9628      register int r;
9629      register mask_bits bits;
9630      int file_d;
9631      extern struct inode *eat_path();
9632
9633      /* See if file descriptor and filp slots are available.  The variable
9634       * 'mode' is 0 for read, 1 for write, 2 for read+write.  The variable
9635       * 'bits' needs to be R_BIT, W_BIT, and R_BIT|W_BIT respectively.
9636       */
9637      if (mode < 0 || mode > 2) return(EINVAL);
9638      if (fetch_name(name, name_length, M3) != OK) return(err_code);
9639      bits = (mask_bits) mode_map[mode];
9640      if ( (r = get_fd(bits, &file_d, &fil_ptr)) != OK) return(r);
9641
9642      /* Scan path name. */
9643      if ( (rip = eat_path(user_path)) == NIL_INODE) return(err_code);
9644
9645      if ((r = forbidden(rip, bits, 0)) != OK) {
9646          put_inode(rip);                 /* can't open: protection violation */
9647          return(r);
9648      }
9649
```

```
9650        /* Opening regular files, directories and special files are different. */
9651        switch (rip->i_mode & I_TYPE) {
9652           case I_DIRECTORY:
9653              if (bits & W_BIT) {
9654                      put_inode(rip);
9655                      return(EISDIR);
9656              }
9657              break;
9658
9659           case I_CHAR_SPECIAL:
9660              /* Assume that first open of char special file is controlling tty. */
9661              if (fp->fs_tty == 0) fp->fs_tty = (dev_nr) rip->i_zone[0];
9662              dev_open((dev_nr) rip->i_zone[0], (int) bits);
9663              break;
9664
9665           case I_BLOCK_SPECIAL:
9666              dev_open((dev_nr) rip->i_zone[0], (int) bits);
9667              break;
9668        }
9669
9670        /* Claim the file descriptor and filp slot and fill them in. */
9671        fp->fp_filp[file_d] = fil_ptr;
9672        fil_ptr->filp_count = 1;
9673        fil_ptr->filp_ino = rip;
9674        return(file_d);
9675     }

9677     /*===========================================================================*
9678      *                              do_close                                      *
9679      *===========================================================================*/
9680     PUBLIC int do_close()
9681     {
9682     /* Perform the close(fd) system call. */
9683
9684        register struct filp *rfilp;
9685        register struct inode *rip;
9686        int rw;
9687        int mode_word;
9688        extern struct filp *get_filp();
9689
9690        /* First locate the inode that belongs to the file descriptor. */
9691        if ( (rfilp = get_filp(fd)) == NIL_FILP) return(err_code);
9692        rip = rfilp->filp_ino;        /* 'rip' points to the inode */
9693
9694        /* Check to see if the file is special. */
9695        mode_word = rip->i_mode & I_TYPE;
9696        if (mode_word == I_CHAR_SPECIAL || mode_word == I_BLOCK_SPECIAL) {
9697             if (mode_word == I_BLOCK_SPECIAL) {
9698                     /* Invalidate cache entries unless special is mounted or ROOT.*/
9699                     do_sync();      /* purge cache */
```

```
9700                        if (mounted(rip) == FALSE) invalidate((dev_nr) rip->i_zone[0]);
9701                }
9702                dev_close((dev_nr) rip->i_zone[0]);
9703        }
9704
9705        /* If the inode being closed is a pipe, release everyone hanging on it. */
9706        if (rfilp->filp_ino->i_pipe) {
9707                rw = (rfilp->filp_mode & R_BIT ? WRITE : READ);
9708                release(rfilp->filp_ino, rw, NR_PROCS);
9709        }
9710
9711        /* If a write has been done, the inode is already marked as DIRTY. */
9712        if (--rfilp->filp_count == 0) put_inode(rfilp->filp_ino);
9713
9714        fp->fp_filp[fd] = NIL_FILP;
9715        return(OK);
9716  }

9718  /*===========================================================================*
9719   *                              do_lseek                                     *
9720   *===========================================================================*/
9721  PUBLIC int do_lseek()
9722  {
9723  /* Perform the lseek(ls_fd, offset, whence) system call. */
9724
9725        register struct filp *rfilp;
9726        register file_pos pos;
9727        extern struct filp *get_filp();
9728
9729        /* Check to see if the file descriptor is valid. */
9730        if ( (rfilp = get_filp(ls_fd)) == NIL_FILP) return(err_code);
9731
9732        /* No lseek on pipes. */
9733        if (rfilp->filp_ino->i_pipe == I_PIPE) return(ESPIPE);
9734
9735        /* The value of 'whence' determines the algorithm to use. */
9736        switch(whence) {
9737                case 0: pos = offset;   break;
9738                case 1: pos = rfilp->filp_pos + offset; break;
9739                case 2: pos = rfilp->filp_ino->i_size + offset; break;
9740                default: return(EINVAL);
9741        }
9742        if (pos < (file_pos) 0) return(EINVAL);
9743
9744        rfilp->filp_ino->i_seek = ISEEK;        /* inhibit read ahead */
9745        rfilp->filp_pos = pos;
9746
9747        reply_l1 = pos;                         /* insert the long into the output message */
9748        return(OK);
9749  }
```

```
9750    /* This file contains the heart of the mechanism used to read (and write)
9751     * files.  Read and write requests are split up into chunks that do not cross
9752     * block boundaries.  Each chunk is then processed in turn.  Reads on special
9753     * files are also detected and handled.
9754     *
9755     * The entry points into this file are
9756     *   do_read:    perform the READ system call by calling read_write
9757     *   read_write: actually do the work of READ and WRITE
9758     *   read_map:   given an inode and file position, lookup its zone number
9759     *   rw_user:    call the kernel to read and write user space
9760     *   read_ahead: manage the block read ahead business
9761     */
9762
9763    #include "../h/const.h"
9764    #include "../h/type.h"
9765    #include "../h/com.h"
9766    #include "../h/error.h"
9767    #include "const.h"
9768    #include "type.h"
9769    #include "buf.h"
9770    #include "file.h"
9771    #include "fproc.h"
9772    #include "glo.h"
9773    #include "inode.h"
9774    #include "param.h"
9775    #include "super.h"
9776
9777    #define FD_MASK           077      /* max file descriptor is 63 */
9778
9779    PRIVATE message umess;               /* message for asking SYSTASK for user copy */
9780
9781    /*===========================================================================*
9782     *                              do_read                                      *
9783     *===========================================================================*/
9784    PUBLIC int do_read()
9785    {
9786      return(read_write(READING));
9787    }


9791    /*===========================================================================*
9792     *                              read_write                                   *
9793     *===========================================================================*/
9794    PUBLIC int read_write(rw_flag)
9795    int rw_flag;                         /* READING or WRITING */
9796    {
9797    /* Perform read(fd, buffer, nbytes) or write(fd, buffer, nbytes) call. */
9798
9799      register struct inode *rip;
```

```
9800        register struct filp *f;
9801        register file_pos bytes_left, f_size;
9802        register unsigned off, cum_io;
9803        file_pos position;
9804        int r, chunk, virg, mode_word, usr, seg;
9805        struct filp *wf;
9806        extern struct super_block *get_super();
9807        extern struct filp *find_filp(), *get_filp();
9808        extern real_time clock_time();
9809
9810        /* MM loads segments by putting funny things in upper 10 bits of 'fd'. */
9811        if (who == MM_PROC_NR && (fd & (~BYTE)) ) {
9812              usr = (fd >> 8) & BYTE;
9813              seg = (fd >> 6) & 03;
9814              fd &= FD_MASK;            /* get rid of user and segment bits */
9815        } else {
9816              usr = who;               /* normal case */
9817              seg = D;
9818        }
9819
9820        /* If the file descriptor is valid, get the inode, size and mode. */
9821        if (nbytes == 0) return(0);    /* so char special files need not check for 0*/
9822        if (who != MM_PROC_NR && nbytes < 0) return(EINVAL);  /* only MM > 32K */
9823        if ( (f = get_filp(fd)) == NIL_FILP) return(err_code);
9824        if ( ((f->filp_mode) & (rw_flag == READING ? R_BIT : W_BIT)) == 0)
9825              return(EBADF);
9826        position = f->filp_pos;
9827        if (position < (file_pos) 0) return(EINVAL);
9828        rip = f->filp_ino;
9829        f_size = rip->i_size;
9830        r = OK;
9831        cum_io = 0;
9832        virg = TRUE;
9833        mode_word = rip->i_mode & I_TYPE;
9834
9835        /* Check for character special files. */
9836        if (mode_word == I_CHAR_SPECIAL) {
9837              if ((r = dev_io(rw_flag, (dev_nr) rip->i_zone[0], (long) position,
9838                                              nbytes, who, buffer)) >= 0) {
9839                    cum_io = r;
9840                    position += r;
9841                    r = OK;
9842              }
9843        } else {
9844              if (rw_flag == WRITING && mode_word != I_BLOCK_SPECIAL) {
9845                    /* Check in advance to see if file will grow too big. */
9846                    if (position > get_super(rip->i_dev)->s_max_size - nbytes )
9847                          return(EFBIG);
9848
9849                    /* Clear the zone containing present EOF if hole about
```

```
9850                      * to be created.  This is necessary because all unwritten
9851                      * blocks prior to the EOF must read as zeros.
9852                      */
9853                     if (position > f_size) clear_zone(rip, f_size, 0);
9854             }
9855
9856             /* Pipes are a little different.  Check. */
9857             if (rip->i_pipe && (r = pipe_check(rip, rw_flag, virg,
9858                                     nbytes, &position)) <= 0) return(0);
9859
9860             /* Split the transfer into chunks that don't span two blocks. */
9861             while (nbytes != 0) {
9862                     off = position % BLOCK_SIZE;     /* offset within a block */
9863                     chunk = MIN(nbytes, BLOCK_SIZE - off);
9864                     if (chunk < 0) chunk = BLOCK_SIZE - off;
9865
9866                     if (rw_flag == READING) {
9867                             if ((bytes_left = f_size - position) <= 0)
9868                                     break;
9869                             else
9870                                     if (chunk > bytes_left) chunk = bytes_left;
9871                     }
9872
9873                     /* Read or write 'chunk' bytes. */
9874                     r=rw_chunk(rip, position, off, chunk, rw_flag, buffer, seg,usr);
9875                     if (r != OK) break;     /* EOF reached */
9876
9877                     /* Update counters and pointers. */
9878                     buffer += chunk;        /* user buffer address */
9879                     nbytes -= chunk;        /* bytes yet to be read */
9880                     cum_io += chunk;        /* bytes read so far */
9881                     position += chunk;      /* position within the file */
9882                     virg = FALSE; /* tells pipe_check() that data has been copied */
9883             }
9884     }
9885
9886     /* On write, update file size and access time. */
9887     if (rw_flag == WRITING) {
9888             if (mode_word != I_CHAR_SPECIAL && mode_word != I_BLOCK_SPECIAL &&
9889                                                     position > f_size)
9890                     rip->i_size = position;
9891             rip->i_modtime = clock_time();
9892             rip->i_dirt = DIRTY;
9893     } else {
9894             if (rip->i_pipe && position >= rip->i_size) {
9895                     /* Reset pipe pointers. */
9896                     rip->i_size = 0;        /* no data left */
9897                     position = 0;           /* reset reader(s) */
9898                     if ( (wf = find_filp(rip, W_BIT)) != NIL_FILP) wf->filp_pos = 0;
9899             }
```

```
9900            }
9901            f->filp_pos = position;
9902
9903            /* Check to see if read-ahead is called for, and if so, set it up. */
9904            if (rw_flag == READING && rip->i_seek == NO_SEEK && position % BLOCK_SIZE == 0
9905                        && (mode_word == I_REGULAR || mode_word == I_DIRECTORY)) {
9906                    rdahed_inode = rip;
9907                    rdahedpos = position;
9908            }
9909            if (mode_word == I_REGULAR) rip->i_seek = NO_SEEK;
9910
9911            return(r == OK ? cum_io : r);
9912    }




9916    /*===========================================================================*
9917     *                              rw_chunk                                     *
9918     *===========================================================================*/
9919    PRIVATE int rw_chunk(rip, position, off, chunk, rw_flag, buff, seg, usr)
9920    register struct inode *rip;     /* pointer to inode for file to be rd/wr */
9921    file_pos position;              /* position within file to read or write */
9922    unsigned off;                   /* off within the current block */
9923    int chunk;                      /* number of bytes to read or write */
9924    int rw_flag;                    /* READING or WRITING */
9925    char *buff;                     /* virtual address of the user buffer */
9926    int seg;                        /* T or D segment in user space */
9927    int usr;                        /* which user process */
9928    {
9929    /* Read or write (part of) a block. */
9930
9931            register struct buf *bp;
9932            register int r;
9933            int dir, n, block_spec;
9934            block_nr b;
9935            dev_nr dev;
9936            extern struct buf *get_block(), *new_block();
9937            extern block_nr read_map();
9938
9939            block_spec = (rip->i_mode & I_TYPE) == I_BLOCK_SPECIAL;
9940            if (block_spec) {
9941                    b = position/BLOCK_SIZE;
9942                    dev = (dev_nr) rip->i_zone[0];
9943            } else {
9944                    b = read_map(rip, position);
9945                    dev = rip->i_dev;
9946            }
9947
9948            if (!block_spec && b == NO_BLOCK) {
9949                    if (rw_flag == READING) {
```

```
9950                    /* Reading from a nonexistent block.  Must read as all zeros. */
9951                    bp = get_block(NO_DEV, NO_BLOCK, NORMAL);      /* get a buffer */
9952                    zero_block(bp);
9953              } else {
9954                    /* Writing to a nonexistent block. Create and enter in inode. */
9955                    if ((bp = new_block(rip, position)) == NIL_BUF)return(err_code);
9956              }
9957        } else {
9958              /* Normally an existing block to be partially overwritten is first read
9959               * in.  However, a full block need not be read in.  If it is already in
9960               * the cache, acquire it, otherwise just acquire a free buffer.
9961               */
9962              n = (rw_flag == WRITING && chunk == BLOCK_SIZE ? NO_READ : NORMAL);
9963              if(rw_flag == WRITING && off == 0 && position >= rip->i_size) n=NO_READ;
9964              bp = get_block(dev, b, n);
9965        }
9966
9967        /* In all cases, bp now points to a valid buffer. */
9968        if (rw_flag == WRITING && chunk != BLOCK_SIZE && !block_spec &&
9969                                        position >= rip->i_size && off == 0)
9970              zero_block(bp);
9971        dir = (rw_flag == READING ? TO_USER : FROM_USER);
9972        r = rw_user(seg, usr, (vir_bytes)buff, (vir_bytes)chunk, bp->b_data+off, dir);
9973        if (rw_flag == WRITING) bp->b_dirt = DIRTY;
9974        n = (off + chunk == BLOCK_SIZE ? FULL_DATA_BLOCK : PARTIAL_DATA_BLOCK);
9975        put_block(bp, n);
9976        return(r);
9977   }



9981   /*===========================================================================*
9982    *                              read_map                                     *
9983    *===========================================================================*/
9984   PUBLIC block_nr read_map(rip, position)
9985   register struct inode *rip;    /* ptr to inode to map from */
9986   file_pos position;             /* position in file whose blk wanted */
9987   {
9988   /* Given an inode and a position within the corresponding file, locate the
9989    * block (not zone) number in which that position is to be found and return it.
9990    */
9991
9992      register struct buf *bp;
9993      register zone_nr z;
9994      register block_nr b;
9995      register long excess, zone, block_pos;
9996      register int scale, boff;
9997      extern struct buf *get_block();
9998
9999      scale = scale_factor(rip);    /* for block-zone conversion */
```

```
10000        block_pos = position/BLOCK_SIZE;       /* relative blk # in file */
10001        zone = block_pos >> scale;    /* position's zone */
10002        boff = block_pos - (zone << scale);   /* relative blk # within zone */
10003
10004        /* Is 'position' to be found in the inode itself? */
10005        if (zone < NR_DZONE_NUM) {
10006                if ( (z = rip->i_zone[zone]) == NO_ZONE) return(NO_BLOCK);
10007                b = ((block_nr) z << scale) + boff;
10008                return(b);
10009        }
10010
10011        /* It is not in the inode, so it must be single or double indirect. */
10012        excess = zone - NR_DZONE_NUM; /* first NR_DZONE_NUM don't count */
10013
10014        if (excess < NR_INDIRECTS) {
10015                /* 'position' can be located via the single indirect block. */
10016                z = rip->i_zone[NR_DZONE_NUM];
10017        } else {
10018                /* 'position' can be located via the double indirect block. */
10019                if ( (z = rip->i_zone[NR_DZONE_NUM+1]) == NO_ZONE) return(NO_BLOCK);
10020                excess -= NR_INDIRECTS;                  /* single indir doesn't count */
10021                b = (block_nr) z << scale;
10022                bp = get_block(rip->i_dev, b, NORMAL);  /* get double indirect block */
10023                z = bp->b_ind[excess/NR_INDIRECTS];      /* z is zone # for single ind */
10024                put_block(bp, INDIRECT_BLOCK);           /* release double ind block */
10025                excess = excess % NR_INDIRECTS;          /* index into single ind blk */
10026        }
10027
10028        /* 'z' is zone number for single indirect block; 'excess' is index into it. */
10029        if (z == NO_ZONE) return(NO_BLOCK);
10030        b = (block_nr) z << scale;
10031        bp = get_block(rip->i_dev, b, NORMAL);          /* get single indirect block */
10032        z = bp->b_ind[excess];
10033        put_block(bp, INDIRECT_BLOCK);                  /* release single indirect blk */
10034        if (z == NO_ZONE) return(NO_BLOCK);
10035        b = ((block_nr) z << scale) + boff;
10036        return(b);
10037 }

10039 /*===========================================================================*
10040  *                              rw_user                                      *
10041  *===========================================================================*/
10042 PUBLIC int rw_user(s, u, vir, bytes, buff, direction)
10043 int s;                          /* D or T space (stack is also D) */
10044 int u;                          /* process number to r/w (usually = 'who') */
10045 vir_bytes vir;                  /* virtual address to move to/from */
10046 vir_bytes bytes;                /* how many bytes to move */
10047 char *buff;                     /* pointer to FS space */
10048 int direction;                  /* TO_USER or FROM_USER */
10049 {
```

```
10050    /* Transfer a block of data.  Two options exist, depending on 'direction':
10051     *    TO_USER:    Move from FS space to user virtual space
10052     *    FROM_USER:  Move from user virtual space to FS space
10053     */
10054
10055      if (direction == TO_USER ) {
10056           /* Write from FS space to user space. */
10057           umess.SRC_SPACE   = D;
10058           umess.SRC_PROC_NR = FS_PROC_NR;
10059           umess.SRC_BUFFER = (long) buff;
10060           umess.DST_SPACE   = s;
10061           umess.DST_PROC_NR = u;
10062           umess.DST_BUFFER = (long) vir;
10063      } else {
10064           /* Read from user space to FS space. */
10065           umess.SRC_SPACE   = s;
10066           umess.SRC_PROC_NR = u;
10067           umess.SRC_BUFFER = (long) vir;
10068           umess.DST_SPACE   = D;
10069           umess.DST_PROC_NR = FS_PROC_NR;
10070           umess.DST_BUFFER = (long) buff;
10071      }
10072
10073      umess.COPY_BYTES = (long) bytes;
10074      sys_copy(&umess);
10075      return(umess.m_type);
10076    }


10079    /*===========================================================================*
10080     *                            read_ahead                                     *
10081     *===========================================================================*/
10082    PUBLIC read_ahead()
10083    {
10084    /* Read a block into the cache before it is needed. */
10085
10086      register struct inode *rip;
10087      struct buf *bp;
10088      block_nr b;
10089      extern struct buf *get_block();
10090
10091      rip = rdahed_inode;             /* pointer to inode to read ahead from */
10092      rdahed_inode = NIL_INODE;       /* turn off read ahead */
10093      if ( (b = read_map(rip, rdahedpos)) == NO_BLOCK) return;    /* at EOF */
10094      bp = get_block(rip->i_dev, b, NORMAL);
10095      put_block(bp, PARTIAL_DATA_BLOCK);
10096    }
```

```
10100   /* This file is the counterpart of "read.c".  It contains the code for writing
10101    * insofar as this is not contained in read_write().
10102    *
10103    * The entry points into this file are
10104    *   do_write:     call read_write to perform the WRITE system call
10105    *   write_map:    add a new zone to an inode
10106    *   clear_zone:   erase a zone in the middle of a file
10107    *   new_block:    acquire a new block
10108    */

10110   #include "../h/const.h"
10111   #include "../h/type.h"
10112   #include "../h/error.h"
10113   #include "const.h"
10114   #include "type.h"
10115   #include "buf.h"
10116   #include "file.h"
10117   #include "fproc.h"
10118   #include "glo.h"
10119   #include "inode.h"
10120   #include "super.h"

10122   /*===========================================================================*
10123    *                              do_write                                      *
10124    *===========================================================================*/
10125   PUBLIC int do_write()
10126   {
10127   /* Perform the write(fd, buffer, nbytes) system call. */
10128     return(read_write(WRITING));
10129   }


10132   /*===========================================================================*
10133    *                              write_map                                     *
10134    *===========================================================================*/
10135   PRIVATE int write_map(rip, position, new_zone)
10136   register struct inode *rip;    /* pointer to inode to be changed */
10137   file_pos position;             /* file address to be mapped */
10138   zone_nr new_zone;              /* zone # to be inserted */
10139   {
10140   /* Write a new zone into an inode. */
10141     int scale;
10142     zone_nr z, *zp;
10143     register block_nr b;
10144     long excess, zone;
10145     int index;
10146     struct buf *bp;
10147     int new_ind, new_dbl;

10149     extern zone_nr alloc_zone();
```

```
10150       extern struct buf *get_block();
10151       extern real_time clock_time();
10152
10153       rip->i_dirt = DIRTY;           /* inode will be changed */
10154       bp = NIL_BUF;
10155       scale = scale_factor(rip);    /* for zone-block conversion */
10156       zone = (position/BLOCK_SIZE) >> scale;       /* relative zone # to insert */
10157
10158       /* Is 'position' to be found in the inode itself? */
10159       if (zone < NR_DZONE_NUM) {
10160             rip->i_zone[zone] = new_zone;
10161             rip->i_modtime = clock_time();
10162             return(OK);
10163       }
10164
10165       /* It is not in the inode, so it must be single or double indirect. */
10166       excess = zone - NR_DZONE_NUM; /* first NR_DZONE_NUM don't count */
10167       new_ind = FALSE;
10168       new_dbl = FALSE;
10169
10170       if (excess < NR_INDIRECTS) {
10171             /* 'position' can be located via the single indirect block. */
10172             zp = &rip->i_zone[NR_DZONE_NUM];
10173       } else {
10174             /* 'position' can be located via the double indirect block. */
10175             if ( (z = rip->i_zone[NR_DZONE_NUM+1]) == NO_ZONE) {
10176                   /* Create the double indirect block. */
10177                   if ( (z = alloc_zone(rip->i_dev, rip->i_zone[0])) == NO_ZONE)
10178                         return(err_code);
10179                   rip->i_zone[NR_DZONE_NUM+1] = z;
10180                   new_dbl = TRUE; /* set flag for later */
10181             }
10182
10183             /* Either way, 'z' is zone number for double indirect block. */
10184             excess -= NR_INDIRECTS; /* single indirect doesn't count */
10185             index = excess / NR_INDIRECTS;
10186             excess = excess % NR_INDIRECTS;
10187             if (index >= NR_INDIRECTS) return(EFBIG);
10188             b = (block_nr) z << scale;
10189             bp = get_block(rip->i_dev, b, (new_dbl ? NO_READ : NORMAL));
10190             if (new_dbl) zero_block(bp);
10191             zp= &bp->b_ind[index];
10192       }
10193
10194       /* 'zp' now points to place where indirect zone # goes; 'excess' is index. */
10195       if (*zp == NO_ZONE) {
10196             /* Create indirect block. */
10197             *zp = alloc_zone(rip->i_dev, rip->i_zone[0]);
10198             new_ind = TRUE;
10199             if (bp != NIL_BUF) bp->b_dirt = DIRTY;  /* if double ind, it is dirty */
```

```
10200                if (*zp == NO_ZONE) {
10201                        put_block(bp, INDIRECT_BLOCK);  /* release dbl indirect blk */
10202                        return(err_code);            /* couldn't create single ind */
10203                }
10204        }
10205        put_block(bp, INDIRECT_BLOCK);               /* release double indirect blk */
10206
10207        /* 'zp' now points to indirect block's zone number. */
10208        b = (block_nr) *zp << scale;
10209        bp = get_block(rip->i_dev, b, (new_ind ? NO_READ : NORMAL) );
10210        if (new_ind) zero_block(bp);
10211        bp->b_ind[excess] = new_zone;
10212        rip->i_modtime = clock_time();
10213        bp->b_dirt = DIRTY;
10214        put_block(bp, INDIRECT_BLOCK);
10215
10216        return(OK);
10217 }

10219 /*===========================================================================*
10220  *                              clear_zone                                   *
10221  *===========================================================================*/
10222 PUBLIC clear_zone(rip, pos, flag)
10223 register struct inode *rip;      /* inode to clear */
10224 file_pos pos;                    /* points to block to clear */
10225 int flag;                        /* 0 if called by read_write, 1 by new_block */
10226 {
10227 /* Zero a zone, possibly starting in the middle.  The parameter 'pos' gives
10228  * a byte in the first block to be zeroed.  Clearzone() is called from
10229  * read_write and new_block().
10230  */
10231
10232        register struct buf *bp;
10233        register block_nr b, blo, bhi;
10234        register file_pos next;
10235        register int scale;
10236        register zone_type zone_size;
10237        extern struct buf *get_block();
10238        extern block_nr read_map();
10239
10240        /* If the block size and zone size are the same, clear_zone() not needed. */
10241        if ( (scale = scale_factor(rip)) == 0) return;
10242
10243
10244        zone_size = (zone_type) BLOCK_SIZE << scale;
10245        if (flag == 1) pos = (pos/zone_size) * zone_size;
10246        next = pos + BLOCK_SIZE - 1;
10247
10248        /* If 'pos' is in the last block of a zone, do not clear the zone. */
10249        if (next/zone_size != pos/zone_size) return;
```

```
10250        if ( (blo = read_map(rip, next)) == NO_BLOCK) return;
10251        bhi = (  ((blo>>scale)+1) << scale)   - 1;
10252
10253        /* Clear all the blocks between 'blo' and 'bhi'. */
10254        for (b = blo; b <= bhi; b++) {
10255                bp = get_block(rip->i_dev, b, NO_READ);
10256                zero_block(bp);
10257                put_block(bp, FULL_DATA_BLOCK);
10258        }
10259     }


10262     /*===========================================================================*
10263      *                           new_block                                       *
10264      *===========================================================================*/
10265     PUBLIC struct buf *new_block(rip, position)
10266     register struct inode *rip;     /* pointer to inode */
10267     file_pos position;              /* file pointer */
10268     {
10269     /* Acquire a new block and return a pointer to it.  Doing so may require
10270      * allocating a complete zone, and then returning the initial block.
10271      * On the other hand, the current zone may still have some unused blocks.
10272      */
10273
10274        register struct buf *bp;
10275        block_nr b, base_block;
10276        zone_nr z;
10277        zone_type zone_size;
10278        int scale, r;
10279        struct super_block *sp;
10280        extern struct buf *get_block();
10281        extern struct super_block *get_super();
10282        extern block_nr read_map();
10283        extern zone_nr alloc_zone();
10284
10285        /* Is another block available in the current zone? */
10286        if ( (b = read_map(rip, position)) == NO_BLOCK) {
10287                /* Choose first zone if need be. */
10288                if (rip->i_size == 0) {
10289                        sp = get_super(rip->i_dev);
10290                        z = sp->s_firstdatazone;
10291                } else {
10292                        z = rip->i_zone[0];
10293                }
10294                if ( (z = alloc_zone(rip->i_dev, z)) == NO_ZONE) return(NIL_BUF);
10295                if ( (r = write_map(rip, position, z)) != OK) {
10296                        free_zone(rip->i_dev, z);
10297                        err_code = r;
10298                        return(NIL_BUF);
10299                }
```

```
10300
10301                    /* If we are not writing at EOF, clear the zone, just to be safe. */
10302                    if ( position != rip->i_size) clear_zone(rip, position, 1);
10303                    scale = scale_factor(rip);
10304                    base_block = (block_nr) z << scale;
10305                    zone_size = (zone_type) BLOCK_SIZE << scale;
10306                    b = base_block + (block_nr)((position % zone_size)/BLOCK_SIZE);
10307            }
10308
10309        bp = get_block(rip->i_dev, b, NO_READ);
10310        zero_block(bp);
10311        return(bp);
10312    }


10315    /*===========================================================================*
10316     *                              zero_block                                    *
10317     *===========================================================================*/
10318    PUBLIC zero_block(bp)
10319    register struct buf *bp;          /* pointer to buffer to zero */
10320    {
10321    /* Zero a block. */
10322
10323        register int n;
10324        register int *zip;
10325
10326        n = INTS_PER_BLOCK;              /* number of integers in a block */
10327        zip = bp->b_int;                /* where to start clearing */
10328
10329        do { *zip++ = 0;}  while (--n);
10330        bp->b_dirt = DIRTY;
10331    }
```

```
10350    /* This file deals with the suspension and revival of processes.  A process can
10351     * be suspended because it wants to read or write from a pipe and can't, or
10352     * because it wants to read or write from a special file and can't.  When a
10353     * process can't continue it is suspended, and revived later when it is able
10354     * to continue.
10355     *
10356     * The entry points into this file are
10357     *   do_pipe:      perform the PIPE system call
10358     *   pipe_check:   check to see that a read or write on a pipe is feasible now
10359     *   suspend:      suspend a process that cannot do a requested read or write
10360     *   release:      check to see if a suspended process can be released and do it
10361     *   revive:       mark a suspended process as able to run again
10362     *   do_unpause:   a signal has been sent to a process; see if it suspended
10363     */

10365    #include "../h/const.h"
10366    #include "../h/type.h"
10367    #include "../h/callnr.h"
10368    #include "../h/com.h"
10369    #include "../h/error.h"
10370    #include "../h/signal.h"
10371    #include "const.h"
10372    #include "type.h"
10373    #include "file.h"
10374    #include "fproc.h"
10375    #include "glo.h"
10376    #include "inode.h"
10377    #include "param.h"

10379    PRIVATE message mess;

10381    /*===========================================================================*
10382     *                              do_pipe                              *
10383     *===========================================================================*/
10384    PUBLIC int do_pipe()
10385    {
10386    /* Perform the pipe(fil_des) system call. */

10388      register struct fproc *rfp;
10389      register struct inode *rip;
10390      int r;
10391      dev_nr device;
10392      struct filp *fil_ptr0, *fil_ptr1;
10393      int fil_des[2];                 /* reply goes here */
10394      extern struct inode *alloc_inode();

10396      /* Acquire two file descriptors. */
10397      rfp = fp;
10398      if ( (r = get_fd(R_BIT, &fil_des[0], &fil_ptr0)) != OK) return(r);
10399      rfp->fp_filp[fil_des[0]] = fil_ptr0;
```

```
10400        fil_ptr0->filp_count = 1;
10401        if ( (r = get_fd(W_BIT, &fil_des[1], &fil_ptr1)) != OK) {
10402             rfp->fp_filp[fil_des[0]] = NIL_FILP;
10403             fil_ptr0->filp_count = 0;
10404             return(r);
10405        }
10406        rfp->fp_filp[fil_des[1]] = fil_ptr1;
10407        fil_ptr1->filp_count = 1;
10408
10409        /* Make the inode in the current working directory. */
10410        device = rfp->fp_workdir->i_dev;       /* inode dev is same as working dir */
10411        if ( (rip = alloc_inode(device, I_REGULAR)) == NIL_INODE) {
10412             rfp->fp_filp[fil_des[0]] = NIL_FILP;
10413             fil_ptr0->filp_count = 0;
10414             rfp->fp_filp[fil_des[1]] = NIL_FILP;
10415             fil_ptr1->filp_count = 0;
10416             return(err_code);
10417        }
10418
10419        rip->i_pipe = I_PIPE;
10420        fil_ptr0->filp_ino = rip;
10421        dup_inode(rip);                 /* for double usage */
10422        fil_ptr1->filp_ino = rip;
10423        rw_inode(rip, WRITING);         /* mark inode as allocated */
10424        reply_i1 = fil_des[0];
10425        reply_i2 = fil_des[1];
10426        return(OK);
10427   }


10430   /*===========================================================================*
10431    *                              pipe_check                                    *
10432    *===========================================================================*/
10433   PUBLIC int pipe_check(rip, rw_flag, virgin, bytes, position)
10434   register struct inode *rip;     /* the inode of the pipe */
10435   int rw_flag;                    /* READING or WRITING */
10436   int virgin;                     /* 1 if no data transferred yet, else 0 */
10437   register int bytes;             /* bytes to be read or written (all chunks) */
10438   register file_pos *position;    /* pointer to current file position */
10439   {
10440   /* Pipes are a little different.  If a process reads from an empty pipe for
10441    * which a writer still exists, suspend the reader.  If the pipe is empty
10442    * and there is no writer, return 0 bytes.  If a process is writing to a
10443    * pipe and no one is reading from it, give a broken pipe error.
10444    */
10445
10446     extern struct filp *find_filp();
10447
10448     /* If reading, check for empty pipe. */
10449     if (rw_flag == READING) {
```

```
10450                 if (*position >= rip->i_size) {
10451                         /* Process is reading from an empty pipe. */
10452                         if (find_filp(rip, W_BIT) != NIL_FILP) {
10453                                 /* Writer exists; suspend rdr if no data already read.*/
10454                                 if (virgin) suspend(XPIPE);      /* block reader */
10455
10456                                 /* If need be, activate sleeping writer. */
10457                                 if (susp_count > 0) release(rip, WRITE, 1);
10458                         }
10459                         return(0);
10460                 }
10461         } else {
10462                 /* Process is writing to a pipe. */
10463                 if (find_filp(rip, R_BIT) == NIL_FILP) {
10464                         /* Tell MM to generate a SIGPIPE signal. */
10465                         mess.m_type = KSIG;
10466                         mess.PROC1 = fp - fproc;
10467                         mess.SIG_MAP = 1 << (SIGPIPE - 1);
10468                         send(MM_PROC_NR, &mess);
10469                         return(EPIPE);
10470                 }
10471
10472                 if (*position + bytes > PIPE_SIZE) {
10473                         suspend(XPIPE); /* stop writer -- pipe full */
10474                         return(0);
10475                 }
10476
10477                 /* Writing to an empty pipe.  Search for suspended reader. */
10478                 if (*position == 0) release(rip, READ, 1);
10479         }
10480
10481     return(1);
10482   }


10485   /*===========================================================================*
10486    *                              suspend                                       *
10487    *===========================================================================*/
10488   PUBLIC suspend(task)
10489   int task;                            /* who is proc waiting for? (PIPE = pipe) */
10490   {
10491   /* Take measures to suspend the processing of the present system call.
10492    * Store the parameters to be used upon resuming in the process table.
10493    * (Actually they are not used when a process is waiting for an I/O device,
10494    * but they are needed for pipes, and it is not worth making the distinction.)
10495    */
10496
10497     if (task == XPIPE) susp_count++;       /* count procs suspended on pipe */
10498     fp->fp_suspended = SUSPENDED;
10499     fp->fp_fd = fd << 8 | fs_call;
```

```
10500      fp->fp_buffer = buffer;
10501      fp->fp_nbytes = nbytes;
10502      fp->fp_task = -task;
10503      dont_reply = TRUE;              /* do not send caller a reply message now */
10504   }


10507   /*===========================================================================*
10508    *                              release                                       *
10509    *===========================================================================*/
10510   PUBLIC release(ip, call_nr, count)
10511   register struct inode *ip;       /* inode of pipe */
10512   int call_nr;                     /* READ or WRITE */
10513   int count;                       /* max number of processes to release */
10514   {
10515   /* Check to see if any process is hanging on the pipe whose inode is in 'ip'.
10516    * If one is, and it was trying to perform the call indicated by 'call_nr'
10517    * (READ or WRITE), release it.
10518    */
10519
10520     register struct fproc *rp;
10521
10522     /* Search the proc table. */
10523     for (rp = &fproc[0]; rp < &fproc[NR_PROCS]; rp++) {
10524           if (rp->fp_suspended == SUSPENDED && (rp->fp_fd & BYTE) == call_nr &&
10525                             rp->fp_filp[rp->fp_fd>>8]->filp_ino == ip) {
10526                   revive(rp - fproc, 0);
10527                   susp_count--;   /* keep track of who is suspended */
10528                   if (--count == 0) return;
10529           }
10530     }
10531   }


10534   /*===========================================================================*
10535    *                              revive                                        *
10536    *===========================================================================*/
10537   PUBLIC revive(proc_nr, bytes)
10538   int proc_nr;                     /* process to revive */
10539   int bytes;                       /* if hanging on task, how many bytes read */
10540   {
10541   /* Revive a previously blocked process. When a process hangs on tty, this
10542    * is the way it is eventually released.
10543    */
10544
10545     register struct fproc *rfp;
10546
10547     if (proc_nr < 0 || proc_nr >= NR_PROCS) panic("revive err", proc_nr);
10548     rfp = &fproc[proc_nr];
10549     if (rfp->fp_suspended == NOT_SUSPENDED) return;
```

```
10550
10551        /* The 'reviving' flag only applies to pipes.  Processes waiting for TTY get
10552         * a message right away.  The revival process is different for TTY and pipes.
10553         * For TTY revival, the work is already done, for pipes it is not: the proc
10554         * must be restarted so it can try again.
10555         */
10556        if (rfp->fp_task == XPIPE) {
10557                /* Revive a process suspended on a pipe. */
10558                rfp->fp_revived = REVIVING;
10559                reviving++;              /* process was waiting on pipe */
10560        } else {
10561                /* Revive a process suspended on TTY or other device. */
10562                rfp->fp_suspended = NOT_SUSPENDED;
10563                rfp->fp_nbytes = bytes; /* pretend it only wants what there is */
10564                reply(proc_nr, bytes);  /* unblock the process */
10565        }
10566   }


10569   /*===========================================================================*
10570    *                              do_unpause                                   *
10571    *===========================================================================*/
10572   PUBLIC int do_unpause()
10573   {
10574   /* A signal has been sent to a user who is paused on the file system.
10575    * Abort the system call with the EINTR error message.
10576    */
10577
10578     register struct fproc *rfp;
10579     int proc_nr, task;
10580     struct filp *f;
10581     dev_nr dev;
10582     extern struct filp *get_filp();
10583
10584     if (who > MM_PROC_NR) return(EPERM);
10585     proc_nr = pro;
10586     if (proc_nr < 0 || proc_nr >= NR_PROCS) panic("unpause err 1", proc_nr);
10587     rfp = &fproc[proc_nr];
10588     if (rfp->fp_suspended == NOT_SUSPENDED) return(OK);
10589     task = -rfp->fp_task;
10590
10591     if (task != XPIPE) {
10592          f = get_filp(rfp->fp_fd);
10593          dev = f->filp_ino->i_zone[0];    /* device on which proc is hanging */
10594          mess.TTY_LINE = (dev >> MINOR) & BYTE;
10595          mess.PROC_NR = proc_nr;
10596          mess.m_type = CANCEL;
10597          if (sendrec(task, &mess) != OK) panic("unpause err 2", NO_NUM);
10598          while (mess.REP_PROC_NR != proc_nr) {
10599                  revive(mess.REP_PROC_NR, mess.REP_STATUS);
```

```
10600                    if (receive(task, &m) != OK) panic("unpause err 3", NO_NUM);
10601            }
10602        revive(proc_nr, EINTR); /* signal interrupted call */
10603    }
10604
10605    return(OK);
10606  }
```

```
10650    /* This file contains the procedures that look up path names in the directory
10651     * system and determine the inode number that goes with a given path name.
10652     *
10653     * The entry points into this file are
10654     *   eat_path:    the 'main' routine of the path-to-inode conversion mechanism
10655     *   last_dir:    find the final directory on a given path
10656     *   advance:     parse one component of a path name
10657     *   search_dir: search a directory for a string and return its inode number
10658     */
10659
10660    #include "../h/const.h"
10661    #include "../h/type.h"
10662    #include "../h/error.h"
10663    #include "const.h"
10664    #include "type.h"
10665    #include "buf.h"
10666    #include "file.h"
10667    #include "fproc.h"
10668    #include "glo.h"
10669    #include "inode.h"
10670    #include "super.h"
10671
10672    /*===========================================================================*
10673     *                              eat_path                                     *
10674     *===========================================================================*/
10675    PUBLIC struct inode *eat_path(path)
10676    char *path;                         /* the path name to be parsed */
10677    {
10678    /* Parse the path 'path' and put its inode in the inode table.  If not
10679     * possible, return NIL_INODE as function value and an error code in 'err_code'.
10680     */
10681
10682      register struct inode *ldip, *rip;
10683      char string[NAME_SIZE];          /* hold 1 path component name here */
10684      extern struct inode *last_dir(), *advance();
10685
10686      /* First open the path down to the final directory. */
10687      if ( (ldip = last_dir(path, string)) == NIL_INODE)
10688          return(NIL_INODE);           /* we couldn't open final directory */
10689
10690      /* The path consisting only of "/" is a special case, check for it. */
10691      if (string[0] == '\0') return(ldip);
10692
10693      /* Get final component of the path. */
10694      rip = advance(ldip, string);
10695      put_inode(ldip);
10696      return(rip);
10697    }
```

```
10700   /*===========================================================================*
10701    *                              last_dir                                     *
10702    *===========================================================================*/
10703   PUBLIC struct inode *last_dir(path, string)
10704   char *path;                      /* the path name to be parsed */
10705   char string[NAME_SIZE];          /* the final component is returned here */
10706   {
10707   /* Given a path, 'path', located in the fs address space, parse it as
10708    * far as the last directory, fetch the inode for the last directory into
10709    * the inode table, and return a pointer to the inode.  In
10710    * addition, return the final component of the path in 'string'.
10711    * If the last directory can't be opened, return NIL_INODE and
10712    * the reason for failure in 'err_code'.
10713    */
10714
10715     register struct inode *rip;
10716     register char *new_name;
10717     register struct inode *new_ip;
10718     extern struct inode *advance();
10719     extern char *get_name();
10720                                  .
10721     /* Is the path absolute or relative?  Initialize 'rip' accordingly. */
10722     rip = (*path == '/' ? fp->fp_rootdir : fp->fp_workdir);
10723     dup_inode(rip);                  /* inode will be returned with put_inode */
10724
10725     /* Scan the path component by component. */
10726     while (TRUE) {
10727           /* Extract one component. */
10728           if ( (new_name = get_name(path, string)) == (char*) 0) {
10729                   put_inode(rip); /* bad path in user space */
10730                   return(NIL_INODE);
10731           }
10732           if (*new_name == '\0') return(rip);     /* normal exit */
10733
10734           /* There is more path.  Keep parsing. */
10735           new_ip = advance(rip, string);
10736           put_inode(rip);          /* rip either obsolete or irrelevant */
10737           if (new_ip == NIL_INODE) return(NIL_INODE);
10738
10739           /* The call to advance() succeeded.  Fetch next component. */
10740           path = new_name;
10741           rip = new_ip;
10742     }
10743   }


10746   /*===========================================================================*
10747    *                              get_name                                     *
10748    *===========================================================================*/
10749   PRIVATE char *get_name(old_name, string)
```

```
10750    char *old_name;                    /* path name to parse */
10751    char string[NAME_SIZE];            /* component extracted from 'old_name' */
10752    {
10753    /* Given a pointer to a path name in fs space, 'old_name', copy the next
10754     * component to 'string' and pad with zeros.  A pointer to that part of
10755     * the name as yet unparsed is returned.  Roughly speaking,
10756     * 'get_name' = 'old_name' - 'string'.
10757     *
10758     * This routine follows the standard convention that /usr/ast, /usr//ast,
10759     * //usr///ast and /usr/ast/ are all equivalent.
10760     */
10761
10762      register int c;
10763      register char *np, *rnp;
10764
10765      np = string;                      /* 'np' points to current position */
10766      rnp = old_name;                   /* 'rnp' points to unparsed string */
10767      while ( (c = *rnp) == '/') rnp++;    /* skip leading slashes */
10768
10769      /* Copy the unparsed path, 'old_name', to the array, 'string'. */
10770      while ( rnp < &user_path[MAX_PATH]  &&  c != '/'   &&  c != '\0') {
10771            if (np < &string[NAME_SIZE]) *np++ = c;
10772            c = *++rnp;                 /* advance to next character */
10773      }
10774
10775      /* To make /usr/ast/ equivalent to /usr/ast, skip trailing slashes. */
10776      while (c == '/' && rnp < &user_path[MAX_PATH]) c = *++rnp;
10777
10778      /* Pad the component name out to NAME_SIZE chars, using 0 as filler. */
10779      while (np < &string[NAME_SIZE]) *np++ = '\0';
10780
10781      if (rnp >= &user_path[MAX_PATH]) {
10782            err_code = E_LONG_STRING;
10783            return((char *) 0);
10784      }
10785      return(rnp);
10786    }



10789    /*===========================================================================*
10790     *                              advance                                       *
10791     *===========================================================================*/
10792    PUBLIC struct inode *advance(dirp, string)
10793    struct inode *dirp;               /* inode for directory to be searched */
10794    char string[NAME_SIZE];           /* component name to look for */
10795    {
10796    /* Given a directory and a component of a path, look up the component in
10797     * the directory, find the inode, open it, and return a pointer to its inode
10798     * slot.  If it can't be done, return NIL_INODE.
10799     */
```

```
10800
10801     register struct inode *rip;
10802     register struct super_block *sp;
10803     register int r;
10804     dev_nr mnt_dev;
10805     inode_nr numb;
10806     extern struct inode *get_inode();
10807
10808     /* If 'string' is empty, yield same inode straight away. */
10809     if (string[0] == '\0') return(get_inode(dirp->i_dev, dirp->i_num));
10810
10811     /* If 'string' is not present in the directory, signal error. */
10812     if ( (r = search_dir(dirp, string, &numb, LOOK_UP)) != OK) {
10813          err_code = r;
10814          return(NIL_INODE);
10815     }
10816
10817     /* The component has been found in the directory.  Get inode. */
10818     if ( (rip = get_inode(dirp->i_dev, numb)) == NIL_INODE) return(NIL_INODE);
10819
10820     if (rip->i_num == ROOT_INODE)
10821          if (dirp->i_num == ROOT_INODE) {
10822               if (string[1] == '.') {
10823                    for (sp = &super_block[1]; sp < &super_block[NR_SUPERS]; sp++) {
10824                         if (sp->s_dev == rip->i_dev) {
10825                              /* Release the root inode.  Replace by the
10826                               * inode mounted on.
10827                               */
10828                              put_inode(rip);
10829                              mnt_dev = sp->s_imount->i_dev;
10830                              rip = get_inode(mnt_dev, sp->s_imount->i_num);
10831                              rip = advance(rip, string);
10832                              break;
10833                         }
10834                    }
10835               }
10836          }
10837     /* See if the inode is mounted on.  If so, switch to root directory of the
10838      * mounted file system.  The super_block provides the linkage between the
10839      * inode mounted on and the root directory of the mounted file system.
10840      */
10841     while (rip->i_mount == I_MOUNT) {
10842          /* The inode is indeed mounted on. */
10843          for (sp = &super_block[0]; sp < &super_block[NR_SUPERS]; sp++) {
10844               if (sp->s_imount == rip) {
10845                    /* Release the inode mounted on.  Replace by the
10846                     * inode of the root inode of the mounted device.
10847                     */
10848                    put_inode(rip);
10849                    rip = get_inode(sp->s_dev, ROOT_INODE);
```

```
10850                            break;
10851                     }
10852              }
10853        }
10854        return(rip);          /* return pointer to inode's component */
10855   }


10858   /*===========================================================================*
10859    *                              search_dir                                   *
10860    *===========================================================================*/
10861   PUBLIC int search_dir(ldir_ptr, string, numb, flag)
10862   register struct inode *ldir_ptr;       /* ptr to inode for dir to search */
10863   char string[NAME_SIZE];               /* component to search for */
10864   inode_nr *numb;                       /* pointer to inode number */
10865   int flag;                             /* LOOK_UP, ENTER, or DELETE */
10866   {
10867   /* This function searches the directory whose inode is pointed to by 'ldip':
10868    * if (flag == LOOK_UP) search for 'string' and return inode # in 'numb';
10869    * if (flag == ENTER)  enter 'string' in the directory with inode # '*numb';
10870    * if (flag == DELETE) delete 'string' from the directory;
10871    */
10872
10873        register dir_struct *dp;
10874        register struct buf *bp;
10875        register int r;
10876        mask_bits bits;
10877        file_pos pos;
10878        unsigned new_slots, old_slots;
10879        block_nr b;
10880        int e_hit;
10881        extern struct buf *get_block(), *new_block();
10882        extern block_nr read_map();
10883        extern real_time clock_time();
10884
10885        /* If 'ldir_ptr' is not a pointer to a searchable dir inode, error. */
10886        if ( (ldir_ptr->i_mode & I_TYPE) != I_DIRECTORY) return(ENOTDIR);
10887        bits = (flag == LOOK_UP ? X_BIT : W_BIT|X_BIT);
10888        if ( (r = forbidden(ldir_ptr, bits, 0)) != OK)
10889             return(r);
10890
10891        /* Step through the directory one block at a time. */
10892        old_slots = ldir_ptr->i_size/DIR_ENTRY_SIZE;
10893        new_slots = 0;
10894        e_hit = FALSE;
10895        for (pos = 0; pos < ldir_ptr->i_size; pos += BLOCK_SIZE) {
10896             b = read_map(ldir_ptr, pos);    /* get block number */
10897
10898             /* Since directories don't have holes, 'b' cannot be NO_BLOCK. */
10899             bp = get_block(ldir_ptr->i_dev, b, NORMAL);    /* get a dir block */
```

```
10900
10901                /* Search a directory block. */
10902                for (dp = &bp->b_dir[0]; dp < &bp->b_dir[NR_DIR_ENTRIES]; dp++) {
10903                        if (++new_slots > old_slots) { /* not found, but room left */
10904                                if (flag == ENTER) e_hit = TRUE;
10905                                break;
10906                        }
10907                        if (flag != ENTER && dp->d_inum != 0
10908                                        && cmp_string(dp->d_name, string, NAME_SIZE)) {
10909                                /* LOOK_UP or DELETE found what it wanted. */
10910                                if (flag == DELETE) {
10911                                        dp->d_inum = 0; /* erase entry */
10912                                        bp->b_dirt = DIRTY;
10913                                        ldir_ptr->i_modtime = clock_time();
10914                                } else
10915                                        *numb = dp->d_inum;     /* 'flag' is LOOK_UP */
10916                                put_block(bp, DIRECTORY_BLOCK);
10917                                return(OK);
10918                        }
10919
10920                        /* Check for free slot for the benefit of ENTER. */
10921                        if (flag == ENTER && dp->d_inum == 0) {
10922                                e_hit = TRUE;   /* we found a free slot */
10923                                break;
10924                        }
10925                }
10926
10927        /* The whole block has been searched or ENTER has a free slot. */
10928        if (e_hit) break;       /* e_hit set if ENTER can be performed now */
10929        put_block(bp, DIRECTORY_BLOCK); /* otherwise, continue searching dir */
10930  }
10931
10932  /* The whole directory has now been searched. */
10933  if (flag != ENTER) return(ENOENT);
10934
10935  /* This call is for ENTER.  If no free slot has been found so far, try to
10936   * extend directory.
10937   */
10938  if (e_hit == FALSE) { /* directory is full and no room left in last block */
10939        new_slots ++;           /* increase directory size by 1 entry */
10940        if (new_slots == 0) return(EFBIG); /* dir size limited by slot count */
10941        if ( (bp = new_block(ldir_ptr, ldir_ptr->i_size)) == NIL_BUF)
10942                return(err_code);
10943        dp = &bp->b_dir[0];
10944  }
10945
10946  /* 'bp' now points to a directory block with space. 'dp' points to slot. */
10947  copy(dp->d_name, string, NAME_SIZE);
10948  dp->d_inum = *numb;
10949  bp->b_dirt = DIRTY;
```

```
10950        put_block(bp, DIRECTORY_BLOCK);
10951        ldir_ptr->i_modtime = clock_time();
10952        ldir_ptr->i_dirt = DIRTY;
10953        if (new_slots > old_slots)
10954                ldir_ptr->i_size = (file_pos) new_slots * DIR_ENTRY_SIZE;
10955        return(OK);
10956    }
```

```
11000   /* This file performs the MOUNT and UMOUNT system calls.
11001    *
11002    * The entry points into this file are
11003    *   do_mount:  perform the MOUNT system call
11004    *   do_umount: perform the UMOUNT system call
11005    */
11006
11007   #include "../h/const.h"
11008   #include "../h/type.h"
11009   #include "../h/error.h"
11010   #include "const.h"
11011   #include "type.h"
11012   #include "buf.h"
11013   #include "file.h"
11014   #include "fproc.h"
11015   #include "glo.h"
11016   #include "inode.h"
11017   #include "param.h"
11018   #include "super.h"
11019
11020   /*===========================================================================*
11021    *                              do_mount                                     *
11022    *===========================================================================*/
11023   PUBLIC int do_mount()
11024   {
11025   /* Perform the mount(name, mfile, rd_only) system call. */
11026
11027     register struct inode *rip, *root_ip;
11028     register struct super_block *xp, *sp;
11029     register dev_nr dev;
11030     register mask_bits bits;
11031     register int r;
11032     int found;
11033     extern struct inode *get_inode(), *eat_path();
11034     extern dev_nr name_to_dev();
11035
11036     /* Only the super-user may do MOUNT. */
11037     if (!super_user) return(EPERM);
11038
11039     /* If 'name' is not for a block special file, return error. */
11040     if (fetch_name(name1, name1_length, M1) != OK) return(err_code);
11041     if ( (dev = name_to_dev(user_path)) == NO_DEV) return(err_code);
11042
11043     /* Scan super block table to see if dev already mounted & find a free slot.*/
11044     sp = NIL_SUPER;
11045     found = FALSE;
11046     for (xp = &super_block[0]; xp < &super_block[NR_SUPERS]; xp++) {
11047             if (xp->s_dev == dev) found = TRUE;      /* is it mounted already? */
11048             if (xp->s_dev == NO_DEV) sp = xp;        /* record free slot */
11049     }
```

```
11050        if (found) return(EBUSY);        /* already mounted */
11051        if (sp == NIL_SUPER) return(ENFILE);   /* no super block available */
11052
11053        /* Fill in the super block. */
11054        sp->s_dev = dev;                 /* rw_super() needs to know which dev */
11055        rw_super(sp, READING);
11056        sp->s_dev = dev;                 /* however, rw_super() overwrites s_dev */
11057
11058        /* Make a few basic checks to see if super block looks reasonable. */
11059        if (sp->s_magic != SUPER_MAGIC || sp->s_ninodes < 1 || sp->s_nzones < 1 ||
11060                        sp->s_imap_blocks < 1 || sp->s_zmap_blocks < 1) {
11061                sp->s_dev = NO_DEV;
11062                return(EINVAL);
11063        }
11064
11065        /* Now get the inode of the file to be mounted on. */
11066        if (fetch_name(name2, name2_length, M1) != OK) {
11067                sp->s_dev = NO_DEV;
11068                return(err_code);
11069        }
11070        if ( (rip = eat_path(user_path)) == NIL_INODE) {
11071                sp->s_dev = NO_DEV;
11072                return(err_code);
11073        }
11074
11075        /* It may not be busy. */
11076        r = OK;
11077        if (rip->i_count > 1) r = EBUSY;
11078
11079        /* It may not be special. */
11080        bits = rip->i_mode & I_TYPE;
11081        if (bits == I_BLOCK_SPECIAL || bits == I_CHAR_SPECIAL) r = ENOTDIR;
11082
11083        /* Get the root inode of the mounted file system. */
11084        root_ip = NIL_INODE;             /* if 'r' not OK, make sure this is defined */
11085        if (r == OK) {
11086                if ( (root_ip = get_inode(dev, ROOT_INODE)) == NIL_INODE) r = err_code;
11087        }
11088
11089        /* Load the i-node and zone bit maps from the new device. */
11090        if (r == OK) {
11091                if (load_bit_maps(dev) != OK) r = ENFILE;        /* load bit maps */
11092        }
11093
11094        /* If error, return the super block and the inodes. */
11095        if (r != OK) {
11096                sp->s_dev = NO_DEV;
11097                put_inode(rip);
11098                put_inode(root_ip);
11099                return(r);
```

```
11100          }
11101
11102          /* File types of 'rip' and 'root_ip' may not conflict. */
11103          if ( (rip->i_mode & I_TYPE) == I_DIRECTORY &&
11104                  (root_ip->i_mode & I_TYPE) != I_DIRECTORY) r = ENOTDIR;
11105
11106          /* If error, return the super block and both inodes. */
11107          if (r != OK) {
11108                  sp->s_dev = NO_DEV;
11109                  put_inode(rip);
11110                  put_inode(root_ip);
11111                  return(r);
11112          }
11113
11114          /* Nothing else can go wrong.  Perform the mount. */
11115          rip->i_mount = I_MOUNT;          /* this bit says the inode is mounted on */
11116          sp->s_imount = rip;
11117          sp->s_isup = root_ip;
11118          sp->s_rd_only = rd_only;
11119          return(OK);
11120  }


11123  /*===========================================================================*
11124   *                              do_umount                                     *
11125   *===========================================================================*/
11126  PUBLIC int do_umount()
11127  {
11128  /* Perform the umount(name) system call. */
11129
11130          register struct inode *rip;
11131          struct super_block *sp, *sp1;
11132          dev_nr dev;
11133          int count;
11134          extern dev_nr name_to_dev();
11135
11136
11137          /* Only the super-user may do UMOUNT. */
11138          if (!super_user) return(EPERM);
11139
11140          /* If 'name' is not for a block special file, return error. */
11141          if (fetch_name(name, name_length, M3) != OK) return(err_code);
11142          if ( (dev = name_to_dev(user_path)) == NO_DEV) return(err_code);
11143
11144          /* See if the mounted device is busy.  Only 1 inode using it should be
11145           * open -- the root inode -- and that inode only 1 time.
11146           */
11147          count = 0;
11148          for (rip = &inode[0]; rip< &inode[NR_INODES]; rip++)
11149                  if (rip->i_count > 0 && rip->i_dev == dev) count += rip->i_count;
```

```
11150          if (count > 1) return(EBUSY); /* can't umount a busy file system */
11151
11152          /* Find the super block. */
11153          sp = NIL_SUPER;
11154          for (sp1 = &super_block[0]; sp1 < &super_block[NR_SUPERS]; sp1++) {
11155                  if (sp1->s_dev == dev) {
11156                          sp = sp1;
11157                          break;
11158                  }
11159          }
11160          if (sp == NIL_SUPER) return(EINVAL);
11161
11162          /* Release the bit maps, sync the disk, and invalidate cache. */
11163          if (unload_bit_maps(dev) != OK) panic("do_umount", NO_NUM);
11164          do_sync();                       /* force any cached blocks out of memory */
11165          invalidate(dev);                 /* invalidate cache entries for this dev */
11166
11167          /* Finish off the unmount. */
11168          sp->s_imount->i_mount = NO_MOUNT;      /* inode returns to normal */
11169          put_inode(sp->s_imount);         /* release the inode mounted on */
11170          put_inode(sp->s_isup);           /* release the root inode of the mounted fs */
11171          sp->s_imount = NIL_INODE;
11172          sp->s_dev = NO_DEV;
11173          return(OK);
11174  }


11177  /*===========================================================================*
11178   *                              name_to_dev                                  *
11179   *===========================================================================*/
11180  PRIVATE dev_nr name_to_dev(path)
11181  char *path;                             /* pointer to path name */
11182  {
11183  /* Convert the block special file 'path' to a device number.  If 'path'
11184   * is not a block special file, return error code in 'err_code'.
11185   */
11186
11187    register struct inode *rip;
11188    register dev_nr dev;
11189    extern struct inode *eat_path();
11190
11191    /* If 'path' can't be opened, give up immediately. */
11192    if ( (rip = eat_path(path)) == NIL_INODE) return(NO_DEV);
11193
11194    /* If 'path' is not a block special file, return error. */
11195    if ( (rip->i_mode & I_TYPE) != I_BLOCK_SPECIAL) {
11196          err_code = ENOTBLK;
11197          put_inode(rip);
11198          return(NO_DEV);
11199    }
```

```
11200
11201     /* Extract the device number. */
11202     dev = (dev_nr) rip->i_zone[0];
11203     put_inode(rip);
11204     return(dev);
11205   }
```

```
11250    /* This file handles the LINK and UNLINK system calls.  It also deals with
11251     * deallocating the storage used by a file when the last UNLINK is done to a
11252     * file and the blocks must be returned to the free block pool.
11253     *
11254     * The entry points into this file are
11255     *   do_link:    perform the LINK system call
11256     *   do_unlink:  perform the UNLINK system call
11257     *   truncate:   release all the blocks associated with an inode
11258     */

11260    #include "../h/const.h"
11261    #include "../h/type.h"
11262    #include "../h/error.h"
11263    #include "const.h"
11264    #include "type.h"
11265    #include "buf.h"
11266    #include "file.h"
11267    #include "fproc.h"
11268    #include "glo.h"
11269    #include "inode.h"
11270    #include "param.h"

11272    /*===========================================================================*
11273     *                              do_link                                       *
11274     *===========================================================================*/
11275    PUBLIC int do_link()
11276    {
11277    /* Perform the link(name, name2) system call. */

11279      register struct inode *ip, *rip;
11280      register int r;
11281      char string[NAME_SIZE];
11282      struct inode *new_ip;
11283      extern struct inode *advance(), *last_dir(), *eat_path();

11285      /* See if 'name' (file to be linked) exists. */
11286      if (fetch_name(name1, name1_length, M1) != OK) return(err_code);
11287      if ( (rip = eat_path(user_path)) == NIL_INODE) return(err_code);

11289      /* Check to see if the file has maximum number of links already. */
11290      r = OK;
11291      if ( (rip->i_nlinks & BYTE) == MAX_LINKS) r = EMLINK;

11293      /* Only super_user may link to directories. */
11294      if (r == OK)
11295            if ( (rip->i_mode & I_TYPE) == I_DIRECTORY && !super_user) r = EPERM;

11297      /* If error with 'name', return the inode. */
11298      if (r != OK) {
11299            put_inode(rip);
```

```
11300                    return(r);
11301            }
11302
11303            /* Does the final directory of 'name2' exist? */
11304            if (fetch_name(name2, name2_length, M1) != OK) return(err_code);
11305            if ( (ip = last_dir(user_path, string)) == NIL_INODE) r = err_code;
11306
11307            /* If 'name2' exists in full (even if no space) set 'r' to error. */
11308            if (r == OK) {
11309                    if ( (new_ip = advance(ip, string)) == NIL_INODE) {
11310                            r = err_code;
11311                            if (r == ENOENT) r = OK;
11312                    } else {
11313                            put_inode(new_ip);
11314                            r = EEXIST;
11315                    }
11316            }
11317
11318            /* Check for links across devices. */
11319            if (r == OK)
11320                    if (rip->i_dev != ip->i_dev) r = EXDEV;
11321
11322            /* Try to link. */
11323            if (r == OK)
11324                    r = search_dir(ip, string, &rip->i_num, ENTER);
11325
11326            /* If success, register the linking. */
11327            if (r == OK) {
11328                    rip->i_nlinks++;
11329                    rip->i_dirt = DIRTY;
11330            }
11331
11332            /* Done.  Release both inodes. */
11333            put_inode(rip);
11334            put_inode(ip);
11335            return(r);
11336    }


11339    /*===========================================================================*
11340     *                              do_unlink                                     *
11341     *===========================================================================*/
11342    PUBLIC int do_unlink()
11343    {
11344    /* Perform the unlink(name) system call. */
11345
11346      register struct inode *rip, *rlast_dir_ptr;
11347      register int r;
11348      inode_nr numb;
11349      char string[NAME_SIZE];
```

```
11350          extern struct inode *advance(), *last_dir();
11351
11352          /* Get the last directory in the path. */
11353          if (fetch_name(name, name_length, M3) != OK) return(err_code);
11354          if ( (rlast_dir_ptr = last_dir(user_path, string)) == NIL_INODE)
11355                  return(err_code);
11356
11357          /* The last directory exists.  Does the file also exist? */
11358          r = OK;
11359          if ( (rip = advance(rlast_dir_ptr, string)) == NIL_INODE) r = err_code;
11360
11361          /* If error, return inode. */
11362          if (r != OK) {
11363                  put_inode(rlast_dir_ptr);
11364                  return(r);
11365          }
11366
11367          /* See if the file is a directory. */
11368          if ( (rip->i_mode & I_TYPE) == I_DIRECTORY && !super_user)
11369                  r = EPERM;                    /* only super_user can unlink directory */
11370          if (r == OK)
11371                  r = search_dir(rlast_dir_ptr, string, &numb, DELETE);
11372
11373          if (r == OK) {
11374                  rip->i_nlinks--;
11375                  rip->i_dirt = DIRTY;
11376          }
11377
11378          /* If unlink was possible, it has been done, otherwise it has not. */
11379          put_inode(rip);
11380          put_inode(rlast_dir_ptr);
11381          return(r);
11382  }


11385  /*===========================================================================*
11386   *                              truncate                                     *
11387   *===========================================================================*/
11388  PUBLIC truncate(rip)
11389  register struct inode *rip;      /* pointer to inode to be truncated */
11390  {
11391  /* Remove all the zones from the inode 'rip' and mark it dirty. */
11392
11393    register file_pos position;
11394    register zone_type zone_size;
11395    register block_nr b;
11396    register zone_nr z, *iz;
11397    register int scale;
11398    register struct buf *bp;
11399    register dev_nr dev;
```

```
11400       extern struct buf *get_block();
11401       extern block_nr read_map();
11402
11403       dev = rip->i_dev;              /* device on which inode resides */
11404       scale = scale_factor(rip);
11405       zone_size = (zone_type) BLOCK_SIZE << scale;
11406       if (rip->i_pipe == I_PIPE) rip->i_size = PIPE_SIZE;   /* pipes can shrink */
11407
11408       /* Step through the file a zone at a time, finding and freeing the zones. */
11409       for (position = 0; position < rip->i_size; position += zone_size) {
11410             if ( (b = read_map(rip, position)) != NO_BLOCK) {
11411                   z = (zone_nr) b >> scale;
11412                   free_zone(dev, z);
11413             }
11414       }
11415
11416       /* All the data zones have been freed.  Now free the indirect zones. */
11417       free_zone(dev, rip->i_zone[NR_DZONE_NUM]);    /* single indirect zone */
11418       if ( (z = rip->i_zone[NR_DZONE_NUM+1]) != NO_ZONE) {
11419             b = (block_nr) z << scale;
11420             bp = get_block(dev, b, NORMAL); /* get double indirect zone */
11421             for (iz = &bp->b_ind[0]; iz < &bp->b_ind[NR_INDIRECTS]; iz++) {
11422                   free_zone(dev, *iz);
11423             }
11424
11425             /* Now free the double indirect zone itself. */
11426             put_block(bp, INDIRECT_BLOCK);
11427             free_zone(dev, z);
11428       }
11429
11430       /* The inode being truncated might currently be open, so certain fields must
11431        * be cleared immediately, even though these fields are also cleared by
11432        * alloc_inode(). The function wipe_inode() does the dirty work in both cases.
11433        */
11434       wipe_inode(rip);
11435 }
```

```
11450   /* This file contains the code for performing four system calls relating to
11451    * status and directories.
11452    *
11453    * The entry points into this file are
11454    *   do_chdir:  perform the CHDIR system call
11455    *   do_chroot: perform the CHROOT system call
11456    *   do_stat:   perform the STAT system call
11457    *   do_fstat:  perform the FSTAT system call
11458    */
11459
11460   #include "../h/const.h"
11461   #include "../h/type.h"
11462   #include "../h/error.h"
11463   #include "../h/stat.h"
11464   #include "const.h"
11465   #include "type.h"
11466   #include "file.h"
11467   #include "fproc.h"
11468   #include "glo.h"
11469   #include "inode.h"
11470   #include "param.h"
11471
11472   /*===========================================================================*
11473    *                              do_chdir                                      *
11474    *===========================================================================*/
11475   PUBLIC int do_chdir()
11476   {
11477   /* Change directory.  This function is  also called by MM to simulate a chdir
11478    * in order to do EXEC, etc.
11479    */
11480
11481     register struct fproc *rfp;
11482
11483     if (who == MM_PROC_NR) {
11484          rfp = &fproc[slot1];
11485          put_inode(fp->fp_workdir);
11486          fp->fp_workdir = (cd_flag ? fp->fp_rootdir : rfp->fp_workdir);
11487          dup_inode(fp->fp_workdir);
11488          fp->fp_effuid = (cd_flag ? SUPER_USER : rfp->fp_effuid);
11489          return(OK);
11490     }
11491
11492   /* Perform the chdir(name) system call. */
11493     return change(&fp->fp_workdir, name, name_length);
11494   }
11495
11496
11497   /*===========================================================================*
11498    *                              do_chroot                                     *
11499    *===========================================================================*/
```

```
11500    PUBLIC int do_chroot()
11501    {
11502    /* Perform the chroot(name) system call. */
11503
11504      register int r;
11505
11506      if (!super_user) return(EPERM);          /* only su may chroot() */
11507      r = change(&fp->fp_rootdir, name, name_length);
11508      return(r);
11509    }


11512    /*===========================================================================*
11513     *                              change                                       *
11514     *===========================================================================*/
11515    PRIVATE int change(iip, name_ptr, len)
11516    struct inode **iip;              /* pointer to the inode pointer for the dir */
11517    char *name_ptr;                  /* pointer to the directory name to change to */
11518    int len;                         /* length of the directory name string */
11519    {
11520    /* Do the actual work for chdir() and chroot(). */
11521
11522      struct inode *rip;
11523      register int r;
11524      extern struct inode *eat_path();
11525
11526      /* Try to open the new directory. */
11527      if (fetch_name(name_ptr, len, M3) != OK) return(err_code);
11528      if ( (rip = eat_path(user_path)) == NIL_INODE) return(err_code);
11529
11530      /* It must be a directory and also be searchable. */
11531      if ( (rip->i_mode & I_TYPE) != I_DIRECTORY)
11532            r = ENOTDIR;
11533      else
11534            r = forbidden(rip, X_BIT, 0);    /* check if dir is searchable */
11535
11536      /* If error, return inode. */
11537      if (r != OK) {
11538            put_inode(rip);
11539            return(r);
11540      }
11541
11542      /* Everything is OK.  Make the change. */
11543      put_inode(*iip);                 /* release the old directory */
11544      *iip = rip;                      /* acquire the new one */
11545      return(OK);
11546    }
```

```
11550   /*===========================================================================*
11551    *                              do_stat                                      *
11552    *===========================================================================*/
11553   PUBLIC int do_stat()
11554   {
11555   /* Perform the stat(name, buf) system call. */
11556
11557     register struct inode *rip;
11558     register int r;
11559     extern struct inode *eat_path();
11560
11561     /* Both stat() and fstat() use the same routine to do the real work.  That
11562      * routine expects an inode, so acquire it temporarily.
11563      */
11564     if (fetch_name(name1, name1_length, M1) != OK) return(err_code);
11565     if ( (rip = eat_path(user_path)) == NIL_INODE) return(err_code);
11566     r = stat_inode(rip, NIL_FILP, name2); /* actually do the work.*/
11567     put_inode(rip);                 /* release the inode */
11568     return(r);
11569   }


11572   /*===========================================================================*
11573    *                              do_fstat                                     *
11574    *===========================================================================*/
11575   PUBLIC int do_fstat()
11576   {
11577   /* Perform the fstat(fd, buf) system call. */
11578
11579     register struct filp *rfilp;
11580     extern struct filp *get_filp();
11581
11582     /* Is the file descriptor valid? */
11583     if ( (rfilp = get_filp(fd)) == NIL_FILP) return(err_code);
11584
11585     return(stat_inode(rfilp->filp_ino, rfilp, buffer));
11586   }


11589   /*===========================================================================*
11590    *                              stat_inode                                   *
11591    *===========================================================================*/
11592   PRIVATE int stat_inode(rip, fil_ptr, user_addr)
11593   register struct inode *rip;     /* pointer to inode to stat */
11594   struct filp *fil_ptr;           /* filp pointer, supplied by 'fstat' */
11595   char *user_addr;                        /* user space address where stat buf goes */
11596   {
11597   /* Common code for stat and fstat system calls. */
11598
11599     register struct stat *stp;
```

```
11600        struct stat statbuf;
11601        int r;
11602        vir_bytes v;
11603
11604        /* Fill in the statbuf struct. */
11605        stp = &statbuf;                  /* set up pointer to the buffer */
11606        stp->st_dev = (int) rip->i_dev;
11607        stp->st_ino = rip->i_num;
11608        stp->st_mode = rip->i_mode;
11609        stp->st_nlink = rip->i_nlinks & BYTE;
11610        stp->st_uid = rip->i_uid;
11611        stp->st_gid = rip->i_gid & BYTE;
11612        stp->st_rdev = rip->i_zone[0];
11613        stp->st_size = rip->i_size;
11614        if (  (rip->i_pipe == I_PIPE) &&       /* IF it is a pipe */
11615             (fil_ptr != NIL_FILP) &&          /* AND it was fstat */
11616             (fil_ptr->filp_mode == R_BIT))  /* on the reading end, */
11617               stp->st_size -= fil_ptr->filp_pos; /* adjust the visible size. */
11618        stp->st_atime = rip->i_modtime;
11619        stp->st_mtime = rip->i_modtime;
11620        stp->st_ctime = rip->i_modtime;
11621
11622        /* Copy the struct to user space. */
11623        v = (vir_bytes) user_addr;
11624        r = rw_user(D, who, v, (vir_bytes) sizeof statbuf, (char *) stp, TO_USER);
11625        return(r);
11626    }
```

```
11650   /* This file deals with protection in the file system.  It contains the code
11651    * for four system calls that relate to protection.
11652    *
11653    * The entry points into this file are
11654    *   do_chmod:  perform the CHMOD system call
11655    *   do_chown:  perform the CHOWN system call
11656    *   do_umask:  perform the UMASK system call
11657    *   do_access: perform the ACCESS system call
11658    *   forbidden: check to see if a given access is allowed on a given inode
11659    */
11660
11661   #include "../h/const.h"
11662   #include "../h/type.h"
11663   #include "../h/error.h"
11664   #include "const.h"
11665   #include "type.h"
11666   #include "buf.h"
11667   #include "file.h"
11668   #include "fproc.h"
11669   #include "glo.h"
11670   #include "inode.h"
11671   #include "param.h"
11672   #include "super.h"
11673
11674   /*===========================================================================*
11675    *                              do_chmod                                      *
11676    *===========================================================================*/
11677   PUBLIC int do_chmod()
11678   {
11679   /* Perform the chmod(name, mode) system call. */
11680
11681     register struct inode *rip;
11682     register int r;
11683     extern struct inode *eat_path();
11684
11685     /* Temporarily open the file. */
11686     if (fetch_name(name, name_length, M3) != OK) return(err_code);
11687     if ( (rip = eat_path(user_path)) == NIL_INODE) return(err_code);
11688
11689     /* Only the owner or the super_user may change the mode of a file.
11690      * No one may change the mode of a file on a read-only file system.
11691      */
11692     if (rip->i_uid != fp->fp_effuid && !super_user)
11693           r = EPERM;
11694     else
11695           r = read_only(rip);
11696
11697     /* If error, return inode. */
11698     if (r != OK) {
11699           put_inode(rip);
```

```
11700                    return(r);
11701            }
11702
11703            /* Now make the change. */
11704            rip->i_mode = (rip->i_mode & ~ALL_MODES) | (mode & ALL_MODES);
11705            rip->i_dirt = DIRTY;
11706
11707            put_inode(rip);
11708            return(OK);
11709        }


11712    /*===========================================================================*
11713     *                              do_chown                                     *
11714     *===========================================================================*/
11715    PUBLIC int do_chown()
11716    {
11717    /* Perform the chown(name, owner, group) system call. */
11718
11719        register struct inode *rip;
11720        register int r;
11721        extern struct inode *eat_path();
11722
11723        /* Only the super_user may perform the chown() call. */
11724        if (!super_user) return(EPERM);
11725
11726        /* Temporarily open the file. */
11727        if (fetch_name(name1, name1_length, M1) != OK) return(err_code);
11728        if ( (rip = eat_path(user_path)) == NIL_INODE) return(err_code);
11729
11730        /* Not permitted to change the owner of a file on a read-only file sys. */
11731        r = read_only(rip);
11732        if (r == OK) {
11733                rip->i_uid = owner;
11734                rip->i_gid = group;
11735                rip->i_dirt = DIRTY;
11736        }
11737
11738        put_inode(rip);
11739        return(r);
11740    }


11743    /*===========================================================================*
11744     *                              do_umask                                     *
11745     *===========================================================================*/
11746    PUBLIC int do_umask()
11747    {
11748    /* Perform the umask(co_mode) system call. */
11749        register mask_bits r;
```

```
11750
11751     r = ~fp->fp_umask;                /* set 'r' to complement of old mask */
11752     fp->fp_umask = ~(co_mode & RWX_MODES);
11753     return(r);                        /* return complement of old mask */
11754   }


11757  /*===========================================================================*
11758   *                              do_access                                     *
11759   *===========================================================================*/
11760  PUBLIC int do_access()
11761  {
11762  /* Perform the access(name, mode) system call. */
11763
11764    struct inode *rip;
11765    register int r;
11766    extern struct inode *eat_path();
11767
11768    /* Temporarily open the file whose access is to be checked. */
11769    if (fetch_name(name, name_length, M3) != OK) return(err_code);
11770    if ( (rip = eat_path(user_path)) == NIL_INODE) return(err_code);
11771
11772    /* Now check the permissions. */
11773    r = forbidden(rip, (mask_bits) mode, 1);
11774    put_inode(rip);
11775    return(r);
11776  }


11779  /*===========================================================================*
11780   *                              forbidden                                     *
11781   *===========================================================================*/
11782  PUBLIC int forbidden(rip, access_desired, real_uid)
11783  register struct inode *rip;     /* pointer to inode to be checked */
11784  mask_bits access_desired;       /* RWX bits */
11785  int real_uid;                   /* set iff real uid to be tested */
11786  {
11787  /* Given a pointer to an inode, 'rip', and the accessed desired, determine
11788   * if the access is allowed, and if not why not.  The routine looks up the
11789   * caller's uid in the 'fproc' table.  If the access is allowed, OK is returned
11790   * if it is forbidden, EACCES is returned.
11791   */
11792
11793    register mask_bits bits, perm_bits, xmask;
11794    int r, shift, test_uid, test_gid;
11795
11796    /* Isolate the relevant rwx bits from the mode. */
11797    bits = rip->i_mode;
11798    test_uid = (real_uid ? fp->fp_realuid : fp->fp_effuid);
11799    test_gid = (real_uid ? fp->fp_realgid : fp->fp_effgid);
```

```
11800          if (super_user) {
11801                perm_bits = 07;
11802          } else {
11803                if (test_uid == rip->i_uid) shift = 6;       /* owner */
11804                else if (test_gid == rip->i_gid ) shift = 3;  /* group */
11805                else shift = 0;                                /* other */
11806                perm_bits = (bits >> shift) & 07;
11807          }
11808
11809          /* If access desired is not a subset of what is allowed, it is refused. */
11810          r = OK;
11811          if ((perm_bits | access_desired) != perm_bits) r = EACCES;
11812
11813          /* If none of the X bits are on, not even the super-user can execute it. */
11814          xmask = (X_BIT << 6) | (X_BIT << 3) | X_BIT;  /* all 3 X bits */
11815          if ( (access_desired & X_BIT) && (bits & xmask) == 0) r = EACCES;
11816
11817          /* Check to see if someone is trying to write on a file system that is
11818           * mounted read-only.
11819           */
11820          if (r == OK)
11821                if (access_desired & W_BIT) r = read_only(rip);
11822
11823          return(r);
11824    }


11827    /*===========================================================================*
11828     *                              read_only                                    *
11829     *===========================================================================*/
11830    PRIVATE int read_only(ip)
11831    struct inode *ip;               /* ptr to inode whose file sys is to be cked */
11832    {
11833    /* Check to see if the file system on which the inode 'ip' resides is mounted
11834     * read only.  If so, return EROFS, else return OK.
11835     */
11836
11837      register struct super_block *sp;
11838      extern struct super_block *get_super();
11839
11840      sp = get_super(ip->i_dev);
11841      return(sp->s_rd_only ? EROFS : OK);
11842    }
```

```
11850   /* This file takes care of those system calls that deal with time.
11851    *
11852    * The entry points into this file are
11853    *   do_utime:  perform the UTIME system call
11854    *   do_time:   perform the TIME system call
11855    *   do_stime:  perform the STIME system call
11856    *   do_tims:   perform the TIMES system call
11857    */
11858
11859   #include "../h/const.h"
11860   #include "../h/type.h"
11861   #include "../h/callnr.h"
11862   #include "../h/com.h"
11863   #include "../h/error.h"
11864   #include "const.h"
11865   #include "type.h"
11866   #include "file.h"
11867   #include "fproc.h"
11868   #include "glo.h"
11869   #include "inode.h"
11870   #include "param.h"
11871
11872   PRIVATE message clock_mess;
11873
11874   /*===========================================================================*
11875    *                              do_utime                                      *
11876    *===========================================================================*/
11877   PUBLIC int do_utime()
11878   {
11879   /* Perform the utime(name, timep) system call. */
11880
11881     register struct inode *rip;
11882     register int r;
11883     extern struct inode *eat_path();
11884
11885     /* Temporarily open the file. */
11886     if (fetch_name(utime_file, utime_length, M1) != OK) return(err_code);
11887     if ( (rip = eat_path(user_path)) == NIL_INODE) return(err_code);
11888
11889     /* Only the owner of a file or the super_user can change its time. */
11890     r = OK;
11891     if (rip->i_uid != fp->fp_effuid && !super_user) r = EPERM;
11892     if (r == OK) {
11893           rip->i_modtime = update_time;
11894           rip->i_dirt = DIRTY;
11895     }
11896
11897     put_inode(rip);
11898     return(r);
11899   }
```

```
11902    /*===========================================================================*
11903     *                              do_time                                       *
11904     *===========================================================================*/
11905    PUBLIC int do_time()
11906
11907    {
11908    /* Perform the time(tp) system call. */
11909
11910      extern real_time clock_time();
11911
11912      reply_l1 = clock_time();         /* return time in seconds */
11913      return(OK);
11914    }


11917    /*===========================================================================*
11918     *                              do_stime                                      *
11919     *===========================================================================*/
11920    PUBLIC int do_stime()
11921    {
11922    /* Perform the stime(tp) system call. */
11923
11924      register int k;
11925
11926      if (!super_user) return(EPERM);
11927      clock_mess.m_type = SET_TIME;
11928      clock_mess.NEW_TIME = (long) tp;
11929      if ( (k = sendrec(CLOCK, &clock_mess)) != OK) panic("do_stime error", k);
11930      return (OK);
11931    }


11934    /*===========================================================================*
11935     *                              do_tims                                       *
11936     *===========================================================================*/
11937    PUBLIC int do_tims()
11938    {
11939    /* Perform the times(buffer) system call. */
11940
11941      real_time t[4];
11942
11943      sys_times(who, t);
11944      reply_t1 = t[0];
11945      reply_t2 = t[1];
11946      reply_t3 = t[2];
11947      reply_t4 = t[3];
11948      return(OK);
11949    }
```

```
11950   /* This file contains a collection of miscellaneous procedures.  Some of them
11951    * perform simple system calls.  Some others do a little part of system calls
11952    * that are mostly performed by the Memory Manager.
11953    *
11954    * The entry points into this file are
11955    *   do_dup:    perform the DUP system call
11956    *   do_sync:   perform the SYNC system call
11957    *   do_fork:   adjust the tables after MM has performed a FORK system call
11958    *   do_exit:   a process has exited; note that in the tables
11959    *   do_set:    set uid or gid for some process
11960    *   do_revive: revive a process that was waiting for something (e.g. TTY)
11961    */
11962
11963   #include "../h/const.h"
11964   #include "../h/type.h"
11965   #include "../h/callnr.h"
11966   #include "../h/com.h"
11967   #include "../h/error.h"
11968   #include "const.h"
11969   #include "type.h"
11970   #include "buf.h"
11971   #include "file.h"
11972   #include "fproc.h"
11973   #include "glo.h"
11974   #include "inode.h"
11975   #include "param.h"
11976   #include "super.h"
11977
11978   /*===========================================================================*
11979    *                              do_dup                                       *
11980    *===========================================================================*/
11981   PUBLIC int do_dup()
11982   {
11983   /* Perform the dup(fd) or dup(fd,fd2) system call. */
11984
11985     register int rfd;
11986     register struct fproc *rfp;
11987     struct filp *dummy;
11988     int r;
11989     extern struct filp *get_filp();
11990
11991     /* Is the file descriptor valid? */
11992     rfd = fd & ~DUP_MASK;          /* kill off dup2 bit, if on */
11993     rfp = fp;
11994     if (get_filp(rfd) == NIL_FILP) return(err_code);
11995
11996     /* Distinguish between dup and dup2. */
11997     if (fd == rfd) {                        /* bit not on */
11998         /* dup(fd) */
11999         if ( (r = get_fd(0, &fd2, &dummy)) != OK) return(r);
```

```
12000          } else {
12001                  /* dup2(fd, fd2) */
12002                  if (fd2 < 0 || fd2 >= NR_FDS) return(EBADF);
12003                  if (rfd == fd2) return(fd2);     /* ignore the call: dup2(x, x) */
12004                  fd = fd2;                   /* prepare to close fd2 */
12005                  do_close();                 /* cannot fail */
12006          }
12007
12008          /* Success. Set up new file descriptors. */
12009          rfp->fp_filp[fd2] = rfp->fp_filp[rfd];
12010          rfp->fp_filp[fd2]->filp_count++;
12011          return(fd2);
12012  }


12015  /*===========================================================================*
12016   *                              do_sync                                      *
12017   *===========================================================================*/
12018  PUBLIC int do_sync()
12019  {
12020  /* Perform the sync() system call.  Flush all the tables. */
12021
12022    register struct inode *rip;
12023    register struct buf *bp;
12024    register struct super_block *sp;
12025    extern real_time clock_time();
12026    extern struct super_block *get_super();
12027
12028    /* The order in which the various tables are flushed is critical.  The
12029     * blocks must be flushed last, since rw_inode() and rw_super() leave their
12030     * results in the block cache.
12031     */
12032
12033    /* Update the time in the root super_block. */
12034    sp = get_super(ROOT_DEV);
12035    sp->s_time = clock_time();
12036    sp->s_dirt = DIRTY;
12037
12038    /* Write all the dirty inodes to the disk. */
12039    for (rip = &inode[0]; rip < &inode[NR_INODES]; rip++)
12040          if (rip->i_count > 0 && rip->i_dirt == DIRTY) rw_inode(rip, WRITING);
12041
12042    /* Write all the dirty super_blocks to the disk. */
12043    for (sp = &super_block[0]; sp < &super_block[NR_SUPERS]; sp++)
12044          if (sp->s_dev != NO_DEV && sp->s_dirt == DIRTY) rw_super(sp, WRITING);
12045
12046    /* Write all the dirty blocks to the disk. */
12047    for (bp = &buf[0]; bp < &buf[NR_BUFS]; bp++)
12048          if (bp->b_dev != NO_DEV && bp->b_dirt == DIRTY) rw_block(bp, WRITING);
12049
```

```
12050        return(OK);              /* sync() can't fail */
12051     }


12054     /*===========================================================================*
12055      *                              do_fork                                      *
12056      *===========================================================================*/
12057     PUBLIC int do_fork()
12058     {
12059     /* Perform those aspects of the fork() system call that relate to files.
12060      * In particular, let the child inherit its parents file descriptors.
12061      * The parent and child parameters tell who forked off whom. The file
12062      * system uses the same slot numbers as the kernel.  Only MM makes this call.
12063      */
12064
12065       register struct fproc *cp;
12066       register char *sptr, *dptr;
12067       int i;
12068
12069       /* Only MM may make this call directly. */
12070       if (who != MM_PROC_NR) return(ERROR);
12071
12072       /* Copy the parent's fproc struct to the child. */
12073       sptr = (char *) &fproc[parent];          /* pointer to parent's 'fproc' struct */
12074       dptr = (char *) &fproc[child];           /* pointer to child's 'fproc' struct */
12075       i = sizeof(struct fproc);                /* how many bytes to copy */
12076       while (i--) *dptr++ = *sptr++;           /* fproc[child] = fproc[parent] */
12077
12078       /* Increase the counters in the 'filp' table. */
12079       cp = &fproc[child];
12080       for (i = 0; i < NR_FDS; i++)
12081             if (cp->fp_filp[i] != NIL_FILP) cp->fp_filp[i]->filp_count++;
12082
12083       /* Record the fact that both root and working dir have another user. */
12084       dup_inode(cp->fp_rootdir);
12085       dup_inode(cp->fp_workdir);
12086       return(OK);
12087     }


12090     /*===========================================================================*
12091      *                              do_exit                                      *
12092      *===========================================================================*/
12093     PUBLIC int do_exit()
12094     {
12095     /* Perform the file system portion of the exit(status) system call. */
12096
12097       register int i;
12098
12099       /* Only MM may do the EXIT call directly. */
```

```
12100          if (who != MM_PROC_NR) return(ERROR);
12101
12102          /* Nevertheless, pretend that the call came from the user. */
12103          fp = &fproc[slot1];              /* get_filp() needs 'fp' */
12104
12105          /* Loop on file descriptors, closing any that are open. */
12106          for (i=0; i < NR_FDS; i++) {
12107                  fd = i;
12108                  do_close();
12109          }
12110
12111          /* Release root and working directories. */
12112          put_inode(fp->fp_rootdir);
12113          put_inode(fp->fp_workdir);
12114
12115          if (fp->fp_suspended == SUSPENDED && fp->fp_task == XPIPE) susp_count--;
12116          fp->fp_suspended = NOT_SUSPENDED;
12117          return(OK);
12118    }


12121    /*===========================================================================*
12122     *                              do_set                                       *
12123     *===========================================================================*/
12124    PUBLIC int do_set()
12125    {
12126    /* Set uid or gid field. */
12127
12128      register struct fproc *tfp;
12129
12130      /* Only MM may make this call directly. */
12131      if (who != MM_PROC_NR) return(ERROR);
12132
12133      tfp = &fproc[slot1];
12134      if (fs_call == SETUID) {
12135            tfp->fp_realuid = (uid) real_user_id;
12136            tfp->fp_effuid =  (uid) eff_user_id;
12137      }
12138      if (fs_call == SETGID) {
12139            tfp->fp_effgid =  (gid) eff_grp_id;
12140            tfp->fp_realgid = (gid) real_grp_id;
12141      }
12142      return(OK);
12143    }


12146    /*===========================================================================*
12147     *                              do_revive                                   *
12148     *===========================================================================*/
12149    PUBLIC int do_revive()
```

```
12150    {
12151    /* A task, typically TTY, has now gotten the characters that were needed for a
12152     * previous read. The process did not get a reply when it made the call.
12153     * Instead it was suspended. Now we can send the reply to wake it up. This
12154     * business has to be done carefully, since the incoming message is from
12155     * a task (to which no reply can be sent), and the reply must go to a process
12156     * that blocked earlier. The reply to the caller is inhibited by setting the
12157     * 'dont_reply' flag, and the reply to the blocked process is done explicitly
12158     * in revive().
12159     */
12160
12161      if (who > 0) return(EPERM);
12162      revive(m.REP_PROC_NR, m.REP_STATUS);
12163      dont_reply = TRUE;              /* don't reply to the TTY task */
12164      return(OK);
12165    }
```

```
12200   /* When a needed block is not in the cache, it must be fetched from the disk.
12201    * Special character files also require I/O.  The routines for these are here.
12202    *
12203    * The entry points in this file are:
12204    *   dev_open:   called when a special file is opened
12205    *   dev_close:  called when a special file is closed
12206    *   dev_io:     perform a read or write on a block or character device
12207    *   do_ioctl:   perform the IOCTL system call
12208    *   rw_dev:     procedure that actually calls the kernel tasks
12209    *   rw_dev2:    procedure that actually calls task for /dev/tty
12210    *   no_call:    dummy procedure (e.g., used when device need not be opened)
12211    */

12213   #include "../h/const.h"
12214   #include "../h/type.h"
12215   #include "../h/com.h"
12216   #include "../h/error.h"
12217   #include "const.h"
12218   #include "type.h"
12219   #include "dev.h"
12220   #include "file.h"
12221   #include "fproc.h"
12222   #include "glo.h"
12223   #include "inode.h"
12224   #include "param.h"

12226   PRIVATE message dev_mess;
12227   PRIVATE major, minor, task;
12228   extern max_major;

12230   /*===========================================================================*
12231    *                              dev_open                                     *
12232    *===========================================================================*/
12233   PUBLIC int dev_open(dev, mod)
12234   dev_nr dev;                     /* which device to open */
12235   int mod;                        /* how to open it */
12236   {
12237   /* Special files may need special processing upon open. */

12239     find_dev(dev);
12240     (*dmap[major].dmap_open)(task, &dev_mess);
12241     return(dev_mess.REP_STATUS);
12242   }


12245   /*===========================================================================*
12246    *                              dev_close                                    *
12247    *===========================================================================*/
12248   PUBLIC dev_close(dev)
12249   dev_nr dev;                     /* which device to close */
```

```
12250     {
12251     /* This procedure can be used when a special file needs to be closed. */
12252
12253       find_dev(dev);
12254       (*dmap[major].dmap_close)(task, &dev_mess);
12255     }


12258     /*===========================================================================*
12259      *                              dev_io                                       *
12260      *===========================================================================*/
12261     PUBLIC int dev_io(rw_flag, dev, pos, bytes, proc, buff)
12262     int rw_flag;                        /* READING or WRITING */
12263     dev_nr dev;                         /* major-minor device number */
12264     long pos;                           /* byte position */
12265     int bytes;                          /* how many bytes to transfer */
12266     int proc;                           /* in whose address space is buff? */
12267     char *buff;                         /* virtual address of the buffer */
12268     {
12269     /* Read or write from a device.  The parameter 'dev' tells which one. */
12270
12271       find_dev(dev);
12272
12273       /* Set up the message passed to task. */
12274       dev_mess.m_type   = (rw_flag == READING ? DISK_READ : DISK_WRITE);
12275       dev_mess.DEVICE   = (dev >> MINOR) & BYTE;
12276       dev_mess.POSITION = pos;
12277       dev_mess.PROC_NR  = proc;
12278       dev_mess.ADDRESS  = buff;
12279       dev_mess.COUNT    = bytes;
12280
12281       /* Call the task. */
12282       (*dmap[major].dmap_rw)(task, &dev_mess);
12283
12284       /* Task has completed.  See if call completed. */
12285       if (dev_mess.REP_STATUS == SUSPEND) suspend(task);      /* suspend user */
12286
12287       return(dev_mess.REP_STATUS);
12288     }


12291     /*===========================================================================*
12292      *                              do_ioctl                                     *
12293      *===========================================================================*/
12294     PUBLIC do_ioctl()
12295     {
12296     /* Perform the ioctl(ls_fd, request, argx) system call (uses m2 fmt). */
12297
12298       struct filp *f;
12299       register struct inode *rip;
```

```
12300        extern struct filp *get_filp();
12301
12302        if ( (f = get_filp(ls_fd)) == NIL_FILP) return(err_code);
12303        rip = f->filp_ino;             /* get inode pointer */
12304        if ( (rip->i_mode & I_TYPE) != I_CHAR_SPECIAL) return(ENOTTY);
12305        find_dev(rip->i_zone[0]);
12306
12307        dev_mess.m_type  = TTY_IOCTL;
12308        dev_mess.PROC_NR = who;
12309        dev_mess.TTY_LINE = minor;
12310        dev_mess.TTY_REQUEST = m.TTY_REQUEST;
12311        dev_mess.TTY_SPEK = m.TTY_SPEK;
12312        dev_mess.TTY_FLAGS = m.TTY_FLAGS;
12313
12314        /* Call the task. */
12315        (*dmap[major].dmap_rw)(task, &dev_mess);
12316
12317        /* Task has completed.  See if call completed. */
12318        if (dev_mess.m_type == SUSPEND) suspend(task);  /* User must be suspended. */
12319        m1.TTY_SPEK = dev_mess.TTY_SPEK;       /* erase and kill */
12320        m1.TTY_FLAGS = dev_mess.TTY_FLAGS;     /* flags */
12321        return(dev_mess.REP_STATUS);
12322    }


12325   /*===========================================================================*
12326    *                              find_dev                                      *
12327    *===========================================================================*/
12328   PRIVATE find_dev(dev)
12329   dev_nr dev;                          /* device */
12330   {
12331   /* Extract the major and minor device number from the parameter. */
12332
12333     major = (dev >> MAJOR) & BYTE;      /* major device number */
12334     minor = (dev >> MINOR) & BYTE;      /* minor device number */
12335     if (major == 0 || major >= max_major) panic("bad major dev", major);
12336     task = dmap[major].dmap_task; /* which task services the device */
12337     dev_mess.DEVICE = minor;
12338    }


12341   /*===========================================================================*
12342    *                              rw_dev                                        *
12343    *===========================================================================*/
12344   PUBLIC rw_dev(task_nr, mess_ptr)
12345   int task_nr;                         /* which task to call */
12346   message *mess_ptr;                   /* pointer to message for task */
12347   {
12348   /* All file system I/O ultimately comes down to I/O on major/minor device
12349    * pairs.  These lead to calls on the following routines via the dmap table.
```

```
12350      */
12351
12352      int proc_nr;
12353
12354      proc_nr = mess_ptr->PROC_NR;
12355
12356      if (sendrec(task_nr, mess_ptr) != OK) panic("rw_dev: can't send", NO_NUM);
12357      while (mess_ptr->REP_PROC_NR != proc_nr) {
12358              /* Instead of the reply to this request, we got a message for an
12359               * earlier request.  Handle it and go receive again.
12360               */
12361              revive(mess_ptr->REP_PROC_NR, mess_ptr->REP_STATUS);
12362              receive(task_nr, mess_ptr);
12363      }
12364  }


12367  /*===========================================================================*
12368   *                              rw_dev2                                       *
12369   *===========================================================================*/
12370  PUBLIC rw_dev2(dummy, mess_ptr)
12371  int dummy;                               /* not used - for compatibility with rw_dev() */
12372  message *mess_ptr;                       /* pointer to message for task */
12373  {
12374  /* This routine is only called for one device, namely /dev/tty.  It's job
12375   * is to change the message to use the controlling terminal, instead of the
12376   * major/minor pair for /dev/tty itself.
12377   */
12378
12379      int task_nr, major_device;
12380
12381      major_device = (fp->fs_tty >> MAJOR) & BYTE;
12382      task_nr = dmap[major_device].dmap_task;          /* task for controlling tty */
12383      mess_ptr->DEVICE = (fp->fs_tty >> MINOR) & BYTE;
12384      rw_dev(task_nr, mess_ptr);
12385  }


12388  /*===========================================================================*
12389   *                              no_call                                       *
12390   *===========================================================================*/
12391  PUBLIC int no_call(task_nr, m_ptr)
12392  int task_nr;                             /* which task */
12393  message *m_ptr;                          /* message pointer */
12394  {
12395  /* Null operation always succeeds. */
12396
12397      m_ptr->REP_STATUS = OK;
12398  }
```

```
12400   /* This file contains a few general purpose utility routines.
12401    *
12402    * The entry points into this file are
12403    *   clock_time:   ask the clock task for the real time
12404    *   cmp_string:   compare two strings (e.g., while searching directory)
12405    *   copy:         copy a string
12406    *   fetch_name:   go get a path name from user space
12407    *   no_sys:       reject a system call that FS does not handle
12408    *   panic:        something awful has occurred;  MINIX cannot continue
12409    */
12410
12411   #include "../h/const.h"
12412   #include "../h/type.h"
12413   #include "../h/com.h"
12414   #include "../h/error.h"
12415   #include "const.h"
12416   #include "type.h"
12417   #include "buf.h"
12418   #include "file.h"
12419   #include "fproc.h"
12420   #include "glo.h"
12421   #include "inode.h"
12422   #include "param.h"
12423   #include "super.h"
12424
12425   PRIVATE int panicking;              /* inhibits recursive panics during sync */
12426   PRIVATE message clock_mess;
12427
12428   /*===========================================================================*
12429    *                              clock_time                                   *
12430    *===========================================================================*/
12431   PUBLIC real_time clock_time()
12432   {
12433   /* This routine returns the time in seconds since 1.1.1970. */
12434
12435     register int k;
12436     register struct super_block *sp;
12437     extern struct super_block *get_super();
12438
12439     clock_mess.m_type = GET_TIME;
12440     if ( (k = sendrec(CLOCK, &clock_mess)) != OK) panic("clock_time err", k);
12441
12442     /* Since we now have the time, update the super block.  It is almost free. */
12443     sp = get_super(ROOT_DEV);
12444     sp->s_time = clock_mess.NEW_TIME;       /* update super block time */
12445     sp->s_dirt = DIRTY;
12446
12447     return (real_time) clock_mess.NEW_TIME;
12448   }
```

```
12451   /*===========================================================================*
12452    *                              cmp_string                                   *
12453    *===========================================================================*/
12454   PUBLIC int cmp_string(rsp1, rsp2, n)
12455   register char *rsp1, *rsp2;        /* pointers to the two strings */
12456   register int n;                    /* string length */
12457   {
12458   /* Compare two strings of length 'n'.  If they are the same, return 1.
12459    * If they differ, return 0.
12460    */
12461
12462     do {
12463           if (*rsp1++ != *rsp2++) return(0);
12464     } while (--n);
12465
12466     /* The strings are identical. */
12467     return(1);
12468   }




12472   /*===========================================================================*
12473    *                              copy                                         *
12474    *===========================================================================*/
12475   PUBLIC copy(dest, source, bytes)
12476   char *dest;                        /* destination pointer */
12477   char *source;                      /* source pointer */
12478   int bytes;                         /* how much data to move */
12479   {
12480   /* Copy a byte string of length 'bytes' from 'source' to 'dest'.
12481    * If all three parameters are exactly divisible by the integer size, copy them
12482    * an integer at a time.  Otherwise copy character-by-character.
12483    */
12484
12485     if (bytes <= 0) return;                  /* makes test-at-the-end possible */
12486
12487     if (bytes % sizeof(int) == 0 && (int) dest % sizeof(int) == 0 &&
12488                                      (int) source % sizeof(int) == 0) {
12489           /* Copy the string an integer at a time. */
12490           register int n = bytes/sizeof(int);
12491           register int *dpi = (int *) dest;
12492           register int *spi = (int *) source;
12493
12494           do { *dpi++ = *spi++; } while (--n);
12495
12496     } else {
12497
12498           /* Copy the string character-by-character. */
12499           register int n = bytes;
```

```
12500             register char *dpc = (char *) dest;
12501             register char *spc = (char *) source;
12502
12503             do { *dpc++ = *spc++; } while (--n);
12504
12505        }
12506   }


12509   /*===========================================================================*
12510    *                              fetch_name                                   *
12511    *===========================================================================*/
12512   PUBLIC int fetch_name(path, len, flag)
12513   char *path;                       /* pointer to the path in user space */
12514   int len;                          /* path length, including 0 byte */
12515   int flag;                         /* M3 means path may be in message */
12516   {
12517   /* Go get path and put it in 'user_path'.
12518    * If 'flag' = M3 and 'len' <= M3_STRING, the path is present in 'message'.
12519    * If it is not, go copy it from user space.
12520    */
12521
12522     register char *rpu, *rpm;
12523     vir_bytes vpath;
12524
12525     if (flag == M3 && len <= M3_STRING) {
12526             /* Just copy the path from the message to 'user_path'. */
12527             rpu = &user_path[0];
12528             rpm = pathname;          /* contained in input message */
12529             do { *rpu++ = *rpm++; } while (--len);
12530             return(OK);
12531     }
12532
12533     /* String is not contained in the message.  Go get it from user space. */
12534     if (len > MAX_PATH) {
12535             err_code = E_LONG_STRING;
12536             return(ERROR);
12537     }
12538     vpath = (vir_bytes) path;
12539     err_code = rw_user(D, who, vpath, (vir_bytes) len, user_path, FROM_USER);
12540     return(err_code);
12541   }


12544   /*===========================================================================*
12545    *                              no_sys                                       *
12546    *===========================================================================*/
12547   PUBLIC int no_sys()
12548   {
12549   /* Somebody has used an illegal system call number */
```

```
12550
12551      return(EINVAL);
12552    }


12555    /*===========================================================================*
12556     *                              panic                                        *
12557     *===========================================================================*/
12558    PUBLIC panic(format, num)
12559    char *format;                       /* format string */
12560    int num;                            /* number to go with format string */
12561    {
12562    /* Something awful has happened.  Panics are caused when an internal
12563     * inconsistency is detected, e.g., a programming error or illegal value of a
12564     * defined constant.
12565     */
12566
12567      if (panicking) return;            /* do not panic during a sync */
12568      panicking = TRUE;                 /* prevent another panic during the sync */
12569      printf("File system panic: %s ", format);
12570      if (num != NO_NUM) printf("%d",num);
12571      printf("\n");
12572      do_sync();                        /* flush everything to the disk */
12573      sys_abort();
12574    }
```

```
12600    /* FS must occasionally print some message.  It uses the standard library
12601     * routine printf(), which calls putc() and flush(). Library
12602     * versions of these routines do printing by sending messages to FS.  Here
12603     * we obviously can't do that, so FS calls the TTY task directly.
12604     */
12605
12606    #include "../h/const.h"
12607    #include "../h/type.h"
12608    #include "../h/com.h"
12609
12610    #define STDOUTPUT          1      /* file descriptor for standard output */
12611    #define BUFSIZE          100      /* print buffer size */
12612
12613    PRIVATE int bufcount;                /* # characters in the buffer */
12614    PRIVATE char printbuf [BUFSIZE];        /* output is buffered here */
12615    PRIVATE message putchmsg;            /* used for message to TTY task */
12616
12617    /*===========================================================================*
12618     *                              putc                                         *
12619     *===========================================================================*/
12620    PUBLIC putc(c)
12621    char c;
12622    {
12623
12624      if (c == 0) {
12625            flush();
12626            return;
12627      }
12628      printbuf[bufcount++] = c;
12629      if (bufcount == BUFSIZE) flush();
12630      if (c == '\n')  flush();
12631    }


12634    /*===========================================================================*
12635     *                              flush                                        *
12636     *===========================================================================*/
12637    PRIVATE flush()
12638    {
12639    /* Flush the print buffer. */
12640
12641      if (bufcount == 0) return;
12642      putchmsg.m_type = TTY_WRITE;
12643      putchmsg.PROC_NR  = 1;
12644      putchmsg.TTY_LINE = 0;
12645      putchmsg.ADDRESS  = printbuf;
12646      putchmsg.COUNT = bufcount;
12647      sendrec(TTY, &putchmsg);
12648      bufcount = 0;
12649    }
```

9

MINIX CROSS REFERENCE LISTING

This chapter lists the principal procedure names, global variables, defined constants, and other macros present in the listing of Appendix E. Local variables and structure members are not listed, as this would have increased the length of this chapter substantially. The **boldface** entries show the lines on which the symbols are defined.

ABS	**0049** 4941 4946 5716 6171
ACCESS	**0130**
ADDRESS	**0211** 2362 2597 3542 3550 3800 3918 4166 7391 12278 12645
ALARM	**0126**
ALARM_ON	**5284** 5799 6616 6617 6709 6711
ALL_MODES	**0072** 9495 9549 11704
ANY	**0154** 1946 2002 2053 2078 2311 2551 3121 3509 4634 5001 5475 9042
AT_SIGN	**3373** 3724
BAD_CYL	**2462** 2822
BAD_SECTOR	**2461** 2822
BASE	**0874** 0903 0973
BEEP_FREQ	**4068** 4244
BIT_MAP_SHIFT	**8626** 8704 8705 8725 8756 8757
BLANK	**4070** 1697 1699 1744 4485
BLOCK_SIZE	**0018** 2387 2590 2599 2644 7540 7542 7543 7544 7546 7566 8310 8311 9097 9098 9138 9190 9216 9220 9862 9863 9864

```
CRMOD              0372 3655 4264 4462
CS_REG             0664 0941 4730
CTL_ACCEPTING      2452 2889
CTL_BUSY           2451 2860
CTRL_S             4073 4146
CURSOR             4091 4336 4355
CUR_SIZE           4089 4487
C_6845             4086 4477
C_RETRACE          4064 4478
C_VID_MASK         4062 4476
D                  0028 0924 0925 0934 0935 0937 0942 0943 0944 0960 1005
                   1994 1998 2004 2005 2055 2056 2362 2672 3467 3489 3834
                   3835 3927 4722 4724 4731 4732 4733 4907 5042 5045 5580
                   5581 5608 5609 5610 5705 5708 5733 5734 5735 5963 5981
                   5999 6004 6151 6152 6153 6154 6156 6171 6329 6361 6362
                   6431 6662 6829 9817 10057 10068 11624 12539
DATA               4088 4418 4420
DATAB              5927 6068
DATA_CHANGED       6277 6348 6369
DELETE             7527 10910 11371
DELTA_TICKS        0200 2994 3157 6707
DELUXE             4097
DEL_CODE           3372 4154
DEVICE             0207 2349 2384 2585 9205 12275 12337 12383
DIRECTION          2450 2855 2888
DIRECTORY_BLO      7604 10916 10929 10950
DIRTY              7530 8139 8224 8439 8516 8568 8732 8764 8844 9217 9599
                   9892 9973 10153 10199 10213 10330 10912 10949 10952 11329 11375
                   11705 11735 11894 12036 12040 12044 12048 12445
DIR_ENTRY_SIZE     7539 7542 10892 10954
DISKINT            0185 1205
DISK_IOCTL         0188 2321 9204
DISK_READ          0186 2319 2351 2366 2559 2669 2804 12274
DISK_WRITE         0187 2320 2560 12274
DIVISOR            2503 2810
DMA_ADDR           2431 2692 2693
DMA_COUNT          2433 2695 2696
DMA_INIT           2436 2698
DMA_M1             2435 2691
DMA_M2             2434 2690
DMA_READ           2475 2669
DMA_TOP            2432 2694
DMA_WRITE          2476 2669
DOR                2428 2725 2748 2959 2960
DST_BUFFER         0229 4937 4947 7289 10062 10070
DST_PROC_NR        0228 4933 7288 10061 10069
DST_SPACE          0227 4935 7287 10060 10068
DS_REG             0663 0942 4731
```

DTL	**2483** 2813
DUMPED	**6481** 6808
DUMP_SIZE	**6479** 6780 6828
DUP	**0133**
DUP_MASK	**7523** 11992
E2BIG	**0263**
EACCES	**0269** 5968 5984 7245 7260 11811 11815
EAGAIN	**0267** 5701 5702 5711 6135
EBADF	**0265** 8921 9825 12002
EBUSY	**0272** 11050 11077 11150
ECHILD	**0266** 5842
ECHO	**0373** 3752 4462
EDOM	**0289**
EEXIST	**0273** 9498 9504 9608 11314
EFAULT	**0270** 4951
EFBIG	**0283** 9847 10187 10940
EINTR	**0260** 3661 4025 6753 6760 10602
EINVAL	**0278** 2322 2561 2590 2599 3519 3990 5958 6496 6592 7302 9637 9740 9742 9822 9827 11062 11160 12551
EIO	**0261** 2586 2644
EISDIR	**0277** 9512 9655
EMFILE	**0280** 8896
EMLINK	**0287** 11291
ENABLE	**0680** 1888 4134 4148 4170
ENABLE_INT	**2454** 2641 2722 2960
ENFILE	**0279** 8404 8465 8909 11051 11091
ENODEV	**0275**
ENOENT	**0258** 6803 9579 10933 11311
ENOEXEC	**0264** 5975 6062 6063 6078 6084
ENOMEM	**0268** 5957 6129 6336 6342 6375 6404 6406 6409
ENOSPC	**0284** 8259
ENOTBLK	**0271** 11196
ENOTDIR	**0276** 10886 11081 11104 11532
ENOTTY	**0281** 12304
ENOUGH	**5425**
ENTER	**7526** 9596 10904 10907 10921 10933 11324
ENXIO	**0262** 2350 2354 2385
EOT_CHAR	**3370** 4470
EPERM	**0257** 5550 6544 6895 6904 9547 10584 11037 11138 11295 11369 11506 11693 11724 11891 11926 12161
EPIPE	**0288** 10469
ERANGE	**0290**
ERASE_CHAR	**3364** 4464
EROFS	**0286** 11841
ERROR	**0256** 8644 12070 12100 12131 12536
ERR_DRIVE	**2496**
ERR_RECALIBRA	**2494** 2933
ERR_SEEK	**2491** 2768 2775 2781 2782 2784 2921

ERR_STATUS   **2493** 2853 2855 2865
ERR_TRANSFER   **2492** 2800 2801 2816 2828 2829 2835
ERR_WR_PROTEC **2495** 2636 2826
ESCAPED   **3435** 3630
ESPIPE   **0285** 9733
ESRCH   **0259** 6633
ES_REG   **0662** 0944 4733
ETXTBSY   **0282**
EXDEV   **0274** 11320
EXEC   **0140** 5462
EXIT   **0102** 5873
EXTERN   **0009 7409 9312**
E_BAD_ADDR   **0306** 1998 2363 3834 3929
E_BAD_BUF   **0301**
E_BAD_CALL   **0293** 5456 9001
E_BAD_DEST   **0297** 1988 1991
E_BAD_FCN   **0305** 4646
E_BAD_PROC   **0307** 4674 4715 4757 4784 4834 4853 4896
E_BAD_SRC   **0298** 1947
E_LOCKED   **0292**
E_LONG_STRING **0294** 10782 12535
E_NO_MESSAGE **0303**
E_NO_PERM   **0304** 1951
E_OVERRUN   **0300** 2010
E_TASK   **0302**
E_TRY_AGAIN   **0299** 3793
F1   **3375** 3592 4526
F10   **3377** 3592
F2   **3376** 4527
FALSE   **0015** 2955 3708 5451 6605 6606 6607 6608 6620 8803 8996
          8997 9700 9882 10167 10168 10894 10938 11045
FDC_DATA   **2430** 2856 2890
FDC_READ   **2468** 2804
FDC_RECALIBRA **2471** 2919
FDC_SEEK   **2467** 2772
FDC_SENSE   **2470** 2779 2925 2967
FDC_SPECIFY   **2472** 2975
FDC_STATUS   **2429** 2852 2854 2859 2887
FDC_WRITE   **2469** 2804
FD_MASK   **9777** 9814
FLOPPY   **0183** 1206 1208 2993 3008 9421
FLOPPY_VECTOR **0673** 0969
FORK   **0103** 5753
FORWARD   **0012**
FROM_USER   **0046** 9971 12539
FSTAT   **0127**
FS_PROC_NR   **0039** 1987 5522 5550 6544 8311 10058 10069
FS_STACK_BYTES **7511** 7819 9332

FULL_DATA_BLO **7609** 9191 9974 10257
FUNC   **0244** 4895
FUNC_TO_CALL   **0201** 2995 3158
F_L_u_s_h   **7383** 7375 7376
GAP   **2482** 2812
GETGID   **0137** 6883
GETPID   **0120** 6888
GETUID   **0124** 6878
GET_TIME   **0173** 3126 12439
GET_TYPE   **4098**
GO_BACKWARD   **4077** 4392
GO_FORWARD   **4076** 4266 4310 4312
HANGING   **5282** 5497 5796 5828 5881 5892 6548 6607 6632
HARDWARE   **0157** 0948 0949 0950 0951 0960 0975 1893 1914 2010 2114
                    2776 2817 2922 2962 5010 5477 6544
HDR_SIZE   **5166** 6044 6062 6089
HIGHEST_ZONE   **0516**
HZ   **0017** 1114 2487 2488 3090 3160 3180 3192 3278 6707
IBM_FREQ   **3095** 3278
IDLE   **0687** 1289 1921 2113
INACTIVE   **3438**
INDEX   **4087** 4417 4419
INDIRECT_BLOCK **7605** 10024 10033 10201 10205 10214 11426
INFO   **8975** 9175 9179 9180 9181
INIT_PROC_NR   **0040** 5141 5523 5577 5676 5742 5887 5891 6602
INIT_PSW   **0655** 0916
INIT_SP   **0656** 0910 0912
INODES_PER_BL   macros
7540   7569 8558 8561
INODE_BLOCK   **7603** 8571
INODE_SIZE   **7541** 7540 8565 8567 9098
INTR_CHAR   **3366** 4466
INTS_PER_BLOCK **7544** 7570 8717 10326
INT_BITS   **8625** 8706 8722 8724 8758 8759
INT_CTL   **0678** 1888 4134 4148 4170
INT_CTLMASK   **0679** 0979
IN_USE   **5280** 5497 5521 5522 5523 5721 5826 5883 6548 6603 6632
                    6655
IOCTL   **0139**
ISEEK   **7887** 9744
I_BLOCK_SPECIA **0067** 9516 9665 9696 9697 9844 9888 9939 11081 11195
I_CHAR_SPECIAL **0069** 9515 9659 9696 9836 9888 11081 12304
I_DIRECTORY   **0068** 9249 9511 9652 9905 10886 11103 11104 11295 11368 11531
I_MAP_BLOCK   **7606** 8680 9218 9219
I_MAP_SLOTS   **7506** 7982 8645
I_MOUNT   **7885** 10841 11115
I_NOT_ALLOC   **0077** 8434
I_PIPE   **7883** 9733 10419 11406 11614

L_REGULAR	**0066**	7243 9495 9507 9905 9909 10411
L_SET_GID_BIT	**0071**	6012
L_SET_UID_BIT	**0070**	6008
L_TYPE	**0065**	7242 9249 9506 9549 9651 9695 9833 9939 10886 11080
		11103 11104 11195 11295 11368 11531 12304
KBIT	**4082**	4123
KB_BUSY	**4096**	
KB_STATUS	**4094**	
KEYBD	**4080**	4121
KEYBOARD_VEC	**0672**	0968
KILL	**0132**	
KILL_CHAR	**3365**	4465
KMEM_DEV	**0180**	2302 2303
KSIG	**0145**	5006 10465
K_STACK_BYTES	**0684**	0717 0949 1164 1278
LAST_FEW	**5674**	5702
LINE_WIDTH	**4071**	4292 4310 4313 4318 4351 4354 4382
LINK	**0110**	
LOOK_UP	**7525**	10812 10887
LOW_USER	**0041**	0907 0953 1950 1987 2110 2137 2163 3261 3663 4896
LSEEK	**0119**	
M1	**0542**	9548 11040 11066 11286 11304 11564 11727 11886
M3	**0543**	9491 9638 11141 11353 11527 11686 11769 12525
M3_STRING	**0545**	0549 12525
M4	**0544**	
M64K	**8974**	9139
MAGIC	**5924**	6063
MAJOR	**0021**	8260 8315 8466 12333 12381
MARKER	**3371**	3639 3682 3753 3854 3856
MASTER	**2449**	2853 2888
MAX	**0501**	
MAX_BLOCK_NR	**0508**	
MAX_ERRORS	**2500**	2604 2611
MAX_FDC_RETR	**2504**	2883
MAX_FILE_POS	**0531**	
MAX_INODE_NR	**0512**	
MAX_ISTACK_BY	**0058**	5156 5158 5943 5957 6184 6200
MAX_LINKS	**0527**	11291
MAX_OVERRUN	**3362**	3445 3446 4486
MAX_PAGES	**5165**	6404 6406
MAX_PATH	**0056**	5155 5158 5945 5958 7814 10770 10776 10781 12534
MAX_P_LONG	**0031**	3165 3215
MAX_RESULTS	**2501**	2518 2851
MAX_ZONES	**7547**	
MEM	**0177**	9209 9420
MEM_BYTES	**0668**	2304
MEM_DEV	**0179**	2304
MEM_PTR	**0245**	4714

MESS_SIZE   **0567** 1997
MILLISEC   **3089** 3090
MIN   **0502** 3842 3843 4385 6170 6828 9863
MINIX   **1153** 1100 1151 1166
MINOR   **0022** 8261 8315 8467 10594 12275 12334 12383
MKNOD   **0114**
MM_PROC_NR   **0038** 1987 2078 4980 5521 5963 5981 5999 6171 6829 9201
                 9811 9822 10468 10584 11483 12070 12100 12131
MM_STACK_BYT   **5156 5158** 5216 7421
MONOCHROME   **4074**
MONO_BASE   **4061** 4480
MOTOR_MASK   **2453** 2747
MOTOR_OFF   **2487** 2642
MOTOR_RUNNIN   **2499** 3007
MOTOR_START   **2488** 2732
MOUNT   **0121**
M_6845   **4085** 4482
M_RETRACE   **4065** 4483
M_VID_MASK   **4063** 4481
NAME_SIZE   **7510** 8004 9571 10683 10705 10751 10771 10779 10794 10863 10908
                 10947 11281 11349
NCALLS   **0100** 5455 7427 8987 9000 9334
NERROR   **0254**
NEW_TIME   **0202** 3180 3192 11928 12444 12447
NIL_BUF   **7585** 8101 8120 8121 8129 8172 8181 8186 8200 8202 8212
                 8213 9130 9131 9142 9145 9955 10154 10199 10294 10298 10941
NIL_FILP   **7711** 8888 8922 8948 9691 9714 9730 9823 9898 10402 10412
                 10414 10452 10463 11566 11583 11615 11994 12081 12302
NIL_HOLE   **6972** 7001 7038 7048 7057 7109 7120 7140 7169 7170
NIL_INODE   **7879** 8390 8403 8405 8429 8472 8477 9008 9575 9579 9581
                 9584 9602 9607 9643 10092 10411 10687 10688 10730 10737 10814
                 10818 11070 11084 11086 11171 11192 11287 11305 11309 11354
                 11359 11528 11565 11687 11728 11770 11887
NIL_MESS   **0568**
NIL_PROC   **0788** 1921 2016 2019 2023 2051 2092 2093 2106 2140 2145
                 2164 2174 2176 2194 2203 4799 4807
NIL_PTR   **0053** 4318 4386 5759 5872 6201 6753 6760
NIL_SUPER   **7992** 11044 11051 11153 11160
NORMAL   **7518** 8149 8560 8650 8655 8837 9184 9214 9951 9962 10022
                 10031 10094 10189 10209 10899 11420
NOT_ESCAPED   **3434** 3609 3618 3626 3642
NOT_REVIVING   **7776** 9034
NOT_SUSPENDED   **7774** 9033 10549 10562 10588 12116
NOT_WAITING   **3442** 3894 3898 4023
NO_BIT   **7522** 8258 8464 8741
NO_BLOCK   **0507** 9125 9156 9948 9951 10006 10019 10029 10034 10093 10250
                 10286 11410
NO_DEV   **0524** 8100 8139 8149 8224 8228 8309 8334 8412 8477 9126

	9240 9951 11041 11048 11061 11067 11071 11096 11108 11142 11172
	11192 11198 12044 12048
NO_ENTRY	**0511**
NO_MAP	**0783** 4683 4737
NO_MEM	**5161** 5711 6147 7019
NO_MOUNT	**7884** 11168
NO_NUM	**0055** 1024 2613 4723 4725 4873 4909 5011 5475 5501 5572
	6000 6147 6172 6714 7038 7239 7319 8121 8646 9038 9042
	9096 9097 9098 9099 9100 9101 9188 9201 9209 9251 9258
	10597 10600 11163 12356 12570
NO_PIPE	**7882** 8435
NO_READ	**7519** 8842 9215 9962 9963 10189 10209 10255 10309
NO_SEEK	**7886** 9904 9909
NO_ZONE	**0515** 8266 8284 8518 9496 10006 10019 10029 10034 10175 10177
	10195 10200 10294 11418
NQ	**0690** 0792 0793
NR_BLOCKS	**2505** 2592
NR_BUFS	**7502** 7581 8117 8333 8643 9100 9122 9124 9131 9135 9143
	9144 9145 9155 12047
NR_BUF_HASH	**7503** 7594 8099 8124 8126 8145 8146 9156
NR_DIR_ENTRIES	**7542** 7567 10902
NR_DRIVES	**2502** 2520 2586 2979
NR_DZONE_NUM	**7538** 7546 7547 10005 10012 10016 10019 10159 10166 10172 10175
	10179 11417 11418
NR_FDS	**7504** 7759 8887 8922 9099 12002 12080 12106
NR_FILPS	**7505** 7709 8899 8942
NR_HEADS	**2481** 2593 2595 2832
NR_HOLES	**6971** 6978 7168 7170
NR_INDIRECTS	**7543** 7547 7568 10014 10020 10023 10025 10170 10184 10185 10186
	10187 11421
NR_INODES	**7508** 7876 8391 11148 12039
NR_PROCS	**0025** 0154 0779 0953 1946 3166 3216 4674 4715 4757 4783
	4798 4834 4853 4896 5004 5277 5477 5701 5702 5720 5743
	5825 5888 6602 7771 9026 9708 10523 10547 10586
NR_RAMS	**2283** 2286 2287 2350 2385
NR_REGS	**0654** 0758 0908
NR_SECTORS	**2480** 2593 2594 2595 2811 2832 2833
NR_SEGS	**0026** 0762 4718 5258 6811 6822
NR_SIGS	**0400** 6496 6564 6592
NR_SUPERS	**7509** 7990 8778 8800 9239 10823 10843 11046 11154 12043
NR_TASKS	**0024** 0715 0779 0787 0796 0907 0909 0910 0914 0931 0948
	0949 0950 0951 1910 1946 2052 2108 2136 2162 3104 3166
	3216 3224 4715 4798 5007 5141
NR_TTYS	**3356** 3431 4459
NR_ZONE_NUMS	**7501** 7538 7866 8015 8517
NULL_DEV	**0181** 2351
OFF_MASK	**4067** 4192
OK	**0255** 1893 1915 1958 1959 2025 2063 2079 2388 2631 2635 2643

	12397
RET_REG	**0686** 1947 1951 1958 1964 4685
REVIVE	**0148** 3571
REVIVING	**7777** 9027 10558
ROOT_DEV	**0061** 8262 8468 8798 9084 9215 9244 9246 9257 12034 12443
ROOT_INODE	**7534** 9084 9246 10820 10821 10849 11086
RUNNING	**3436** 3660 3675 4024 4196
RWX_MODES	**0073** 11752
R_BIT	**0074** 9474 9707 9824 10398 10463 11616
S	**0029** 0926 0927 0928 0931 0936 0937 3466 3488 4908 5042
	5045 5582 5583 5611 5612 5613 5706 5708 5734 5735 5876
	5996 6139 6154 6155 6156 6330 6362
SAFETY	**0872** 0913 0951
SCHED_RATE	**3090** 3101 3244
SCR_LINES	**4072** 4313 4351 4354
SECONDS_LEFT	**0204** 3160 6715
SECTOR_SIZE	**2479** 2591 2810 2835
SEEK_ST0	**2460** 2781 2929
SEND	**0151** 1179 1956 1958
SENDING	**0784** 2012 2057 4796
SEP	**5925** 6064
SEPARATE	**5285** 5584 5877 6019 6064 6069 6085 6140 6360 6403
SERVER_Q	**0692** 2093 2137 2163
SETGID	**0136** 6014 6902 6907 12138
SETUID	**0123** 6010 6893 6898 12134
SET_ALARM	**0171** 2992 3125 6705
SET_TIME	**0174** 3127 11927
SIGALRM	**0415** 3226 6615
SIGBUS	**0411**
SIGEMT	**0408**
SIGFPE	**0409**
SIGHUP	**0402**
SIGILL	**0405**
SIGINT	**0403** 3659 6565
SIGIOT	**0407**
SIGKILL	**0410** 6497
SIGNAL	**0138**
SIGNUM	**0243** 4894
SIGPIPE	**0414** 10467
SIGQUIT	**0404** 3659 6565
SIGSEGV	**0412** 6436
SIGSYS	**0413**
SIGTERM	**0416**
SIGTRAP	**0406**
SIG_DFL	**0421** 6504
SIG_IGN	**0422** 6501
SIG_MAP	**0247** 5008 6550 10467
SIG_PUSH_BYTES	**0057** 4622 4905 6661

SIZES	**0875**
SPEC1	**2484** 2976
SPEC2	**2485** 2977
SQUARE_WAVE	**3096** 3281
SRC_BUFFER	**0226** 4936 4942 7285 10059 10067
SRC_PROC_NR	**0225** 4932 7284 10058 10066
SRC_SPACE	**0224** 4934 7283 10057 10065
SS_REG	**0665** 0943 4732
ST0	**2439** 2781 2828 2929
ST0_BITS	**2455** 2781 2828 2929
ST1	**2440** 2782 2822 2824 2829
ST2	**2441** 2822 2829
ST3	**2442**
ST3_FAULT	**2456**
ST3_READY	**2458**
ST3_WR_PROTEC	**2457**
STACK_CHANGE	**6278** 6356 6370
STACK_FAULT	**0418** 6554
STACK_PTR	**0241** 4756 4836
STAT	**0118**
STDOUTPUT	**12610**
STD_OUTPUT	**7359**
STIME	**0125**
STOPPED	**3437** 3669 4147
ST_CYL	**2443** 2832
ST_HEAD	**2444** 2833
ST_PCN	**2446** 2929
ST_SEC	**2445** 2834
SUPER_BLOCK	**7533** 8650 8653 8837 8842 9184
SUPER_MAGIC	**7514** 9187 9250 11059
SUPER_SIZE	**7545** 8838 8843 9097
SUPER_USER	**0019** 6566 6605 6609 6801 6894 6903 11488
SUSPEND	**0197** 3830 12285 12318
SUSPENDED	**7775** 10498 10524 12115
SU_UID	**7515** 8996
SYNC	**0131** 7321
SYSTASK	**0159** 4724 4907
SYSTEM_TIME	**0234** 4858
SYS_ABORT	**0168** 4643
SYS_COPY	**0165** 4645
SYS_EXEC	**0166** 4639
SYS_FORKED	**0163** 4637
SYS_GETSP	**0161** 4641
SYS_GID	**7517** 9090 9091
SYS_NEWMAP	**0164** 4638
SYS_SIG	**0162** 4644
SYS_TIMES	**0167** 4642
SYS_UID	**7516** 9088 9089

SYS_VECTOR	**0675** 0966
SYS_XIT	**0160** 4640
S_IEXEC	**0475**
S_IFBLK	**0468**
S_IFCHR	**0467**
S_IFDIR	**0466**
S_IFMT	**0465**
S_IFREG	**0469**
S_IREAD	**0473**
S_ISGID	**0471**
S_ISUID	**0470**
S_ISVTX	**0472**
S_IWRITE	**0474**
T	**0027** 0922 0923 0932 0933 0935 0941 3466 3488 4730 5041
	5044 5578 5579 5605 5606 5607 5705 5715 5732 5733 5877
	5878 6003 6140 6141 6148 6149 6150 6163 6361
TAB_MASK	**3361** 4280
TAB_SIZE	**3360**
TASK_Q	**0691** 1921 2092 2137 2163
TASK_REPLY	**0149** 2326 2565 3518 3793 3806 3897 3994 4025
TASK_STACK_BY	**0683** 0714 0913
TEXTB	**5926** 6067
TIME	**0113**
TIMER0	**3093** 3282 3283
TIMER2	**4078** 4440 4441
TIMER3	**4079** 4439
TIMER_MODE	**3094** 3281
TIMES	**0135**
TIOCGETC	**0379** 3978
TIOCGETP	**0377** 3970
TIOCSETC	**0380** 3961
TIOCSETP	**0378** 3954
TOP_ROW	**3378** 3711 3716
TOTB	**5929** 6077
TO_USER	**0045** 9971 10055 11624
TRANS_ST0	**2459** 2828
TRUE	**0014** 2309 2549 2864 2895 2931 3120 3508 4495 4633 5444
	5774 5830 5839 6569 6604 6609 6632 6728 8798 8801 8992
	8996 9832 10180 10198 10503 10726 10904 10922 11047 12163 12568
TTY	**0190** 3835 4167 7393 9423 9424 12647
TTY_BUF_SIZE	**3359** 3447 3835 3843
TTY_CHAR_INT	**0192** 3512 4165
TTY_FLAGS	**0217** 3958 3967 4046 12312 12320
TTY_IN_BYTES	**3357** 3382 3596 3649 3684 3773 3850
TTY_IOCTL	**0196** 3515 12307
TTY_LINE	**0214** 3510 7390 10594 12309 12644
TTY_O_DONE	**0193** 3517
TTY_RAM_WOR	**3358** 3389 4293

alloc_zone   **8235** 10149 10177 10197 10283 10294
allowed   **7224** 5966 6796 6797
alt   **3449** 3722 3734 4154
b_data   **7588** 8311 8838 8843 9137 9185 9216 9972
b_dir   **7589** 10902 10943
b_ind   **7590** 10023 10032 10191 10211 11421
b_inode   **7591** 8561
b_int   **7592** 8658 8659 8716 8717 8724 8761 8763 10327
beep   **4427** 4244
begbss   **1339**
block   **1384** 2582 2591 2592 2593 2594 2595 8079 8081 8099 8102
                    8143
boot_time   **3099** 3180 3192
buf_count   **7362** 7374 7375 7387 7392 7394
buf_pool   **9107** 9077
bufcount   **12613** 12628 12629 12641 12646 12648
buffer   **7903** 1502 1691 1693 1697 9031 9838 9874 9878 10500 11585
bufs_in_use   **7598** 8104 8117 8118 8178 8643 8660 8679 9120
build_sig   **1612** 1360 1371 1594 1605 1612 4902
busy_map   **0795** 1895 1899 1904 1905 1915
capslock   **3448** 3710 3715 3735
cause_sig   **4960** 3226 3663
cd_flag   **7904** 11486 11488
change   **11515** 11493 11507
check_sig   **6577** 6523 6566
child   **7905** 5849 5850 5866 5867 5870 5871 5872 5876 5877 5878
                    5881 5883 12074 12079
chuck   **3761** 3610 3619
cleanup   **5849** 5794 5829 5894
clear_zone   **10222** 9853 10302
clock_int   **1217** 0891 0967 1114 1124 1215 1217
clock_mess   **2986** 2642 2732 11872 11927 11928 11929 12426 12439 12440 12444
                    12447
clock_task   **3109** 5134 5143
clock_time   **12431** 8512 8515 9808 9891 10151 10161 10212 10883 10913 10951
                    11910 11912 12025 12035
cmp_string   **12454** 10908
co_mode   **7906** 11752
color   **4102** 0890 0957 1363 1364 1378 1671 1675 1678 1679 1688
                    1694 1699 1712 1714 1717 4474
console   **4178** 4463
control   **3449** 1602 3711 3716 3723 3733 4146 4154
copy   **12475** 1364 1405 1413 1433 1435 1436 1439 1440 1441 1477
                    1507 1508 1509 1511 1512 1647 1695 1696 1711 1717 1732
                    1745 8565 8567 8838 8843 9185 9216 10947
copy_mess   **7219** 7283 7284 7285 7287 7288 7289 7291 7292 7293
cp_mess   **1490** 1354 1370 1475 1481 1490 2004 2055
cret   **1660** 1362 1371 1634 1637

csv	**1638** 1361 1371 1634 1636 1646 1649 1650 1657
cur_proc	**0707** 0990 1132 1178 1289 1378 1653 1921 2105 2108 2110 2113
del_slot	**7072** 7012 7112 7123
dev_close	**12248** 9702
dev_io	**12261** 8311 9837
dev_mess	**12226** 12240 12241 12254 12274 12275 12276 12277 12278 12279 12282 12285 12287 12307 12308 12309 12310 12311 12312 12315 12318 12319 12320 12321 12337
dev_open	**12233** 9518 9662 9666
disk_int	**1203** 0891 0969 1113 1124 1201 1203
dma_setup	**2653** 2624
do_abort	**4868** 4643
do_access	**11760** 9324 9368
do_alarm	**6679** 7424 7455
do_brk	**6283** 7423 7445
do_brk2	**5534** 7425 7495
do_cancel	**4003** 3516
do_charint	**3528** 3512
do_chdir	**11475** 9324 9347
do_chmod	**11677** 9324 9350
do_chown	**11715** 9324 9351
do_chroot	**11500** 9324 9396
do_clocktick	**3199** 3128
do_close	**9680** 9325 9341 12005 12108
do_copy	**4922** 4645
do_creat	**9479** 9325 9343
do_dup	**11981** 9325 9376
do_exec	**4746 5934** 4639 7423 7487
do_exit	**12093** 9325 9336
do_fork	**4658 5683 12057** 4637 7423 7430 9325 9337
do_fstat	**11575** 9325 9363
do_get_time	**3175** 3126
do_getset	**6867** 7423 7448 7451 7452 7474 7475
do_getsp	**4825** 4641
do_ioctl	**3941 12294** 3515 9326 9389
do_kill	**6519** 7424 7465
do_ksig	**6530** 7425 7493
do_link	**11275** 9326 9344
do_lseek	**9721** 9326 9354
do_mem	**2337** 2319 2320
do_mknod	**9541** 9326 9349
do_mm_exit	**5767** 7423 7429
do_mount	**11023** 9326 9356
do_newmap	**4698** 4638
do_open	**9622** 9326 9340
do_pause	**6723** 7424 7457
do_pipe	**10384** 9327 9377
do_rdwt	**2576** 2559 2560

do_read	**3784 9784** 3513 9327 9338
do_revive	**12149** 9327 9403
do_set	**12124** 9327 9358 9381
do_set_time	**3187** 3127
do_setalarm	**3142** 3125
do_setup	**2377** 2321
do_sig	**4880** 4644
do_signal	**6488** 7424 7476
do_stat	**11553** 9327 9353
do_stime	**11920** 9327 9360
do_sync	**12018** 9328 9371 9699 11164 12572
do_time	**11905** 9328 9348
do_times	**4844** 4642
do_tims	**11937** 9328 9378
do_umask	**11746** 9328 9395
do_umount	**11126** 9328 9357
do_unlink	**11342** 9328 9345
do_unpause	**10572** 9329 9401
do_utime	**11877** 9329 9365
do_wait	**5809** 7423 7435
do_write	**3905 10125** 3514 9329 9339
do_xit	**4771** 4640
dont_reply	**5202 7803** 5451 5461 5774 5830 5839 6569 6632 6728 8997 9006 10503 12163
dump_core	**6774** 6672
dup_inode	**8579** 9086 9254 10421 10723 11487 12084 12085
eat_path	**10675** 9631 9643 11033 11070 11189 11192 11283 11287 11524 11528 11559 11565 11683 11687 11721 11728 11766 11770 11883 11887
echo	**3746** 3611 3612 3613 3620 3621 3631 3662 3687
eff_grp_id	**7907** 12139
eff_user_id	**7908** 12136
erki	**7909** 3947 3952 3974 3985 3994
err_code	**5212 7817** 5452 8259 8404 8465 8921 9491 9497 9548 9551 9579 9601 9610 9615 9638 9643 9691 9730 9823 9955 10178 10202 10297 10416 10782 10813 10942 11040 11041 11068 11072 11086 11141 11142 11196 11286 11287 11304 11305 11310 11353 11355 11359 11527 11528 11564 11565 11583 11686 11687 11727 11728 11769 11770 11886 11887 11994 12302 12535 12539 12540
escape	**4362** 4236
exec_len	**5303** 5958 5963
exec_name	**5302** 5961
fd	**7910** 5942 5966 5968 5972 5974 5983 5991 6003 6004 6005 6030 6031 6062 6089 6216 6217 6235 7233 7238 7239 7244 7249 7257 7259 9030 9691 9714 9811 9812 9813 9814 9823 10499 11583 11992 11997 12004 12107
fd2	**7911** 11999 12002 12003 12004 12009 12010 12011
fdc_out	**2872** 2772 2773 2774 2779 2805 2806 2807 2808 2809 2810 2811 2812 2813 2919 2920 2925 2967 2975 2976 2977

fdc_results   **2843** 2780 2820 2926 2968

fetch_name   **12512** 9491 9548 9638 11040 11066 11141 11286 11304 11353
11527 11564 11686 11727 11769 11886

find_dev   **12328** 12239 12253 12271 12305

find_filp   **8930** 9807 9898 10446 10452 10463

finish   **3884** 3661 4210

floppy   **2508** 1203 2520 2580 2587 2654 2704 2758 2793 2844 2904
2952 2965 2979

floppy_task   **2540** 5134 5142

flush   **4326 12637** 3754 4202 4243 4287 4293 4350 12625 12629 12630

forbidden   **11782** 9508 9517 9645 10888 11534 11773

free_bit   **8747** 8288 8479 8536

free_inode   **8525** 8436

free_mem   **7026** 5878 6141

free_slots   **6982** 7038 7041 7087 7088 7172

free_zone   **8275** 10296 11412 11417 11422 11427

fs_call   **7813** 9000 9003 9029 9045 10499 12134 12138

fs_init   **9069** 8989

fstack   **7819** 9331 9332

func   **5304** 2986 2988 2995 6501 6504 6510

func_key   **4519** 3593

get_block   **8079** 8553 8560 8639 8650 8655 8832 8837 8842 9176 9184
9214 9215 9936 9951 9964 9997 10022 10031 10089 10094 10150
10189 10209 10237 10255 10280 10309 10881 10899 11400 11420

get_byte   **1759** 1365 1371 1751 1755 1759 4197

get_chrome   **1673** 0890 0957 1363 1371 1668 1673

get_fd   **8871** 9492 9640 10398 10401 11999

get_filp   **8916** 9688 9691 9727 9730 9807 9823 10582 10592 11580 11583
11989 11994 12300 12302

get_inode   **8379** 8458 8477 9075 9084 9235 9246 10806 10809 10818 10830
10849 11033 11086

get_name   **10749** 10719 10728

get_super   **8771** 8245 8254 8282 8287 8459 8462 8532 8535 8554 8557
8640 8642 8676 8678 8815 8817 9806 9846 10281 10289 11838
11840 12026 12034 12437 12443

get_work   **5471 9016** 5446 8993

group   **7913** 11734

grpid   **5305** 6903 6905 6906 6907

hole_head   **6981** 7000 7042 7051 7082 7083 7138 7171

idle   **1319** 1289 1290 1317 1321

in_char   **3581** 3559

inform   **4987** 2078 4980

initialized   **2529** 2611 2643

int_mess   **0710** 1132 1205 1206 1219 1220

interleave   **2535** 2594

interrupt   **1878** 1103 1105 1106 1111 1112 1113 1114 1128 1189 1198
1206 1210 1220 1224 1263 1321 1322 1603 1604 1782 1789
1796 1810 4167

mode_map	**9474** 9639
motor_goal	**2526** 2641 2722 2723 2725 2726 2747 2748 2749 2958
motor_status	**2525** 2723 2724 2726 2747 2749 2801 2957
mounted	**8789** 9700
move_to	**4343** 4248 4252 4256 4260 4269 4273 4398 4489
name	**7918** 9491 9638 11141 11353 11493 11507 11686 11769
name1	**7919** 9548 11040 11286 11564 11727
name1_length	**7922** 9548 11040 11286 11564 11727
name2	**7920** 11066 11304 11566
name2_length	**7923** 11066 11304
name_length	**7921** 9491 9638 11141 11353 11493 11507 11686 11769
name_to_dev	**11180** 11034 11041 11134 11142
namelen	**5307**
nbytes	**7924** 9032 9821 9822 9838 9846 9858 9861 9863 9879 10501
need_reset	**2528** 2621 2775 2816 2864 2882 2895 2921 2931 2955
new_block	**10265** 9936 9955 10881 10941
new_mem	**6097** 5988
new_node	**9557** 9488 9496 9550
next_alarm	**3100** 3165 3167 3213 3215 3233 3234
next_pid	**5676** 5742 5744 5748 5760
no_call	**12391** 9329 9420 9421 9422 9423 9424 9425
no_sys	**7298 12547** 7425 7428 7431 7432 7433 7434 7436 7437 7438 7439 7440 7441 7442 7443 7444 7446 7447 7449 7450 7453 7454 7456 7458 7459 7460 7461 7462 7463 7464 7466 7467 7468 7469 7470 7471 7472 7473 7477 7478 7479 7480 7481 7482 7483 7484 7485 7486 7488 7489 7490 7491 7494 7496 7497 9329 9335 9342 9346 9352 9355 9359 9361 9362 9364 9366 9367 9369 9370 9372 9373 9374 9375 9379 9380 9382 9383 9384 9385 9386 9387 9388 9390 9391 9392 9393 9394 9397 9398 9400 9402 9404
numlock	**3448** 3712 3717 3736
offset	**7925** 1418 1420 1502 1504 1691 1695 1710 1758 1764 4188 4192 4193 4197 4199 4205 4308 4313 4315 4318 9737 9738 9739
olivetti	**3450** 3708 4495
out_char	**4217** 3753 4198 4264 4279 4512
owner	**7926** 11733
panic	**1012 7309 12558** 0990 1128 1233 1375 1646 1650 1656 2313 2553 2613 2684 2686 2969 2972 3129 4723 4725 4873 4909 5011 5475 5477 5501 5717 6000 6147 6172 6714 7038 7239 8117 8121 8646 8762 8782 9038 9042 9096 9097 9098 9099 9100 9101 9188 9201 9209 9251 9258 10547 10586 10597 10600 11163 11929 12335 12356 12440
panicking	**12425** 12567 12568
parent	**7927** 4778 4781 4783 4785 5861 5867 5882 12073
patch_ptr	**6183** 5997
pathname	**7928** 12528
phys_copy	**1387** 0961 1056 1353 1370 1382 1385 1387 2367 2369 3868

	4726 4910 4952
pick_proc	**2086** 0976 1922 2168 2204
pid	**5308** 4667 4672 4684 6523
pipe_check	**10433** 9857
port_in	**1547** 1356 1370 1544 1546 1547 2852 2854 2856 2859 2887 4121 4122 4442
port_out	**1529** 0979 1355 1370 1525 1527 1529 1888 2690 2691 2692 2693 2694 2695 2696 2698 2725 2748 2890 2959 2960 3281 3282 3283 4123 4124 4134 4148 4170 4417 4418 4419 4420 4439 4440 4441 4443 4445
prev_motor	**2527** 2723 2727
prev_proc	**0708** 2105 3261
prev_ptr	**3102** 2044 2062 2065 3243 3245 6997 7012 7016 7036 7058 7063 7064 7065 7072 7073 7085 8096 8124 8125 8129 8130 8131 8134 8170 8180 8181 8182 8187 8189
print_buf	**7363** 7374 7391
printbuf	**12614** 12628 12645
printf	**0695 5169 7549** 1001 1002 1003 1004 1023 1024 1025 1027 2825 5566 5567 5568 5569 5570 5572 7318 7319 7320 8263 8265 8314 8469 8471 9212 9221 9224 12569 12570 12571
pro	**7929** 6736 6737 6748 6753 6760 6765 10585
proc_addr	**0787** 0953 0960 0975 1945 1989 1990 2047 2114 2361 2672 3159 3831 3835 3924 4675 4678 4679 4716 4717 4724 4758 4785 4786 4835 4854 4897 4907 4944 4949 4977 5000 5004
procs_in_use	**5203** 5524 5701 5702 5725 5884
put_block	**8157** 8571 8680 8681 8848 9191 9218 9219 9975 10024 10033 10095 10201 10205 10214 10257 10916 10929 10950 11426
put_inode	**8421** 9525 9550 9583 9597 9600 9614 9646 9654 9712 10695 10729 10736 10828 10848 11097 11098 11109 11110 11169 11170 11197 11203 11299 11313 11333 11334 11363 11379 11380 11485 11538 11543 11567 11699 11707 11738 11774 11897 12112 12113
putc	**4503 7369 12620**
putch_msg	**7364** 7388 7389 7390 7391 7392 7393
putchmsg	**12615** 12642 12643 12644 12645 12646 12647
ram_limit	**2287** 2303 2304 2356 2358 2387
ram_origin	**2286** 2302 2355 2386
rd_chars	**3813** 3566 3804
rd_only	**7930** 11118
rdahedpos	**7806** 9907 10093
read_ahead	**10082** 9008
read_header	**6030** 5972
read_map	**9984** 9937 9944 10093 10238 10250 10282 10286 10882 10896 11401 11410
read_only	**11830** 11695 11731 11821
read_write	**9794** 9786 10128
ready	**2122** 0915 2007 2058 4738 4763
real_grp_id	**7914** 12140
real_user_id	**7931** 12135

realtime	**0703** 3160 3161 3180 3192 3210 3213 3219
reboot	**1780** 1366 1367 1371 1776 1780 1785 1794 4154
recalibrate	**2903** 2768 2784
release	**10510** 1111 9708 10457 10478
reply	**5485 9053** 5463 5759 5872 6753 6760 9007 10564
reply_i1	**5318 7944** 5499 10424
reply_i2	**7945** 10425
reply_l1	**7943** 9747 11912
reply_p1	**5319** 5500
reply_t1	**7946** 11944
reply_t2	**7947** 11945
reply_t3	**7948** 11946
reply_t4	**7949** 11947
reply_type	**5317 7942** 5498 9062
request	**7932**
res_ptr	**5214** 5463 6305
reset	**2945** 2621
restart	**1288** 0980 1107 1117 1125 1181 1190 1199 1211 1225 1234 1243 1286 1288 1289
restore	**1587** 1251 1294 1295 1296 1297 1298 1305 1306 1307 1308 1312 1359 1362 1370 1453 1454 1455 1456 1457 1458 1459 1460 1461 1462 1514 1515 1516 1517 1518 1519 1520 1537 1538 1539 1557 1558 1559 1584 1587 1589 1627 1628 1629 1662 1663 1664 1735 1736 1737 1738 1739 1740 1741 1768 1769 1784 1791 1807 2146 2179 2195 2205
result2	**5213** 5463 6880 6885 6890
resvec	**1797** 1784 1791
revive	**10537** 10526 10599 10602 12162 12361
reviving	**7805** 9024 9035 10559
rw_block	**8295** 8139 8149 8225 12048
rw_chunk	**9919** 9874
rw_dev	**12344** 9408 9420 9421 9422 9423 9425 12384
rw_dev2	**12370** 9408 9424
rw_inode	**8543** 8412 8439 9593 10423 12040
rw_super	**8824** 9245 11055 12044
rw_user	**10042** 9972 11624 12539
s_call	**1173** 0891 0966 1110 1125 1171 1173
save	**1249** 1104 1162 1174 1188 1197 1204 1218 1232 1241 1247 1256 1257 1264 1268 1270 1271 1272 1273 1274 1275 1361 1388 1390 1391 1392 1393 1394 1395 1396 1397 1398 1431 1491 1492 1493 1495 1497 1498 1499 1530 1532 1533 1548 1550 1551 1568 1570 1613 1615 1616 1642 1643 1704 1705 1706 1707 1708 1724 1760 1762
scale_factor	**8810** 9999 10155 10241 10303 11404
scan_code	**3451** 1132 1162 4495
sched	**2186** 3243
sched_ticks	**3101** 3242 3244
scroll_screen	**4304** 4266 4392

search_dir	**10861** 9596 10812 11324 11371
seconds	**5309** 6686
seek	**2757** 2630
send_mess	**3003** 2718 2732
set_6845	**4403** 4319 4336 4355 4487 4488
set_alarm	**6695** 5799 6687
set_map	**5593**
set_vec	**1036** 0964 0965 0966 0967 0968 0969 0970 0973
sh	**3464** 3710 3711 3712 3716
shift1	**3448** 3710 3715 3731
shift2	**3448** 3710 3715 3732
sig	**5310 7933** 1605 3588 3659 3663 4889 4894 4902 6496 6497 6498
sig_proc	**6640** 6436 6627
sig_procs	**0709** 2078 4978 5009
sig_stuff	**4622** 1605 1617 1620 1622 1624 1626 4898 4902
size_ok	**6382** 6087 6361
sizes	**1330** 0889 0904 0925 0927 0928 0932 0934 0935 0936 0937 1046 1054 1133 1330 2297 2303
slot1	**7934** 11484 12103 12133
stack_bytes	**5311** 5956
stack_fault	**6418** 6555
stack_ptr	**5312** 5979
start_motor	**2703** 2627 2918
stat_inode	**11592** 11566 11585
status	**5313** 2848 2852 2853 2854 2855 2856 2857 2859 2860 2951 2970 2971 4031 4035 4045 5773
steps_per_cyl	**2530** 2612 2615 2774 2782
stop_motor	**2740** 2581 2642
super_user	**7802** 8996 9547 11037 11138 11295 11368 11506 11692 11724 11800 11891 11926
surprise	**1231** 0892 0964 1115 1125 1229 1231
susp_count	**7804** 10457 10497 10527 12115
suspend	**10488** 10454 10473 12285 12318
sys_call	**1929** 1128 1180
sys_task	**4627** 5134 5143
task	**12227** 0890 0914 1107 1110 1117 1181 1205 1219 1264 1288 1313 1653 1808 1878 1879 1892 1893 1896 1900 5141 10488 10489 10497 10502 10579 10589 10591 10597 10600 12240 12254 12282 12285 12315 12318 12336
task_mess	**0796** 1900 1914
tot_mem	**5428** 5517 5518 5563
tp	**7935** 11928
transfer	**2792** 2634
trap	**0997** 1103 1105 1128 1242
trp	**1240** 0892 0965 1116 1125 1238 1240
truncate	**11388** 8433 9508
tty_buf	**3447** 3835 3845

tty_copy_buf	**3446** 3543 3555
tty_driver_buf	**3445** 4157 4160 4161 4162 4166 4486
tty_init	**4453** 3507
tty_int	**1187** 0891 0968 1111 1124 1185 1187
tty_reply	**4031** 3518 3571 3793 3806 3897 3994 4025
tty_struct	**3380** 3431 3505 3510 3539 3562 3587 3590 3747 3762 3785 3814 3885 3906 3942 4004 4144 4145 4147 4179 4218 4305 4327 4344 4363 4457 4459 4473 4485 4489 4512
tty_task	**3500** 5135 5142
umap	**5021** 0893 0960 2346 2362 2667 2672 3827 3834 3835 3913 3927 4619 4722 4724 4907 4908 4944 4949
umess	**9779** 10057 10058 10059 10060 10061 10062 10065 10066 10067 10068 10069 10070 10073 10074 10075
unexpected_int	**0987** 1128 1233
unload_bit_maps	**8669** 11163
unlock	**1578** 1358 1370 1575 1578 2697 2728 2961 3552 4446
unm24	**3475** 3715
unpause	**6736** 6623 7425
unready	**2153** 2013 2073 4789
unsh	**3454** 3710
update_time	**7936** 11893
user_path	**7814** 9496 9550 9643 10770 10776 10781 11041 11070 11142 11287 11305 11354 11528 11565 11687 11728 11770 11887 12527 12539
usr_id	**5314** 6894 6896 6897 6898
utime_file	**7937** 11886
utime_length	**7938** 11886
vid_base	**4105** 4318 4332 4386 4475 4480
vid_copy	**1701** 1364 1371 1685 1691 1701 4318 4332 4386
vid_mask	**4106** 4311 4313 4476 4481
vid_port	**4107** 4417 4418 4419 4420 4477 4482
vid_retrace	**4104** 4385 4478 4483
whence	**7939** 9736
who	**5208** **7812** 5447 5463 5476 5477 5550 5731 5752 5753 5826 5963 5965 5981 5999 6010 6014 6022 6157 6235 6303 6544 6687 6889 6898 6907 8995 9007 9028 9044 9811 9816 9822 9838 10584 11483 11624 11943 12070 12100 12131 12161 12308 12539
whom	9053 9054
wipe_inode	**8503** 8493 11434
wreboot	**1787** 1028 1367 1372 1776 1787
write_map	**10135** 10295
zero_block	**10318** 9952 9970 10190 10210 10256 10310

INDEX

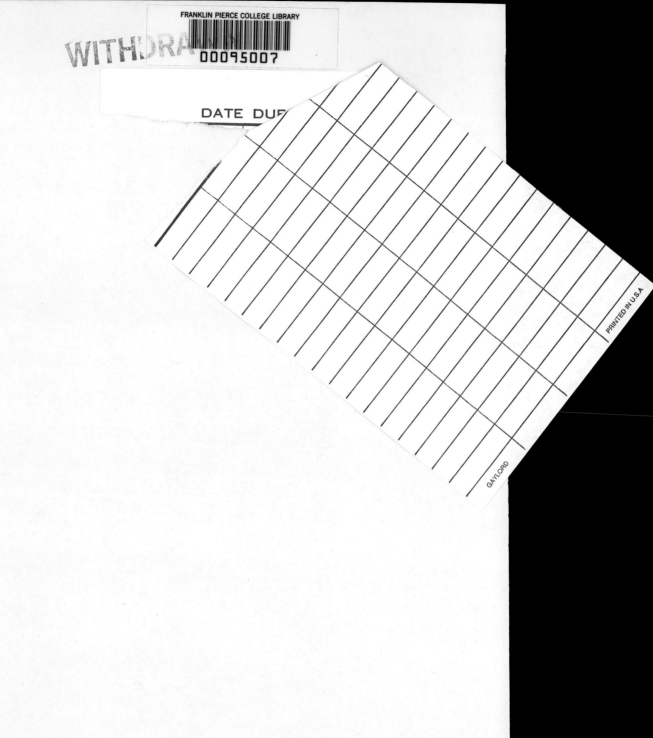